A BIBLIOGRAPHY OF
FINANCE AND INVESTMENT

A BIBLIOGRAPHY OF FINANCE AND INVESTMENT

Compiled by Richard A. Brealey and Connie Pyle

The MIT Press
Cambridge, Massachusetts

Published in Great Britain 1973 by
Elek Books Limited

Copyright © 1973 by R. A. Brealey and C. Pyle

First MIT Press edition, 1973

Library of Congress catalog card number: 73-5340
ISBN 0-262-02105-6

Printed in Great Britain

CONTENTS

To

David Brealey

who was unwittingly
responsible for this book

ACKNOWLEDGMENTS

From its youthful beginnings as a short private reading list this work has developed into a large and comprehensive bibliography. Many people have contributed to this development. In particular we should like to express our appreciation to Mr John Whittaker for access to his bibliographic material, and to Mrs Gira Gratier, Mrs Eileen Thesiger, and Miss Mary Jane Morser for their help in compilation. We are equally grateful for the help and advice provided by our two spouses.

Introduction

The considerable growth in the output of books, articles and dissertations on the theory and practice of finance has produced a need for a relatively comprehensive bibliography. It is this need which we have attempted to alleviate. We list below our criteria for inclusion of a work and describe the lay-out of the book.

CRITERIA FOR INCLUSION

We have referenced works that fall under the broad subject headings of corporate finance, and of the securities and other speculative markets. The boundaries to this domain are, however, ill-defined and we were continuously forced to make arbitrary rulings lest we encroach on the kingdoms of accounting or monetary economics. As a result we are likely to have provided less comprehensive coverage of such topics as 'the interpretation of financial statements' or 'the foreign exchange markets' that lie on the borders of our subject.

Our second main criterion for inclusion was that the work should be concerned with questions of lasting importance. We have not limited our selection to the publications of any one country. Although approximately nine-tenths of the works are American in origin, we have included a substantial number of British works and a few from other countries. With rare exceptions all works are written in the English language.

We have sought to avoid obtruding our own opinion of a work's merits. Indeed, in the case of the two leading professional journals (Financial Analysts Journal in the USA and Investment Analyst in the UK) and of seventeen academic journals, we have included all articles that fall within the broad subject area. In other cases we have been swayed by the importance of the subject matter, the reputation of the publisher or the extent to which a work has been referenced by other authors.

Dissertations raise a minor problem in that they may be published subsequently in part or in entirety. Where we know that the dissertation and published work are essentially identical we have included only the published work. In all other cases we have included both.

Another difficulty arises with unpublished papers. Some such papers have had wide circulation and are frequently quoted. We have, therefore, resisted the suggestion that we do not incorporate such papers and have included interesting papers of which we are aware. In particular, with the long publication delays, there are a number of such papers that are important and that will undoubtedly be published. By including these papers we hope to protect this bibliography a little against the ravages of time.

We have not restricted the selection to recent works. Our earliest included article is Bernoulli's famous paper of 1730. Nevertheless, only one-sixth of the references date from before 1960. This reflects the growth in the number of studies in recent years and the fact that a fully comprehensive coverage of principal sources has been limited to the past ten to twenty years. Our latest entries are works published at the end of 1972.

This bibliography contains over 3,600 entries. Almost 200 book publishers and a similar number of periodicals are represented. It would be disingenuous to pretend that we have been able to avoid errors. These may be of three kinds. First, in cases where we have been forced to rely on a reference in another article, the volume number or page numbers may be missing. It seemed small-minded to exclude works on these grounds and we have simply required that the reader should have enough information to identify and locate the article. Secondly, there are some simple errors of commission. Sample checks suggest that these are most frequent in the case of page numbers and of dissertation dates. We estimate that no more than 1% of entries contain such errors and they are mostly of a minor nature. The third kind of error is the mis-allocation of subjects in cases where we are not sufficiently well acquainted with the work. It is difficult to assess the prevalence of these errors, but it is probably the case that on average less than one entry per subject heading has been clearly mis-classified.

LAY-OUT OF BIBLIOGRAPHY

Works are listed under two principal files. One of these consists of an alphabetical listing by first author. Cross-references are included for works by more than one author.

The other file consists of a subject index. Entries have been divided into 150 subject areas. Thus on average about 25 entries are included under each subject heading and in no case does the number exceed one hundred and fifty. Within each subject, entries have been listed by year of publication. A list of the subject headings is provided on pp. 18-24. The choice of headings was pragmatic. Articles stubbornly refused to fit into our *a priori* classes. To prevent undue length, articles have rarely been filed under more than one subject heading. The user is therefore advised to consult entries under related headings. Conversely, we attempted to provide subject entries for all works even though this meant stretching the definition of the subject. However, in one or two cases, such as Victor Niederhoffer's article on the alphabetical properties of stocks, we were insufficiently ingenious to imagine any broad subject under which it might be included.

Ideally, perhaps, all works should be accompanied by a brief abstract. However, not only would such a book be prohibitively expensive but the authors confess to having read only a small proportion of the works referenced. We have, however, attempted to do the next best thing by including a short introduction to each subject that both defines the subject area and, where necessary, suggests some initial reading for the incognoscenti.

There are differences between British and American financial terminology. We have sought in our introductory material to employ terms that would be fully comprehensible on both sides of the Atlantic even though they may not be the most commonly used. In cases where no such means of communication exists we have written in both languages.

Guide to Publishers' Abbreviations

Addison—Wes	Addison-Wesley Publishing Co. Inc.	Reading, Mass.
Alexander	Alexander and Alexander Inc.	Chicago
Allen	Allen (George) & Unwin Ltd	London
Allyn	Allyn & Bacon Inc.	Boston
Am Ent	American Enterprise Institute for Public Policy Research	Washington, D.C.
Am Mgmt	American Management Assn	New York
Am Pr	American Press, The	New York
Am Res Co	American Research Council	Larchmont, N.J.
Analytical Inv	Analytical Investors	New York
Anbar	Anbar Publications Ltd	London
Anthoensen	The Anthoensen Press	Portland, Ma.
Appleton	Appleton-Century-Crofts Inc.	New York
Arco	Arco Publishing Company Inc.	New York
Asia	Asia Publishing House	New York
BAI	Bank Administration Institute	Park Ridge, Ill.
Bankers	Bankers Publishing Company	Boston
Basic	Basic Books	New York
BEA	Bureau of Economic Affairs	Washington, D.C.
Bernhard	Arnold Bernhard & Co.	New York
Blackwell	Blackwell (Basil)	Oxford
Boardman	Boardman Clark Co.	New York
Bombay U Pr	Bombay University Press	Bombay
Bourse	Business Bourse, The	New York
Bowes	Bowes and Bowes Publishers Ltd	Cambridge, England
Brackenburg	Brackenburg (M.C.) & Co.	London
Brookings	Brookings Institution, The	Washington, D.C.
Brown U Pr	Brown University Press	Providence, R.I.
Business Bks	Business Books Ltd	London
Butterworth	Butterworth & Co.	London
Carswell	The Carswell Co. Ltd	Toronto
Cass	Cass (Frank) & Co.	London
Chapman	Chapman & Hall Ltd	London

Chatto	Chatto & Windus Ltd	London
Clarendon	Clarendon Press	Oxford
Columbia U Pr	Columbia University Press	New York
Commerce	Commerce Clearing House Inc.	New York
Commodities	Commodities Press	Wilmette, Ill.
Commodity R	Commodity Research Bureau Inc.	New York
Convertible S Pr	Convertible Securities Press	New York
Crown	Crown Publishers Inc.	New York
Dartmouth C Trust	Dartmouth College, Trustees of	Hanover, N.H.
Dennis	Dennis & Co.	Buffalo, N.Y.
Dial	Dial Press Inc.	New York
Dickens	Dickens Press, The	London
Doubleday	Doubleday & Company Inc.	New York
Dow Jones—Irwin	Dow Jones—Irwin Inc.	Homewood, Ill.
Duke	Duke University Press	Durham, N.C.
Dunod	Dunod	Paris
Econ Affairs	Economic Affairs, Institute of	London
Edinburgh U Pr	Edinburgh University Press	Edinburgh
Effingham	Effingham Wilson	London
Elek	Elek Books Ltd	London
Eyre & S	Eyre & Spottiswoode (Publishers) Ltd	London
Fed Tax Pr	Federal Tax Press Inc.	Boston
Fed Tst	Federal Trust for Education and Research	London
Fin Exec	Financial Executive Research Foundation	New York
Forbes BC	Forbes (B.C.) & Sons Publishing Co. Ltd.	New York
Ford	Ford Foundation	New York
Fordham	Fordham University Press	New York
Fraser	Fraser Publishing Company	Burlington, Vt.
Free Pr	Free Press	New York
Funk	Funk (Wilfred) Inc.	New York
Gee	Gee & Co. (Publishers) Ltd	London
Gollancz	Gollancz (Victor) Ltd	London
Gower	Gower Press	London

4

Greenwood	Greenwood Press Inc.	Westport, Conn.
Griffin	Griffin (Charles) & Co. Ltd	London
Griffith	Griffith (W.P.) & Sons Ltd	London
Gulf Pub	Gulf Publishing Company	Houston, Tex.
Guthstead	Guthstead	Liverpool, England
Hamilton	Hamilton (Hamish) Ltd	London
HarBraceJ	Harcourt Brace Johanovich Inc.	New York
Harrap	Harrap (George G.) & Co. Ltd	London
Har-Row	Harper & Row Publishers Inc.	New York
Harvard Busn	Harvard Business School, Division of Research	Boston
Harvard U Pr	Harvard University Press	Cambridge, Mass.
Heath	Heath (D.C.) & Company	Indianopolis, Ind.
Heineman	Heineman (James H.) Inc.	New York
HM	Houghton Mifflin Co.	Boston
HMSO	Her Majesty's Stationery Office	London
HR & W	Holt, Rinehart & Winston Inc.	New York
Hutchinson	Hutchinson Publishing Group, Ltd	London
Hutton	Hutton Publishing Company	New York
IC FC	Industrial and Commercial Finance Corporation, Ltd	London
Ind U Busn Res	Indiana University Bureau of Business Research	Bloomington, Ind.
Inst Econ Aff	Institute of Economic Affairs	London
Inst Real Est Mgmt	Institute of Real Estate Management	Chicago
Int Econ	International Economic Publishers	Washington, D.C.
Intext	Intext Educational Pubs	Scranton, Pa.
Intl Pubn Serv	International Publication Service	New York
Inv Bankers	Investment Bankers Assn. of America	Washington, D.C.
Inv Int	Investors Intelligence	Larchmont, N.Y.
Inv Pr	Investors' Press	Palisades Park, N.J.
Iowa St Busn	Bureau of Business and Economic Research, Iowa State University	Iowa City, Iowa
Iowa St U Pr	Iowa State University Press	Ames, Iowa

Irwin	Irwin (Richard D.) Inc.	Homewood, Ill.
Jahnssonin	Yrjö Jahnssonin Säätiö	Helsinki, Finland
Johnsen	Johnsen Publishing Co.	Lincoln, Neb.
Johns Hopkins	Johns Hopkins Press	Baltimore, Md.
Kelley	Kelley (August M.) Publishers	East Orange, N.J.
Kyklos	Kyklos-Verlag	Basel, Switzerland
Lakeside	Lakeside Press	Chicago
Law Book	Law Book Co. Ltd	Sydney, Australia
Little	Little, Brown & Company	Boston
Littlefield	Littlefield, Adams & Co.	Totowa, N. J.
Liverpool U Pr	Liverpool University Press	Liverpool, England
Longman	Longman Group Ltd	London
Lybrand	Lybrand, Ross Bros. & Montgomery	New York
McGill-Queens U Pr	McGill-Queens University Press	Montreal
McGraw	McGraw-Hill Book Company	New York
Macmillan	Macmillan Company	New York
Macmillan Int	Macmillan International Ltd	London
Magee	Magee, John, Inc.	Springfield, Mass.
Man U Pr	Manchester University Press	Manchester, England
Merrill	Merrill (Charles E.) Publishing Company	Columbus, Ohio
Metcalf	Metcalf Press	Boston
Methuen	Methuen & Co. Ltd	London
Mich St U Busn	Graduate School of Business Administration, Michigan State University	East Lansing, Mich.
Mimir	Mimir Publishers	Madison, Wis.
MIT Pr	M.I.T. Press	Cambridge, Mass.
Morrow	William Morrow & Company Inc.	New York
Natl Bur Econ Res	National Bureau of Economic Research Inc.	New York
Natl Ind Conf Bd	National Industrial Conference Board	New York
Nedlaw	Nedlaw Finance & Publishing Co. Ltd	Sanderstead, England
N Holland	North-Holland Publishing Co.	Amsterdam

6

Norton	Norton W. W. & Co.	New York
Nostrand	Van Nostrand Reinhold Company	New York
Oliver	Oliver & Boyd	Edinburgh
Oregon Busn	University of Oregon, Bureau of Business and Economic Research	Eugene, Or.
Oxford U Pr	Oxford University Press	London
P-H	Prentice-Hall Inc	Englewood Cliffs, N.J.
Parker Pub	Parker Publishing Co.	West Nyack, N.Y.
Paul, Trench	K. Paul, Trench, Trubner and Co.	London
Penguin	Penguin Books Ltd	Harmondsworth, England
Pergamon	Pergamon Press Ltd	Oxford
Pitman	Pitman (Sir Isaac) & Sons Ltd	London
Praeger	Praeger Publishers	New York
Presidents	Presidents Publishing House	New York
Princeton U Intl Fin	Princeton University International Finance Section	Princeton, N.J.
Princeton U Pr	Princeton University Press	Princeton, N.J.
Principia Pr	Principia Press Inc.	Granville, Ohio
Pr Law Inst	Practising Law Institute	New York
Profit Sharing	Profit Sharing Research Foundation	Evanston, Ill.
Programmed	Programmed Press	Elmont, N.Y.
Pub Affairs	Public Affairs Press	Washington, D.C.
Putnam	Putnam's, G.P., Sons	New York
Queen Anne	Queen Anne Press Ltd	London
Random	Random House Inc.	New York
Reidel	Reidel, D.	Dordrecht, Holland
RHM	RHM Associates	New York
Ronald	Ronald Press Company	New York
Routledge	Routledge & Kegan Paul Ltd	London
Russell Sage	Russell Sage Foundation	New York
Rutgers U Pr	Rutgers University Press	New Brunswick, N.J.
Simmons—B	Simmons—Boardman	New York
Skinner	Skinner (Thomas) Directories	London
Soc Sci Res	Social Science Research Council	New York

S & P	Standard & Poor's Corp.	New York
S & S	Simon & Schuster Inc.	New York
Stanford U Pr	Stanford University Press	Stanford, Calif.
Staples	Staples Press Ltd	London
St Martin	St Martin's Press, Inc.	New York
Sweet	Sweet & Maxwell Ltd	London
SW Pub	South-Western Publishing Co.	Cincinnati, Ohio
Syracuse U Pr	Syracuse University Press	Syracuse, N.Y.
Taxation	Taxation Publishing Co. Ltd	London
Textbooks	Textbooks Ltd	Harpenden, England
Times	Times Newspapers Ltd	London
Twentieth Fund	Twentieth Century Fund Inc.	New York
Twentieth Press	Twentieth Century Press Inc.	Chicago
UCLA Busn	University of California, Los Angeles, Bureau of Business and Economic Research	Los Angeles, Calif.
U of Cal Pr	University of California Press	Berkeley, Calif.
U of Chicago Pr	University of Chicago Press	Chicago
U of Fla Pr	University of Florida Press	Gainesville, Fla.
U of Ill Bur of Busn	University of Illinois, Bureau of Economics and Business Research	Urbana, Ill.
U of Ill Pr	University of Illinois Press	Urbana, Ill.
U of Ky Pr	University of Kentucky Press	Lexington, Ky.
U of Mich Busn Res	University of Michigan, Graduate School of Business Administration, Bureau of Business Research	Ann Arbor, Mich.
U of Mich Pr	University of Michigan Press	Ann Arbor, Mich.
U of Minn Pr	University of Minnesota Press	Minneapolis, Minn.
U of NC Busn	University of North Carolina, School of Business Administration	Chapel Hill, N.C.
U of Pa Pr	University of Pennsylvania Press	Philadelphia, Pa
U Pr of Va	University Press of Virginia	Charlottesville, Va.
U of Queensland Pr	University of Queensland Press	Brisbane, Australia

8

. Tex Busn	University of Texas, Bureau of Business Research	Austin, Tex.
U of Toronto Pr	University of Toronto Press	Toronto, Canada
U of Wash Pr	University of Washington Press	Seattle, Wash.
U of Wis Busn	University of Wisconsin, School of Commerce, Bureau of Business Research	Madison, Wis.
US Govt	U.S. Government Printing Office	Washington, D.C.
Van N—Rein	Van Nostrand Reinhold Company	New York
Vantage	Vantage Press Inc.	New York
Wadsworth Pub	Wadsworth Publishing Company Inc.	Belmont, Calif.
Wayne St U Pr	Wayne State University Press	Detroit, Mich.
Weidenfeld & N	Weidenfeld (George) & Nicolson Ltd	London
Wiley	Wiley (John) & Sons Inc.	New York
Wilson	Wilson, H.W.	New York
Winston	Winston, The John C., Co.	Philadelphia, Pa.
World Pub	World Publishing Co.	New York
Yale U Pr	Yale University Press	New Haven, Conn.

Guide to Journal Abbreviations

A	Accountancy
ABQR	Amsterdamsche Bank Quarterly Review
AE	Applied Economics
AEP	Australian Economic Papers
AER	American Economic Review
AFR	Appalachian Financial Review
AIGC	Arquito de Instituto Gulbenkian de Cience
AJ	Analysts Journal (see also FAJ)
AJAE	American Journal of Agricultural Economics
AJP	American Journal of Psychology
AJS	Australian Journal of Statistics
AmE	The American Economist
AMJ	Academy of Management Journal
AR	The Accounting Review
AS	Applied Statistics
B	Barron's
Banker	The Banker
BC	Business Conditions, Federal Reserve Bank of Chicago
BE	Business Economics
BellJ	Bell Journal of Economics and Management Science
BellSys	Bell Systems Technical Journal
BEQB	Bank of England Quarterly Bulletin
BH	Business Horizons
BIB	Bank of Israel Bulletin
BL	Business Lawyer
BLJ	The Banking Law Journal
BM	The Bankers' Magazine
BNLQR	Banca Nazionale di Lavoro Quarterly Review
BR	Business Ratios
BS	Behavioral Science
BT	Business Topics (Michigan State University)
CFC	Commercial and Financial Chronicle
CJE	Canadian Journal of Economics
CMR	California Management Review

DBR	District Bank Review
EBR	European Business Review
Ec	Economica
EE	Engineering Economist
EI	Economia Internazionale
EJ	Economic Journal
Em	Econometrica
ER	The Economic Record
ERA	Empirical Research in Accounting: Selected Studies
F	Fortune
FAJ	Financial Analysts Journal (See also AJ)
FE	Financial Executive
Forbes	Forbes
FRIS	Food Research Institute Studies
HBR	Harvard Business Review
HLR	Harvard Law Review
IA	Investment Analyst
IC	Investors' Chronicle and Stock Exchange Gazette
II	Institutional Investor
IJE	Indian Journal of Economics
IMF	Staff Papers, International Monetary Fund
IMR	Industrial Management Review
IntER	International Economic Review
JA	Journal of Accountancy
JAR	Journal of Accounting Research
JASA	American Statistical Association, Journal
JB	Journal of Business
JBF	Journal of Business Finance
JBR	Journal of Bank Research
JEP	Journal of Experimental Psychology
JES	Journal of Economic Studies
JF	Journal of Finance
JFE	Journal of Farm Economics
JFQA	Journal of Financial and Quantitative Analysis
JI	Journal of Insurance
JIA	Journal of the Institute of Actuaries

11

JIASS	Journal of the Institute of Actuaries Students' Society
JIE	Journal of Industrial Economics
JIEng	Journal of Industrial Engineering
JLE	Journal of Law and Economics
JMCB	Journal of Money, Credit and Banking
JMS	Journal of Management Studies
JPE	Journal of Political Economy
JRSS	Royal Statistical Society, Journal
KanBR	Kansas Business Review
Kyk	Kyklos
LBR	Lloyds Bank Review
LCP	Law and Contemporary Problems
LRP	Long Range Planning
MA	Management Accounting
MarqBR	Marquette Business Review
MBA	The Magazine of Bank Administration
MBR	Monthly Business Review, Federal Reserve Bank of Cleveland
Met	Metroeconomica
Mich Law Rev	Michigan Law Review
Moorgate	Moorgate and Wall Street
Mo Rev F R Bk Kansas City	Monthly Review Federal Reserve Bank of Kansas City
Mo Rev F R Bk New York	Monthly Review Federal Reserve Bank of New York
Mo Rev F R Bk San Francisco	Monthly Review Federal Reserve Bank of San Francisco
Mo Rev F R Bk St Louis	Monthly Review Federal Reserve Bank of St Louis
MR	Monthly Review
MS	Manchester School of Economic and Social Studies
MSci	Management Science
MServ	Management Services
MVJBE	Mississippi Valley Journal of Business and Economics
NAA	NAA Bulletin
NBR	National Banking Review
NRLQ	Naval Research Logistics Quarterly
NTJ	National Tax Journal

OEP	Oxford Economic Papers
OIS	Oxford University: Institute of Economics and Statistics Bulletin
OR	Operations Research
ORQ	Operational Research Quarterly
PB	Psychological Bulletin
PF	Public Finance
PNAS	Proceedings National Academy of Science, USA
PSQ	Political Science Quarterly
PUF	Public Utilities Fortnightly
QJE	Quarterly Journal of Economics
QREB	Quarterly Review of Economics and Business
REStat	Review of Economics and Statistics
REStud	Review of Economic Studies
RSE	Review of Social Economy
SAJE	South African Journal of Economics
SAkt	Skandinavisk Aktuarietidskrift
Sc	Science
SEJ	Southern Economic Journal
SJB	Southern Journal of Business
SJE	Swedish Journal of Economics
SJPE	Scottish Journal of Political Economy
ST	Statsøkonomist Tiddskrift
SWSSQ	Southwestern Social Science Quarterly
Taxes	Taxes
TBR	Three Banks Review
TE	Trusts and Estates
U of Chicago Law Rev	University of Chicago Law Review
U of Pa Law Rev	University of Pennsylvania Law Review
UWBR	University of Washington Business Review
WA	Weltswirtschaftliches Archiv
WEJ	Western Economic Journal
Wheat	Wheat Studies of the Food Research Institute
YB	Yorkshire Bulletin of Economic and Social Research
YEE	Yale Economic Essays
YLJ	Yale Law Journal

Guide to Abbreviations of Universities and Colleges

Am U	The American University
Arizona St U	Arizona State University
Boston C	Boston College
Brown U	Brown University
Carnegie IT	Carnegie Institute of Technology (see Carnegie-Mellon U)
Carnegie-Mellon U	Carnegie-Mellon University (see Carnegie IT)
Case IT	Case Institute of Technology (see Case WR U)
Case WR U	Case Western Reserve University (see Case IT)
City U of NY	The City University of New York
Claremont	Claremont Graduate School and University Center
Columbia U	Columbia University
Cornell U	Cornell University
Cranfield IT	Cranfield Institute of Technology
Dartmouth C	Dartmouth College
Duke U	Duke University
Edinburgh U	Edinburgh University
Fla St U	Florida State University
Georgetown U	Georgetown University
Georgia St C	Georgia State College
G Wash U	George Washington University
Harvard Bus	Harvard Business School
Harvard U	Harvard University
Hebrew U	Hebrew University of Jerusalem
Ill IT	Illinois Institute of Technology
Indiana U	Indiana University
Johns Hopkins U	Johns Hopkins University
Kent St U	Kent State University
La St U	Louisiana State University
LSE	London School of Economics
Manchester Bus	Manchester Business School
Man U	Manchester University
Mich St U	Michigan State University

MIT	Massachusetts Institute of Technology
Northwestern U	Northwestern University
N Tex St U	North Texas State University
NYU	New York University
Ohio St U	Ohio State University
Pa St U	Pennsylvania State University
Princeton U	Princeton University
Purdue U	Purdue University
Rensselaer	Rensselaer Polytechnic Institute
Rice U	Rice University
S Methodist U	Southern Methodist University
Stanford U	Stanford University
St Louis U	St Louis University
St U NY Buffalo	State University of New York at Buffalo
Swansea U	Swansea University
UCLA	University of California, Los Angeles
U of Ala	University of Alabama
U of Arizona	University of Arizona
U of Ark	University of Arkansas
U of Aston	University of Aston in Birmingham
U of BC	University of British Columbia
U of Cal Berkeley	University of California, Berkeley
U of Cal Irvine	University of California, Irvine
U of Cal Santa Barbara	University of California, Santa Barbara
U of Chicago	University of Chicago
U of Cincinnati	University of Cincinnati
U of Fla	University of Florida
U of Ga	University of Georgia
U of Ill	University of Illinois
U of Iowa	University of Iowa
U of Ky	University of Kentucky
U of London	University of London
U of Mich	University of Michigan
U of Minn	University of Minnesota
U of Miss	University of Mississippi
U of Mo	University of Missouri

U of NC	University of North Carolina
U of Nebr	University of Nebraska
U of Nottingham	University of Nottingham
U of Ok	University of Oklahoma
U of Oreg	University of Oregon
U of Pa	University of Pennsylvania
U of Pittsburgh	University of Pittsburgh
U of Reading	University of Reading
U of Rochester	University of Rochester
U of Santa Clara	University of Santa Clara
U of S Cal	University of Southern California
U of S Dak	University of South Dakota
U of Tenn	University of Tennessee
U of Tex	University of Texas
U of Wash	University of Washington
U of Wis	University of Wisconsin
Wash St U	Washington State University
Yale U	Yale University

Guide to Other Abbreviations

diss	dissertation
dist	distributed
ed	edition
Ed	Editor
ff	following
jr	junior
ms	manuscript
nd	not dated
no.	number
pseud	pseudonym
qtr	quarter
rev	revised
suppl	supplement
unp	unpublished
vol	volume
wkg paper	working paper

Guide to Subject Headings

Figures in parentheses indicate page numbers in bibliography.

19

22

Part 27. TAXATION

SUBJECT INDEX

In the following pages works are classified according to the subject headings shown on pages 18-24. Within each subject heading works are listed in order of year of publication beginning with the most recent date. Where several works were published in the same year they are listed in alphabetical order of author. As far as possible the publication date for a book is that of the latest revised edition. Undated works are listed at the end of each section.

Part 1 Works of Reference and Anthologies

1a BIBLIOGRAPHIES

This section lists several bibliographies. The Bower & Wippern compilation complements the present collection, being less comprehensive but including short summaries of articles.

Bower, R. S. & Wippern, R. F. (Eds).   Analytical and Quantitative Research in Finance: a Bibliography of Selected Journals, Jan 1962 to Mar 1967. Unp, 1970

Pratt, S. P.   Bibliography on Risks and Rates of Return for Common Stocks. FAJ, 24 (May-Jun, 1968), 151-166

Williamson, J. P.   Selected Bibliography for those Concerned with Administration of College and University Endowment Funds. Unp, Oct 1968

Society of Investment Analysts.   A Bibliography for Investment and Economic Analysis. London: Society of Investment Analysts, 1965

Donaldson, G. & Stubbs, C.   Corporate and Business Finance: a Classified Bibliography. Baker Library, Harvard Bus, 1964

European Federation of Financial Analysts Societies.   A Concise Bibliography for Investment Analysis in Europe. Paris: The Federation, 1963

National Industrial Conference Board.   Bibliography on Diversification and Mergers. Natl Ind Conf Bd, 1962

Masui, M.   Bibliography of Finance. Kobe University of Commerce, 1935

1b BOOKS OF READINGS—GENERAL

We have listed here only general books of readings on corporate finance and investment and have classified more specialised works under the appropriate topic. Comprehensive books of readings on the modern study of investment are exemplified by Fredrikson, Wu & Zakon, Elton & Gruber and Lorie & Brealey. Corresponding collections in the field of corporate finance include Van Horne, Brigham & Ricks, Archer & D'Ambrosio, Ball & Melnyk and the two books by Weston & Woods.

Elton, E. & Gruber, M. J. (Eds).   Security Evaluation and Portfolio Analysis. P-H, 1972

Lorie, J. H. & Brealey, R. A. (Eds).   Modern Developments in Investment Management: a Book of Readings. Praeger, 1972

Szego. G. P. & Shell, K. (Eds).   Mathematical Methods in Investment and Finance. N-Holland, 1972

Brigham, E. F. & Ricks, M. B. (Eds).   Reading in the Essentials of Managerial Finance, 2nd ed. HR & W, 1971

Fredrikson, E. B. (Ed).   Frontiers of Investment Analysis, rev ed. Intext, 1971

Chartered Financial Analysts, Institute of.   C.F.A. Readings in Financial Analysis. Irwin, 1970

Lishan, J. M. & Crary, D. T. (Eds).   The Investment Process. Intext, 1970

Taylor, B. F. (Ed).   Investment Analysis and Portfolio Management: Readings from British Publications. Elek, 1970

Carsberg, B. V. & Edey, H. C. (Eds).   Modern Financial Management: Selected Readings. Penguin, 1969
Archer, S. H. & D'Ambrosio, C. A. (Eds).   The Theory of Business Finance: A Book of Readings. Macmillan, 1967
Ball, R. E. & Melnyk, Z. L. (Eds).   Theory of Managerial Finance: Selected Readings. Allyn, 1967
Chen, H–C (Ed).   Frontiers of Managerial Finance. Gulf Pub, 1967
Hester, D. D. & Tobin, J. (Eds).   Financial Markets and Economic Activity. Wiley, 1967
Hester, D. D. & Tobin, J. (Eds).   Risk Aversion and Portfolio Choice. Wiley, 1967
Hester, D. D. & Tobin, J. (Eds).   Studies of Portfolio Behavior. Wiley, 1967
Weston, J. F. & Woods, D. H. (Eds).   Basic Financial Management: Selected Readings. Wadsworth Pub, 1967
Weston, J. F. & Woods, D. H. (Eds).   Theory of Business Finance: Advanced Readings. Wadsworth Pub, 1967
Van Horne, J. C. (Ed).   Foundations for Financial Management: A Book of Readings. Irwin, 1966
Wolf, H. A. & Richardson, L. (Eds).   Readings in Finance. Appleton, 1966
Ball, R. E. (Ed).   Readings in Investments. Allyn, 1965
Wu, H-K & Zakon, A. J. (Eds).   Elements of Investments: Selected Readings. HR & W, 1965
Mock, E. J. (Ed).   Readings in Financial Management. Intext, 1964
Lerner, E. M. (Ed).   Readings in Financial Analysis and Investment Management. Irwin, 1963
Solomon, E. (Ed).   The Management of Corporate Capital. Free Pr, 1959
Weston, J. F. (Ed).   Readings in Finance from Fortune. HR & W, 1958

1c CASES—GENERAL

This section includes only general books of cases in the fields of corporate finance and investment management. Collections in more limited areas have been classified under the appropriate heading. The Brigham and Butters books are good examples of corporate finance cases. There is a great shortage of recent case books in the portfolio investment field, the nearest approach being the Robichek & Coleman book on institutions.

Committe, T. C.   Managerial Finance for the Seventies. McGraw, 1972
Brigham, E. F.   Cases in Managerial Finance. HR & W, 1970
Butters, J. K. (Ed).   Case Problems in Finance. Irwin, 1969
Bush, R. C. et al.   Case Problems in Financial Management. Appleton, 1968
Hunt, P. & Andrews, V. L.   Financial Management: Cases and Readings. Irwin, 1968
Norgaard, R. L. & Vaughn, D. E.   Cases in Financial Decision Making. P-H, 1967
Robichek, A. A. & Coleman, A. B.   Management of Financial Institutions: Notes and Cases. HR & W, 1967
Fenlon, P. E.   Financial Management Decisions: Case Problems. Allyn, 1964
Howard, B. B. & Jones, S. L. (Eds).   Managerial Problems in Finance: Cases in Decision Making. McGraw, 1964

Mock, E. J.   Short Problems in Business Finance and Financial Management. Intext, 1964

Norgaard, R. L. & Longstreet, J. R.   Cases in Financial Management, 2nd ed. Wadsworth Pub, 1964

Vandell, R. F. & Coleman, A. B.   Case Problems in Finance, 4th ed. Irwin, 1962

Longstreet, J. R.   Cases in Financial Management. Wadsworth Pub, 1961

Masson, R. L. ; Hunt P. & Anthony, R.N.   Cases in Financial Management. Irwin, 1960

Bates, G. E.   Investment Management: a Casebook. McGraw, 1959

Calkins, F. J.   Cases and Problems in Investments. P-H, 1955

Part 2   Securities Markets

2a SECURITIES MARKETS—UK

This section contains publications on the structure of the British securities
markets. Some useful background material is provided in 'Beginners
Please'. Most of the other books are aimed principally at the layman, and
there is a scarcity of good analytical work on the British market. Relevant
books that are listed in subsequent sections are those of Morgan & Thomas,
Hamilton and Briston.

See also:

  3e   Institutions—General
  4a   Investment Management—General
  19c Government Bonds

Thomas, W. A.   Jobbing in the Regional Stock Exchanges. BM, 206 (Aug,
1968), 90-94
Grant, A. T. K.   A Study of the Capital Market in Britain from 1919-1936.
Cass, 1967
Hartley, R.   No Mean City: a Guide to the Economic City of London.
Queen Anne, 1967
Investors Chronicle.   Beginners Please. Eyre & S, 1967
Hobson, O.   How the City Works. Dickens, 1966
Ferris, P.   The City, rev ed. Penguin, 1965
Macrae, N.   The London Capital Market. Staples, 1964
Armstrong, F. E.   The Book of the Stock Exchange, 5th ed. Pitman, 1961
Paukert, F.   The Value of Stock Exchange Transactions in Non-Govern-
ment Securities, 1911-1959. Ec, 28 (Aug, 1961), 303-309
Thomas, W. A.   An Analysis of the Part Played by the Stock Exchange
in the Postwar Financial System. MA Thesis, Swansea U, 1961
Hirst, F. W.   The Stock Exchange: A Short Study of Investment and
Speculation, 4th ed. Oxford U Pr, 1948

2b SECURITIES MARKETS—USA

This section contains a variety of works on the structure of the securities
markets in the USA. A useful background book is Robbins (1966). A vast
amount of more detailed material is provided in the SEC Institutional Investor Report. Many of the more recent articles (e.g. by Jones, Davant,
Farrar and Smidt) are concerned with discussion of the reforms proposed
by the SEC and Martin reports. Finally, the articles by Black and Treynor
(Bagehot) raise some basic questions about criteria for market efficiency
and the extent to which they are satisfied by existing or alternative systems.

See also:

  2e   Securities Markets—Regulation
  3e   Institutions—General
  4a   Investment Management—General
  19c Government Bonds

Feuerstein, D. M.   Toward a National System of Securities Exchanges: The Third and Fourth Markets. FAJ, 28 (Jul-Aug, 1972), 57ff

Freund, W. C.   Issues Confronting the Stock Markets in a Period of Rising Institutionalization. JFQA, 7 (Suppl, Mar, 1972), 1687-1690

Friend, I.   Effect of Institutionalization of Savings on the Long-Term for the Securities Industry. JFQA, 7 (Suppl, Mar, 1972), 1691-1695

Jones, L. D.   Some Contributions of the Institutional Investor Study. JF, 27 (May, 1972), 305-318

Tinic, S. M. E.   The Economics of Liquidity Services. QJE, 86 (Feb, 1972), 79-93.

Tinic, S. M. E. & West, R. R.   Competition and the Pricing of Dealer Service in the Over-the-Counter Market. JFQA, 7 (Jun, 1972), 1707-1728

Wagner, W. H. & Cuneo, L. J.   Stock Trading Costs. Paper for the Seminar on the Analysis of Security Prices, U of Chicago, May 1972

Weedin D. E.   Competition: Key to Market Structure. JFQA, 7 (Suppl, Mar, 1972), 1696-1701

Bagehot, W. (pseud for Treynor, J. L.)   The Only Game in Town. FAJ, 27 (Mar-Apr, 1971), 12ff

Baker, G.   The Martin Report: Blueprint for Constructive Reform. FAJ, 27 (Nov-Dec, 1971), 20 ff

Black, F.   Toward a Fully Automated Stock Exchange.
Part 1: FAJ, 27 (Jul-Aug, 1971), 29-35,
Part 2: FAJ, 27 (Nov-Dec, 1971), 24 ff

Davant, J. W.   The Martin Report: An Answer to the Critics. FAJ, 27 (Nov-Dec, 1971), 14ff

Farrar, D. E.   Wall Street's Proposed 'Great Leap Backward'. FAJ, 27 (Sep-Oct, 1971), 14ff

Fortune.   The Higher Meaning of NASDAQ. F, 83 (Apr, 1971), 141 ff

Martin, W. McC., Jr.   The Securities Markets. A Report with recommendations submitted to the Board of Governors of the New York Stock Exchange, Aug 5, 1971

Maynard, J.   The Most Rapidly Changing Industry of All. FAJ, 27 (Nov-Dec, 1971), 41-47

Schreiner, J.   Graphical Comparisons of Actual and Proposed Brokerage Commission Schedules. FAJ, 27 (Jul-Aug, 1971), 75-84

Securities & Exchange Commission.   Institutional Investor Study Report of the Securities and Exchange Commission. US Govt, 1971

Smidt, S.   Which Road to an Efficient Stock Market? FAJ, 27 (Sep-Oct, 1971), 18ff

West, R. R.   Institutional Trading and the Changing Stock Market. FAJ, 27 (May-Jun, 1971), 17ff

West, R. R. & Tinic, S. M. E.   The Economics of the Stock Market. Praeger, 1971

Dougall, H. E.   Capital Markets and Institutions, 2nd ed. P-H, 1970

Tinic, S. M. E.   The Value of Time Preferences and the Behavior of Liquidity Costs in the New York Stock Exchange. PhD diss, Cornell U, 1970

Heinze, D. C.   Price Spreads on the Over-the-Counter Securities Market. DBA diss, Arizona St U, 1969

Youngblood, C. E.   A Publicly Owned Stock Exchange? FAJ, 25 (Nov-Dec, 1969), 104A-104D

Demsetz, H.   The Cost of Transacting. QJE, 82 (Feb, 1968), 33-53

Studness, C. M.   New York Stock Exchange Trading in Perspective. FAJ, 24 (Nov-Dec, 1968), 26-36

Willett, E. F.　Fundamentals of Securities Markets. Appleton, 1968

Doede, R. W.　The Monopoly Power of the New York Stock Exchange. PhD diss, U of Chicago, 1967

Loll, L. M. & Buckley, J.　Over-the-Counter Securities Markets, 2nd ed. P-H, 1967

Mayer, M.　Wall Street: Men and Money, rev ed. Macmillan, 1966

Robbins, S. M.　The Securities Markets, Operations and Issues. Free Pr, 1966

Baumol, W. J.　Stock Market and Economic Efficiency. Fordham, 1965

Evans, M. D.　Arbitrage in Domestic Securities in the U.S. Parker Pub, 1965

Jennings, R. W.　The New York Stock Exchange and the Commission Rate Struggle. BL, (Nov, 1965), 159-183

Cohen, M. F. & Rabin, J. J.　Broker-Dealer Selling Practice Standards: the Importance of Administrative Adjudication in their Development. LCP, (Jun, 1964), 694-710

Cooke, G. W.　The Stock Markets. Simmons-B, 1964

Malkiel, B. G.　Problems in the Structure of Financial Markets. PhD diss, Princeton U, 1964

Murray, R. F.　Urgent Questions About the Stock Market. HBR, 42 (Sep-Oct, 1964), 53-59

National Bureau of Economic Research.　Research in the Capital Markets. JF, 19 (Suppl, May, 1964) 1-43

Robinson, R. I.　Money and Capital Markets. McGraw, 1964

Wyckoff, P.　Dictionary of Stock Market Terms. P-H, 1964

Leffler, G. L., rev. by Farwell, L. C.　The Stock Market, 3rd ed. Ronald, 1963

Schultz, B. E.　The Securities Market, and How It Works, rev ed. Har-Row, 1963

Securities & Exchange Commission.　Report of the Special Study of the Securities Markets. US Govt, 1963

Axelrad, L. I.　Over-the-Counter Market: Its Organization, Its Problems. FAJ, 18 (Nov-Dec, 1962), 71-73

Cormier, F.　Wall Street's Shady Side. Pub Affairs, 1962

Fuller, J. G.　The Money Changers. Dial, 1962

James, R. & E.　Disputed Role of the Stock Exchange Specialists. HBR, 40 (May-Jun, 1962), 133-146

Ludtke, J. B.　The American Financial System: Markets and Institutions, 2nd ed. Allyn, 1961

Duesenberry, J. S.　Criteria for Judging the Performance of Capital Markets. Commission on Money and Credit Memorandum, April 10, 1960

Robbins, S. M. & Terleckyj, N. E.　Money Metropolis; a Locational Study of Financial Activities in the New York Region. Harvard U Pr, 1960

Friend, I., Hoffman, G. W. & Winn, W. J.　The Over-the-Counter Securities Markets. McGraw, 1958

Walter, J. E.　The Role of Regional Security Exchanges. U of Cal Pr, 1957

Pinney, A.　The Plight of the Stock Exchange. AJ, 10 (Aug, 1954) 99-102

Securities & Exchange Commission.　Stock Trading on the New York Stock Exchange. US Govt, Sep 3 1946

Pecora, F.　Wall Street Under Oath. S & S, 1939

Simpson, K. & Ballinger, W.　The Feasibility and Advisability of the Complete Separation of the Functions of Dealer and Broker. Washington DC: Securities and Exchange Commission, 1936

Twentieth Century Fund.　The Security Markets. Twentieth Fund, 1935

2c SECURITIES MARKETS—OTHER

This section contains a variety of studies of capital markets other than those of the USA and UK. The books by Spray and the Eitemans provide comparative analyses.

Baker, J. C.   The German Stock Market. Praeger, 1970

Basch, A. & Kybal, M.   Capital Markets in Latin America. Praeger, 1970

Ishaq, T.   The Capital Market in Pakistan. PEJ, 2 (Jan, 1969), 102-111

Eiteman, W. J. & S. C.   Nine Leading Stock Exchanges. Michigan International Business Studies No. 12, Graduate School of Business Administration, U of Mich, 1968

Ferris, P.   Men and Money: Financial Europe Today. Hutchinson, 1968

Noritake, Y.   The Japanese Capital Market. BM 205 (May, 1968), 287-291

OECD Committee for Invisible Transactions. Functioning of capital markets. OECD 1968

Misawa, M.   The Historical and Comparative Study of the Post-War Japanese Securities Markets in the Light of Law and Business Practice. PhD diss, U of Mich, 1967

OECD Committee for Invisible Transactions.   Capital Markets Study: Utilisation of Savings. OECD, 1967

Richebächer, K.   Structural Weaknesses of Europe's Capital Markets. Banker, 117 (Dec, 1967), 1048-1055

Rolfe, S. E.   Capital Markets in Atlantic Economic Relationships. The Atlantic Institute, 1967

Amsterdam-Rotterdam Bank & Others.   Capital Markets in Europe: A Study of Markets in Belgium, West Germany, the Netherlands and the UK. The Bank, 1966

Eiteman, D. K.   Stock Exchanges in Latin America. U of Mich Pr, 1966

Palmer, G. F. D.   The Majority and Minority Reports of the Commission of Inquiry into the Stock Exchange. SAJE, 34 (Jun, 1966), 93-112

Sarnat, M.   The Development of the Securities Market in Israel. Kyklos, 1966

Wilson, J. S. G.   Some Aspects of the Development of Capital Markets. BNLQR, 19 (Dec, 1966), 263-310

Eiteman, W. J. & Eiteman, D. K.   Leading World Stock Exchanges: Trading Practices and Organisation. U of Mich Pr, 1964

Federal Reserve Bank of Chicago.   Capital Markets—United States and Europe. Bus Cond F R Bk Chicago (Sep, 1964), 9-16

Spray, D. E. (Ed).   The Principal Stock Exchanges of the World—Their Operation, Structure and Development. Int Econ, 1964

Treasury Department et al.   A Description and Analysis of Certain European Capital Markets, prepared for the Joint Economic Committee by the Treasury Dept and various European consulates. US Govt, 1964

Doodha, K. D.   Stock Exchanges in a Developing Economy. Bombay U Pr, 1962

New York University.   The Capital Market in Japan. New York University, C. J. Devine Institute of Finance, 1962

Manes, P.   The Structure of the Italian Stock Market. BNLQR, 53 (Jun, 1960), 171-208

Walter, J. E. & Williamson, J. P.   Organized Securities Exchanges in Canada. JF, 15 (Sep. 1960), 307-324

Gordon, M. J.   European Stock Exchanges. AJ, 15 (May, 1959), 31-34

OECD Committee for Invisible Transactions. The Supply of Capital Funds for Industrial Development in Europe: Resources, Structure and Methods. OECD, 1957

2d HISTORY OF SECURITIES MARKETS

This section contains a small selection of works on the history of the securities markets. Sobel (1965) and Morgan & Thomas provide general histories. Galbraith and Brooks (1969) offer entertaining but more limited studies.

Morgan, E. V. & Thomas, W. A. The Stock Exchange, Its History and Functions, 2nd ed. Elek, 1970

Brooks, J. Once in Golconda. Har-Row, 1969

Sobel, R. The Great Bull Market: Wall Street in the 1920's. Norton, 1968

Sobel, R. Panic on Wall Street: a History of America's Financial Disasters. Macmillan, 1968

Cowing, C. B. Populists, Plungers and Progressives: a Social History of Stock and Commodity Speculation. Princeton U Pr, 1965

Sobel, R. The Big Board, A History of the New York Stock Market. Free Pr, 1965

Greenleaf, R. W. Forces in the Stock Market 1949-1959. DBA diss, Indiana U, 1961

Brooks, J. The 7 Fat Years: Chronicles of Wall Street. Magee, 1958

Galbraith, J. K. The Great Crash. HM, 1955

Neill, H. B. The Inside Story of the Stock Exchange. Forbes B C, 1950

Mottram, R. H. A History of Financial Speculation. Chatto, 1929

2e SECURITIES MARKETS—REGULATION

This section lists a small selection of works on securities regulation—notably in the USA. Clare's book provides a useful background to regulatory practice.

See also:

2b   Securities Markets—USA
3e   Institutions—General

Gillis, J. G. A Prospectus is a Prospectus. FAJ, 27 (Sep-Oct, 1971), 6ff

Gillis, J. G. The Tippee in Transition. FAJ, 27 (Jan-Feb, 1971), 6-16

West, R. R. Conflicts of Interest: Substance or Subterfuge? FAJ, 27 (Nov-Dec, 1971), 31-39

Clare, R. L., Jr. (Ed). The Law, Disclosure and the Securities Market. Pr Law Inst, 1970

Manne, H. G. (Ed). Economic Policy and the Regulation of Corporate Securities. Am Ent, 1969

Naylor, G. Guide to Shareholders' Rights. Allen, 1969

Singhvi, S. S. Disclosure to Whom? Annual Financial Reports to Stockholders and to the Securities and Exchange Commission. JB, 41 (Jul, 1968), 347-351

Manne, H. G. Insider Trading and the Stock Market. Free Pr, 1966

Sowards, H. L.   Comments, Cases and Materials on Securities Regulation. Dennis, 1966

Mundheim, R. H. (Ed).   Conference on Securities Regulation. Commerce, 1965

Robinson, R. I. & Bartell, R., Jr.   Uneasy Partnership: SEC/NYSE. HBR, 43 (Jan-Feb, 1965), 76-88

Schneider, C. W.   SEC Filings—Their Content and Use. FAJ, 21 (Mar-Apr, 1965), 42-48

Spacek, L.   Are Double Standards Good Enough for Investors But Unacceptable to the Securities Industry? FAJ, 21 (Mar-Apr, 1965), 17 ff

Tyler, P. (Ed).   Securities, Exchanges and the S.E.C. Wilson, 1965

Cary, W. L.   Administrative Agencies and the Securities and Exchange Commission. LCP, 29 (Jun, 1964), 653-662

Cary, W. L.   A Review of the Work of the Securities and Exchange Commission. The Record of the Association of the Bar of the City of New York, (Nov, 1964)

De Bedts, R. F.   The New Deal's S.E.C.: The Formative Years. Columbia U Pr, 1964

Friend, I. & Herman, E. F.   The S.E.C. Through a Glass Darkly. JB, 37 (Oct, 1964), 382-403

Heller, H.   Integration of the Dissemination of Information Under the Securities Act of 1933 and the Securities Act of 1934. LCP, 29 (Jun, 1964), 749-776

Henshaw, R. C., Jr.; Olson, A. C. & O'Donnell, J. L.   The Case for Public Regulation of the Securities Markets. BT, (Autumn, 1964), 69-77

Jennings, R. W.   Self-Regulation in the Securities Industry: The Role of the Securities and Exchange Commission. LCP, 29 (Jun, 1964), 663-690

Knaus, R. L.   A Reappraisal of the Role of Disclosure. Mich Law Rev, (Feb, 1964), 607-648

Robbins, S. M. & Werner, W.   Professor Stigler Revisited. JB, 37 (Oct, 1964), 406-413

Silberman, L.   Critical Examination of S.E.C. Proposals. HBR, 42 (Nov-Dec, 1964), 121-132

Stigler, G. J.   Public Regulation of the Securities Markets. JB, 37 (Apr, 1964), 117-142

Wise, T. A.   Wall Street's Main Event: S.E.C. vs. the Specialist. F, 76 (May, 1964), 149-152

Guthmann, H. G.   The Jenkins Report—English Corporation Law Scrutinized for Reform, *in* Lerner, E. M. (Ed), Readings in Financial Analysis and Investment Management. Irwin, 1963

Rappaport, L. H.   S.E.C. Accounting Practice and Procedure, 3rd ed. Ronald, 1963

Rose, H. B.   Disclosure in Company Accounts (Eaton Paper No. 1). Econ Affairs, 1963

Whitney, J. M., II.   The S.E.C. and the Financial Analyst. FAJ, 19 (Jul-Aug, 1963), 11-16

Black, H.   The Watchdogs of Wall Street. Morrow, 1962

Gies, T. G.   Portfolio Regulations of Selected Financial Intermediaries: Some Proposals for Change. JF, 17 (May, 1962), 302-310

Berman, A.   Regulation of Unlisted Securities; Has Time Come to End the Double Standard? FAJ, 17 (Jul-Aug, 1961), 45-54

Loss, L.   Securities Regulation, Vols. 1-3. Little, 1961

Securities & Exchange Commission.   A 25 Year Summary of the Activities of the Securities and Exchange Commission, 1934-1959. US Govt, 1961

Williamson, J. P.   Securities Regulation in Canada. U of Toronto Pr,
   1960
Choka, A. D.   An Introduction to Securities Regulation. Twentieth Press,
   1958
Bernstein, M. H.   Regulating Business by Independent Commission.
   Princeton U Pr, 1955

2f LISTING

These works are concerned with the impact of listing on securities prices.
The articles by Furst and Van Horne provide a useful introduction. Some
evidence on differences in the properties of listed and unlisted stocks is
provided under subject heading 5a-'Realised Returns on Equities'.

Furst, R. W.   Does Listing Increase the Market Price of Common Stocks?
   JB, 43 (Apr, 1970), 174-180
Van Horne, J. C.   New Listings and their Price Behavior. JF, 25 (Sep,
   1970), 783-794
Furst, R. W.   Does Listing on the Big Board Really Increase Market
   Price? FE, 37 (Apr, 1969)
O'Donnell, J. L.   Case Evidence on the Value of a New York Stock
   Exchange Listing. BT, 17 (Summer, 1969)
Furst, R. W.   An Investigation into the Effect of Listing on the Market
   Price of Common Stocks. DBA diss, U of Wash, 1968
Merjos, A.   Going on the Big Board. B, (May 1, 1967), 9-10
Newbould, G. D.   The Benefits and Costs of a Stock Exchange Quotation.
   BM, 203, (Jun, 1967), 359-365
OTC Information Bureau.   Supplement to Considerations in Listing on a
   Stock Exchange. New York: Arthur Schmidt & Associates, Inc, 1966
Adams, D. F.   The Effect on Stock Price from Listing on the New York
   Stock Exchange. MBA thesis, NYU, 1965
OTC Information Bureau.   Considerations in Listing on a Stock Exchange.
   New York: Arthur Schmidt & Associates Inc, 1965
Forbes.   That Post-Listing Tired Feeling. Forbes, (Nov 1, 1964)
Cobleigh, I. A. & King, H. J.   Difference Between Listed and Over-the-
   Counter Trading. CFC, (Oct 10, 1963), 39 ff
Merjos, A.   Like Money in the Bank: Big Board Listing, the Record
   Suggests, is a Valuable Asset. B, (Jul 8, 1963), 94ff
Merjos, A.   Going on the Big Board: Stocks Act Better Before Listing
   than Right Afterward. B, (Jan 29, 1962), 54ff
New York Stock Exchange.   Comparative Price Performance of New
   1959 and 1960 Listings on the New York Stock Exchange. New York
   Stock Exchange, Department of Research and Statistics, 1962

Part 3 Investment Institutions & the Ownership of Securities

3a OWNERSHIP

This section lists some analyses of share ownership. Discussions of institutional ownership are listed under 3e — 'Institutions—General', and works on private investment behaviour are listed under 3b — 'Personal Investment'. Studies of British shareownership are provided in the surveys by the Stock Exchange and Stone et al. Works on the characteristics of stockholders in the USA are exemplified by Larner, Cox (1963), and the New York Stock Exchange surveys.

Moyle, J. The Pattern of Ordinary Share Ownership 1957-1960. Cambridge U Pr, 1971

Redwood, H. The Fisons Shareholder Survey LRP, 3 (Apr, 1971), 2-6

Berle, A. A. & Means, G. C. The Modern Corporation and Private Property, rev ed. HarBraceJ, 1969

Baker, J. C. Shareownership in Germany. BT, (Winter 1968), 46-52

British Market Bureau Limited. How does Britain Save?—a Summary of the Results of a Survey Conducted for the London Stock Exchange. London: Stock Exchange, 1966

Ladendorf, J. W. The Stockholder Interest: a Study of Over-the-Counter Corporations. PhD diss, Harvard U, 1966

Larner, R. J. Ownership and Control in the 200 Largest Nonfinancial Corporations, 1929 and 1963. AER, 56 (Sep, 1966), 777-787

Stone, R; Revell, J. & Moyle, J. The Ownership of Quoted Ordinary shares—a Survey for 1963. Chapman, 1966

Brown, J. A. The Decade Ahead in Shareownership Research. Proceedings of the Business and Economic Statistics Section, American Statistical Association, 1963

Brown, J. A. Techniques for Measuring Share Ownership. Proceedings of the American Statistical Association, Dec, 1963

Cox, E. B. Trends in the Distribution of Stock Ownership. U of Pa Pr, 1963

Crockett, J. & Friend, I. Characteristics of Stock Ownership. Proceedings of the American Statistical Association, 1963, 146-168

Donaldson, G. Financial Goals: Management vs Stockholders. HBR, 41 (May-Jun, 1963), 116-129

New York Stock Exchange. The 17 Million: 1962 Census of Shareowners in America. The New York Stock Exchange, 1962

Cox, E. B. Changes in the Size Distribution of Dividend Income. JASA, 56 (Jun, 1961), 250-260

Jacobs, D. P. The Marketable Security Portfolios of Non-Financial Corporations, Investment Practices and Trends. JF, 15 (Sep, 1960), 341-352

Kreinin, M. E. Factors Associated with Stock Ownership. REStat, 41 (Feb, 1959), 12-23

Dartmouth Economic Research Council. Broadening the Base of Stock Ownership. Amos Tuck School of Business Administration, Dartmouth C, 1956

Gilbert, L. D. Dividends and Democracy. Am Res Co, 1956

Crum, W. L. Analysis of Stock Ownership. HBR, 31 (May-Jun, 1953), 36-54

Kimmel, L. H.   Share Ownership in the United States; A Study Prepared
at the Request of the New York Stock Exchange. Brookings, 1952

3b PERSONAL INVESTMENT

This section contains some miscellaneous studies on the investment activities of individuals. Other information on the size of individual holdings is
provided under 3a—'Ownership', and a little material on trading activities
is listed under 13b—'Odd-Lot Trading'. Finally section 10k on 'Dynamic
Portfolio Theory' lists studies concerned with the allocation of wealth
between consumption and investment.

Vernon, R. A; Middleton, M. & Harper, D. G.   Who Owns the Blue Chips?
A Study of Shareholding in a Leading Company. Gower, forthcoming
Barrett, R. J; Gray, M. R. & Parkin, J. M.   The Demand for Financial
Assets by the Personal Sector of the U.K. Economy. U of Manchester
mimeo, Jun 1972
Hamburger, M. J.   Household Demand for Financial Assets. Em, 36 (Jan,
1968), 97-118
Nicholson, G. A., Jr., & O'Hara, T. E.   Investment Clubs. FAJ, 24
(May-Jun, 1968), 141-146
Morgan, J; Barlow R. & Brazer, H.   A Survey of Investment Management
and Working Behavior among High-Income Individuals. AER, 55
(May, 1965), 252-264
Naess, R. D.   Changing Patterns of Individual Equity Investment.   FAJ, 20
(Jul, 1964), 74-83
Loomis, C. J.   Fortune's Guide to Personal Investing. McGraw, 1963
Wilson, S. J.   Public Participation in the Stock Market: an Analysis of
Long-Term Market Trends. Fraser, 1962
Atkinson, T. R.   The Pattern of Financial Asset Ownership: Wisconsin
Individuals. (Dist by Princeton U Pr) Natl Bur Econ Res, 1956

3c FLOW OF FUNDS THROUGH THE CAPITAL MARKETS

This section lists several works on the flow of funds through the capital
markets. Goldsmith's analysis of the US market is a useful contribution.

See also:

> 2a   Securities Markets—UK
> 2b   Securities Markets—USA
> 3e   Institutions—General

Hendershott, P. H.   A Flow of Funds Model. JMCB, (1971), 815-832
Stewart, S. S.   An Econometric Model of the Stock Market. PhD diss,
Stanford U, 1970
Cohen, J. B. & L'Esperance, W. L.   An Econometric Analysis of the Flow
of Funds in the Stock Market. Paper delivered at the Econometric
Society meeting, New York, Dec 1965
Goldsmith, R. W.   The Flow of Capital Funds in the Postwar Economy.
(Dist by Columbia U Pr) Natl Bur Econ Res, 1965
Minto, G. S.   The Flow of Funds Through the Capital Market. IA, 9
(Sep, 1964), 11-20

Mayer, R. W.   Analysis of the Flow of Funds Through the Capital Market.
FAJ 17 (Jan, 1961) 71-76

Freund, W. C.   An Appraisal of the Sources and Uses of Funds: Approach
to the Analysis of Financial Markets. JF, 13 (May, 1958), 275-294

3d THEORY OF FINANCIAL INTERMEDIATION

The works in this section, notably those of Pyle, are concerned with explaining the existence of financial intermediaries.

Pyle, D. H.   On the Theory of Financial Intermediation. JF, 26 (Jun, 1971)
737-747

Hakansson, N. H.   An Induced Theory of the Firm Under Risk: The Pure
Mutual Fund. JFQA, 5 (Jun, 1970), 155-178

Pyle, D. H.   On the Theory of Financial Intermediation. PhD diss, MIT,
1968

Michaelsen, J. B., & Goshay, R. C.   Portfolio Selection in Financial Intermediaries: A New Approach. JFQA, 2 (Jun, 1967), 166-199

3e INSTITUTIONS—GENERAL

This section lists some general works on the role of institutions. The
importance of institutions in the USA is illustrated by the studies of
Soldofsky, Safer & Levine, and the SEC. The Bank of England and Leach
provide similar information for the UK. Other evidence on institutional
ownership is listed under 3a — 'Ownership'.

General studies of the nature and role of institutions are exemplified by the
British Radcliffe Report and the works of Sheppard and Clarke. Polakoff
and Goldsmith (1968) provide examples of texts on American institutions.
Other relevant works are listed under the sections on the securities
markets or on specific classes of institution.

See also:

3c   Flow of Funds through the Capital Markets
3d   Theory of Financial Intermediation

Bank of England.   The Financial Institutions.
Part 1: BEQB, 10 (Dec, 1970), 419-431,
Part 2: BEQB, 11 (Mar, 1971), 48-71,
Part 3: BEQB, 11 (Jun, 1971), 199-210

Freund, W. C.   Will Institutional Demands Outrun the Supply of Common
Stock in the '70s? FAJ, 27 (Jul-Aug, 1971), 37-44.

Hunt Commission Report.   The Report of the President's Commission
on Financial Structure and Regulation (The Hunt Commission Report).
Washington, DC: Supt. of Documents, Dec 1971.

Krooss, H. E. & Blyn, M. R.   A History of Financial Intermediaries.
Random, 1971.

Leach, J. H. C.   The Role of Institutions in the UK Ordinary Share Market. IA, 31 (Dec, 1971), 33-35

Securities & Exchange Commission.   Institutional Investor Study Report
of the Securities and Exchange Commission. US Govt, 1971

Sheppard, D. K.   The Growth and Role of U.K. Financial Institutions 1880-1962. Methuen, 1971.

Smith, P. F.   Economics of Financial Institutions and Markets. Irwin, 1971

Soldofsky, R. M.   Institutional Holdings of Common Stock 1900-2000. U of Mich Busn Res, 1971

Baldwin, R.   Conventional Principal and Income Accounting and Its Effect on Institutional Investment Policy. FAJ, 25 (Mar-Apr, 1970), 60-67

Kirkham, P. G.   The Portfolio Behavior of Selected Canadian Financial Intermediaries: An Econometric Analysis. PhD diss, Princeton U. 1970

Polakoff, M. E. et al.   Financial Institutions and Markets. HM, 1970

Safer, A. E. & Levine, J. M.   How Fast Are the Institutions Accumulating Equity Shares? FAJ, 26 (Jul-Aug, 1970), 74-86

Silber, W. L.   Portfolio Behavior of Financial Institutions. HR & W, 1970

Leach, J. H. C.   Institutional Role in United Kingdom Ordinary Share Market. FAJ, 25 (Jul-Aug, 1969), 163-166

Gentry, J. A.   Do Institutional Investors Buy and Sell Common Stocks with Similar Characteristics? QREB, 8 (Winter, 1968), 21-29

Goldsmith, R. W.   Financial Institutions. Random, 1968

Kopp, B. S.   Conglomerates in Portfolio Management. FAJ, 24 (Mar-Apr, 1968), 145-148

Mennis, E. A.   New Trends in Institutional Investing. FAJ, 24 (July-Aug, 1968) 133-138

Schneider, T. H.   The Smaller Institution. FAJ, 24 (Sep-Oct, 1968), 9-11

West, D. A.   The Investor in a Changing Economy. P-H, 1968

Woods, D. H.   Decision-Making in Investment Management Institutions. FAJ, 23 (Jul-Aug, 1967), 73-75

Baum, D. J. & Stiles, N. B.   The Silent Partners—Institutional Investors and Corporate Control. Syracuse U Pr, 1965

Clarke, W. M.   The City in the World Economy. Econ Affairs, 1965

Hayes, D. A.   Institutional Investors and Selection Criteria. FAJ, 21 (Jul, 1965), 86-87

Ketchum, M. D. & Kendall, L. T. (Eds).   Readings in Financial Institutions. HM, 1965

Blease, J. G.   Institutional Investors and the Stock Exchange. DBR, 151 (Sep, 1964), 38-64

Krainer, R. E.   Financial Institutions and the Struggle for Primary Securities. SEJ, 30 (Apr, 1964), 362-376

New York Stock Exchange.   Institutional Shareownership. The New York Stock Exchange. Jun 1964

Seligman, D., & Wise, T. A.   New Forces in the Stock Market. F, 69 (Feb, 1964), 92 ff

Commission on Money & Credit.   Private Financial Institutions: a Series of Research Studies Prepared for the Commission. P-H, 1963

Hanson, W. C.   Capital Sources and Major Investing Institutions. Simmons-B, 1963

Clayton, G.   British Financial Intermediaries in Theory and Practice. EJ, 72 (Dec, 1962), 869-886

Cooke, G. W. et al.   Financial Institutions: Their Role in the American Economy. Simmons-B, 1962

Mayer, T.   Is the Portfolio Control of Financial Institutions Justified? JF, 17 (May, 1962), 311-317

Rozen, M. E.   The Changing Structure of Financial Institutions. QREB, 2 (Nov, 1962), 69-80

Sheppard, D. K.   The Growth and Role of UK Financial Institutions, 1880-
    1962. Methuen, 1962
Lombourne, R. W.   Institutional Investing. FAJ, 17 (Nov-Dec, 1961), 61-70
McDiarmid, F. J.   Investing for a Financial Institution. New York: Life
    Office Management Association Institute, 1961
Robinson, R. I.; Boehmler, E. W.; Gane, F. H. & Farwell, L. C. (Eds).
    Financial Institutions, 3rd ed. Irwin, 1960
Committee on the Working of the Monetary System.   Report Command
    827 (The Radcliffe Report) HMSO, 1959
Goldsmith, R. W.   Financial Intermediaries in the American Economy
    Since 1900. Princeton U Pr, 1958
Murray, R. F.   Institutional Influences on the Stock Market. AJ, 14 (May,
    1958), 15-16
Neenan, W. B.   Review of Institutional Activity in the Equity Market,
    1951-54. JF, 12 (Dec, 1957), 468-488
Sprowls, J. S.   Short Term Investment Practices of Large Non-Financial
    Corporations. Masters thesis, U of Pittsburgh, 1953
Schmidt, C. H. & Stockwell, E. J.   The Changing Importance of Institutional
    Investors in the American Capital Markets. LCP, 17 (Winter, 1952),
    3-25
Prochnow, H. V. (Ed).   American Financial Institutions. P-H, 1951
Menippus (Pseud)   Some Self-Criticism of Institutional Investing. AJ, 6
    (4th Qtr, 1950) 29-31
Maine, R. F.   My Attitude Toward Institutional Investment Attitudes.
    AJ, 4 (Suppl, 2nd Qtr, 1948), 31-36

3f BANKS

This section lists a variety of publications on the banking industry, with
particular emphasis on investment activities. Works on bank asset portfolio models are listed under a separate section, 10g—'Models for the
Selection of Bank Assets'. Basic general works on banking are exemplified by Sayers (1967) and Dacey for the UK, and by Prather and Fischer
for the USA. Beckhart and Crick provide comparative analyses. Cohen &
Hammer, and Wolf & Doenges have compiled useful books of readings.

See also:

3e Institutions—General

Aigner, D. J. & Bryan, W. R.   A Model of Short-Run Bank Behavior.
    QJE, 85 (Feb, 1971), 97-118
Gies, T. G. & Apilado, V. P. (Eds).   Banking Markets and Financial Institu-
    tions. Irwin, 1971
Renwick, F. B. et al.   Portfolio Management for Commercial Banks.
    Presidents, 1971
Watson, R. D.   Tests of Maturity Structures for Commercial Bank Securi-
    ties Portfolios—a Simulation Approach. DBA diss, Indiana U, 1971
Larkin, E. L., Jr.   Accounting for the Realities of Bank Portfolio Manage-
    ment. New York: Haskins & Sells, Feb 1970
Melnik, A.   Short Run Determinants of Commercial Bank Investment
    Portfolios: An Empirical Analysis. JF, 25 (Jun, 1970), 639-649
Nevin, E. & Davis, E. W.   The London Clearing Banks. Elek, 1970

Reed, E. W. & Woodland, D. L.   Cases in Commercial Banking. Appleton, 1970

Emery, J. T.   Risk, Return and the Competitive Structure of Commercial Banking. DBA diss, U of Wash, 1969

Prather, C. L.   Money and Banking, 9th ed. Irwin, 1969

Wolf, C. R.   A Model for Selecting Commercial Bank Government Security Portfolios. REStat, 51 (Feb, 1969), 40-52

Fischer, G. C.   American Banking Structure. Columbia U Pr, 1968

Neveu, R. P.   Constraints on the Risk Behavior of Commercial Banks. PhD diss, U of Pittsburgh, 1968

Whittlesey, C. R., & Wilson, J. S. G. (Eds).   Essays in Money and Banking, in honour of R. S. Sayers. Oxford U Pr, 1968

Wolf, H. A. & Doenges, R. C. (Eds).   Readings in Money and Banking. Appleton, 1968

Bryan, W. R. & Carleton, W. T.   Short-Run Adjustments of an Individual Bank. Em, 35 (Apr, 1967), 321-347

Guttentag, J. M. & Herman, E. S.   Banking Structure and Performance. NYU, 1967

Ruffin, R. J.   Free Reserves, Vault Cash, and the Portfolio Behavior of Banks. JPE, 75 (Dec, 1967), 889-892

Sayers, R. S.   Modern Banking. Oxford U Pr, 1967

Scott, R. H.   A Conditional Theory of Banking Enterprise, *in* Pontecorvo, G. et al (Eds), Issues in Banking and Monetary Analysis. HR & W, 1967

Thomson, T. D.   The Demand of Commercial Banks for Cash Assets: a Cross Sectional Analysis. PhD diss, U of Chicago, 1967

Cohen, K. J. & Hammer, F. S. (Eds).   Analytical Methods in Banking. Irwin, 1966

Cotter, R. V.   Capital Adequacy and Commercial Bank Failures. PhD diss, U of Oreg, 1966

Frazer, W. J. & Yohe, W. P.   Introduction to the Analytics and Institutions of Money and Banking. Van N-Rein, 1966

Hahn, P. J.   The Capital Adequacy of Commercial Banks. Am Pr, 1966

Hester, D. D. & Zoellner, J. F.   The Relation Between Bank Portfolios and Earnings: an Econometric Analysis. REStat, 48 (Nov, 1966), 372-386

Morrison, G. R.   Liquidity Preference of Commercial Banks. U of Chicago Pr, 1966

Wasson, H. C.   Some Investment Policies for Commercial Banks. FAJ, 22 (May-Jun, 1966), 83-91

Crick, W. F. (Ed).   Commonwealth Banking Systems. Oxford U Pr, 1965

Meigs, J. A.   The Changing Role of Banks in the Market for Equities. JF, 20 (May, 1965), 368-378

Wolf, C. R.   The Management of Commercial Bank Government Bond Portfolios. PhD diss, Harvard U, 1965

Beckhart, B. H. (Ed).   Banking Systems: a Definitive Comparison and Authoritative Account of the Banking Systems of Sixteen Countries. Columbia U Pr, 1964

Dacey, W. M.   The British Banking Mechanism. Hutchinson, 1964

Russell, W. R.   Commercial Bank Portfolio Adjustments. AER, 56 (May, 1964), 547-550

Russell, W. R.   Commercial Bank Portfolio Adjustments. PhD diss, U of Washington, 1964

Silverberg, S.   Bank Trust Investments: Their Size and Significance. NBR, (Jun, 1964), 577-598

Galbraith, J. A.   The Economics of Banking Operations: a Canadian Study.
    McGill-Queens U Pr, 1963
Hodgman, D. R.   Commercial Bank Loan and Investment Policy. U of Ill
    Pr, 1963
Reed, E. W.   Commercial Bank Management. Har-Row, 1963
Williams, C. M.   Senior Securities—Boon for Banks. HBR, 41 (Jul-Aug,
    1963), 82-94
American Bankers Association.   The Commercial Banking Industry: a
    Monograph Prepared for the Commission on Money and Credit. P-H,
    1962
Crosse, H. D.   Management Policies for Commercial Banks. P-H, 1962
Luckett, D. G.   Compensatory Cyclical Bank Asset Adjustments. JF, 17
    (Mar, 1962), 53-62
Munn, G. G.   Encyclopedia of Banking and Finance, 6th ed. Bankers, 1962
Robinson, R. I.   The Management of Bank Funds, 2nd ed. McGraw, 1962
Sayers, R. S. (Ed).   Banking in Western Europe. Oxford U Pr, 1962
Bogen, J. I.   The Changing Composition of Bank Assets. Graduate School
    of Business Administration, NYU, 1961
Edwards, W.   Study of the Management of Investment and Loan Portfolios
    of Selected Commercial Banks. DBA diss, Harvard Bus, 1961
Lyon, R. A.   Investment Portfolio Management in the Commercial Bank.
    Rutgers U Pr, 1961
Federal Reserve Bank of Kansas City.   Bank Reactions to Security Losses.
    Mo Rev F R Bk Kansas City, (Jun, 1960)
Federal Reserve Bank of Kansas City.   Commercial Bank Investments in
    Recession and Expansion. Mo Rev F R Bk Kansas City, (Mar, 1959)
Goldsmith, R. W. & Shapiro, E.   An Estimate of Bank-Administered Per-
    sonal Trust Funds. JF, 14 (Mar, 1959), 11-17
Parks, R. H.   Portfolio Operations of Commercial Banks and the Level
    of Treasury Security Prices. JF, 14 (Mar, 1959), 52-66
Parks, R. H.   Income and Tax Aspects of Commercial Bank Portfolio
    Operations in Treasury Securities. NTJ, 11 (Mar, 1958), 21-34
Scott, I. O.   The Changing Significance of Treasury Bill Obligations in
    Commercial Bank Portfolios. JF, 12 (May, 1957), 213-222
McEvoy, R. H.   Variation in Bank Asset Portfolios. JF, 11 (Dec, 1956),
    463-473
Coleman, G. W.   Lending and Investment Practices of Commercial Banks.
    LCP, 17 (Winter, 1952), 108-127
Hunt, P.   Portfolio Policies of Commercial Banks in the United States
    1920-1939. Harvard Busn, 1940

3g MERCHANT BANKS

Sandra Mason's article provides a useful introduction to the role of the
merchant banker.

    See also:

        3e Institutions—General

Mason, S.   Merchant Banking Today and in the Future. JBF, 3 (Winter,
    1971), 4-28
Kellett, R.   The Merchant Banking Arena. Macmillan Int, 1967
Wechsberg, J.   The Merchant Bankers. Weidenfeld & N, 1967

Young, G. K. Merchant Banking: Practice and Prospects. Weidenfeld & N, 1966

3h INSURANCE COMPANIES

Studies of the institutional role of insurance companies in the UK and USA are exemplified by Clayton and Brimmer. A general discussion of the investment policies of British insurance firms is provided by Clayton & Osborn and the Jones and Walter books perform a similar function for the USA.

See also:

3e Institutions—General

Chartered Financial Analysts, Institute of. Property and Liability Insurance Investment Management. Irwin, 1971

Clayton, G. British Insurance. Elek, 1971

Schlarbaum, G. G. The Investment Performance of Stock Property—Liability Insurance Companies: 1948-1967. PhD diss, U of Pa, 1971

Haugen, R. A. & Kroncke, C. A Portfolio Approach to Optimizing the Structure of Assets and Claims of a Stock Insurance Company. JRI, 37 (Mar, 1970), 41-48

Jackson, D. F. The Variable Annuity and Its Investment Performance. PhD diss, U of Tex, 1968

Jones, L. D. Investment Policies of Life Insurance Companies. Harvard Busn, 1968

Leverett, E. J., Jr. A Simulation of the Financial Operations of a Life Insurance Company under Various Operating Assumptions with Special Emphasis on Solvency and Paid-in Surplus and Capital. DBA diss, Indiana U, 1967

Gentry, J. A. An Analysis of the Characteristics of the Common Stocks Purchased and Sold by Six Life Insurance Companies and Six Balanced Investment Companies in 1963 and 1964. DBA diss, Indiana U, 1966

Schutt, L. D. Investment Policy and Portfolio Considerations for a Mutual Life Insurance Company. FAJ, 22 (Mar-Apr, 1966), 105-112

Barton, C. E. Equity Investment and Participating Life Assurance. JIASS, 17 (Jul, 1965)

Clayton, G. & Osborn, W. T. Insurance Company Investment, Principles and Policy. Allen, 1965

Hart, O. H. Life Insurance Companies and the Equity Capital Markets. JF, 20 (May, 1965), 358-367

Ferrari, J. R. Quantitative Decision-Making for Life Insurance Company Investments: Possibilities and Limitations. PhD diss, U of Pa, 1964

Wherry, R. H. & Newman, M. Insurance and Risk. HR & W, 1964

Federal Reserve Bank of Cleveland. Investment Patterns of Fire and Casualty Insurance Companies. MBR, (May, 1963)

Bailey, W. G. Some Points on Equity-Linked Contracts. JIA, 88 (1962)

Brimmer, A. F. Life Insurance Companies in the Capital Markets. Mich St U Busn, 1962

Fraine, H. G. Valuation of Securities Holdings of Life Insurance Companies. Irwin, 1962

Life Insurance Association of America. Life Insurance Companies as Financial Institutions. P-H, 1962

Rejda, G. E.   Dollar Averaging and Other Formula Plans: Their Role in the Investment Operations of Insurance Companies. PhD diss, U of Pa, 1962

Rejda, G. E.   The Role of Dollar Averaging in the Common Stock Investment Operations of Life Insurance Companies. JI, (Dec, 1962)

Walter, J. E.   The Investment Process, as Characterized by Leading Life Insurance Companies. Harvard Busn, 1962

Davis, S. C.   How US Fire and Casualty Companies Invest. FAJ, 17 (Nov-Dec, 1961), 19-24

Wehrle, L. S.   Life Insurance Investment: the Experiences of Four Companies. YEE, 1 (Spring, 1961), 70-136

Wright, K. M.   Gross Flows of Funds through Life Insurance Companies. JF, 15 (May, 1960), 140-156

Fricke, C. V.   The Variable Annuity: its Impact on the Savings-Investment Market. U of Mich Pr, 1959

Federal Reserve Bank of New York.   Life Insurance Companies in the Postwar Capital Markets. Mo Rev F R Bk New York, (Sep, 1958)

Wehrle, L. S.   A Theory of Life Insurance Portfolio Selection. Cowles Foundation Discussion Paper No. 60, Dec 1958

Blunt, R. H. & Lane, L. H.   Variable Annuities. JIASS, 14 (Jul, 1957)

Brimmer, A. F.   Some Studies in Monetary Policy, Interest Rates and the Investment Behavior of Life Insurance Companies. DBA diss, Harvard Bus, 1956

Torrance, G.   Investing Life Insurance Funds. AJ, 11 (Feb, 1955), 45-48

Patrick, R. B.   The Life Insurance Company Portfolio. AJ, 10 (Jun, 1954), 54-57

McCahan, D. (Ed).   Investment of Life Insurance Funds. Irwin, 1953

Federal Reserve Bank of New York.   Life Insurance Companies and the Security Markets.
Part 1: Mo Rev FR Bk New York (Mar, 1952),
Part 2: Mo Rev FR Bk New York (Apr, 1952)

Davis, S. C.   Investments in Common Stocks by Life Insurance Companies. AJ, 1 (Jul, 1945), 3-13

McDiarmid, F. J.   Some Broader Aspects of the Insurance Investment Problem. AJ, 1 (3rd Qtr, 1945), 39-48

3i   PENSION FUNDS

This section contains studies of the role and management of pension funds. We have excluded works that are concerned principally with the design of pension plans. Analyses of fund performance that are largely concerned with measurement technique are listed under 14b—'Performance Measurement—Pension Funds'. The studies by Holland and Polakoff provide some basic background material. Important questions on possible conflicts in objectives are raised by Treynor speaking with the voice of Walter Bagehot.

See also:

3e   Institutions—General

Bagehot, W. (pseud for Treynor, J. L.)   Risk and Reward in Corporate Pension Funds. FAJ, 28 (Jan-Feb, 1972), 80-84

O'Brien, J. & Tito, D.   The Implications of Pension Fund Investment Policy. Paper for the Seminar on the Analysis of Security Prices, U of Chicago, Nov 1972

Voorheis, F. L.   Bank Trustees and Pension Performance. FAJ, 28 (Jul-Aug, 1972), 60-64

Gumperz, J.   Pension Funds in an Age of Discontinuity. FAJ, 26 (Nov-Dec, 1970), 20ff

Schoeplein, R. N.   The Effect of Pension Plans on Other Retirement Saving. JF, 25 (Jun, 1970), 633-638

Beier, E.   An Analysis of Pension Plan Management and Its Public Policy Implications. PhD diss, U of Wis, 1969

Chartered Financial Analysts, Institute of. Pension Fund Investment Management. Irwin, 1969

Innocenti, R. E.   The Stock-Bond Split Decision for Pension Funds. FAJ, 25 (Nov-Dec, 1969), 97-101

Keeley, R. H.   Pension Plan Decisions and Corporate Financial Policy. PhD diss, Stanford U, 1969

Larson, R. C.   Self-Administered Pension Funds and Performance. FAJ, 25 (Jul-Aug, 1969) 135-137

Gibb, W. T.   Critical Evaluation of Pension Plans. JF, 23 (May, 1968), 337-343

Hewitt Associates.   1968 Report on the Investment Performance of Retirement Funds. Chicago: The Associates, 1968

Mennis, E. A.   Investment Policy for a Growing Pension Fund. FAJ, 24 (Mar-Apr, 1968), 122-131

Murray, R. F.   Economic Aspects of Pensions: A Summary Report. (Dist. by Columbia U Pr) Natl Bur Econ Res, 1968

Murray, R. F.   Pension Funds in the American Economy. JF, 23 (May, 1968), 331-336

Welles, C.   The Unions: $ 4 Billion Goes to Work. II, 2 (Jun, 1968)

Antliff, J. C. & Freund, W. C.   Some Basic Research Into Historical Results Under Pension Plans with Benefits Based on Common Stock Performance. JF, 22 (May, 1967), 169-191

Rogers, A. Y.   Management of Trusteed Pension Funds; Review of Fiduciary Responsibility. TE, (Mar, 1967)

Root, C. D., Jr.   Importance of Investment Yield (in Pension and Profit-Sharing Plans). TE (Jul, 1967)

Rose, P. J.   Some Aspects of Private Pension Funds and the Capital Market. ER, 43 (Sep, 1967), 354-370

Wrightsman, D.   Pension Funds and Economic Concentration. QREB, 7 (Winter, 1967), 29-36

Holland, D. M.   Private Pension Funds: Projected Growth. (Dist by Columbia U Pr) Natl Bur Econ Res, 1966

Polakoff, M. E.   Public Pension Funds. FAJ, 22 (May-Jun, 1966), 75-81

Trowbridge, C. L.   ABC's of Pension Funding. HBR, 44 (Mar-Apr, 1966), 115-126

Voorheis, F. L.   Investment Policy and Performance of Bank Administered Pooled Equity Funds for Employee Benefit Plans. PhD diss, Mich St U, 1966

Cagan, P.   Effect of Pension Plans on Aggregate Saving. Evidence from a Sample Survey. (Dist by Columbia U Pr) Natl Bur Econ Res, 1965

Nursaw, W. G.   Principles of Pension Fund Investment. Hutchinson, 1965

Sieff, J. A.   Construction of a Retirement Fund Portfolio. FAJ, 21 (Jul-Aug, 1965), 89-94

Bernstein, M. C.   The Future of Private Pensions. Free Pr, 1964

Cramer, J. J., Jr.   Accounting and Reporting Requirements of the Private Pension Trust. DBA diss, Indiana U, 1964

Mundheim, R. H. & Henderson, G. D. Applicability of the Federal Securities Laws to Pension and Profit Sharing Plans. LCP, 29 (Jun, 1964), 795-841

Anderson, W. M. Group Accumulation Through Equities for Pensions. JF, 17 (May, 1962), 194-202

McGill, D. M. Fulfilling Pension Expectations. Irwin, 1962

Andrews, V. L. The Supply of Loanable Funds from Non-Insured Corporate State-, and City-Administered Employee Pension Funds. JF, 16 (May, 1961), 328-350

Miller, E. Trends in Private Pension Funds. JF, 16 (May, 1961), 313-327

Andrews, V. L. Pension Funds in the Securities Markets. HBR, 37 (Nov-Dec, 1959), 90-102

Harbrecht, P. P. Pension Funds and Economic Power. Twentieth Fund, 1959

Howell, P. L. Common Stocks and Pension Fund Investing. HBR, 36 (Nov-Dec, 1958), 92-106

Howell, P. L. A Re-examination of Pension Fund Investment Policies. JF, 13 (May, 1958), 261-274

Steinhaus, H. W. The Effect of Pension Fund Investments on Common Stock Funds. AJ, 14 (Feb, 1958), 63-64

Greeley, R. E. What Are the Investment Objectives of Private Pension Plans? AJ, 13 (Nov, 1957), 75-76

Wren, P. I. The Pension Fund Portfolio. AJ, 10 (Jun, 1954), 58-59

3j ENDOWMENT AND TRUST FUNDS

Useful background material to the investment of endowment funds is provided by Nelson's book. The Ford Foundation Report constitutes an interesting discussion of the issues confronting the manager of such funds. A number of works in this section are concerned with the design of appropriate spending policies for endowments. The studies by K. Jensen and Meckling & M. Jensen are well worth reading.

See also:

3e Institutions—General

Harris (Louis) & Associates. Managing Endowment Funds. New York: Louis Harris & Associates, 1972

Institutional Investor. Can Our Non-Profit Institutions be Saved?—Special Issue. II, 6 (Aug, 1972), 33 ff.

Davidson H. A. College Endowment Fund Management. FAJ, 27 (Jan-Feb, 1971), 69-74

Sims, E. C. A Critical Analysis of Yields and Rates of Return Received from the Investment of Educational Endowments. PhD diss, U of Mo, 1971

Meckling, W. H. & Jensen, M. C. University Endowments and Spending Policies. U of Rochester, Jan 1970

Advisory Committee on Endowment Management. Managing Educational Endowments: Report to the Ford Foundation. Ford, 1969

Cary, W. L. & Bright, C. B. The Law and the Lore of Endowment Funds. Ford, 1969

Endowment Conference. Managing Endowment Capital. New York: Donaldson, Lufkin & Jenrette, Inc, 1969

Malkiel, B. G. et al.   The Definition of Endowment Income. Report of a special faculty-administrative committee, Princeton U, unp 1969

Meck, J. F.   A New Investment Concept: Total Returns. Dartmouth Alumni Magazine, (Jul, 1969)

Bowen, W. G.   The Economics of Major Universities. Berkeley, Cal: Carnegie Commission on Higher Education, 1968

Chartered Financial Analysts, Institute of.   Personal Trust Investment Management. Proceedings, C.F.A. Research Seminar, May 4-6, 1967, Charlottesville, Va. Irwin, 1968

Dreze, J. H.   Endowment Income, Risk Preference and the Cost of Capital in Non-Profit Institutions. Unp ms, Apr 1968

Jensen, K. R.   A Critical Analysis of Measures of Income for the Endowment Funds of Universities and Colleges Invested in Common Stock: their Empirical Utility and Accounting Acceptability. Unp ms, Mar 1968

Nelson, R. L.   The Investment Policies of Foundations. Russell Sage, 1967

Welles, C.   University Endowments: Revolution Comes to the Ivory Tower. II, (Sep, 1967)

Freeman, R. A.   Crisis in College Finance? Washington, DC: Institute for Social Science Research, 1965

Boylan, W. A.   Endowment Funds-Collision of Corporate and Trust Standards. BL, 18 (Apr, 1963), 807-818

Duncan, R. R.   The Trustee's Dilemma in Growth Stock Investing. CFC, (Jun 29, 1961)

Buek, C. W.   Managing Our Trusts as Prudent Men Would Do. CFC, (Mar 3, 1960)

Elsom, H. B.   The Law of Trust Investment. FAJ, 16 (Jul-Aug, 1960), 27-33

Jehring, J. J.   The Investment and Administration of Profit Sharing Trust Funds: A Research Study of 208 Profit Sharing Trust Funds. Profit Sharing, 1957

Hall, L. W.   Security Analysis from the Point of View of a Trust Company. AJ, 9 (May, 1953), 123-124

3k UNIT TRUSTS, MUTUAL FUNDS AND CLOSED-END FUNDS

Useful background reading, particularly to the British unit trust industry, is provided by Burton & Corner. The 1962 SEC Study and the book by Friend, Blume & Crockett are important sources of information on the American industry. Empirical studies of mutual fund performance are listed principally under 14a - 'Performance Measurement—General'.

See also:

3e   Institutions—General

Levy, H. & Sarnat, M.   Investment Performance in an Imperfect Securities Market and the Case for Mutual Funds. FAJ, 28 (Mar-Apr, 1972), 77-81

Simonson, D. G.   The Speculative Behavior of Mutual Funds. JF, 27 (May, 1972), 381-391

Lehane, J. F.   Comparative Analyses of the Underlying Characteristics for Risk-Performance Measures of No-Load Mutual Funds in the 1950-1969 Period. PhD diss, U of Santa Clara, 1971

Chartered Financial Analysts, Institute of. Investment Company Portfolio Management. Irwin, 1970

Fleming, M. The Investment Trust Company. JBF, 2 (Spring, 1970), 42-45

Friend, I; Blume, M. & Crockett, J. Mutual Funds and Other Institutional Investors. McGraw, 1970

Spitz, A. E. Mutual Fund Performance and Cash Inflows. AE, 2 (Aug, 1970), 141-145

Carlson, R. S. & Campanella, F. B. No Load Mutual Funds—a Serendipity to Date. Harvard Bus, Jan, 1969

Spitz, A. E. Some Determinants of Investing in Load or No-Load Mutual Funds: A Statistical Analysis. PhD diss, U of Ky, 1969

Burton, H, & Corner, D. C. Investment and Unit Trusts in Britain and America. Elek, 1968

Friend, I. The Effect of Mutual Funds on Market Performance. Paper for the Seminar on the Analysis of Security Prices, U of Chicago, May 1968

Allerdice, F. B. & Farrar, D. E. Factors that Affect Mutual Fund Growth. JFQA, 2 (Dec, 1967), 365-382

Baum, D. J. Should the Size of Mutual Funds Be Limited? II, 1 (Apr, 1967)

Greeley, R. E. What's Happening to Mutual Fund Management Companies? FAJ, 23 (Sep-Oct, 1967), 75-82

Investment Company Institute. The Money Managers: Professional Investment Through Mutual Funds. McGraw, 1967

Little, A. D., Inc. Studies of the Mutual Fund Industry. Report to the Investment Company Institute, Jun, 1967

Straley, J. A. What About Mutual Funds? Har-Row, 1967

Birmingham, J. M., Jr. The Quest for Performance (Keynote Review). FAJ 22 (Sep-Oct, 1966), 93-94

Federal Bar Association. Conference on Mutual Funds, San Francisco, California, Mar 1966. Federal Bar Association, 1966

Gentry, J. A. An Analysis of the Characteristics of the Common Stocks Purchased and Sold by Six Life Insurance Companies and Six Balanced Investment Companies in 1963 and 1964. DBA diss, Indiana U, 1966

Meyerholz, J. C. Competition and Investment Management. FAJ, 22 (Jan-Feb, 1966), 97-105

Perez, R. C. A Critical Appraisal of the Marketing Structure and Techniques Used in Distributing Mutual Fund Shares to the Investing Public. PhD diss, NYU, 1966

Securities & Exchange Commission. Public Policy Implications of Investment Company Growth. US Govt, 1966

Merriman, C. O. H. Mutual Funds and Unit Trusts; a Global View. Pitman, 1965

Qureshi, M. A. Mutuality as a Factor in the Growth of the Mutual Fund Industry. PhD diss, U of S Cal, 1965

Richardson, D. Investment Companies Throughout the Free World. FAJ, 21 (Jan-Feb, 1965), 90-91

Fischer, G. C. & Minet, L. J. No-Load Mutual Funds. FAJ, 20 (Jan, 1964), 64-68

Jaretzki, A., Jr. Duties and Responsibilities of Directors of Mutual Funds. LCP, 29 (Jun, 1964), 777-794

Stutchbury, O. P. The Management of Unit Trusts. Skinner, 1964

Brown, E. E. & Vickers, D. Mutual Funds Portfolio Activity, Performance and Market Impact. JF, 18(May, 1963), 377-391

Herman, E.S.   Mutual Fund Management Fee Rates. JF, 18(May, 1963), 360-376

Palance, D.   Mutual Funds—Legal Pickpockets? Vantage, 1963

Smith, R.L.   The Grim Truth about Mutual Funds. Putnam, 1963

Crysler, E.W, Jr.   Growth of the Mutual Fund Industry. FAJ, 18(Jan, 1962), 31-38

Gilbert, J.C.   British Investment and Unit Trusts Since the War. YB, 14 (May, 1962), 3-13

Investment Company Institute.   Management Investment Companies. P-H, 1962

Securities & Exchange Commission.   Study of Mutual Funds Prepared for the Securities and Exchange Commission by the Wharton School of Finance and Commerce. House Report No 2274. US Govt, 1962

Armstrong, J.B.   The Case for Mutual Fund Management. FAJ, 16(May 1960), 33-38

Renshaw, E.F. & Feldstein, P.J.   The Case for an Unmanaged Investment Company. FAJ, 16 (Jan-Feb, 1960), 43-46

Bullock, H.   The Story of Investment Companies. Columbia U Pr, 1959

Pierce, S.   Mutual Funds — a Growth Business. AJ, 7(4th Qtr, 1951), 23-25

Carter, W.D.   Quality of Mutual Fund Portfolio Supervision. AJ, 6 (4th Qtr, 1950), 32-36

31 HEDGE FUNDS

Little has been published on the role of hedge funds. The reader is referred particularly to the SEC Institutional Investor Report listed elsewhere.

See also:

> 3e Institutions—General

Fortune.   Hedge-Fund Miseries. F, 83(May 1971), 269 ff.

Loomis, C.J.   Hard Times Come to the Hedge Funds. F, 81 (Jan, 1970), 100 ff.

Sosnoff, M.T.   Hedge Fund Management. FAJ, 22(Jul-Aug, 1966), 105-108

3m SPLIT TRUSTS AND DUAL FUNDS

The works in this section are predominantly concerned with the valuation of British split trusts or the equivalent American dual funds.

See also:

> 3e Institutions—General
> 3k Unit Trusts, Mutual Funds and Closed-End Funds

Brew, J.M.   The Analysis of Split Trusts. IA, 25(Dec, 1969), 14-20

Gentry, J.A. & Pike, J.R.   Dual Funds Revisited. FAJ, 24(Mar-Apr, 1968), 149-157

Johnston, G.S.; Curley, M.L. & McIndoe, R.A.   Dual Purpose Funds Undervalued? FAJ, 24(Nov-Dec, 1968), 157-164

Netter, J., II.   Dual-Purpose Funds. FAJ, 23, (Jul-Aug, 1967), 85-87

Shelton, J.P.; Brigham, E.F. & Hofflander, A.E. Jr.   Dual Funds. FAJ, 23 (May-Jun 1967), 131-139

Part 4   Investment Management

4a   INVESTMENT MANAGEMENT—GENERAL

This section contains a sample of general articles and textbooks on investment management. Important examples of the latter are the works of Graham & Dodd and of Cohen & Zinbarg, which survey both the workings of the American securities markets and propose some general principles of investment management. The books by Briston and Weaver seek to provide similar studies for the British market. Ellis's book offers an interesting discussion of investment strategy as seen by an institutional investor.

See also:

4b   Quantitative Texts on Investment Management

Block, F. E.   Time Horizon. FAJ, 28(Sep-Oct, 1972), 30ff
Bolten, S.   Security Analysis and Portfolio Management. HR & W, 1972
Stern, W. P. & Norby, W. C.   Investment Research and Market Structure—Today and Tomorrow. FAJ, 28(Jan-Feb, 1972), 24ff
Briston, R. J.   The Stock Exchange and Investment Analysis. Allen, 1971
Ellis, C. D.   Institutional Investing. Dow Jones-Irwin, 1971
Ellis, C. D.   Portfolio Operations. FAJ, 27 (Sep-Oct, 1971), 36-46
Loeb, G. M.   Battle for Stock Market Profits. S&S, 1971
Mason, S.   Information for Investment Decisions. How Efficiently is it Used? IA, 30(Sep, 1971), 3-16
Renwick, F. B.   Introduction to Investments and Finance: Theory and Analysis. Macmillan, 1971
Weaver, D.   Investment Analysis. Longman, 1971
Amling, F.   Investments: an Introduction to Analysis and Management, 2nd ed. P-H, 1970
Smith, K. V. & Goudzwaard, M. B.   Survey of Investment Management: Teaching Versus Practice. JF, 25(May, 1970), 329-348
Block, F. E.   Elements of Portfolio Construction. FAJ, 25(May-Jun, 1969), 123-129
Clendenin, J. C.   Introduction to Investments, 5th ed. McGraw, 1969.
Chottiner, S.   An Investigation of Stock Market Interactions via Computer Simulation of a Model of Idealized Behavior. PhD diss, NYU, 1968
Corley, L.   Practical Investment. Arco, 1968
Dougall, H. E.   Investments, 8th ed. P-H, 1968
Ellis, C. D.   Will Success Spoil Performance Investing? FAJ, 24 (Sep-Oct, 1968), 117-119
Fisch, G. G.   Management in Financial Analysis. FAJ, 24(Jul-Aug, 1968), 43-49
Howard, G. G.   Investment Research in the 1970's. FAJ, 24(May-Jun, 1968), 120-123
Maledon, E. N., Jr.   Toward a Theory of Investment Decision Making. PhD diss, U of Tex, 1968
Smith, A. (pseud).   The Money Game. Random, 1968
Badger, R. E. & Coffman P. B.   The Complete Guide to Investment Analysis. McGraw, 1967
Bauman, W. S.   Investment Analysis: Science or Fiction? FAJ, 23(Jan-Feb, 1967), 93-97
Bing, R. A.   Scientific Investment Analysis. FAJ, 23(May-Jun, 1967), 97-98

Cohen, J. B. & Zinbarg, E. D.   Investment Analysis and Portfolio Management. Irwin, 1967

Hayes, D. A.   The Undervalued Issue Strategy. FAJ, 23(May-Jun, 1967), 121-127

Helfert, E. A.   Techniques of Financial Analysis, rev ed. Irwin, 1967

Hoffland, D. L.   The Folklore of Wall Street. FAJ, 23 (May-Jun, 1967), 85-88

Marks, L. J.   In Defense of Performance. FAJ, 23 (Nov-Dec, 1967) 135-137

Miles, J. E.   Investment Management: Strategies in Ferment. FAJ, 23 (Sep-Oct, 1967), 147-154

Sauvain, H. C.   Investment Management, 3rd ed. P-H, 1967

Smith, K. V.   Needed: A Dynamic Approach to Investment Management. FAJ, 23 (May-Jun, 1967), 115-117

Vaughn, D. E.   Combining the Undervaluation, Fundamental, and Technical Approaches to Security Selection. SWSSQ, 48 (Jun, 1967), 79-85

Vaughn, D. E.   Survey of Investments. HR & W, 1967

Abbott, C. C. (Ed).   Basic Research in Finance: Needs and Prospects. U Pr of Va, 1966

Bowyer, J. W.   Investment Analysis and Management, 3rd ed. Irwin, 1966.

Fanning, J. E.   How to Improve Investment Decisions. HBR, 44 (Jan-Feb, 1966), 156-168

Freund, W. C.   Investment Fundamentals. New York: American Bankers Association, 1966

Hall, J. P. III.   Toward Effective Portfolio Management. FAJ, 22 (Jan, 1966), 91-95

Hayes, D. A.   The Dimensions of Analysis. FAJ, 22 (Sep-Oct, 1966), 81-83

Hayes, D. A.   Investments: Analysis and Management, 2nd ed. Macmillan, 1966.

Sauvain, H. C.   Investment Management (A Review). FAJ, 22 (Jul-Aug, 1966), 91-92

Block, F. E.   Theory, Performance and Practice. FAJ, 21 (Nov-Dec, 1965), 94-95

Fredrikson, E. B.   Security Analysis and the Multinational Corporation. FAJ, 21 (Sep-Oct, 1965), 109-117

Graham, B.   The Intelligent Investor, 4th ed. Har-Row, 1965

Loeb, G. M.   The Battle for Investment Survival. S & S, 1965

Sauvain, H. C.   Problems of Portfolio Policy. FAJ, 21 (May-Jun, 1965), 88-89

Schneider, C. W.   S.E.C. Filings—Their Use to the Professional. FAJ, 21 (Jan-Feb, 1965), 33-38

Vaughn, D. E.   Investment Principles, Practices and Techniques. HR & W, 1965

Crane, B.   The Sophisticated Investor, rev ed. S & S, 1964

Morrison, R. J.   The Bullish Bias. FAJ, 20 (Mar-Apr, 1964), 77-78

Graham, B.   The Future of Financial Analysis. FAJ, 19 (May, 1963) 65-70

Harper, A. D.   How a Professional Investor Seeks Investment Opportunities. FAJ, 19 (Nov-Dec, 1963), 47-52

Nursaw, W. G.   The Art and Practice of Investment. Hutchinson, 1963

Rix, M. S.   Stock Market Economics. Pitman, 1963

Graham, B.; Dodd, D. L. & Cottle, S.   Security Analysis: Principles and Technique, 4th ed. McGraw, 1962

Wise, T. A. & the editors of Fortune.   The Insiders. Doubleday, 1962

Bauman, W. S.   Investment Experience With Less Popular Stocks. DBA diss, Indiana U, 1961

Plum, L. V.; Humphrey, J. H. & Bowyer, J. W.   Investment Analysis and Management. Irwin, 1961

Norr, D.   Investment Theories and Applications. FAJ, 16 (Jul-Aug, 1960), 121-124

Graham, B.   The New Speculation in Common Stocks. AJ, 14 (Jun, 1958), 17-21

Renshaw, E. F.   Foundations of Security Analysis. AJ, 14 (Feb, 1958), 57-61

Weston, J. F.   The Stock Market in Perspective. HBR, 34 (Mar-Apr, 1956), 71-80

Graham, B.   Toward a Science of Security Analysis. AJ, 8 (Aug, 1952), 96-99

Naess, R. D.   The Enigma of Investment Management, AJ, 5 (3rd Qtr, 1949), 5-9

Bookbinder, A. I. A.   Investment Decision-Making, Programmed, 1948.

Edwards, W. F.   Techniques of Investment Management. AJ, 4 (Suppl, 2nd Qtr, 1948), 83-88

Bender, W.   Horizons of Security Analysis. AJ, 3 (3rd Qtr, 1947), 50-54

Langmuir, D.   Common Sense and Investment Techniques. AJ, 3 (1st Qtr, 1947), 3-10

Graham, B.   On Being Right in Security Analysis. AJ, 2 (1st Qtr, 1946), 18-21

Graham, B.   The Hippocratic Method in Security Analysis. AJ, 2 (2nd Qtr, 1946), 47-50

Graham, B.   The S.E.C. Method of Security Analysis. AJ, 2 (3rd Qtr, 1946), 32-35

Popovic, M. D.   A Case for Security Analysis. AJ, 2 (1st Qtr, 1946), 31-36

4b QUANTITATIVE TEXTS ON INVESTMENT MANAGEMENT

This section lists a number of general texts which have drawn principally on modern quantitative research into investment management and the behaviour of security prices. Most of these texts provide relatively little discussion of institutional considerations. In general they are aimed at the non-numerate reader. An exception is the Fama-Miller work which provides a rigorous unified analysis of portfolio investment and corporate finance.

See also:

4a   Investment Management—General

Fama, E. F. & Miller, M. H.   The Theory of Finance. HR & W, 1972

Francis, J. C.   Investments Analysis and Management. McGraw, 1972

Levy, H. & Sarnat, M.   Investment and Portfolio Analysis. Wiley, 1972

Brealey, R. A.   Security Prices in a Competitive Market: More About Risk and Return from Common Stocks. MIT Pr, 1971

Latané, H. A. & Tuttle, D. L.   Security Analysis and Portfolio Management. Ronald, 1971

Smith, K. V.   Portfolio Management. HR & W, 1971

Williamson, J. P.   Investments, New Analytic Techniques. Praeger, 1971

Brealey, R. A.   An Introduction to Risk and Return from Common Stocks. MIT Pr, 1969

4c INVESTMENT MANAGEMENT—THE PROFESSION

This section consists principally of articles from the Financial Analysts Journal on the profession of investment analysis.

Crum, M. C.   Performance Investing and the Breakdown of Respect for Authority. FAJ, 25 (May-Jun, 1969), 142-147

Rosen, L. R.   Go Where the Money is: a Guide to Understanding and Entering the Securities Business. Dow Jones-Irwin, 1969

Browne, D. E.   Analyst, Analyse Thyself! FAJ, 24 (Nov-Dec, 1968), 23-24

Hamilton, J. D.   Stockbroking Today. Macmillan Int, 1968

Norby, W. C.   Some Contrary Views on the Professional Status of Financial Analysis. FAJ, 24 (Mar-Apr, 1968), 11-13

Norby, W. C.   Profile of the Financial Analyst. FAJ, 24 (Jul-Aug, 1968), 11-15

Ketchum, M. D.   Is Financial Analysis a Profession? FAJ, 23 (Nov-Dec, 1967), 33-37

Sheppard, C. S.   The Professionalization of the Financial Analysts. FAJ, 23 (Nov-Dec, 1967), 39-41

Wendt, P. F.   What Should We Teach in an Investment Course? JF, 21 (May, 1966), 416-422

Hooper, L. O.   The Specialist Should Be a Generalist Too. FAJ, 21 (Nov-Dec, 1965), 33-35

Porter, S.   Regulation of Financial Analysis. FAJ, 19 (May-Jun, 1963), 104

Ward, K.   Number of Analysts Increasing in Field of Investment Research. FAJ, 19 (Jul, 1963), 84-85

Hayes, D. A.   Ethical Considerations in the Professional Stature of Analysts. FAJ, 18 (Sep-Oct, 1962), 53-56

Randell, D. H.   Evolution of the Analyst. FAJ, 17 (Mar-Apr, 1961), 67-75

Mennis, E. A.   The Investment Manager of the Future. FAJ, 16 (Mar, 1960), 23-24

Squier, A. P.   Training Prospective Security Analysts. AJ, 10 (May, 1954), 39

Hooper, L. O.   Should Security Analysts Have a Professional Rating? The Negative Case. AJ, 1 (1st Qtr, 1945), 41-44

4d INVESTMENT MANAGEMENT—SOME BEHAVIOURAL CONSIDERATIONS

This section contains a diverse selection of works that emphasise some of the behavioural considerations in investment management. Noteworthy is Clarkson's book on simulating the actions of a trust manager.

Slovic, P.   Psychological Study of Human Judgment: Implications for Investment Decision Making. JF, 27 (Sep, 1972), 779-800

Slovic, P.; Fleissner, D. & Baumann, W. S.   Analysing the Use of Information in Investment Decision Making: a Methodological Proposal. JB, 45 (Apr, 1972), 283-301

Copeman, R. C.   Attitude to Stockmarket Investment Decisions in the City of London, August to October, 1971. Discussion paper No 33, Graduate Centre for Mgmt Studies, U of Aston, Nov 1971

Smith, R. G. E.   Uncertainty, Information and Investment Decisions. JF, 26 (Mar, 1971), 67-82

Zeikel, A.   Group Dynamics. FAJ, 27 (Jan-Feb, 1971), 30-34

Wilcox, J. W.   Market Participant Cognitive Maps for Individual Common
    Stocks.   PhD diss, MIT, 1970
Keller, F. R.   The Behavior of Individuals in Security Investment Decisions.
    DBA diss, Harvard Bus, 1967
Rose, A. M.   A Social Psychological Approach to the Study of the Stock
    Market. Kyk, 19 (1966), 267-287
Clarkson, G. P. E.   Portfolio Selection: A Simulation of Trust Investment.
    P-H, 1962
Clarkson, G. P. E., & Meltzer, A. H.   Portfolio Selection: A Heuristic
    Approach. JF, 15 (Dec, 1960), 465-480

4e COMPUTERS IN INVESTMENT MANAGEMENT

The growing usage of computers and the construction in the early 1960s
of several files of financial data prompted a certain amount of discussion
about the possible impact of these developments on investment practice.
The following articles predominantly reflect this concern.

Kahl, A. L.   Investment Management and the Computer: Limitations and
    Prospects. PhD diss, U of Fla, 1969
Winthrop, J.   Layman's View of Computer Power. FAJ, 25 (Sep-Oct, 1969),
    101-103
Blake, C. W. & Riegle, D. W.   Data Processing Key to Investment Success.
    FAJ, 24 (Jan-Feb, 1968), 134-146
Feuerstein, A. E. & Maggi, P. G.   Computer Investment Research. FAJ, 24
    (Jan-Feb, 1968), 154-158
Stone, D. E.   Computer-Aided Financial Analysis. FAJ, 24 (Jan-Feb, 1968),
    149-153
Bower, R. S.; Myers, B. C.; Nugent, C. E. & Williamson, J. P.   A Language for
    the Aid of Financial Fact Finders. FAJ, 23 (Jan-Feb, 1967), 121-129
Bower, R. S.; Williamson, J. P. & Wippern, H. F.   Financial Research, In-
    vestment Analysis and the Computer: Work Done at the Amos Tuck
    School. Tuck Bulletin 31, The Amos Tuck School, Dartmouth C, 1967
Gumperz, J.   Machines that Analyse—or Analysts? FAJ, 23 (Jan-Feb, 1967),
    113-115
Chase, R. H., Jr. et al.   Computer Applications in Investment Analysis.
    Dartmouth C, 1966
Clay, L. T.   Computers in Investment Analysis. FAJ, 22 (Jan, 1966), 70-71
Gal, J. G.   Man—Machine Interactive Systems and their Application to
    Financial Analysis. FAJ, 22 (May-Jun, 1966), 126-136
Shelton, J. P.   The New Research and the Investment Profession. FAJ,
    22 (Nov-Dec, 1966), 65-67
Moynihan, E. O.   The Financial Analyst and the Computer. FAJ, 20 (Mar-
    Apr, 1964), 115-119
Coughtry, L. S.   Computers—A Tool in Security Analysis. FAJ, 19 (Jan-
    Feb, 1963), 53-55
Blease, J. G.   Computers as an Aid to Investment Analysis. IA, 1 (Nov,
    1961), 12-26
Rischer, G.   Computers and the Stock Market. FAJ, 17 (Jul-Aug, 1961),
    91-93
Heiser, H. C.   The Application of Computers to Scientific Management. AJ,
    14 (Jun, 1958), 70-72
Rosenfeld, L.   Electronic Computers and Their Place in Security Analysis.
    AJ, 13 (Feb, 1957), 51-53

4f MANAGEMENT GAMES

This section lists three articles on the application of management games to the study of finance. The Barish & Siff article provides a general formulation of a stock selection game, the Brealey & Hodges paper is concerned with a portfolio selection game, and the paper by Gordon et al. describes an investment-consumption game designed to reveal attitudes to risk.

See also:

9b Utility Functions—Some Empirical Studies

Brealey, R. A. & Hodges, S. D.   Playing with Portfolios. FAJ, forthcoming

Gordon, M. J.; Paradis, G. E. & Rorke, C. H.   Experimental Evidence on Alternative Portfolio Decision Rules. AER, 62 (Mar, 1972), 107-118

Barish, N. N. & Siff, F. H.   Operational Gaming Simulation with Application to a Stock Market. MSci, 15 (Jun, 1969), B530-B541

Part 5   Market Indexes & the Return on Equities

5a REALISED RETURNS ON EQUITIES

This section contains some studies of historical rates of return on equities. Comprehensive analyses for the USA are provided by Fisher & Lorie (see especially their 1968 and 1970 articles). Merrett & Sykes provide less detailed information on the British market.

Pinches, G. E. & Simon, G.   An Analysis of Portfolio Accumulation Strategies Employing Low-Priced Common Stocks. JFQA, 7 (Jun, 1972), 1773-1796

Robichek, A. A.; Cohn, R. A. & Pringle, J. J.   Returns on Alternative Investment Media and Implications for Portfolio Construction. JB, 45 (Jul, 1972), 427-443

Reilly, F. K.   Price Changes in NYSE, Amex and OTC Stocks Compared. FAJ, 27 (Mar-Apr, 1971), 54-59

Fisher, L. & Lorie, J. H.   Some Studies of Variability of Returns on Investments in Common Stocks. JB, 43 (Apr, 1970), 99-134

Stitzel, T. E.   Investing in Intrastate Issues of Common Stock. JFQA, 4 (Jan, 1970), 697-706

Brigham, E. F. & Pappas, J. L.   Rates of Return on Common Stock. JB, 42 (Jul, 1969), 302-316

Fairbairn, I. J. & McShane, R. W.   The Return on Equities and Fixed Interest Securities on the Australian Capital Market. ER, 45 (Mar, 1969), 116-123

Fisher, L. & Lorie, J. H.   Rates of Return on Investments in Common Stock. The Year by Year Record, 1926-65. JB, 41 (Jul, 1968), 291-316

Ben-Shahar, H. & Sarnat, M.   Reinvestment and the Rate of Return on Common Stocks. JF, 21 (Dec, 1966), 737-742

Merrett, A. J. & Sykes, A.   Return on Equities and Fixed Interest Securities: 1919-1966. DBR, 158 (Jun, 1966), 29-45

Barnes, L.   What Difference Does Knowledge Make to Investors ? FAJ, 21 (Sep-Oct, 1965), 60-68

Fisher, L.   Outcomes for 'Random' Investments in Common Stocks Listed on the New York Stock Exchange. JB, 38 (Apr, 1965), 149-161

Latané, H. A. & Tuttle, D. L.   Annual Changes in Prices of Equity Securities. Paper presented at Southern Economic Association Meeting, Miami, Florida, 1965

Lorie, J. H. & Fisher, L.   Knowledge Makes a Difference—a Reply to Dr Leo Barnes. FAJ, 21 (Nov-Dec, 1965), 118-120

Soldofsky, R. M.   Growth Yields on Common Stock Since 1900. QREB, 5 (Winter, 1965), 51-61

Fisher, L. & Lorie, J. H.   Rates of Return on Investments in Common Stocks. JB, 37 (Jan, 1964), 1-17

Ortner, R.   The Concept of Yield on Common Stock. JF, 19 (May, 1964), 186-198

Merrett, A. J. & Sykes, A.   Return on Equities and Fixed Interest Securities 1919-1963. DBR, (Dec, 1963)

Eiteman, W. J. & D. S.   Common Stock Values and Yields 1950-61. U of Mich Busn Res, 1962

Tatham, C.   Common Stock Dividend Yields and Total Return. New York: Bache & Co., 1961

Lerner, E. M.   Rate of Return on Common Stocks. FAJ, 16 (Sep-Oct, 1960), 47-50

Eiteman, W. J.   Yield on Common Stock Investments. AJ, 13 (Feb, 1957), 13-14

Haney, L. H.   Different Values of Income from Short Loans, Bonds, and Stocks. AJ, 10 (Feb, 1954), 9-13

Walker, W. B.   A Re-examination of Common Stocks as Long Term Investments. Anthoensen, 1954

Eiteman, W. J. & Smith, F. P.   Common Stock Values and Yields. U of Mich Pr, 1953

Kemmerer, D. L.   For Long-Term Investment: Stocks or Bonds. CFC, (Feb 1, 1951)

Cowles, A. et al.   Common Stock Indexes 1871-1937. Principia Pr, 1938

Bosland, C. C.   The Common Stock Theory of Investment. Ronald, 1937

Harold, G.   A Reconsideration of the Common-Stock Theory. JB, 7 (Jan, 1934), 42-59

Smith, E. L.   Common Stocks as Long Term Investments. Macmillan, 1924

5b MARKET INDEXES

Most of the articles in this section describe and assess the construction of specific market indexes. Fisher in his article on investment performance indexes discusses some of the general desirable characteristics of market indexes. This is also the subject of the very readable article by Cootner.

Marks, P. & Stuart, A.   An Arithmetic Version of the FT Index. JIA, 97 (Dec, 1971), 297-324

Rose, H. B.   Share Price Indices and the Measurement of Investment Performance. IA, 31 (Dec, 1971), 3-9

Conlong, A.   The First Eight Years of the FT Actuaries All Share Index. IA, 27 (Sep, 1970), 3-18

Elliott, D. C.   A New Index of Equity Values. FAJ, 25 (May-Jun, 1969), 101-104

Tuttle, D. L.   The Implications for Portfolio Management of Different Measures of Market Performance. Paper for the Seminar on the Analysis of Security Prices, University of Chicago, Nov 1969

Cavaco Silva, A. A.   Contribution to the Study of the Influence of Each of the 30 Dow-Jones Industrial Stocks on the Average. AIGC, 3 (1968), 15-48

Carter, E. E. & Cohen, K. J.   Stock Averages, Stock Splits, and Bias. FAJ, 23 (May-Jun, 1967), 77-81

Kekish, B. J.   Moody's Averages. FAJ, 23 (May-Jun, 1967), 65-69

Molodovsky, N.   Building a Stock Market Measure—A Case Story. FAJ, 23 (May-Jun, 1967), 43-46

Reilly, F. K.   Our Misnamed Stock Price Indicators. Kan BR, 20 (Jan, 1967), 4-9

Schellbach, L. L.   When Did the DJIA Top 1200? FAJ, 23 (May-Jun, 1967), 71-73

Schoomer, B. A., Jr.   American Stock Exchange Index System. FAJ, 23 (May-Jun, 1967), 57-61

West, S. & Miller, N.   Why the NYSE Common Stock Indexes? FAJ, 23 (May-Jun, 1967), 49-54

Carter, E. E. & Cohen, K. J.   Bias in the DJIA Caused by Stock Splits. FAJ, 22 (Nov-Dec, 1966), 90-94

Cootner, P. H.   Stock Market Indexes—Fallacies and Illusions. CFC (Sep 29, 1966)

Fisher, L.   Some New Stock-Market Indexes. JB, 39 (Suppl, Jan, 1966), 191-225

Milne, R. D.   The Dow-Jones Industrial Average Re-examined. FAJ, 22 (Nov-Dec, 1966), 83-88

Comer, H. D.   Is the 'Dow' Already Above 1200? FAJ, 20 (May-Jun, 1964), 69-70

Haycocks, H. W. & Plymen, J.   The Design, Application and Future Development of the Financial Times Actuaries Index. JIA, 90, (Dec, 1964)

The Times.   The Times Share Indices. Times Publishing, 1964

Drakatos, C.   London Share Price Indices. BM, 193 (Jun, 1962), 465-473

Financial Times.   Guide to the FT-Actuaries Share Indices. London: Financial Times, 1962

Kendall, M. G. & Stuart, A.   Measuring Share Price Changes. Times (Apr 20, 1960), 13

St Laurent, A. G.   A Stochastic Model for the Behavior of a Set of Price Index-Numbers and its Application. Michigan St U Research memo No. 37, 1957

Smerling, S. A.   Found: a Realistic Market Measure. AJ, 13 (May, 1957), 59-62

Haycocks, H. W. & Plymen, J.   Investment Policy and Index Numbers. JIA, 82 (1956), 359

Shaw, R. B.   The Dow-Jones Industrials vs the Dow-Jones Industrial Average. AJ, 11 (Nov, 1955), 37-40

Decker, M. G. & Butler, H. L., Jr.   A Security Check on the Dow-Jones Industrial Average. AJ, 9 (Feb, 1953), 37-45

Schloss, W. J.   The Dow-Jones Industrial Average Amended. AJ, 9 (Feb, 1953), 35-36

Gaubis, A.   Which is the Best Stock Average from a Practical Standpoint? AJ, 8 (Nov, 1952), 70-73

Rich, C. D.   The Rationale of the Use of the Geometric Average as an Investment Index. JIA, 74 (1948), 338-339

Mitchell, W. C.   A Critique of Index Numbers of the Prices of Stocks. JPE, 24 (Jul, 1916), 685

5c AVERAGES, RATES OF RETURN AND BIASES

This section contains some miscellaneous articles concerning biases arising from calculations of rates of return. The Working and Rosenberg articles discuss the effect of averaging on serial correlations. Cheng & Deets are concerned with biases that arise from annualizing rates of return or from using overlapping data.

Cheng, P. L. & Deets, M. K.   Statistical Biases and Security Rates of Return. JFQA, 6 (Jun, 1971), 977-994

Rosenberg, B.   Statistical Analysis of Price Series Obscured by Averaging Measures. JFQA, 6 (Sep, 1971), 1083-1094

Daniels, H. E.   Autocorrelation between First Differences of Mid-Ranges. Em, 34 (Jan, 1966), 215-219

Edwards, C. E. & Hilton, J. G.   High-Low Averages as an Estimator of Annual Average Stock Prices. JF, 21 (Mar, 1966), 112-115

Marris, R. & Singh, A.   A Measure of a Firm's Average Share Price.
  JRSS, 129 Series A, Part I (1966), 74-97
Working, H.   Note on the Correlation of First Differences of Averages
  in a Random Chain. Em, 28 (Oct, 1960), 916-918

Part 6   The Economy & the Stock Market

6a ECONOMICS—GENERAL

The following works consist principally of general observations on the role
of economics and the economist in the field of portfolio investment. Rose's
book on the economic background approaches being a general textbook on
investment.

Moor, R. E.   The Use of Economics in Investment Analysis. FAJ, 27
  (Nov-Dec, 1971), 63-69
Ferretti, A. P.   The Economist's Role and the Stock Market. FAJ, 25
  (Jan-Feb, 1969), 35-37
Mennis, E. A.   New Tools for Profits Analysis. FAJ, 25 (Jan-Feb, 1969),
  25-33
Bonham, H. B., Jr.   The Use of Input-Output Economics in Common Stock
  Analysis. FAJ, 23 (Jan-Feb, 1967), 19-28
Cropper, P. J.   The Economist in the Investment Business, *in* Alexander,
  K. J. W. et al. (Eds), The Economist in Business. Blackwell, 1967
Ahearn, D. S.   Investment Management and Economic Research. FAJ, 20
  (Jan-Feb, 1964), 15-20
Rose, H. B.   The Economic Background to Investment. Cambridge U Pr,
  1960
Fisher, G. H.   The Input-Output Technique as an Aid to Security Analysis.
  AJ, 9 (Feb, 1953), 85-92
Leonard, W. R. & Shapiro, L. A.   Heavy-Duty Tools for the Market Analyst.
  AJ, 8 (May, 1952), 73-76

6b BUSINESS CYCLES AND STOCK PRICES

The following articles are concerned with the relationship between the
business cycle and share prices, with heavy emphasis on the use of National
Bureau leading indicators. The interesting Shiskin paper has a somewhat
wider coverage. A discussion of the increasing sensitivity of profits to
changes in GNP is contained in Andersen's article.

Levin, J.   Prophetic Leaders. FAJ, 26 (Jul-Aug, 1970), 87-90
Cullity, J. P.   Stock Price Recoveries After Post-War Recessions. FAJ,
  23 (Sep-Oct, 1967), 98-100
Moore, G. H. & Shiskin, J.   Indicators of Business Expansion and Contrac-
  tions. (Dist by Columbia U Pr) Natl Bur Econ Res, 1967
Shiskin, J.   Systematic Aspects of Stock Price Fluctuations. Paper for the
  Seminar on the Analysis of Security Prices, U of Chicago, May 1967
Lempert, L. H.   The Use of Composite Indicators. FAJ, 21 (Nov-Dec, 1965),
  57-59
Leeuw, F. De.   Financial Markets in Business Cycles: a Simulation Study.
  AER, 54 (May, 1964), 309-323
Andersen, T. A.   Trends in Profit Sensitivity. JF, 28 (Dec, 1963), 637-646
Lempert, L. H.   Forecasting the Leading Indicator of Stock Prices. FAJ,
  17 (Sep-Oct, 1961), 13-21
Storer, R. W. & Conn, M. V.   Stock Market Leading Indicators. FAJ, 17
  (Sep-Oct, 1961), 61-64

Mennis, E. A.   Security Prices and Business Cycles. AJ, 11 (Feb, 1955), 79-86

6c INFLATION AND STOCK PRICES

This section is concerned with the effect of inflation on the equity market. The articles by Kessel & Alchian are directed at the relative impact of inflation on net creditor or debtor companies. The work by Nichols and Hanna is concerned principally with the adequacy of depreciation provisions. The section also includes several more general attempts (e.g. by Johnson et al.) to identify an inflation effect. Studies of the effect of inflation on interest rates are listed under 18c-'Inflation and the Rate of Interest'.

Van Horne, J. C. & Glassmire, W.   The Impact of Unanticipated Changes in Inflation on the Value of Common Stocks. JF, forthcoming

Oudet, B. A.   Returns on Financial Assets in Periods of Inflation. PhD diss, Indiana U, 1972

Johnson, G. L.; Reilly, F. K. & Smith, R. E.   Individual Common Stocks as Inflation Hedges. JFQA, 6 (Jun, 1971), 1015-1024

Fukasawa, S.   A Variable Lag Pattern in the Formation of Expected Price Changes. PhD diss, Columbia U, 1970

Homer, S.   Inflation and the Capital Markets. FAJ, 25 (Jul-Aug, 1969), 143-145

Nichols, D. A.   A Note on Inflation and Common Stock Values. JF, 23 (Sep, 1968), 655-657

Kessel, R. A. & Alchian, A. A.   Inflation and Stock Prices. Paper for the Seminar on the Analysis of Security Prices, U of Chicago, May 1965

Hanna, M.   A Study of Inadequate Depreciation for 1956 Due to Inflation Based Upon External Reports of Fifteen Corporations Selected from the Dow-Jones Industrial Average. PhD diss, U of NC, 1963

Kessel, R. A. & Alchian, A. A.   Effects of Inflation. JPE, 70 (Dec, 1962), 521-537

Greenhut, M. L.   Full Employment, Inflation and Common Stock. Pub Affairs, 1961

Archer, S. H.   Common Stocks as an Inflation Hedge. FAJ, 16 (Sep-Oct, 1960), 41-45

Alchian, A. A. & Kessel, R. A.   Redistribution of Wealth through Inflation. Sc, 130 (Sep 4, 1959), 535-539

Tilney, N. S.   Security Selection During a Period of Inflation. Bernhard, 1959

Dedalus, A. I.   The Effect of Inflation on the Stock Market. AJ, 14 (Aug, 1958), 73-76

6d MONEY AND STOCK PRICES

This section consists principally of studies of the apparent link between changes in the money supply and stock prices. Sprinkel's books provide good examples of this work.

See also:

18b Interest Rates—General

Hamburger, M. J. & Kochin, L. A.   Money and Stock Prices: the Channels of Influence. JF, 27 (May, 1972), 231-250

Malkiel, B. G. & Quandt, R. E.   The Supply of Money and Common Stock
    Prices: Comment. JF, 27 (Sep, 1972), 921-926
Rudolph, J. A.   The Money Supply and Common Stock Prices. FAJ, 28
    (Mar-Apr, 1972), 19-25
Homa, K. E. & Jaffee, D. M.   The Supply of Money and Common Stock
    Prices. JF, 26 (Dec, 1971), 1045-1066
Keran, M. W.   Expectations, Money and the Stock Market. Mo Rev F R
    Bk St Louis (Jan, 1971), 16-31
Pepper, N. A.   The Money Supply and Demand Determinants of Stock
    Prices. PhD diss, UCLA, 1971
Pepper, N. A. & Zwick, B.   Liquidity and Income Effects of Monetary
    Changes on Stock Prices. UCLA, (1971), Mimeo
Sprinkel, B. W.   Money and Markets. Irwin, 1971
Palmer, M.   Money Supply, Portfolio Adjustments and Stock Prices.
    FAJ, 26 (Jul-Aug, 1970), 19-22
Walters, A. A.   Monetary Policy, Gilts and Equities. IA, 28 (Dec, 1970),
    3-6
Foster, E. M.   Analysis of Common Stock Prices. PhD diss, NYU, 1969
Nightingale, R. D.   Money Supply and the Stock Market. IA, 23 (Jun, 1969),
    5-10
Leveson, S. M.   Money and Stock Prices. BE, 3 (Summer, 1968)
Baron, D. C.   The Interrelationship between Money Supply, Interest Rates
    and Stock Prices. SM thesis, MIT, 1967
Bolton, A. H.   Money and Investment Profits. Dow Jones-Irwin, 1967
Brickman, M.   New Federal Reserve Series Is Valuable Forecasting Tool.
    FAJ, 23 (Sep-Oct, 1967), 88-92
Sprinkel, B. W.   Money and Stock Prices. Irwin, 1964
Schumacher, A. C.   The Relationship of Money Forces to Equity Prices.
    AJ, 11 (Feb, 1955), 15-18

6e MARGIN REQUIREMENTS, PRIME RATES AND STOCK PRICES

This section is concerned with the impact of Federal Reserve actions on
the market. Studies of the effect on stock prices are exemplified by Waud
and Niederhoffer & Bossell. Cohen and Largay also provide some evidence
of the effect on activity and variability.

Largay, J. A.   100% Margins: Combating Speculation in Individual Security
    Issues. JF, forthcoming
Largay, J. A.   Some Tests of the Relationship between Margin Require-
    ments and Stock Market Activity. PhD diss, Cornell U, 1971
Waud, R. N.   Public Interpretation of Discount Rate Changes: Evidence
    on the 'Announcement' Effect. Em, 38 (Mar, 1970), 231-250
Niederhoffer, V. & Bossell, S.   Effect of Quantitative Federal Reserve
    Actions on the Bond and Stock Market. Paper for the Seminar on the
    Analysis of Security Prices, U of Chicago, Nov 1969
Stoffels, J. D.   The Use of Margin Credit in the Trading of Securities.
    PhD diss, Mich St U, 1969
Tersine, R. J.   Analysis of the Effect of 100 Per Cent Margin Require-
    ment on Certain Common Stocks in 1967 Listed on the New York Stock
    Exchange. DBA diss, Fla St U, 1969
Bolster, R. L.   The Relationship of Monetary Policy to the Stock Market:
    the Experience with Margin Requirements. PhD diss, Am U, 1966

Cohen, J.   Federal Reserve Margin Requirements and the Stock Market. JFQA, 1 (Sep, 1966), 30-54

Moore, T. G.   Stock Market Margin Requirements. JPE, 74 (Apr, 1966), 158-167

Elsom, H. B.   Common Stocks and the Short Term Interest Rate. FAJ, 17 (Mar-Apr, 1961), 21-26

Bogen, J. I. & Krooss, H. E.   Security Credit, Its Economic Role and Regulation. P-H, 1960

Spiegelglas, S.   Changes in Margin Requirements and Stock Market Prices. FAJ, 16 (Nov-Dec, 1960), 35-37

Harris, R. E.   Federal Reserve Margin Requirements: a Selective Instrument of Monetary Policy. PhD diss, U of Pa, 1958

Murray, R. F.   Interest Rates and their Influence on Equity Prices. AJ, 12 (Jun, 1956), 15-17

6f RESEARCH AND DEVELOPMENT AND STOCK PRICES

The following articles are concerned with the relationship between stock prices and expenditures on research and development.

Gumperz, J.   Scientific Input and Economic Output. FAJ, 24 (Nov-Dec, 1968), 111-113

Kolb, B. A.   Research, Development and Common Stock Values. FAJ, 18 (Sep-Oct, 1962), 9-16

Lazarcik, G.   Scientific Research and Its Relation to Earnings and Stock Prices. FAJ, 18 (Jan-Feb, 1962), 49-53

Morgner, A.   Security Analysis in a Science-Oriented Society. AJ, 11 (Aug, 1955), 59-61

Part 7 The Valuation of Equities

7a SHARE VALUATION—GENERAL

This section contains a rather heterogeneous collection of studies on the determinants of share prices.

See also:

4a Investment Management—General
7b Share Valuation—Present Value Theory and Growth Stocks
7c Share Valuation—Cross-Sectional Analyses

Zweig, M.   An Investor Expectations Stock Price Predictive Model Using Closed-End Fund Premiums. JF, forthcoming

Bing, R. A.   Survey of Practitioners' Stock Evaluation Methods. FAJ, 27 (May-Jun, 1971), 55-60

Black, F. & Scholes, M.   Dividend Yields and Common Stock Returns: a New Methodology. Paper for the Seminar on the Analysis of Security Prices, U of Chicago, Nov 1970

Boness, A. J. & Jen, F. C.   A Model of Information Diffusion, Stock Market Behavior, and Equilibrium Price. JFQA, 5 (Sep, 1970), 279-296

Haugen, R. A.   Expected Growth, Required Return, and the Variability of Stock Prices. JFQA, 5 (Sep, 1970), 297-308

Weisman, B. B.   An Empirical Study of 21 Investment Criteria Employed in Common Stock Selection. PhD diss, NYU, 1970

Hubbard, C. L. & Hawkins, C. A.   Theory of Valuation. Intext, 1969

Breen, W. J. & Savage, J.   Portfolio Distributions and Tests of Security Selection Models. JF, 23 (Dec, 1968), 805-819

Eiteman, D. K.   A Computer Program for Common Stock Valuation. FAJ, 24 (Jul-Aug, 1968), 107-111

Hoppes, H. N.   An Evaluation of Selected Normative Models of Equity Valuation. PhD diss, Am U, 1968

Sloane, W. R. & Reisman, A.   Stock Evaluation Theory: Classification, Reconciliation and General Model. JFQA, 3 (Jun, 1968), 171-203

Smith, R. G. E.   The Appraisement, Valuation and Selection of Security Investments and the Theory of Price Determination in Securities Markets. DBA diss, La St U, 1968

Baty, G. B.   Optimum Linear Prediction in Speculative Markets. PhD diss, MIT, 1967

Hammel, J. E. & Hodes, D. A.   Factors Influencing P/E Multiples. FAJ, 23 (Jan-Feb, 1967), 90-92

Keenan, W. M.   Towards a Positive Theory of Equity Valuation. PhD diss, Carnegie IT, 1967

Sloane, W. R.   Earnings, Dividends and Stock Prices: Review and General Model. Marq BR, (Fall, 1967)

Smith, R. G. E.   The 'Marginal Opinion' Theory of Stock Prices. FAJ, 23 (Nov-Dec, 1967), 127-132

Adamson, A. & Coorey, M. G.   The Valuation of Company Shares and Businesses. Law Book, 1966

Baynes, T. A. H.   Share Valuations. Heinemann, 1966

Griffith, R.   The Valuation of Life Insurance Stocks. PhD diss, U of Tex, 1966

Gruber, M. J.   Determinants of Common Stock Prices. PhD diss, Columbia U, 1966

Hagin, R. L.   An Empirical Evaluation of Selected Hypotheses Related to Price Changes in the Stock Market. PhD diss, UCLA, 1966

Helfert, E. A.   Valuation: Concepts and Practice. Wadsworth Pub, 1966

Bauman, W. S.   The Less Popular Stocks versus the Most Popular Stocks. FAJ, 21 (Jan-Feb, 1965), 83-89

Birmingham, J. M., Jr.   Stock Values and Stock Prices. FAJ, 21 (Mar-Apr, 1965), 88-89

Lerner, E. M.   Model of Security Price Determination. Paper for the Seminar on the Analysis of Security Prices, University of Chicago, Nov 1965

Tuttle, D. L.   An Analysis of Annual Changes in Prices of Equity Securities. PhD diss, U of NC, 1965

Walter, J. E.   The Information Content of Stock Prices. BE, 1 (Summer, 1965)

Bauman, W. S.   Investment Experience With Less Popular Common Stocks. FAJ, 20 (Mar-Apr, 1964), 79-88

Bodenhorn, D.   A Cash-Flow Concept of Profit. JF, 19 (Mar, 1964), 16-31

Bosland, C. C.   Valuation Theories and Decisions of the SEC. Simmons-B, 1964

Eisenstadt, S.   A Mathematical Formulation of the Behavior of Stocks During the Postwar Period. Value Line Investment Survey, 19 (April, 1964), 1-4

Sjogren, P. H.   Enterprise Valuation by the Securities and Exchange Commission under Chapter X of the Bankruptcy Act. PhD diss, Columbia U, 1964

Agrawal, K. P.   Share Prices and Corporate Dividends. IJE, 43 (1963), 347-362

Hirsch, J. H.   Improved Yardstick of Common Stock Value. FAJ, 19 (Sep-Oct, 1963), 60-69

Jicha, O.   A Conceptual Approach to Securities Valuation and Analysis. PhD diss, U of Mich, 1963

Kourday, M.   A Method of Outperforming the Market. FAJ, 19 (Nov-Dec, 1963), 35-44

Rosett, R. N.   Estimating Time Horizons and Expected Yields: A Comment. IntER, 4 (Jan, 1963), 105-107

Bosland, C. C.   The Valuation of Public Utility Enterprises by the Securities and Exchange Commission. JF, 16 (Mar, 1961), 52-64

Hirsch, J. H.   An Effective Yardstick of Common Stock Value. FAJ, 17 (May-Jun, 1961), 13-20

Ortner, R.   An Estimate of the Time Horizon and Expected Yield for a Selected Group of Common Shares, 1935-1955. IntER, 2 (May, 1961), 179-198

Hale, I.   The Stock Selection 'Game Theory'. FAJ, 16 (Mar, 1960), 53-56

Bernhard, A.   The Evaluation of Common Stocks. S & S, 1959

Walter, J. E.   A Discriminant Function for Earnings Price Ratios of Large Industrial Corporations. REStat, 41 (Feb, 1959), 44-52

Bell, W. E.   The Price-Future Earnings Ratio. AJ, 14 (Aug, 1958), 25-28

Florence, P. S.   Tests of the Validity of Some Stock Exchange Folk-Lore. TBR, 37 (Mar, 1958), 3-20

Graham, B.   Two Illustrative Approaches to Formula Valuations of Common Stocks. AJ, 13 (Nov, 1957), 11-15

Tucker, R. D.   A Discussion of Benjamin Graham's Central Value Concept. AJ, 13 (May 1957), 93-95

Bernstein, P. L.   Growth Companies vs. Growth Stocks. HBR, 34 (Sep-Oct, 1956), 87-98

Scoville, J. A.   An Exercise in Common Stock Selection. AJ, 12 (Nov, 1956), 99-103

Jarislowsky, S. A. & Brown, J. J.   A Statistical Approach to Security Analysis. AJ, 10 (Nov, 1954), 79-83

Latané, H. A.   Price Changes in Equity Securities. JF, 9 (Sep, 1954), 252-264

Litts, R. N.   Another Interesting Tool for Stock Appraisal. AJ, 10 (Nov, 1954), 59-62

Oxenfeldt, A. R.   Valuation of Untraded and Closely Held Securities. AJ, 9 (Aug, 1953), 33-37

Bernhard, A.   The Valuation of Listed Stocks. AJ, 5 (2nd Qtr, 1949), 20-24

Bedford, G. L.   A Method of Estimating Price-Earnings Ratios. AJ, 3 (3rd Qtr, 1947), 14-19

Comer, H. D.   Low Priced Versus High Priced Stocks. AJ, 1 (2nd Qtr, 1945), 15-20

Tinbergen, J.   The Dynamics of Share Price Formation. REStat, 21 (Nov, 1939), 153-160

7b SHARE VALUATION—PRESENT VALUE THEORY AND GROWTH STOCKS

The following articles discuss share valuation within the context of present value theory. An early and notable exposition is that of Williams (1938) and a more complete statement is to be found in Miller & Modigliani. Malkiel's article provides a good example of empirical analysis using the present value framework. Other articles, notably by Molodovsky, envisage the formal use of such models for security analysis.

See also:

7a   Share Valuation—General
7d   Determinants of the Market Level

Bierman, H., Jr.; Downes, D. H. & Hass, J. E.   Closed-Form Stock Price Models. JFQA, 7 (Jun, 1972), 1797-1808

Beidleman, C. R.   Limitations of Price-Earnings Ratios. FAJ, 27 (Sep-Oct, 1971), 86-91

Beidleman, C. R.   On Growth in Share Values. JBF, 3 (Summer, 1971), 51-56

Bierman, H., Jr. & Hass, J.   Normative Stock Models. JFQA, 6 (Sep, 1971), 1135-1146

Robichek, A. A. & Bogue, M. C.   A Note on the Behavior of Expected Price/Earnings Ratios over Time. JF, 26 (Jun, 1971), 731-736

Foster, E. M.   Price-Earnings Ratio and Corporate Growth. FAJ, 26 (Jan-Feb, 1970), 96-103

Foster, E. M.   Price-Earnings Ratio and Corporate Growth: A Revision. FAJ, 26 (Jul-Aug, 1970), 115-118

Merrett, A. J.   Valuation of Ordinary Shares. Gower, 1970

Bauman, W. S.   Investment Returns and Present Values. FAJ, 25 (Nov-Dec, 1969), 107-120

Beidleman, C. R.   A Study of the Influence of Growth on the Valuation of Equity. PhD diss, U of Pa, 1969

Elton, E. J. & Gruber, M. J.   Prediction and Market Evaluation of Growth. Wkg paper, NYU Busn, 1969

Hakansson, N. H.   On the Dividend Capitalization Model under Uncertainty. JFQA, 4 (Mar, 1969), 65-87

Winer, L.   Growth Rate Graph and Nomograph. FAJ, 25 (Jan-Feb, 1969), 105-108

Bierman, H., Jr.   The Growth Period Decision. MSci, 14 (Feb, 1968), B302-B309

Jones, C. H., Jr.   The Growth Rate Appraiser. FAJ, 24 (Sep-Oct, 1968), 109-111

Mampe, E. P., Jr.   The Impact of Interest Rates on Share Prices: the Influence of Expectation, Growth and Leverage. PhD diss, U of Ill, 1968

Margoshes, S. L.   Profitability, Probability and 'The Modified Present Value Profile'. FAJ, 24 (Mar-Apr, 1968), 97-104

Molodovsky, N.   Selecting Growth Stocks. FAJ, 24 (Sep-Oct, 1968), 103-106

Molodovsky, N.   Stock Values and Stock Prices. FAJ, 24 (Nov-Dec, 1968), 134-148

Christy, G. A.   A Rationalization of the Stock Bond Yield Spread. QREB, 7 (Spring, 1967), 63-70

Soldofsky, R. M. & Murphy, J. T.   Growth Yields on Common Stock: Theory and Tables. Iowa St Busn, 1967

Brigham, E. F. & Pappas, J. L.   Duration of Growth, Changes in Growth Rates, and Corporate Share Prices. FAJ, 22 (May-Jun, 1966) 157-162

Mao, J. C. T.   The Valuation of Growth Stocks. JF, 21 (Mar, 1966), 95-102

Soldofsky, R. M.   The Industry of Bond Tables and Stock Valuation Models. JF, 21 (Mar, 1966), 103-111

Bauman, W. S.   The Investment Value of Common Stock Earnings and Dividends. FAJ, 21 (Nov-Dec, 1965), 98-104

Eiteman, D. K.   A Graphic Framework for Growth Stock Selection. CMR, 8 (Winter, 1965), 39-50

Huang, S. S. C.   Study of the Performance of Rapid Growth Stocks. FAJ, 21 (Jan-Feb, 1965), 58-59

Hubbard, C. L.   An Operational Stock Valuation Model Based on Multiple Growth Horizons. PhD diss, St U NY Buffalo, 1965

Molodovsky, N; May, C. & Chottiner, S.   Common Stock Valuation.
Part 1: FAJ, 21 (Mar-Apr, 1965), 104-123,
Part 2: FAJ, 21 (Sep-Oct, 1965), 135

Reisman, A.   On the Valuation of Growth Equity Shares. Paper for the 12th International Meeting of TIMS, Vienna, Sep, 1965

Wendt, P. F.   Current Growth Stock Valuation Methods. FAJ, 21 (Mar-Apr, 1965), 91-103

Bing, R. A.   Appraising Our Methods of Stock Appraisal. FAJ, 20 (May-Jun, 1964), 118-124

Friend, I.   Equity Yields, Growth and the Structure of Share Prices: Comment. AER, 54 (Dec, 1964), 1029-1035

Guild, S. E.   The Case for Stock Value Tables. FAJ, 20 (Sep-Oct, 1964), 80-97

Hayes, D. A.   Some Reflections on Techniques for Appraising Growth Rates. FAJ, 20 (Jul-Aug, 1964), 96-101

Bauman, W. S.   Estimating the Present Value of Common Stocks by the Variable Rate Method. U of Mich Busn Res, 1963

Malkiel, B. G.   Equity Yields, Growth and the Structure of Share Prices. AER, 53 (Dec, 1963), 1004-1031

Molodovsky, N.   'Its Good to Own Growth Stocks.' FAJ, 19 (Mar-Apr, 1963), 75 ff

Holt, C. C.   The Influence of Growth Duration on Share Prices. JF, 17 (Sep, 1962), 465-475

Kotler, P.   Elements in a Theory of Growth Stock Valuation. FAJ, 18 (May-Jun, 1962), 35-44

Ferguson, R.   A Nomograph for Valuing Growth Stocks. FAJ, 17 (May-Jun, 1961), 29-34

Margoshes, S. L.   'Present Value' Techniques of Common Stock Valuation. FAJ, 17 (Mar, 1961), 37-42

Miller, M. H. & Modigliani, F.   Dividend Policy, Growth and the Valuation of Shares. JB, 34 (Oct, 1961), 411-433

Soldofsky, R. M.   Growth Yields. FAJ, 17 (Sep-Oct, 1961), 43-47

Bohmfalk, J. F.   The Growth Stock Philosophy. FAJ, 16 (Nov-Dec, 1960), 113-123

Buckley, J. G.   A Method of Evaluating Growth Stocks. FAJ, 16 (Mar-Apr, 1960), 19-21

Burrell, O. K.   A Mathematical Approach to Growth Stock Valuation. FAJ, 16 (May-Jun, 1960), 69-76

Dake, L. E.   Are Analysts' Techniques Adequate for Growth Stocks? FAJ, 16 (Nov-Dec, 1960), 45-49

Kennedy, R. E., Jr.   Growth Stocks: Opportunity or Illusion. FAJ, 16 (Mar, 1960), 27-31

Margoshes, S. L.   Price-Earnings Ratio in Financial Analysis. FAJ, 16 (Nov, 1960), 125-130

Molodovsky, N.   Stock Values and Stock Prices.
Part 1: FAJ, 16 (May-Jun, 1960), 9 ff,
Part 2: FAJ, 16 (Jul-Aug, 1960), 53-54

Clendenin, J. C.   Price-Level Variations and the Tenets of High Grade Investment. JF, 14 (May, 1959), 245-262

Molodovsky, N.   Valuation of Common Stocks. AJ, 15 (Jan-Feb, 1959), 23-44

Conklin, G. H.   Growth Stocks—A Critical View. AJ, 14 (Feb, 1958), 49-52

Heilbrunn, R.   A Practical Approach to Common Stock Valuation. AJ, 14 (May, 1958), 49-51

Adderley, T. E. & Hayes, D. A.   The Investment Performance of Selected Growth Stock Portfolios: 1939-55. AJ, 13 (May, 1957), 65-76

Clendenin, J. C.   Theory and Technique of Growth Stock Valuation. UCLA Busn, 1957

Clendenin, J. C.   Dividend Growth as Determinant of Common Stock Values. TE, (Feb, 1957)

Durand, D.   Growth Stocks and the Petersburg Paradox. JF, 12 (Sep, 1957), 348-363

Kennedy, R. E., Jr.   An Approach to Pricing Growth Stocks. AJ, 13 (Aug, 1957), 31-33

Maynard, W.   Problems of Investing in Growth Stocks. AJ, 12 (Aug, 1956), 27-28

Palmer, G. A.   An Approach to Stock Valuation, AJ, 12 (May, 1956), 17-19

Howard, E. D.   The Relative Vulnerability of Growth and Income Stocks. AJ, 11 (Aug, 1955), 19-23

Molodovsky, N.   Stock Prices and Current Earnings. AJ, 11 (Aug, 1955), 83-94

Clendenin, J. & Van Cleave, M.   Growth and Common Stock Values. JF, 9 (Sep, 1954), 365-376

Molodovsky, N.   Some Aspects of Price-Earnings Ratios. AJ, 9 (May, 1953), 65-78

69

Molodovsky, N.   A Theory of Price-Earnings Ratios. AJ, 9 (Nov, 1953), 65-80

Clendenin, J.C.   Quality versus Price as Factors Influencing Common Stock Price Fluctuations. JF, 6 (Dec, 1951), 398-405

Jenks, J.C.   Investing in Growth Stock. AJ, 3 (2nd Qtr, 1947), 38-53

Mackintosh, G.   A Method of Valuing Growth Stocks. AJ, 1 (1st Qtr, 1945), 6-14

Williams, J.B.   The Theory of Investment Value. Harvard U Pr, 1938

7c SHARE VALUATION—CROSS-SECTIONAL ANALYSES

The following articles are concerned with cross-sectional regression models of share prices. Some, such as those of Bower & Bower, Arditti, Nerlove, Crowell or Benishay, are positive in character. The papers by Whitbeck & Kisor, Ahlers and Weaver & Hall exemplify the use of these models for normative purposes, an application which is strongly criticised by Keenan and Malkiel & Cragg.

See also:

7a   Share Valuation—General

Chase, D.D.   An Asset Portfolio Preference Model of Equity Valuation with an Empirical Investigation. DBA diss, Arizona St U, 1972

McKibben, W.   Econometric Forecasting of Common Stock Investment Returns: a New Methodology Using Fundamental Operating Data. JF, 27 (May, 1972), 371-380

Bower, D.H. & R.S.   Test of a Stock Valuation Model. JF, 25 (May, 1970), 483-492

Keenan, M.   The State of the Finance Field Methodology Models of Equity Valuation: The Great Serm Bubble. JF, 25 (May, 1970), 243-274

Malkiel, B.G. & Cragg, J.G.   Expectations and the Structure of Share Prices. AER, 60 (Sep, 1970), 601-617

Bower, R.S. & D.H.   Risk and the Valuation of Common Stock. JPE, 77 (May-Jun, 1969), 349-362

Hall, M.G.   Portfolio Management Using a Computer. Unp ms, 1969.

Ahlers, D.M. & Steglitz, M.   The Use and Misuse of Security Evaluation Models. Paper for the Seminar on the Analysis of Security Prices, U of Chicago, May 1968

Bauman, W.S. & Klein, T.A.   Investment Profit Correlation. U of Mich Busn Res, 1968

Bomford, M.D.   Changes in the Evaluation of Equities. IA, 22 (Dec, 1968), 3-12

Nerlove, M.   Factors Affecting Differences among Rates of Return on Investments in Individual Common Stocks. REStat, 50 (Aug, 1968), 312-331

Whitbeck, V.S.   An Iterative Version of a Stock Valuation Model. Paper for the Seminar on the Analysis of Security Prices, U of Chicago, May 1968

Arditti, F.D.   Risk and the Required Return on Equity. JF, 22 (Mar, 1967), 19-36

Crowell, R.A.   Earnings Expectations, Security Valuation and the Cost of Equity Capital. PhD diss, MIT, 1967

Kisor, M., Jr. & Feuerstein, A.   Towards a Valuation Model Employing Historical Constructs as Proxies for Analysts' Expectations. Paper for the Seminar on the Analysis of Security Prices, U of Chicago, May 1967

Weaver, D. & Hall, M.G.   The Evaluation of Ordinary Shares Using a Computer. JIA, 93 (1967), 165-203

Ahlers, D.M.   SEM: a Security Evaluation Model *in* Cohen K.J. & Hammer F.S. (Eds), Analytical Methods in Banking. Irwin, 1966

Drzycimski, E.F.   A Study of the Determinants of Common Stock Prices and Price-Relatives for a Selected Sample of Large Commercial Banks. PhD diss, Mich St U, 1966

Whitbeck, V.S. & Kisor, M., Jr.   A New Tool in Investment Decision Making. FAJ, 19 (May-Jun, 1963), 55-62

Benishay, H.   Variability in Earnings-Price Ratios: Reply. AER, 52 (Mar, 1962), 209-216

Gordon, M.J.   Variability in Earnings-Price Ratios: Comment. AER, 52 (Mar, 1962), 203-209

Scott, M.F.G.   Relative Share Prices and Yields. OEP, 14 (Oct, 1962), 218-250

Benishay, H.   Variability in Earnings-Price Ratios of Corporate Equities. AER, 51 (Mar, 1961), 81-94

Benishay, H.   Determinants of Variability in Earnings Price Ratio of Corporate Equity. PhD diss, U of Chicago, 1960

7d DETERMINANTS OF THE MARKET LEVEL

The following studies are representative of the very sparse literature on the determination of the overall market level. Solomon and Rose provide general discussions of the relationship between stock prices and economic growth, and Shiskin (listed elsewhere) and Pattison cite some empirical evidence. The paper by Coen et al. offers interesting, but highly controversial, reading on the relationship between market levels and a large number of economic variables.

See also:

4a   Investment Management—General
6b   Business Cycles and Stock Prices
6d   Money and Stock Prices
7a   Share Valuation—General

Fanning, J.E.   A Four-Indicator System for Forecasting the Market. FAJ, 27 (Sep-Oct, 1971), 49-56

Leroy, S.F.   The Determination of Stock Prices. PhD diss, U of Pa, 1971

Light, J.U.   The Effect of News of General Interest on Stock Market Prices. PhD, U of Wash, 1971

Pattison, J.C.   Stock Market Prices and Economic Activity: an Empirical Examination. JBF, 3 (Autumn, 1971), 13-17

McCue, G.A.   An Econometric Equity-Market Model: Cobwebs in the Stock Market. PhD diss, U of Cal Irvine, 1970

Coen, P.J.; Gomme, E.D. & Kendall, M.G.   Lagged Relationships in Economic Forecasting. JRSS, 31 (1969), A133-A163

Henderson, R.H.   Ruminations on Performance. FAJ, 25 (Nov-Dec, 1969), 103 ff

Renshaw, E. F.   Estimating the Return on S & P's Industrial Price Index
 FAJ, 25 (Jan-Feb, 1969), 121-123
Rose, H. B.   Reflections on the Equity Boom, 1966-69. TBR, 82 (Jun, 1969),
 4-24
Rose, H. B.   Price Earnings Multiples and Long Term Rates of Return.
 IA, 21 (Oct, 1968), 15-23
Whittaker, J.   How High is High?—the Market's Required Return in
 America and in Britain. IA, 20 (Jun, 1968), 15-19
Whittaker, J.   What Level for Share Prices? LBR, 87 (Jan, 1968), 1-14
Arena, J. J.   Postwar Stock Market Changes and Consumer Spending.
 REStat, 47 (Nov, 1965), 379-391
Helmer, B.   Perspective on Timing Equity Investments. FAJ, 21 (May-
 Jun, 1965), 21-25
Wyckoff, P. G.   The Psychology of Stock Market Timing. P-H, 1963
Molodovsky, N.   The Many Aspects of Yields. FAJ, 18 (Mar-Apr, 1962),
 49 ff
Sauvain, H. C.   Common Stock Prices in the Sixties. BH, 3 (Fall, 1960)
Lamberton, D. L.   Economic Growth and Stock Prices: the Australian
 Experience. JB, 31 (Jul, 1958), 200-212
Friend, I. & Parker, S.   A New Slant on the Stock Market. F, 68 (Sep, 1956)
Von Szeliski, V.   Predicting Stock Market Trends by Structure Analysis.
 AJ, 12 (May, 1956), 51-61
Solomon, E.   Economic Growth and Common-Stock Value. JB, 28 (Jul,
 1955), 213-221
La Farge, F. W.   Timing Common Stock Purchases and Sales. AJ, 10
 (Feb, 1954), 47-49
Storer, R. W.   A Stock-Price Yardstick. AJ, 10 (Aug, 1954), 51-56
Cottle, S. & Whitman, W. T.   Investment Timing. McGraw, 1953
Ray, H. C.   Pros and Cons of Timing Methods. AJ, 9 (Jun, 1953), 52-54
Farr, F. W. E.   The Future Level of Industrial Stock Prices. AJ, 5 (3rd
 Qtr, 1949), 26-27
Brown, B.   Common-Stock Price Ratios and Long-term Interest Rates.
 JB, 21 (Jul, 1948), 180-182
Knodel, H. W.   A Method of Appraising the Stock Market. AJ, 4 (4th Qtr,
 1948), 43-53
Rotnem, R. A.   Methods for Determining Stock Market Trends. AJ, 2 (3rd
 Qtr, 1946), 12-21
La Farge, F. W.   Methods of Evaluating Future Price Levels of the Dow-
 Jones Industrial Average. AJ, 1 (Oct, 1945), 49-55

Part 8 The Behaviour of Accounting Numbers & Their Effect on Stock Prices

8a THE TIME SERIES BEHAVIOUR OF EARNINGS

The notion that earnings growth is 'higgledy piggledy' was suggested by Little, first in his 1962 article and subsequently in his book with Rayner. The studies of Ball & Watts and Lintner & Glauber exemplify American studies of the topic. The time series behaviour of quarterly earnings is the subject of the controversy between Green & Segall and Brown in conjunction with Niederhoffer and Kennelly.

Ball, R. J. & Watts, R. Some Time Series Properties of Accounting Income. JF, 27 (Jun, 1972), 663-682

Brown, P. & Kennelly, J. W. The Informational Content of Quarterly Earnings: an Extension and Some Further Evidence. JB, 45 (Jul, 1972), 403-415

Youssef, A. A. The Predictive Power of Corporate Interim Earnings Reports. PhD diss, U of Minn, 1971

Beaver, W. H. The Time Series Behavior of Earnings. ERA, (1970), 62-107

Green, D., Jr. & Segall, J. Return of Strawman. JB, 43 (Jan, 1970), 63-65

Niederhoffer, V. The Predictive Content of First-Quarter Earnings Reports. JB, 43 (Jan, 1970), 60-62

Lintner, J. & Glauber, R. R. Further Observations on Higgledy Piggledy Growth. Paper for the Seminar on the Analysis of Security Prices, U of Chicago, May 1969

Simmons, J. K. & Gray, J. An Investigation of the Effect of Differing Accounting Frameworks on the Prediction of Net Income. AR, 44 (Oct, 1969), 757-776

Werner, F. A Study of the Predictive Significance of Two Income Measures. JAR, 7 (Spring, 1969), 123-136

Brown, P. & Niederhoffer, V. The Predictive Content of Quarterly Earnings. JB, 41 (Oct, 1968), 488-497

Green, D., Jr. & Segall, J. Brickbats and Straw Men: A Reply to Brown and Niederhoffer. JB, 41 (Oct, 1968), 498-502

Trent, R. H. Corporate Growth Rates: An Analysis of Their Intertemporal Association. PhD diss, U of NC, 1968

Brealey, R. A. The Character of Earnings Changes. Paper for the Seminar on the Analysis of Security Prices, U of Chicago, May 1967

Green, D., Jr. & Segall, J. The Predictive Power of First Quarter Earnings Reports. JB, 40 (Jan, 1967), 44-55

Lintner, J. & Glauber, R. R. Higgledy Piggledy Growth in America. Paper for the Seminar on the Analysis of Security Prices, U of Chicago, May 1967

Little, I. M. D. & Rayner, A. C. Higgledy Piggledy Growth Again. Blackwell, 1966

Murphy, J. Relative Growth of Earnings per Share—Past and Future. FAJ, 22 (Nov-Dec, 1966), 73-76

Hall, M. G. Some Thoughts on 'Higgledy Piggledy Growth'. IA, 5 (May, 1963), 3-10

Little, I. M. D. Higgledy Piggledy Growth. OIS, 24 (Nov, 1962), 387-412

8b THE FACTOR STRUCTURE OF FINANCIAL STATEMENTS

The articles in this section are principally concerned with measuring common and industry factors in earnings changes. Exceptions are the Williams & Goodman and Schwartz & Aronson articles which identify an industry component in balance sheet ratios.

See also:

10a Factor Structure of Rates of Return
10n Accounting and Market Determined Risk Measures

Gonedes, N. J.   Properties of Accounting Numbers: Models and Tests. Working Paper No 64-71-2, Graduate School of Industrial Administration, Carnegie-Mellon U, Jan 1972

Brealey, R. A.   Some Implications of the Co-movement of American Company Earnings. AE, 3 (1971), 183-196

Williams, W. H. & Goodman, M. L.   A Statistical Grouping of Corporations by their Financial Characteristics. JFQA, 6 (Sep, 1971), 1095-1104

Ball, R. & Brown, P.   Some Preliminary Findings on the Association Between the Earnings of a Firm, Its Industry and the Economy. ERA, (1967), 55-57

Schwartz, E. & Aronson, J. R.   Some Surrogate Evidence in Support of the Concept of Optimal Financial Structure. JF, 22 (Mar, 1967), 10-18

8c THE CHARACTERISTICS OF FINANCIAL STATEMENTS—GENERAL

This section contains miscellaneous papers on the behaviour of earnings and on the character and interpretation of financial statements. The implications of financial ratios for credit analysis are considered under 26g-'Bankruptcy and Reorganisations'.

See also:

8a The Time Series Behaviour of Earnings
8b The Factor Structure of Financial Statements
8d Earnings and Dividend Announcements and Stock Prices

Elliott, J. W.   Forecasting and Analysis of Corporate Financial Performance with an Econometric Model of the Firm. JFQA, 7 (Mar, 1972), 1499-1526

Gonedes, N. J.   Efficient Capital Markets and External Accounting. AR, 47 (Jan, 1972)

Kinney, W. R.   Predicting Earnings: Entity versus Subentity Data. JAR, 9 (Spring, 1971), 127-136

Murphy, J. E., Jr. & Nelson, J. R.   Five Principles of Financial Relationships. FAJ, 27 (Mar-Apr, 1971), 38-52

Murphy, J. E., Jr. & Nelson, J. R.   Random and Nonrandom Relationships Among Financial Variables: a Financial Model. JFQA, 6 (Mar, 1971), 875-886

Newell, G. E.   Revisions of Reported Quarterly Earnings. JB, 44 (Jul, 1971), 282-285

Whittington, G.   The Prediction of Profitability and Other Studies of Company Behaviour. Cambridge U Pr, 1971

Babcock, G. C.   The Concept of Sustainable Growth. FAJ, 26 (May-Jun, 1970), 108-114

Babcock, G. C.   The Trend and Stability of Earnings per Share. Paper for the Seminar on the Analysis of Security Prices, U of Chicago, Nov 1970

Solomon, E. & Laya, J. C.   Measuring Profitability. P-H, 1970

Cushing, B. E.   The Effects of Accounting Policy Decisions on Trends in Reported Corporate Earnings per Share. PhD diss, Mich St U, 1969

Dunning, J. H.   Profitability, Productivity and Measures of Business Performance. IA, 23 (Jun, 1969), 22-34

Mascia, J. S.   Corporate Earnings Predictions. FAJ, 25 (Jul-Aug, 1969), 107-110

Rolen, C. O.   An Analysis and Evaluation of Earnings per Share. PhD diss, U of Ark, 1969

Theil, H.   The Use of Information Theory Concepts in the Analysis of Financial Statements. MSci, 15 (May, 1969), 459-481

Johnson, A. W.   The Interpretation of Financial Statements. FAJ, 24 (Nov-Dec, 1968), 75 ff

Olsen, J. A. & Blaney, T. A.   Forecasting by Probabilities: the Copper Industry. FAJ, 24 (Mar-Apr, 1968), 36-40

Singh, A. & Whittington, G.   Growth, Profitability and Valuation: A Study of United Kingdom Quoted Companies. Cambridge U Pr, 1968

Whittall, D.   A Simulation Model for Estimating Earnings. FAJ, 24 (Nov-Dec, 1968), 115-118

Greenball, M. N.   The Concept, Relevance and Estimation of the Permanent Earnings of the Firm. PhD diss, U of Chicago, 1967

Taylor, B. F.   Financing Tables and the Future. IA, 19 (Dec, 1967), 29-35

Goodfriend, H. E.   Adjustment and Projection of Life Insurance Company Earnings Utilizing a Computer. FAJ, 22 (Nov-Dec, 1966), 57-63

Vatter, W. J.   Income Models, Book Yield, and Rate of Return. AR, 41 (Oct, 1966), 681-698

Smith, J. M., Jr.   Financial Information Conversion: Analysis and Evaluation. PhD diss, Stanford U, 1965

Block, F. E.   The Place of Book Value in Common Stock Evaluation. FAJ, 20 (Mar-Apr, 1964), 29-33

Block, F. E.   A Study of the Price to Book Relationship. FAJ, 20 (Sep-Oct, 1964), 108-117

Eiteman, D. K.   A Computer Program for Financial Statement Analysis. FAJ, 20 (Nov-Dec, 1964), 61-68

Kisor, M., Jr.   The Financial Aspects of Growth. FAJ, 20 (Mar-Apr, 1964), 46-51

Taylor, R. G.   An Examination of the Evolution, Content, Utility and Problems of Published Interim Reports. PhD diss, U of Chicago, 1964

Sorter, G. H. & Benston, G.   Appraising the Defensive Position of a Firm: The Interval Measure. AR, 35 (Oct, 1960), 633-640

Spacek, L.   Business Success Requires an Understanding of Unsolved Problems of Accounting and Financial Reporting. Address presented at Harvard U, Sep, 1959

Alten, K. W.   A New Tool for Security Analysis. AJ, 12 (Aug, 1956), 78-83

8d EARNINGS AND DIVIDEND ANNOUNCEMENTS AND STOCK PRICES

This section consists principally of empirical evidence concerning the impact on security prices of earnings announcements. Such, for example, are the studies of Ball & Brown, Beaver and Benston. A more dramatic but less rigorous analysis is that of Niederhoffer & Regan. The Treynor and Revsine papers have a different theme and raise some important general questions about the relevance for security analysts of accounting income numbers.

See also:

7a Share Valuation—General
7b Share Valuation—Present Value Theory and Growth Stocks

Niederhoffer, V. & Regan, P. J. Earnings Changes, Analysts' Forecasts and Stock Prices. FAJ. 28 (May-Jun, 1972), 65-71

Treynor, J. L. The Trouble with Earnings FAJ, 28 (Sep-Oct, 1972), 41-43

Gonedes, N. J. Some Evidence on Investor Actions and Accounting Messages.
Part 1: AR, 46 (Apr, 1971), 320-328,
Part 2: AR, 46 (Jul, 1971), 535-551

Jordan, R. J. An Empirical Investigation of the Adjustment of Stock Prices to New Quarterly Earnings Data. PhD diss, NYU, 1971

Kiger, J. E. An Empirical Investigation of the Use of Interim Reports. PhD diss, U of Mo, 1971

Revsine, L. Predictive Ability, Market Prices and Operating Flows. AR, 46 (Jul 1971), 480-489

Murphy, J. E., Jr. & Nelson, J. R. A Note on the Stability of P/E Ratios. FAJ, 25 (Mar-Apr, 1969), 77-80

Newell, G. E. Published Quarterly Financial Data: Their Adequacy for Investment Decision Making. PhD diss, Mich St U, 1969

Ball, R. J. & Brown, P. An Empirical Evaluation of Accounting Income Numbers. JAR, 6 (Autumn, 1968), 159-178

Beaver, W. H. The Information Content of Annual Earnings Announcements. ERA, (1968), 67-100

Fredman, A. J. The Relative Significance of Earnings and Dividends as Determinants of Stock Prices over Time and among Industries. PhD diss, UCLA, 1968

Green, V. M. Stock Prices and Subsequent Corporate Income. PhD diss, U of Wis, 1968

Murphy, J. E., Jr. Earnings Growth and Price Changes in the Same Time Period. FAJ, 24 (Jan-Feb, 1968), 97-99

O'Donnell, J. L. Relationships between Reported Earnings and Stock Prices in the Electric Utility Industry. AR, 43 (Jul, 1968), 549-553

Staubus, G. J. Earnings Periods for Common Share Analysis. JB, 41 (Oct, 1968), 472-476

Benston, G. J. Published Corporate Accounting Data and Stock Prices. ERA, (1967), 1-54

Latané, H. A. & Tuttle, D. L. An Analysis of Common Stock Price Ratios. SEJ, 33 (Jan, 1967), 343-354

Murphy, J. E., Jr. & Stevenson, H. W. Price/Earnings Ratios and Future Growth of Earnings and Dividends. FAJ, 23 (Nov-Dec, 1967), 111-114

Black, J. B., Jr. The Pattern of Accumulation of Common Equity Capital Relative to Price Earnings Relationships for Common Stocks. DBA diss, Indiana U, 1965

Smilen, K. B. & Safian, K. Relative Earnings: a Fresh Approach. FAJ, 20 (Sep-Oct, 1964), 104-107

Ashley, J. W. Stock Prices and Changes in Earnings and Dividends: Some Empirical Results. JPE, 70 (Feb, 1962), 82-85

Cottle, S. & Whitman, W. T.   Corporate Earning Power and Market Valuation, 1935-1955. Duke, 1959

Zinbarg, E. D.   Price-Earnings Ratios and Yields. AJ, 15 (Aug, 1959), 35-42

Wilcoxen, L. C.   The Price-Earnings-Variable Characteristics. AJ, 11 (Aug, 1955), 41-45

8e ACCOUNTING METHODS AND STOCK PRICES

This section is concerned with the effect on stock prices of differences in accounting methods. The articles by Ball, and Kaplan & Roll exemplify work in the area. Studies of the relevance to investors of accounting numbers are listed under 8d—'Earnings and Dividend Announcements and Stock Prices'.

Ball, R. J.   Risk, Return and Disequilibrium: an Application to Changes in Accounting Techniques. JF, 27 (May, 1972), 343-354

Barrett, M. E.   A.P.B. Opinion Number 18: a Move Toward Preferences of Users. FAJ, 28 (Jul-Aug, 1972), 47-55

Beaver, W. H. & Dukes, R. E.   Interperiod Tax Allocation, Earnings Expectations and the Behavior of Security Prices. AR, 47 (Apr, 1972), 320-332

Cattanach, R. L.   An Inquiry into the Informational Needs of Stockholders and Potential Investors. DBA diss, Arizona St U, 1972

Kaplan, R. S. & Roll, R.   Investor Evaluation of Accounting Information: some Empirical Evidence. JB, 45 (Apr, 1972), 225-257

Backer, M.   Financial Reporting and Security Investment Decisions. FAJ, 27 (Mar-Apr, 1971), 67 ff

Martin, A.   The Decision-Relevance of Reported Accounting Information: an Empirical Perspective. PhD diss, Northwestern U, 1971

Crooch, G. M.   An Investigation of Investors' Financial Statement Knowledge. PhD diss, Mich St U, 1970

McKenzie, P. B.   The Relative Usefulness to Investors of Price-Level Adjusted Financial Statements: an Empirical Study. PhD diss, Mich St U, 1970

Pankoff, L. D. & Virgil, R. L.   Some Preliminary Findings from a Laboratory Experiment on the Usefulness of Financial Accounting Information to Security Analysts. ERA, (1970), 1-61

Dyckman, T. R.   Investment Analysis and General Price-Level Adjustments: a Behavioral Study. Studies in Accounting Research No 1. Evanston, Ill: American Accounting Association, 1969

Mlynarczyk, F. A., Jr.   An Empirical Study of Accounting Methods and Stock Prices. ERA, (1969), 63-89

Greenball, M. N.   Evaluation of the Usefulness to Investors of Different Accounting Estimators of Earnings: a Simulation Approach. ERA, (1968), 27-58

Simmons, J. K.   Comparability in Financial Reporting: the Concept and its Application to Financial Analysts. PhD diss, Ohio St U, 1967

Jensen, R. E.   An Experimental Design for Study of Effects of Accounting Variations in Decision Making. JAR, 4 (Autumn, 1966), 224-238

8f EARNINGS FILTERS

Some evidence has been produced to suggest that the recent earnings history provides some information about a stock's subsequent performance.

This view is exemplified in the work of Kisor and Jones & Litzenberger.

See also:

8g   Performance of Low P/E Ratio Stocks

Litzenberger, R. H.; Joy, O. M. & Jones, C. P.   Ordinal Predictions and the Selection of Common Stocks. JFQA, 6 (Sep, 1971), 1059-1068

Jones, C. P. & Litzenberger, R. H.   Quarterly Earnings Reports and Intermediate Stock Price Trends. JF, 25 (Mar, 1970), 143-148

Latané, H. A.; Joy, O. M. & Jones, C. P.   Quarterly Data, Sort-Rank Routines, and Security Evaluation. JB, 43 (Oct, 1970), 427-438

Gould, A. & Buchsbaum, M.   A Filter Approach Using Earnings Relatives. FAJ, 25 (Nov-Dec, 1969), 61 ff

Jones, C. P.   The Value of Quarterly Information in Predicting Future Stock Price Changes. PhD diss, U of NC, 1969

Kisor, M., Jr. & Messner, V. A.   The Filter Approach and Earnings Forecasts. FAJ, 25 (Jan-Feb, 1969), 109-116

Myers, T. S.   A leading Indicator Approach to Stock Selection. Financial Research, Investment Analysis and the Computer, the Amos Tuck School, Dartmouth C, 1967

Kisor, M., Jr.   Quantitative Approaches to Common Stock Selection. BE, 2 (Spring, 1966)

Peck, L. G.   A Critique of the Filter Technique. FAJ, 22 (May-Jun, 1966), 156

8g   PERFORMANCE OF LOW P/E RATIO STOCKS

Some evidence has been adduced which suggests that low P/E ratio stocks provide superior rates of return. The articles by Nicholson and McWilliams were important contributions to this belief. Some further discussion of the subject is contained in articles listed under 8f—'Earnings Filters'.

Joy, O. M. & Jones, C. P.   Predictive Value of P/E Ratios. FAJ, 26 (Sep-Oct, 1970), 61-68

Nicholson, S. F.   Price-Earnings Ratios. FAJ, 16 (Jul-Aug, 1970), 43-45

Latané, H. A., Tuttle, D. L. & Jones, C. P.   E/P Ratios v Changes in Earnings. FAJ, 25 (Jan-Feb, 1969), 117-120

Breen, W. J.   Low Price-Earnings Ratios and Industry Relatives. FAJ, 24 (Jul-Aug, 1968), 125-127

Fluegel, F. K.   The Rate of Return on High and Low P/E Ratio Stocks. FAJ, 24 (Nov-Dec, 1968), 130-133

Nicholson, S. F.   Price Ratios in Relation to Investment Results. FAJ, 24 (Jan-Feb, 1968), 105-109

Miller, P. F., Jr. & Beach, T. E.   Recent Studies of P/E Ratios—A Reply. FAJ, 23 (May-Jun, 1967), 109-110

Molodovsky, N.   Recent Studies of P/E Ratios.   FAJ, 23 (Mar-Apr, 1967), 101-108

McWilliams, J. D.   Prices, Earnings and P-E Ratios. FAJ, 22 (May-Jun, 1966), 137-142

Part 9 Decisions Under Uncertainty & General Equilibrium Conditions

9a UTILITY THEORY

This section contains a small selection from the vast literature on utility theory. Grayson (listed elsewhere) provides a very readable introduction to the subject and Ozga a useful synthesis of the literature. We would draw particular attention to Arrow's 1965 lectures on utility and to the historically important works of Bernoulli, Ramsey, de Finetti, Savage and Menger.

See also:

    9b Utility Functions—Some Empirical Studies
    9c Decisions Under Uncertainty—General
    9d Equilibrium Under Uncertainty—General
    10k Dynamic Portfolio Theory

Fama, E. F.   Ordinal and Measurable Utility *in* Jensen, M. C. (Ed), Studies in the Theory of Capital Markets, Praeger, 1972

Luce, R. D. & Krantz, D. H.   Conditional Expected Utility. Em, 39 (Mar, 1971), 253-272

Jamison, D.   Time Preference and Utility: A Comment. EJ, 80 (Mar, 1970), 179-180

Shackle, G. L. S.   Decision Order and Time in Human Affairs, 2nd ed. Cambridge U Pr, 1970

Zeckhauser, R. & Keeler, E.   Another Type of Risk Aversion. Em, 38 (Sep, 1970), 661-665

Stiglitz, J. E.   Behavior Towards Risk with Many Commodities. Em, 37 (Oct, 1969), 660-667

Borch, K.   The Economics of Uncertainty. Princeton U Pr, 1968

Enzer, H.   An Utility Measure Based on Time Preference. EJ, 78 (Dec, 1968), 888-897

Fishburn, P. C.   Methods of Estimating Additive Utilities. MSci, 13 (Mar, 1967), 435-453

Lloyd C; Rohr, R. J. & Walker, M.   A Calculus Proof of the Existence of a Continuous Utility Function. Met, 19 (1967), 103-112

Borch, K.   A Utility Function Derived from a Survival Game. MSci, 12 (Apr, 1966), B287-B295

Swalm, R. O.   Utility Theory-Insights into Risk Taking. HBR, 44 (Nov-Dec, 1966), 123-136

Arrow, K. J.   Aspects of the Theory of Risk Bearing.   Jahnssonin, 1965

Ozga, S. A.   Expectations in Economic Theory. Weidenfeld & N, 1965

Rosett, R. N.   Gambling and Rationality. JPE, 73 (Dec, 1965), 595-607

Yaari, M. E.   Convexity in the Theory of Choice under Risk. QJE, 79 (May, 1965), 278-290

Pratt, J. W.   Risk Aversion in the Small and in the Large. Em, 32 (Jan-Apr, 1964), 122-136

Borch, K.   A Note on Utility and Attitudes to Risk. MSci, 9 (Jul, 1963), 697-700

Ellsberg, D.   Risk, Ambiguity and the Savage Axioms: Reply. QJE, 77 (May, 1963), 336-342

Roberts, H. V.   Risk, Ambiguity and the Savage Axioms: Comment. QJE, 77 (May, 1963), 327-336

Massé, P.   Optimal Investment Decisions: Rules for Action and Criteria for Choice. Translated by Scripta Technica, Inc, P-H, 1962

Pollak, R.A.   Additive Von Neumann-Morgenstern Utility Functions. Em, 30 (Oct, 1962), 729-743

Quirk, J.P. & Saposnik, R.   Admissibility and Measurable Utility Functions. REStud, 29 (Feb, 1962), 140-146

Eisenberg, E.   Aggregation of Utility Functions. MSci, 7 (Jul, 1961), 337-350

Ellsberg, D.   Risk, Ambiguity and the Savage Axioms. QJE, 75 (Nov, 1961), 643-669

Raiffa, H.   Risk, Ambiguity and the Savage Axioms: Comment. QJE, 74 (Nov, 1961), 690-694

Suppes, P.   Behavioristic Foundations of Utility. Em, 29 (Apr, 1961) 186-202

Chipman, J.S.   The Foundations of Utility. Em, 28 (Apr, 1960), 193-224

Koopmans, T.C.   Stationary Ordinal Utility and Impatience. Em, 28 (Apr, 1960), 287-309

Majumdar, T.   The Measurement of Utility. St Martin, 1958

Shackle, G.L.S.   Uncertainty in Economics and Other Reflections. Cambridge U Pr, 1955

Ellsberg, D.   Classic and Current Notions of 'Measurable Utility'. EJ, 64 (Sep, 1954)

Savage, L.J.   The Foundations of Statistics. Wiley, 1954

Alchian, A.A.   The Meaning of Utility Measurement. AER, 43 (Mar, 1953), 26-50

Herstein, I.N. & Milnor, J.   An Axiomatic Approach to Measurable Utility. Em, 21 (Apr, 1953), 291-297

Strotz, R.H.   Cardinal Utility. AER, 43 (May, 1953), 390-391

Friedman, M. & Savage, L.J.   The Expected Utility Hypothesis and the Measurability of Utility. JPE, 60 (Dec, 1952), 463-475

Markowitz, H.M.   The Utility of Wealth. JPE, 60 (Apr, 1952), 151-158

Samuelson, P.A.   Probability, Utility and the Independence Axiom. Em, 20 (Oct, 1952)

Hurwicz, L.   Optimality Criteria for Decision Making Under Ignorance. Cowles Commission Discussion Paper, No. 370 (1951)

Marschak, J.   Rational Behavior, Uncertain Prospects and Measurable Utility. Em, 18 (Apr, 1950), 111-141

Stigler, G.J.   The Development of Utility Theory. JPE, 58 (Aug, 1950), 307-327

Shackle, G.L.S.   Expectations in Economics. Cambridge U Pr, 1949

Armstrong, W.E.   Uncertainty and the Utility Function. EJ, 58 (Mar, 1948), 1-10

Friedman, M. & Savage, L.J.   The Utility Analysis of Choices Involving Risk. JPE, 56 (Aug, 1948), 279-304

Vickrey, W.S.   Measuring Marginal Utility by Reactions to Risk. Em, 13 (Oct, 1945), 319-333

Tintner, G.   A Contribution to the Non-Static Theory of Choice. QJE, 55 (Feb, 1942), 274-306

Tintner, G.   The Theory of Choice Under Subjective Risk and Uncertainty. Em, 9 (Jul-Oct, 1941), 298-304

Finetti, B. De.   La Prévision: ses Lois Logiques, ses Sources Subjectives. Annales de l'Institut Henri Poincaré, 7 (1937), 1-68. Translated into English *in* Kyburg, H.E., Jr. & Smokler H.E., Studies in Subjective Probability, Wiley, 1964

Menger, K.   Das Unsicherheitsmoment in der Wertlehre Zeitschrift für
    Nationalökonomie, 51 (1934), 459-485
Ramsey, F. P.   Truth and Probability, *in* The Foundations of Mathematics
    and Other Logical Essays. Paul Trench, 1931
Bernoulli, D.   Exposition of a New Theory on the Measurement of Risk.
    Papers of the Imperial Academy of Science in Petersburg, 2 (1730),
    175-192. Translated into English by Sommer, L., Em, (Jan, 1954), 23-36

9b UTILITY FUNCTIONS—SOME EMPIRICAL STUDIES

The following publications are concerned with attempts to quantify individuals' utility functions, usually by forcing them to choose between hypothe-
tical gambles. Important early works are those of Grayson and Mosteller
& Nogee, with the former providing a readable general introduction to
utility theory.

See also:

Gordon, M. J.; Paradis, G. E. & Rorke, C. H.   Experimental Evidence on
    Alternative Portfolio Decision Rules. AER, 62 (Mar, 1972), 107-118
Alderfer, C. P. & Bierman, H., Jr.   Choices with Risk: Beyond the Mean
    and Variance. JB, 43 (Jul, 1970), 341-353
Becker, S. W. & Weil, R. L.   Experimental Determination of Risk Pre-
    ferences for Portfolio Selection. Paper for the Seminar on the Analysis
    of Security Prices, U of Chicago, Nov 1970
Green, P. E. & Maheshwari, A.   Common Stock Perception and Preference:
    an Application of Multi-Dimensional Scaling. JB, 42 (Oct, 1969),
    439-457
Feldstein, M. S.   On the Measurement of Risk Aversion. SEJ, 35 (Jul,
    1968), 58-59
Kogan, N. & Wallach, M. A.   Risk Taking: a Study in Cognition &
    Personality. HR & W, 1964
De Groot, M. H.   Some Comments on the Experimental Measurement of
    Utility. BS, 8 (Apr, 1963), 146-149
Green, P. E.   The Derivation of Utility Functions in a Large Industrial
    Firm. Paper for the First Joint National Meeting of the Operations
    Research Society of America and the Institute of Management Sciences,
    1961
Coombs, C. H. & Pruitt, D. G.   Components of Risk in Decision-Making:
    Probability and Variance Preferences. JEP, 60 (1960), 265-277
Grayson, C. J.   Decisions Under Uncertainty: Drilling Decisions by Oil and
    Gas Operators. Harvard Bus, 1960
Latané, H. A.   Individual Risk Preference in Portfolio Selection. JF, 15
    (Mar, 1960), 45-52
Edwards, W.   Variance Preferences in Gambling. AJP, 67 (1954), 441-452
Edwards, W.   Probability Preferences in Gambling. AJP, 66 (Jul, 1953),
    349-364
Mosteller, F. & Nogee, P.   An Experimental Measurement of Utility.
    JPE, 59 (Oct, 1951), 371-404

Somewhat artificially we have attempted to distinguish between articles on utility theory and those on the problem of decision making under uncertainty with particular reference to financial decision making. We draw attention to Von Neumann & Morgenstern's classical work on game theory, the exposition by Pratt et al. of the foundations of Bayesian decision theory and the works by Hirshleifer and Myers on state preference and choice theoretic approaches.

See also:

9a Utility Theory
9d Equilibrium Under Uncertainty—General
10b The Measurement of Risk

Diamond, P. A. & Yaari, M. E.   Implications of the Theory of Rationing for Consumer Choice Under Uncertainty. AER, 62 (Jun, 1972), 333-343

Kamien, M. I. & Schwartz, N. L.   A Direct Approach to Choice Under Uncertainty. MSci, 18 (Apr, 1972), B470-B477

Hakansson, N. H.   An Induced Theory of the Firm Under Risk: The Pure Mutual Fund. JFQA, 5 (Jun, 1970), 155-178

Machol, R. E. & Lerner, E. M.   Risk, Ruin and Investment Analysis. JFQA, 4 (Dec, 1969), 473-492

Bierman, H., Jr.   Using Investment Portfolios to Change Risk. JFQA, 3 (Jun, 1968), 151-156

Borch, K.   Indifference Curves and Uncertainty. SJE, 70 (Mar, 1968), 19-24

Borch, K. & Mossin, J. (Eds).   Risk and Uncertainty: Proceedings of a Conference by the International Economic Association. Macmillan Int, 1968

Buff, J. H.; Biggar, G. G., Jr. & Burkhead, J. G.   The Application of New Decision Analysis Techniques to Investment Research. FAJ, 24 (Nov-Dec, 1968), 123-128

Freimer, M. & Gordon, M. J.   Investment Behavior with Utility a Concave Function of Wealth, *in* Borch, K. and Mossin, J. (Eds), Risk and Uncertainty. Macmillan Int, 1968

Hammond, J. S., III   Towards Simplifying the Analysis of Decisions Under Uncertainty Where Preference is Non-Linear. DBA diss, Harvard Bus, 1968

Hodges, S. D. & Moore, P. G.   The Consideration of Risk in Project Selection. JIA, 94 (1968), 355-378

Latané, H. A. & Tuttle, D. L.   Framework for Forming Probability Beliefs. FAJ, 24 (Jul-Aug, 1968) 51-61

Maccrimmon, K. R.   Descriptive and Normative Implications of the Decision-Theory Postulates, *in* Borch, K., & Mossin, J. (Eds), Risk and Uncertainty. Macmillan Int, 1968

Mossin, J.   Studies in the Theory of Risk-bearing. PhD diss, Carnegie-Mellon U, 1968

Myers, S. C.   Effects of Uncertainty on the Valuation of Securities and the Financial Decisions of the Firm. JF, 23 (Mar, 1968), 205-206

Myers, S. C.   A Time-State Preference Model of Security Valuation. JFQA, 3 (Mar, 1968), 1-34

Raiffa, H.   Decision Analysis: Introductory Lectures on Choices Under Uncertainty. Addison-Wes, 1968

Rosett, R. N. Measuring the Perception of Risk, *in* Borch, K., & Mossin, J. (Eds), Risk and Uncertainty. Macmillan Int, 1968

Borch, K. The Theory of Risk. JRSS, 29 (1967), B432-B452

Chen, A. H-Y. Valuation Under Uncertainty. JFQA, 2 (Sep, 1967), 313-326

Hammond, J. S., III Better Decisions with Preference Theory. HBR, 45 (Nov-Dec, 1967), 123-141

Myers, S. C. Effects of Uncertainty on the Valuation of Securities and the Financial Decisions of the Firm. PhD diss, Stanford U, 1967

Puu, T. Some Reflections on the Theories of Choice Between Alternative Investment Opportunities. Weltwirtsch Archiv, 99 (1967), 107-123

Royama, S. & Hamada, K. Substitution and Complementarity in the Choice of Risky Assets, *in* Hester, D. D. & Tobin, J. E. (Eds), Risk Aversion and Portfolio Choice. Wiley, 1967

Hirshleifer, J. Investment Decision Under Uncertainty: Applications of the State-Preference Approach. QJE, 80 (May, 1966), 252-277

Latané, H. A. & Tuttle, D. L. Decision Theory and Financial Management. JF, 21 (May 1966), 228-244

Nevins, A. J. Some Effects of Uncertainty: Simulation of a Model of Price. QJE, 80 (Feb, 1966), 73-87

Robichek, A. A., & Myers, S. C. Valuation of the Firm: Effects of Uncertainty in the Market Context. JF, 21 (May, 1966), 215-227

Thompson, H. E. & Beranek, W. The Efficient Use of an Imperfect Forecast. MSci, 13 (Nov, 1966), 233-243

Brewer, K. R. W. & Fellner, W. The Slanting of Subjective Probabilities-Agreement on some Essentials. QJE, 79 (Nov, 1965), 657-663

Fellner, W. Probability and Profit. Irwin, 1965

Hirshleifer, J. Investment Decision Under Uncertainty: Choice-Theoretic Approaches. QJE 79 (Nov, 1965), 509-536

Naslund, B. Mathematical Programming under Risk. SJE, 67 (Sep, 1965), 240-255

Roberts, H. V. Probabilistic Prediction. JASA, 60 (Mar, 1965), 50-62

Archer, S. H. The Structure of Management Decision Theory. AMJ, (Dec, 1964), 269-287

Becker, S. W. & Brownson, F. O. What Price Ambiguity? Or the Role of Ambiguity in Decision Making. JPE, 72 (Feb, 1964), 62-73

Boehm, G. A. W. The Science of Being Almost Certain. F, 76 (Feb, 1964), 104 ff.

Brown, R. Measuring Uncertainty in Business Investigations. JMS, 1 (Sep, 1964), 143-163

Cootner, P. H. Rationality and Risk in Financial Decision Making, *in* Fisk, G. (Ed), The Frontiers of Management Psychology. Har-Row, 1964

Naslund, B. & Whinston, A. Model of Decision-Making under Risk. Met, 16 (May-Aug, 1964), 81-94

Pratt, J. W.; Raiffa, H. & Schlaifer, R. The Foundations of Decision Under Uncertainty. JASA, 59 (Jun, 1964), 353-375

Brewer, K. R. W. Decisions Under Uncertainty: Comment. QSE, 77 (Feb, 1963), 159-161

Fellner, W. Slanted Subjective Probabilities and Randomization: Reply to Howard Raiffa and K. R. W. Brewer. QJE, 77 (Nov, 1963), 676-690

Hemsted, J. R. Probability in the Investment Field. IA, 5 (May, 1963), 11-15

Tisdell, C. Notes Upon some of the Present Theories of Choice under Uncertainty. Met, 15 (Aug-Dec, 1963), 125-135

Fellner, W.   Distortion of Subjective Probabilities as a Reaction to Uncertainty. QJE, 75 (Nov, 1961), 670-689

Smith, V. L.   Time Preference and Risk in Investment Theory. AER, 51 (May, 1961), 124-127

Angell, J. W.   Uncertainty, Likelihoods and Investment Decisions. QJE, 74 (Feb, 1960), 1-28

Egerton, R. A. D.   Investment Decisions under Uncertainty. Liverpool U Pr, 1960

Haring, J. E. & Smith, G. C.   Utility Theory, Decision Theory, and Profit Maximization. AER, 49 (Sep, 1959), 566-583

Bowman, M. J. (Ed).   Expectations, Uncertainty, and Business Behavior. Soc Sci Res, 1958

Carter, C. F.; Meredith, G. P. & Shackle, G. L. S. (Eds).   Uncertainty and Business Decisions: The Logic, Philosophy and Psychology of Business Decision-Making Under Uncertainty: A Symposium, 2nd ed. Liverpool U Pr, 1957

Redlich, F.   Towards a Better Theory of Risk. Explorations in Entrepreneurial History, (Oct, 1957), 33-39

Freund, R. J.   The Introduction of Risk Into a Programming Model. Em, 24 (Jul, 1956), 253-263

Egerton, R. A. D.   Investment, Uncertainty and Expectations. REStud, 22 (Summer 1955), 143-150

Kenadjian, V. H.   Constant Safety Versus Sound Profitability. AJ, 11 (Aug, 1955), 77-80

Edwards, W.   The Theory of Decision Making. PB, (Jul, 1954), 380-417

Gorski, R. S.   Investment Security in an Uncertain World. AJ, 10 (Aug, 1954), 33-36

Von Neumann, J. & Morgenstern, O.   Theory of Games and Economic Behavior. Princeton U Pr, 1953

Arrow, K. J.   Alternative Approaches to the Theory of Choice in Risk Taking Situations. Em, 19 (Oct, 1951), 404-437

Hart, A. G.   Risk, Uncertainty and the Unprofitability of Compounding Probabilities, *in* Studies in Mathematical Economics and Econometrics. U of Chicago Pr, 1942

Steindl, J.   On Risk. OEP, (Jun, 1941), 43-53

Hart, A. G.   Anticipations, Uncertainty, and Dynamic Planning. U of Chicago Pr, 1940

Kalecki, M.   The Principle of Increasing Risk. Ec, 4 (Nov, 1937), 440-447

Knight, F. H.   Risk, Uncertainty and Profit. Kelley, 1921

Haynes, J.   Risk as an Economic Factor. QJE, 9 (Jul, 1895), 409-449

Clark, J. B.   Insurance and Business Profit. QJE, 6 (Oct, 1892), 40-54

9d EQUILIBRIUM UNDER UNCERTAINTY—GENERAL

The works in this section are principally concerned with the theory of the existence and optimality of competitive equilibrium in an uncertain world. The development of much of the analysis stems from Arrow (1964) and Debreu (1959). Radner's 1970 article provides a useful brief survey and discussion of the topic.

See also

9a   Utility Theory
9c   Decisions Under Uncertainty—General

Long, J. B., Jr.   Wealth, Welfare and the Price of Risk. JF, 27 (May, 1972), 419-433

Long, J. B., Jr. & Jensen, M. C.   Corporate Investment Under Uncertainty and Pareto Optimality in the Capital Market. Bell J, 3 (Apr, 1972)

Stiglitz, J. G.   On the Optimality of Stock Market Allocation. QJE, 86 (Feb, 1972), 25-60

Fama, E. F. & Laffer, A. B.   Perfect Competition and the Market Value Rule in the Two Parameter Model. Unp ms, U of Chicago, Oct 1971

Imai, Y.   An Integration of Neo-classical Theory of Optimal Accumulation and Corporate Financial Theory. PhD diss, Rice U, 1971

Radner, R.   Problems in the Theory of Markets under Uncertainty. AER, 60 (May, 1970), 454-464

Sandmo, A.   Equilibrium and Efficiency in Loan Markets. Ec, 37 (Feb, 1970), 23-38

Schmeidler, D.   Competitive Equilibria in Markets with a Continuum of Traders and Incomplete Preferences. Em, 37 (Oct. 1969), 578-585

Stignum, B. P.   Competitive Equilibria under Uncertainty. QJE, 83 (Nov, 1969), 533-561

Borch, K.   General Equilibrium in the Economics of Uncertainty, *in* Risk and Uncertainty, Borch, K., & Mossin, J., (Eds). Macmillan Int, 1968

Radner, R.   Competitive Equilibrium Under Uncertainty. Em, 36 (Jan, 1968), 821-824

Borch, K.   The Economic Theory of Insurance. The Astin Bulletin, (Jul, 1967), 252-264

Diamond, P. A.   The Role of a Stock Market in a General Equilibrium Model with Technological Uncertainty. AER, 57 (Sep, 1967), 759-776

Ferber, R. (Ed).   Determinants of Investment Behavior. Natl Bur Econ Res, 1967

Aumann, R. J.   Existence of Competitive Equilibria in Markets with a Continuum of Traders. Em, 34 (Jan, 1966), 1-17

Arrow, K. J.   The Role of Securities in the Optimal Allocation of Risk-Bearing. REStud, 46 (Apr, 1964), 91-96

Arrow, K. J.   Uncertainty and the Welfare Economics of Medical Care. AER, 53 (Dec, 1963), 941-973

Debreu, G.   New Concepts and Techniques for Equilibrium Analysis. IntER, 3 (1962), 257-273

Debreu, G.   Theory of Value: an Axiomatic Analysis of Economic Equilibrium. Wiley, 1959

McKenzie, L. W.   On the Existence of General Equilibrium for a Competitive Market. Em, 27 (Jan, 1959), 54-71

Hicks, J. R.   Value and Capital: An Inquiry Into Some Fundamental Principles of Economic Theory, 2nd ed. Oxford U Pr, 1946

9e SPECULATION AND STABILITY

The following articles are concerned with the stabilising effects of speculation. The exchange between Baumol and Telser and the paper by Friedman exemplify this work. In rather different vein is Muth's article on the implications for prices of a particular model of expectations. Black's paper offers a test of the Muth model.

See also:

9d   Equilibrium Under Uncertainty—General

Black, S. W.   The Use of Rational Expectations in Models of Speculation. REStat, 54 (May, 1972), 161-165

Gray, R. W.   Price Effects of a Lack of Speculation. FRIS, 7 (Suppl, 1967), 177-194

Farrell, M. J.   Profitable Speculation. Ec, 46 (May, 1966), 183-193

Glahe, F. R.   Professional and Nonprofessional Speculation, Profitability, and Stability. SEJ, 33 (Jul, 1966), 43-44

Aliber, R. Z.   Speculation and Price Stability Once Again. JPE, 72 (Dec, 1964), 607-609

Fishman, G. S.   Price Behavior Under Alternative Forms of Price Expectations. QJE, 78 (May, 1964), 281-298

Kemp, M. C.   Speculation, Profitability and Price Stability. REStat, 45 (May, 1963), 185-189

Muth, J. F.   Rational Expectations and the Theory of Price Movements. Em, 29 (Jul, 1961), 315-335

Stein, J. L.   Destabilizing Speculative Activity Can be Profitable. REStat, 43 (Aug, 1961), 301-302

Friedman, M.   In Defense of Destabilizing Speculation, *in* Prouts, R. W. (Ed), Essays in Economics and Econometrics. U of NC Pr, 1960

Telser, L. G.   A Theory of Speculation Relating Profitability and Stability. REStat, 41 (Aug, 1959), 295-301

Baumol, W. J.   Speculation, Profitability and Stability. REStat, 39 (Aug, 1957), 263-271

Meade, J.   Degrees of Competitive Speculation. REStud, 17 (1949-1950)

Kaldor, N.   Speculation and Economic Stability. REStud, 7 (Oct, 1939), 13-16

Williams, J. B.   Speculation and the Carry Over. QJE, 50 (May, 1936)

Part 10 Portfolio Selection & Capital Asset Pricing Theory

10a FACTOR STRUCTURE OF RATES OF RETURN

This section is concerned with the identification of market and industry factors in rates of return. King's 1966 article constituted an important contribution. The subject has major implications for topics discussed under heading 10b—'The Measurement of Risk'.

Hall, M. G. Industries or Shares—a Controversial Problem in Portfolio Management. IA, 33 (Sep, 1972), 12-23

Tysseland, M. S. Further Tests of the Validity of the Industry Approach to Investment Analysis. JFQA, 6 (Mar, 1971), 835-848

Meyers, S. L. A Factor Analysis Approach to Studying the Structure of the Stock Market. PhD diss, U of Penn, 1970

Ewart-James, D. O. A Factor Analysis of Stock Market Prices. MBA thesis, Manchester Bus, 1969

Feeney, G. J. & Hester, D. D. Stock Market Indices: a Principal Components Analysis, *in* Hester, D. D. & Tobin, J. (Eds), Risk Aversion and Portfolio Choice. Wiley, 1967

King, B. F. Market and Industry Factors in Stock Price Behavior. JB, 39 (Jan, 1966), 139-190

King, B. F. The Latent Statistical Structure of Security Price Changes. PhD diss, U of Chicago, 1964

Yohn, C. B. An Investigation of the Covariance of Stock Prices. SB thesis, MIT, 1962

Durand, D. Bank Stocks and the Analysis of Covariance. Em, 23 (Jan, 1955), 30-45

10b THE MEASUREMENT OF RISK

This section is devoted to works on objective estimates of stock market risk, particularly systematic risk. Several of the articles (exemplified by Blume (1971)) examine the stationarity of ordinary least squares estimates of beta. Others, such as Kantor, Fisher & Kamin and Sharpe examine alternative regression procedures. A good illustration of institutional attitudes to such measures is to be found in Welles.

See also:

> 9c Decisions Under Uncertainty—General
> 10l Capital Asset Pricing Theory
> 10n Accounting and Market Determined Risk Measures

Schwartz, R. A. & Altman, E. I. Volatility Behavior of Industrial Stock Price Indices. JF, forthcoming

Babcock, G. C. A Note on Justifying Beta as a Measure of Risk. JF, 27 (Jun, 1972), 699-702

Beja, A. On Systematic and Unsystematic Components of Financial Risk. JF, 27 (Mar, 1972), 37-46

Campanella, F. B. The Measurement of Portfolio Risk Exposure, the Use of the Beta Coefficient. Heath, 1972

Blume, M. E. On the Assessment of Risk. JF, 26 (Mar, 1971), 1-10

Fisher, L. & Kamin, J. Good Betas and Bad Betas. Paper for the Seminar on the Analysis of Security Prices. University of Chicago, Nov 1971

Jacob, N. L. The Measurement of Systematic Risk for Securities and Portfolios: Some Empirical Results. JFQA, 6 (Mar, 1971), 815-834

Kantor, M. Market Sensitivities. FAJ, 27 (Jan-Feb, 1971), 64-68

Levy, R. A. On the Short Term Stationarity of Beta Coefficients. FAJ, 27 (Nov-Dec, 1971), 55-62

Mokkelbost, P. B. Unsystematic Risk Over Time. JFQA, 6 (Mar, 1971), 785-796

Mumey, G. A. & Korkie, R. M. Balance Sheet Additivity of Risk Measures. JFQA, 6 (Sep, 1971), 1123-1134

Pinches, G. E. & Kinney, W. R. The Measurement of the Volatility of Common Stock Prices. JF, 26 (Mar, 1971), 119-126

Sharpe, W. F. Mean-Absolute-Deviation Characteristic Lines for Securities and Portfolios. MSci, 18 (Oct, 1971), B1-B13

Welles, C. The Beta Revolution: Learning to Live with Risk. II, 5 (Sep, 1971), 21 ff

Zdanowicz, J. S. Investment Risk Considering Intraperiod Liquidation: a Reevaluation of Price Variance. PhD diss, Mich St U, 1971

Altman, E. I. & Schwartz, R. A. Common Stock Price Volatility Measures and Patterns. JFQA, 4 (Jan, 1970), 603-626

Campanella, F. B. The Measurement and Use of Systematic Risk. DBA diss, Harvard Bus, 1970

Jacob, N. L. The Measurement of Market Similarity for Securities under Uncertainty. JB, 43 (Jul, 1970), 328-340

Joyce, J. M. & Vogel, R. C. The Uncertainty in Risk: Is Variance Unambiguous? JF, 25 (Mar, 1970), 127-134

Brealey, R. A. The Impact of the Market on British Share Prices. IA, 24 (Oct, 1969), 3-9

Drzycimiski, E. F. & Yudelson, J. Problems in the Measurement of Risk. FE, 37 (Sep, 1969), 32-36

Blume, M. E. The Assessment of Portfolio Performance—An Application to Portfolio Theory. PhD diss, U of Chicago, 1968

Breen, W. J. Homogeneous Risk Measures and the Construction of Composite Assets. JFQA, 3 (Dec, 1968), 405-414

Fisher, E. More About Stability of Measures of Volatility of Individual Stocks. Paper for the Seminar on the Analysis of Security Prices, U of Chicago, Nov 1968

Rosenberg, M. A Study of the Risk Factor Implicit in Security Prices. PhD diss, Columbia U, 1968

Treynor, J. L.; Priest, W. W., Jr.; Fisher, L. & Higgins, C. A. Using Portfolio Composition to Estimate Risk. FAJ, 24 (Sep-Oct, 1968), 93-100

Renshaw, E. F. Stock Market Instability. FAJ, 23 (Jul-Aug, 1967), 80-83

Tuite, M. F. An Analysis of Variables which are Associated with the Sensitivity of Common Stock Prices to News. DBA diss, Indiana U, 1967

West, D. A. Risk Analysis in the Sixties. FAJ, 23 (Nov-Dec, 1967), 124-126

Fanning, J. E., & Steglitz, M. A Risk Measure for Common Stock Portfolios. Paper for the Seminar on the Analysis of Security Prices, U of Chicago, Nov, 1966

Ferreira, C. G.   Quantification and Measurement of Risk: An Empirical
    Study of Selected Common Stocks. DBA diss, U of Wash, 1966
Gould, E.   Laggards and Swingers—Investors Should Know More About
    the Volatility of Stocks. B, (May 23, 1966), 9
Heins, A. J. & Allison, S. L.   Some Factors Affecting Stock Price Varia-
    bility. JB, 39 (Jan, 1966), 19-23
Clark, J. N., Jr.   Common Stock Price Fluctuations. FAJ, 20 (May-Jun,
    1964), 71-74
Edwards, N. D.   Significance of Price Fluctuations in Securities. AJ,
    14 (May, 1958), 87-90
Hood, O.   The Science of Volatility. AJ, 14 (Aug, 1958), 35-37
Barnes, L.   Is the Stock Market Getting More Stable? AJ, 12 (Feb,
    1956), 21-22
Spear, R. E.   Constant Dividends Plus Good Appreciation through Fast
    Stocks versus Slow Stocks. AJ, 7 (3rd Qtr, 1951), 47-50
Fischer, R. M.   Measuring Stability. AJ, 4, (3rd Qtr, 1948), 19-25
Tomlinson, L.   Appraising the Risk Factor in Investment Company
    Leverage Shares. AJ, 2 (1st Qtr, 1945), 52-62
Fritzemeier, L. H.   Relative Price Fluctuations of Industrial Stocks in
    Different Price Groups. JB, 9 (Apr, 1936), 133-154

10c MEAN-VARIANCE PORTFOLIO THEORY AND PORTFOLIO SELECTION—GENERAL

The basis for mean-variance portfolio theory was established by Markowitz (1952, 1959) and simplified quadratic and linear models were developed by Sharpe (1963 and 1967). Useful general texts are those of Sharpe
and Francis & Archer. Some of the implications of portfolio theory for
the security analyst are considered by Treynor, Treynor & Black and
Brealey. The reader is also advised to consult other sections in Part 10.

Brealey, R. A. & Hodges, S. D.   Playing with Portfolios. FAJ, forthcoming
Treynor, J. L. & Black, F.   Using Security Analysis to Improve Port-
    folio Selection. JB, forthcoming
Brealey, R. A.   Managing the Research Department. Paper for the
    Seminar on the Analysis of Security Prices, U of Chicago, Nov 1972
Hodges, S. D. & Brealey, R. A.   Portfolio Selection in a Dynamic and Un-
    certain World. FAJ, 28 (Nov-Dec, 1972), 58-70
Jacob, N. L. & Smith, K. V.   The Value of Perfect Market Forecasts in
    Portfolio Selection. JF, 27 (May, 1972), 355-370
Breen, W. J. & Jackson, R.   An Efficient Algorithm for Solving Large-
    Scale Portfolio Problems. JFQA, 6 (Jan, 1971), 627-638
Cheng, P. L.   Efficient Portfolio Selections beyond the Markowitz Fron-
    tier. JFQA, 6 (Dec, 1971), 1207-1234
Francis, J. C. & Archer, S. H.   Portfolio Analysis. P-H, 1971
Frankfurter, G. M.; Phillips, H. E. & Seagle, J. P.   Portfolio Selection:
    the Effects of Uncertain Means, Variances, and Covariances. JFQA,
    6 (Dec, 1971), 1251-1262
Hodges, S. D. & Moore, P. G.   Mathematical Models in Portfolio Selec-
    tion. JBF, 3 (Spring, 1971)
Jones-Lee, M. W.   Some Portfolio Adjustment Theorems for the Use of
    Non-Negativity Constraints on Security Holdings. JF, 26 (Jun, 1971),
    763-776

Kalymon, B. A.   Estimation Risk in the Portfolio Selection Model. JFQA, 6 (Jan, 1971), 559-582

Levy, H. & Sarnat, M.   A Note on Portfolio Selection and Investors' Wealth. JFQA, 6 (Jan, 1971), 639-642

Levy, H. & Sarnat, M.   Two-Period Portfolio Selection and Investors Discount Rates. JF, 26 (Jun, 1971), 757-762

Remaley, W. A.   Suboptimization in Mean-Variance Efficient Set Analysis. PhD diss, NYU, 1971

Sharpe, W. F.   A Linear Programming Approximation for the General Portfolio Analysis Problem. JFQA, 6 (Dec, 1971), 1263-1276

Sharpe, W. F.   Portfolio Theory and Capital Markets. McGraw, 1971

Stevens, G. G. V.   Two Problems in Portfolio Analysis: Conditional and Multiplicative Random Variables. JFQA, 6 (Dec, 1971), 1235-1250

Treynor, J. L.   The Coming Revolution in Investment Management. Unp ms, 1971

Wippern, R. F.   Utility Implications of Portfolio Selection and Performance Appraisal Models. JFQA, 6 (Jun, 1971), 913-924

Blume, M. E.   Portfolio Theory: A Step Toward Its Practical Application. JB, 43 (Apr, 1970), 152-173

Evans, J. L.   An Analysis of Portfolio Maintenance Strategies. JF, 25 (Jun, 1970), 561-572

Fried, J.   Forecasting and Probability Distributions for Models of Portfolio Selection. JF, 25 (Jun, 1970), 539-554

Hanoch, G., & Levy, H.   Efficient Portfolio Selection with Quadratic and Cubic Utility. JB, 43 (Apr, 1970), 181-189

Hodges, S. D. & Brealey, R. A.   Using the Sharpe Model. IA, 27 (Sep, 1970) 41-50

Krouse, C. G.   Portfolio Balancing Corporate Assets and Liabilities with Special Application to Insurance Management. JFQA, 5 (Mar, 1970), 77-104

Levy, H. & Sarnat, M.   Portfolio Selection and Investors' Utility: a Graphical Analysis. AE, 2 (1970), 113-120

Mao, J. C. T.   Essentials of Portfolio Diversification Strategy. JF, 25 (Dec, 1970), 1109-1122

Pogue, J. A.   An Extension of the Markowitz Portfolio Selection Model to Include Variable Transaction Costs, Short Sales, Leverage Policies and Taxes. JF, 25 (Dec, 1970), 1005-1028

Samuelson, P. A.   The Fundamental Approximation Theorem of Portfolio Analysis in Terms of Means, Variances and Higher Moments. REStud, 37 (Oct, 1970), 537-542

Schreiner, J. C.   Historically Successful Portfolio Selection Rules. PhD, diss, UCLA, 1970

Bickel, S. H.   Minimum Variance and Optimal Asymptotic Portfolios. MSci, 16 (Nov, 1969), 221-226

Feldstein, M. S.   Mean-Variance Analysis in the Theory of Liquidity Preference and Portfolio Selection. REStud, 36 (Jan, 1969)

Fried, J.   A Generalized Markowitz Model of Bank Portfolio Selection. PhD diss, Northwestern U, 1969

Hakansson, N. H.   Risk Disposition and the Separation Property in Portfolio Selection. JFQA, 4 (Dec, 1969), 401-416

Roll, R.   Bias in Fitting the Sharpe Model to Time Series Data. JFQA, 4 (Sep, 1969), 271-289

Smith, K. V.   Stock Price and Economic Indexes for Generating Efficient Portfolios. JB, 42 (Jul, 1969), 326-336

Young, W. E.   Common Stock Ex Post Holding Period Returns and Port-
      folio Selection. PhD diss, U of NC, 1969
Breen, W.   Specific versus General Models of Portfolio Selection. OEP,
      20 (Nov, 1968), 361-368
Friend, I. & Vickers, D.   Re-evaluation of Alternative Portfolio Selection
      Models. JB, 41 (Apr, 1968), 174-179
Handa, J. C.   A New Approach to the Theory of Portfolio Selection. PhD
      diss, Johns Hopkins U, 1968
Smith, K. V.   Alternative Procedures for Revising Investment Port-
      folios. JFQA, 3 (Dec, 1968), 371-403
Thornber, E. H. & Lynch, M.   A Workable Procedure for Optimizing the
      Value of a Portfolio. Paper for the Seminar on the Analysis of
      Security Prices, U of Chicago, Nov 1968
Cohen, K. J. & Elton, E. J.   Inter-Temporal Portfolio Analysis Based on
      Simulation of Joint Returns. MSci, 13 (Sep, 1967), 5-18
Cohen, K. J. & Pogue, J. A.   An Empirical Evaluation of Alternative Port-
      folio-Selection Models. JB, 40 (Apr, 1967), 166-193
Hester, D. D.   Efficient Portfolios with Short Sales and Margin Holdings,
      in Hester, D. D. & Tobin, J. (Eds), Risk Aversion and Porfolio Choice.
      Wiley, 1967
Hicks, J. R.   The Pure Theory of Portfolio Selection, in Hicks, J. R.,
      Critical Essays in Monetary Theory. Oxford U Pr, 1967
Pogue, J. A.   An Adaptive Model for Investment Management. PhD diss,
      Carnegie IT, 1967
Pye, G.   Portfolio Selection and Security Prices. REStat, 49 (Feb, 1967),
      111-115
Renshaw, E. F.   Portfolio Balance Models in Perspective: Some
      Generalizations that can be Derived from the Two-Asset Case.
      JFQA, 2 (Jun, 1967), 123-149
Schrock, N. W.   Asset Choice Under Uncertainty with Borrowing Intro-
      duced. WEJ, (Mar, 1967), 201-209
Sharpe, W. F.   A Linear Programming Algorithm for Mutual Fund Port-
      folio Selection. MSci, 13 (Mar, 1967), 499-510
Sharpe, W. F.   Portfolio Analysis. JFQA, 2 (Jun, 1967), 76-84
Smith, K. V.   Selection and Revision Decision Rules for Portfolio
      Management. PhD diss, Purdue U, 1967
Smith, K. V.   A Transition Model for Portfolio Revision. JF, 22 (Sep,
      1967), 425-439
Wallingford, B. A.   A Survey and Comparison of Portfolio Selection
      Models. JFQA, 2 (Jun, 1967), 85-106
Baumol, W. J.   Mathematical Analysis of Portfolio Selection. FAJ, 22
      (Sep-Oct, 1966), 95-99
Breen, W. J.   Markowitz, Sharpe, et al.: A Dissenting View. Paper for the
      Seminar on the Analysis of Security Prices, U of Chicago, Nov 1966
Mao, J. C. T. & Särndal, C. E.   A Decision Theory Approach to Portfolio
      Selection. MSci, 12 (Apr, 1966), B323-B333
Paine, N. R.   A Case Study in Mathematical Programming of Portfolio
      Selection. AS, 15 (1966), 24-36
McFarlane, D. D.   Application of the Markowitz Portfolio Selection
      Model as a Managerial Tool. DBA diss, Indiana U, 1965
Sharpe, W. F.   Addendum to 'A Simplified Model for Portfolio Analysis'.
      MSci, 9 (Apr, 1963), 498
Sharpe, W. F.   Mathematical Investment Portfolio Selection: Some Early
      Results. UWBR (Apr, 1963)

Sharpe, W. F. A Simplified Model for Portfolio Analysis. MSci, 9 (Jan, 1963), 277-293

Farrar, D. E. The Investment Decision Under Uncertainty. P-H, 1962

Markowitz, H. M. Portfolio Selection: Efficient Diversification of Investments. Wiley, 1959

Tobin, J. Liquidity Preference as Behavior Toward Risk. REStud, 25 (Feb, 1958), 65-86

Markowitz, H. M. The Optimization of a Quadratic Function Subject to Linear Constraints. NRLQ (Mar-Jun, 1956), 111-133

Martin, A. D. Jr. Mathematical Programming of Portfolio Selections. MSci, 1 (Jan, 1955) 152-166

Weston, J. F. & Beranek, W. Programming Investment Portfolio Construction. AJ, 11 (May, 1955), 51-55

Markowitz, H. M. Portfolio Selection. JF, 7 (Mar, 1952), 77-91

10d PORTFOLIO SELECTION IN PARETO LEVY MARKETS

The following two articles extend mean-variance theory to cover cases where the distribution of returns is non-Gaussian Pareto Levy.

Samuelson, P. A. Efficient Portfolio Selection for Pareto-Levy Investments. JFQA, 2 (Jun, 1967), 107-122

Fama, E. F. Portfolio Analysis in a Stable Paretian Market. MSci, 11 (Jan, 1965), 404-419

10e DIVERSIFICATION

This section is concerned with the effects of diversification on risk. Sharpe's article provides a simple exposition of the topic in the context of mean-variance portfolio theory, whereas a general and rigorous justification for diversified portfolios is provided in Samuelson's paper. The Fisher-Lorie paper is notable among the empirical studies of the effect of diversification. Other relevant material (notably Markowitz (1952) and Fama (1965)) is listed under 10c — 'Mean-Variance Portfolio Theory and Portfolio Selection—General' and 10d — 'Portfolio Selection in Pareto Levy Markets'.

Sarnat, M. The Gains from Risk Diversification on the London Stock Exchange. JBF, 4 (Autumn, 1972), 54-64

Sharpe, W. F. Risk, Market Sensitivity and Diversification. FAJ, 28 (Jan-Feb, 1972), 74-79

Jennings, E. H. An Empirical Analysis of Some Aspects of Common Stock Diversification. JFQA, 6 (Mar, 1971), 797-814

Wagner, W. H. & Lau, S. C. The Effect of Diversification on Risk. FAJ, 27 (Nov-Dec, 1971), 48-53

Fisher, L. & Lorie, J. H. Some Studies of Variability of Returns on Investments in Common Stocks. JB, 43 (Apr, 1970), 99-134

Whitmore, G. A. Diversification and the Reduction of Dispersion: a Note. JFQA, 5 (Jun, 1970), 263-264

Evans, J. L. Diversification and the Reduction of Dispersion: An Empirical Analysis. DBA diss, U of Wash, 1968

Evans, J. L. & Archer, S. H. Diversification and the Reduction of Dispersion: An Empirical Analysis. JF, 23 (Dec, 1968), 761-767

Aranyi, J.   Portfolio Diversification. FAJ, 23 (Sep-Oct, 1967), 133-139

Gaumnitz, J. E.   Investment Diversification under Uncertainty: An Examination of the Number of Securities in a Diversified Portfolio. PhD diss, Stanford U, 1967

Samuelson, P. A.   General Proof that Diversification Pays. JFQA, 2 (Mar, 1967), 1-13

Archer, S. H.   Diversification and Risk Reduction. UWBR, (Apr-Jun, 1964), 19-25

Milne, R. D.   Benchmarks for a Diversified Portfolio. AJ, 14 (Nov, 1958), 51-54

Morris, W. T.   Diversification. MSci, 4 (Jul, 1958), 382-391

10f SAFETY FIRST, CHANCE CONSTRAINED PORTFOLIOS AND MINIMAX

This section is concerned with various specifications of safety first or chance constrained portfolio policies. It includes Roy's pioneering work on safety first and Baumol's proposed E—kV objective function.

See also:

    9a Utility Theory
    25d Capital Budgeting Under Uncertainty

Levy, H. & Sarnat, M.   Safety First—an Expected Utility Principle. JFQA 7 (Jun, 1972), 1829-1834

Pye, G.   Minimax Portfolio Policies. FAJ, 28 (Mar-Apr, 1972), 56-60

Pyle, D. H. & Turnovsky, S. J.   Risk Aversion in Chance Constrained Portfolio Selection. MSci, 18 (Nov, 1971), 218-225

Burnham, J. M.   Conditional Chance-Constrained Programming Techniques in Portfolio Selection. PhD diss, U of Texas, 1970

Pyle, D. H. & Turnovsky, S. J.   Safety-First and Expected Utility Maximization in Mean-Standard Deviation Portfolio Analysis. REStat, 52 (Feb, 1970), 75-81

Agnew, N. H. et al.   An Application of Chance Constrained Programming to Portfolio Selection in a Casualty Insurance Firm. MSci, 15 (Jun, 1969), B512-B520

Hanssmann, F.   Probability of Survival as an Investment Criterion. MSci, 15 (Sep, 1968), 33-48

Russell, W. R. & Smith, P. E.   A Comment on Baumol (E, L) Efficient Portfolios. MSci, 12 (Mar, 1966), 619-621

Baumol, W. J.   An Expected Gain-Confidence Limit Criterion for Portfolio Selection. MSci, 9 (Oct, 1963), 174-182

Naslund, B. & Whinston, A.   A Model of Multi-Period Investments Under Uncertainty. MSci, 8 (Jan, 1962), 184-200

Egerton, R. A. D.   The Holding of Assets: Gambler Preference or 'Safety First'? OEP, 8 (Feb, 1956), 51-59

Telser, L.   Safety-First and Hedging. REStud, 23 (1955-1956), 1-16

Roy, A. D.   Safety First and the Holding of Assets. Em, 20 (Jul, 1952), 431-449

10g MODELS FOR THE SELECTION OF BANK ASSETS

This section is concerned predominantly with linear programming models for the management of bank assets. The Cohen & Hammer article is a good introduction to the subject.

See also:

>   3f Banks
>   10c Mean-Variance Portfolio Theory and Portfolio Selection—
>   General
>   10f Safety First, Chance Constrained Portfolios and Minimax

Booth, G. G.   Programming Bank Portfolios Under Uncertainty: an Extension. JBR, (Winter, 1972), 28-40

Cohen, K. J.   Dynamic Balance Sheet Management: a Management Science Approach. JBR, (Winter, 1972), 9-19

Booth, G. G.   The Management of a Commercial Bank Portfolio: a Programming Approach. PhD diss, U of Mich, 1971

Cohen, K. J. & Rutenberg, D. P.   Toward a Comprehensive Framework for Bank Financial Planning. JBR, 2 (Winter, 1971), 41-57

Crane, D. B.   A Stochastic Programming Model for Commercial Bank Bond Portfolio Management. JFQA, 6 (Jun, 1971), 955-976

Cohen, K. J. & Thore, S.   Programming Bank Portfolios Under Uncertainty. JBR, 1 (Spring, 1970), 42-61

Frey, T. L.   Optimal Asset and Liability Decisions for a Rural Bank: an Application of Multi-Period Linear Programming. PhD diss, U of Ill, 1970

Fried, J. S.   Bank Portfolio Selection. JFQA, 5 (Jun, 1970), 203-228

Gray, K. B., Jr.   Managing the Balance Sheet: a Mathematical Approach to Decision Making. JBR, (Spring, 1970), 35-42

Supel, T. M.   A Two-Period Balance Sheet Model for Banks. PhD diss, U of Minn, 1969

Charnes, A. & Littlechild, S. C.   Intertemporal Bank Asset Choice with Stochastic Dependence. Paper at the TIMS/ORSA Joint Meeting, San Francisco, May 1968

Klein, M. A.   Differential Commercial Bank Portfolio Allocation. PhD diss, Northwestern U, 1968

Cohen, K. J. & Hammer, F. S.   Linear Programming and Optimal Bank Asset Management Decisions. JF, 22 (May, 1967), 147-165

Cohen, K. J.; Hammer, F. S. & Schneider, H. M.   Harnessing Computers for Bank Asset Management. BM, 150 (Summer, 1967), 72-80

Pierce, J. L.   An Empirical Model of Commercial Bank Portfolio Management, *in* Hester, D. D. & Tobin, J. (Eds), Studies of Portfolio Behavior. Wiley, 1967

Roskamp, K. W.   Factors Influencing Portfolio Selection: a Simple Model. Kyk, 20 (1967), 502-510

Haydon, R. B. & Wicks, J. H.   A Model of Commercial Bank Earning Assets Selection. JFQA, 1 (Jun, 1966) 99-113

Hulett, D. T.   A Short-Run Model of Commercial Bank and Portfolio Behavior. PhD diss, Stanford U, 1966

Wacht, R. F.   The Derivation and Testing of a Normative Portfolio Balance Model for Allocating Commercial Bank Funds among Alternative Assets. PhD diss, U of NC, 1966

Beazer W. F.   Optimization of Bank Portfolios and Response to Monetary Policy. PhD diss, Northwestern U, 1965

Kane, E. J. & Malkiel, B. G.   Bank Portfolio Allocation, Deposit Variability and the Availability Doctrine. QJE, 79 (Feb, 1965), 113-134
Chambers, D. J. & Charnes, A.   Intertemporal Analysis and Optimization of Bank Portfolios. MSci, 7 (Jul, 1961), 393-410
Porter, R. C.   A Model of Bank Portfolio Selection. YEE, 1 (Fall, 1961), 323-359

10h PORTFOLIO SELECTION AND STOCHASTIC DOMINANCE

Hadar & Russell provide important background reading to the concept of stochastic dominance and the article by Porter & Gaumnitz offers an introduction to the implications for portfolio selection.

See also:

10c Mean-Variance Portfolio Theory and Portfolio Selection—
General

Porter, R. B. & Gaumitz, J. E.   Stochastic Dominance vs. Mean-Variance Portfolio Analysis: an Empirical Evaluation. AER, 62 (Jun, 1972), 438-446
Sarnat, M.   A Note on the Prediction of Portfolio Performance from Ex Post Data. JF, 27 (Sep, 1972), 903-906
Porter, R. B.   Application of Stochastic Dominance Principles to the Problem of Asset Selection Under Risk. PhD diss, Purdue U, 1971
Levy, H. & Hanoch, G.   Relative Effectiveness of Efficiency Criteria for Portfolio Selection. JFQA, 5 (Mar, 1970), 63-76
Levy, H. & Sarnat, M.   Alternative Efficiency Criteria: an Empirical Analysis. JF, 25 (Dec, 1970), 1153-1158
Hadar, J. & Russell, W. R.   Rules for Ordering Uncertain Prospects. AER, 59 (Mar, 1969), 25-34
Hanoch, G. & Levy, H.   The Efficiency Analysis of Choices Involving Risk. REStud, 36 (Jul, 1969), 335-346
Quirk, J. P. & Saposnik, R.   Admissibility and Measurable Utility Functions. REStud, 29 (Feb, 1962), 140-146

10i INTERNATIONALLY DIVERSIFIED PORTFOLIOS

The studies of Lessard and Levy & Sarnat are principally concerned with the extension of normative portfolio theory to international investment. The studies by Agmon and Modigliani et al. are primarily concerned with the implications for equilibrium theory and the Grubel, Grubel & Fadner and Miller & Whitman articles with explaining capital flows.

See also:

10c Mean-Variance Portfolio Theory and Portfolio Selection—
General
21b Forward Currency Markets

Cohn, R. A. & Pringle, J.   Imperfections in International Financial Markets: Implications for Risk Premia and the Cost of Capital to Firms. JF, forthcoming
Lessard, D.   International Portfolio Diversification: a Multivariate Analysis for a Group of Latin American Companies. JF, forthcoming

Agmon, T.   The Relations Among Equity Markets: a Study of Share Price Co-Movements in the United States, United Kingdom, Germany and Japan. JF, 27 (Sep, 1972), 839-856

Makridakis, S. G. & Wheelwright, S. C.   Predicting European Stock Indices from Movements in the New York Stock Exchange Index. JBF, 4 (Autumn, 1972), 65-69

Modigliani, F. et al.   Efficiency of European Capital Markets and Comparison with American Markets. Unp ms, 1972

Agmon, T. B.   Interrelationships Among Equity Markets—a Study of Share Price Movements in the United States, United Kingdom, Germany and Japan. PhD diss, U of Chicago, 1971

Grubel, H. G. & Fadner, K.   The Interdependence of International Equity Markets. JF, 26 (Mar, 1971), 89-94

Lessard, D. R.   Multinational Portfolio Diversification for Developing Countries. PhD diss, Stanford U, 1970

Levy, H. & Sarnat, M.   International Diversification of Investment Portfolios. AER, 60 (Sep, 1970), 668-675

Miller, N. C. & Whitman, M. v. N.   A Mean-Variance Analysis of United States Long-Term Portfolio Foreign Investment. QJE, 84 (May, 1970), 175-196

Grubel, H. G.   Internationally Diversified Portfolios: Welfare Gains and Capital Flows. AER, 58 (Dec, 1968), 1299-1314

10j THE GROWTH OPTIMUM MODEL

A number of writers have advocated maximising the geometric mean return as a portfolio strategy. Important examples are those of Latané (1959), Breiman and Kelly. The weaknesses of the growth optimum model are argued by Samuelson. The implications for equilibrium theory are examined by Litzenberger & Budd, Fama and Roll. Because the model has attractive dynamic properties, readers should also consult references listed under 10k—'Dynamic Portfolio Theory', notably the articles by Hakansson.

See also:

10c Mean-Variance Portfolio Theory and Portfolio Selection—General

Fama, E. F.   Risk and Rate of Return in the Long Run. Paper for the Seminar on the Analysis of Security Prices, U of Chicago, Nov 1972

Hakansson, N. H.   Capital Growth and the Mean-Variance Approach to Portfolio Selection. JFQA, 6 (Jan, 1971), 517-558

Litzenberger, R. H. & Budd, A. P.   A Note on Geometric Mean Portfolio Selection and the Market Prices of Equities. JFQA, 6 (Dec, 1971), 1263-1276

Roll, R.   Some Preliminary Evidence on the 'Growth Optimum' Model. Wkg Paper No 3-71-2, Graduate School of Industrial Administration, Carnegie-Mellon U, Jul 1971

Samuelson, P. A.   The 'Fallacy' of Maximizing the Geometric Mean in Long Sequences of Investing or Gambling. PNAS (Oct, 1971), 2493-2496

Hakansson, N. H. & Liu, T-C.   Optimal Growth Portfolios When Yields are Serially Correlated. REStat, 52 (Nov, 1970), 385-394

Renshaw, E. F. & Renshaw, V. D.   Some Notes on the Rationality Model.
  SEJ, 36 (Jan, 1970), 244-251
Latané, H. A. & Young, W. E.   Test of Portfolio Building Rules. JF, 24
  (Sep, 1969), 595-612
Young, W. E. & Trent, R. H.   Geometric Mean Approximations of Individual
  Security and Portfolio Performance. JFQA, 4 (Jun, 1969), 179-200
Latané, H. A. & Tuttle, D. L.   Criteria for Portfolio Building. JF, 22 (Sep,
  1967), 360-361
Latané, H. A.   Investment Criteria—A Three Asset Portfolio Balance
  Model. REStat, 45 (Nov, 1963), 427-430
Breiman, L.   Investment Policies for Expanding Businesses' Optimal
  in a Long-Run Sense. NRLQ, 7 (Dec, 1960), 647-651
Latané, H. A.   Criteria for Choice among Risky Ventures. JPE, 67 (Apr,
  1959), 144-155
Latané, H. A.   Rational Decision Making in Portfolio Management. PhD
  diss, U of NC, 1957
Kelly, J.   A New Interpretation of Information Rate. Bell Sys, 35 (Jul,
  1956), 917-926

10k DYNAMIC PORTFOLIO THEORY

Work on multi-period portfolio theory has centred heavily on the conditions
under which myopia and separation hold and hence on additive iso-elastic
utility functions. Leland's dissertation provides a useful introduction to the
subject and the articles by Samuelson, Mossin and Fama constitute important related reading. Hakansson's strong advocacy of the average compound
growth model with its induced power utility function is exemplified in his
1971 Journal of Finance article. Finally, we have listed a selection of
studies (notably by Friedman, and Modigliani & Brumberg) that are principally concerned with the consumption function.

See also:

  10c Mean-Variance Portfolio Theory and Portfolio Selection—
       General
  10j The Growth Optimum Model

Hakansson, N. H.   Mean-Variance Analysis of Average Compound Returns.
  Unp ms, 1971
Hakansson, N. H.   Multi-Period Mean-Variance Analysis: Toward a
  General Theory of Portfolio Choice. JF, 26 (Sep, 1971), 857-884
Hakansson, N. H.   On Optimal Myopic Portfolio Policies with and without
  Serial Correlation of Yields. JB, 44 (Jul, 1971), 324-334
Holbrook, R. & Stafford, F.   The Propensity to Consume Separate Types of
  Income: a Generalized Permanent Income Hypothesis. Em, 39 (Jan,
  1971), 1-22
Mirman, L. J.   Uncertainty and Optimal Consumption Decisions.
  Em, 36 (Jan, 1971), 177-183
Rentz, W. F.   Optimal Consumption and Investment Policies. PhD diss,
  U of Rochester, 1971
Wippern, R. F.   Portfolio Selection: the Multiperiod Case. Wkg paper,
  Amos Tuck School of Business Administration, Dartmouth C, Apr 1971
Fama, E. F.   Multi-Period Consumption-Investment Decisions. AER, 60
  (Mar, 1970), 163-174

Hakansson, N. H.   Optimal Investment and Consumption Strategies under Risk for a Class of Utility Function. Em, 38 (Sep, 1970), 587-607

Holmes, J. M.   A Direct Test of Friedman's Permanent Income Hypothesis. JASA, 65 (Sep, 1970), 1159-1162

Pogue, G. A.   An Inter-Temporal Model for Investment Management. JBR, 1 (Spring, 1970), 17-34

Black, F.   Lifetime Investment Strategies for Individuals. Paper for the Seminar on the Analysis of Security Prices, U of Chicago, Nov 1969

Hakansson, N. H.   Optimal Investment and Consumption Strategies Under Risk, an Uncertain Lifetime and Insurance. IntER, 10 (Oct, 1969), 443-466

Levhari, D. & Srinivasan, T. N.   Optimal Savings and Uncertainty. REStud, 36 (Apr, 1969), 363-379

Merton, R. C.   Lifetime Portfolio Selection under Uncertainty. REStat, 51 (Aug, 1969), 247-257

Samuelson, P. A.   Lifetime Portfolio Selection by Dynamic Stochastic Programming. REStat, 51 (Aug, 1969), 239-246

Leland, H. E.   Dynamic Portfolio Theory. PhD diss, Harvard U, 1968

Mossin, J.   Optimal Multiperiod Portfolio Policies. JB, 41 (Apr, 1968), 215-229

Sandmo, A.   Portfolio Choice in a Theory of Saving. SJE, 70 (1968), 106-122

Hakansson, N. H.   Optimal Investment and Consumption Strategies for a Class of Utility Functions. PhD diss, UCLA, 1966

Liviatan, N.   Multiperiod Future Consumption as an Aggregate. AER, 56 (Sep, 1966), 828-840

Tobin, J.   The Theory of Portfolio Selection, *in* Hahn, F. H. & Brechling, F. P. R. (Eds), The Theory of Interest Rates. Macmillan Int, 1966

Midler, J. L.   A Dynamic Portfolio Selection Model. Paper for the Seminar on the Analysis of Security Prices, U of Chicago, Nov 1965

Yaari, M. E.   Uncertain Lifetime, Life Insurance and the Theory of the Consumer. REStud, 32 (1965), 137-150

Naslund, B. & Whinston, A.   A Model of Multi-Period Investment Under Uncertainty. MSci, 8 (Jan, 1962), 184-200

Phelps, E. S.   The Accumulation of Risky Capital: a Sequential Utility Analysis. Em, 30 (Oct, 1962), 729-743

Friedman, M.   A Theory of the Consumption Function. (Dist by Princeton U Pr) Natl Bur Econ Res, 1957

Modigliani & Brumberg, R.   Utility Analysis and the Consumption Function: an Interpretation of Cross Section Data, *in* Kurihara, K. (Ed), Post-Keynsian Economics. Rutgers U Pr, 1954

10*l* CAPITAL ASSET PRICING THEORY

This section is concerned with the implications of mean-variance portfolio theory for equilibrium prices. Important pioneering papers on the subject are those of Sharpe (1964), Treynor and Lintner (1965). Subsequent work has primarily been concerned with testing the theory's empirical validity (see especially Black, Jensen & Scholes, and Sharpe & Cooper) and with examining some of the more unrealistic assumptions (see the more recent articles of Lintner, Merton, Black, Brennan and Vasicek). A useful textbook exposition of capital asset pricing theory is provided by Sharpe.

See also:

Blume, M. E. & Friend, I.   A New Look at the Capital Asset Pricing Model.
JF, forthcoming
Levy, H.   The Demand for Assets Under Conditions of Risk. JF, forth-
coming
Lintner, J.   Security Market Equilibrium with Increasing Costs of Debt,
Restrictions on Total Debt and Imperfect Markets for Short Sales.
JFQA, forthcoming
Black, F.   Capital Market Equilibrium with Restricted Borrowing. JB,
45 (Jul, 1972), 444-455
Black, F.   Equilibrium in the Creation of Investment Goods Under Un-
certainty, *in* Jensen, M. C. (Ed), Studies in the Theory of Capital
Markets. Praeger, 1972
Black, F; Jensen, M. C. & Scholes, M.   The Capital Asset Pricing Model:
Some Empirical Tests, *in* Jensen, M. C. (Ed), Studies in the Theory of
Capital Markets. Praeger, 1972
Heckerman, D. G.   Portfolio Selection and the Structure of Capital Asset
Prices when Relative Prices of Consumption Goods May Change. JF,
27 (Mar, 1972), 47-60
Jensen, M. C.   The Foundations and Current State of Capital Market
Theory, *in* Jensen, M. C. (Ed), Studies in the Theory of Capital Markets.
Praeger, 1972
Jensen, M. C. (Ed).   Studies in the Theory of Capital Markets. Praeger,
1972
Levy, H.   Portfolio Performance and the Investment Horizon. MSci, 18
(Aug, 1972), B645-B653
Litzenberger, R. H. & Budd, A. P.   Secular Trends in Risk Premiums.
JF, 27 (Sep, 1972), 857-864
Long, J. B. Jr.   Consumption-Investment Decisions and Equilibrium in
the Securities Market, *in* Jensen, M. C. (Ed), Studies in the Theory of
Capital Markets. Praeger, 1972
Masson, R. T.   The Creation of Risk Aversion by Imperfect Capital
Markets. AER, 62 (Mar, 1972), 77-86
Mayers, D.   Non-Marketable Assets and Capital Market Equilibrium under
Uncertainty, *in* Jensen, M. C. (Ed), Studies in the Theory of Capital
Markets. Praeger, 1972
Merton, R. C.   An Intertemporal Capital Asset Pricing Model. Wkg paper
No 588-72, Alfred P. Sloan School of Management. MIT, Feb 1972
Miller, M. H. & Scholes, M.   Rates of Return in Relation to Risk: a Re-
examination of some Recent Findings, *in* Jensen, M. C. (Ed), Studies in
the Theory of Capital Markets. Praeger, 1972
Reilly, F. K.   Evidence Regarding a Segmented Stock Market. JF, 27
(Jun, 1972), 607-626
Sharpe, W. F. & Cooper, G. M.   Risk-Return class of New York Stock
Exchange Common Stocks, 1931-1967. FAJ, 28 (Mar-Apr, 1972), 46ff
Black, F. & Scholes, M.   Capital Market Equilibrium and the Pricing of
Corporate Liabilities. Unp paper, 1971

Brennan, M. J.   Capital Market Equilibrium with Divergent Borrowing and Lending Rates. JFQA, 6 (Dec, 1971), 1197-1206

Fama, E. F.   Risk, Return and Equilibrium. JPE, 79 (Jan-Feb, 1971), 30-55

Lintner, J.   The Effects of Short Selling and Margin Requirements in Perfect Capital Markets. JFQA, 6 (Dec, 1971), 1173-1196

Mao, J. C. T.   Security Pricing in an Imperfect Capital Market. JFQA, 6 (Sep, 1971), 1105-1116

Sharpe, W. F.   Portfolio Theory and Capital Markets. McGraw, 1971

Vasicek, O. A.   Capital Asset Pricing Model with no Riskless Borrowing. Unp ms, Wells Fargo Bank, 1971

Adler, M.   On Risk-Adjusted Capitalization Rates and Valuation by Individuals. JF, 25 (Sep, 1970), 819-836

Brennan, M. J.   Capital Asset Pricing and the Structure of Security Returns. Unp ms, U of BC, 1970

Gaumnitz, J. E.   Appraising Performance of Investment Portfolios. JF, 25 (Jun, 1970), 555-560

Gentry, J. & Pike, J.   An Empirical Study of the Risk-Return Hypothesis Using Common Stock Portfolios of Life Insurance Companies. JFQA, 5 (Jun, 1970), 179-186

Lambert, W. R.   Evidence of Risk Aversion in the Stock Market. DBA diss, U of Indiana, 1970

Lintner, J.   The Market Price of Risk, Size of Market and Investor's Risk Aversion. REStat, 52 (Feb, 1970), 87-99

Merton, R. C.   A Dynamic General Equilibrium Model of the Asset Market and its Application to the Pricing of the Capital Structure of the Firm. Wkg Paper 497-70, Alfred P. Sloan School of Management. MIT, Dec 1970

Rie, D.   Preliminary Test of a Theory of Market Returns when Capitalization Rates are Variable. Unp ms, Wharton School of Finance and Commerce, U of Pa, 1970

Stone, B. K.   Risk, Return and Equilibrium. MIT Pr, 1970

Upson, R. B. & Jessup, P. F.   Risk-Return Relationships in Regional Securities. JFQA, 4 (Jan, 1970), 677-696

Adler, M.   On the Risk-Return Trade-Off in the Valuation of Assets. JFQA, 4 (Dec, 1969), 493-512

Borch, K.   Equilibrium, Optimum and Prejudices in Capital Markets. JFQA, 4 (Mar, 1969), 1-14

Brealey, R. A.   Investment Uncertainty and British Equities: a Comment. IA, 23 (Jun, 1969), 40-41

Briscoe, G.; Samuels, J. M. & Smyth, D. J.   The Treatment of Risk in the Stock Market. JF, 24 (Sep, 1969), 707-714

Douglas, G. W.   Risk in the Equity Markets: an Empirical Appraisal of Market Efficiency. YEE, 9 (Spring, 1969), 3-45

Jensen, M. C.   Risk, the Pricing of Capital Assets, and the Evaluation of Investment Portfolios. JB, 42 (Apr, 1969), 167-247

Jones-Lee, M. W.   A Risk Model of Equilibrium Equity Price Determination. JES, 4 (Nov, 1969)

Lintner, J.   The Aggregation of Investors' Diverse Judgments and Preferences in Purely Competitive Security Markets. JFQA, 4 (Dec, 1969), 347-400

Litzenberger, R. H.   Equilibrium in the Equity Market under Uncertainty. JF, 24 (Sep, 1969), 663-671

Mossin, J.   Security Pricing and Investment Criteria in Competitive Markets. AER, 59 (Dec, 1969), 749-756

Robichek, A. A. Risk and the Value of Securities. JFQA, 4 (Dec, 1969) 513-538

Sandmo, A. Capital Risk, Consumption and Portfolio Choice. Em, 37 (Oct, 1969), 586-599

Treynor, J. L.; Shelton, J. & Kantor, M. Is Rate of Return Influenced More by Systematic Risk than by Unique Risk? An Empirical Test of the Asset-Pricing Model. Paper for the Seminar on the Analysis of Security Prices, U of Chicago, Nov 1969

Fama, E. F. Risk, Return, and Equilibrium: Some Clarifying Comments. JF, 23 (Mar, 1968), 29-40

Russell, A. & Taylor, B. F. Investment Uncertainty and British Equities. IA, 22 (Dec, 1968), 13-22

Soldofsky, R. M. Yield-Risk Performance Measurements. FAJ, 24 (Sep-Oct, 1968), 130-139

Soldofsky, R. M. & Biderman, R. Yield-Risk Measurements of the Performance of Common Stocks. JFQA, 3 (Mar, 1968), 59-74

Arditti, F. D. Risk and the Required Return on Equity. JF, 22 (Mar, 1967), 19-36

Douglas, G. W. Risk in the Equity Market: An Empirical Appraisal of Market Efficiency. PhD diss, Yale U, 1967

Hastie, K. L. The Determination of Optimal Investment Policy. MSci, 13 (Aug, 1967), B757-B774

Pratt, S. P. Relationship between Risk and Rate of Return for Common Stocks. DBA diss, Indiana U, 1967

Pratt, S. P. Relationship between Variability of Past Rates of Return and Levels of Future Rates of Return for Common Stocks—1926-1960. Paper for the Seminar on the Analysis of Security Prices, U of Chicago, May 1967

Summers, R. A Peek at the Trade off Relationship between Expected Return and Risk. QJE, 81 (Aug, 1967), 437-456

Friend, I. & Taubman, P. Risk and the Rate of Return on Common Stock. Paper for the Seminar on the Analysis of Security Prices, U of Chicago, Nov 1966

Mossin, J. Equilibrium in a Capital Asset Market. Em, 34 (Oct, 1966), 768-783

Sharpe, W. F. Security Prices, Risk and Maximal Gains from Diversification: Reply. JF, 21 (Dec, 1966), 743-744

Bierwag, G. O. & Grove, M. A. On Capital Asset Prices: Comment. JF, 20 (Mar, 1965), 89-93

Lintner, J. Security Prices and Risk: The Theory and a Comparative Analysis of A.T. & T., and Leading Industrials. Paper at the Conference on 'The Economics of Regulated Public Utilities', Sponsored by the Bell System and U of Chicago Business School, Jun 1965

Lintner, J. Security Prices, Risk and Maximal Gains from Diversification. JF, 20 (Dec, 1965), 587-615

Lintner, J. The Valuation of Risk Assets and the Selection of Risky Investments in Stock Portfolios and Capital Budgets. REStat, 47 (Feb, 1965), 13-37

Mayer, R. W. Business Risk and the Earnings Multiplier. FAJ, 21 (Sep-Oct, 1965), 19-21

Sharpe, W. F. Reply (to Bierwag and Grove). JF, 20 (Mar, 1965), 94-95

Sharpe, W. F. Risk-Aversion in the Stock Market: Some Empirical Evidence. JF, 20 (Sep, 1965), 416-422

Repsold, G. J.   The Relationship Between the Rate of Return and Risk.
Unp ms, May 1964

Sharpe, W. F.   Capital Asset Prices: A Theory of Market Equilibrium
Under Conditions of Risk. JF, 19 (Sep, 1964), 425-442

Amoroso, L.   Do Shares Reach Equity at the Market Rate of Interest?
EI, 14 (May, 1961), 189-196

Treynor, J. L.   Towards a Theory of Market Value of Risky Assets. Unp
ms, nd

10m SKEWNESS, CUBIC UTILITY AND ASSET PRICES

This section lists a small sample of articles that provide evidence of investor preference for skewness and that examine its implications for portfolio selection and equilibrium.

See also:

9a   Utility Theory

Stone, B. K.   A General Class of Three-Parameter Risk Measures. JF,
forthcoming

Arditti, F. D.   Another Look at Mutual Fund Performance. JFQA, 6 (Jun,
1971), 909-912

Jean, W. H.   The Extension of Portfolio Analysis to Three or More
Parameters. JFQA, 6 (Jan, 1971), 505-516

Alderfer, C. P. & Bierman, H., Jr.   Choices with Risk: Beyond the Mean
and Variance. JB, 43 (Jul, 1970), 341-353

Rosett, R. N.   Estimating the Utility of Wealth from Call Option Transactions, *in* Hester, D. D. & Tobin, J. (Eds), Risk Aversion and Portfolio
Choice. Wiley, 1967

Poensgen, O. H.   The Valuation of Convertible Bonds.
Part I IMR, 7 (Fall, 1965), 77-92,
Part II IMR, 7 (Spring, 1966), 83-98

10n ACCOUNTING AND MARKET DETERMINED RISK MEASURES

The works in this section are concerned with the relationship between
stock market risk and measures derived from financial statements.

See also:

8b   The Factor Structure of Financial Statements
10o   Relationship between Accounting Measures of Risk and Return
19f   Bond and Stock Ratings
26g   Bankruptcy and Reorganisations

Pettit, R. R. & Westerfield, R.   A Model of Capital Asset Risk. JFQA, 7
(Mar, 1972), 1649-1668

Gonedes, N. J.   Evidence on the Information Content of Accounting Numbers: Accounting-Based and Market-Based Estimates of Systematic
Risk. Report No. 7115. Center for Mathematical Studies in Business
and Economics, U of Chicago, Mar 1971

Beaver, W.; Kettler, P. & Scholes, M.   The Association Between Market-
Determined and Accounting-Determined Risk Measures. AR, 45 (Oct,
1970), 654-682

Mayer, R.W.   Analysis of Internal Risk in the Individual Firm. AJ, 15
(Sep, 1959), 91-95

10o RELATIONSHIP BETWEEN ACCOUNTING MEASURES OF RISK AND RETURN

This section is concerned with the return on corporate assets as a function of risk. Cootner & Holland is an important, if slightly ageing, contribution.

See also:

Dunn, M.F.   Measurement of Firm Risk and Rate of Return. PhD diss,
UCLA, 1971

Norgaard, R.L.   Evaluating Intercorporate Risk, Returns, and Trends.
JFQA, 6 (Sep, 1971), 1069-1082

Rush, D.F.   Corporate Risk-Rate of Return Performance 1948-1966.
DBA diss, Indiana U, 1971

Fisher, I.N. & Hall, G.R.   Risk and Corporate Rates of Return. QJE, 83
(Feb, 1969), 79-92

Conrad, G.R. & Plotkin, I.H.   Risk/Return: U.S. Industry Pattern. HBR, 46
(Mar-Apr, 1968), 90-99

Stubbs, F.G., Jr.   An Evaluation of the Risk Management Practices in
Selected Corporations. PhD diss, U of Ill, 1966

Cootner, P.H. & Holland, D.M.   Risk and Rate of Return, rev ed. MIT
Pr, 1964

Fellner, W.   Profit as the Risk-Taker's Surplus: A Probabilistic Theory.
REStat, 45 (May, 1963), 173-184

Florence, P.S.   Reward for Risk-Bearing by Shareholders in Large
Companies. JIE, 5 (1957), 81-111

Part 11   Market Efficiency & the Random Walk Hypothesis

11a THE ADJUSTMENT OF STOCK PRICES TO NEW INFORMATION

Some general articles on market efficiency are listed under 11c—'Random Walk Hypothesis'. The articles in this section are principally concerned with the efficiency with which the market reacts to specific items of information. Niederhoffer's work fits only indirectly into this pattern and is concerned largely with the relationship between the magnitude of market movements and the importance of world events. Finally, the articles by Stigler and Fama & Laffer are concerned with the economics of information.

Pettit, R. R.   Dividend Announcements, Security Performance and Capital Efficiency. JF, forthcoming

Scholes, M.   The Market for Securities: Substitution versus Price Pressure and the Effects of Information on Share Prices. JB, 45 (Apr, 1972), 179-211

Fama, E. F. & Laffer, A. B.   Information and Capital Markets. JB, 44 (Jul, 1971), 289-298

Niederhoffer, V.   The Analysis of World Events and Stock Prices. JB, 44 (Apr, 1971), 193-219

Waud, R. N.   Public Interpretation of Discount Rate Changes: Evidence on the 'Announcement' Effect. Em, 38 (Mar, 1970), 231-250

Fama, E. F.; Fisher, L.; Jensen, M. C. & Roll, R.   The Adjustment of Stock Prices to New Information. IntER, 10 (Feb, 1969), 1-21

Joy, O. M.   The Value of Limited Monthly Information in Forecasting Airline Price Relatives. PhD diss, U of NC, 1969

Niederhoffer, V.   World Events and Stock Prices: a Study of Large New York Times Headlines and Subsequent Movements in the Standard and Poor's Composite Index. PhD diss, U of Chicago, 1969

Scholes, M.   A Test of the Competitive Market Hypothesis: the Market for New Issues and Secondary Offerings. PhD diss, U of Chicago, 1969

Ball, R. J. & Brown, P.   An Empirical Evaluation of Accounting Income Numbers. JAR, 6 (Autumn, 1968), 159-178

Davis, J. V.   The Adjustment of Stock Prices to New Information. PhD diss, Cornell U, 1967

Ashley, J. W.   Stock Prices and Changes in Earnings and Dividends: Some Empirical Results. JPE, 70 (Feb, 1962), 82-85

Merjos, A.   Lunch at the Analysts. B, (Oct 9, 1961), 5ff

Mindell, J.   How News Affects Market Trends. FAJ, 17 (Jan-Feb, 1961), 17-22

Stigler, G. J.   The Economics of Information. JPE, 69 (Jun, 1961), 213-225

Ferber, R.   Short-Run Effects of Stock Market Services on Stock Prices. JF, 13 (Mar, 1958), 80-95

11b FREQUENCY DISTRIBUTION OF SUCCESSIVE RETURNS

The bulk of the articles in this section are concerned with the controversy (prompted by Mandelbrot) as to whether successive, continuously compounded, rates of return best approximate the normal or non-normal members of the stable Paretian family of distributions. Fama's 1963 article is a good introduction to the issues involved. Fama (1965) and Works exemplify the conflicting empirical evidence. We have also included in this section Aitchison & Brown's standard work on the log-normal distribution together with some articles on the properties of non-Gaussian stable distributions (notably the articles by Gnedenko & Kolmogorov, Fama & Roll and Blattberg & Sargent). Because the Paretian family constitutes the limiting distribution for random processes, section 11c on the 'Random Walk Hypothesis' contains a number of other discussions of the topic. Roll's dissertation and book (listed elsewhere) discuss the subject in the context of the treasury bill market.

Praetz, P. D.   The Distribution of Price Changes. JB, 45 (Jan, 1972), 49-55

Barnea, A. & Downes, D. H.   A Re-examination of the Empirical Distribution of Stock Price Changes. Unp ms, 1971

Blattberg, R. & Sargent, T.   Regression with Non-Gaussian Disturbances: Some Sampling Results. Em, 39 (May, 1971), 501-510

Clark, P. K.   A Subordinated Stochastic Process Model with Finite Variance for Speculative Prices. Discussion paper No 1, Center for Economic Research, U of Minn, Apr 1971

Fama, E. F. & Roll, R.   Parameter Estimates for Symmetric Stable Distributions. JASA, 66 (Jun, 1971), 331-338

Fielitz, B. D.   Stationarity of Random Data: Some Implications for the Distribution of Stock Price Changes. JFQA, 6 (Jun, 1971), 1025-1034

Teichmoeller, J.   A Note on the Distribution of Stock Price Changes. JASA, 66 (Jun, 1971), 282-284

Brealey, R. A.   The Distribution and Independence of Successive Rates of Return in the U.K. Equity Market. JBF, 2 (Summer, 1970), 29-40

Brown, K. C.   Estimating Frequency Functions from Limited Data. JFQA, 5 (Mar, 1970), 139-148

Fama, E. F. & Roll, R.   Some Properties of Symmetric Stable Distributions. JASA, 63 (Sep, 1968), 817-836

Gnedenko, B. V. & Kolmogorov, A. N.   Limit Distributions for Sums of Independent Random Variables. Addison-Wes, 1968

Granger, C. W. J.   Some Aspects of the Random Walk Model of Stock Market Prices. IntER, 9 (Jun, 1968), 253-257

Mandelbrot, B.   Some Aspects of the Random Walk Model of Stock Market Prices: Comment. IntER, 9 (Jun, 1968), 258-259

Renwick, F. B.   Theory of Investment Behavior and Empirical Analysis of Stock Market Price Relatives. MSci, 15 (Sep, 1968), 57-71

Works, J. W.   Analysis of Distributions of First Differences in Price of Electric Utility Common Stocks as the Time Interval between Differences is Increased for Tendency to Gaussian Normality. PhD diss, Northwestern U, 1968

Mandelbrot, B.   The Variation of Some Other Speculative Prices. JB, 40 (Oct, 1967), 393-413

Mandelbrot, B. & Taylor, H. M.   On the Distribution of Stock Price Differences. OR, (Nov-Dec, 1967), 1057-1062

Press, S. J.   A Compound Events Model for Security Prices. JB, 40 (Jul, 1967), 317-335

Stalker, A. C.   Frequency Distributions of Investment Index Yields. JIA, 93 (1967), 113-118

Brada, J. C.; Ernst, H. & Van Tassel, J.   The Distribution of Stock Price Differences: Gaussian After All? OR, 14 (Apr, 1966), 334-340

Fama, E. F.   The Behavior of Stock Market Prices. JB, 38 (Jan, 1965), 34-105

Renwick, F. B.   Economic Growth and Distributions of Change in Stock Market Prices. IMR, 9 (Spring, 1965), 39-68

Fama, E. F.   The Distribution of the Daily Differences of the Logarithms of Stock Prices. PhD diss, U of Chicago, 1964

Fama, E. F.   Mandelbrot and the Stable Paretian Hypothesis. JB, 36 (Oct, 1963), 420-429

Mandelbrot, B.   New Methods in Statistical Economics. JPE, 71 (Oct, 1963), 421-440

Mandelbrot, B.   The Stable Paretian Income Distribution when the Apparent Exponent is Near Two. IntER, 4 (Jan, 1963), 111-115

Mandelbrot, B.   The Variation of Certain Speculative Prices. JB, 36 (Oct, 1963), 394-419

Wise, J.   Linear Estimators for Linear Regression Systems Having Infinite Variances. Paper presented at the Berkeley-Stanford Mathematical Economics Seminar, Oct 1963

Mandelbrot, B.   Paretian Distributions and Income Maximization. QJE, 76 (Oct, 1962), 57-85

Niederhoffer, V.   Clustering of Stock Prices. OR, 13 (1959), 258-265

Aitchison, J. & Brown, J. A. C.   The Lognormal Distribution. Cambridge U Pr, 1957

11c RANDOM WALK HYPOTHESIS

Two useful introductions to the random walk hypothesis are provided by Fama. His 1965 Financial Analysts Journal article provides a readable non-technical exposition and his 1970 review article places the issue in the wider context of efficient market theory.

Cootner's book combines a valuable collection of the earlier essays on the subject with useful editorial comment. Among the later works, we should perhaps single out Samuelson's theoretical explanation for random price movements and Fama's 1965 Journal of Business article with its important statistical evidence.

Distributional evidence for the random walk hypothesis is largely listed under 11b—'Frequency Distribution of Rates of Return'. Other subject headings are concerned with tests for particular kinds of dependence (e.g. relative strength and filter rules). Finally the sections on other speculative markets provide evidence of randomness in future markets.

Some of the more important evidence relating to the semi-strong form of the efficient market hypothesis is listed under 11a—'The Adjustment of Stock Prices to New Information'. Evidence for the strong form is to be found under 14a—'Performance Measurement—General', 15c—'The Accuracy of Share Price Forecasts' and 13c—'Insider Trading'.

Black, F.   Implications of the Random Walk Hypothesis for Portfolio Management. FAJ, 27 (Mar-Apr, 1971), 16-22

Cheng, P. L. & Deets, M. K.   Portfolio Returns and the Random Walk Theory. JF, 26 (Mar, 1971), 11-30

Kemp, A. G. & Reid, G. C.   The Random Walk Hypothesis and the Recent Behaviour of Equity Prices in Britain. Ec, 38 (1971), 28-51

Mandelbrot, B. When can Price be Arbitraged Efficiently? A Limit to the Validity of the Random Walk and Martingale Models. ReStat, 53 (Aug, 1971), 225-236

Niarchos, N. A. Statistical Analysis of Transactions of the Athens Stock Exchange. PhD diss, Nottingham U, 1971

Vasicek, O. A. & McQuown, J. A. The Efficient Market Model. FAJ, 28 (Sep-Oct, 1971), 71-84

Young, W. E. Random Walk of Stock Prices: a Test of the Variance-Time Function. Em, 39 (Sep, 1971), 797-812

Broyles, J. E. A Stochastic Model of New York Stock Exchange Transactions. PhD diss, LSE, 1970

Dryden, M. M. A Statistical Study of U.K. Share Prices. SJPE, 17 (Nov, 1970), 369-389

Drzycimski, E. F. & Frederickson, D. R. A Relative-to-Market Test of the Random Walk Theory. MVJBE, 6 (1970), 33-47

Fama, E. F. Efficient Capital Markets: a Review of Theory and Empirical Work. JF, 25 (May, 1970), 383-417

Granger, C. W. J. & Morgenstern, O. Predictability of Stock Market Prices. Heath, 1970

Renshaw, E. F. & V. D. Test of the Random Walk Hypothesis. FAJ, 26 (Sep-Oct, 1970), 51-60

Semah, J.; Serres, C. & Tessier, B. L'Ordinateur Speculateur. Dunod, 1970

West, R. R. Simulating Securities Markets Operations; some Examples, Observations, and Comments. JFQA, 5 (Mar, 1970), 115-138

Black, F. Differences in Ability among Professional Portfolio Managers. Financial Note 5A, (Sep 15, 1969), unp

Cox, R. A Counter-Example to the Random Walk Hypothesis of Stock Market Prices. PhD diss, Columbia U, 1969

Dryden, M. M. Share Price Movements: A Markovian Approach. JF, 24 (Mar, 1969), 49-60

Fielitz, B. D. On the Behavior of Stock Price Relatives as a Random Process with an Application to New York Stock Exchange Prices. DBA diss, Kent St U, 1969

Praetz, P. D. Australian Share Prices and the Random Walk Hypothesis. AJS, 11 (1969) 123-129

Evans, J. L. The Random Walk Hypothesis, Portfolio Analysis and the Buy-and-Hold Criterion. JFQA, 3 (Sep, 1968), 327-342

Hey, J. D. Spectral Analysis of Stock Market Prices. MSc diss, Edinburgh U, 1968

Owen, J. Analysis of Variance Tests for Local Trends in the Standard and Poor's Index. JF, 23 (Jun, 1968), 509-514

Renshaw, E. F. The Random Walk Hypothesis, Performance Measurement and Portfolio Theory. FAJ, 24 (Mar-Apr, 1968), 114-119

Rinfret, P. A. Investment Managers are Worth their Keep. FAJ, 24 (Mar-Apr, 1968), 163-170

Smidt, S. A New Look at the Random Walk Hypothesis. JFQA, 3 (Sep, 1968) 235-262

Levy, R. A. The Theory of Random Walks: A Survey of Findings. AmE 11 (Fall, 1967), 34-48

Osborne, M. F. M. Some Quantitative Tests for Stock Price Generating Models and Trading Folklore. JASA, 62 (Jun, 1967), 321-340

Mandelbrot, B. Forecasts of Future Prices, Unbiased Markets, and Martingale Models. JB, 39 (Suppl, Jan, 1966), 242-255

Niederhoffer, V. & Osborne, M. F. M.   Market Making and Reversal on the Stock Exchange. JASA, 61 (Dec, 1966), 897-916

Owen, J.   An Investor in the Stock Market. PhD diss, Harvard U, 1966

Smith, E. P.   Markov Processes and Investment Behavior. Met, 18 (Jan-Apr, 1966), 15-30

Fama, E. F.   The Behavior of Stock Market Prices. JB, 38 (Jan, 1965), 34-105

Fama, E. F.   Random Walks in Stock Market Prices. FAJ, 21 (Sep-Oct, 1965), 55-59

Howrey, E. P.   Are Stock Prices Random or Predictable? BE, 1 (Summer, 1965)

Osborne, M. F. M.   The Dynamics of Stock Trading. Em, 33 (Jan, 1965), 88-113

Samuelson, P. A.   Proof That Properly Anticipated Prices Fluctuate Randomly. IMR, 6 (Spring, 1965), 41-49

Alexander, S. S.   Price Movements in Speculative Markets: Trends or Random Walks, Number 2. IMR, 5 (Spring, 1964), 25-46

Borch, K.   Price Movements in the Stock Market. SAkt, 47 (1964), 41-50

Cootner, P. H. (Ed).   The Random Character of Stock Market Prices. MIT Pr, 1964

Godfrey, M. D.; Granger, C. W. J. & Morgenstern, O.   The Random Walk Hypothesis of Stock Market Behavior. Kyk, 17 (1964), 1-30

Jackson, J. T. R.   Some Speculative Strategies in the Stock Market. PhD diss, Case IT, 1964

Mandelbrot, B.   Is there Persistence in Stock Price Movements? Paper for the Seminar on the Analysis of Security Prices, U of Chicago, Nov 1964.

Moore, A. B.   Some Characteristics of Changes in Common Stock Prices, *in* Cootner, P. H. (Ed), The Random Character of Stock Market Prices. MIT Pr, 1964

Steiger, W.   A Test of Nonrandomness in Stock Price Changes, *in* Cootner, P. H. (Ed), The Random Character of Stock Market Prices. MIT Pr, 1964

Granger, C. W. J. & Morgenstern, O.   Spectral Analysis of New York Stock Market Prices. Kyk, 16 (1963), 1-27

Steiger, W.   Non-Randomness in the Stock Market: A New Test on an Existent Hypothesis. SM diss, MIT, 1963

Weintraub, R. E.   On Speculative Prices and Random Walks: A Denial JF, 18 (Mar, 1963), 59-66

Cootner, P. H.   Stock Prices: Random Walks vs Finite Markov Chains IMR, 3 (Spring, 1962), 24-25

Moore, A. B.   A Statistical Analysis of Common Stock Prices. PhD diss, U of Chicago, 1962

Osborne, M. F. M.   Periodic Structure in the Brownian Motion of Stock Prices. OR, 10 (May-Jun, 1962), 345-379

Alexander, S. S.   Price Movements in Speculative Markets: Trends or Random Walks, IMR, 2 (May, 1961), 7-26

Cowles, A.   A Revision of Previous Conclusions Regarding Stock Price Behavior. Em, 28 (Oct, 1960), 909-915

Osborne, M. F. M.   Brownian Motion in the Stock Market. OR, 7 (Mar-Apr, 1959), 145-173

Roberts, H. V.   Stock Market 'Patterns' and Financial Analysis: Methodological Suggestions. JF, 14 (Mar, 1959), 1-10

St Laurent, A. G.   Comments on 'Brownian Motion in the Stock Market'. OR, 7 (1959), 806-807

Working, H.   A Theory of Anticipatory Prices. AER, 48 (May, 1958), 188-199

Samuelson, P. A.   Intertemporal Price Equilibrium: a Prologue to the Theory of Speculation. WA, 79 (1957), 181-221

Working, H.   New Ideas and Methods for Price Research. JFE, 38 (1956), 1427-1436

Brinegar, C. S.   Statistical Analysis of Speculative Price Behavior. PhD diss, Stanford U, 1954

Kendall, M. G.   The Analysis of Economic Time Series, Part I. JRSS, 96 (1953), 11-25

Working, H.   The Investigation of Economic Expectations. AER, 39 (May, 1949), 150-166

Cowles, A. & Jones, H. E.   Some A Posteriori Probabilities in Stock Market Action. Em, (Jul, 1937), 280-294

Working, H.   A Random Difference Series for Use in the Analysis of Time Series. JASA, 29 (Mar, 1934), 11-24

Taussig, F. W.   Is Market Price Determinate? QJE, 35 (May, 1921), 394-411

Bachelier, L.   Théorie de la Speculation. Docteur des Sciences Mathematiques diss, U. of Paris, 1900. Originally published in Annales de l'Ecole Normale Superieure, Sec. 3, 1900, 21-86. English translation by A. J. Boness: Theory of Speculation, *in* Cootner, P. H. (Ed), The Random Character of Stock Market Prices. MIT Pr, 1964

Part 12 Technical Analysis

12a TECHNICAL ANALYSIS—GENERAL

This section brings together a number of general expositions of technical analysis. The article by Seligman is a good introduction to the subject and the books by Granville and Edwards & Magee provide more extensive discussions. Studies of specific technical tools are allocated to other sections in Parts 12 and 13.

See also:

11c Random Walk Hypothesis

Helm, H. M., Jr.   Technical Analysis as Applied to the 1961-1962 Stock Market Price Cycle. PhD diss, U of Tex, 1968

Patni, N. K.   Empirical Evaluation of Combined Fundamental and Technical Models for Stock Prices. SM thesis, MIT 1968

Damant, D.   Some Aspects of Technical Analysis (II). IA, 19 (Dec, 1967), 24-28

Freeman, P.   Some Aspects of Technical Analysis. IA, 18 (Oct, 1967), 9-19

Ellinger, A. G.   Security Price Behaviour. IA, 14 (May, 1966), 42-43

Levy, R. A.   Conceptual Foundations of Technical Analysis. FAJ, 22 (Jul-Aug, 1966), 83-89

Cootner, P. H.   Technicians' Contribution in Selecting Undervalued Stocks. CFC, (Sep 16, 1965), 5 ff

Edwards, R. D. & Magee, J.   Technical Analysis of Stock Trends, 5th ed. Magee, 1964

Krow, H. A.   Forecasting Stock Market Fluctuations by Technical Methods. PhD diss, U of Pittsburgh, 1964

Stewart, T. H.   Can Technical Analysis Help? IA, 8 (May, 1964), 29-34

Tabell, E. W. & A. W.   The Case for Technical Analysis. FAJ, 20 (Mar-Apr, 1964), 67-76

Granville, J. E.   New Key to Stock Market Profits. P-H, 1963

Tabell, E. W. & Tabell, A. W.   An Introduction to Technical Analysis. IA, 6 (Sep, 1963), 15-26

Jiler, W. L.   How Charts Can Help You in the Market. Commodity R, 1962

Seligman, D.   The Mystique of Point-and-Figure. F, 67 (Mar, 1962)

Seligman, D.   Playing the Market with Charts. F, 67 (Feb, 1962)

Granville, J. E.   A Strategy of Daily Stock Market Timing for Maximum Profit. P-H, 1960

Kreag, M. A.   The Market as a Function of Time, Price and Volume. AJ, 9 (Jul-Aug, 1953), 81-86

Tabell, E. W.   Technical Approach to the Market. AJ, 7 (2nd Qtr, 1951) 49-56

Gartley, H. M.   Modern Approaches to Stock Market Analysis. AJ, 4 (Suppl 2nd Qtr, 1948), 3-7

12b SEASONAL PATTERNS IN THE STOCK MARKET

The majority of these studies are concerned with the identification of seasonals in rates of return. They are exemplified by Shiskin's paper. The Jones & Litzenberger article is an exception in that it is concerned with earnings seasonality. Works on the seasonality of interest rates are listed under 18d—'Interest Rates—Cyclical and Seasonal Effects'.

Moses, E. A.   Seasonal Variations in Common Stock Prices. PhD diss, U of Ga, 1971

Jones, C. P. & Litzenberger, R. H.   Earnings Seasonality and Stock Prices. FAJ, 25 (Nov-Dec, 1969), 57-59

Shiskin, J.   Systematic Aspects of Stock Price Fluctuations. Paper for the Seminar on the Analysis of Security Prices, U of Chicago, May 1967

Fortune.   Buying Stocks by the Calendar. F, 71 (Jun, 1965)

Zinbarg, E. D. & Harrington, J. J.   The Stock Market's Seasonal Pattern. FAJ, 20 (Jan-Feb, 1964), 53-56

Osborne, M. F. M.   Periodic Structure in the Brownian Motion of Stock Prices. OR, 10 (May-Jun, 1962), 345-379

Leffler, G. L.   Seasonal Patterns. B, (Mar 30, 1953), 27

12c FILTER RULES AND THE DOW THEORY

This section contains several descriptive articles on the Dow Theory, one of the most influential of technical aids. Students of the random walk hypothesis have been interested in the merits of the so-called filter rule, which has much in common with the Dow Theory. This work includes Alexander's historically important articles and Fama & Blume's careful assessment of the profitability of filter rules. Dryden has examined the profitability of such rules in the UK context.

     See also:

         11c Random Walk Hypothesis
         12a Technical Analysis—General

Dryden, M. M.   Filter Tests of U.K. Share Prices. AE, 1 (Jan, 1970), 261-276

Dryden, M. M.   A Source of Bias in Filter Tests of Share Prices. JB, 42 (Jul, 1969), 321-325

Gould, A. & Buchsbaum, M.   A Filter Approach to Stock Selection. FAJ, 25 (Nov-Dec, 1969), 61 ff

Greiner, P. P. & Whitcomb, H. C.   The Dow Theory and the 70 Year Forecast Record. Inv Int, 1969

Woodward, B. M.   The Dow Theory and the Management of Portfolios. PhD diss, U of Fla, 1969

Fama, E. F. & Blume, M. E.   Filter Rules and Stock Market Trading. JB, 39 (Jan, 1966), 226-241

Alexander, S. S.   Price Movements in Speculative Markets: Trends or Random Walks, Number 2. IMR, 5 (Spring, 1964), 25-46

Helpern, S. R.   An Analysis of Stock Price Movements Using Stop Orders. SB thesis, MIT, 1962

Levine, S.   Heuristic Determination of Optimum Filters for Use in a Rule for Speculative Market Action. SM thesis, MIT, 1962

Alexander, S. S.   Price Movements in Speculative Markets: Trends or Random Walks. IMR, 2 (May, 1961), 7-26

Bishop, G. W., Jr.   Evolution of the Dow Theory. FAJ, 17 (Sep-Oct, 1961) 23-26

Bishop, G. W. Jr.   Charles H. Dow and the Dow Theory. Appleton, 1960

Barbour, J. F.   An Analysis of the Conclusions of the Cowles Studies with Respect to the Dow Theory. AJ, 4 (4th Qtr, 1948), 11-20

12d RELATIVE STRENGTH AND MOVING AVERAGES

A number of technical rules have been devised that require the investor to purchase stocks that have been appreciating unusually fast. The controversy surrounding relative strength analysis is well summarised in the 1967 exchange between Levy and Jensen. Jensen & Bennington offer a rigorous assessment of the performance of a relative strength rule and James provides an analysis of a similar rule based on moving averages.

See also:

11c Random Walk Hypothesis
12a Technical Analysis—General

Griffiths, R. J. Relative Strength-an Indicator for Investment in the Equity Market. MSc thesis, Cranfield IT, 1970

Jensen, M. C. & Bennington, G. A. Random Walks and Technical Theories: Some Additional Evidence. JF, 25 (May, 1970), 469-482

Levy, R. A. & Kripotos, S. L. Sources of Relative Price Strength. FAJ, 25 (Nov-Dec, 1969), 60 ff

Peet, C. H. Relative Strength—a Review and Some New Results. Paper delivered to the Financial Analysts Federation, Baltimore, Oct 21, 1969

James, F. E. Jr. Monthly Averages—An Effective Investment Tool? JFQA, 3 (Sep, 1968), 315-326

Levy, R. A. Random Walks: Reality or Myth—Reply. FAJ, 24 (Jan-Feb, 1968), 129-133

Levy, R. A. The Relative Strength Concept of Common Stock Price Forecasting. Inv Int, 1968

Seelenfreund, A.; Parker, G. G. C. & Van Horne, J. C. Stock Price Behavior and Trading. JFQA, 3 (Sep, 1968), 263-282

Van Horne, J. C.; & Parker, G. G. C. Technical Trading Rules: A Comment. FAJ, 24 (Jul-Aug, 1968), 128-132

James, F. E. Jr. The Implications of Trend Persistency in Portfolio Management. PhD diss, Rensselaer, 1967

Jensen, M. C. Random Walks: Reality or Myth—Comment. FAJ, 23 (Nov-Dec, 1967), 77-85

Levy, R. A. The Principle of Portfolio Upgrading. IMR, 7 (Fall, 1967), 82-96

Levy, R. A. Random Walks: Reality or Myth. FAJ, 23 (Nov-Dec, 1967), 69-77

Levy, R. A. Relative Strength as a Criterion for Investment Selection. JF, 22 (Dec, 1967), 595-610

Van Horne, J. C. & Parker, G. G. C. The Random Walk Theory: An Empirical Test. FAJ, 23 (Nov-Dec, 1967), 87-92

Levy, R. A. An Evaluation of Selected Application of Stock Market Timing Techniques, Trading Tactics and Trend Analysis. PhD diss, Am U, 1966

Barney, W. An Investigation of Parametric Variations in a Moving Average Investment Rule. SM thesis, MIT, 1964

12e DIFFUSION INDEXES

Under this heading have been grouped all discussions of breadth of market indicators, advance decline ratios and diffusion indexes of security price changes.

112

The studies broadly fall into two groups. The first, exemplified by the articles of Dryden, Theil & Leenders and Fama, is concerned with the relationships between successive values of the advance-decline ratio. The second group of studies is concerned with the relationship between breadth of market indicators and subsequent market changes. The Zakon & Pennypacker article provides a useful introduction to this question.

See also:

11c Random Walk Hypothesis
12a Technical Analysis—General

Dryden, M. M.   Short-term Forecasting of Share Prices: An Information Theory Approach. SJPE, 15 (Nov, 1968), 227-249

Harlow, C. V.   An Analysis of the Predictive Value of Stock Market 'Breadth' Measurements. DBA diss, U of S Cal, 1968

Harlow, C. V.   An Analysis of the Predictive Value of Stock Market 'Breadth' Measurements. Inv Int, 1968

Zakon, A. J. & Pennypacker, J. C.   An Analysis of the Advance-Decline Line as a Stock Market Indicator. JFQA, 3 (Sep, 1968), 229-314

Cullity, J. P.   An Alternative Measure of the Diffusion of Stock Prices. QREB, 7 (Autumn, 1967), 47-55

Fama, E. F.   Tomorrow on the New York Stock Exchange. JB, 38 (Jul, 1965), 285-299

Theil, H. & Leenders, C. T.   Tomorrow on the American Exchange. JB, 38 (Jul, 1965), 277-284

Bauer, J.   A Diffusion Index As Applied to Price Movement in the Stock Market. SM thesis, MIT, 1964

Freeman, G. K.   Advance-Decline Line a Clue to the Underlying Strength or Weakness of the Market. B, (Jan 21, 1963)

Mennis, E. A. & Birmingham, J. M., Jr.   Diffusion Analysis as an Investment Guide. AJ, 13 (May, 1957), 47-56

12f FORMULA PLANS

A number of formula plans have been devised in the hope of allocating assets more efficiently between cash and equities. Pye's article provides an interesting justification for dollar averaging plans.

See also:

12a Technical Analysis—General

Pye, G.   Minimax Policies for Selling an Asset and Dollar Averaging. MSci, 17 (Mar, 1971), 379-393

Cranshaw, E. T.   Is Pound-Averaging a Hoax? IA, 28 (Dec, 1970), 12-13

Persons, R. H.   Handbook of Formula Plans in the Stock Market. Am Res Co, 1967

Dince, R. R.   Portfolio Income: A Test of a Formula Plan. JFQA, 1 (Sep, 1966), 90-107

Dince, R. R.   Another View of Formula Planning. JF, 19 (Dec, 1964), 678-688

Dince, R. R.   Formula Planning. FAJ, 17 (Mar-Apr, 1961), 59-64

Ascher, L. W.   Dollar Averaging in Theory and Practice. FAJ, 16 (Sep-Oct, 1960), 51-53

Vawter, J.   The Role of Formula Timing Plans in Investment Analysis. AJ, 15 (Feb, 1959), 67-68

Renshaw, E. F.   A Note on Behavior in the Stock Market. AJ, 14 (Aug, 1958) 19-23

Szatrowski, Z.   A Statistical Approach to Formula Planning. AJ, 11 (May, 1955), 65-69

Warren, R. A.   Formula Plan Investing. HBR, 31 (Jan-Feb, 1953), 57 ff

Sitt, I.   Mechanical Investment Plans versus Judgment. AJ, 2 (2nd Qtr, 1946), 30-38

Carpenter, H. G.   Investment Timing by Formula Plans. Har-Row, 1943

12g TECHNICAL SYSTEMS—MISCELLANEOUS

This section lists studies of some miscellaneous specific technical tools.

See also:

11c Random Walk Hypothesis
12a Technical Analysis—General

Levy, R. A.   The Predictive Significance of Five-Point Chart Patterns. JB, 44 (Jul, 1971), 316-323

Gaumnitz, J. E. & Salabar, C. A.   The Barron's Confidence Index: an Examination of its Value as a Market Indicator. FAJ, 25 (Sep-Oct, 1969) 16 ff

Besser, D. E.   Tick Volume as a Means of Common Stock Selection. SM thesis, MIT, 1968

Collins, C. J.   Effect of Sunspot Activity on the Stock Market. FAJ, 21 (Nov-Dec, 1965), 45-56

Smith, E. L.   Low Tide in Sunspots-1964. FAJ, 19 (Jul-Aug, 1963), 91-92

Part 13   Volume & Unusual Market Activity

13a VOLUME

This section is primarily concerned with the implications of variations in volume for changes in the stock price.

Crouch, R. L.   Market Volume and Price Changes. FAJ, 26 (Jul-Aug, 1970), 104-109

Reilly, F. K.   First Look at O-T-C Volume. FAJ, 25 (Jan-Feb, 1969), 124-128

Ying, C. C.   Stock Market Prices and Volume of Sales. Em, 34 (Jul, 1966), 676-685

Ying, C. C.   Are There Any Relationships Between Stock Price and Volume? DBA diss, Harvard U, 1964

13b ODD-LOT TRADING

The writings of Drew expound the theory that investment performance can be enhanced by the study of odd lot trading data. Other works in this section, including the interesting early study by Hardy, are concerned with testing this theory. More general studies of personal investing are listed under 3a—'Ownership' and 3b—'Personal Investment'.

See also:

12a Technical Analysis—General

Wu, H-K.   Odd-Lot Trading in the Stock Market and its Market Impact. JFQA, 7 (Jan, 1972), 1321-1342

Kaish, S.   Odd Lotter Trading of High and Low Quality Stocks. FAJ, 25 (Mar-Apr, 1969), 88-91

Kaish, S.   Odd Lot Profit and Loss Performance. FAJ, 25 (Sep-Oct, 1969), 83-92

Kewley, T. J. & Stevenson, R. A.   The Odd-Lot Theory for Individual Stocks: A Reply. FAJ, 25 (Jan-Feb, 1969), 99-104

Kisor, M., Jr. & Niederhoffer, V.   Odd-Lot Short Sales Ratio: It Signals a Market Rise. B, (Sep 1, 1969), 8

Aby, C. D.   An Investigation of the Concept of Public Participation as a Basis for Forecasting Stock Market and Security Trends. PhD diss, La St U, 1968

Synott, T. W., III.   Time Series Analysis for Investment Decisions. Paper for the Seminar on the Analysis of Security Prices, U of Chicago, Nov 1968

Drew, G. A.   A Clarification of the Odd-Lot Theory. FAJ, 23 (Sep-Oct, 1967) 107-108

Kewley, T. J. & Stevenson, R. A.   The Odd-Lot Theory as Revealed by Purchase and Sales Statistics for Individual Stocks. FAJ, 23 (Sep-Oct, 1967), 103-106

Klein, D. J.   The Odd-Lot Stock Trading Theory. PhD diss, Mich St. U, 1964

Drew, G. A.   New Methods for Profit in the Stock Market. Metcalf, 1955

Whitney, A. D.   Odd Lot Trading as a Market Barometer. AJ, 4 (1st Qtr, 1948), 58-66

Hardy, C. O.   Odd Lot Trading on the New York Stock Exchange. Brookings, 1939

13c INSIDER TRADING

The works in this section are concerned principally with the performance of stocks traded by insiders. These studies are exemplified by the papers of Lorie & Niederhoffer, and Pratt & De Vere. Some publications on the regulation of insider trading are listed under 2e—'Securities Markets—Regulation'.

Edwards, K. B.   Insider Trading. A, 81 (Jan, 1970), 46-49

Lorie, J. H. & Niederhoffer, V.   Predictive and Statistical Properties of Insider Trading. JLE, 11 (Apr, 1968), 35-53

Pratt, S. P. & DeVere, C. W.   Relationship between Insider Trading and Rates of Return for NYSE Common Stocks, 1960-1966. Paper for the Seminar on the Analysis of Security Prices, U of Chicago, May 1968

Glass, G. A.   Extensive Insider Accumulation as an Indication of Near-Term Stock Price Performance. PhD diss, Ohio St U, 1966

Fischer, M. C.   The Relationship between Insiders' Transactions, the Price of the Common Stock of their Respective Companies, the Standard and Poor's Stock Price Index and Price Stability. PhD diss, Am U, 1965

Rogoff, D. L.   The Forecasting Properties of Insiders' Transactions. DBA diss, Mich St U, 1964

Wu, H-K.   Corporate Insider Trading, Profitability and Stock Price Movement. PhD diss, U of Pa, 1963

Hamada, R. S.   An Analysis of Diffusion Indices of Insiders' Transactions. SM thesis, MIT, 1961

O' Donnell, T. M.   The Stock Market Activity of the Corporate Insider and Future Price Movements of the Stock. MBA thesis, U of Pa, 1960

Driscoll, T. E.   Some Aspects of Corporate Insider Stock Holdings and Trading Under Section 16(b) of the Securities Exchange Act. MBA thesis, U of Pa, 1956

Smith, F. P.   Management Trading, Stock Market Prices and Profits. Yale U Pr, 1941

13d SHORT SELLING

The books by Frederick and Bruner exemplify the odium heaped on short sellers who were held largely responsible for the 'great crash'. In this vein Macaulay & Durand are primarily interested in testing whether short selling has been destabilising.

Many general manuals on technical analysis (notably Granville (1960)) have advocated the study of short interest data and most of the more recent articles in this section are concerned with testing the value of this maxim. The articles by Mayor and Seneca are good instances of this work.

See also:

12a Technical Analysis—General

McDonald, J. G. & Baron, D.   Risk and Return on Short Position in Common Stocks. JF, forthcoming

Whitmarsh, T. F.   When to Sell Securities Short Against the Box. FAJ, 28 (May-Jun, 1972), 80ff

McEnally R. W. & Dyl, E. A.   Risk of Selling Short. FAJ, 25 (Nov-Dec, 1969), 73-77

Hanna, M.   Short Interest: Bullish or Bearish?—Comment. JF, 23 (Jun, 1968), 520-523

Mayor, T. H.   Short Trading Activities and the Price of Equities: Some Simulation and Regression Results. JFQA, 3 (Sep, 1968), 283-298

Seneca, J. J.   Short Interest: Bullish or Bearish?—Reply. JF, 23 (Jun, 1968), 524-527

Smith, D.   Short Interest and Stock Market Prices. FAJ, 24 (Nov-Dec, 1968), 151-154

Seneca, J. J.   Short Interest: Bullish or Bearish? JF, 22 (Mar, 1967), 67-70

Biggs, B. M.   The Short Interest—a False Proverb. FAJ, 22 (Jul-Aug, 1966), 111-116

Weaver, M.   The Technique of Short Selling. Inv Pr, 1963

Wyckoff, P. G.   The Method and Motives of Selling Short. AJ, 15 (May, 1959), 101-104

Macaulay, F. R., & Durand, D.   Short Selling on the New York Stock Exchange. Twentieth Fund, 1951

Field, M. J.   Security Prices and Stock Exchange Holidays in Relation to Short Selling. JB, 7 (Oct, 1934), 328

Bruner, D. McD.   Short Selling the USA. Winston, 1933

Frederick, J. G.   The Real Truth about Short Selling. Bourse, 1932

Part 14 Performance Measurement

14a PERFORMANCE MEASUREMENT—GENERAL

There has been considerable interest in recent years in the development of risk-adjusted performance measures and the subject occupies much of this section. Noteworthy are the articles of Treynor (1965), Sharpe (1966) and Jensen (1968), and the somewhat cautionary paper by Friend & Blume. Fama's paper extends these analyses to consider the components of performance. One particular component, market timing, is the topic of Treynor & Mazuy, and Jensen (1971). Empirical studies of unit trust and mutual fund performance are mainly listed below. Those of other institutional portfolios are classified by institution.

See also:

10c Mean-Variance Portfolio Theory and Portfolio Selection—General

10l Capital Asset Pricing Theory

14b Performance Measurement—Pension Funds

Fama, E. F.   Components of Investment Performance. JF, 27 (Jun, 1972), 551-568

Arditti, F. D.   Another Look at Mutual Fund Performance. JFQA, 6 (Jun, 1971), 909-912

Jensen, M. C.   Optimal Utilization of Market Forecasts and the Evaluation of Investment Performance. Unp ms, 1971

Williamson, J. P.   Performance of Canadian Mutual Funds 1961-1970. Unp ms, Mar, 1971

Bogle, J. C.   Mutual Fund Performance Evaluation. FAJ, 26 (Nov-Dec, 1970), 25ff

Bower, R. S; Williamson, J. P. & Wippern, R. F.   Portfolio Selection and Performance Appraisal Models: the Multiperiod Case. Paper for the Seminar on the Analysis of Security Prices, U of Chicago, Nov 1970.

Brew, J. M.   The Trustees' Meeting—a City Daydream. IA, 28 (Dec, 1970), 14-17

Carlson, R. S.   Aggregate Performance of Mutual Funds. JFQA, 5 (Mar, 1970), 1-32

Friend, I. & Blume, M.   Measurement of Portfolio Performance under Uncertainty. AER, 60 (Sep, 1970), 561-575

Jones, I. E.   Performance Measurement: Are We Lacking Critical Data? Paper for the Seminar on the Analysis of Security Prices, U of Chicago, Nov 1970

Mills, H. D.   On the Measurement of Fund Performance. JF, 25 (Dec, 1970), 1125-1132

Minto, G. S.   Some Suggestions Relating to the Assessment of Investment Performance in Multi-Asset Funds Subject to Decentralised Control. IA, 28 (Dec, 1970), 7-11

O'Brien, J. W.   How Market Theory Can Help Investors Set Goals, Select Investment Managers and Appraise Investment Performance. FAJ, 26 (Jul-Aug, 1970), 91-103

Samuels, J. M.   The Measurement of the Performance of Unit Trusts. IA, 27 (Sep, 1970), 34-40

Spitz, A. E.   Mutual Fund Performance and Cash Inflows. AE, 2 (Aug, 1970), 141-145

Bower, R. S. & Wippern, R. F.   Risk-Return Measurement in Portfolio Selection and Performance Appraisal Models: Progress Report. JFQA, 4 (Dec, 1969), 417-448

Rutherford, R. W.   Ranking Correlation of Unit Trust Performance 1963-1968. IA, 25 (Dec, 1969), 21-24

Schneider, T. H.   Measuring Performance. FAJ, 25 (May-Jun, 1969), 105-111

Simon, J. L.   Does 'Good Portfolio Management' Exist? MSci, 15 (Feb, 1969), B308-B319

Smith, K. V., & Tito, D. A.   Risk-Return Measures of Ex Post Portfolio Performance. JFQA, 4 (Dec, 1969), 449-472

Way, P. & Ferguson, R.   The Role of Simulation in Measuring Investment Performance. Paper for the Seminar on the Analysis of Security Prices, U of Chicago, Nov 1969

Bauman, W. S.   Evaluation of Prospective Investment Performance. JF, 23 (May, 1968), 276-295

Cohen, K. J. & Pogue, J. A.   Some Comments Concerning Mutual Fund versus Random Portfolio Performance. JB, 41 (Apr, 1968), 180-190

Fiske, H. S.   Performance Fees: Should a Manager Get a Piece of the Action? II, 2 (Mar, 1968), 23ff

Jensen, M. C.   The Performance of Mutual Funds in the Period 1945-1964. JF, 23 (May, 1968), 389-416

Levy, R. A.   Measurement of Investment Performance. JFQA, 3 (Mar, 1968), 35-57

Samuels, J. M.   The Performance of Unit Trusts. BM, 206 (Aug, 1968), 80-87

Sharpe, W. F.   Mutual Fund Performance and the Theory of Capital Asset Pricing: Reply. JB, 41 (Apr, 1968), 235-236

Stern, W. P.   Performance—Transitory or Real? FAJ, 24 (Jan-Feb, 1968), 110-113

West, R. R.   Mutual Fund Performance and the Theory of Capital Asset Pricing: Some Comments. JB, 40 (Apr, 1968), 230-234

Briggs, G. C.   Performance and Portfolio Management. FAJ, 23 (Sep-Oct, 1967), 123-127

Levy, R. A.   Is Performance Fund Trading Gainful or Wasteful? II, 1 (Dec, 1967)

Wood, R. N.   Measurement of Investment Performance. Alexander, 1967

Bingham, A. Y.   Relative Performance—Nonsense. FAJ, 22 (Jul-Aug, 1966), 101-104

Block, F. E.   Risk and Performance. FAJ, 22 (Mar-Apr, 1966), 65-74

Cohen, K. J. & Fitch, B.   The Average Investment Performance Index. MSci, 12 (Feb, 1966), B195-B215

Horowitz, I.   Popularity Versus Performance: The Mutual Funds. QREB, 6 (Spring, 1966), 45-57

Horowitz, I.   The 'Reward-to-Variability' Ratio and Mutual Fund Performance. JB, 39 (Oct, 1966), 485-488

McQuown, J. A.   The Nature, Measurement, and Meaning of Investment Performance. Paper for the Seminar on the Analysis of Security Prices, U og Chicago, May 1966

Mayer, R. W.   Performance and Its Measurement. FAJ, 22 (Mar-Apr, 1966), 54-55

Sharpe, W. F.   Mutual Fund Performance. JB, 39 (Jan, 1966), 119-138

Sherman, J. C.   A Device to Measure Portfolio Performance. FAJ, 22 (Jan-Feb, 1966), 106-108

Sieff, J. A. Measuring Investment Performance: the Unit Approach. FAJ, 22 (Jul-Aug, 1966), 93-99

Treynor, J. & Mazuy, K. Can Mutual Funds Outguess the Market? HBR, 44 (Jul-Aug, 1966), 131-136

Friend, I. & Vickers, D. Portfolio Selection and Investment Performance. JB, 20 (Sep, 1965), 391-415

Horowitz, I. A Model for Mutual Fund Evaluation. IMR, 6 (Spring, 1965), 81-92

Horowitz, I. A Rating of Mutual Fund Managements' Investment Ability. IMR, 7 (Fall, 1965), 65-76

Treynor, J. L. How to Rate Management of Investment Funds. HBR, 43 (Jan-Feb, 1965), 63-75

Horowitz, I. The Varying (?) Quality of Investment Trust Management. JASA, 58 (Dec, 1963), 1011-1032

Horowitz, I. & Higgins, H. B. Some Factors Affecting Investment Fund Performance. QREB, 3 (Spring, 1963), 41-50

Gilliland, A. B. Measuring Ordinary Share Portfolio Performance. IA, 3 (Aug, 1962), 30-35

Mead, S. B. Mutual Fund and Investment Company Performance in the 1950's. Mich St U Busn, 1962

Securities And Exchange Commission. Study of Mutual Funds prepared for the Securities Exchange Commission by the Wharton School of Finance and Commerce. House Report No. 2274. US Govt, 1962

Ball, M. Investment Company Performance. FAJ, 17 (Sep-Oct, 1961), 51-58

Hochmuth, W. P. & Bowes, A. S. Investment Companies: Performance vs Charges. FAJ, 17 (Jan-Feb, 1961), 43-49

Hayes, D. A. Evaluating the Investment Management Record of Fire Insurance Companies. AJ, 14 (Jul-Aug, 1958), 57-59

Heness, S. Measuring Investment Performance of Balanced Funds. AJ, 7 (4th Qtr, 1951), 59-60

14b PERFORMANCE MEASUREMENT—PENSION FUNDS

A significant volume of published work has been specifically concerned with the measurement of pension fund performance, though much of the analysis has wider application. The Financial Analysts Journal articles of Dietz, McCandlish and Bower & Williamson are useful introductions. The Bank Administration Institute report provides an authoritative and detailed blueprint for the measurement of pension fund performance.

See also:

> 10c Mean-Variance Portfolio Theory and Portfolio Selection—General
> 10l Capital Asset Pricing Theory
> 14a Performance Measurement—General

Robinson, R. S. Measuring the Risk Dimension of Investment Performance. JF, 25 (May, 1970), 455-468

Schneider, T. H. A Worksheet Technique for Measuring Performance. FAJ, 25 (May-Jun, 1969), 105-111

Bank Administration Institute. Measuring the Investment Performance of Pension Funds. BAI, 1968

Dietz, P. O. Components of a Measurement Model: Rate of Return, Risk and Timing. JF, 23 (May, 1968), 267-275

Dietz, P. O. Investment Goals: A Key to Measuring Performance of Pension Funds. FAJ, 24 (Mar-Apr, 1968), 133-137

Fiske, H. S. The Banks Learn to Live with Report Cards. II, 2 (May, 1968)

Fox, E. A. Comparing Performance of Equity Pension Trusts. FAJ, 24 (Sep-Oct, 1968), 121-129

Fox, G. R. Measuring Pension Fund Performance. MBA, (Jan, 1968), 6ff

Lorie, J. H. NABAC Study on Measuring Investment Performance of Pension Funds. FAJ, 24 (Mar-Apr, 1968), 139-143

Miller, F. B. & Robinson, R. S. A Management Summary of 'Measuring the Investment Performance of Pension Funds'. BAI, 1968

McCandlish, R. W., Jr. Portfolio Evaluation: An Approach. FAJ, 23 (Nov-Dec, 1967), 147-150

Bower, R. S. & Williamson, J. P. Measuring Pension Fund Performance: Another Comment. FAJ, 22 (May-Jun, 1966), 143-149

Dietz, P. O. Pension Fund Investment Performance—What Method to Use When. FAJ, 22 (Jan-Feb, 1966), 83-86

Dietz, P. O. Pension Funds: Measuring Investment Performance. Free Pr, 1966

Dietz, P. O. Evaluating the Investment Performance of Noninsured Pension Funds. PhD diss, Columbia U, 1965

McCandlish, R. W., Jr. Some Methods for Measuring Performance of a Pension Fund. FAJ, 21 (Nov-Dec, 1965), 105-110

Wood, R. N. Measuring the Investment Yield of Pension Funds. Alexander, 1965

14c PERFORMANCE MEASUREMENT—ANALYSTS

This section is devoted to the measurement of analysts' performance, with the Ramsey & Behrens paper providing a useful discussion of the extension of risk adjusted fund performance measures to the case of the individual analyst.

Mastrapasqua, F. & Bolten, S. A Note on Financial Analyst Evaluation: a Statistical Approach. JF, forthcoming

Mattlin, E. How Do You Measure an Analyst's Performance? II, 3 (Jul, 1969), 37ff

Ramsey, C. M. & Behrens, C. Analysing the Performance of Security Analysts. Paper for the Seminar on the Analysis of Security Prices, U of Chicago, Nov 1969

Gray, W. S. Measuring the Analysts' Performance. FAJ, 22 (Mar-Apr, 1966), 56-63

Templeton, J. M. Practical Methods to Test Analysts' Ability to Select Stocks for Appreciation. AJ, 2 (3rd Qtr, 1946), 51-52

Part 15 The Accuracy of Forecasts

15a THE ACCURACY OF ECONOMIC FORECASTS

We have listed below a small selection of articles on the accuracy of general economic forecasts. Zarnowitz's 1967 study is a useful introduction.

Jorgenson, D. W., Hunter, J. & Nadiri, M. I.   The Predictive Performance of Economic Models of Quarterly Investment Behavior. Em, 38 (Mar, 1970), 213-224

Stekler, H. O.   Economic Forecasting. Praeger, 1970

Mincer, J. (Ed).   Economic Forecasts and Expectations: Analyses of Forecasting Behavior and Performance. (Dist by Columbia U Pr) Natl Bur Econ Res, 1969

Stekler, H. O.   An Evaluation of Quarterly Judgmental Economic Forecasts. JB, 41 (Jul, 1968), 329-339

Zarnowitz, V.   Prediction and Forecasting, Economic, *in* International Encyclopedia of the Social Sciences, Vol. 12. Macmillan, 1968

Zarnowitz, V.   An Appraisal of Short-Term Economic Forecasts. Natl Bur Econ Res, Occasional Paper No. 104, 1967

Butler, W. F. & Kavesh, R. A. (Eds).   How Business Economists Forecast. P-H, 1966

Andrew, S. L. & Flinn, H. M.   Appraisal of Economic Forecasts. JASA (Suppl Mar, 1930), 36-41

15b THE ACCURACY OF EARNINGS FORECASTS

This section is concerned with empirical studies of the accuracy of earnings forecasts. Noteworthy is Cragg & Malkiel's analysis of the characteristics of five year forecasts and Elton & Gruber's assessment of short term forecasts.

Dev, S. & Webb, M.   The Accuracy of Company Profit Forecasts. JBF, 4 (Autumn, 1972), 26-39

Elton, E. J. & Gruber, M. J.   Earnings Estimates and the Accuracy of Expectational Data. MSci, 18 (Apr, 1972), B409-B424

Westwick, C. A.   The Accuracy of Profit Forecasts in Bid Situations. A, 83 (Jul, 1972), 10-16

Brealey, R. A.   Some Implications of the Comovement of American Company Earnings. AE, 3 (1971), 183-196

McEnally, R. W.   An Investigation of the Extrapolative Determinants of Short-Run Earnings Expectations. JFQA, 6 (Mar, 1971), 687-706

Cragg, J. G. & Malkiel, B. G.   The Consensus and Accuracy of Some Predictions of the Growth of Corporate Earnings. JF, 23 (Mar, 1968), 67-84

Crowell, R. A.   An Analysis of Expected Earnings. Paper for the Seminar on the Analysis of Security Prices, U of Chicago, May 1967

Continental Illinois National Bank Of Chicago.   The Computer Looks at the Analyst. Report prepared by D. A. Monteith and J. D. McWilliams. Chicago: Continental Illinois National Bank, 1966

Continental Illinois National Bank of Chicago.   The Reliability of Earnings Forecasts. Chicago: Continental Illinois National Bank, 1963

15c THE ACCURACY OF SHARE PRICE FORECASTS

This section is concerned with empirical studies of the merits of share recommendations and price forecasts. None is comprehensive, but the Ferber and Firth articles are useful introductions to the material.

Diefenbach, R. E.   How Good is Institutional Brokerage Research? FAJ, 28 (Jan-Feb, 1972), 54-60

Firth, M.   The Performance of Share Recommendations Made by Investment Analysts and the Effects on Market Efficiency. JBF, 4 (Summer, 1972), 58ff

Cheney, H. L.   How Good are Investment Advisory Services? FE, 37 (Nov, 1969), 30-35

Hausman, W. H.   A Note on 'The Value Line Contest: A Test of the Predictability of Stock Price Changes'. JB, 42 (Jul, 1969), 317-320

Money Which.   Share Tipsters. Money Which, (Sep, 1968)

Shelton, J. P.   The Value Line Contest: A Test of the Predictability of Stock Price Changes. JB, 40 (Jul, 1967), 251-269

Stoffels, J. D.   Stock Recommendations by Investment Advisory Services: Immediate Effects on Market Pricing. FAJ, 22 (Mar-Apr, 1966), 77-86

Colker, S. S.   An Analysis of Security Recommendations by Brokerage Houses. QREB, 3 (Summer, 1963), 19-28

Ruff, R. T.   The Effect of Selection and Recommendation of a Stock of the Month. FAJ, 19 (Mar-Apr, 1963), 41-43

Ferber, R.   Short-Run Effects of Stock Market Services on Stock Prices. JF, 13 (Mar, 1958), 80-95

Fischer, R. M.   The Accuracy of Forecasts. AJ, 10 (Feb, 1954), 73-78

Spano, A. T.   The Accuracy of Stock Market Forecasts, 1947-52. Senior thesis, Princeton U, 1954

Underwood, E. F. & Nelkin, M. C.   Brokerage House Opinion at Turning Points in the Stock Market. FAJ, 2 (4th Qtr, 1946), 39-43

Cowles, A.   Stock Market Forecasting. Em, 12 (Jul-Oct, 1944), 206-214

Goehring, E. E.   An Appraisal of Some Security Price Forecasting Services. MA thesis, U of Chicago, 1938

Kerchner, D. H.   Some Limitations on the Usefulness of Investors' Services. PhD diss, U of Chicago, 1936

Cowles, A.   Can Stock Market Forecasters Forecast? Em, (Jul, 1933)

Part 16 Sales of Stock & Changes in Issued Capital

16a NEW EQUITY ISSUES BY UNSEASONED COMPANIES

This section contains material on companies going public for the first time. Useful background material for the UK is provided by Merrett et al. and for the USA by Friend et al. Many of the articles and dissertations are concerned with the price behaviour of the stocks. Useful reading here is the exchange between Stigler and Friend & Herman and the articles by Shaw and McDonald & Fisher.

See also:

16b Equity Issues by Seasoned Companies

Ibbotson, R.   Price Performance of New Unseasoned Common Stock Issues. Paper for the Seminar on the Analysis of Security Prices, U of Chicago, Nov 1972

McDonald, J. G. & Fisher, A. K.   New Issue Stock Price Behavior. JF, 27 (Mar, 1972), 97-102

Blaser, A. L.   Dynamic Price Movements: the New Issue Aftermarket. DBA diss, U of Oregon, 1971

Blum, J. D.   An Analysis of the Price Behavior of Initial Common Stock Offerings. PhD diss, Mich St U, 1971

Logue, D. E.   An Empirical Appraisal of the Efficiency of the Market for First Public Offerings of Common Stock. PhD diss, Cornell U, 1971

Robinson, G. J.   Going Public—Successful Securities Underwriting, 2nd ed. Boardman, 1971

Shaw, D. C.   The Performance of Primary Common Stock Offerings: a Canadian Comparison. JF, 26 (Dec, 1971), 1101-1114

Brown, J. M.   Post-Offering Experience of Companies Going Public. JB, 43 (Jan, 1970), 10-18

Stoll, H. R. & Curley, A. J.   Small Business and the New Issues Market for Equities. JFQA, 5 (Sep, 1970), 309-322

Reilly, F. K. & Hatfield, K.   Experience with New Stock Issues. FAJ, 25 (Sep-Oct, 1969), 73-82

Friend, I; Longstreet, J. R; Mendelson, M; Miller, E. & Hess, A. P., Jr. Investment Banking and the New Issues Market. World Pub, 1967

Lehr, M. E. & Newbould, G. D.   New Issues—Activity and Pricing Performance 1964-1967. IA, 18 (Oct, 1967), 20-23

McLaughlin, C. W.   An Analysis of the First Public Stock Issues of New Technical Enterprises. SM thesis, MIT, 1967

Merrett, A. J.; Howe, M. & Newbould, G. D.   Equity Issues and the London Capital Market. Longman, 1967

Murphy G. W. & Prussman, D. F.   Equity Issues and the London Capital Market. MS, 35 (May, 1967), 167-184

Ben-Shahar, H. & Sarnat, M.   New Issues and Profitability of Investment in Common Stock, 1959-1964. BIB, 25 (Apr, 1966), 3-31

Merrett, A. J. & Newbould, G. D.   The Comparative Efficiency of Methods of Issues. MS, 34 (Jan, 1966), 1-14

Faerber, L. G.   The Cost of External Common Stock Equity Capital for Small Business: An Empirical Study of New Common Stock Offerings. PhD diss, U of Wash, 1964

Friend, I. & Herman, E. S.   The SEC Through a Glass Darkly. JB, 37 (Oct, 1964), 382-403

Ghandhi, J. K. S.   Some Aspects of the Provincial New Issue Market. OIS, (Aug, 1964), 239-263

Stigler, G. J.   Public Regulation in the Securities Market. JB, 37 (Apr, 1964), 117-142

Winter, E. L.   Cost of Going Public. FE, 31 (Sep, 1963)

Flink, S. J.   Equity Financing for Small Business. New York: Simmons-B, 1962

Israels, C. L. & Duff, G. M., Jr., (Eds).   When Corporations Go Public. Pr Law Inst, 1962

Klein, S.   How to Play the New Issues Game. F, 74 (Jan, 1962)

Taylor, L. H.   When to Go Public for the Acquisition of Capital. CFC, (Feb 1, 1962)

Winter, E. L.   A Complete Guide to Making a Public Stock Offering. P-H, 1962

Nevin, E.   Some Reflections on the New York New Issue Market. OEP, 13 (Feb, 1961), 84-102

Waterman, M. H.   Investment Banking Functions, their Evolution and Adaption to Business Finance. U of Mich Busn Res, 1958

Securities & Exchange Commission.   Cost of Flotation of Corporate Securities, 1951-1955. US Govt, 1957

Henderson, R. F.   The New Issue Market and the Finance of Industry. Bowes, 1951

16b EQUITY ISSUES BY SEASONED COMPANIES

This section lists studies of rights offerings and placements of stock by seasoned firms. Again Friend et al. provide good background material. Scholes's 1972 Journal of Business article (listed elsewhere) and Boden-hammer's dissertation provide evidence on the price effects of rights offerings.

See also:

Thompson, H.   A Note on the Value of Rights in Estimating the Investor Capitalization Rate. JF, forthcoming

Keane, S. M.   The Significance of the Issue Price in Rights Issues. JBF, 4 (Autumn, 1972), 40-45

Bodenhammer, L.   The Effect of the Size of Public Offerings of Common Stocks upon Pre-Offering Stock Prices. PhD diss, Harvard U, 1968

Friend, I.; Longstreet, J. R.; Mendelson, M.; Miller, E. & Hess, A. P., Jr.   Investment Banking and the New Issues Market. World Pub, 1967

Soldofsky, R. M. & Johnson, C. R.   Rights Timing. FAJ, 23 (Jul-Aug, 1967), 101-104

Kuehner, C. D.   Underwritten Common Stock Rights Offers, 1955-64; Considerations and Descriptive Under-pricing Model. PhD diss, NYU, 1966

Block, F. E.   Per Share Adjustments for Rights. FAJ, 21 (May, 1965), 58-60

Edge, S. K.   Shareholders' Reaction to Rights Issues. MS, 33 (Sep, 1965), 263-284

Edge, S. K.   Sources of Funds from Rights Issues and their Cost. JES (Winter, 1965)

Rose, H. B.   Industry, New Issues and the Equity Market. DBR, 149 (Mar, 1964), 19-37

Harris, J. R.   Earnings per Share, Adjusted for New Issues. IA, 5 (May, 1963), 23-27

Sarachman, E. T.   A Study of Rights Offerings on the New York Stock Exchange from 1950 to 1961. MBA thesis, NYU, 1963

Nelson, J. R.   The Role of Stock Rights in Corporate Financial Policy. PhD diss, UCLA, 1962

Beranek, W.   Common Stock Financing, Book Values and Stock Rights: the Theory and the Evidence. U of Wis Busn, 1961

Weller, K. J.   An Analysis and Appraisal of Rights Offerings as a Method of Raising Equity Capital. PhD diss, U of Mich, 1961

Investment Bankers Association of America.   A Study of the Market Effects of Cash Equity Financing, Jan 1, 1958-Jun 30, 1960. Report of the Industrial Securities Committee, 1960

Hartill, C.   Stock Rights Make Sense. AJ, 14 (May, 1958), 63-65

Langer, L. C. R.   The Use of Stock Subscription Rights in the Financing of Gas and Electric Utility Companies. DBA diss, Harvard Bus, 1958

Greene, N. R.   Are Stock Rights Obsolete? AJ, 13 (Nov, 1957), 41-43

Leffler, G. L.   Stock Rights. B, (Sep 16, 1957), 15ff

Stevenson, H. W.   Common Stock Financing. U of Mich Busn Res, 1957

Archer, S. H.   The Theoretical Value of a Stock Right. JF, 11 (Sep, 1956), 363-366

Weaver, R. A., Jr.   Equity Financing for the Small Firm. HBR, 34 (Mar-Apr, 1956), 91-102

Evans, G. H., Jr.   The Theoretical Value of a Stock Right. JF, 10 (Mar, 1955), 55-61

Barry, E. P.   The Financing of Stock Issues with Pre-emptive Rights, 1943-1948. New York: Shields & Co, 1948

Myers, J. H.   The Effect of Issuing Securities for New Capital upon the Company's Common Stock Price. CFC, (Nov 18, 1943), 1991ff

Myers, J. H.   The Effect of Raising New Capital by Security Issues upon the Company's Common Stock Price. PhD diss, Northwestern U, 1943

Dolley, J. C.   The Price-Effect of Stock Right Issues. JB, 7 (Apr, 1934), 133-160

Mears E. G.   Stockholders' Privileged Subscriptions, 1906-1911 Inclusive: their Effect on the Market Price of the Stocks. MBA thesis, Harvard Bus, 1912

16c SCRIP ISSUES, STOCK SPLITS AND STOCK DIVIDENDS

Background material on the use of stock dividends is contained in Sussman. Many of the other works are concerned with the effect of splits and stock dividends on stock prices. Notable here is the paper of Fama, Fisher, Jensen & Roll.

Briston, R. J. & Herbert, P. J. A.   The Measurement of Underwriting Performance in a Depressed Market. JBF, 4 (Summer, 1972) 88-95

Millar, J. A.   The Effect of Stock Splits and Stock Dividends on the Monthly Price Relatives of Common Stocks. Phd diss, U of Ok, 1971

West, R. R. & Brouillette, A. B.   Reverse Stock Splits—Harbinger of Bad Times or Valid Management Technique? FE (Jan, 1970) 12-17

Fama, E. F.; Fisher, L.; Jensen, M. C. & Roll, R.   The Adjustment of Stock Prices to New Information. IntER, 10 (Feb, 1969), 1-21

de Marco, M. A.   A Computer-Aided Analysis of the Impact of Stock Dividends and Splits on Share Price Change. SM thesis, MIT, 1967

Thornton, J. E.   Financial Characteristics of Firms Following a Policy of Paying Small, Periodic Stock Dividends. PhD diss, U of NC, 1967

Johnson, K. B.   Stock Splits and Price Change. JF, 21 (Dec, 1966), 675-686

Kimball, P. & Papera, D. R.   Effect of Stock Splits on Short-Term Market Prices. FAJ, 20 (May-Jun, 1964), 75-80

Eiteman, D. S.   Are There Two Kinds of Stock Dividends? NAA, 45 (Oct, 1963), 53-58

Johnson, K. B.   An Analysis of the Permanent Price Change Associated with Common Stock Splits. PhD diss, U of Wash, 1963

Poe, J. B.   An Analysis of the Stock Dividend Distributions of New York Stock Exchange Listed Corporations. PhD diss, Harvard U, 1963

Merjos, A.   Reverse Stock Splits. B (May 28, 1962)

Sussman, M. R.   The Stock Dividend. U of Mich Busn Res, 1962

Sosnick, S. H.   Stock Dividends Are Lemons, Not Melons. CMR, 3 (Winter, 1961), 61-82

Seghers, P. D; Reinhart, W. J. & Nimaroff, S.   Essentially Equivalent to a Dividend. Ronald, 1960

Barker, C. A.   Price Changes of Stock Dividend Shares at Ex-Dividend Dates. JF, 14 (Sep, 1959), 373-378

Bellemore, D. H. & Blucher, Mrs L.   A Study of Stock Splits in the Post-war Years. AJ, 15 (Nov, 1959), 19-26

Barker, C. A.   Evaluation of Stock Dividends. HBR, 36 (Jul-Aug, 1958), 99-114

Barker, C. A.   Stock Splits in a Bull Market. HBR, 35 (May-Jun, 1957), 72-79

Jaffe, L. H.   A Study of Stock Splits, 1946-1956. MBA thesis, NYU, 1957

Barker, C. A.   Effective Stock Splits. HBR, 34 (Jan-Feb, 1956), 101-106

Green, D., Jr.   Taxable Stock Dividends. JB, 26 (Oct, 1953), 224-230

Bothwell, J. C., Jr.   Periodic Stock Dividends. HBR, 28 (Jan, 1950), 89-100

Burrell, O. K.   Price Effects of Stock Dividends and Split-ups. CFC (Dec 2, 1948), 10ff

Livermore, S.   Value of Stock Dividends. AER, 20 (Dec, 1930), 687-691

16d STOCK REPURCHASE

This section is concerned with stock repurchase and its effect on the stock price. Little empirical evidence is available. Most of the theoretical issues are discussed in the Elton & Gruber article. A more extensive discussion of repurchase is provided by Ellis & Young (1971).

Ellis, C. D. & Young, A. E.   The Repurchase of Common Stock. Ronald, 1971

Eckel, L. G.   The Regulation of Treasury Stock Transactions. PhD diss, U of Mich, 1969

Young, A. E.   Financial, Operating and Security Market Parameters of Repurchasing. FAJ, 25 (Jul-Aug, 1969), 123-128

Elton, E. J. & Gruber, M. J.   The Cost of Retained Earnings—Implications of Share Repurchase. IMR, 9 (Spring, 1968), 87-104

Elton, E. J. & Gruber, M. J.   The Effect of Share Repurchases on the Value of the Firm. JF, 23 (Mar, 1968), 135-149

Elton, E. J. & Gruber, M. J.   The Effect of Share Repurchases on the Value of the Firm: Reply. JF 23 (Dec, 1968), 870-874

Marshall, W. S. & Young, A. E.   A Mathematical Model for Re-Acquisition of Small Shareholdings. JFQA, 3 (Dec, 1968), 463-470

Rueschhoff, N. G.   Treasury Stock Practices of Industrial Corporations with Listed Common Stocks. PhD diss, U of Neb, 1968

Guthart, L. A.   Why Companies Are Buying Back Their Own Stock. FAJ, 23 (Mar-Apr, 1967), 105-110

Young, A. E.   Managerial, Market and Investor Problems Associated with the Cash Tender Offers of Corporations for Their Own Common Stocks. PhD diss, Columbia U, 1967

Young. A. E.   The Performance of Common Stocks Subsequent to Repurchase. FAJ, 23 (Sep-Oct, 1967), 117-121

Bierman, H., Jr. & West, R. R.   Acquisition of Common Stock by the Corporate Issuer. JF, 21 (Dec, 1966), 687-696

Guthart, L. A.   Corporate Repurchases of Already Outstanding Common Stock. PhD diss, Harvard U, 1966

Rapp, W. A.   The Role of Reacquired Common Stock in Financial Management. PhD diss, Northwestern U, 1966

Woods, D. H. & Brigham, E. F.   Stockholder Distribution Decisions: Share Repurchases or Dividends. JFQA, 1 (Mar, 1966), 15-25

Ellis, C. D.   Repurchase Stock to Revitalize Equity. HBR, 43 (Jul-Aug, 1965), 119-129

Guthart, L. A.   More Companies are Buying Back Their Stock. HBR, 43 (Mar-Apr, 1965), 41ff

Brigham, E. F.   The Profitability of a Firm's Repurchase of its Own Shares. CMR, 7 (Winter, 1964), 67-75

Merjos, A.   Into the Treasury. B (Aug 17, 1964), 9-12

Merjos, A.   Treasury Stock: Many Companies Are Regular Buyers of Their Own shares. B (Aug 29, 1960), 11-12

16e BLOCK TRADING AND THE SECONDARY DISTRIBUTION

This section is concerned with market liquidity and the effect on stock prices of the sale of large blocks of stock. Notable contributions are the articles of Scholes and Kraus & Stoll.

Kraus, A. & Stoll, H.   Price Impacts of Block Trading on New York Stock Exchange. JF, 27 (Jun, 1972), 569-588

Scholes, M.   The Market for Securities: Substitution versus Price Pressure and the Effects of Information on Share Prices. JB, 45 (Apr, 1972), 179-211

Lyons, J. F.   What Happens When Liquidity Disappears? II, 3 (Nov, 1969), 29 ff

Scholes, M.   A Test of the Competitive Market Hypothesis: the Market for New Issues and Secondary Offerings. PhD diss, U of Chicago, 1969

Fredman, A. J. & Wert, J. E.   An Analysis of Secondary Distributions. FAJ, 24 (Nov-Dec, 1968), 165-168

Hubbard, P. M., Jr.   Hard Look at Securities. B (Nov. 23, 1964) 18

Hubbard, P. M., Jr.   Short Term Impact of Secondary Distributions. CFC, (Apr 28, 1960), 11ff

Part 17 Options & Convertible Securities

17a OPTIONS

The Malkiel & Quandt book provides a useful institutional background to the
put and call market. There are a number of empirical studies of the profitability of option trading such as those of Boness, Kruizenga, Katz and Black
& Scholes (1972). Finally, Black & Scholes (forthcoming) provide a theory
of option pricing with wide implications both for other forms of option contract and for corporate liabilities.

See also:

17b Warrants
17c Convertible Bonds and Preferred Stock
19h Call Provisions, Sinking Funds and Bond Refunding

Black, F. & Scholes, M. J.   Capital Market Equilibrium and the Pricing of
Corporate Liabilities. JPE, forthcoming

Black, F. & Scholes, M. J.   The Valuation of Option Contracts and a Test
of Market Efficiency. JF, 27 (May, 1972), 399-417

Filer, H.   Understanding Put and Call Options. Magee, 1972

Klemkosky, R. R.   An Analysis of a Strategy for Purchasing Straddle
Options. PhD diss, Mich St U, 1971

McGuigan, J. R.   Timing Strategies in the Call Option Market. PhD diss,
U of Pittsburgh, 1971

Meyer, R. L.   The Rationale and an Empirical Test of a Model to Determine the Intrinsic Value of Call Options. PhD diss, U of Wis, 1971

Wilburn, D. S.   A Model of the Put and Call Option Market. SM thesis,
Alfred P. Sloan School of Management, MIT, 1970

Hubbard, C. L. & Johnson, T.   Writing Calls with Convertible Bonds. FAJ,
25 (Nov-Dec, 1969), 78-89

Malkiel, B. G. & Quandt, R. E.   Strategies and Rational Decisions in the
Securities Option Market. MIT Pr, 1969

Snyder, G. L.   Alternative Forms of Options. FAJ, 25 (Sep-Oct, 1969),
93-100

Stoll, H. R.   The Relationship between Put and Call Option Prices. JF,
24 (Dec, 1969), 801-824

Sullivan, J. W.   A Central Market for Stock Options: the Problems and the
Promise. Paper for the Seminar on the Analysis of Security Prices, U
of Chicago, Nov 1969

Zieg, K. C., Jr.   A Study of Common Stock Options from the Standpoint of
the Returns Accruing to the Buying and Selling Sides. PhD diss, Ohio
St U, 1969

Zweig, M. E.   An Analysis of Risk and Return on Put and Call Option
Strategies. PhD diss, Mich St U, 1969

Bracken, J.   Models for Call Options. FAJ, 24 (Sep-Oct, 1968), 149-151

Hausman, W. H. & White, W. L.   Theory of Option Strategy Under Risk
Aversion. JFQA, 3 (Sep, 1968), 343-358

Malkiel, B. G. & Quandt, R. E.   Can Options Improve an Institution's Performance? II, 2 (Nov, 1968), 55ff

Smith, K. V.   Option Writing and Portfolio Management. FAJ, 24 (May-
Jun, 1968), 135-138

Bierman, H., Jr.   The Valuation of Stock Options. JFQA, 2 (Sep, 1967),
327-334

Rosett, R. Estimating the Utility of Wealth from Call Option Transactions, *in* Hester, D. D. & Tobin J. (Eds), Risk Aversion & Portfolio Choice. Wiley, 1967

Snyder, G. L. A Look at Options. FAJ, 23 (Jan-Feb, 1967), 100-103

Taylor, H. M. Evaluating a Call Option and Optimal Timing Strategy on the Stock Market. MSci, 14 (Sep, 1967), 111-120

Williams, D. E. Profitability of Writing 6-Month 10-Day Calls. MBA thesis, NYU, 1967

Gup, B. E. The Economics of the Security Option Markets. PhD diss, U of Cincinnati, 1966

Van Alstyne, D. T. Models of Option Writer Portfolios. PhD diss, Northwestern U, 1966

Rosen, M. N. Strategies for Writers of Puts and Calls. SM thesis, MIT, 1965

Boness, A. J., Jr. Elements of a Theory of Stock Option Value. JPE, 72 (Apr, 1964), 163-175

Boness, A. J., Jr. Some Evidence on the Profitability of Trading in Put and Call Options, *in* Cootner, P. H. (Ed), The Random Character of Stock Market Prices. MIT Pr, 1964

Katz, R. C. The Profitability of Put and Call Option Writing. IMR, 5 (Fall, 1963), 55-69

Boness, A. J. Jr. A Theory and Measurement of Stock Option Value. PhD diss, U of Chicago, 1962

Katz, R. C. Profitability of Put and Call Option Writing. SM thesis, MIT, 1962

Investors' Chronicle All About Options.
Part 1: IC, (Sep 1, 1961),
Part 2: IC, (Sep 8, 1961),
Part 3: IC, (Sep 15, 1961)

Securities & Exchange Commission. Report on Put and Call Options. US Govt, 1961

Platt, S. D. & Rosen, D. A. Put and Call Options Under Section 16 of the Securities Exchange Act. YLJ, (Apr, 1960)

Cresson, G. V. The Writing of Options. AJ, 15 (May, 1959), 43-46

Franklin, C. B. & Colberg, M. R. Comment on 'Puts and Calls: A Factual Survey': Reply. JF, 14 (Mar, 1959), 71-74

Kruizenga, R. J. Comment on 'Puts and Calls: A Factual Survey'. JF, 14 (Mar, 1959), 67-70

Whiting, R. Profitable Trading with Puts and Calls. RHM, 1959

Franklin, C. B. & Colberg, M. R. Puts and Calls: A Factual Survey. JF, 13 (Mar, 1958), 21-34

Kruizenga, R. J. Put and Call Options: A Theoretical and Market Analysis. PhD diss, MIT, 1956

Filer, H. Investing in Options. AJ, 11 (Feb, 1955), 77-78

Hartnett, J. H. A Survey of the Put and Call Market with a Statistical Analysis of Factors Affecting Contract Premiums. SB thesis, MIT, 1955

King, M. J. Puts, Calls and Straddles: a Study. MBA thesis, NYU, 1954

Higgins, L. R. The Put-and-Call. Effingham, 1906

Bachelier, L. Théorie de la Speculation. Unpublished Docteur des Sciences Mathematiques dissertation, University of Paris, 1900. Originally published in Annales de l'Ecole Normale Superieure, Ser. 3, 1900, 21-86. English trans by A. J. Boness, Theory of Speculation, *in* Cootner, P. H. (Ed), The Random Character of Stock Market Prices. MIT Pr, 1964

17b WARRANTS

Kaplan and Hayes & Reiling provide some information of an institutional character on the use of warrants. Most of the other works are concerned with warrant valuation. Important contributions include those of Samuelson (1965), Sprenkle and Kassouf (notably in his dissertation).

See also:
    17a Options
    17c Convertible Bonds and Preferred Stock
    19h Call Provisions, Sinking Funds and Bond Refunding

Bird, A. P.   Evaluating Warrants. IA, 31 (Dec, 1971), 17-32

Giles, L. G.   The Function of Stock Purchase Warrants in Corporate Financing. PhD diss, U of Ill, 1971

Miller, J. D.   Effects of Longevity on Values of Stock Purchase Warrants. FAJ, 27 (Nov-Dec, 1971), 78-85

Stone, D. G.   A Price Model for Common Stock Warrants. PhD diss, NYU, 1971

Chen, A. H-Y.   A Model of Warrant Pricing in a Dynamic Market. JF, 25 (Dec, 1970), 1041-1060

Schwartz, W.   Warrants: a Form of Equity Capital. FAJ, 26 (Sep-Oct, 1970), 87-101

Flynn, J.; Joseph, S.; Parker, D. & Stacey, D.   An Examination of the Common Stock Warrant and a New Valuation Model. MBA thesis, Harvard Bus, 1969

Hayes, S. L., III & Reiling, H. B.   Sophisticated Financing Tool: the Warrant. HBR, 47 (Jan-Feb, 1969), 137-150

Kassouf, S. T.   An Econometric Model for Option Price With Implications for Investors' Expectations and Audacity. Em, 37 (Oct, 1969), 685-694

Samuelson, P. A. & Merton, R. C.   A Complete Model of Warrant Pricing that Maximizes Utility. IMR, 10 (Winter, 1969), 17-46

Van Horne, J. C.   Warrant Valuation in Relation to Volatility and Opportunity Costs. IMR, 10 (Spring, 1969) 19-32

Chen, A. H-Y.   A Dynamic Programming Approach to the Valuation of Warrants. PhD diss, U of California Berkeley, 1968

Kassouf, S. T.   Stock Price Random Walks: Some Supporting Evidence. REStat, 50 (May, 1968), 275-278

Kassouf, S. T.   Warrant Price Behavior, 1945-1964. FAJ, 24 (Jan-Feb, 1968), 123-126

Shelton, J. P.   The Relation of the Price of a Warrant to the Price of the Associated Stock.
Part I, FAJ, 23 (May-Jun, 1967), 149-151,
Part II, FAJ, 23 (Jul-Aug, 1967), 88-99

Thorp, E. O. & Kassouf, S.   Beat the Market. Random, 1967

Whittaker, J.   The Evaluation of Warrants. IA, 18 (Oct, 1967), 39-47

Kassouf, S. T.   The Evaluation of Convertible Securities. Analytical Inv, 1966

Plum, L. V. & Martin, T. J.   The Significance of Conversion Parity in Valuing Common Stock Warrants. FR, 1 (Feb, 1966), 21-31

Kaplan, S. A.   Piercing the Corporate Boilerplate: Anti-Dilution Clauses in Convertible Securities. U of Chicago Law Rev, 33 (Autumn, 1965), 1-30

Kassouf, S. T.   A Theory and an Econometric Model for Common Stock Purchase Warrants. PhD diss, Columbia U, 1965

Samuelson, P. A.   Rational Theory of Warrant Pricing. IMR, 6 (Spring, 1965), 13-31

Ayres, H. F.   Risk Aversion in the Warrant Markets. IMR, 4 (Fall, 1963), 45-53

Cheng, P. L. & Savage, D. T.   Short-Run Manipulative Aspects of Common Stock Warrants. QREB, 3 (Summer, 1963), 102-107

Harbaugh, A. W.   Operations Research in the Stock Market. El Segunda, Cal: Computer Sciences Corporation, 1963

Pease, F.   The Warrant—Its Powers and Its Hazards. FAJ, 19 (Jan-Feb, 1963), 25-32

Fox, J. S.   The Price Relationship between Purchase Warrants and Common Stock. SB thesis, MIT, 1961

Fried, S.   The Speculative Merits of Warrants. RHM, 1961

Sprenkle, C. M.   Warrant Prices as Indicators of Expectations and Preferences. YEE, 1 (Fall, 1961), 179-231

Giguère, G.   Warrants, A Mathematical Method of Evaluation. AJ, 14 (Nov, 1958), 17-25

Morrison, R. J.   The Warrants or the Stock. AJ, 13 (Nov, 1957), 51-52

Armstrong, T. H.   Stock Option Warrants. AJ, 10 (May, 1954), 89-91

Hallingby, P., Jr.   Speculative Opportunities in Stock Purchase Warrants. AJ, 3 (3rd Qtr, 1947), 41-49

17c CONVERTIBLE BONDS AND PREFERRED STOCK

Useful background material on the usage of convertibles is provided by Pilcher, Pinches and Hayes & Reiling. Important contributions to the topic of convertible valuation include the single period models of Poensgen and Baumol, Malkiel & Quandt and the dynamic models of Duvel and Tennican. Some evidence on realised returns from convertibles is provided by Soldofsky and Vinson.

See also:

17a Options
17b Warrants
19i Preferred Stock

Walter, J. E. & Que, A.   The Valuation of Convertible Bonds. JF, forthcoming

Brealey, R. A. & Hodges, S. D.   The Valuation of British Convertibles, *in* Szego, G. P. & Shell, K. (Eds), Mathematical Methods in Investment and Finance. N-Holland, 1972

Choi, K. S.   A Theoretical and Empirical Analysis of Convertible Bond Financing and Investment. PhD diss, U of Cincinnati, 1971

Frank, W. G. & Weygandt, J. T.   A Prediction Model for Convertible Debentures. JAR, 9 (Spring, 1971), 116-126

Miller, A. B.   The Standby Purchase Agreement. FAJ, 27 (Jul-Aug, 1971), 71ff

Moore, D. M.   The Price Behavior of Convertible Preferred Stock. DBA diss, Georgia St U, 1971

Soldofsky, R. M.   Yield-Risk Performance of Convertible Securities. FAJ, 27 (Mar-Apr, 1971), 61ff

Sprecher, C. R.   A Note on Financing Mergers with Convertible Preferred Stock. JF, 26 (Jun, 1971), 683-686

Johnson, R. D. The Extinguishment of Convertible Bonds: a Theoretical and Empirical Analysis. PhD diss, St U NY Buffalo, 1970

Lavely, J. A. Comparative Usage of Bond-Warrant and Convertible Bond Issues. PhD diss, U of Iowa, 1970

Pinches, G. E. Financing with Convertible Preferred Stock, 1960-1967. JF, 25 (Mar, 1970), 53-63

Tennican, M. L. The Valuation of Convertible Debentures. DBA diss, Harvard Bus, 1970

Vinson, C. E. Rates of Return on Convertibles. FAJ, 26 (Jul-Aug, 1970), 110-114

Bacon, P. W. & Winn, E. L. The Impact of Forced Conversion on Stock Prices. JF, 24 (Dec, 1969), 871-874

Cretien, P. D., Jr. Convertible Bond Premiums as Predictors of Common Stock Price Changes. FAJ, 25 (Nov-Dec, 1969), 90-95

Fried, S. Investing and Speculating with Convertibles. Crown, 1969

Hayes, S. L. III & Reiling, H. B. Sophisticated Financing Tool: the Warrant. HBR, 47 (Jan-Feb, 1969), 137-150

Lerner, E. M. & Auster, R. Does the Market Discount Potential Dilution? FAJ, 25 (Jul-Aug, 1969), 118-121

McCullers, L. D. Convertible Securities—Debt or Equity? PhD diss, U of Fla, 1969

Sparrow, J. Convertible Loan Stocks. JBF, 1 (Spring, 1969), 24-31

Vinson, C. E. Investing and Hedging Techniques in the Convertible Bond Market. PhD diss, N Tex St U, 1969

Duvel, D. A Dynamic Programming Model for the Evaluation of Convertible Bonds. Paper for the Seminar on the Analysis of Security Prices, U of Chicago, May 1968

Lutgert, S. Risk and Convertible Bonds. Unp ms, U of Chicago, 1968

Meyer, A. H. Designing a Convertible Preferred Issue. FE, 36 (Apr, 1968), 42ff

Pinches, G. E. Financing Corporate Mergers and Acquisitions with Convertible Preferred Stock. PhD diss, Mich St U, 1968

Stone, G. R. An Analysis of the Investment Nature of Convertible Bonds. PhD diss, Stanford U, 1968

Weil, R. L.; Segall, J. E. & Green, D., Jr. Premiums on Convertible Bonds. JF, 23 (Jun, 1968), 445-463

Foster, J. H. & Morgan, R. Evaluation of Convertible Bonds. Financial Research, Investment Analysis and the Computer, Bulletin 31, Hanover, N.H: The Amos Tuck School, 1967

Schwartz, W. Convertibles Get Realistic Image. FAJ, 23 (Jul-Aug, 1967) 55-57

Strauss Turnbull. A Technical Study of Convertible Euro-bonds. London: Strauss Turnbull, Mar 1967

Baumol, W. J.; Malkiel, B. G. & Quandt, R. E. The Valuation of Convertible Securities. QJE, 80 (Feb, 1966), 48-59

Bladen, A. Techniques for Investing in Convertible Bonds. New York: Salomon Bros & Hutzler, 1966

Bladen, A. Time to Buy? B, (Oct 10, 1966), 9ff

Bown, C. C. Convertible Bonds and the Cost of Capital: Some Theoretical Considerations and Empirical Findings. Paper for the Second Annual Meeting of the Western Finance Association, 1966

Brigham, E. F. An Analysis of Convertible Debentures: Theory and Some Empirical Evidence. JF, 21 (Mar, 1966), 35-54

Hershey, R. D. Bond Men Start Hunting. New York Times, Aug 21, 1966, 1ff

Jensen, J. E.   A Pricing Model for the Convertible Debenture: A Selective Study. PhD diss, U of Pittsburgh, 1966

Kassouf, S. T.   The Evaluation of Convertible Securities. Analytical Inv, 1966

McKenzie, R. R.   Convertible Debentures, 1956-65. QREB, (Winter, 1966), 41-51

Poensgen, O. H.   The Valuation of Convertible Bonds.
Part I: IMR, 7 (Fall, 1965), 77-92
Part II: IMR, 7 (Spring, 1966), 83-98

Kaplan, S. A.   Piercing the Corporate Boilerplate: Anti-Dilution Clauses in Convertible Securities. U of Chicago Law Rev, 33 (Autumn, 1965), 1-30

Brand, L.   Investing for Profit in Convertible Bonds. S & P, 1964

Mock, E. J.   An Evaluation of Borrower Risk in Industrial Companies Employing Convertible Subordinated Debentures. PhD diss, Ohio St U, 1964

Pain, R. H.   Convertible Debentures. IA, 9 (Sep, 1964), 21-25

Broman, K. L.   The Use of Convertible Subordinated Debentures by Industrial Firms, 1949-1959. QREB, 3 (Spring, 1963), 65-75

Gagan, L. J.   A Decision Model for Evaluating Convertible Bonds. SM thesis, MIT, 1962

Kriss, H.   The Convertible Bond as a Capital Raising Instrument. SM thesis, MIT, 1961

Moody, P. E.   The Market Price of Convertible Loan Stocks. JIASS, 15 (Mar, 1959), 295-298

Skelly, W. S.   Convertible Bonds: A Study of the Suitability for Commercial Bank Bonds Portfolios. New York: Salomon Bros & Hutzler, 1959

Johnson, R. W.   Subordinated Debentures: Debt that Serves as Equity. JF, 10 (Mar, 1955), 1-16

Pilcher, J. C.   Raising Capital with Convertible Securities. U of Mich Pr, 1955

Davenport, M. W.   Appreciation with Safety in Convertibles. AJ, 10 (Aug, 1954), 37-39

Schwartz, W. & Spillman, J.   Guide to Convertible Securities. Convertible S Pr, nd

17d EXECUTIVE STOCK OPTIONS

The following works are concerned principally with the degree of incentive provided by stock options and with the reporting requirements. The Hayes and Holland & Lewellen articles provide useful introductions.

Calkins, D. O.   An Empirical Study of Executive Stock Options and Company Performance. DBA diss, U of S Cal, 1969

Smith, E. P.   Reporting Requirements and Standards for Stock Option Plans. FAJ, 25 (Sep-Oct, 1969), 64-68

Call, D. V.   Accounting and Management Considerations Relative to Stock Options. PhD diss, UCLA, 1966

Hayes, S. L. III   New Interest in Incentive Financing. HBR, 44 (Jul-Aug, 1966), 99-112

Dean, J.   Outside Directors Appraise Stock Options. FAJ, 19 (Mar-Apr, 1963), 25-31

Holland, D. M. & Lewellen, W. G.   Probing the Record of Stock Options. HBR, 40 (Mar-Apr, 1962), 132-150

Jones, D. L.   Stock Options—An Incentive in Reverse? FAJ, 18 (Nov, 1962), 33-39

Campbell, E. D.   Stock Options Should Be Valued. HBR, 39 (Jul-Aug, 1961), 52-58

Wallace, E.   Appraisal of Stock Options as an Incentive Device—A Study of Their Use and Abuse. PhD diss, Columbia U, 1961

Hardee, C.   Stock Options and the 'Insider Trading' Provisions of the Securities Exchange Act. HLR, 65 (1952)

Part 18 Interest Rates

18a LIQUIDITY PREFERENCE

Normative analyses of cash holdings are listed under 25a—'Management of Cash and Working Capital'. This section is confined to positive studies of the desire for liquidity. Important contributions include Keynes, Hicks, Tobin, Patinkin (1956) and Arrow. Other discussions of liquidity preference, including empirical analyses, are listed under 18f—'Interest Rates—Term Structure'.

See also:

18b Interest Rates—General

Pesek, B.　Equilibrium Level of Transaction Services of Money. JF, forthcoming

Tsiang, S. C.　The Rationale of the Mean-Standard Deviation Analysis, Skewness Preference and the Demand for Money. AER, 62 (Jun, 1972), 354-371

Krainer, R. E.　Liquidity Preference and Stock Market Speculation. JFQA, 4 (Mar, 1969), 89-98

Douglas, A. J.　A Theory of Saving and Portfolio Selection. REStud, 35 (Oct, 1968), 453-463

Sandmo, A.　Portfolio Choice in a Theory of Saving. SJE, 70 (1968) 106-122

Breen, W. J.　Liquidity Preference, Degree of Risk Aversion and the Expected Utility Hypothesis. Unp ms, 1967

Patinkin, D.　An Indirect-Utility Approach to the Theory of Money, Assets and Savings, *in* Hahn, F. H. & Brechling, F. P. R. (Eds), The Theory of Interest Rates. Macmillan Int, 1966

Diamond, P. A.　On the Asset Demand for Money. Wkg Paper No 75, Institute of Business and Economic Research, U of Cal Berkeley, 1965

Diamond, P. A.　Risk Aversion and Savings. Wkg Paper No 70, Institute of Business and Economic Research, U of Cal Berkeley, 1965

Diamond, P. A.　Savings Decisions under Uncertainty. Wkg Paper No. 71, Institute of Business and Economic Research, U of Cal Berkeley, 1965

Arrow, K. J.　Comment on the Portfolio Approach to the Demand for Money and Other Assets. REStat 45 (Suppl, Feb, 1963), 24-27

Duesenberry, J. S.　The Portfolio Approach to the Demand for Money and Other Assets. REStat, 45 (Suppl, Feb, 1963), 9-24

Freeman, J. F.　Liquidity Preference v. Loanable Funds: a New Approach to the Problem. EJ, 73 (Dec, 1963), 681-688

Hicks, J. R.　Liquidity. EJ, 72 (Dec, 1962), 787-802

Tobin, J.　Liquidity Preference as Behavior Toward Risk. REStud, 25 (Feb, 1958), 65-86

Patinkin, D.　Money, Interest and Prices, 2nd ed. Har-Row, 1956

Keynes, J. M.　A Treatise on Money. Macmillan Int, 1930

18b INTEREST RATES—GENERAL

This section lists miscellaneous articles on the level of interest rates. It includes the historically important contributions of Fisher, Lutz and Joan

Robinson, and two useful books of readings by Hahn & Brechling and Guttentag.

Guttentag, J. M. (Ed).   Essays on Interest Rates, Vol. 2. (Dist by Columbia U Pr) Natl Bur Econ Res, 1971

Hamburger, M. J.   Expectations, Long-Term Interest Rates and Monetary Policy in the United Kingdom. BEQB, 11 (Sep, 1971), 354-372

Pierson, G.   Why Have Interest Rates Risen? REStat, 53 (Feb, 1971), 89-100

Bonello, F. J.   The Formulation of Expected Interest Rates: an Examination of Alternative Hypotheses. Mich St U Busn, 1970

Feldstein, M. & Eckstein, O.   The Fundamental Determinants of the Interest Rate. REStat, 52 (Nov, 1970), 363-375

Van Horne, J. C.   The Function and Analysis of Capital Market Rates. P-H, 1970

Grossman, H. I.   Expectations, Transactions Costs, and Asset Demands. JF, 24 (Jun, 1969), 491-506

Guttentag, J. M. & Cagan, P. (Eds).   Essays in Interest Rates, Vol. 1. (Dist by Columbia U Pr) Natl Bur Econ Res, 1969

Homer, S. & Johannesen, R.   The Price of Money, 1946-1969: an Analytical Study of United States and Foreign Interest Rates. Rutgers U Pr, 1969

Zwick, B.   An Equilibrium Model of Interest Rate Determination. PhD diss, Carnegie-Mellon U, 1969

Lutz, F. A.   The Theory of Interest. Reidel, 1968

Ford, J. L. & Stark, T.   Long- and Short-Term Interest Rates. Blackwell, 1967

Hendershott, P. H.   Structure of International Interest Rates: the US Treasury Bill Rate and the Eurodollar Deposit Rate. JF, 22 (Sep, 1967), 455-465

Lee, T. H.   Alternative Interest Rates and the Demand for Money: the Empirical Evidence. AER, 57 (Dec, 1967), 1168-1181

OECD Committee for Invisible Transactions.   Capital Markets Study: Structure of Interest Rates in some OECD Countries. OECD, 1967

Conard, J. W.   The Behavior of Interest Rates: a Progress Report (Dist by Columbia U Pr) Natl Bur Econ Res, 1966

Diulio, E. A.   Fund Mobility in the Capital Markets: Interest Rate Differentials as a Measure. PhD diss, Columbia U, 1966

Hahn, F. H. & Brechling, F. P. R. (Eds).   The Theory of Interest Rates. Macmillan Int, 1966

Laidler, D.   The Rate of Interest and the Demand for Money—Some Empirical Evidence. JPE, 74 (Dec, 1966), 543-555

Paish, F. W.   Long-Term and Short-Term Interest Rates in the United Kingdom. Man U Pr, 1966

Ball, R. J.   Some Econometric Analyses of the Long-Term Rate of Interest in the United Kingdom 1921-1961. MS, 33 (Jan, 1965), 45-96

Brown, C. V.   A Theory of Interest Rates or Asset Prices? SJPE, 12 (Nov, 1965), 297-308

Bottomly, A.   The Determination of Pure Rates of Interest in Under-developed Rural Areas. REStat, 46 (Aug, 1964), 301-304

Freund, W. C. & Zinbarg, E. D.   Application of Flow of Funds to Interest Rate Forecasting. JF, 18 (May, 1963), 231-248

Holland, T. E.   Forecasting Interest Rate Movements: Time Series Analyses and Functional Relationships. PhD diss, Duke U, 1963

Homer, S.   A History of Interest Rates. Rutgers U Pr, 1963

Horwick, G.   Real Assets and the Theory of Interest. JPE, 70 (Apr, 1962), 157-169

Paish, F. W.   Factors Determining the Long-Term Rate of Interest. IA, 4 (Dec, 1962), 20-23

Lerner, A. P.   A Note on the Rate of Interest and the Value of Assets. EJ, 71 (Sep, 1961), 539-543

Conard, J. W.   An Introduction to the Theory of Interest. U of Cal Pr, 1959

Sauvain, H. C.   Changing Interest Rates and Investment Portfolio. JF, 14 (May, 1959), 230-244

Samuelson, P. A.   An Exact Consumption-Loan Model of Interest With or Without the Social Contrivance of Money. JPE, 66 (Dec, 1958), 467-482

Alchian, A. A.   The Rate of Interest, Fisher's Rate of Return over Cost and Keynes' Internal Rate of Return. AER, 45 (Dec, 1955), 938-943

Robinson, R. I.   Forecasting Interest Rates. JB, 27 (Jan, 1954), 87-100

Robinson, J.   The Rate of Interest. Em, 19 (Apr, 1951), 92-111

Hicks, J. R.   Mr Hawtrey on Bank Rates and the Long Term Rate of Interest. MS, 10 (No 1, 1939), 21-37

Hawtrey, R. G.   A Century of Bank Rates. Longmans, 1938

Fisher, I.   The Theory of Interest: as Determined by Impatience to Spend Income and Opportunity to Invest it. Kelley, 1930

De Zoete & Gorton.   Changes in Bank Rate since 1964 and Movements in Long Term Interest Rates since 1731. London: de Zoete & Gorton, nd

18c INFLATION AND THE RATE OF INTEREST

This section lists studies that are predominantly concerned with the Fisher hypothesis (see Fisher, I., 1930) that the rate of interest changes to reflect anticipated changes in the rate of inflation. The papers of Gibson and Roll provide useful entries into the controversy.

See also:

18b Interest Rates—General

Fand, D. I.   High Interest Rates and Inflation in the U.S.: Cause or Effect? BNLQR, 25 (Mar, 1972), 23-64

Pyle, D. H.   Observed Price Expectations and Interest Rates. REStat, 54 (Aug, 1972), 275-280

Roll, R.   Interest Rates on Monetary Assets and Commodity Price Index Changes. JF, 27 (May, 1972), 251-278

Pyle, D. H.   Asset Substitution, Inflation and Interest Rates. Wkg paper No 2, Institute of Business and Economic Research, U of Cal, Berkeley, 1971

Sargent, T. J.   Interest Rates and Prices in the Long Run: a Study of the Gibson Paradox. Unp ms, 1971

Feldstein, M. S.   Inflation, Specification Bias and the Impact of Interest Rates. JPE, 78 (Nov-Dec, 1970), 1325-1339

Gibson, W. E.   Price Expectations Effects on Interest Rates. JF, 25 (Mar, 1970), 19-34

Gupta, S. B.   The Portfolio Balance Theory of the Expected Rate of Change of Prices. REStat, 37 (Apr, 1970), 187-203

Hicks, J. R.   Inflation and Interest. BNLQR, 23 (Sep, 1970), 261-275

Sargent, T. J.   Commodity Price Expectations and the Interest Rate.
QJE, 83 (Feb, 1969), 127-140

Yohe, W. P. & Karnosky, D. W.   Interest Rates and Price Level Changes
1952-69. Mo Rev F R Bk St Louis, (Dec, 1969), 18-38

Aharoni, Y. & Ophir, T.   Accounting for Linked Loans. JAR, 5 (Spring,
1967), 1-26

Ball, R. J.   Inflation and the Theory of Money. Allen, 1964

Meiselman, D.   Bond Yields and the Price Level: the Gibson Paradox
Regained *in* Carson, D. (Ed), Banking and Monetary Studies. Irwin,
1963

Mundell, R.   Inflation and Real Interest. JPE, 71 (Jun, 1963), 280-283

Kennedy, C. M.   Inflation and the Bond Rate. OEP, 12 (Oct, 1960), 269-273

Wright, D. M.   Inflation and the Rate of Interest. FAJ, 16 (May-Jun, 1960),
45-47

18d INTEREST RATES—CYCLICAL AND SEASONAL EFFECTS

The Cagan and Diller books are good examples of work on cyclical and
seasonal patterns in interest rates. Studies of cyclical effects on the term
structure (notably by Kessel) and of the implications of seasonal patterns
for term structure (notably by Macaulay (1938)) are listed elsewhere.

Sargent, T.   Expectations at the Short End of the Yield Curve: an
Application of Macaulay's Test, *in* Guttentag, J. M. (Ed), Essays on
Interest Rates, Vol 2. (Dist by Columbia U Pr) Natl Bur Econ Res,
1971

Diller, S.   The Seasonal Variation of Interest Rates. Natl Bur Econ Res,
1970

Cagan, P.   Changes in the Cyclical Behavior of Interest Rates. (Dist
by Columbia U Pr) Natl Bur Econ Res, 1966

Cagan, P.   Changes in the Cyclical Behavior of Interest Rates. REStat, 48
(Aug, 1966), 219-250

Holland, T. E.   Cyclical Movements of Interest Rates, 1948-61. JB, 37 (Oct,
1964), 364-369

Federal Reserve Bank of St Louis.   The Seasonal Pattern of Interest
Rates. Mo Rev F R Bk St Louis, (Nov, 1960)

18e INTEREST RATES—MEASURING THE TERM STRUCTURE

The following works are concerned with measuring the yield curve or term
structure. Durand's studies derive freehand yield curves for the USA.
Other articles develop regression estimates of the yield curve or (in the
case of McCulloch) of the term structure.

See also:

18f Interest Rates—Term Structure
19b Expected and Realised Return on Bonds

Gray, J.   New Evidence on the Term Structure of Interest Rates: 1884-
1900. JF, forthcoming

McCulloch, J. H.   Measuring the Term Structure of Interest Rates. JB, 44
(Jan, 1971), 19-31

Masera, R. S.   Least-Squares Construction of the Yield Curves for Italian
Government Securities, 1957-1967
Part 1, BNLQR, 22 (Dec, 1969), 347-371
Part 2, BNLQR, 23 (Mar, 1970), 82-102

Cohen, K. J.; Kramer, R. L. & Waugh, W. H.   Regression Yield Curves for
U.S. Government Securities. MSci, 13 (Dec, 1966), B168-B175

Durand, D.   A Quarterly Series of Corporate Basic Yields 1952-1957 and
some Attendant Reservations. JF, 13 (Sep, 1958), 348-356

Durand, D. & Winn, W. J.   Basic Yields of Bonds 1920-1947: Their
Measurement and Pattern. Natl Bur Econ Res, 1947

Durand, D.   Basic Yields of Corporate Bonds 1900-1942. Natl Bur Econ
Res (Technical Paper No. 3), 1942

18f INTEREST RATES—TERM STRUCTURE

This section is concerned with attempts to explain interest rates as a
function of maturity. The books by Kessel and Malkiel offer useful introductions to the subject. Two of the most important contributions are provided by the books of Meiselman and Roll.

See also:

18b Interest Rates—General
18e Interest Rates—Measuring the Term Structure

Masera, R. S.   The Term Structure of Interest Rates—an Expectations
Model Tested on Post-War Italian Data. OUP, 1972

Nelson, C. R.   The Term Structure of Interest Rates. Basic, 1972

Smith, V. K. & Marcis, R. G.   A Time Series Analysis of Post-Accord
Interest Rates. JF, 27 (Jun, 1972), 589-606

Terrell, W. T. & Frazer, W. J.   Interest Rates, Portfolio Behavior and
Marketable Government Securities. JF, 27 (Mar, 1972), 1-36

Crouch, R. L.   Tobin vs Keynes on Liquidity Preference. REStat, 53
(Nov, 1971), 368-371

Diller, S.   The Expectations Component of the Term Structure, *in* Guttentag, J. M. (Ed), Essays on Interest Rates, Vol. 2. (Dist by Columbia
U Pr) Natl Bur Econ Res, 1971

Roll, R.   Investment Diversification and Bond Maturity. JF, 26 (Mar, 1971)
51-66

Sargent, T.   Expectations at the Short End of the Yield Curve: an
Application of Macaulay's Test, *in* Guttentag, J. M. (Ed), Essays on
Interest Rates, Vol 2. (Dist by Columbia U Pr) Natl Bur Econ Res,
1971

Sinkey, J. F.   The Term Structure of Interest Rates: Theory, Models of
Interest-Rate Forecasting, and Empirical Evidence. PhD diss,
Boston C, 1971

Buse, A.   Expectations, Prices, Coupons and Yields. JF, 25 (Sep, 1970),
809-818

Kane, E. J.   The Term Structure of Interest Rates: An Attempt to Reconcile Teaching with Practice. JF, 25 (May, 1970), 361-374

Nelson, C. R.   A Model of the Term Structure of Interest Rates. JASA,
65 (Sep, 1970), 1163-1179

Pierson, G.   Effect of Economic Policy on the Term Structure of Interest
Rates. REStat, 52 (Feb, 1970), 1-11

Roll, R.   The Behavior of Interest Rates: an Application of the Efficient Market Model to US Treasury Bills. Basic, 1970

Rowan, D. C. & O'Brien, R. J.   Expectations, the Interest Rate Structure and Debt Policy, *in* Hilton, K. & Heathfield, D. F., The Econometric Study of the United Kingdom. Macmillan Int, 1970

Vanderford, D. E.   An Econometric Evaluation of Alternative Models of the Term Structure of Interest Rates. PhD diss, U of Cal Berkeley, 1970

Diller, S.   Expectations in the Term Structure of Interest Rates, *in* Mincer, J. (Ed), Economic Forecasts and Expectations. Natl Bur Econ Res, 1969

Malkiel, B. G. & Kane, E. J.   Expectations and Interest Rates: a Cross-sectional Test of the Error-learning Hypothesis. JPE, 77 (Jul-Aug, 1969), 453-470

Mauer, L. J.   Commercial Bank Maturity Demand for United States Government Securities and the Determinants of the Term Structure of Interest Rates. JFQA, 4 (Mar, 1969), 37-52

Meek, P.   Open Market Operations. New York: Federal Reserve Bank, 1969

Pye, G.   On the Tax Structure of Interest Rates. QJE, 83 (Nov, 1969), 562-579

Taylor, J. H.   Wartime Finance and the Term Structure of Interest Rates. PhD diss, Iowa St U, 1969

Wood, J. H.   Expectations and the Demand for Bonds. AER, 59 (Sep, 1969), 522-530

Anderson, R. C.   The Term Structure of Interest Rates: A Portfolio Analysis. PhD diss, Claremont, 1968

Bonello, F. J.   The Term Structure of Interest Rates, the Expectations Hypothesis, and the Formulation of Expected Interest Rates. PhD diss, Mich St U, 1968

Granger, C. W. J. & Rees, H. J. B.   Spectral Analysis of the Term Structure of Interest Rates. REStat, 50 (Jan, 1968)

Naylor, J. A.   Some Theoretical and Empirical Considerations Relative to the Term Structure of Interest Rates. PhD diss, U of Ill, 1968

Pierson, G.   The Effect of Economic Policy on the Term Structure of Interest Rates. PhD diss, U of Mich, 1968

Roll, R.   The Efficient Market Model Applied to US Treasury Bill Rates. PhD diss, U of Chicago, 1968

Sargent, T. J.   The Structure of Interest Rates. PhD diss, Harvard U, 1968

Sutch, R. C.   Expectation, Risk and the Term Structure of Interest Rates. PhD diss, MIT, 1968

Walters, A. A.   The Demand for Money, Expectations, and Short and Long Rates, *in* Wolfe, J. N. (Ed), Value, Capital and Growth. Edinburgh U Pr, 1968

Ben-Shahar, H.   The Structure of Interest Rates, Government Financing and Economic Growth. Kyk, 20 (1967), 492-500

Bierwag, G. O. & Grove M. A.   A Model of the Term Structure of Interest Rates. REStat, 49 (Feb, 1967), 50-62

Buse, A.   Interest Rates, the Meiselman Model and Random Numbers. JPE, 75 (Feb, 1967), 49-62

Buse, A.   The Structure of Interest Rates and Recent British Experience: A Comment. Ec, 34 (May, 1967), 298-308

Ford, J. L. & Stark, T.   Long- and Short-term Interest Rates. Blackwell, 1967

Green, H. A. J. Uncertainty and the 'Expectations Hypothesis'. REStud, 34 (Oct, 1967), 387-398

Grossman, H. I. Risk Aversion, Financial Intermediation and the Term Structure of Interest Rates. JF, 22 (Dec, 1967), 611-622

Johnson, R. E. Term Structures of Corporate Bond Yields as a Function of Risk of Default. JF, 22 (May, 1967), 313-345

Kane, E. J. & Malkiel, B. G. The Term Structure of Interest Rates: an Analysis of a Survey of Interest Rate Expectations. REStat, 49 (Aug, 1967), 343-355

Luckett, D. G. Multi-Period Expectations and the Term Structure of Interest Rates. QJE, 81 (May, 1967), 321-329

Mauer, L. J. The Term Structure of Interest Rates. PhD diss, U of Tenn, 1967

Modigliani, F. & Sutch, R. Debt Management and the Term Structure of Interest Rates. JPE, 75 (Suppl Aug, 1967), 569-589

Telser, L. G. A Critique of Some Recent Empirical Research on the Explanation of the Term Structure of Interest Rates. JPE, 75 (Suppl, Aug, 1967), 546-561

Wallace, N. Term Structure of Interest Rates and the Maturity Composition of the Federal Debt. JF, 22 (May, 1967), 301-312

Brew, J. M. Gilt-Edged Yield Curves. IA, 16 (Dec, 1966), 3-22

Cohen, K. J.; Kramer, R. L. & Waugh, W. W. Regression Yield Curves for US Government Securities. MSci, 13 (Dec, 1966), B168-B175

Fisher, D. A British Test of Recent Developments in Term Structure Theory. PhD diss, U of Chicago, 1966

Fisher, D. Expectations, the Term Structure of Interest Rates and Recent British Experience. Ec, 46 (Aug, 1966), 319-329

Jen, F. C. & Wert, J. E. Imputed Yields of Sinking Fund Bonds and the Term Structure of Interest Rates. JF, 21 (Dec, 1966), 697-714

Malkiel, B. G. The Term Structure of Interest Rates: Expectations and Behavior Patterns. Princeton U Pr, 1966

Modigliani, F. & Sutch, R. Innovations in Interest Rate Policy. AER, 56 (May, 1966), 178-197

Pye, G. A Markov Model of the Term Structure. QJE, 80 (Feb, 1966), 60-72

Struble, F. M. The Current Debate on the Term Structure of Interest Rates. Mo Rev F R Bk Kansas City, (Jan-Feb, 1966)

Van Horne, J. C. Interest-Rate Expectations, the Shape of the Yield Curve, and Monetary Policy. REStat, 48 (May, 1966), 211-215

Weaver, A. R. H. The Uncertainty of the Expectations Theory of the Term Structure of Interest Rates. WEJ, 4 (1966), 122-134

Culbertson, J. M. The Interest Rate Structure: Towards Completion of the Classical System, *in* Hahn, F. H. & Brechling, F. P. R. (Eds), the Theory of Interest Rates. Macmillan Int, 1965

Kessel, R. A. The Cyclical Behavior of the Term Structure of Interest Rates. (Dist by Columbia U Pr) Natl Bur Econ Res, 1965

Michaelsen, J. B. The Term Structure of Interest Rates and Holding-Period Yields on Government Securities. JF, 20 (Sep, 1965), 444-463

Scott, R. H. Liquidity and the Term Structure of Interest Rates. QJE, 79 (Feb, 1965), 135-145

Van Horne, J. C. Interest-Rate Risk and the Term Structure of Interest Rates. JPE, 73 (Aug, 1965), 344-351

Fisher, D. The Structure of Interest Rates: A Comment. Ec, 44 (Nov, 1964), 412-418

Grant, J. A. G.   Meiselman on the Structure of Interest Rates: a British Test. Ec, 44 (Feb, 1964), 51-71

Malkiel, B. G.   The Term Structure of Interest Rates. AER, 54 (May, 1964), 532-543

Wallace, N.   The Term Structure of Interest Rates and the Maturity Composition of the Federal Debt. PhD diss, U of Chicago, 1964

Wood, J. H.   The Expectations Hypothesis, the Yield Curve and Monetary Policy.   QJE, 78 (Aug, 1964), 457-470

Bowers, D. A.   Investor Preference and the Structure of Interest Rates in the US Government Securities Market, 1953-1961. PhD diss, S Methodist U, 1963

Michaelsen, J. B.   The Term Structure of Interest Rates: a Comment. QJE, 77 (Feb, 1963), 166-174

Wood, J. H.   Expectations, Errors, and the Term Structure of Interest Rates. JPE, 71 (Apr, 1963), 160-171

Malkiel, B. G.   Expectations, Bond Prices and the Term Structure of Interest Rates. QJE, 76 (May, 1962), 197-218

Meiselman, D.   The Term Structure of Interest Rates. P-H, 1962

Wood, J. H.   The Term Structure of Interest Rates: A Theoretical and Empirical Study.   PhD diss, Purdue U, 1962

Federal Reserve Bank of Kansas City.   Taxes and the Term Structure of Yields. Mo Rev F R Bk Kansas City, (Dec, 1960)

Goode, R. & Birnham, E. A.   The Relation between Long-term and Short-term Interest Rates in the United States. IMF (Oct, 1959), 224-243

Luckett, D. G.   Professor Lutz and the Structure of Interest Rates. QJE, 73 (Feb, 1959), 131-144

Culbertson, J. M.   The Term Structure of Interest Rates. QJE, 71 (Nov, 1957), 485-517

Stetson, W. B.   Price-Yield Relationships. AJ, 10 (Nov, 1954), 67-68

Walker, C. E.   Federal Reserve Policy and the Structure of Interest Rates on Government Securities. QJE, 68 (Feb, 1954), 19-42

Segall, J. E.   The Effect of Maturity on Price Fluctuations. JB, 29 (1950), 202-206

Lusher, D. W.   The Structure of Interest Rates and the Keynsian Theory of Interest. JPE, 50 (Apr, 1942), 272-279

Lutz, F. A.   The Structure of Interest Rates. QJE, 55 (1940-1941), 36-63

18g DURATION

This section includes Macaulay's classical work on the concept of duration and Fisher & Weil's demonstration of its relevance for predicting bond returns. Holt and Whittaker are principally concerned with the relevance of duration for equity prices.

Fisher, L. & Weil, R. L.   Coping with the Risk of Interest Rate Fluctuations: Returns to Bondholders from Naive and Optimal Strategies. JB, 44 (Oct, 1971), 408-431

Whittaker, J.   The Relevance of Duration. JBF, 2 (Spring, 1970), 34-41

Block, F. E.   The Same Maturity? FAJ, 25 (Jul-Aug, 1969), 184

Frostman, L.   The Concept of Time Centre in Investment Theory and its Relation to the Average Period of Investment. SJE, 67 (Jun, 1965), 125-150

Holt, C. C.　The Influence of Growth Duration on Share Prices. JF, 17 (Sep, 1962), 465-475

Macaulay, F. R.　Some Theoretical Problems Suggested by the Movements of Interest Rates, Bond Yields, and Stock Prices in the United States since 1856. Natl Bur Econ Res, 1938

Part 19 Bonds & Preferred Stock

19a BONDS—GENERAL

The section lists some general works on the bond market. It includes an interesting study by Scholes which examines bond prices within the context of capital asset pricing theory.

Ascher, L. W.   Selecting Bonds for Capital Gains. FAJ, 27 (Mar–Apr, 1971), 74–79

Scholes, M.   The Relationship Between the Returns on Bonds and the Returns on Common Stocks. Paper for the Seminar on the Analysis of Security Prices. U of Chicago, Nov 1971

Williamson, J. P.   Bond Switching and the Computer. FAJ, 26 (Jul-Aug, 1970), 65–73

Miles, J. E.   Formulas for Pricing Bonds and Their Impact on Prices. FAJ, 25 (Jul—Aug, 1969), 156–161

Pettway, R. H. & Weinraub, H. J.   Profitable Bond Trading Among Bonds of the Same Risk Class and Maturity. FAJ, 25 (Nov-Dec, 1969), 125–128

Deslattes, V. L.   The Demand for Savings Bonds in the United States— with Emphasis on the Significance of Interest Rates in the Postwar Period. PhD diss, La St U, 1968

Harris, J. T.   A Comparison of Long Term Deep Discount and Current Coupon Bonds. FAJ, 24 (Jul-Aug, 1968), 81–85

Homer, S.   Distortions Within Bond and Money Markets. FAJ, 24 (Jul-Aug, 1968), 77–79

Homer, S.   Stocks Versus Bonds: A Comparison of Supply and Demand Factors. II, 2 (Aug, 1968), 45ff

Johannesen, R. I., Jr.   The Effect of Coupon on Bond Price Fluctuations. FAJ, 24 (Sep-Oct, 1968), 89–91

Schilbred, C. M.   Bond Evaluation as a Decision under Certainty, Risk or Uncertainty. SJE, 70 (May, 1968), 43–56

Thompson, E. A.   Debt Instruments in Both Macroeconomic Theory and Capital Theory. AER, 57 (Dec, 1967), 1196–1210

Bierman, H., Jr.   The Bond Issue Size Decision. JFQA, 1 (Dec, 1966), 1–14

Cootner, P. H.   The Stochastic Theory of Bond Prices. Paper presented at the Econometric Society Meeting, Dec, 1966

Miles, J. E.   Discount Bonds. PhD diss, NYU, 1966

Puu, T.   A Simple Graphic Method of Estimating the Yield of Bonds, *in* Hahn F. H. & Brechling, F. P. R. (Eds), The Theory of Interest Rates Macmillan Int, 1966

Halford, F. A.   Income Bonds. FAJ, 20 (Jan-Feb, 1964), 73–79

Sloane, P. E.   Determinants of Bond Yield Differentials 1954-59. YEE, 3 (Spring, 1963), 3–55

Cheng, P. L.   Optimum Bond Portfolio Selection. MSci, 8 (Jul, 1962), 490–499

Fullerton, D. H.   The Bond Market in Canada. Carswell, 1962

Latané, H. A.   Portfolio Balance—the Demand for Money, Bonds and Stock. SEJ, 29 (Oct, 1962), 71–76

Spencer, M. H.   Studies in the Determination of Specific Interest Rates. EE, 8 (Oct-Nov, 1962), 17–32

Homer, S.   A Dynamic Approach to Institutional Investment. New York: Salomon Bros & Hutzler, 1961

Robson, P.   Index-Linked Bonds. REStud, 28 (Oct, 1960), 57-68

Baldwin, R. R.   An Approximate Formula for the Yield on Bonds Selling Close to Par. AJ, 14 (Aug, 1958), 77

Storer, R. W.   The Effects of the Yield-Maturity Curve on True Yields. AJ, 5 (2nd Qtr, 1949), 29-33

19b EXPECTED AND REALISED RETURNS ON BONDS

The following studies provide information on both yields to maturity and realised returns on bonds. They include Weil's useful study of returns on US corporates.

See also:

18b Interest Rates—General
18e Interest Rates—Measuring the Term Structure
19g Bonds—Return as a Function of Default Risk

De Zoete & Gorton.   Equity & Fixed Interest Investment 1919-1970. London: de Zoete & Gorton, 1970

Weil, R. L.   Realized Interest Rates and Bondholders' Returns. AER, 60 (Jun, 1970), 502-511

Baskin, E. F. & Crooch, G. M.   Historical Rates of Return on Investments in Flat Bonds. FAJ, 24 (Nov-Dec, 1968), 95-97

Cohan, A. B.   Yields on Corporate Debt Directly Placed. (Dist by Columbia U Pr) Natl Bur Econ Res, 1967

Merrett, A. J. & Sykes, A.   Return on Equities and Fixed Interest Securities: 1919-1966. DBR, 158 (Jun, 1966), 29-45

Herzog, J. P.   Investor Experience in Corporate Securities. JF, 19 (Mar, 1964), 46-62

Merrett, A. J. & Sykes, A.   Return on Equities and Fixed Interest Securities 1919-1963. DBR, (Dec, 1963)

Cohan, A. B.   Yields on New Underwritten Corporate Bonds, 1935-58. JF, 17 (Dec, 1962), 585-605

Kaplan, M.   Yields on Recently Issued Corporate Bonds: A New Index. JF, 17 (Mar, 1962), 81-109

Macaulay, F. R.   Some Theoretical Problems suggested by the Movement of Interest Rates, Bond Yields and Stock Prices in the United States since 1856. Natl Bur Econ Res, 1938

19c GOVERNMENT BONDS

Scott's book provides a useful introduction to the institutional structure of the US government market and Chalmers and Pember & Boyle offer a similar service for the UK (Chalmers at a fairly elementary level). Most of the remaining works are concerned with an analysis of the ownership of government bonds.

See also:

3e Institutions—General
3f Banks
19a Bonds—General
20b Treasury Bills
20c Federal Funds

Pember & Boyle.   British Government Securities in the 20th Century; Supplement 1950-1972. London: Pember and Boyle, 1972

Wolfe, C. R.   Bank Preferences and Government Security Yields. QJE, 85 (May, 1971), 283-303

Colby, W. G.   The Management of Dealer Positions in US Government Securities. PhD diss, Yale U, 1970

Federal Reserve Bank of Kansas City.   Corporate Participation in the Government Securities Market. Mo Rev F R Bk Kansas City (Dec, 1970)

Kramer, R. L.   Arbitrage in U.S. Government Bonds: a Management Science Approach. JBR, 1 (Summer, 1970), 30-44

Chalmers, E. R.   The Gilt-edged Market: a Study of the Background Factors. Griffith, 1967

Eagly, R. V.   On Government Issuance of an Index Bond. PF, 22 (1967), 268-284

Wendel, H. F.   Short-Run Interest-Rate Expectations in the Government Securities Market. PhD diss, Columbia U, 1967

Levy, M. E.   Cycles in Government Securities: Determinants of Changes in Ownership. Natl Ind Conf Bd, 1965

Scott, I. O., Jr.   Government Securities Markets. McGraw, 1965

Berney, R. E.   The Auction of Long-Term Government Securities. JF, 19 (Sep, 1964), 470-482

Entine, A. D.   Government Securities Holdings of Selected Financial Intermediaries, 1954-1962. JF, 19 (Dec, 1964), 644-651

Federal Reserve Bank of New York.   The Financing of Government Securities Dealers. Mo Rev F R Bk New York, (Jun, 1964)

Pepper, G. T.   The Selection and Maintenance of a Gilt-Edged Portfolio. JIA, 90 (1964)

Bloch, E.   Short Cycles in Corporate Demand for Government Securities. AER, 53 (Dec, 1963), 1058-1077

Grant, J. A. G.   A Study of the London Government Securities Market. PhD diss, London U, 1963

Grant, A. T. K.   Switching of British Government Securities. IA, 3 (Aug, 1962), 14-29

Levy, M. E.   Cycles in Government Securities: Federal Debt and its Ownership. Natl Ind Conf Bd, 1962

Bower, J.   Investment in United States Government Securities by State Governments. NTJ, 13 (Jun, 1960), 127-140

Meltzer, A. H. & Von Der Linde, G.   A Study of the Dealer Market for Federal Government Securities. US Govt, 1960

Frazer, W. J.   Large Manufacturing Corporations as Suppliers of Funds to the United States Government Securities Market. JF, 13 (Dec, 1958), 499-509

Campbell, C. D.   Investment in United States Government Securities by State and Local Government. NTJ, 10 (Mar, 1957), 78-87

Scott, I. O., Jr.   The Implications of the Changing Ownership of Federal Securities. Proceedings of the Business and Economic Statistics Section, American Statistical Association, 1957, 154-158

Childs, C. F.   Concerning US Government Securities. Lakeside, 1947

19d LOCAL GOVERNMENT AND MUNICIPAL BONDS

The following works are concerned with local authority, state and municipal bonds. The books by Robinson and Calvert provide some useful background material on the American market, underwriting costs are examined by both Kessel and West, and the determinants of municipal bond yields are discussed by Horton and Hastie.

See also:

19a Bonds—General
19e Corporate Bonds
19f Bond and Stock Ratings

Bonner, J.   Local Authority Investment and Debt Financing. SJPE, 19 (Jun, 1972), 135-150

Hastie, K. L.   Determinants of Municipal Bond Yields. JFQA, 7 (Jun, 1972), 1729-1748

Treynor, J. L.   On the Quality of Municipal Bonds. Paper for the Seminar on the Analysis of Security Prices, U of Chicago, Nov 1972

Hempel, G. H.   The Postwar Quality of State and Local Debt. Columbia U Pr, 1971

Kessel, R. A.   A Study of the Effects of Competition in the Tax-Exempt Bond Market. JPE, 79 (Jul-Aug, 1971), 706-738

Hastie, K. L.   The Determinants of Municipal Bond Yields. PhD diss, Cornell U, 1970

Horton, J. J. Jr.   Statistical Classification of Municipal Bonds. JBR, 1 (Autumn, 1970), 29-40

Robinson, R. I.   Postwar Market for State and Local Government Securities. Princeton U Pr, 1970

Calvert, G. L. (Ed).   Fundamentals of Municipal Bonds, 7th ed. Inv Bankers, 1969

Horton, J. J. Jr.   A Statistical Rating Index for Municipal Bonds. FAJ, 25 (Mar-Apr, 1969), 72-75

Smith, W. P.   Commercial Bank Entry into Revenue Bond Underwriting: an Appraisal of the Public Benefits of S 1306. Washington, D.C.: Dept. of Banking and Currency, Office of the Controller of the Currency, 1967

West, R. R.   Determinants of Underwriters' Spreads on Tax Exempt Bond Issues. JFQA, 2 (Sep, 1967), 241-263

Cohen, K. J. & Hammer, F. S.   Optimal Level Debt Schedules for Municipal Bonds. MSci, 13 (Nov, 1966), 161-166

West, R. R.   More on the Effects of Municipal Bond Monopsony. JB, 39 (Apr, 1966), 305-308

Cohen, K. J. & Hammer, F. S.   Optimal Coupon Schedules for Municipal Bonds. MSci, 12 (Sep, 1965), 68-82

Diamond, P. A.   On the Cost of Tax-Exempt Bonds. JPE, 73 (Aug, 1965), 399-403

West, R. R.   New Issue Concessions on Municipal Bonds: a Case of Monopolistic Pricing. JB, 38 (Apr, 1965), 135-148

West, R. R.   Should Commercial Banks Be Allowed to Underwrite Municipal Bonds? NBR 3 (Sep, 1965), 35-44

Heins, A. J.   The Interest Rate Differential between Revenue Bonds and General Obligations: a Regression Model. NTJ, 15 (Dec, 1962), 399-405

Gottlieb, M.   Cyclical Timing of Municipal Bond Issues. QREB, 1 (May, 1961), 67-75

19e CORPORATE BONDS

The somewhat ageing works by Hickman and Cohan provide important background material on the American corporate bond market. We would also draw attention to Christenson's book on optimal bidding strategies and to some useful papers in Guttentag's book of readings (listed elsewhere).

See also:

Pinches, G. E. & Mingo, K.   A Multivariate Analysis of Industrial Bond Ratings. JF, forthcoming

Litzenberger, R. H. & Rutenberg, D. P.   Size and Timing of Corporate Bond Flotations. JFQA, 7 (Jan, 1972), 1343-1360

Frankena, M. W.   The Influency of Call Provisions and Coupon Rate on the Yields of Corporate Bonds, *in* Guttentag, J. M. (Ed), Essays on Interest Rates, Vol 2. (Dist by Columbia U Pr) Natl Bur Econ Res, 1971

Morris, E. L.   Agent-Aided Private Placements. FAJ, 27 (May-Jun, 1971), 83-88

Peters, J. R.   Economics of the Canadian Corporate Bond Market. McGill-Queen's U Pr, 1971

Tuttle, D. L. & Wilbur, W. L.   A Multivariate Time-Series Investigation of Annual Returns on Highest Grade Corporate Bonds. JFQA, 6 (Mar, 1971), 707-722

Conard, J. W. & Frankena, M. W.   The Yield Spread Between New and Seasoned Corporate Bonds, 1952-62, *in* Guttentag, J. M. & Cagan, P. (Eds), Essays on Interest Rates, Vol. 1. (Dist by Columbia U Pr) Natl Bur Econ Res, 1969

Zaentz, N.   Relative Price Performance Among Coupon Areas in Corporate Bonds. FAJ, 25 (Jul-Aug, 1969), 146-155

Kaufman, H.   The Changing Dimensions of the Corporate Bond Market. New York: Salomon Bros & Hutzler, 1967

Van Horne, J. C.   A Linear Programming Approach to Evaluating Restrictions Under Bond Indenture or Loan Agreement. JFQA, 1 (Jun, 1966), 68-83

Christenson, C. J.   Strategic Aspects of Competitive Bidding for Corporate Securities. Harvard Busn, 1965

Federal Reserve Bank of Cleveland.   Direct Placement of Corporate Debt. MBR, (Mar, 1965)

Williams, C. M.   Senior Securities—Boon for Banks. HBR, 41 (Jul-Aug, 1963), 82-94

Christenson, C. J.   Optimal Strategies in Sealed Bidding for Corporate Debt Securities. PhD diss, Harvard U, 1961

Cohan, A. B.   Cost of Flotation of Long-Term Corporate Debt Since 1935. U of NC Busn, 1961

Cohan, A. B.   Private Placements and Public Offerings: Market Shares Since 1935. U of NC Busn, 1961

Stuebner, E. A.   The Role of the Investment Banker in Arranging Private Financing. BL (Jan, 1961)

Hickman, W. B.   Statistical Measures of Corporate Bond Financing Since 1900. (Dist by Princeton U Pr) Natl Bur Econ Res, 1960

Soldofsky, R. M.   The Size and Maturity of Direct-Placement Loans. JF, 15 (Mar, 1960), 32-44

Shapiro, E.   The Postwar Market for Corporate Securities: 1946-55. JF, 14 (May, 1959), 196-217

Percus, J. & Quinto, L.   The Application of Linear Programming to Competitive Bond Bidding. Em, 24 (Oct, 1956), 413-429

Robbins, S. M.   A Bigger Role for Income Bonds. HBR, 33 (Nov-Dec, 1955), 100-115

Hickman, W. B.   The Volume of Corporate Bond Financing Since 1900. Princeton U Pr, 1953

Conklin, G. T., Jr.   Direct Placements. JF, 6 (Jun, 1951), 85-118

Corey, E. R.   Direct Placements of Corporate Securities. Harvard Busn, 1951

Hickman, W. B.   Trends and Cycles in Corporate Bond Financing. Natl Bur Econ Res, 1950

National Bureau of Economic Research.   Corporate Bond Project: Organization and Methods. Parts 1-5, 1942-1944

19f BOND AND STOCK RATINGS

With the exception of Stevenson, all authors in this section are concerned with corporate and municipal bond ratings. Hoffland is principally concerned with the relationship between rating and market price and Horrigan, West and Pogue & Soldofsky with the predictability of ratings. Harold provides an early analysis of the relationship between rating and risk of default. Further information on this topic is provided under 19g—'Bonds—Return as a Function of Default Risk' (notably in the works of Hickman, Atkinson and Fisher).

See also:

19d Local Government and Municpial Bonds
19e Corporate Bonds
26g Bankruptcy and Reorganisations

Hoffland, D. C.   The Price-Rating Structure of the Municipal Bond Market. FAJ, 28 (Mar-Apr, 1972), 65-70

West, R. R.   An Alternative Approach to Predicting Bond Ratings. JAR, 8 (Spring, 1970), 118-125

Pogue, T. F. & Soldofsky, R. M.   What's in a Bond Rating? JFQA, 4 (Jun, 1969), 201-228

Goodman, R. M.   Municipal Bond Rating Testimony. FAJ, 24 (May-Jun, 1968), 59-65

Harries, B. W.   Standard and Poor's Corporation New Policy in Rating Municipal Bonds. FAJ, 24 (May-Jun, 1968), 68-71

Horrigan, J. O.   An Evaluation of Financial Ratio Analysis. PhD diss, U of Chicago, 1968

Packer, S. R.   Municipal Bond Ratings. FAJ, 24 (Jul-Aug, 1968), 93-97

Riehle, R. C.   Moody's Municipal Ratings. FAJ, 24 (May-Jun, 1968), 71-73

Horrigan, J. O.   The Determination of Long-Term Credit Standing with Financial Ratios. ERA, (1966), 44-62

Stevenson, R. A.   The Variability of Common Stock Quality Ratings. FAJ, 22 (Nov-Dec, 1966), 97-101

Standard & Poor's Corporation. Bond Quality Ratings. AJ, 2 (1st Qtr, 1946), 9-17

Harold, G. Bond Ratings as an Investment Guide. Ronald, 1938

19g BONDS—RETURN AS A FUNCTION OF DEFAULT RISK

The following studies seek to explain the risk premium on corporate bonds. They include the important empirical studies of Hickman and Fisher and the interesting theoretical paper by Black & Scholes on the valuation of corporate liabilities.

See also:

19e Corporate Bonds
19f Bond and Stock Ratings
26g Bankruptcy and Reorganisations

Black, F. & Scholes, M. Capital Market Equilibrium and the Pricing of Corporate Liabilities. JPE, forthcoming

Silvers, J. B. An Alternative to the Yield Spread as a Measure of Risk. JF, forthcoming

Silvers, J. B. An Alternative Analysis of Bond Risk. PhD diss, Stanford U, 1971

Soldofsky, R. M. & Miller, R. L. Risk Premium Curves for Different Classes of Long-Term Securities, 1950-1966. JF, 24 (Jun, 1969), 429-445

Atkinson, T. R. Trends in Corporate Bond Quality. (Dist by Columbia U Pr) Natl Bur Econ Res, 1967

Sloane, P. E. Determinants of Bond Yield Differentials. YEE, 3 (Spring, 1963), 3-55

Fraine, H. G. & Mills, R. H. Effect of Defaults and Credit Deterioration on Yields of Corporate Bonds. JB, 34 (Sep, 1961), 423-434

Brimmer, A. F. Credit Conditions and Price Determination in the Corporate Bond Market. JF, 15 (Sep, 1960), 353-370

Fisher, L. Determinants of Risk Premiums on Corporate Bonds. JPE, 67 (Jun, 1959), 217-237

Hickman, W. B. Corporate Bond Quality and Investor Experience. (Dist by Princeton U Pr) Natl Bur Econ Res, 1958

Hickman, W. B. Corporate Bonds: Quality and Investment Performance. Natl Bur Econ Res, 1957

19h CALL PROVISIONS, SINKING FUNDS AND BOND REFUNDING

Studies of the value of the call privilege are exemplified by the work of Pye, Jen & Wert and Hess & Winn. In a second article Jen & Wert also provide some discussion of the effects of sinking funds. On the subject of bond refunding Bowlin offers a useful discussion of current practice and of the appropriate discount rates, while Weingartner, Kalymon, and to a lesser extent Bierman, are concerned with normative multi-period decision rules.

See also:

18f Interest Rates—Term Structure
19a Bonds—General
19d Local Government and Municipal Bonds
19e Corporate Bonds

Elton, E. J. & Gruber, M. J.   The Economic Value of the Call Option. JF, 27 (Sep, 1972), 891-902

Joehnk, M. D.   The Call-Risk Protection of the Seasoned Issue. PhD diss, U of Arizona, 1971

Kalymon, B. A.   Bond Refunding with Stochastic Interest Rates. MSci, 18 (Nov, 1971), 171-183

Demetriou, P. A.   The Present Value of Investments in Sinking Funds. MSci, 13 (Jan, 1967), 336-343

Jen, F. C. & Wert, J. E.   Effect of Call Risk on Corporate Yields. JF, 22 (Dec, 1967), 637-651

Jen, F. C. & Wert, J. E.   The Effect of Sinking Fund Provisions on Corporate Bond Yields. FAJ, 23 (Mar-Apr, 1967), 125-131

Johnson, R. L.   The Value of the Call Privilege. FAJ, 23 (Mar-Apr, 1967), 134-140

Pye, G.   Value of Call Deferment on a Bond: Some Empirical Results. JF, 22 (Dec, 1967), 623-636

Sherr, L. A.   The Value of the Delayed Call Provision. PhD diss, U of Mich, 1967

Thompson, F. C. & Norgaard R. L.   Sinking Funds. Fin Exec, 1967

Weingartner, H. M.   Optimal Timing of Bond Refunding. MSci, 13 (Mar, 1967), 511-524

Bierman, H., Jr.   The Bond Refunding Decision as a Markov Process. MSci, 12 (Aug, 1966), B545-B551

Bowlin, O. D.   The Refunding Decision. JF, 21 (Mar, 1966), 55-68

Jen, F. C. & Wert, J. E.   The Value of the Deferred Call Privilege. NBR, (Mar, 1966)

Pye, G.   The Value of a Call Option on a Bond. JPE, 74 (Apr, 1966), 200-205

Wahlstrom, K.   A Study and Analysis of the Bond Market in 1962 and 1963 Concerning the Value Placed on the Call Privilege. U of S Dak, Unp monograph, 1966

Williams, B. S. & Letwat, M.   Underwritten Calls of Industrial Securities, 1950-1961. QREB, 3 (Winter, 1963), 71-77

Hess, A. C. & Winn, W. J.   The Value of the Call Privilege. U of Pa Pr, 1962

Hess, A. C. & Winn, W. J.   The Value of the Call Privilege. JF, 14 (May, 1959), 182-195

19i PREFERRED STOCK

Useful background material on the American market in preferred stock is provided by Fischer & Wilt's general study and Elsaid's survey of issuers.

See also:

17c Convertible Bonds and Preferred Stock

Curran, W. S.   Preferred Stock in Public Utility Finance—a Reconsideration. FAJ, 28 (Mar-Apr, 1972), 71-76

Stevenson, R. A.　Retirement of Non-Callable Preferred Stock. JF, 25 (Dec, 1970), 1143-1152

Elsaid, H. H.　The Function of Preferred Stock in the Corporate Financial Plan. FAJ, 25 (Jul-Aug, 1969), 112-117

Hawk, S. L.　Comparative Investment Performance of Preferred Stocks and Bonds. PhD diss, U of Wis, 1969

Niendorf, R. J.　Changes in the Price Relationship between Investment-Grade Bonds and Preferred Stocks. PhD diss, U of Wis, 1969

Fischer, D. E. & Wilt, G. A., Jr.　Non-Convertible Preferred Stock as a Financing Instrument, 1950-1965. JF, 23 (Sep, 1968), 611-624

Bonner, G. R.　Some Notes on the Rehabilitation of Preferred Stock. AFR, (Spring, 1966), 32-37

New York Stock Exchange.　Understanding Preferred Stocks and Bonds. The Stock Exchange, 1966

Fischer, D. E.　An Analysis and Evaluation of the Role of Preferred Stock in Electric Utility Financing. PhD diss, U of Wash, 1965

Horwitz, R. M.　Arrearages on Cumulative Preferred Stocks Listed on the New York Stock Exchange: an Analysis of Experiences, 1935-1962. PhD diss, Mich St U, 1964

Donaldson, G.　In Defense of Preferred Stock. HBR, 40 (Jul-Aug, 1962), 123-136

Olson, A. C.　An Analysis of the Impact of Valuation Requirements on the Preferred Stock Investment Policies of Life Insurance Companies. PhD diss, U of Minn, 1962

Santow, L. J.　Ultimate Demise of Preferred Stock as a Source of Corporate Capital. FAJ, 18 (May-Jun, 1962), 47-54

Fergusson, D. A.　Preferred Stock Valuation in Recapitalizations. JF, 13 (Mar, 1958), 48-69

Davenport, M. W.　Measuring Earnings Protection for Preferred Stocks. AJ, 12 (Aug, 1956), 31-34

Ballam, S. H., Jr.　Preferred Stocks—They Can Be Attractive Investments. AJ, 11 (Nov, 1955), 53-57

Fergusson, D. A.　Recent Developments in Preferred Stock Financing. JF, 7 (Sep, 1952), 447-462

Part 20 Money Market & International Capital Markets

20a MONEY MARKET—GENERAL

This section contains general studies of the money market and articles on certificates of deposit and commercial paper. The book by Nadler et al. provides a somewhat ageing introduction to the US money market. Einzig's book offers a useful survey of the London money market, and a comparison with overseas markets. Background material on the American and British CD markets is provided by the Heth and Baker articles.

Einzig, P. Parallel Money Markets, 2 vols. Macmillan Int, 1972

Cohen, B. C. Money Market Development and the Demand for Money. JFQA, 6 (Sep, 1971), 1155-1158

Baker, A. W. Sterling Certificates of Deposit. IA, 28 (Dec, 1970), 23-26

Schadrack, F. C., Jr. Demand and Supply in the Commercial Paper Market. JF, 25 (Sep, 1970), 837-852

Clarke, W. M. Money Markets of the City: What the Future may Bring. London: Laurie, Milbank, 1969

Cohan, S. B. The Determinants of Supply and Demand for Certificates of Deposit. PhD diss, U of Mich, 1969

Baxter, N. D. Marketability, Default Risk and Yields on Money Market Instruments. JFQA, 3 (Mar, 1968), 75-86

Cloos, G. W. A Larger Role for Commercial Paper. BC, (Dec, 1968), 2-12

Heth, M. The CD in American Banking: Retrospect and Prospect. BNLQR, 21 (Mar, 1968), 48-74

Johnston, R. Rebirth of Commercial Paper. Mo Rev F R Bk San Francisco, (Jul, 1968), 137-142

Scammell, W. M. The London Discount Market. Elek, 1968

Struble, F. M. The Commercial Paper Boom in Perspective. Mo Rev F R Bk Kansas City, (Nov, 1968), 3-10

Mendelsohn, M. S. London's Many Money Markets. Banker, 117 (May, 1967), 411-417

Wilson, J. S. G. Monetary Policy & the Development of Money Markets. Allen, 1966.

Federal Reserve Bank of Chicago. Bankers' Acceptance Used More Widely. BC, (May, 1965), 9-16

Stone, R. W. The Changing Structure of the Money Markets. JF, 20 (May, 1965), 229-238

Baxter, N. D. The Commercial Paper Market. Econometric Research Program Memorandum 69, Princeton U, 1964

Bratten, H. Is the CD a Deposit or a Loan? Banking, (Mar, 1964), 46-47

Morgan Guaranty Trust Company. Money Market Investments, the Risk and the Return. New York: Morgan Guaranty Trust Company 1964

Bigosinski, J. T. The Swiss Money Market. PhD diss, NYU, 1963

Federal Reserve Bank of New York. Certificate of Deposits. Mo Rev F R Bk, New York, (Jun, 1963), 82-87

Law, W. & Crum, C. New Trend in Finance, the Negotiable Certificate of Deposit. HBR, 41 (Jan-Feb, 1963), 113-126

Selden, R. T. Trends and Cycles in the Commercial Paper Market. (Dist by Columbia U Pr) Natl Bur Econ Res, 1963

Brimmer, A. F. Foreign Banking Institutions in the United States Money
Market. REStat, 44 (Feb, 1962)

Reierson, R. L. New Forces in the Money Market. JF, 17 (May, 1962),
220-229

Wilson, J. S. G. The New Money Markets. LBR, 64 (Apr, 1962), 31-45

Hagemann, H. F. Money Market Forces. FAJ, 16 (Aug-Sep, 1960), 81-84

Nadler, M; Heller, S. & Shipman, S. S. The Money Market and Its Institutions. Ronald, 1955

Riefler, W. W. Money Rates and Money Markets in the United States.
Har-Row, 1930

20b TREASURY BILLS

Most of the works in this section are concerned either with an assessment
of the US 'bills only' policy or with the auction market for treasury bills
(with particular reference to Friedman's criticism of marketing methods).
Works on the term structure of treasury bill yields (notably by Roll) are
listed under section 18f—'Interest Rates—Term Structure'.

See also:

3f Banks
20a Money Market—General
20c Federal Funds

Bolten, S. Treasury Bill Auction Procedures: an Empirical Investigation.
JF, forthcoming

Griffiths, B. The Determination of the Treasury Bill Tender Rate. Ec,
38 (May, 1971), 180-191

Robichek, A. A. & Niebuhr, W. D. Tax-Induced Bias in Reported Treasury
Yields. JF, 25 (Dec, 1970), 1081-1090

Rieber, M. Bids, Bid Patterns and Collusion in the Auction Market for
Treasury Bills. JLE, 10 (Oct, 1967), 149-168

Fand, D. A Time-Series Analysis of the 'Bills-only' Theory of Interest
Rates. REStat, 48 (Nov, 1966), 361-371

Rieber, M. Collusion in the Auction Market for Treasury Bills. JPE,
72 (Oct, 1964), 509-512

Rieber, M. The Primary Market for United States Treasury Bills. PhD
diss, MIT, 1963

Brimmer, A. F. Price Determination in the United States Treasury Bills
Market. REStat, 44 (May, 1962), 178-183

Goldstein, H. N. The Friedman Proposal for Auctioning Treasury Bills.
JPE, 70 (Aug, 1962), 386-392

Goldstein, H. N. Should the Treasury Auction Long-Term Securities?
JF, 17 (Sep, 1962), 444-464

Luckett, D. G. Bills Only: a Critical Appraisal. REStat, 41 (Aug, 1960),
301-306

Young, R. A. & Yager, C. A. The Economics of 'Bills Preferably'. QJE,
74 (Aug, 1960), 341-373

Friedman, M. A Program for Monetary Stability. Fordham, 1959

Roosa, R. V. Federal Reserve Operations in the Money and Government
Securities Markets. New York: Federal Reserve Bank, 1956

20c FEDERAL FUNDS

Dorothy Nichols's study provides useful background material on the market for Federal Funds, and Platt's article a discussion of the determinants of the Funds rate.

See also:

3f Banks
20a Money Market—General

Platt, R. B.   The Interest Rate on Federal Funds: an Empirical Approach. JF, 25 (Jun, 1970), 585-598

Nichols, D. M.   Trading in Federal Funds. Washington, D.C.: Board of Governors of the Federal Reserve System, 1965

Willis, P. B.   The Federal Funds Market. The Federal Reserve Bank of Boston, 1964

Federal Reserve Bank of Cleveland.   Trading in Federal Funds. MBR, (Oct, 1961)

Federal Reserve Bank of St Louis.   The Federal Funds Market. Mo Rev F R Bk St Louis, (Apr, 1960)

Federal Reserve System, Board of Governors.   The Federal Funds Market. Washington DC: Board of Governors, Federal Reserve System, 1959

Turner, B,   The Federal Funds Market. P-H, 1931

20d INTERNATIONAL MONEY MARKETS

The following articles are principally concerned with the development of the Euro-dollar market, though we have sought to exclude articles whose principal concern is the effect of the market on international capital flows. Useful introductory reading is provided by Klopstock (1965) and Einzig (1967).

See also:

20e International Long-Term Capital Markets

Hugon, J. H.   Past and Future of the Euro-Money Market. FAJ, 27 (Sep-Oct, 1971), 21-24

Bank of England.   The Euro-Currency Business of Banks in London. BEQB, 10 (Mar, 1970), 31-49

Chalmers, E. R. (Ed).   Readings in the Euro-Dollar. Griffith, 1969

Friedman, M.   The Euro-dollar Market. Morgan Guaranty Survey, Oct 1969

Kindleberger, C. P.   The Euro-Dollar and the Internationalization of United States Monetary Policy. BNLQR, 22 (Mar, 1969), 3-15

Paxson, D. A.   The International Monetary Fund for Commercial Banks. DBA diss, Harvard Bus, 1969

Clendenning, E. W.   Euro-dollars: the Problem of Control. Banker, 118 (Apr, 1968), 321-329

Klopstock, F. H.   The Euro-Dollar Market: Some Unresolved Issues. International Finance Section, Princeton U, Mar 1968

Madden, J. T. & Nadler, M.   The International Money Markets. Greenwood, 1968

Swoboda, A. K.   The Euro-Dollar Market: An Interpretation. Princeton U
Intl Fin, Feb 1968

Altman, O. L.   Euro-dollars. Finance and Development, International
Monetary Fund, 1967

Christie, H.   Eurodollars and the Balance of Payments. Banker 117
(Jan, 1967), 34-45

Einzig, P.   The Euro-Dollar System, Practice and Theory of International
Interest Rates, 3rd ed. Macmillan Int, 1967

Bloch, E.   Eurodollars: an Emerging International Money Market. Bulletin No. 39, Institute of Finance, NYU, Apr 1966

Saunders, P., Jr.   American Banks in London's Eurodollar Market. NBR,
(Sep, 1966)

Van Houten, J. F.   The Euro-Dollar Market and Monetary Policy. PhD
diss, Georgetown U, 1966

Altman, O. L.   Euro-dollars: some Further Comments. IMF, 12 (Mar,
1965), 1-16

Klopstock, F. H.   The International Money Market: Structure, Scope and
Instruments. JF, 20 (May, 1965), 182-208

Stein, J. L.   International Short-Term Capital Movements. AER, 55 (Mar,
1965), 40-66

Einzig, P.   Some Recent Changes in the Euro-Dollar System. JF, 19
(Sep, 1964), 443-449

Johnson, N. O.   Euro-dollars in the New International Money Market.
New York: First National City Bank, 1964

Martenson, G. C.   The Euro-dollar Market. Bankers, 1964

Parker, H. J.   The Euro-Dollar Market. Detroit: City National Bank of
Detroit, 1964

Reierson, R. L.   The Euro-Dollar Market. New York: Bankers Trust Co.,
1964

Gemmill, R. F.   Interest Rates and Foreign Dollar Balances. JF, 16
(Sep, 1961), 363-376

Holmes, A. R. & Klopstock, F. H.   The Market for Dollar Deposits in
Europe. Mo Rev F R Bk New York, (1960)

20e INTERNATIONAL LONG-TERM CAPITAL MARKETS

This section is principally concerned with the development of the Eurobond
market. Chown & Valentine provide a valuable introduction to the workings
of the market and the Bank of England article a useful brief study of its
growth.

See also:

20d International Money Markets

Bank of England.   The International Capital Markets of Europe. BEQB,
10 (Sep, 1970), 295-307

Park, Y. S.   Financing Operations of U.S. firms in the Euro-bond market.
DBA diss, Harvard Bus, 1970

Cheng, H-S.   International Bond Issues of the Less-Developed Countries:
Diagnosis and Prescription. Iowa St U Pr, 1969

Einzig, P.   The Euro-bond Market. Macmillan Int, 1969

Lockhart, J. A.   The Eurobond Market Today. FAJ, 25 (Mar-Apr, 1969),
128-132

Chown, J. F. & Valentine, R. The International Bond Market in the 1960's. Praeger, 1968

Bolton, G. et al. The European Capital Market. Fed Tst, 1967

Genillard, R. L. The Eurobond Market. FAJ, 23 (Mar-Apr, 1967), 144-151

Heller, H. R. Foreign Bond Issues in Europe. LBR, 86 (Oct, 1967), 49-62

Rolfe, S. E. Capital Markets in Atlantic Economic Relationships. The Atlantic Institute, 1967

Strauss Turnbull. A Technical Study of Convertible Euro-bonds. London: Strauss Turnbull, Mar 1967

Weiner, J. M. Developing a European Capital Market. LBR, 85 (Jul, 1967), 16-28

Williams, D. Foreign Currency Issues on European Security Markets. IMF, 14 (Mar, 1967), 43-79

European Economic Community. The Development of a European Capital Market: Report of a Group of Experts Appointed by the EEC Commission. Brussels: EEC, 1966

Scott, I. O., Jr. European Capital Markets. NBR, (Dec, 1966), 131-144

Altman, O. L. The Integration of European Capital Markets. JF, 20 (May 1965), 209-221

Basch, A. Capital Markets of the European Economic Community: Problems of Integration. U of Mich Busn Res, 1965

Williams, D. The Development of Capital Markets in Europe. IMF, 12 (Mar, 1965), 37-62

American Management Association. Sources and Methods of International Financing: Practical Guide for U.S. Investors and Traders. Am Mgmt, 1961

Part 21 Other Speculative Markets

21a COMMODITIES, FUTURES MARKETS AND HEDGING

In addition to specific studies of the commodity market, we have included general works on futures markets and hedging. General introductory books include those of Rees and Teweles et al. Weymar and Labys & Granger provide somewhat more analytical studies. Tests of market efficiency are exemplified by Houthakker (1961), Larson (FRIS, 1960), Smidt (1965) and Stevenson & Bear. Discussions of the theory of normal backwardation are exemplified by Telser (1958), Cootner (1960) and Rockwell (1967).

See also:

11c Random Walk Hypothesis
18f Interest Rates—Term Structure
21b Forward Currency Markets

Harlow, C. V. & Teweles, R. J.   Commodities and Securities Compared. FAJ, 28 (Sep-Oct, 1972), 64-70

Leuthold, R. M.   Random Walk and Price Trends: the Live Cattle Futures Market. JF, 27 (Sep, 1972), 879-890

Hieronymus, T. A.   Economics of Futures Trading: for Commercial and Personal Profit. Commodity R, 1971

Labys, W. C.; Rees, H. J. B. & Elliott, C. M.   Copper Price Behaviour and the London Metal Exchange. AE, 3 (Jun, 1971), 99-114

Rees, G. L.   Britain's Commodity Markets. Elek, 1971

Bear, R. M.   Martingale Movements in Commodity Futures. PhD diss, U of Iowa, 1970

Dalrymple, B. B.   Risk Analysis Applied to Commodity Speculations. PhD diss, La St U, 1970

Labys, W. C. & Granger, C. W. J.   Speculation, Hedging and Commodity Price Forecasts. Heath, 1970

Poole, W.   McKinnon on Futures Markets and Buffer Stocks. JPE, 78 (Sep-Oct, 1970), 1185-1190

Stevenson, R. A. & Bear, R. M.   Commodity Futures: Trends or Random Walks? JF, 25 (Mar, 1970), 65-81

Ehrich, R. L.   Cash-Futures Price Relationships for Live Beef Cattle. AJAE, 51 (Feb, 1969), 26-39

McCain, W. G.   Price Effects of Margin Changes in Commodity Futures Markets. PhD diss, Stanford U, 1969

Teweles, R. J.; Harlow, C. V. & Stone, H. L.   The Commodity Futures Trading Guide. McGraw, 1969

Labys, W. C.   Commodity Price Fluctuations: A Short-Term Explanation for Selected Commodities on the American Market. PhD diss, U of Nottingham, 1968

Snape, R. H.   Price Relationships on the Sydney Wool Futures Market. Ec, 35 (May, 1968)

Weymar, F. H.   The Dynamics of the World Cocoa Market. MIT Pr, 1968

Belveal, L. D.   Commodity Speculation: With Profits in Mind. Commodities Pr, 1967

Cootner, P. H.   Speculation and Hedging. FRIS, 7 (Suppl, 1967), 65-105

Kogiku, K. C.   A Model of the Raw Materials Market. IntER, 8 (Feb, 1967), 116-120

Larson, A. B.   Price Prediction on the Egg Futures Market. FRIS, 7 (Suppl, 1967), 49-64

McKinnon, R. I.   Futures Markets, Buffer Stocks and Income Stability for Primary Producers. JPE, 75 (Dec, 1967), 844-861

Nimrod, V. L. & Bower, R. S.   Commodities and Computers. JFQA, 2 (Mar, 1967), 58-73

Radner, R.   Equilibrium of Spot and Futures Markets Under Uncertainty. Technical Report No. 24, Center for Research in Management Science. U of Cal Berkeley, Apr 1967

Rockwell, C. S.   Normal Backwardation, Forecasting and the Returns to Commodity Futures Traders. FRIS, 7 (Suppl, 1967) 107-130

Schrock, N. W.   A Portfolio Analysis of Straddle Operations in the Futures Markets: An Application of the Expected Returns-Variance of Returns Hypothesis. PhD diss, U of Oreg, 1967

Telser, L. G.   The Supply of Speculative Services in Wheat, Corn and Soybeans. FRIS, 7 (Suppl, 1967), 131-176

Working, H.   Tests of a Theory Concerning Floor Trading on Commodity Exchanges. FRIS, 7 (Suppl, 1967), 5-48

Brackenburg & Co.   Dealing on the London Metal Exchange. Brackenburg, 1966

Gaumnitz, E. A. (Ed).   Futures Trading Seminar: a Commodity Marketing Forum for College Teachers of Economics. Mimir, 1966

Gold, G.   Modern Commodity Futures Trading, 4th ed. Commodity R, 1966

Miller, N. C.   The Great Salad Oil Swindle. Gollancz, 1966

Phillips, J.   The Theory and Practice of Futures Trading. Review of Marketing and Agricultural Economics, (Jun, 1966)

Powers, M. J.   An Economic Analysis of the Futures Market for Pork Bellies. PhD diss, U of Wis, 1966

Weymar, F. H.   The Supply of Storage Revisited. AER, 56 (Dec, 1966), 1226-1234

Beckmann, M. J.   On the Determination of Prices in Futures Markets, *in* Brennan, M.J. (Ed), Patterns of Market Behavior. Brown U Pr, 1965

Jarrett, F. G.   Short Term Forecasting of Australian Wool Prices. AEP 4 (Jun-Dec, 1965), 93-102

Jiler, H. (Ed).   Guide to Commodity Price Forecasting. Commodity R, 1965

Samuelson, P. A.   A Random Theory of Futures Prices. IMR, 6 (Jun, 1965)

Smidt, S.   A Test of the Serial Independence of Price Changes in Soybean Futures. FRIS, 5 (1965), 117-136

Snape, R. H. & Yamey, B. S.   Test of the Effectiveness of Hedging. JPE, 73 (Oct, 1965), 540-544

Venkataramanan, L. S.   The Theory of Futures Trading. Asia, 1965

Ashby, A. W.   On Forecasting Commodity Prices by the Balance-Sheet Approach. JFE, 46 (Aug, 1964), 633-743

Gray, R. W.   The Attack upon Potato Futures Trading in the United States. FRIS, 4 (1964), 97-121

Houck, J. P.   A Statistical Model of the Demand for Soybeans. JFE, 46 (May, 1964), 366-374

Rockwell, C. S.   Profit, Normal Backwardation, and Forecasting in Commodity Futures. PhD diss, U of Cal Berkeley, 1964

Gray, R. W.   Fundamental Price Behavior Characteristics in Commodity Futures, *in* Futures Trading Seminar. Mimir, 1963

Working, H.   Futures Markets Under Renewed Attack. FRIS, 5 (Feb, 1963), 13-24

Gardner, R. L.   How to Make Money on the Commodity Market. P-H, 1962

160

Smidt, S. & Johnson, A.   Expectations and Information: A Study of Past Inventory Behavior. Graduate School of Business and Public Administration, Cornell U, 1962

Working, H.   New Concepts Concerning Futures Markets and Prices. AER, 52 (Jun, 1962), 431-459

Cootner, P. H.   Common Elements in Futures Markets for Commodities and Bonds. AER, 51 (May, 1961), 173-183

Gray, R. W.   The Relationship among Three Futures Markets: an Example of the Importance of Speculation. FRIS, 2 (Feb, 1961), 21-32

Gray, R. W.   The Search for a Risk Premium. JPE, 69 (Jun, 1961), 250-260

Houthakker, H. S.   Systematic and Random Elements in Short-Term Price Movements. AER, 51 (May, 1961), 164-172

Larson, A. B.   Estimation of Hedging and Speculative Positions in Futures Markets. FRIS, 2 (Nov, 1961), 203-212

Stein, J. L.   The Simultaneous Determination of Spot and Futures Prices. AER, 51 (Dec, 1961), 1012-1025

Cootner, P. H.   Returns to Speculators: Telser Versus Keynes. JPE, 68 (Aug, 1960), 396-404

Gray, R. W.   The Characteristic Bias in Some Thin Futures Markets. FRIS, 1 (Nov, 1960), 296-312

Johnson, L. L.   The Theory of Hedging and Speculation in Commodity Futures. REStud, 27 (Jun, 1960), 139-151

Larson, A. B.   Evidence on the Temporal Dispersion of Price Effects of New Market Information. PhD diss, Stanford U, 1960

Larson, A. B.   Measurement of a Random Process in Futures Prices. FRIS, 1 (Nov, 1960), 313-324

Peston, M. H. & Yamey, B. S.   Inter-Temporal Price Relationships with Forward Markets: a Method of Analysis. Ec 27 (Nov, 1960), 355-367

Working, H.   Price Effects of Futures Trading. FRIS, 1 (Feb, 1960), 3-31

Working, H.   Speculation on Hedging Markets. FRIS, 1 (May, 1960), 185-220

Houthakker, H. S.   The Scope and Limits of Futures Trading, *in* Abromovitz, M. (Ed), Allocation of Economic Resources. Stanford U Pr, 1959

Telser, L. G.   A Theory of Speculation Relating Profitability and Stability. REStat, 41 (Aug, 1959), 295-301

Telser, L. G.   Futures Trading and the Storage of Cotton and Wheat. JPE, 66 (Jun, 1958), 233-255

Brennan, M. J.   The Supply of Storage. AER, 47 (Mar, 1957), 50-72

Glick, I. O.   A Social Psychological Study of Futures Trading. PhD diss, U of Chicago, 1957

Houthakker, H. S.   Can Speculators Forecast Prices? REStat, 39 (May, 1957), 143-151

Houthakker, H. S.   Restatement of the Theory of Normal Backwardation. Cowles Foundation Discussion Paper, No. 44, (18 Dec, 1957)

Johnson, L. L.   Hedging and Speculation and Futures Trading in the Futures Market since World War II. PhD diss, Yale U, 1957

Johnson, L. L.   Price Instability, Hedging and Trade Volume in the Coffee Market. JPE, 65 (Aug, 1957)

Telser, L. G.   The Supply of Stocks, Cotton and Wheat. PhD diss, U of Chicago, 1956

Houthakker, H. S.   Commodity Futures IV: an Empirical Test of the Theory of Normal Backwardation. Cowles Commission Discussion Paper, Economics, No 2124, (22 Jun, 1955)

Working, H.   Price Effects of Scalping and Day Trading. Proceedings of the Chicago Board of Trade Annual Symposium, (1954), 114-139

Working, H.   Whose Markets? Evidence on Some Aspects of Futures Trading. JM, 19 (Jul, 1954)

Graf, T. F.   Hedging—How Effective Is It? JFE, 35, (Aug, 1953), 398-413

Working, H.   Futures Trading and Hedging. AER, 43 (Jun, 1953), 314-343

Working, H.   Hedging Reconsidered. JFE, 35, (Nov, 1953), 314-343

Houthakker, H. S. & Telser, L. G.   Commodity Futures II: Gain and Losses of Hedgers and Futures Speculators. Cowles Commission Discussion Paper, Economics, No 2090 (7 Dec, 1952)

Yamey, B. S.   An Investigation of Hedging on an Organized Produce Exchange. MS, 19 (Sep, 1951)

Anderson, M. A.   Fundamentals and Technicalities of Commodity Futures Trading. Hutton, 1949

Baer, J. B. & Saxon, O. G.   Commodity Exchanges and Futures Trading. Har-Row, 1949

Schultz, T. W.   Spot and Futures Prices as Production Guides. AER, 39 (May, 1949)

Stewart, B.   An Analysis of Speculative Trading in Grain Futures. US Dept of Agriculture Technical Bulletin No. 1001, Oct 1949

Working, H.   Memorandum on Measurement of Cycles in Speculative Prices. Food Research Institute, Stanford U, 1949

Howell, L. D.   Analysis of Hedging and Other Operations in Grain Futures. US Dept of Agriculture Technical Bulletin No 971, Aug, 1948

Vaile, R.   Inverse Carrying Charges in Futures Markets. JFE, 30 (Aug, 1948), 574-575

Working, H.   Theory of the Inverse Carrying Charge in Futures Markets. JFE, 30 (1948), 1-28

Johnson, D. G.   Forward Prices for Agriculture. U of Chicago Pr, 1947

Vance, L.   Grain Market Forces in the Light of Inverse Carrying Charges. JFE, 28 (Nov, 1946), 1036-1040

Blau, G.   Some Aspects of the Theory of Futures Trading. REStud, 12 (1944)

Vaile, R.   Cash and Futures Price of Corn. JM, 9 (Jul, 1944)

Working, H.   Quotations on Commodity Futures as Price Forecasts. Em, 10 (1942), 30-52

Hawtrey, R. G.   A Symposium on the Theory of the Forward Market: III Mr Kaldor on the Forward Market. REStud, 7 (Jun, 1940), 196-205

Hoos, S. & Working, H.   Price Relations of Liverpool Wheat Futures with Special Reference to the December-March Spread. Wheat Studies of the Food Research Institute, 16 (Nov, 1940), 101-143

Kaldor, N.   A Note on the Theory of the Forward Markets. REStud, 7 (Oct, 1939), 196-201

Irwin, H. S.   Seasonal Cycles in Aggregates of Wheat Futures Contracts. JPE, 43 (1935), 278-288

Working, H.   Price Relations between July and September Wheat Futures at Chicago, since 1885. Wheat, 9 (1933), 187-238

Working, H.   Cycles in Wheat Prices. Wheat, 7 (Nov, 1931)

Working, H.   Financial Results of Speculative Holdings in Wheat. Wheat, 7 (Jul, 1931)

Working, H.   The Post Harvest Depression of Wheat Prices. Wheat, 5 (Nov, 1929)

Emery, H. C.   Legislation Against Futures. PSQ (Mar, 1895)

This section is concerned with speculation in the forward exchange market. It is not principally concerned with the establishment of foreign exchange parities or with mechanisms for dealing with dis-equilibrium in the exchange markets. Einzig's books provide useful institutional material. Articles by Tsiang, Feldstein and Canterbury exemplify theoretical discussions of the stabilising effects of speculation in the exchange markets. Poole and Pippenger provide empirical evidence that flexible exchange rates resemble speculative prices.

See also:

9e Speculation and Stability
10i Internationally Diversified Portfolios
21a Commodities, Futures Markets and Hedging

Canterbery, E. R. A Theory of Foreign Exchange Speculation Under Alternative Systems. JPE, 79 (May-Jun, 1971), 407-436

Haas, R. D. A Portfolio Model of International Capital Flows. PhD diss, Duke U, 1971

Lietaer, B. A. Financial Management of Foreign Exchange. MIT Pr, 1971

Einzig, P. Foreign Exchange Crisis: an Essay in Economic Pathology, 2nd ed. Macmillan Int, 1970

Einzig, P. The History of Foreign Exchange. Macmillan Int, 1970

Branson, W. H. The Minimum Covered Interest Differential Needed for International Arbitrage Activity. JPE, 77 (Nov-Dec, 1969), 1028-1035

Einzig, P. A Textbook of Foreign Exchange, 2nd ed. Macmillan Int, 1969

Arndt, S. W. International Short Term Capital Movements: a Distributed Lag Model of Speculation in Foreign Exchange. Em, 36 (Jan, 1968), 59-70

Feldstein, M. S. Uncertainty and Forward Exchange Speculation. REStat, 50 (May, 1968), 182-192

Stoll, H. An Empirical Study of the Forward Exchange Market under Fixed and Flexible Exchange Rate Systems. CJE, 1 (Feb, 1968), 55-78

Van Den Dool, P. Forward Exchange Transactions and Some Theoretical Implications. DBA diss, U of Oreg, 1968

Einzig, P. A Dynamic Theory of Forward Exchange. Macmillan Int, 1967

Frevert, P. W. A Theoretical Model of the Forward Exchange.
Part 1: IntER, 8 (Jun, 1967), 307-326,
Part 2: IntER, 8 (Oct, 1967), 153-167

Glahe, F. R. An Empirical Study of the Foreign Exchange Market: Test of a Theory. Princeton U Pr, 1967

Obst, N. P. A Connection Between Speculation and Stability in the Foreign Exchange Market. SEJ, 34 (Jul, 1967), 146-149

Poole, W. Speculative Prices as Random Walks: an Analysis of Ten Time Series of Flexible Exchange Rates. SEJ, 33 (Apr, 1967), 468-478

Schilling, D. J. Devaluation Risk and Interest Rate Parity Theory. PhD diss, U of NC, 1967

Stoll, H. R. The Determinants of Forward Exchange Rates. PhD diss U of Chicago, 1967

Evitt, H. E. A Manual of Foreign Exchange, 6th ed. Pitman, 1966

Grubel, H. G. Forward Exchange, Speculation and the International Flow of Capital. Stanford U Pr, 1966

Pippenger, J. E. The Behavior of Flexible Exchange Rates: Theory and Evidence. PhD diss, UCLA, 1966

Sohmen, E. The Theory of Forward Exchange. International Finance Section, Department of Economics. Princeton U, 1966

Grubel, H. G. Profits from Forward Exchange Speculation. QJE, 79 (May, 1965), 248-262

Frevert, P. W. A Model of the Spot and Forward Markets for Foreign Exchange. PhD diss, Purdue U, 1964

Goldstein, H. N. The Implications of Triangular Arbitrage for Forward Exchange Policy. JF, 19 (Sep, 1964), 544-551

Grubel, H. G. Triangular Arbitrage and Forward Exchange Policy: Reply. JF, 19 (Sep, 1964), 552-554

Aliber, R. Z. More about Counter-Speculation in the Forward Exchange Market. JPE, 71 (Dec, 1963), 588-590

Grubel, H. G. A Neglected Aspect of Forward Exchange Theory and Policy. JF, 18 (Sep, 1963), 537-548

Stein, J. L. The Optimum Foreign Exchange Market. AER, 53 (Jun, 1963), 384-402

White, W. H. Interest Rate Differences, Forward Exchange Mechanism and Scope for Short-Term Capital Movements. IMF, (Nov, 1963)

Stein, J. L. The Nature and Efficiency of the Foreign Exchange Market. Princeton U Intl Fin, Oct 1962

Aliber, R. Z. Speculation in the Foreign Exchanges: the European Experience, 1919-1926. PhD diss, Yale U, 1961

Auten, J. H. Counter-Speculation and the Forward Exchange Market. JPE, 69 (Feb, 1961), 49-55

Auten, J. H. Monetary Policy and the Forward Exchange Market. JF, (Dec, 1961) 546-558

Sohmen, E. Flexible Exchange Rates. Theory and Controversy, rev ed. U of Chicago Pr, 1961

Reading, B. The Forward Pound, 1951-1959. EJ, 70 (Jun, 1960), 304-319

Tsiang, S. C. A Theory of Foreign-Exchange Speculation under a Floating Exchange System. JPE, 66 (Oct, 1958), 399-418

21c REAL ESTATE

This section contains a small selection of articles on the mortgage market and direct investment in real estate. Wendt & Cerf exemplify the general textbooks on property investment. Some very fragmentary evidence on returns from such investment is proffered by Wendt & Wong, Chisholm, Ricks and Friedman.

Olney, P. Some Observations on Pension Fund Property Unit Trusts. IA, 33 (Sep, 1972), 32-41

Pellatt, P. G. K. The Analysis of Real Estate Investments Under Uncertainty. JF, 27 (May, 1972), 459-472

Friedman, H. C. Real Estate Investment and Portfolio Theory. JFQA, 6 (Mar, 1971), 861-874

Schulkin, P. A. Real Estate Investment Trusts. FAJ, 27 (May-Jun, 1971), 33ff

Ring, A. A. The Valuation of Real Estate. P-H, 1970

Hoagland, H. E. & Stone, L. D. Real Estate Finance, 4th ed. Irwin, 1969

Ricks, R. B. Imputed Returns on Real Estate Financed with Life Insurance Company Loans. JF, 24 (Dec, 1969), 921-937

Wendt, P. F. & Cerf, A. R. Real Estate Investment Analysis and Taxation. McGraw, 1969

Chisholm, R. K.   The Rate of Return to Investment in Farm Land. PhD diss, U of Chicago, 1968

Jones, O.   Private Secondary Market Facilities. JF, 23 (May, 1968), 359-366

Kost, W. E.   Rates of Return for Farm Real Estate and Common Stock. AJAE, 50 (May, 1968), 213-224

Hayes, S. L., III & Harlan, L. M.   Real Estate as a Corporate Investment. HBR, 45 (Jul-Aug, 1967), 144-160

Kahn, S. R.   An Evaluation of the Real Estate Investment Trust. PhD diss, U of Cincinnati, 1967

McCloy, H. F.   Managing Corporate Real Estate. Am Mgmt, 1967

McMichael, S. L.   How to Operate a Real Estate Business, rev ed. P-H, 1967

McMichael, S. L. & O'Keefe, P. T.   How to Finance Real Estate, 3rd ed. P-H, 1967

Hanford, L. D.   Investing in Real Estate. Inst Real Est Mgmt, 1966

Pringle, J. M.   The Mortgage Market and Its Relationship to Markets for Government, High-Grade Corporate and Municipal Bonds. FAJ, 22 (May-Jun, 1966), 105-106

Ricks, R. B. & Weston, J. F.   Land as a Growth Investment. FAJ, 22 (Jul-Aug, 1966), 69-78

Maisel, S. J.   Financing Real Estate. McGraw, 1965

Wendt, P. F. & Wong, S. N.   Investment Performance: Common Stocks Versus Apartment Houses. JF, 20 (Dec, 1965), 633-646

Edwards, E. E.   Changing Character of the Real Estate Mortgage Markets. JF, 19 (May, 1964), 313-320

Leach, W. A. & Wenman, E. G.   Investments in Land and Property: a Guide for Investors and Those Responsible for Investment Policy. Estates Gazette, 1964

O'Connor, J. J.   An Investment Analysis of the Office Building. PhD diss, NYU, 1964

Page, A. N.   The Variation of Mortgage Interest Rates. JB, 37 (Jul, 1964), 280-294

Ricks, R. B.   Recent Trends in Institutional Real Estate Investment. Research Report 23, Center for Real Estate and Urban Economics, U of Cal Berkeley, 1964

Kahn, S. R; Case, F. E. & Schimmel, A.   Real Estate Appraisal and Investment. Ronald, 1963

Vidger, L. P.   Selected Cases and Problems in Real Estate. Wadsworth Pub, 1963

Bryant, W. R.   Mortgage Lending: Fundamentals and Practice, 2nd ed. McGraw, 1962

Turvey, R.   The Economics of Real Property: an Analysis of Property Values and Patterns of Use. Allen, 1957

Wheeler, A. C. & K. A. C.   Some Views on Property Investment. JIASS, 12 (Nov, 1953)

21d AUCTIONS, GAMBLES AND OTHER SPECULATIONS

Pankoff's article in this section provides interesting evidence of the information content of experts' recommendations on football bets.

See also:

15c The Accuracy of Share Price Forecasts

Niarchos, N. & Granger, C. W. J.   The Gold Sovereign Market in Greece—an Unusual Speculative Market. JF, forthcoming

Pankoff, L. D.   Market Efficiency and Football Betting. JB, 41 (Apr, 1968), 203-214

Pankoff, L. D.   The Quantification of Judgment: A Case Study. PhD diss, U of Chicago, 1967

Butler, E. B.   Auction Prices: Estimated and Realised. EJ, 71 (Mar, 1961), 114-120

Part 22 Corporate Finance–General

22a CORPORATE FINANCE—GENERAL

This section consists principally of general texts on corporate finance.
The two Van Horne books offer good introductory material, and Mao's
book constitutes a useful, more quantitative text. An important and rigorous
theoretical study is provided by Fama & Miller.

Rubinstein, M.   A Synthesis of Corporate Financial Theory. JF, forthcoming

Archer, S. H. & D'Ambrosio, C. A.   Business Finance: Theory and
Management, 2nd ed. Macmillan, 1972

Brandt, L. K.   Analysis for Financial Management. P-H, 1972

Fama, E. F. & Miller, M. H.   The Theory of Finance. HR & W, 1972

Dobrovolsky, S. P.   The Economics of Corporation Finance. McGraw,
1971

Elton, E. J.   Studies in Financial Theory. PhD diss, Carnegie-Mellon U,
1971

Elton, E. J. & Gruber, M. J.   Dynamic Programming Applications in
Finance. JF, 26 (May 1971), 473-506

Hunt, P; Williams, C. M. & Donaldson, G.   Basic Business Finance: Text
and Cases, 4th ed. Irwin, 1971

Johnson, R. W.   Financial Management, 4th ed. Allyn, 1971

Lerner, E. M.   Managerial Finance: a Systems Approach. HarBrace J,
1971

Van Horne, J. C.   Financial Management and Policy, 2nd ed. P-H, 1971

Van Horne, J. C.   Fundamentals of Financial Management. P-H, 1971

Curran, W. S.   Principles of Financial Management. McGraw, 1970

Grunewald, A. E. & Nemmers, E. E.   Basic Managerial Finance. HR & W
1970

Jackson, A. S. & Townsend, E. C.   Financial Management. Harrap, 1970

Jean, W. H.   The Analytical Theory of Finance: a Study of the Investment
Decision Process of the Individual and the Firm. HR & W, 1970

Newbould, G. D.   Business Finance. Harrap, 1970

Stapleton, R. C.   The Theory of Corporate Finance. Harrap, 1970

Whitmore, G. A.   Market Demand Curve for Common Stock and the Maximization of Market Value. JFQA, 5 (Mar, 1970), 105-114

Wright, M. G.   Financial Management. McGraw, 1970

Bierman, H., Jr.; Fouraker, L. E., & Jaedicke, R. K.   Quantitative Analysis
for Business Decisions, 3rd ed. Irwin, 1969

Bradley, J. F.   Administrative Financial Management, 2nd ed. HR & W,
1969

Clarkson, G. P. E. & Elliott, B. J.   Managing Money and Finance. Gower,
1969

Donaldson, E. F. & Pfahl, J. K.   Corporate Finance: Policy and Management, 3rd ed. Ronald, 1969

Flink, S. J. & Grunewald, D.   Managerial Finance. Wiley, 1969

Kent, R. P.   Corporate Financial Management, 3rd ed. Irwin, 1969

Mao, J. C. T.   Quantitative Analysis of Financial Decisions. Macmillan,
1969

Midgley, K. & Burns, R. G.   Business Finance and the Capital Market.
Macmillan Int, 1969

Peterson, D. E. & Haydon, R. B.   A Quantitative Framework for Financial Management. Irwin, 1969

Weston, J. F. & Brigham, E. F.   Managerial Finance, 3rd ed. HR & W, 1969

Childs, J. F.   Profit Goals and Capital Management. P-H, 1968

Moore, B. J.   An Introduction to the Theory of Finance—Assetholder Behaviour under Uncertainty. Free Pr, 1968

Paish, F. W.   Business Finance, 4th ed. Pitman, 1968

Van Arsdell, P. M.   Corporation Finance. Ronald, 1968

Zausner, M.   Corporate Policy and the Investment Community. Ronald, 1968

Carleton, W. T. & Lerner, E. M.   Measuring Corporate Profit Opportunities, JFQA, 2 (Sep, 1967), 225-240

Chambers, R. J.   Financial Management. Law Book, 1967

Cooke, G. W. & Bomeli, E. C.   Business and Financial Management. HM, 1967

Lindsay, R. & Sametz, A. W.   Financial Management: an Analytical Approach, rev ed. Irwin, 1967

Mock, E. J.   Financial Decision Making. Intex, 1967

Robichek, A. A. (Ed).   Financial Research and Management Decisions. Wiley, 1967

Abbott, C. C. (Ed).   Basic Research in Finance: Needs and Prospects. U Pr of Va, 1966

Carson, D. (Ed).   Money and Finance. Wiley, 1966

Cohen, J. B. & Robbins, S. M.   The Financial Manager—Basic Aspects of Financial Administration. Har-Row, 1966

Friedland, S.   The Economics of Corporate Finance. P-H, 1966

Hastings, P. G.   The Management of Business Finance. VanN Rein, 1966

Husband, W. H. & Dockeray, J. C.   Modern Corporation Finance, 6th ed. Irwin, 1966

Lerner, E. M. & Carleton, W. T.   A Theory of Financial Analysis. Har-Brace J, 1966

Page, C. S. & Canaway, E. E.   Finance for Management. Heinemann, 1966

Brandt, L. K.   Business Finance, a Management Approach. P-H, 1965

Osborn, R. C.   Business Finance: the Management Approach. Appleton, 1965

Robinson, R. I. & Johnson, R. W.   Self-Correcting Problems in Finance. Allyn, 1965

Walker, E. W.   Essentials of Financial Management. P-H, 1965

Bogen, J. I. & Shipman, S. S. (Eds).   Financial Handbook, 4th ed. Ronald, 1964

Burtchett, F. F. et al.   Corporation Finance, rev ed. Johnsen, 1964

Dauten, C. A. & Welshans, M. T.   Principles of Finance: Functions, Problems, Institutions, 3rd ed. SW Pub, 1964

Gordon, M. J.   The Investment, Financing and Valuation of the Corporation. Irwin, 1964

Marting, E. & Finley, R. E. (Eds).   The Financial Manager's Job. Am Mgmt, 1964

Prather, C. L.   Financing Business Firms, 3rd ed. Irwin, 1964

Taylor, M.   General Financing Knowledge: the Principles and Practice of Finance. Textbooks, 1964

Walker, E. W. & Baughn, W. H.   Financial Planning and Policy. Har-Row, 1964

Corrigan, F. J. & Ward, H. A. (Eds).   Financial Management: Policies and Practices. HM, 1963

Solomon, E.   The Theory of Financial Management. Columbia U Pr, 1963
Guthmann, H. G. & Dougall, H. E.   Corporate Financial Policy, 4th ed. P-H, 1962
Kimball, M.   Corporate Finance. Littlefield, 1962
O'Donnell, J. L. & Goldberg, M. S. (Eds).   Elements of Financial Administration. Merrill, 1962
Schwartz, E.   Corporation Finance. Macmillan Int, 1962
Summers, G. W.   Financing and Initial Operations of New Firms. P-H, 1962
Childs, J. F.   Long-Term Financing. P-H, 1961
Lintner, J.   The Financing of Corporations, *in* Mason, E. S. (Ed), The Corporation in Modern Society. Harvard U Pr, 1961
Whyte, L. G.   Some Basic Principles of Investment. Cambridge U Pr, 1961
Mathews, R.   Inflation and Company Finance. AR, 35 (Jan, 1960), 8-18
Prentice-Hall Editorial Staff.   Encyclopedic Dictionary of Business Finance. P-H, 1960
Welfling, W.   Financing Business Enterprise. New York: American Institute of Banking, 1960
Bradley, J. F.   Fundamentals of Corporation Finance, rev ed. HR & W, 1959
Gerstenberg, C. W.   Financial Organisation and Management of Business, 4th ed. P-H, 1959
Osborn, R. C.   Corporation Finance. Har-Row, 1959
Solomon, E. (Ed).   The Management of Corporate Capital. Free Pr, 1959
Tew, B. & Henderson, R. F. (Eds).   Studies in Company Finance. Cambridge U Pr, 1959
Dauten, C. A.   Business Finance: The Fundamentals of Financial Management, 2nd ed. P-H, 1956
Dewing, A. S.   The Financial Policy of Corporations, 2 vols, 5th ed. Ronald, 1953
Howard, B. B. & Upton, M.   Introduction to Business Finance. McGraw, 1953
Evans, G.   Financial Life Cycle of Corporations, *in* Conference in Research in Business Finance. Natl Bur Econ Res, 1952
Dean, J.   Managerial Economics. P-H, 1951
Lutz, F. A. & V. C.   The Theory of Investment of the Firm. Princeton U Pr, 1951
Starkweather, L. P.; Otto, E. A. & Kreger, H. R.   Policies and Practices in Corporate Finance; an Application of Principles and Techniques. New York: New York University Book Store, 1951

22b CAPITAL THEORY

This section lists a few works concerned with the amorphous subject of capital theory. Vickers and Turnovsky provide an interesting attempt to integrate production and money assets into a theoretical framework.

See also:

9d   Equilibrium Under Uncertainty—General

Turnovsky, S. J.   Financial Structure and the Theory of Production. JF, 25 (Dec, 1970), 1061-1080

Vickers, D.   The Theory of the Firm; Production, Capital and Finance. McGraw, 1968

Dewey, D.   Modern Capital Theory. Columbia U Pr, 1965

Lamberton, D. M.   The Theory of Profit. Blackwell, 1965

Jorgenson, D. W.   Capital Theory and Investment Behavior. AER, 53 (May, 1963), 247-259

Kuh, E.   Capital Stock Growth: A Micro-econometric Approach. N Holland, 1963

Lutz, F. A. & Hague, D. C. (Eds).   The Theory of Capital. Macmillan, 1963

Solow, R. M.   Capital Theory and the Rate of Return. N Holland, 1963

Haavelmo, T.   A Study in the Theory of Investment. U of Chicago Pr, 1960

Machlup, F.   The Stock Market, Credit and Capital Formation. Translated from a revised version of the German edition by V. C. Smith. Macmillan, 1940

Samuelson, P. A.   Some Aspects of the Pure Theory of Capital. QJE, 51 (1937), 469-496

Fisher, I.   The Nature of Capital and Income. Macmillan, 1906

22c FINANCIAL PLANNING MODELS

This section is concerned with general financial planning models involving either simulation or optimising techniques. The articles by Gershefski, Carleton and Warren & Shelton exemplify this work.

See also:

25c Capital Budgeting—General

Chambers, D. J.   Dividend Plans and Balance Sheet Management. JBF, 4 (Autumn, 1972), 17-25

Krouse, C. G.   A Model for Aggregate Financial Planning. MSci, 18 (Jun, 1972), B555-B566

Carlson, C. R.   A Financial Efficiency Model. PhD diss, Mich St U, 1971

Horiguchi, Y.   Corporate Financial Decisions: General Equilibrium Approach. PhD diss, Rice U, 1971

Warren, J. M. & Shelton, J. P.   A Simultaneous Equation Approach to Financial Planning. JF, 26 (Dec, 1971), 1123-1142

Boulden, J. B. & Buffa, E. S.   Corporate Models: On Line, Real Time Systems. HBR, 48 (Jul-Aug, 1970), 65-83

Carleton, W. T.   An Analytical Model for Long-Range Financial Planning. JF, 25 (May, 1970), 291-315

Schrieber, A. N. (Ed).   Corporate Simulation Models. U of Washington Pr, 1970

Gershefski, G. W.   Building a Corporate Financial Model. HBR, 47 (Jul-Aug, 1969), 61-72

Krouse, C. G.   Financial Planning: a Dynamic Multiobjective Framework. PhD diss, UCLA, 1969

Wagle, B.   The Use of Models for Environmental Forecasting and Corporate Planning. ORQ, 20 (Sep, 1969), 327-336

Chambers, D. J.   Programming the Allocation of Funds Subject to Restriction on Reported Results. ORQ, 18 (Dec, 1967), 407-432

Moag, J. S, Carleton, W. T. & Lerner, E. M.   Defining the Finance Function: a Model-Systems Approach. JF, 22 (Dec, 1967), 543-555

McKenzie, R. R.   A Computer Simulation Used to Evaluate Alternative Financial Strategies. PhD diss, UCLA, 1965

Mattessich, R.   Simulation of a Firm through a Budget Computer Program. Irwin, 1964

Ijiri, Y; Levy, F.K. & Lyon, R.C.   A Linear Programming Model for Budgeting and Financial Planning. JAR, 1 (Autumn, 1963), 198-212

Mattessich, R.   Budgeting Models and System Simulation. AR, 36 (Jul, 1961), 384-397

Part 23 Capital Structure

23a TRENDS IN CAPITAL FORMATION

This section contains some general material on long-term trends in capital formation.

See also:

23b Corporate Choice Among Alternative Sources of Finance.

Stigler, G. J.   Capital and Rates of Return in Manufacturing. (Dist by Princeton U Pr) Natl Bur Econ Res, 1963

Deane, P.   Long-Term Trends in Capital Formation and Financing. EJ, 72 (Dec, 1962), 926-930

Kuznets, S.   Capital in the American Economy: Its Formation and Financing. (Dist by Princeton U Pr) Natl Bur Econ Res, 1961

Creamer, D.; Dobrovolsky, S. P. & Borenstein, I.   Capital in Manufacturing and Mining. Princeton U Pr, 1960

23b CORPORATE CHOICE AMONG ALTERNATIVE SOURCES OF FINANCE

This section is concerned with positive studies of firms' capital structure as opposed to the normative works listed under 23c—'Leverage and Optimal Capital Structure'. The Baxter & Cragg article is a good example of the few general attempts that have been made to explain company actions in this field. The articles by Baumol et al. and Whittington are concerned with the somewhat different subject of the extent to which profitability varies with source of finance.

See also:

16b Equity Issues by Seasoned Companies
19e Corporate Bonds
23a Trends in Capital Formation

Litzenberger, R. H. & Rutenberg, D. P.   Size and Timing of Corporate Bond Flotations. JFQA, 7 (Jan, 1972), 1343-1360

Whittington, G.   The Profitability of Retained Earnings. REStat, 54 (May, 1972), 152-160

Baumol, W. J.; Heim, P.; Malkiel, B. G. & Quandt, R. E.   Earnings Retention, New Capital and the Growth of Firms. REStat, 52 (Nov, 1970), 345-355

Baxter, N. D. & Cragg, J. G.   Corporate Choice Among Long-Term Financing Instruments. REStat, 52 (Aug, 1970), 225-235

Cragg, J. G. & Baxter, N. D.   The Issuing of Corporate Securities. JPE, 78 (Nov-Dec, 1970), 1310-1324

McKeon, J. J.   Structure of Corporate External Financing. FAJ, 25 (Sep-Oct, 1969), 25-28

Bray, J. N.   The Risk and Use of Debt Financing. PhD diss, UCLA, 1967

Carter, P.   Capital Structure Changes over the Life Cycle of Corporations. MBA thesis, U of Cal Berkeley, 1967

Fogler, H. R.   An Explanation of the Relative Decline in Common Stock Financing, 1946-1963. PhD diss, Columbia U, 1967

Gupta, M. C.   A Synchronic Study of Corporate Financial Structures 1961-62. PhD diss, UCLA, 1967

Freytag, D. C.   An Investigation of the Relationship between the Rate of
Growth for the Gross National Product and the Debt to Equity Ratio
for Nonfinancial Business. PhD diss, U of Cincinnati, 1966

Heron, J. P.   The Capital Gearing of Companies. IA, 10 (Dec, 1964), 11-18

Sametz, A. W.   Trends in the Volume and Composition of Equity Finance.
JF, 19 (Sep, 1964), 450-469

Zinbarg, E. D.   Supply and Demand Factors in the Stock Markets. FAJ,
20 (Jul-Aug, 1964), 84-88

Miller, M. H.   The Corporation Income Tax and Corporate Financial
Policies, *in* Stabilization Policies, CMC Supporting Papers. P-H, 1963

Donaldson, G.   New Framework for Corporate Debt Policy. HBR, 40 (Mar-
Apr, 1962), 117-131

Farrell, M. J.   On the Structure of the Capital Market. EJ, 72 (Dec, 1962),
830-844

Donaldson, G.   Corporate Debt Capacity: A Study of Corporate Debt
Policy and the Determination of Corporate Debt Capacity. Harvard
Busn, 1961

Smith, W. L.   Debt Management in the United States, Study Paper No. 19.
Paper prepared for the Joint Economic Committee, Congress of the
United States, January, 1960

Durand, D.   Cost of Debt and Equity Funds for Business: Trends and
Problems of Measurement, *in* Conference on Research in Business
Finance. Natl Bur Econ Res, 1952

Jacoby, N. H. & Weston, J. F.   Factors Influencing Managerial Decisions
in Determining Forms of Business Financing. An Exploratory Study.
Conference on Research in Business Finance, Natl Bur Econ Res, 1952

Association of Certified & Chartered Accountants. Sources of Capital. The
Association, nd

23c LEVERAGE AND OPTIMAL CAPITAL STRUCTURE

Many of the studies in this section were prompted by Modigliani & Miller's
important 1958 article on the cost of debt. We draw attention to Gordon's
criticisms of this work, to M. & M.'s own empirical tests published in 1966
and Hamada's discussion of the topic in the context of capital asset pricing
theory.

See also:

7c   Share Valuation—Cross-Sectional Analyses
23b Corporate Choice Among Alternative Sources of Finance
23d Cost of Capital
24b Dividend Policy and the Cost of Capital

Kraus, A. & Litzenberger, R. H.   A State-Preference Model of Optimal
Financial Leverage. JF, forthcoming

Krouse, C. G.   Optimal Financing and Capital Structure Programs for
the Firm. JF, forthcoming

Bierman, H., Jr. & Thomas, L. J.   Ruin Considerations and Debt Issuance.
JFQA, 7 (Jan, 1972), 1361-1378

Hamada, R. S.   The Effect of the Firm's Capital Structure on the Systematic Risk of Common Stocks. JF, 27 (May, 1972), 435-452

Rao, N. K.   Equivalent-Risk Class Hypothesis. JFQA, 7 (Jun, 1972), 1763-
1772

Smith, V. L.   Default Risk, Scale, and the Homemade Leverage Theorem.
AER, 62 (Mar, 1972), 66-76

Williams, E. E.   Cost of Capital Functions and the Firm's Optimal Level of Gearing. JBF, 4 (Summer, 1972), 78-83

Beechy, T. H.   The Effects of Financial Variables on the Cost of Capital. DBA diss, U of Wash, 1971

Frankfurter, G. M.   The Dynamics of Corporate Debt Management. PhD diss, St U NY Buffalo, 1971

Haugen, R. A. & Pappas, J. L.   Equilibrium in the Pricing of Capital Assets, Risk-Bearing Debt Instruments and the Question of Optimal Capital Structure. JFQA, 6 (Jun, 1971), 943-954

Korsvold, P. E.   The Cost of Raising New Private Debt Capital and Capital Market Efficiency. JBF, 3 (Summer, 1971), 3-9

Rao, C. U. & Litzenberger, R. H.   Leverage and the Cost of Capital in a Less Developed Capital Market: Comment. JF, 26 (Jun, 1971), 777-782

Schall, L. D.   Firm Financial Structure and Investment. JFQA, 6 (Jun, 1971), 925-942

Beach, P. R.   Equity Values and Corporate Debt in the Capital Structure. PhD diss, Brown U, 1970

Ben-Shahar, H.   On the Capital Structure Theorem: Reply. JF, 25 (Jun, 1970), 678-681

Bierman, H., Jr.   Financial Policy Decisions. Macmillan, 1970

DeFelice, F.   Security and Investment: More Evidence. JF, 25 (Sep, 1970), 803-808

Haugen, R. A. & Pappas, J. L.   A Comment on the Capital Structure and the Cost of Capital: a Suggested Exposition. JF, 25 (Jun, 1970), 674-677

Kumar, P.   Market Power, Growth, Leverage and the Valuation of the Firm. PhD diss, U of Wis, 1970

Litzenberger, R. H. & Jones, C. P.   The Capital Structure and the Cost of Capital: Comment. JF, 25 (Jun, 1970), 669-673

Resek, R. W.   Multidimensional Risk and the Modigliani-Miller Hypothesis. JF, 25 (Mar-Apr, 1970), 47-51

Scott, D. F.   An Inquiry into the Existence of Optimum Financial Structures. PhD diss, U of Fla, 1970

Tinsley, P. A.   Capital Structure, Precautionary Balances, and Valuation of the Firm: The Problem of Financial Risk. JFQA, 5 (Mar, 1970), 33-64

Walter, R. G.   The Effects of Corporate Financial Policy on Shareholder Expectations. PhD diss, Mich St U, 1970

Wong, C-H.   Capital Structure and Investment Behavior. PhD diss, U of Minn, 1970

Borch, K.   The Capital Structure of a Firm. SJE, 71 (Mar, 1969)

Ellis, C. D.   New Thoughts on an Old Argument: Rebuttal to M & M. FE, (Sep, 1969), 68-74

Goldsmith, R. W.   Financial Structure and Development. Yale U Pr, 1969

Gonedes, N. J.   A Test of the Equivalent-Risk Class Hypothesis. JFQA, 4 (Jun, 1969), 159-178

Hamada, R. S.   Portfolio Analysis, Market Equilibrium and Corporation Finance. JF, 24 (Mar, 1969), 13-31

Levy, H.   Portfolio Selection and Optimal Capital Structure. PhD diss, Hebrew U, 1969

Mumey, G. A.   Theory of Financial Structure. HR & W, 1969

Sarma, L. & Rao, K.   Leverage and the Value of the Firm. JF, 24 (Sep, 1969), 673-677

Stiglitz, J. E.   A Re-Examination of the Modigliani-Miller Theorem. AER, 59 (Dec, 1969), 784-793

Baldwin, W. L. & Velk, T. J.   Uncertainty of the Income Stream in the Modigliani-Miller Model. QREB, 8 (Winter, 1968), 39-43

Barges, A.   Growth Rates and Debt Capacity. FAJ, 24 (Jan-Feb, 1968), 100-104

Ben-Shahar, H.   Capital Structure and the Cost of Capital. JF, 23 (Sep, 1968), 639-653

Bierman, H., Jr.   Risk and the Addition of Debt to the Capital Structure. JFQA, 3 (Dec, 1968), 415-426

Brigham, E. F. & Gordon, M. J.   Leverage, Dividend Policy, and the Cost of Capital. JF, 23 (Mar, 1968), 85-103

Brown, K. C.   The Significance of Dummy Variables in Multiple Regressions Involving Financial and Economic Data. JF, 23 (Jun, 1968), 515-517

Harkins, E. P. & Walsh, F. J., Jr.   Corporate Debt Management. Natl Ind Conf Bd, 1968

Haugen, R. A.   Effects of Leverage and Dividend Policy on the Value of Equity Capital. PhD diss, U of Ill, 1968

Lüthi, J. E.   The Problem of Corporate Debt Capacity. SM thesis, MIT 1968

Murphy, J. E., Jr.   Some Effects of Leverage. FAJ 24 (Jul-Aug, 1968), 121-123

Wippern, R. F.   The Significance of Dummy Variables in Multiple Regressions Involving Financial and Economic Data: Reply. JF, 23 (Jun, 1968), 518-519

Baumol, W. J. & Malkiel, B. G.   The Firm's Optimal Debt-Equity Combination and the Cost of Capital. QJE, 81 (Nov, 1967), 547-578

Baxter, N. D.   Leverage, Risk of Ruin and the Cost of Capital. JF, 22 (Sep, 1967), 395-403

Braun, M. E.   Optimum Debt Financing Policy: A Linear Programming Approach. PhD diss, Ohio St U, 1967

Carson, R. L.   A Note on the 'Cost of Capital'. WEJ (Jun, 1967)

Crockett, J. & Friend, I.   Some Estimates of the Cost of Capital to the Electric Utility Industry, 1954-57: Comment. AER, 57 (Dec, 1967), 1258-1267

Gordon, M. J.   Some Estimates of the Cost of Capital to the Electric Utility Industry, 1954-57: Comment. AER, 57 (Dec, 1967), 1267-1278

Miller, M. H. & Modigliani, F.   Some Estimates of the Cost of Capital to the Electric Utility Industry, 1954-1957: Reply. AER, 57 (Dec, 1967), 1288-1300

Morgan, B. W.   Corporate Debt and Stockholder Portfolio Selection. YEE, (Fall, 1967), 201-261

Robichek, A. A.; McDonald, J. G. & Higgins, R. C.   Some Estimates of the Cost of Capital to the Electric Utility Industry, 1954-57: Comment. AER, 57 (Dec, 1967), 1278-1288

Schwartz, E.   Some Surrogate Evidence in Support of the Concept of Optimal Financial Structure. JF, 22 (Mar, 1967), 10-18

Stigler, J.   Imperfections in the Capital Market. JPE, 75 (Jun, 1967), 287-292

Vickers, D.   Elasticity of Capital Supply, Monopsonistic Discrimination and Optimal Capital Structure. JF, 22 (Mar, 1967), 1-9

Ghandhi, J. K. S.   On the Measurement of Leverage. JF, 21 (Dec, 1966), 715-726

Haley, C. W.   A Note on the Cost of Debt. JFQA, 1 (Dec, 1966), 72-93

Hållsten, B. A.   A Note on Modigliani and Miller's Extension of the Theory of Investment and Financing. SJE, 68 (Jun, 1966)

Miller, M. H. & Modigliani, F. Some Estimates of the Cost of Capital to the Electric Utility Industry, 1954-57. AER, 56 (Jun, 1966), 333-391

Morgan, B. W. Corporate Debt and the Evaluation of Corporate Earnings. PhD diss, Yale U, 1966

Robichek, A. A. & Myers, S. C. Problems in the Theory of Optimal Capital Structure. JFQA, 1 (Jun, 1966), 1-35

Seager, S. E. Leverage and the Cost of Capital. NBR, (Jun, 1966), 497-508

Sykes, A. Optimum Company Financing—Debt Versus Equity. IA, 15 (Sep, 1966), 3-9

Wippern, R. F. Financial Structure and the Value of the Firm. JF, 21 (Dec, 1966), 615-634

Wippern, R. F. A Note on the Equivalent Risk Class Assumption. EE (Spring, 1966), 13-22

Wright, F. K.; Young, I. C. & Barton, A. D. The Effect of Financial Structure on the Market Value of Companies. AEP, (Jun, 1966), 21-34

Beranek, W. The Effect of Leverage on the Market Value of Common Stock. U of Wis Busn, 1965

Brewer, D. E. & Michaelsen, J. B. The Cost of Capital, Corporation Finance and the Theory of Investment: Comment. AER, 55 (Jun, 1965), 516-524

Lerner, E. M. & Carleton, W. T. The Capital Structure Problem of a Regulated Public Utility. PUF, 76 (Jul 8, 1965), 24-32

Robichek, A. A. & Myers, S. C. Optimal Financing Decision. P-H, 1965

Boness, A. J. A Pedagogic Note on the Cost of Capital, JF, 19 (Mar, 1964), 99-106

Gordon, M. J. Security and Investment: Theory and Evidence. JF, 19 (Dec, 1964), 607-618

Theilman, W. A General Theory of the Optimum Plan of Financing. PhD diss, U of Ill, 1964

Wippern, R. F. Earnings Variability, Financial Structure and the Value of the Firm. PhD diss, Stanford U, 1964

Woods, I. R. Financial 'Leverage' and 'Gearing' in Perspective. SAJE, 32 (Mar, 1964), 26-35

Barges, A. The Effect of Capital Structure on the Cost of Capital. P-H, 1963

Brownlee, O. H. & Scott, I. O. Utility, Liquidity and Debt Management. Em, 31 (Jul, 1963), 349-362

Gordon, M. J. Optimal Investment and Financing Policy. JF, 18 (May, 1963), 264-272

Modigliani, F. & Miller, M. H. Corporate Income Taxes and the Cost of Capital: A Correction. AER, 53 (Jun, 1963), 433-443

Petersen, H. Risk and the Capital Structure of the Firm. PhD diss, Brown U, 1963

Santow, L. J. Cost of Long-Term Capital from a Corporate Point of View. FAJ, 19 (May-Jun, 1963), 43-50

Solomon, E. Leverage and the Cost of Capital. JF, 18 (May, 1963), 273-279

White, W. L. The Debt-Equity Ratio, the Dividend-Payment Ratio, Growth and the Rate at which Earnings are Capitalized. An Empirical Study. PhD diss, MIT, 1963

Gordon, M. J. The Savings, Investment and Valuation of a Corporation. REStat, 44 (Feb, 1962), 37-51

Gordon, M. J. Security and a Financial Theory of Investment: Reply. QJE, 76 (May, 1962), 315-319

Margoshes, S. L.   Debt Financing and Investment Value of Common Stock. FAJ, 18 (Jul-Aug, 1962), 67-72

Mendelson, M.   Security and a Financial Theory of Investment: Comment. QJE, 76 (May, 1962), 311-315

Hunt, P.   A Proposal for Precise Definitions of 'Trading on the Equity' and 'Leverage'. JF, 16 (Sep, 1961), 377-386

Neilsen, E. S.   Market Value and Financial Structure in the Railroad Industry. PhD diss, MIT, 1961

Neilsen, E. S.   Market Value and Financial Structure in the Railroad Industry.
The Travelers Insurance Company, Occasional Paper No. 4, Mar, 1961

Quirk, J. P.   The Capital Structure of Firms and the Risk of Failure. IntER, 2 (May, 1961), 210-228

Gordon, M. J.   Risk, Debt and Share Prices. Paper presented at the meeting of the Econometric Society, MIT, Dec, 1960

Gordon, M. J.   Security and a Financial Theory of Investment. QJE, 74 (Aug, 1960), 472-492

Usher, D.   The Debt/Equity Ratio. PhD diss, U of Chicago, 1960

Durand, D.   The Cost of Capital, Corporation Finance and the Theory of Investment: Comment. AER, 49 (Sep, 1959), 639-655

Miller, M. H. & Modigliani, F.   The Cost of Capital, Corporation Finance, and the Theory of Investment: Reply. AER, 49 (Sep, 1959), 655-668

Rose, J. R.   The Cost of Capital, Corporation Finance, and the Theory of Investment: Comment. AER, 49 (Sep, 1959), 638-639

Schwartz, E.   Theory of the Capital Structure of the Firm. JF, 14 (Mar, 1959), 18-39

Modigliani, F. & Miller, M. H.   The Cost of Capital, Corporation Finance and the Theory of Investment. AER, 48 (Jun, 1958), 261-297

Smith, R.   Cost of Capital in the Oil Industry. Hectograph, Carnegie IT, 1955

Walter, J. E.   The Use of Borrowed Funds. JB, 28 (Apr, 1955), 138-147

Allen, F. B.   Does Going into Debt Lower the 'Cost of Capital'? AJ, 10 (Aug, 1954), 57-61

Weston, J. F.   Norms for Debt Levels. JF, 9 (May, 1954), 124-135

23d COST OF CAPITAL

This section is concerned with general works on the cost of capital. The short book by Lewellen is a useful introduction. Litzenberger & Rao and Budd & Litzenberger offer some consideration of the cost of capital within the context of portfolio theory.

See also:

10*l* Capital Asset Pricing Theory
23c Leverage and Optimal Capital Structure
25c Capital Budgeting—General

Brennan, M. J.   Valuation and the Cost of Capital for Regulated Industries. JF, forthcoming

Budd, A. P. & Litzenberger, R.   Changes in the Supply of Money, the Firm's Market Value and Cost of Capital. JF, forthcoming

Levy, H. & Arditti, F. D.   Valuation, Leverage, and the Cost of Capital in the Cost of Depreciable Assets. JF, forthcoming

Tepper, I.   Revealed Preference Methods and the Pure Theory of the Cost of Capital. JF, forthcoming

Litzenberger, R. H. & Rao, C. U.   Portfolio Theory and Industry Cost-of-Capital Estimates. JFQA, 7 (Mar, 1972), 1443-1462

Elton, E. J. & Gruber, M. J.   Valuation and the Cost of Capital for Regulated Industries. JF, 26 (Jun, 1971), 661-670

Haugen, R. A. & Kroncke, C. O.   Rate Regulation and the Cost of Capital in the Insurance Industry. JFQA, 6 (Dec, 1971), 1283-1305

Litzenberger, R. H. & Rao, C. U.   Estimates of the Marginal Rate of Time Preference and Average Risk Aversion of Investors in Electric Utility Shares, 1960-1966. BellJ, (Spring, 1971), 265-277

Caltagirone, J., Jr.   An Econometric Analysis of Risks and Returns to Common Stock Holders: Behavior of a 65 Company Cross-Section between 1952 and 1965. PhD diss, NYU, 1970

Lockett, A. G. & Tomkins, C.   The Discount Rate Problem in Capital Rationing Situations: a Comment. JFQA, 5 (Jun, 1970), 245-260

Schwartz, E.   The Cost of Capital and Investment Criteria in the Public Sector. JF, 25 (Mar, 1970), 135-142

Vickers, D.   The Cost of Capital and the Structure of the Firm. JF, 25 (Mar, 1970), 35-46

Lewellen, W. G.   The Cost of Capital. Wadsworth Pub, 1969

Sampson, A. A.   Measuring the Rate of Return on Capital. JF, 24 (Mar, 1969), 61-74

Wentz, A. G.   Intrinsic Value and Its Use as a Determinant of Cost of Capital: A Test. PhD diss, Ohio St U, 1969

Fenix y Pil, A. V. J., Jr.   Development Finance and the Cost of Capital. PhD diss, MIT, 1968

Keefe, W. C.   Cost of Capital—Rate of Return. FAJ, 24 (Jul-Aug, 1968), 113-116

Murphy, J. S.   An Empirical Investigation of the Relationship between Interest Rates and Changes in the Stock of Money. PhD diss, St U NY Buffalo, 1968

Samuels, J. M.   An Empirical Study of the Cost of Equity Capital. BR, (Summer, 1968), 12-15

McDonald, J. G.   Valuation of Common Stock and the Cost of Equity Capital. PhD diss, Stanford U, 1967

Mumey, G. A.   Earnings Probabilities and Capital Costs. JB, 40 (Oct, 1967), 450-461

Oster, R. J.   The Cost of Capital and Investment Behavior: A Study of the Opportunity Cost of Investment, Its Determinants, and Its Determination of Business Investment Behavior. PhD diss, U of Cal Berkeley, 1967

Wenglowski, G. M.   Estimates of the Cost of Capital and the Market's Valuation of the Average Utility Firms 1954-1964. PhD diss, U of Pa, 1967

Wright, F. K.   Investment Criteria and the Cost of Capital. JMS, 4 (Oct, 1967), 251-269

Krainer, R. E.   Interest Rates, Investment Decisions and External Financing. OEP, 18 (Nov, 1966), 304-312

Lerner, E. M. & Carleton, W. T.   Financing Decisions of the Firm. JF, 21 (May, 1966), 202-214

Merrett, A. J. & Sykes, A.   Rates of Return Standards: The Cost of Capital. A, 77 (Jan, 1966), 7-14

Ochs, J. N.   The Appropriate Set of Discount Rates for Public Investment Decisions. PhD diss, Indiana U, 1966

Robichek, A. A. & Myers, S. C.   Conceptual Problems in the Use of Risk-Adjusted Discount Rates. JF, 21 (Dec, 1966), 727-730

Latané, H. A. & Tuttle, D. L.   Pure Risk Yields and the Cost of Capital. Paper presented at the Eastern TIMS meeting, Oct 1965

Jeynes, P. H.   Evaluating Cost of Capital. FAJ, 20 (Jul-Aug, 1964), 102-108

Richardson, L. K.   Misconception About Earnings Dilution in Electric Utility Analysis. FAJ, 20 (Sep-Oct, 1964), 58-62

Lintner, J.   The Cost of Capital and Optimal Financing of Corporate Growth. JF, 18 (May, 1963), 302-310

Margoshes, S. L.   Cost of Capital. FAJ, 19 (Jul-Aug, 1963), 49-53

Van Arsdell, P. M.   Considerations Underlying Cost of Capital. FAJ, 19 (Nov-Dec, 1963), 69-76

Weston, J. F.   A Test of Cost of Capital Propositions. SEJ, 30 (Oct, 1963), 105-112

Weston, J. F.   An Appraisal of Recent Contributions to the Theory of the Cost of Capital. Proceedings of the 34th Annual Conference of the Western Economic Association, 1959, 19-22

Cunningham, N.   Business Investment and the Marginal Cost of Funds. Met, (Dec, 1958), 155-181

Dobrovolsky, S. P.   Economics of Corporate Internal and External Financing. JF, 13 (Mar, 1958), 35-47

Durand, D.   Bank Stock Prices and the Bank Capital Problem. Natl Bur Econ Res, 1957

Gordon, M. J. & Shapiro, E.   Capital Equipment Analysis: the Required Rate of Profit. MSci, 3 (Oct, 1956), 102-110

Solomon, E.   Measuring a Company's Cost of Capital. JB, 28 (Oct, 1955), 240-252

Soule, R. P.   Trends in the Cost of Capital. HBR, 31 (Mar-Apr, 1953), 33-47

Part 24 Dividend Policy

24a DIVIDEND DETERMINANTS

Many of the articles in this section were stimulated by Lintner's distributed lag model of dividend payments. Brittain's book provides a good example of a test of the model with aggregate data and the Fama & Babiak article performs a similar service with individual firm data. Watts's article employs the Lintner model to test for a dividend information effect.

Watts, R. The Information Content of Dividends. JB, forthcoming

Higgins, R. C. The Corporate Dividend-Saving Decision. JFQA, 7 (Mar, 1972), 1477-1494

Pogue, T. F. A Cross-Section Study of the Relationship between Dividends and Investment. YEE, 11 (1971), 181-218

Feldstein, M. S. Corporate Taxation and Dividend Behaviour, REStud, 37 (Jan, 1970), 57-72

Shin, S. K. Relative Importance of Cash Flow as a Criterion of Dividend Policy. PhD diss, U of Ill, 1970

Laporte, L. Dividend Policy in the Smaller Company. Natl Ind Conf Bd, 1969

Fama, E. F. & Babiak, H. Dividend Policy: an Empirical Analysis. JASA, 63 (Dec, 1968), 1132-1161

Pogue, T. F. The Corporate Dividend Decision: A Cross-section Study of the Relationship Between Dividends and Investment. PhD diss, Yale U, 1968

Dhrymes, P. J. & Kurz, M. Investment, Dividend, and External Finance Behavior of Firms, *in* Ferber, R. (Ed), Determinants of Investment Behavior. Natl Bur Econ Res, 1967

Jääkeläinen, V. Growth of Earnings and Dividend Distribution Policy. SJE, 69 (Sep, 1967), 184-195

Turnovsky, S. J. The Allocation of Corporate Profits between Dividends and Retained Earnings. REStat, 49 (Nov, 1967), 583-589

Brittain, J. A. Corporate Dividend Policy. Brookings, 1966

Kartchner, E. C. A Distributed Lag Analysis of the Dividends Earnings Relationship of Some Listed, Non-Financial U.S. Corporations. PhD diss, U of Wash, 1966

Waud, R. N. Small Sample Bias Due to Misspecification in the 'Partial Adjustment' and 'Adaptive Expectations' Models. JASA, 61 (Dec, 1966), 1130-1152

Borch, K. Dividend Policies. ST, 79 (Dec, 1965), 183-201

Dhrymes, P. J. & Kurz, M. On the Dividend Policy of Electric Utilities. REStat, 46 (Feb, 1964), 76-81

Thompson, G. C. & Walsh, F. J., Jr. Companies Stress Dividend Consistency. Natl Ind Conf Bd Management Record, 25 (Jan, 1963), 30-36

Dobrovolsky, S. P. Corporate Income Retention, 1915-1943. Natl Bur Econ Res, 1962

Michaelsen, J. B. The Determinants of Dividend Policies: A Theoretical and Empirical Study. PhD diss, U of Chicago, 1961

Stevens, G. Corporation Dividend Payout Ratios and Target Ratios. Cowles Foundation Discussion Paper, Cowles Commission for Research in Economics, Dept of Economics, Yale U, 1961

Darling, P. G.   The Influence of Expectations and Liquidity on Dividend
    Policy. JPE, 65 (Jun, 1957), 209-224
Lintner, J.   Distribution of Incomes of Corporations Among Dividends,
    Retained Earnings and Taxes. AER, 46 (May, 1956), 97-113
Darling, P. G.   A Surrogative Measure of Business Confidence and its
    Relation to Stock Prices. JF, 10 (Dec, 1955), 442-458
Lintner, J.   The Determinants of Corporate Savings, *in* Heller, W. W. et al,
    Savings in the Modern Economy. U of Minn Pr, 1953
Tinbergen, J.   Statistical Testing of Business Cycle Theories II; Business
    Cycles in the United States of America, 1919-1932. Geneva: League of
    Nations Economic Intelligence Service, 1939, (No. 6 in 1939 Volume)
Hart, P. E.   The Time Response of Dividends to Profit. U of Reading,
    Discussion Papers in Economics, No. 3, nd

24b DIVIDEND POLICY AND THE COST OF CAPITAL

Most of the articles in this section were stimulated by Miller & Modigliani's
1961 article on the cost of dividends. Reading should probably include the
two articles by Lintner and the 1959 Gordon article. Brennan's short paper
places the M. & M. hypothesis in the context of capital asset pricing theory.
Porterfield's article constitutes a readable presentation of the M. & M. case.

    See also:

Higgins, R. C.   Dividend Policy and Increasing Discount Rates. JFQA,
    forthcoming
Wallingford, B. A.   An Inter-Temporal Approach to the Optimization of
    Dividend Policy with Predetermined Investments. JF, 27 (Jun, 1972),
    627-636
Brennan, M. J.   A Note on Dividend Irrelevance and the Gordon Valuation
    Model. JF, 26 (Dec, 1971), 1115-1122
Krainer, R. E.   A Pedagogic Note on Dividend Policy. JFQA, 6 (Sep, 1971),
    1147-1154
Magen, S. D.   Cost of Capital and Dividend Policies in Commercial Banks.
    JFQA, 6 (Mar, 1971), 733-746
Mantripragada, K. G.   Stable Dividends and Share Prices. PhD diss, U of
    Minn, 1971
Van Horne, J. C. & McDonald, J. G.   Dividend Policy and New Equity
    Financing. JF, 26 (May, 1971), 507-520
Black, F. & Scholes, M.   Dividend Yield and Common Stock Returns: a New
    Methodology. Paper for the Seminar on the Analysis of Security
    Prices, U of Chicago, Nov 1970
Brennan, M. J.   Investor Taxes, Market Equilibrium and Corporate
    Finance. PhD diss, MIT, 1970
Briston, R. J. & Tomkins, C. R.   Dividend Policy, Shareholder Satisfaction
    and the Valuation of Shares. JBF, 2 (Spring, 1970), 17-24
Edwards, C. E. & Hilton, J. G.   Some Comments on Short-Run Earnings
    Fluctuation Bias. JFQA, 5 (Jun, 1970), 187-202
Higgins, R. C.   Dividend Policy and the Valuation of Corporate Shares
    under Uncertainty. PhD diss, Stanford U, 1969

Plattner, R. H.   Fund Administration and Dividend Policy. QREB, 9 (Summer, 1969), 21-29

Esslen, R.   How Do Dividends Affect Price/Earnings Ratios? FE, (Feb, 1968), 45-50

Loomis, C. J.   A Case for Dropping Dividends. F, (Jun 15, 1968), 181ff

West, R. R. & Bierman, H., Jr.   Corporate Dividend Policy and Preemptive Security Issues. JB, 41 (Jan, 1968), 71-75

Bicksler, J. L.   Empirical Test of the Compatibility of Selected Equity Price Equations with a Descriptive Dividend Model. PhD diss, NYU, 1967

Diamond, J. J.   Earnings Distribution and the Evaluation of Shares: Some Recent Evidence. JFQA, 2 (Mar, 1967), 14-29

Murphy, J. E., Jr.   Return, Payout and Growth. FAJ, 23 (May-Jun, 1967), 91-96

Walter, J. E.   Dividend Policy and Enterprise Valuation. Wadsworth Pub, 1967

Wilson, R.   A Pareto-Optimal Dividend Policy. MSci, 13 (May, 1967), 756-764

Lawson, G. H.   The Cost of Ploughed-Back Profits. BM, 201 (Feb, 1966), 103-113

Kolin, M.   The Relative Price of Corporate Equity with Particular Attention to Investor Valuation of Retained Earnings and Dividends: Tests on Cross-Sections of Industrials, 1951-1957. PhD diss, U of Chicago, 1965

Rubner, A.   The Ensnared Shareholder. Macmillan Int, 1965

Friend, I. & Puckett, M.   Dividends and Stock Prices. AER, 54 (Sep, 1964), 656-682

Lintner, J.   Optimal Dividends and Corporate Growth Under Uncertainty. QJE, 78 (Feb, 1964), 68-71

Baumol, W. J.   On Dividend Policy and Market Imperfection. JB, 36 (Jan, 1963), 112-115

Miller, M. H., & Modigliani, F.   Dividend Policy and Market Valuation: A Reply. JB, 36 (Jan, 1963), 116-119

Walter, J. E.   Dividend Policy: its Influence on the Value of the Enterprise. JF, 18 (May, 1963), 280-291

White, W. L.   The Debt-Equity Ratio, the Dividend Payment Ratio, Growth and the Rate at which Earnings are Capitalized. An Empirical Study. PhD diss, MIT, 1963

Lintner, J.   Dividends, Earnings, Leverage, Stock Prices and the Supply of Capital to Corporations. REStat, 44 (Aug, 1962), 243-269

Fisher, G. R.   Some Factors Influencing Share Prices. EJ, 71 (Mar, 1961), 121-141

Miller, M. H., & Modigliani, F.   Dividend Policy, Growth, and the Valuation of Shares. JB, 34 (Oct, 1961), 411-433

Gordon, M. J.   The Optimum Dividend Rate, *in* Churchman, C. W. & Verhulst, M. (Ed), Management Science, Models and Techniques. Pergamon, 1960

Gordon, M. J.   Dividends, Earnings and Stock Prices. REStat, 41 (May, 1959), 99-105

Porterfield, J. T. S.   Dividends, Dilution and Delusion. HBR, 37 (Nov-Dec, 1959), 56-61

Clendenin, J. C.   What Do Stockholders Like? CMR, 1 (Fall, 1958), 47-55

Shaw, R. B.   Justifiable Invasion of Principal. AJ, 12 (Nov, 1956), 65-67

Walter, J. E.   Dividend Policies and Common Stock Prices. JF, 11 (Mar, 1956), 29-41

Taff, C.   Dividend Omission as a Buying Signal. AJ, 10 (Feb, 1954), 67-70

Harkavy, O.   The Relationship between Retained Earnings and Common Stock Prices for Large Listed Corporations. JF, 8 (Sep, 1953), 283-297

Burrell, O. K.   Dividends vs Retained Earnings as Market Force. CFC, 176 (Aug 21, 1952), 29-30

Robinson, F. A., Jr.   An Inquiry into the Dividend Practices of Industrial Corporations. PhD diss, NYU, 1952

Johnson, L. R.; Shapiro, E. & O'Meara, J.   Valuation of Closely-Held Stock for Federal Tax Purposes: Approach to an Objective Method. U of Pa Law Rev, 100 (Nov, 1951), 166-195

Pastoriza, H.   Valuing Utility Earnings, Distributed and Retained. AJ, 1 (Jul, 1945), 11-15

Kulp, C. A.   The Discounting of Dividends by the Stock Market. U of Pa Pr, 1924

24c EX-DIVIDEND BEHAVIOUR

The magnitude of the price decline on xd dates offers some clue as to the tax status of investors. The most comprehensive study is that of Elton & Gruber, who investigate the relationship between implied tax rate and payout.

See also:

27a Taxation—General

Brealey, R. A.   The Distribution and Independence of Successive Rates of Return in the UK Equity Market. JBF, 2 (Summer, 1970), 29-40

Elton, E. J. & Gruber, M. J.   Marginal Stockholder Tax Rates and the Clientele Effect. REStat, 52 (Feb, 1970), 68-74

Woods, I. R.   Price Behaviour of Ordinary Shares on Ex Div Dates on the Johannesburg Stock Exchange, July 1, 1959 to June 30, 1961. SAJE, 31 (Mar, 1963), 38-59

Durand, D. & May, A. M.   The Ex-Dividend Behavior of American Telephone and Telegraph Stock. JF, 15 (Mar, 1960), 19-31

Readett, P. B. Jr.   The Price Behavior of Stocks on their Ex-Dividend Dates. SM thesis, MIT, 1956

Campbell, J. A. & Beranek, W.   Stock Price Behavior on Ex-Dividend Dates. JF, 10 (Dec, 1955), 425-429

Part 25 Asset Management

25a CASH AND WORKING CAPITAL MANAGEMENT

Useful introductions to these topics are provided by the Orgler, Orr and Beranek books. Important contributions to the theory of cash management include articles by Tobin, Baumol and Miller & Orr (1966).

See also:

18a Liquidity Preference

Chen, A. H-Y.; Jen, C. F. & Zionts, S.   Portfolio Models with Stochastic Cash Demands. JF, forthcoming

Eppen, G. D. & Fama, E. F.   Three Asset Cash Balance and Dynamic Portfolio Problems. MSci, 17 (Jan, 1971), 320-336

Orr, D.   Cash Management and the Demand for Money. Praeger, 1971

Saving, T. R.   Transactions Costs and the Demand for Money. AER, 61 (Jun, 1971), 407-420

Frost, P. A.   Banking Services, Minimum Cash Balances and the Firm's Demand for Money. JF, 25 (Dec, 1970), 1029-1039

Hill, R. W.   Cash Management Techniques. Am Mgmt, 1970

Neave, E. H.   The Stochastic Cash Balance Problem with Fixed Costs for Increases and Decreases. MSci, 16 (Mar, 1970), 472-490

Orgler, Y. E.   Cash Management, Methods and Models. Wadsworth Pub, 1970

Sastry, A. S. R.   The Effect of Credit on Transactions Demand for Cash. JF, 25 (Sep, 1970), 777-781

Eppen, G. & Fama, E. F.   Cash Balance and Simple Dynamic Portfolio Problems with Proportional Costs. IntER, 10 (Jun, 1969), 119-133

Orgler, Y. E.   An Unequal-Period Model for Cash Management Decisions. MSci, 16 (Oct, 1969), B77-B92

Sprenkle, C. M.   The Uselessness of Transaction Demand Models. JF, 24 (Dec, 1969), 835-847

Calman, R. F.   Linear Programming and Cash Management—Cash Alpha. MIT Pr, 1968

Eppen, G. & Fama, E. F.   Solutions for Cash Balance and Simple Dynamic Portfolio Problems.   JB, 41 (Jan, 1968), 94-112

Girgis, N. M.   Optimal Cash Balance Levels. MSci, 15 (Nov, 1968), 130-140

Miller, M. H. & Orr, D.   The Demand for Money by Firms: Extensions of Analytical Results. JF, 23 (Dec, 1968), 735-759

Whalen, E. L.   Extension of the Baumol-Tobin Approach to the Transactions Demand for Cash. JF, 23 (Mar, 1968), 113-134

Baird, B. F.   A Simulated Sensitivity Analysis of Normative Cash Management. PhD diss, U of NC, 1967

Mock, E. J.   The Investment of Corporate Cash. MServ, 4 (Sep-Oct, 1967)

Orgler, Y. E.   Cash Budgeting, the Payment Schedule and Short Term Financing by Business Firms. PhD diss, Carnegie-Mellon U, 1967

Archer, S. H.   A Model for the Determination of Firm Cash Balances. JFQA, 1 (Mar, 1966), 1-11

Baumol, W. J.   The Transactions Demand for Cash: An Inventory Theoretic Approach. QJE, 80 (Feb, 1966), 48-59

Beranek, W.   Working Capital Management.   Wadsworth Pub, 1966

Girgis, N. M.   Optimal Cash Balance Levels. PhD diss, U of Cal Berkeley, 1966

Levy, F. K.   An Application of Heuristic Problem Solving to Accounts
    Receivable Management. MSci, 12 (Feb, 1966), B236-B244
Miller, M. H. & Orr, D.   A Model of the Demand for Money by Firms.
    QJE, 80 (Aug, 1966), 413-435
Orgler, Y. E.   Joint Demand and Time Deposits: an Application of
    Inventory Control. NBR, 14 (Sep, 1966), 73-80
Robichek, A. A.; Teichroew, D. & Jones, J. M.   Optimal Short-Term
    Financing Decision.   MSci, 12 (Sep, 1965), 1-36
Burton, J. C.   The Management of Corporate Liquid Assets. PhD diss,
    Columbia U, 1962
Heston, A. W.   Corporate Cash and Securities Holdings: an Empirical
    Study of Cash, Securities and Other Current Accounts of Large
    Corporations. PhD diss, Yale U, 1962
Heston, A. W.   An Empirical Study of Cash, Securities, and Other Current
    Accounts of Large Corporations. YEE, 2 (Spring, 1962), 116-168
McCall, J. J.   Difference between the Personal Demand for Money and the
    Business Demand for Money. JPE, 68 (Aug, 1960), 358-368
Tobin, J.   The Interest Elasticity of Transactions Demand for Cash.
    REStat, 38 (Aug, 1956), 241-247

25b INTERNAL RATE OF RETURN

The articles in this section are principally concerned with the uniqueness of
the internal rate of return. We draw attention to the pioneering articles of
Samuelson and Lorie & Savage. Fisher and Kaplan (1967) are concerned
with the computation of exact rates of return assuming uniqueness and
Weingartner with the generalised rate of return where interest rates are
not constant.

Norstrøm, C. J.   A Mathematical Connection Between the Present Value
    the Rate of Return and the Scale of an Investment. JBF, 4 (Summer,
    1972), 75-77
Norstrøm, C. J.   A Sufficient Condition for Nonnegative Internal Rate of
    Return. JFQA, 7 (Jun, 1972), 1835-1840
Arrow, K. J. & Levhari, D.   Uniqueness of the Internal Rate of Return with
    Variable Life of Investment. EJ, 79 (Sep, 1969), 560-566
Jean, W. H.   On Multiple Rates of Return. JF, 23 (Mar, 1968), 187-191
Bernhard, R. H.   On the Consistency of the Soper and Sturm-Kaplan
    Conditions for Uniqueness of the Internal Rate of Return. JIEng, 18
    (Aug, 1967), 498
Kaplan, S.   Computer Algorithms for Finding Exact Rates of Return.
    JB, 40 (Oct, 1967), 389-392
Fisher, L.   An Algorithm for Finding Exact Rates of Return. JB, 39
    (Suppl Jan, 1966), 111-118
Kaplan, S.   Solution of the Lorie-Savage and Similar Integer Programming
    Problems by the Generalized Lagrange Multiplier Method. OR, 14
    (Nov-Dec, 1966), 1130-1136
Weingartner, H. M.   The Generalized Rate of Return. JFQA, 1 (Sep, 1966),
    1-29
Kaplan, S.   A Note on a Method for Precisely Determining the Uniqueness
    or Non-uniqueness of the Internal Rate of Return for a Proposed
    Investment. JIEng, 16 (Jan-Feb, 1965)

Teichroew, D; Robichek, A. A. & Montalbano, M.　Mathematical Analysis of Rates of Return Under Certainty.　MSci, 11 (Jan, 1965), 395-403

Bernhard, R. H.　Discount Methods for Expenditure Evaluation—A Clarification of Their Assumptions. JIEng, (Jan-Feb, 1962), 19-27

Lorie, J. H. & Savage, L. J.　Three Problems in Rationing Capital. JB, 28 (Oct, 1955), 229-239

Arnstein, M. G.　A Yardstick for Determining Rate of Return. AJ, 10 (May, 1954), 41-44

Samuelson, P. A.　Some Aspects of the Pure Theory of Capital. QJE, 51 (1937), 469-496

25c CAPITAL BUDGETING—GENERAL

The following section is concerned with general works on capital budgeting. Related studies are listed under sections 25d—'Capital Budgeting Under Uncertainty' and 25e— 'Capital Budgeting with Interrelated Projects'. Useful general textbooks are those of Quirin and Bierman & Smidt, and two British texts on the subject are authored by Merrett & Sykes.

See also:

Dudley, C. L., Jr.　A Note on Reinvestment Assumptions in Choosing between Net Present Value and Internal Rate of Return. JF, 27 (Sep, 1972), 907-916

Pye, G.　Preferential Tax Treatment of Capital Gains, Optimal Dividend Policy and Capital Budgeting. QJE, 86 (May, 1972), 226-242

Wilkes, F. M.　Inflation and Capital Budgeting Decisions. JBF, 4 (Autumn, 1972), 46-53

Bierman, H., Jr. & Smidt, S.　The Capital Budgeting Decision, 3rd ed. Macmillan, 1971

Bierman, H., Jr.　Discounted Cash Flows, Price Level Adjustments and Expectations. AR, 46 (Oct, 1971), 693-699

Jean, W. H.　Terminal Value or Present Value in Capital Budgeting Programs. JFQA, 6 (Jan, 1971), 649-652

Mendelson, M.　A Comment on Payback. JFQA, 6 (Sep, 1971), 1159-1160

Schirger, J. F.　Accounting Constraints on the Capital Budgeting Decision. PhD diss, NYU, 1971

Van Horne, J. C.　A Note on Biases in Capital Budgeting Introduced by Inflation. JFQA, 6 (Jan, 1971), 653-658

Johnson, R. W.　Capital Budgeting. Wadsworth Pub, 1970

Nichols, A.　The Optimal Rate of Investment in a Firm: Comment. JF, 25 (Jun, 1970), 683-684

Oakford, R. V.　Capital Budgeting—a Quantitative Evaluation of Investment Alternatives. Ronald, 1970

Ungar, M.　Rational Entrepreneurial Behavior and the Demand for Investment and Borrowing. PhD diss, Columbia U, 1970

Bromwich, M.　Inflation and the Capital Budgeting Process. JBF, 1 (Autumn, 1969), 39-46

Hirshleifer, J.　Investment, Interest and Capital. P-H, 1969

Jean, W. H.   Capital Budgeting: the Economic Evaluation of Investment Projects. Intex, 1969

Moag, J. S. & Lerner, E. M.   Capital Budgeting Decisions Under Imperfect Market Conditions—a Systems Framework. JF, 24 (Sep, 1969), 613-622

Sarnat, M. & Levy, H.   The Relationship of Rules of Thumb to the Internal Rate of Return: a Restatement and Generalization. JF, 24 (Jun, 1969), 479-490

Schwab, B. & Lusztig, P.   A Comparative Analysis of the Net Present Value and the Benefit-Cost Ratio as Measures of the Economic Desirability of Investments. JF, 24 (Jun, 1969), 507-516

Weingartner, H. M.   Some New Views on the Payback Period and Capital Budgeting Decisions. MSci, 15 (Aug, 1969), B594-B607

Bailey, A. D. & Gray, J.   A Study of the Importance of the Planning Horizon on Reports Utilizing Discounted Future Cash Flows. JAR, 6 (Spring, 1968), 98-105

Bierman, H., Jr.   The Growth Period Decision. MSci, 14 (Feb, 1968), B302-B309

Gupta, S. K. & Rosenhead, J.   Robustness in Sequential Investment Decisions. Msci, 15 (Oct, 1968), B18-B29

Haley, C. W.   The Evaluation of Investment Proposals: An Application to de-novo Branch Offices of Commercial Banks. PhD diss, Stanford U, 1968

House, W. C.   Sensitivity Analysis in Making Capital Investment Decisions. National Association of Accountants, 1968

Kolb, B. A.   Problems and Pitfalls in Capital Budgeting. FAJ, 24 (Nov-Dec, 1968), 170-174

Lerner, E. M. & Rappaport, A.   Limit DCF in Capital Budgeting. HBR, 46 (Sep-Oct, 1968), 133-139

Levy, H.   A Note on the Payback Method. JFQA, 3 (Dec, 1968), 433-444

Maw, J. G.   Return on Investment; Concept and Application. Am Mgmt, 1968

Murdick, R. G. & Deming, D. D.   The Management of Capital Expenditures. McGraw, 1968

Parr, A. F.   Theory of the Capital Decision in the Regulated Firm. PhD diss, U of Ok, 1968

Richardson, R. A.   Financial Forecasting for Capital Budgeting. PhD diss, U of S Cal, 1968

Rockley, L. E.   Capital Investment Decisions: a Manual for Profit Planning. Business Bks, 1968

Sutton, S. S.   An Evaluation of Investment Criteria. PhD diss, G Wash U, 1968

Valenta, J. R.   Capital Equipment Decisions: A Model for Optimal Systems Interfacing. SM thesis, MIT, 1968

Wright, M. G.   Discounted Cash Flow. McGraw, 1968

Brown, G. C.   Discounted Cash Flow Method: Circumstantial Behavior in Capital Budgeting Applications. PhD diss, Ohio St U, 1967

Chambers, D. J.   An Approach to Capital Budgeting. EBR, (May, 1967), 7-11

Diggory, T. G. & Wade, E.   Capital Expenditure. Anbar, 1967

Gould, J. P.   Market Value and the Theory of Investment of the Firm. AER, 57 (Sep, 1967), 910-913

Ijiri, Y.   On the Convergence of Periodic Reinvestments by an Amount Equal to Depreciation. MSci, 13 (Jan, 1967), 321-335

Innes, J. T.   The Role of Capacity Utilization in the Investment Decision. PhD diss, U of Oregon, 1967

Lawson, G. H. & Windle, D. W. Capital Budgeting in the Corporation Tax Regime. JMS, 4 (May, 1967), 189-203

Lawson, G. H. & Windle, D. W. Capital Budgeting and the Use of DCF Criteria in the Corporation Tax Regime. Oliver, 1967

Lerner, E. M. & Carleton, W. T. The Integration of Capital Budgeting and and Stock Valuation: Reply. AER, 57 (Mar, 1967), 220-221

Manne, A. S. (Ed). Investments for Capacity Expansion: Size, Location, and Time-phasing. Allen, 1967

Mathur, G. Investment Criteria in a Platinum Age. OEP, 19 (Jul, 1967), 199-214

National Economic Development Corporation. Investment Appraisal, 2nd ed. HMSO, 1967

Quirin, G. D. The Capital Expenditure Decision. Irwin, 1967

Robichek, A. A. & Van Horne, J. C. Abandonment Value and Capital Budgeting. JF, 22 (Dec, 1967), 577-589

Taylor, D. H. Capital Budgeting Theory as Applied to the Leasing or Purchasing of Capital Assets—with the Emphasis on Computer Equipment. PhD diss, La St U, 1967

Alberts, W. W. Capital Investment by the Firm in Plant and Equipment. JF, 21 (May, 1966), 178-201

Blecke, C. J. Financial Analysis for Decision-Making. P-H, 1966

Ferrara, W. L. Should Investment and Financing Decisions be Separated? AR, 41 (Jan, 1966), 106-114

Jack, A. B. The Capital Expenditure Function. MS, 34 (May, 1966), 133-158

Laya, J. C. A Cash Flow Model and the Rate of Return: the Effect of Price Level Change and Other Factors on Book Yield. PhD diss, Standford U, 1966

Lucas, W. H. An Entity Theory of Capital Budgeting. PhD diss, U of Ala, 1966

Mayer, R. R. Financial Analysis of Investment Alternatives. Allyn, 1966

Meredith, G. G. Capital Investment Decisions: a Manual for Managerial Planning and Control. U of Queensland Pr, 1966

Merrett, A. J. & Sykes, A. Capital Budgeting and Company Finance. Longman, 1966

P. A. Management Consultants Ltd. Expenditure Evaluation Using Discounted Cash Flows: a Course of Programmed Instruction. Business Bks, 1966

Poore, D. M. A Behavioral Analysis of the Short-Range Capital Budgeting Decision Process. PhD diss, U of Pittsburgh, 1966

Vickers, D. Profitability and Reinvestment Rates: A Note on the Gordon Paradox. JB, 39 (Jul, 1966), 366-370

Wilkinson, J. W. An Investment Decision Model for Electric Utility Distribution Facilities. DBA diss, U of Oreg, 1966

Williams, A. C. & Nassar, J. I. Financial Measurement of Capital Investments. MSci, 12 (Jul, 1966), 851-864

Zobian, S. P. Investment Decision Modelling. FAJ, 22 (May-Jun, 1966), 151-155

Duvall, R. M. & Bulloch, J. Adjusting Rate of Return and Present Value for Price Level Changes. AR, 40 (Jul, 1965), 569-573

Hirschmann, W. B. & Brauweiler, J. R. Investment Analysis: Coping with Change. HBR, 43 (May-Jun, 1965), 62-72

Hunt, P. Financial Analysis in Capital Budgeting. Harvard Busn, 1965

Merrett, A. J. Net Present Value versus the Internal Rate of Return Yet Again. SJPE, 12 (Feb, 1965), 116-118

Porterfield, J. T. S. Investment Decisions and Capital Costs. P-H, 1965

Priest, W. W., Jr. Rate of Return as a Criterion for Investment Decisions. FAJ, 21 (Jul-Aug, 1965), 109-113

Sihler, W. W. The Capital Investment Analysis and Decision Process at the Plant Level of a Large, Diversified Corporation. PhD diss, Harvard U, 1965

Teichroew, D.; Robichek, A. A. & Montalbano, M. An Analysis of Criteria for Investment and Financing Decisions Under Certainty. MSci, 11 (Nov, 1965), 151-179

Williams, B. R. & Scott, W. P. Investment Proposals and Decisions. Allen, 1965

Wright, J. F. Some Further Comments on the Ambiguity and Usefulness of Marginal Efficiency as an Investment Criterion. OEP, 17 (Mar, 1965), 81-89

Anderson, W. H. L. Corporate Finance and Fixed Investment: an Econometric Study. Harvard Busn, 1964

Cheng, P. L. & Shelton, J. P. Capital Budgeting: Reply. JF, 19 (Dec, 1964), 671-672

Dyckman, T. R. On the Investment Decision. AR, 39 (Apr, 1964), 285-295

Harvard Business Review. Capital Investment Decisions. (15 articles reprinted from Harvard Business Reviews, 1954 to 1964) Harvard U, 1964

Kohlmeier, J. M. An Analysis of Some Aspects of Capital Budgeting Policy, a Simulation Approach. PhD diss, Harvard U, 1964

Lerner, E. M. & Carleton, W. T. The Integration of Capital Budgeting and Stock Valuation. AER, 54 (Sep, 1964), 681-702

Theil, H. Optimal Decision Rules for Government and Industry. N Holland, 1964

Williams, B. R. Information and Criteria in Capital Expenditure Decisions. JMS, 1 (Sep, 1964), 116-127

Beranek, W. Analysis for Financial Decisions. Irwin, 1963

Kennedy, M. A Critique of Game Theory for Capital Budgeting. NAA, 44 (May, 1963)

Marglin, S. A. Approach to Dynamic Investment Planning. N Holland, 1963

Merrett, A. J. & Sykes, A. The Finance and Analysis of Capital Projects. Longman, 1963

Peterson, D. E. Corporate Investment Decisions and Financial Planning. PhD diss, U of Ill, 1963

Solomon, M. B. Investment Decisions in Small Business. U of Ky Pr, 1963

Turvey, R. Present Value versus Internal Rate of Return: an Essay in the Theory of the Third Best. EJ, 73 (Mar, 1963), 93-98

Wright, J. F. Notes on the Marginal Efficiency of Capital. OEP, 15 (Jul, 1963), 124-129

Gort, M. Systematic Errors in Budgeting Capital Outlays. REStat, 44 (Feb, 1962), 72-75

Nelson, W. G. Could Game Theory Aid Capital Budgeting? NAA, 43 (Jun, 1962)

Reisman, A. & Buffa, E. S. A General Model for Investment Policy. MSci, 8 (Apr, 1962), 304-310

Vandell, R. F. & Vancil, R. F. Cases in Capital Budgeting. Irwin, 1962

Davidson, S. & Drake, D. F. Capital Budgeting and the 'Best' Tax Depreciation Method. JB, 34 (Oct, 1961), 442-452

Fraser, H. W.   A Theory of the Optimum Time Rate of Growth of the Firm. PhD diss, Princeton U, 1961

Haring, J. E.   The Investment Horizon. Met, 13 (Aug, 1961), 77-93

Sunbury, D. H. & Thompson, G. C.   Improving Control over Capital Expenditures. Natl Ind Conf Bd, Conference Board Business Record, 18 (Oct, 1961), 22-33

Walker, R. G.   The Judgment Factor in Investment Decisions. HBR, 39 (Mar-Apr, 1961), 93-99

Anthony, R. N.   Some Fallacies in Figuring Return on Investment. NAA, 42 (Dec, 1960), 5-13

Dean, J.   Management of Capital Expenditures. U of Tex Busn, 1960

Dryden, M. M.   The MAPI Urgency Rating as an Investment Ranking Criterion. JB, 33 (Oct, 1960), 327-341

Kuh, E.   Capital Theory and Capital Budgeting. Met, 12 (Aug-Dec, 1960), 64-80

Ravenscroft, E. A.   Return on Investment: Fit the Method to Your Need. HBR, 38 (Mar-Apr, 1960), 97-109

Terborgh, G. W.   Studies in the Analysis of Business Investment Projects. Machinery and Allied Products Institute and Council for Technological Advancement, 1960-1961

Bailey, M. J.   Formal Criteria for Investment Decisions. JPE, 67 (Oct, 1959), 476-488

Baldwin, R. H.   How to Assess Investment Proposals. HBR, 37 (May-Jun, 1959), 98-104

Bodenhorn, D.   On the Problem of Capital Budgeting. JF, 14 (Dec, 1959), 473-492

Charnes, A.; Cooper, W. W. & Miller, M. H.   Application of Linear Programming to Financial Budgeting and the Costing of Funds. JB, 32 (Jan, 1959), 20-46

Wright, J. F.   The Marginal Efficiency of Capital. EJ, 69 (Dec, 1959), 813-816

Hirshleifer, J.   On the Theory of Optimal Investment Decisions. JPE, 66 (Aug, 1958), 329-352

McLean, J. G.   How to Evaluate New Capital Investments. HBR, 36 (Nov-Dec, 1958), 59-69

Terborgh, G. W.   An Introduction to Business Investment Analysis. Machinery and Allied Products Institute and Council for Technological Advancement, 1958

Bierman, H., Jr. & Smidt, S.   Capital Budgeting and the Problem of Reinvesting Cash Proceeds. JB, 30 (Oct, 1957), 276-279

Osborn, R.   The Mathematics of Investment. Har-Row, 1957

Renshaw, E. F.   A Note on the Arithmetic of Capital Budgeting Decisions. JB, 30 (Jul, 1957), 193-201

Reul, R. I.   Profitability Index for Investments. HBR, 35 (Jul-Aug, 1957), 116-132

Bennion, E. G.   Capital Budgeting and Game Theory. HBR, 34 (Nov-Dec, 1956), 115-123

Solomon, E.   The Arithmetic of Capital Budgeting Decisions. JB, 29 (Apr, 1956), 124-129

Anthony, R. N.   Re: Depreciation in Investment Decisions. HBR, 33 (Jan-Feb, 1955), 75-76

Gordon, M. J.   The Pay-Off Period and the Rate of Profit. JB, 28 (Oct, 1955)

Hill, H. G., Jr.   Capital Expenditures Management. JB, 28 (Oct, 1955), 285-290

Mayer, T.& Sonenblum, S.   Lead Times for Fixed Investment. REStat, 37 (Aug, 1955), 300-304

Norton, F. E.   Administrative Organization in Capital Budgeting. JB, 28 (Oct, 1955), 291-295

Shillinglaw, G.   Residual Values in Investment Analysis. JB, 28 (Oct, 1955), 275-284

Dean, J.   Measuring the Productivity of Capital. HBR, 32 (Jan-Feb, 1954), 120-130

Hoover, E. M.   Some Institutional Factors in Business Investment Decisions. AER, 44 (May, 1954), 201-213

Dean, J.   Capital Budgeting; Top-Management Policy on Plant, Equipment and Product Development. Columbia U Pr, 1951

25d CAPITAL BUDGETING UNDER UNCERTAINTY

Works in this section fall into several groups. The articles by Hertz, Hillier and Paine exemplify the development of simple probabilistic models. Those by Hausmann and Byrne et al. formally incorporate risk into the model in the shape of constraints (for other works on chance constrained programming the reader should consult section 10f—'Safety First, Chance Constrained Portfolios and Minimax'). Finally, other studies, notably that of Hamada, draw on portfolio theory or equilibrium theory to examine the effect of covariance between projects.

See also:

> 23d Cost of Capital
> 25c Capital Budgeting—General
> 25e Capital Budgeting with Interrelated Projects

Bierman, H., Jr. & Hass, J. E.   Capital Budgeting Under Uncertainty—a Reformulation. JF, forthcoming

Schwab, B. & Lustig, P.   A Note on Investment Evaluation in the Light of Uncertain Future Opportunities. JF, forthcoming

Bailey, M. J. & Jensen, M. C.   Risk and the Discount Rate for Public Investment, *in* Jensen, M. C. (Ed), Studies in the Theory of Capital Markets. Praeger, 1972

Bierman, H., Jr. & Hausman, W. H.   The Resolution of Investment Uncertainty through Time. MSci, 18 (Aug, 1972), B654-B662

Keeley, R. & Westerfield, R.   A Problem in Probability Distribution Techniques for Capital Budgeting. JF, 27 (Jun, 1972), 703-710

Greer, W. R.   Sub-Optimization in Capital Investment Decisions Due to Excessive Risk Aversion. PhD diss, U of Mich, 1971

Hamada, R. S.   Investment Decisions with a General Equilibrium Mean-variance Approach. QJE, 85 (Nov, 1971)

Larson, R. B.   The Optimal Choice of Corporate Growth Plans Under Risk. PhD diss, Case WR U, 1971

Laughhunn, D. J. & Peterson, D. E.   Computational Experience with Capital Expenditure Programming Models under Risk. JBF, 3 (Winter, 1971), 43-48

Litzenberger, R. H. & Joy, O. M.   Target Rates of Return and Corporate Asset and Liability Structure under Uncertainty. JFQA, 6 (Mar, 1971), 675-686

Peterson, D. E. & Laughhunn, D. J.   Capital Expenditure Programming and Some Alternative Approaches to Risk. MSci, 17 (Jan, 1971), 320-336

Stapleton, R. C.   Portfolio Analysis, Stock Valuation and Capital Budgeting Decision Rules for Risky Projects. JF, 26 (Mar, 1971), 95-118

Whitmore, G. A. & Darkazanli, S.   A Linear Risk Constraint in Capital Budgeting. MSci, 18 (Dec, 1971), B155-B157

Hammonds, T. M. & Padberg, D. I.   The Risk Factor in Investment Decisions. JASA, 65 (Jun, 1970), 602-612

Kabak, I. W. & Owen, J.   Random Variables, the Time Value of Money and Capital Expenditures. MSci, 17 (Nov, 1970), 142-145

Litzenberger, R. H. & Budd, A. P.   Corporate Investment Criteria and the Valuation of Risk Assets. JFQA, 5 (Dec, 1970), 395-420

Mao, J. C. T.   Models of Capital Budgeting, E-V vs E-S. JFQA, 4 (Jan, 1970), 657-676

Townsend, E. C.   Investment and Uncertainty: a Practical Guide. Oliver, 1970

Jones-Lee, M.   Portfolio Adjustment and Capital Budgeting Criteria JBF, 1 (Autumn, 1969), 47-54

Litzenberger, R. H.   Allocation of Corporate Capital under Uncertainty. PhD diss, U of NC, 1969

Van Horne, J. C.   The Analysis of Uncertainty Resolutions in Capital Budgeting for New Products. MSci, 15 (Apr, 1969), B376-B386

Ziemba, W. T.   A Myopic Capital Budgeting Model. JFQA, 4 (Sep, 1969), 305-328

Bower, R. S.   Comments on 'Capital Budgeting Under Uncertainty'. SJB, (Apr, 1968), 132-138

Hanssman, F.   Operations Research Techniques for Capital Investment. Wiley, 1968

Hanssman, F.   Probability of Survival as an Investment Criterion. MSci, 15 (Sep, 1968), 33-48

Hertz, D. B,   Investment Policies that Pay Off. HBR, 46 (Jan-Feb, 1968), 96-103

Huefner, R. J.   Capital Investment Decisions and Uncertainty: Sensitivity Analysis of the Present Value Model and Evaluation of the Treatment of Uncertainty. PhD diss, Cornell U, 1968

Manne, A. S.   Optimal Dividend and Investment Policies for a Self Financing Business Enterprise. MSci, 15 (Nov, 1968), 119-129

Myers, S. C.   Procedures for Capital Budgeting Under Uncertainty. IMR, 9 (Spring, 1968), 1-20

Salazar, R. C. & Sen, S. K.   A Simulation Model of Capital Budgeting Under Uncertainty. MSci, 15 (Dec, 1968), B161-B179

Spetzler, C. S.   The Explicit Consideration of Uncertainty in Capital Investment Analysis. PhD diss, Ill IT, 1968

Tuttle, D. L. & Litzenberger, R. H.   Capital Budgeting under Uncertainty. SJB, (April, 1968), 119-131

Tuttle, D. L. & Litzenberger, R. H.   Leverage, Diversification and Capital Market Effects on a Risk-Adjusted Capital Budgeting Framework. JF, 23 (Jun, 1968), 427-443

Vaughn, D. E. & Bennett, H.   Adjusting for Risk in the Capital Budget of a Growth-Oriented Company. JFQA, 3 (Dec, 1968), 445-462

Byrne, R.; Charnes, A.; Cooper, W. W. & Kortanek, K.   A Chance Constrained Approach to Capital Budgeting with Portfolio Type Payback and Liquidity Constraints and Horizon Posture Controls. JFQA, 2 (Dec, 1967), 339-364

Harvey, R. K.   A Portfolio Model of Capital Budgeting under Risk. DBA diss, Indiana U, 1967

Klevorick, A. K.   Capital Budgeting Under Risk: a Mathematical-programming Approach. PhD diss, Princeton U, 1967

Naslund, B.   A Model of Capital Budgeting Under Risk. JB, 39 (Apr, 1966), 257-271

Solomon, M. B., Jr.   Uncertainty and its Effect on Capital Investment Analysis. MSci, 12 (Apr, 1966), B334-B339

Van Horne, J. C.   Capital-Budgeting Decisions Involving Combinations of Risky Investments. MSci, 13 (Oct, 1966), B84-B92

Woodfield, L. W.   An Experiment in Application of Monte Carlo Method for Simulating Capital Budgeting Decisions under Uncertainty. PhD diss, Mich St U, 1966

Adelson, R. M.   Criteria for Capital Investment: an Approach through Decision Theory. ORQ, 16 (Mar, 1965), 19-50

Gaver, D. P.   Models for Appraising Investments Yielding Stochastic Returns. MSci, 11 (Jul, 1965), 815-830

Hespos, R. F. & Strassmann, P. A.   Stochastic Decision Trees for the Analysis of Investment Decisions. MSci, 12 (Aug, 1965), B244-B259

Hillier, F. S.   Supplement to the Derivation of Probabilistic Information for the Evaluation of Risky Investments. MSci, 11 (Jan, 1965), 485-487

Iglehart, D. L.   Capital Accumulation and Production for the Firm: Optimal Dynamic Policies. MSci, 11 (Nov, 1965)

Cord, J.   A Method of Allocating Funds to Investment Projects When Returns Are Subject to Uncertainty. MSci, 10 (Jan, 1964), 335-341

Dryden, M. M.   Capital Budgeting: Treatment of Uncertainty and Investment Criteria. SJPE, 11 (Nov, 1964), 235-259

Dyckman, T. R.   Allocating Funds to Investment Projects When Returns are Subject to Uncertainty: a Comment. MSci, 10 (Nov, 1964), 348

Hertz, D. B.   Risk Analysis in Capital Investment. HBR, 42 (Jan-Feb, 1964), 95-106

Hirshleifer, J.   Efficient Allocation of Capital in an Uncertain World. AER, 54 (May, 1964), 77-85

Magee, J. F.   How to Use Decision Trees in Capital Investment. HBR, 42 (Sep-Oct, 1964), 79-96

Paine, N. R.   Uncertainty and Capital Budgeting. AR, 39 (Apr, 1964), 330-332

Hillier, F. S.   Derivation of Probabilistic Information for the Evaluation of Risky Investments. MSci, 9 (Apr, 1963), 443-457

Kaufman, G. M.   Sequential Investment Analysis under Uncertainty. JB, 36 (Jan, 1963), 39-65

Fisher, J. L.   A Class of Stochastic Investment Problems. OR, 9 (Jan-Feb, 1961), 53-65

Hirshleifer, J.   Risk, the Discount Rate, and Investment Decisions. AER, 51 (May, 1961), 112-120

Breiman, L.   Investment Policies for Expanding Businesses'Optimal in a Long-Run Sense. NRLQ, 7 (Dec, 1960), 647-651

25e CAPITAL BUDGETING WITH INTERRELATED PROJECTS

This section embraces both interrelated projects and the special problem of capital rationing. We draw attention to the classical works of Lorie & Savage and Weingartner (1963).

See also:
25c Capital Budgeting—General

Amey, L. R.   Interdependencies in Capital Budgeting: a Survey. JBF, 4 (Autumn, 1972), 70-86

Gould, J. R.   On Investment Criteria for Mutually Exclusive Projects. Ec, 39 (Feb, 1972), 70-77

Myers, S. C.   A Note on Linear Programming and Capital Budgeting. JF, 27 (Mar, 1972), 89-92

Elton, E. J.   Capital Rationing and External Discount Rates. JF, 25 (Jun, 1970) 573-584

Bernhard, R. H.   Mathematical Programming Models for Capital Budgeting-a Survey, Generalization and Critique. JFQA, 4 (Jun, 1969), 111-158

Carleton, W. T.   Linear Programming and Capital Budgeting Models: A New Interpretation. JF, 24 (Dec, 1969), 825-833

Alexander, M. J.   Dynamic Programming and Capital Budgeting Analysis. PhD diss, Georgia St C, 1968

Lusztig, P. & Schwab, B.   A Note on the Application of Linear Programming to Capital Budgeting. JFQA, 3 (Dec, 1968), 427-432

Mao, J. C. T. & Wallingford, B. A.   An Extension of Lawler and Bell's Method of Discrete Optimization with Examples from Capital Budgeting. MSci, 15 (Oct, 1968), B51-B60

Weingartner, H. M.   Capital Budgeting of Interrelated Projects: Survey and Synthesis. MSci, 12 (Mar, 1966), 485-516

Weingartner, H. M.   Criteria for Programming Investment Project Selection. JIE, 15 (Nov, 1966), 65-76

Baumol, W. J. & Quandt, R. E.   Investment and Discount Rates under Capital Rationing—a Programming Approach. EJ, 75 (Jun, 1965), 317-329

Schwartz, E.   A Contribution to the Theory of Capital Budgeting—the Multi-Investment Case—a Comment. JF, 19 (Dec, 1964), 668-670

Cheng, P. L. & Shelton, J. P.   A Contribution to the Theory of Capital Budgeting—the Multi-Investment Case. JF, 18 (Dec, 1963), 622-636

Weingartner, H. M.   Mathematical Programming and the Analysis of Capital Budgeting Problems. P-H, 1963

Hetrick, J. C.   Mathematical Models in Capital Budgeting. HBR, 39 (Jan-Feb, 1961), 49-64

Lorie, J. H. & Savage, L. J.   Three Problems in Rationing Capital. JB, 28 (Oct, 1955), 229-239

25f CAPITAL BUDGETING—POSITIVE STUDIES

In contrast to the normative works in the preceding three sections, the following studies are concerned with explaining observed patterns in corporate investment behaviour. They fall into two broad groups. The first, exemplified by Meyer & Glauber, Meyer & Kuh, and Jorgenson & Siebert, consists of econometric studies of the amount of capital expenditures. The second group consists of investigations of the techniques that firms employ to assess expenditure proposals. The Klammer article is a good introduction to this work.

Klammer, T.   Empirical Evidence of the Adoption of Sophisticated Capital Budgeting Techniques. JB, 45 (Jul, 1972), 387-397

Mao, J. C. T.   Survey of Capital Budgeting: Theory and Practice. JF, 25 (May, 1970), 349-360

Carter, E. E.   A Behavioral Theory Approach to Firm Investment and Acquisition Decisions. PhD diss, Carnegie-Mellon U, 1969

Jorgenson, D. W. & Siebert, C. D.   A Comparison of Alternative Theories of Corporate Investment Behavior. AER, 58 (Sep, 1968), 681-772

Jorgenson, D. W. & Siebert, C. D.   Optimal Capital Accumulation and Corporate Investment Behavior. JPE, 76 (Nov-Dec, 1968), 1123-1151

Jorgenson, D. W. & Siebert, C. D.   Theories of Corporate Investment Behavior. AER, 58 (Sep, 1968), 681-712

La Noue, B. E.   Analysis of the Factors which Affect the Investment Decision: a Case Study. PhD diss, St Louis U, 1968

Evans, M. K.   A Study of Industry Investment Decisions. REStat, 49 (May, 1967), 151-164

Terborgh, G. W.   Business Investment Management. Machinery and Allied Products Institute and Council for Technological Advancement, 1967

Christy, G. A.   Capital Budgeting—Current Practices and their Efficiency. Oregon Busn, 1966

Meyer, J. R. & Glauber, R. R.   Investment Decisions, Economic Forecasting and Public Policy. Harvard Busn, 1964

Istvan, D. F.   Capital Expenditures Decisions: How They Are Made in Large Corporations. Ind U Busn Res, 1961

Meyer, J. R. & Kuh, E.   The Investment Decision: An Empirical Study. Harvard U Pr, 1957

Eisner, R.   Determinants of Capital Expenditures: an Interview Study. U of Ill, Bur of Busn, 1956

White, W. H.   Interest Inelasticity of Investment Demand: The Case from Business Attitude Surveys Re-examined. AER, 46 (Sep, 1956), 565-587

25g LEASING

The following works are concerned with the lease-buy decision. Vancil's article makes a good introduction.

Johnson, R. W. & Lewellen, W. G.   Analysis of the Lease-or-Buy Decision. JF, 27 (Sep, 1972), 815-824

Mitchell, G. B.   After-Tax Cost of Leasing. AR, 45 (Apr, 1970), 308-314

Beechy, T. H.   Quasi-Debt Analysis of Financial Leases. AR, 44 (Apr, 1969), 375-381

Bower, R. S.; Herringer, F. C. & Williamson, J. P.   Lease Evaluation. AR, 41 (Apr, 1966), 257-265

Pettway, R. H.   Interest Rates on Direct Leases and Secured Term Loans. NBR, 3 (Jun, 1966), 533-537

Vancil, R. F.   Lease or Borrow—New Method of Analysis. HBR, 39 (Sep, 1961), 122-136

Part 26 Mergers, Bankruptcies & Reorganisations

26a MERGERS AND ACQUISITIONS—GENERAL

The following works fall principally into three groups. The first consists of empirical studies of the extent and nature of merger activity. These are exemplified by the books by Nelson and McCarthy for the USA and by those of Newbould and Singh for the UK. Other studies, e.g. by Gort and Mossin, represent theoretical attempts to explain the occurrence of mergers. Finally, the section includes a number of works, e.g. the Mace & Montgomery book, which might be regarded as directed at those contemplating acquisition. Two collections of papers on mergers are provided by Alberts & Segall and Samuels.

See also:

26b Mergers and Acquisitions—Profitability
26c Conglomerate Mergers and Corporate Diversification
26d Mergers and Acquisitions—Accounting Issues

Buckley, A.   The Takeover in the Context of a Capital Budgeting Framework. JBF, 4 (Summer, 1972), 37-46

Reddaway, W. B.   An Analysis of Take-Overs. LBR, (Apr, 1972), 8-19

Samuels, J. M. (Ed).   Readings on Mergers and Takeovers. Elek, 1972

Shick, R. A.   The Analysis of Mergers and Aquisitions. JF, 27 (May, 1972), 495-502

Tzoannos, J. & Samuels, J.   Mergers and Takeovers—the Financial Characteristics of Companies Involved. JBF, 4 (Autumn, 1972), 5-16

Jervis, F. R.   The Economics of Mergers. Routledge, 1971

Ramanathan, K. V. & Rappaport, A.   Size, Growth Rates and Merger Valuation. AR, 46 (Oct, 1971), 733-745

Singh, A.   Take-overs: their Relevance to the Stock Market and the Theory of the Firm. Cambridge U Pr, 1971

Jackson, R.   The Consideration of Economies in Merger Cases. JB, 43 (Oct, 1970), 439-447

MacDougal, G. E. & Malek, F. V.   Master Plan for Merger Negotiations. HBR, 48 (Jan-Feb, 1970), 71-82

Newbould, G. D.   Management and Merger Activity. Guthstead, 1970

Woods, D. H. & Caverly, T. A.   Development of a Linear Programming Model for the Analysis of Merger/Acquisition Situations. JFQA, 4 (Jan, 1970), 627-642

Eis, C.   The 1919-1930 Merger Movement in American Industry. JLE, 12 (Oct, 1969), 267-296

Gort, M.   An Economic Disturbance Theory of Mergers. QJE, 83 (Nov, 1969), 624-642

Hunter, A.   Mergers and Industry Concentration in Britain. BNLQR, 22 (Dec, 1969), 372-394

Adaniya, G. A.   Mergers and Acquisitions in Technically-Based Enterprises. SM thesis, MIT, 1968

Eis, C.   The 1919-1930 Merger Movement in American Industry. PhD diss, City U of NY, 1968

Hutchinson, G. S. (Ed).   The Business of Acquisitions and Mergers. Presidents, 1968

Linowes, D. F.   Managing Growth Through Acquisition. Am Mgmt, 1968

Melicher, R. W. An Analysis of Changes in the Merger Valuation Processes of Listed Industrial Corporations During the Current Merger Movement (1950-1966). DBA diss, U of Wash, 1968

Moon, R. W. Business Mergers and Take-Over Bids: a Study of the Post War Pattern of Amalgamations and Reconstructions of Companies, 3rd ed. Gee, 1968

Mossin, J. Merger Agreements: Some Game-theoretic Considerations. JB, 41 (Oct, 1968), 460-471

Parker, J. A. An Investigation of the Ten Most Active Acquisitors in the Paper and Allied Products Industry, 1950-1965. PhD diss, U of Ok, 1968

Pratten, C. F. The Merger Boom in Manufacturing Industry. LBR, 90 (Oct, 1968), 39-55

Silberman, I. H. A Note on Merger Valuation. JF, 23 (Jun, 1968), 528-534

Weston, J. F. A Note on Merger Valuation: Reply. JF, 23 (Jun, 1968), 535-536

Wyatt, A. R. & Kieso, D. E. Mergers, Acquisitions and Considerations. Intext, 1968

Arnfield, R. V. (Ed). Company Mergers and Acquisitions. Proceedings of a National Conference organised by the University of Strathclyde and the Financial Times, Glasgow, Mar, 1967

Hichens, A. Valuing a Company for Acquisition. IA, 17 (May, 1967), 3-10

Holmes, L. M. Corporate Acquisition Patterns. SM thesis, MIT, 1967

Rose, H. B. & Newbould, G. D. The 1967 Take-over Boom. Moorgate, (Autumn, 1967)

Short, R. A. Business Mergers: How and When to Transact Them. P-H 1967

Taussig, R. A. & Hayes, S. L., III. Are Cash Takeover Bids Unethical? FAJ, 23 (Jan-Feb, 1967), 107-111

Alberts, W. W. & Segall, J. E. (Eds). The Corporate Merger. U of Chicago Pr, 1966

Dellenbarger, L. E., Jr. Common Stock Valuation in Industrial Mergers. U of Fla Pr, 1966

Hennessy, J. H. Acquiring and Merging Businesses. P-H, 1966

Merjos, A. Broken Mergers: A Security Analyst Adds Up the Gains and Losses. B, 36 (Mar 21, 1966), 5ff

National Industrial Conference Board. Mergers and Markets: An Economic Analysis of the First Fifteen Years Under the Merger Act of 1950, 5th ed. Natl Ind Conf Bd, 1966

Stacey, N. A. H. Mergers in Modern Business. Hutchinson, 1966

Manne, H. G. Merger and the Market for Corporate Control. JPE, 73 (Apr, 1965), 110-120

Shelton, J. P. An Evaluation of Merger Hedges. FAJ, 21 (Mar-Apr, 1965), 49-52

Wakefield, B. R. Mergers and Acquisitions. HBR, 43 (Sep-Oct, 1965), 6 ff

Young, G. R. et al. Mergers and Acquisitions: Planning and Action. Routledge, 1965

Scharf, C. A. Techniques for Buying, Selling and Merging Businesses. P-H, 1964

American Management Association Report No. 75. Corporate Growth Through Merger and Acquisition. Am Mgnt, 1963

Dellenbarger, L. E. A Study of Relative Common Equity Values in Fifty Mergers of Listed Industrial Corporations, 1950-57. JF, 18 (Sep, 1963), 564-565

Drayton, C. I., Jr.; Emerson, C. & Griswald, J. D. Mergers and Acquisitions: Planning and Action. Fin Exec, 1963

Heflebower, R. B.   Corporate Mergers: Policy and Economic Analysis. QJE, 77 (Nov, 1963), 537-558

Holsen, R. C.   Another Look at Business Combinations. JA, 116 (Jul, 1963), 67

Kinard, H. Y.   Financing Mergers and Acquisitions. FE, 31 (Aug, 1963), 13-16

McCarthy, G. D.   Acquisitions and Mergers. Ronald, 1963

Weinberg, M. A.   Take-overs and Amalgamations. Sweet, 1963

Ansoff, H. I. & Weston, J. F.   Merger Objectives and Organizational Structure. QREB, 2 (Aug, 1962), 51-52

Folz, D. F. & Weston, J. F.   Looking Ahead in Evaluating Proposed Mergers. NAA, 43 (Apr, 1962), 17-27

Healy, K. T.   The Merger Movement in Transportation. AER, 52 (May, 1962), 436-444

Mace, M. L. & Montgomery, G. E., Jr.   Management Problems of Corporate Acquisitions. Harvard Busn, 1962

Reilly, F. K.   What Determines the Ratio of Exchange in Corporate Mergers. FAJ, 18 (Nov-Dec, 1962), 47-50

Wright, L. T.   Some Financial Aspects of Recent Corporation Mergers and Consolidations. PhD diss, Am U, 1962

McCarthy, G. D.   Premeditated Merger. HBR, 39 (Jan-Feb, 1961), 74-82

Cook, P. W.   Thinking Ahead: Trends in Merger Activity. HBR, 37 (Mar-Apr, 1959), 15-20

Graichen, R. E.   Buying and Selling a Corporate Business. JA, 107 (Apr, 1959), 45-53

Kottke, F. J.   Mergers of Large Manufacturing Companies: 1951 to 1959. REStat, 41 (Nov, 1959), 430-433

Nelson, R. L.   Merger Movements in American Industry 1895-1956. (Dist by Princeton U Pr) Natl Bur Econ Res, 1959

American Management Association.   Report No. 4. Corporate Mergers and Acquisitions: Basic Financial, Legal and Policy Aspects. Am Mgmt, 1958

Sommers, H. M.   Estate Taxes and Business Mergers. JF, 13 (May, 1958), 201-210

American Management Association.   Financial Management Series, No. 114. Legal, Financial and Tax Aspects of Mergers and Acquisition. Am Mgmt, 1957

American Management Association.   Financial Management Series, No. 115. A Case Study in Corporate Acquisition. AM Mgmt, 1957

Mueller, W. F.   A Comment on the FTC's Report on Mergers with Special Reference to Dairy Mergers. JFE, 39 (Feb, 1957), 140-152

Berman, D. S.   Using Tax Laws to Help Finance Corporate Acquisitions. AJ, 12 (May, 1956), 119-121

Stigler, G. J.   The Statistics of Monopoly and Merger. JPE, 64 (Feb, 1956), 33-40

Abbott, C. C.   Fundamental Factors Causing Bank Mergers and Branch Banking. AJ, 11 (Jun, 1955), 151-153

Bosland, C. C.   Stock Valuation in Recent Mergers. TE, 94 (Jun, 1955), 516 ff

Kaplan, A. D. H.   The Current Merger Movement Analysed. HBR, 33 (May-Jun, 1955), 391-398

Nutter, G. W.   Growth by Merger. JASA, 49 (Sep, 1954), 448-466

Weston, J. F.   The Role of Mergers in the Growth of Large Firms. U of Cal Pr, 1953

Weston, J. F.   The Recent Merger Movement. JB, 25 (Jan, 1952), 30-38
Butters, J. K.; Lintner, J. & Cary, W. L.   Effects of Taxation on Corporate
Mergers. Harvard Busn, 1951
Stigler, G. J.   Monopoly and Oligopoly by Merger. AER, 40 (May, 1950)
United States Trade Commission.   The Merger Movement: A Summary
Report. US Govt, 1948
United States Trade Commission.   Present Trend of Corporate Mergers
and Aquisitions. US Govt, 1947

26b MERGERS AND ACQUISITIONS—PROFITABILITY

The following studies provide empirical evidence of the profitability of
growth through merger. Good examples of this work are the articles by
Hogarty and Lev & Mandelker.

See also:

26a Mergers and Acquisitions—General

Haugen, R. A. & Udell, J. G.   Rates of Return to Stockholders of Acquired
Companies. JFQA, 7 (Jan, 1972), 1387-1398
Lev, B. & Mandelker, G.   The Microeconomic Consequences of Corporate
Mergers. JB, 45 (Jan, 1972), 85-104
Gort, M. & Hogarty, T. F.   New Evidence on Mergers. JLE, 13 (Apr, 1970),
167-184
Hogarty, T. F.   The Profitability of Corporate Mergers. JB, 43 (Jul, 1970),
317-327
Briloff, A. J.   The 'Funny-Money' Game. FAJ, 25 (May-Jun, 1969), 73-79
Johnson, H. W. & Simon, J. L.   The Success of Mergers: the Case of Adver-
tising Agencies. OIS, 31 (1969), 139-144
Kuehn, D. A.   Stock Market Valuation and Acquisitions: an Empirical
Test of One Component of Managerial Utility. JIE, 17 (Apr, 1969), 132-
144
Block, S. B.   The Effect of Mergers and Acquisitions on the Market Value
of Common Stock. PhD diss, La St U, 1968
Reid, S. R.   Mergers, Managers, and the Economy. McGraw, 1968
Segall, J. E.   Merging for Fun and Profit. IMR, 9 (Winter, 1968), 17-30
Bacon, P. W.   An Analysis of Bank Mergers in Marion County, Indiana,
1945 to 1960. DBA diss, U of Indiana, 1967
Kelly, E. M.   The Profitability of Growth Through Mergers. Pa St U,
Center for Research of the College of Business Administration, 1967
Kitching, J.   Why Do Mergers Miscarry? HBR, 45 (Nov-Dec, 1967), 84-101
Cohen, K. J. & Reid, S. R.   The Benefits and Costs of Bank Mergers.
JFQA, 1 (Dec, 1966), 15-57
Weiss, L. W.   An Evaluation of Mergers in Six Industries. REStat, 47
(May, 1965), 172-181
Sapienza, S. R.   Business Combinations: A Case Study. AR, 91 (Jan, 1963),
91-101
Reid, S. R.   Corporate Mergers and Acquisitions Involving Firms in
Missouri: Some Economic Results and Administrative Policies and
Procedures. PhD diss, St Louis U, 1962
Cook, P. L.   Effects of Mergers: Six Studies. Allen, 1958
Markham, J. W.   Survey of the Evidence and Findings on Mergers, *in*
Business Concentration and Price Policy. (Dist by Princeton U Pr)
Natl Bur Econ Res, 1955

Livermore, S.   The Success of Industrial Mergers. QJE, 49 (Nov, 1935), 68-95

Dewing, A. S.   A Statistical Test of the Success of Consolidations. QJE, 36 (Nov, 1921), 84-101

26c CONGLOMERATE MERGERS AND CORPORATE DIVERSIFICATION

Many of the studies in this section are concerned with the rationale for corporate diversification. Good instances of this work are the articles by West, Levy & Sarnat and Lewellen. Empirical studies of the performance of conglomerates are exemplified by Lorie & Halpern and Lynch.

See also:

Schall, L. D.   Asset Valuation, Firm Investment, and Firm Diversification. JB, 45 (Jan, 1972), 11-28

Hutchins, R. C.   Measurement of Multicompany Diversification. PhD diss, U of S Cal, 1971

Lewellen, W. G.   A Pure Financial Rationale for the Conglomerate Merger. JF, 26 (May, 1971), 521-537

Lynch, H. H.   Financial Performance of Conglomerates. Harvard Busn, 1971

Treadway, P. T.   An Explanation of the Conglomerate Merger Movement—the Conglomerate as a Result of Forces Arising in the Capital Markets. PhD diss, U of NC, 1971

Wood, T. D.   A Study of the Behavioral Characteristics of Conglomerates. PhD diss, U of Fla, 1971

Alberts, W. W.   The Profitability of Conglomerate Investment Mergers: Sources and Prospects. UWBR, (Winter, 1970), 13-27

Levy, H. & Sarnat, M.   Diversification, Portfolio Analysis and the Uneasy Case for Conglomerate Mergers. JF, 25 (Sep, 1970), 795-802

Lorie, J. H. & Halpern, P.   Conglomerates: The Rhetoric and the Evidence. JLE, 13 (Apr, 1970), 149-166

Pratten, C. F.   A Case Study of a Conglomerate Merger. Moorgate, (Spring, 1970), 27-54

Rankin, D. F.   Security-based Conglomerate Acquisitions: the Effect on Residual Ownership. PhD diss, U of Miss, 1970

Shapiro, D. L.   Conglomerate Mergers and Optimal Investment Policy. JFQA, 4 (Jan, 1970), 643-656

Betty, W. P.   The Valuation of Conglomerate Companies. PhD diss, N Tex St U, 1969

Goudzwaard, M. B.   Conglomerate Mergers, Convertibles and Cash Dividends. QREB, 9 (Spring, 1969), 53-62

Mueller, D. C.   A Theory of Conglomerate Mergers. QJE, 83 (Nov, 1969), 643-659

Smith, K. V. & Schreiner, J. C.   A Portfolio Analysis of Conglomerate Diversification. JF, 35 (Jun, 1969), 413-427

Westerfield, R.   The Capital Asset Pricing Model: an Analysis of the Performance of Conglomerates. U of Pa Pr, 1969

May, M. M.   The Earnings Per Share Trap. FAJ, 24 (May-Jun, 1968), 113-117

Renshaw, E. F.   The Theory of Financial Leverage and Conglomerate
   Mergers. CMR, 11 (Fall, 1968), 79-84
Narver, J. C.   Conglomerate Mergers and Market Competition. U of Cal
   Pr, 1967
O'Hanlon, T.   The Odd News about Conglomerates. F, (Jun 15, 1967),
   175-177
West, R. R.   'Homemade' Diversification vs Corporate Diversification.
   JFQA, 2 (Dec, 1967), 417-420
Turner, D. F.   Conglomerate Mergers and Section 7 of the Clayton Act.
   HLR, 78 (May, 1965), 1313-1395
Schachner, L. L.   Corporate Diversification Policies. PhD diss, NYU, 1964
Gort, M.   Diversification and Integration in American Industry. Princeton
   U Pr, 1962
Hamman, R. L.   Theory of Investment of the Diversified Corporation.
   PhD diss, Harvard U, 1961
Ansoff, H. I.   A Model for Diversification. MSci, 4 (1958)

26d MERGERS AND ACQUISITIONS—ACCOUNTING ISSUES

This section contains a small selection of articles on the accounting aspects
of mergers, notably on the purchase/pooling decision.

   See also:

      26a Mergers and Acquisitions—General

Fraedrich, K. E.   Accounting for Business Combinations. PhD diss, U of
   Wis, 1969
Lauver, R. C.   The Case for Pooling. AR, 41 (Jan, 1966), 65-74
Parker, W. M.   Business Combinations and Accounting Valuation. JAR, 4
   (Autumn, 1966), 149-154
Schachner, L. L.   Equitable Accounting for Goodwill Upon Merger. FE, 34
   (Mar, 1966), 53-54
Terrell, J. H.   Mergers and Consolidations: The Role of Accounting in the
   Management-Decision Process. PhD diss, U of Tex, 1966
Maher, C. L.   Corporate Acquisitions—Tax Accounting Consequences.
   NAA, 46 (Mar, 1965), 50-54
Mosich, A. N.   Impact of Merger Accounting on Post-Merger Financial
   Records. MA, 97 (Dec, 1965), 21-28
Jaenicke, H. R.   Business Combinations: The Criteria for Distinguishing
   Purchases from Poolings of Interests and their Present Day Applica-
   bility. PhD diss, U of Pa, 1963
Mosich, A. N.   An Evaluation of Purchase and Pooling Concepts of Account-
   ing for Corporate Mergers and Acquisitions. PhD diss, UCLA, 1963
Wyatt, A. R.   A Critical Study of Accounting for Business Combinations,
   Accounting Research Study No. 5. New York: American Institute of
   Certified Public Accountants, 1963
Jaenicke, H. R.   Management's Choice to Purchase or Pool. AR, 37 (Oct,
   1962), 758-765
Lee, R. E., Jr.   Acquisition of a Business: Accounting and Financial As-
   pects. Taxes, 49 (Feb, 1962), 147-152
Sapienza, S. R.   Distinguishing Between Purchase and Pooling. JA, 111
   (Jun, 1961), 35-40
Barr, A.   Accounting for Business Combinations. AR, 34 (Apr, 1959), 175-
   181

Blough, C. M.　Business Combination: 'Pooling' or Purchase? JA, 104
(Jul, 1957), 55-56

26e TENDER OFFERS

The following theses are concerned with predicting or assessing the price
effects of cash tender offers.

See also:

26a Mergers and Acquisitions—General

Yamashita, G. A.　Cash Tender Offers: a Predictive Model. PhD diss
Columbia U, 1970

Oliver, R. B.　Cash Tender Offers. MBA thesis, NYU, 1969

26f SIZE OF COMPANY

The bulk of the works in this section are concerned with the effect on profitability of company size. UK studies are exemplified by Samuels & Smyth
and Whittington. The studies by Stekler and Hall & Weiss are good examples
of US work.

See also:

26c Conglomerate Mergers and Corporate Diversification

Elliott, J. W.　Control, Size, Growth and Financial Performance in the Firm.
JFQA, 7 (Jan, 1972), 1309-1320

Whittington, G.　The Prediction of Profitability and Other Studies of
Company Behaviour. Cambridge U Pr, 1971

Gupta, M. C.　The Effect of Size, Growth, and Industry on the Financial
Structure of Manufacturing Companies. JF, 24 (Jun, 1969), 517-529

Marcus, M.　Profitability and Size of the Firm: Some Further Evidence.
REStat, 51 (1969), 104-107

Samuels, J. M. & Smyth, D. J.　Profits, Variability of Profits and Firm
Size. Ec, 35 (May, 1968), 127-139

Hall, M. & Weiss, L. W.　Firm Size and Profitability. REStat, 49 (Aug,
1967), 319-331

Mermelstein, D.　Large Industrial Corporations and Asset Share Maintenance, 1909-1964. PhD diss, Columbia U, 1967

Archer, S. H. & Faerber, L. G.　Firm Size and the Cost of Equity Capital.
JF, 21 (Mar, 1966), 69-83

Quandt, R. E.　On the Size Distribution of Firms. AER, 56 (Jun, 1966),
416-432

Dyckman, T. R. & Stekler, H. O.　Firm Size and Variability. JIE, 13 (Jun,
1965), 214-218

Steindl, J.　Random Processes and the Growth of Firms. Griffin, 1965

Stekler, H. O.　The Variability of Profitability with Size of Firm, 1947-
1958. JASA, 59 (Dec, 1964), 1183-1193

Stekler, H. O.　Profitability and the Size of Firm. U of Cal Pr, 1963

Hart, P. E.　The Size and Growth of Firms. Ec, 42 (Feb, 1962), 29-39

Morgan, E. V. & Taylor, C.　The Relationship between Size of Joint Stock
Companies and the Yield of their Shares. Ec, 24 (1957), 116-127

Prais, S. J. The Financial Experience of Giant Companies. EJ, 67 (Jun, 1957), 249-264

Osborn, R. C. Efficiency and Profitability in Relation to Size. HBR, 29 (Mar, 1951), 82-94

Osborn, R. C. Effects of Corporate Size on Efficiency and Profitability. U of Ill Bur of Busn, 1950

Osborn, R. C. The Relative Profitability of Large, Medium Sized and Small Business. AR, (Oct, 1950)

Alexander, S. S. The Effect of Size of Manufacturing Corporations on the Distribution of Rate of Return. REStat, 17 (Aug, 1949), 229-235

Blair, J. M. The Relation Between Size and Efficiency of Business. REStat, 24 (Aug, 1942), 125-135

Crum, W. S. Corporate Size and Earning Power. Harvard U Pr, 1939

Somers, H. B. A Comparison of Rates of Earnings of Large Scale and Small Scale Industries. QJE, 46 (May, 1932), 465-479

Epstein, R. H. Profits and the Size of the Firm in the Automobile Industry, 1919-1927. AER, 21 (Dec, 1931)

26g BANKRUPTCY AND REORGANISATIONS

This section is principally concerned with the predictions of corporate bankruptcy. The articles by Beaver and Altman (1968) are good instances of this work. Altman's later articles also provide some information on the performance of the stocks of bankrupt companies.

See also:

10n Accounting and Market Determined Risk Measures
19f Bond and Stock Ratings
19g Bonds—Return as a Function of Default Risk

Dascher, P. E. The Penn Central Revisited: a Predictable Situation. FAJ, 28 (Mar-Apr, 1972), 61-64

Edmister, R. O. An Empirical Test of Financial Ratio Analysis for Small Business Failure Prediction. JFQA, 7 (Mar, 1972), 1477-1494

Gordon, M. J. Towards a Theory of Financial Distress. JF, 26 (May, 1971), 347-356

Edmister, R. O. Financial Ratios as Discriminant Predictors of Small Business Failure. PhD diss, Ohio St U, 1970

Meyer, P. A. & Pifer, H. W. Prediction of Bank Failures. JF, 25 (Sep, 1970), 853-868

Altman, E. I. Bankrupt Firms' Equity Securities As an Investment Alternative. FAJ, 25 (Jul-Aug, 1969), 129-133

Altman, E. I. Corporate Bankruptcy Potential, Stockholder Returns and Share Valuation. JF, 24 (Dec, 1969), 887-900

Altman, E. I. Financial Ratios, Discriminant Analysis and the Prediction of Corporate Bankruptcy. JF, 23 (Sep, 1968), 589-609

Altman, E. I. The Prediction of Corporate Bankruptcy: a Discriminant Analysis. PhD diss, UCLA, 1968

Beaver, W. H. Market Prices, Financial Ratios and the Prediction of Failure. JAR, 6 (Autumn, 1968), 179-192

Beaver, W. H. Financial Ratios as Predictors of Business Failure. PhD diss, U of Chicago, 1966

Laughlin, E. J. Creditors' Rights in Corporate Reorganization: a Financial Approach. PhD diss, U of Ill, 1965

Nadler, M. Corporate Consolidations and Reorganizations. New York: Alexander Hamilton Institute, 1930

26h PROXY CONTESTS

The Duvall & Austin article provides an interesting attempt to discriminate between successful and unsuccessful proxy contests.

Duvall, R. M. & Austin, D. V. Predicting the Results of Proxy Contests. JF, 20 (Sep, 1965), 464-471

Austin, D. V. The Causes of Proxy Contests: An Empirical Study, 1959-1960. PhD diss, U of Indiana, 1964

Von Mehren, R. B. & McCarroll, J. C. The Proxy Rules: A Case Study in Administrative Process. LCP, 29 (Jun, 1964), 728-748

Part 27 Taxation

27a TAXATION—GENERAL

We have sought to confine Part 27 to works in which the principal interest
is the effect of taxation on financial decision making. Incidental discussions
of taxation are listed according to the context of the discussion. Jolivet's
evidence on investor tax rates is supplemented by material listed under
24c—'Ex-Dividend Behaviour'. Useful material on the effect of taxes on
investors is provided by Holland and Butters et al. Some interesting evidence of the response of corporations to changes in tax structure is provided by Feldstein, Feldstein & Flemming and Hall & Jorgenson.

Rose, H. B.   Some Aspects of the New Tax System. IA, 33 (Sep, 1972), 3-11

Colin, J. W. & Dyl, E. A.   Calculation of Tax Effective Yields: a Correction.
JFQA, 6 (Sep, 1971), 1163-1164

Feldstein, M. S. & Flemming, J. S.   Tax Policy, Corporate Saving and Investment Behaviour in Britain. REStud, 38 (1971), 415-434

Christensen, L. R.   Tax Policy and Investment Expenditures in a Model of
General Equilibrium. AER, 60 (May, 1970), 18-22

Whittaker, J.   Minimising the Burden of the Dollar Premium. IA, 24
(Oct, 1969), 26-33

Hall, R. E. & Jorgenson, D. W.   Tax Policy and Investment Behavior. AER,
57 (Jun, 1967), 391-414

Henderson-Stewart, D. J.   Implications of Personal Taxation for Corporate
Investment Decisions. SM thesis, MIT, 1967

Lepper, S. J.   Effects of Alternative Tax Structures on Individuals' Holdings of Financial Assets, *in* Hester, D. D. & Tobin, J. E. (Eds), Risk
Aversion and Portfolio Choice. Wiley, 1967

Reeves, J. P.   Tax Aspects of Corporate Mergers, Exchanges, Redemptions, Liquidations, and Reorganisations. Vantage, 1967

Bittker, B. I.   Federal Income Taxation of Corporations and Shareholders,
2nd ed. Fed Tax Pr, 1966

Edwards, J. W.   The Effects of Federal Income Taxes on Capital Budgeting. PhD diss, Mich St U, 1966

Jolivet, V.   The Weighted Average Marginal Tax Rate on Dividends Received by Individuals in the U.S. AER, 56 (Jun, 1966), 473-477

Schneider, H. M. & Wintrub, W. G.   Tax Savings Opportunities in Securities
Transactions. Lybrand, 1966

Barnes, L.   Tax Relativity: The Missing 'X' Factor in Stock and Portfolio
Evaluation. FAJ, 21 (Jan-Feb, 1965), 70-74

Brittain, J. A.   The Tax Structure and Corporate Dividend Policy. AER,
54 (May, 1964), 272-287

Ott, D. J. & Meltzer, A. H.   Federal Tax Treatment of State and Local
Securities. Brookings, 1963

Riggs, H. E.   The Economics of 'Tax Switching'. FAJ, 19 (Sep, 1963), 25-31

Wakely, M. A. H. et al. (Eds).   Federal Income Taxation of Banks and
Financial Institutions. Boston: The Banking Law Journal, 1963

Holland, D. M.   Dividends under the Income Tax. Princeton U Pr, 1962

Smeets, M. J. H.   The Influence of Taxes on the Capital Market. ABQR, 133
(1961), 3-16

Holland, D. M.   The Income-Tax Burden on Stockholders. (Dist by Princeton U Pr) Natl Bur Econ Res, 1958

American Management Association. Management and Taxes Report Series, No. 10. Growth Expansion From the Tax Viewpoint. Am Mgmt, 1956

Butters, J. K. Taxation Incentives and Financial Capacity. AER, 44 (May, 1954), 504-519

Lintner, J. Effect of Taxation on Real Investment. AER, 44 (May, 1954), 520-534

Stockfisch, J. A. Common Stock Financing and Tax Capitalization. NTJ, 7 (Jun, 1954), 182-186

Butters, J. K.; Thompson, L. E. & Bollinger, L. L. Effects of Taxation on Investments by Individuals. Harvard Busn, 1953

Smith, D. T. Effects of Taxation: Corporate Financial Policy. Harvard Busn, 1952

27b THE EFFECT OF TAXATION ON RISK TAKING

The articles in this section derive from Domar & Musgrave's early suggestion that a proportional tax increases risk taking. We draw attention to the contributions of Richter, Mossin, Feldstein and Leland (listed elsewhere).

See also:

27a Taxation—General

Stiglitz, J. Taxation, Risk Taking and the Allocation of Investment in a Competitive Economy, *in* Jensen, M. C. (Ed), Studies in the theory of Capital Markets. Praeger, 1972

Feldstein, M. S. The Effects of Taxation on Risk Taking. JPE, 77 (Jul-Aug, 1969), 755-764

Shibata, A. N. Effects of Taxation on Risk Taking. AER, 59 (May, 1969), 553-561

Mossin, J. Taxation and Risk-Taking: an Expected Utility Approach. Ec, 35 (Feb, 1968), 74-82

Naslund, B. Some Effects of Taxes on Risk Taking. REStat, 35 (1968), 289-306

Bierwag, G. O. & Grove, M. A. Portfolio Selection and Taxation. OEP, 19 (Jul, 1967), 215-221

Penner, R. G. A Note on Portfolio Selection and Taxation. REStud, 31 (Jan, 1964), 83-86

Richter, M. K. Cardinal Utility, Portfolio Selection and Taxation. REStud, 27 (Jun, 1960), 152-166

Brown, E. C. Mr Kaldor on Taxation and Risk Bearing. REStud, 25 (1957), 49-52

Streeten, P. The Effect of Taxation on Risk-Bearing. OEP, 5 (1953), 271-287

Domar, E. D. & Musgrave, R. A. Proportional Income Taxation and Risk-Taking. QJE, 58 (May, 1944), 388-422

27c CORPORATION TAX

A number of the works in this section are concerned with the extent to which firms can shift the burden of corporation tax. The article by Cragg et al. is a useful introduction. Most of the remainder are concerned with the effect of corporation tax on investment activities.

See also:

27a Taxation—General

Oakland, W. H. Corporate Earnings and Tax Shifting in U.S. Manufacturing, 1930-1968. REStat, 54 (Aug, 1972), 235-244

Tambini, L. Financial Policy and the Corporation Income Tax. PhD diss U of Chicago, 1968

Cragg, J. G.; Harberger, A. C. & Mieszkowski, P. Empirical Evidence on the Incidence of the Corporation Income Tax. JPE, 75 (Dec, 1967), 811-821

Rose, H. B. Corporation Tax and Share Prices—Some Reflections on 'Supply' Factors. IA, 19 (Dec, 1967), 3-9

Krzyzaniak, M. (Ed). Effects of Corporation Income Tax. Wayne St U Pr, 1966

Alessi, L. De. The Incidence of Corporate Income Tax: the Stock Price Approach. PF, 20 (1965), 263-271

Krzyzaniak, M. & Musgrave, R. A. The Shifting of the Corporation Income Tax: an Empirical Study of the Short Run Effect upon the Rate of Return. Johns Hopkins, 1963

Harberger, A. C. The Incidence of the Corporation Income Tax. JPE, 70 (Jun, 1962), 215-240

Clark, C. D. A Note on Investment Activities and the Graduated Corporate Tax. JF, 12 (Mar, 1957), 44-50

Smith, D. T. Corporate Taxation and Common Stock Financing. NTJ, 6 (Sep, 1953), 209-225

27d CAPITAL GAINS TAX

Most of the following articles are concerned with the lock-in effects of capital gains tax. The work is exemplified by Rose in the UK and by Sprinkel & West and Holt & Shelton (1962) in the USA

See also:

27a Taxation—General

Haugen, R. A. & Wichern, D. The Diametric Effects of the Capital Gains Tax on the Stability of Stock Prices. JF, forthcoming

De Wulf, L. Taxation of Unrealised Capital Gains: Theoretical and Empirical Analysis. PhD diss, Clark U, 1970

Brown, H. A. Jr. & Nichols, D. R. A Deterrent to Investment Mobility. FAJ, 25 (May-Jun, 1969), 131-137

Hughes, P. F. & Tingley, K. R. Taxation of Capital Gains, 2nd ed. Taxation, 1969

Rose, H. B. Investment Policy and Capital Gains Tax. IA, 20 (Jun, 1968), 3-14

Marshall, D. C. Federal Income Tax Treatment of Capital Gains and Losses. PhD diss, La St U, 1967

Sophian, T. J. The Taxation of Capital Gains. Butterworths, 1967

Joseph, A. W. The Yield on a Loan Subject to Capital Gains Tax. JIASS, 18 (Oct, 1966)

McClung, N. The Distribution of Capital Gain on Corporate Shares by Holding Time. REStat, 48 (Feb, 1966), 40-50

Bizley, M. T. L. Yields on Redeemable Securities Subject to Capital Gains Tax. JIASS, 17 (1965)

Merrett, A. J.   The Capital Gains Tax. LBR, 78 (Oct, 1965), 1-14

Vowels, R. C.   An Evaluation of Equity and Economic Effects in Capital Gains Taxation. PhD diss, Am U, 1964

Malkiel, B. G. & Kane, E. J.   U.S. Tax Law and the Locked-In Effect. NTJ, 16 (Dec, 1963), 389-396

Holt, C. C. & Shelton, J. P.   The Lock-In Effect of the Capital Gains Tax. NTJ, 15 (Dec, 1962), 337-352

Shelton, J. P.   Influence of the Six-Month Capital Gains Rule on Short Term Transactions. FAJ, 18 (Sep, 1962), 99-101

Sprinkel, B. W. & West, B. K.   Effects of Capital Gains Taxes on Investment Decisions. JB, 35 (Apr, 1962), 122-134

Holt, C. C. & Shelton, J. P.   The Implications of the Capital Gains Tax for Investment Decisions. JF, 16 (Dec, 1961), 559-580

Steiger, W.   The Taxation of Unrealized Capital Gains and Losses: A Statistical Study. NTJ, 10 (Sep, 1957)

Gemmill, R. F.   The Effect of the Capital Gains Tax on Asset Prices. NTJ, 9 (1956)

AUTHOR INDEX

In the following pages works are listed in alphabetical order of first authors. Where several works are by the same author they are listed in alphabetical order of title. Cross-references are included for works by multiple authors. Appended to each reference is the number of the subject heading under which the work has been classified.

Abbott, C. C. (Ed).   Basic Research in Finance: Needs and Prospects. U Pr of Va, 1966; -4a, 22a

    Fundamental Factors Causing Bank Mergers and Branch Banking. AJ, 11 (Jun, 1955), 151-153; -26a

Aby, C. D.   An Investigation of the Concept of Public Participation as a Basis for Forecasting Stock Market and Security Trends. PhD diss, La St U, 1968; -13b

Adams, D. F.   The Effect on Stock Price from Listing on the New York Stock Exchange. MBA thesis, NYU, 1965; -2f

Adamson, A. & Coorey, M. G.   The Valuation of Company Shares and Businesses. Law Book, 1966; -7a

Adaniya, G. A.   Mergers and Acquisitions in Technically-Based Enterprises. SM thesis, MIT, 1968; -26a

Adderley, T. E. & Hayes, D. A.   The Investment Performance of Selected Growth Stock Portfolios: 1939-55, AJ, 13 (May, 1957), 65-76; -7b

Adelson, R. M.   Criteria for Capital Investment: an Approach Through Decision Theory. ORQ, 16 (Mar, 1965), 19-50; -25d

Adler, M.   On Risk-Adjusted Capitalization Rates and Valuation by Individuals. JF, 25 (Sep, 1970), 819-836; -10l

    On the Risk-Return Trade-Off in the Valuation of Assets. JFQA, 4 (Dec, 1969), 493-512; -10l

Advisory Committee on Endowment Management.   Managing Educational Endowments: Report to the Ford Foundation. Ford, 1969; -3j

Agmon, T. B.   Interrelations Among Equity Markets—a Study of Share Price Movements in the United States, United Kingdom, Germany and Japan. PhD diss, U of Chicago, 1971; -10i

    The Relations Among Equity Markets: a Study of Share Price Co-Movements in the United States, United Kingdom, Germany and Japan. JF, 27 (Sep, 1972), 839-856; -10i

Agnew, N. H., et al.   An Application of Chance Constrained Programming to Portfolio Selection in a Casualty Insurance Firm. MSci, 15 (Jun, 1969), B512-B520; -10f

Agrawal, K. P.   Share Prices and Corporate Dividends. IJE, 43 (1963), 347-362; -7a

Aharoni, Y. & Ophir, T.   Accounting for Linked Loans. JAR, 5 (Spring, 1967), 1-26; -18c

Ahearn, D. S.   Investment Management and Economic Research. FAJ, 20 (Jan-Feb, 1964), 15-20; -6a

Ahlers, D. M.   SEM: a Security Evaluation Model, *in* Cohen, K. J. & Hammer, F. S. (Eds), Analytical Methods in Banking. Irwin, 1966; -7c

    & Steglitz, M.   The Use and Misuse of Security Evaluation Models. Paper for the Seminar on the Analysis of Security Prices, U of Chicago, May, 1968; -7c

Aigner, D. J. & Bryan, W. R.   A Model of Short-Run Bank Behavior. QJE, 85 (Feb, 1971), 97-118; -3f

Aitchison, J. & Brown, J. A. C.   The Lognormal Distribution. Cambridge U Pr, 1957; -11b

Alberts, W. W.   Capital Investment by the Firm in Plant and Equipment. JF, 21 (May, 1966), 178-201; -25c

    The Profitability of Conglomerate Investment Mergers: Sources and Prospects. UWBR, (Winter, 1970), 13-27; -26c

    & Segall, J. E.   The Corporate Merger. U of Chicago Pr, 1966; -26a

Alchian, A. A.   The Meaning of Utility Measurement. AER, 43 (Mar, 1953), 26-50; -9a

The Rate of Interest, Fisher's Rate of Return over Cost and Keynes' Internal Rate of Return. AER, 45 (Dec, 1955), 938-943; -18b

& Kessel, R. A.   Redistribution of Wealth Through Inflation. Sc, 130 (Sep 4, 1959), 535-539; -6c

See also **Kessel, R. A. & Alchian, A. A.**

Alderfer, C. P., & Bierman, H. Jr.   Choices with Risk: Beyond the Mean and Variance. JB, 43 (Jul, 1970), 341-353; -9b, 10m

Alessi, L. De.   The Incidence of Corporate Income Tax: the Stock Price Approach. PF, 20 (1965), 263-271; -27c

Alexander, M. J.   Dynamic Programming and Capital Budgeting Analysis. PhD diss, Georgia St C, 1968; -25e

Alexander, S. S.   The Effect of Size of Manufacturing Corporations on the Distribution of Rate of Return. REStat, 17 (Aug, 1949), 229-235; -26f

Price Movements in Speculative Markets: Trends or Random Walks. IMR, 2 (May, 1961), 7-26; -11c

Price Movements in Speculative Markets: Trends or Random Walks, Number 2. IMR, 5 (Spring, 1964), 25-46; -11c

Aliber, R. Z.   More about Counter-Speculation in the Forward Exchange Markets. JPE, 71 (Dec, 1963), 589-590; -21b

Speculation and Price Stability Once Again. JPE, 72 (Dec, 1964), 607-609; -9e

Speculation in the Foreign Exchanges: the European Experience, 1919-1926. PhD diss, Yale U, 1961; -21b

Allen, F. B.   Does Going into Debt Lower the 'Cost of Capital'? AJ, 10 (Aug, 1954), 57-61; -23c

Allerdice, F. B. & Farrar, D. E.   Factors that Affect Mutual Fund Growth. JFQA, 2 (Dec, 1967), 365-382; -3k

Allison, S. L.

See **Heins, A. J. & Allison, S. L.**

Alms, E. W.

See **Warren, J. P. & Alms, E. W.**

Alten, K. W.   A New Tool for Security Analysis. AJ, 12 (Aug, 1956), 78-83; -8c

Altman, E. I.   Bankrupt Firms' Equity Securities as an Investment Alternative. FAJ, 25 (Jul-Aug, 1969), 129-133; -26g

Corporate Bankruptcy Potential, Stockholder Returns and Share Valuation. JF, 24 (Dec, 1969), 887-900; -26g

Financial Ratios, Discriminant Analysis and the Prediction of Corporate Bankruptcy. JF, 23 (Sep, 1968), 589-609; -26g

The Prediction of Corporate Bankruptcy: a Discriminant Analysis. PhD diss, UCLA, 1968; -26g

& Schwartz, R. A.   Common Stock Price Volatility Measures and Patterns. JFQA, 4 (Jan, 1970), 603-626; -10b

Altman, O. L.   Euro-dollars. Finance and Development, IMF, 1967; -20d

Euro-dollars: Some Further Comments. IMF, 12 (Mar, 1965), 1-16; -20d

The Integration of European Capital Markets. JF, 20 (May, 1965), 209-221; -20e

American Bankers Association.   The Commercial Banking Industry: a Monograph Prepared for the Commission on Money and Credit. P-H, 1962; -3f

American Management Association.   Financial Management Series,

No. 115: A Case Study in Corporate Acquisition. Am Mgmt, 1957; -26a

Report No. 75. Corporate Growth Through Merger and Acquisition. Am Mgmt, 1963; -26a

Report No. 4. Corporate Mergers and Acquisitions: Basic Financial, Legal and Policy Aspects. Am Mgmt, 1958; -26a

Management and Taxes Report Series, No. 10. Growth Expansion From the Tax Viewpoint. Am Mgmt, 1956; -27a

Financial Management Series, No. 114. Legal, Financial and Tax Aspects of Mergers and Acquisitions. Am Mgmt, 1957; -26a

Sources and Methods of International Financing: Practical Guide for U.S. Investors and Traders. Am Mgmt, 1961; -20e

Amey, L. R.   Interdependencies in Capital Budgeting: a Survey. JBF, 4 (Autumn, 1972), 70-86; -25e

Amling, F.   Investments: an Introduction to Analysis and Management, 2nd ed. P-H, 1970; -4a

Amoroso, L.   Do Shares Reach Equity at the Market Rate of Interest? EI, 14 (May, 1961), 189-196; -10l

Amsterdam-Rotterdam Bank & Others.   Capital Markets in Europe: a Study of Markets in Belgium, West Germany, the Netherlands and the UK. The Banks, 1966; -2c

Andersen, T. A.   Trends in Profit Sensitivity. JF, 18 (Dec, 1963), 637-646; -6b

Anderson, M. A.   Fundamentals and Technicalities of Commodity Futures Trading. Hutton, 1949; -21a

Anderson, R. C.   The Term Structure of Interest Rates: a Portfolio Analysis. PhD diss, Claremont, 1968; -18f

Anderson, W. H. L.   Corporate Finance and Fixed Investment: an Econometric Study. Harvard Busn, 1964; -25c

Anderson, W. M.   Group Accumulation Through Equities for Pensions. JF, 17 (May, 1962), 194-202; -3i

Andrew, S. L. & Flinn, H. M.   Appraisal of Economic Forecasts. JASA (Suppl Mar, 1930), 36-41; -15a

Andrews, V. L.   Pension Funds in the Securities Markets. HBR, 37 (Nov-Dec, 1959), 90-102; -3i

The Supply of Loanable Funds from Non-Insured Corporate State- and City-Administered Employee Pension Funds. JF, 16 (May, 1961), 328-350; -3i

See also **Hunt, P. & Andrews, V. L.**

Angell, J. W.   Uncertainty, Likelihoods and Investment Decisions. QJE, 74 (Feb, 1960), 1-28; -9c

Ansoff, H. I.   A Model for Diversification. MSci, 4 (1958); -26c

& **Weston, J. F.**   Merger Objectives and Organizational Structure. QREB, 2 (Aug, 1962), 51-52; -26a

Anthony, R. N.   Some Fallacies in Figuring Return on Investment. NAA, 42 (Dec, 1960), 5-13; -25c

Re: Depreciation in Investment Decisions. HBR, 33 (Jan-Feb, 1955), 75-76; -25c

See also **Masson, R. L.; Hunt, P. & Anthony, R. N.**

Antliff, J. C. & Freund, W. C.   Some Basic Research into Historical Results Under Pension Plans with Benefits Based on Common Stock Performance. JF, 22 (May, 1967), 169-191; -3i

Apilado, V. P.

See **Gies, T. G. & Apilado, V. P.**

Aranyi, J. Portfolio Diversification. FAJ, 23 (Sep-Oct, 1967), 133-139; -10e

Archer, S. H. Common Stocks as an Inflation Hedge. FAJ, 16 (Sep-Oct, 1960), 41-45; -6c

Diversification and Risk Reduction. UWBR, (Apr-Jun, 1964), 19-25; -10e

A Model for the Determination of Firm Cash Balances. JFQA, 1 (Mar, 1966), 1-11; -25c

The Structure of Management Decision Theory. AMJ, (Dec, 1964), 269-287; -9c

The Theoretical Value of a Stock Right. JF, 11 (Sep, 1956), 363-366; -16b

& **D'Ambrosio, C. A.** Business Finance: Theory and Management, 2nd ed. Macmillan, 1972; -22a

& **D'Ambrosio, C. A. (Eds).** The Theory of Business Finance: A Book of Readings. Macmillan, 1967; -1b

& **Faerber, L. G.** Firm Size and the Cost of Equity Capital. JF, 21 (Mar, 1966), 69-83; -26f

See also **Evans, J. L. & Archer, S. H.**

See also **Francis, J. C. & Archer, S. H.**

Arditti, F. D. Another Look at Mutual Fund Performance. JFQA, 6 (Jun, 1971), 909-912; -10m, 14a

Risk and the Required Return on Equity. JF, 22 (Mar, 1967), 19-36; -7c, 10*l*

See also **Levy, H. & Arditti, F. D.**

Arena, J. J. Postwar Stock Market Changes and Consumer Spending. REStat, 47 (Nov, 1965), 379-391; -7d

Armstrong, F. E. The Book of the Stock Exchange, 5th ed. Pitman, 1961; -2a

The Case for Mutual Fund Management. FAJ, 16 (May, 1960), 33-38; -3k

Armstrong, T. H. Stock Option Warrants. AJ, 10 (May, 1954), 89-91; -17b

Armstrong, W. E. Uncertainty and the Utility Function. EJ, 58 (Mar, 1948), 1-10; -9a

Arndt, S. W. International Short Term Capital Movements: a Distributed Lag Model of Speculation in Foreign Exchange. Em, 36 (Jan, 1968), 59-70; -21b

Arnfield, R. V. (Ed). Company Mergers and Acquisitions. Proceedings of a National Conference organised by the University of Strathclyde and the Financial Times, Glasgow, Mar, 1967; -26a

Arnstein, M. G. A Yardstick for Determining Rate of Return. AJ, 10 (May, 1954), 41-44; -25b

Aronson, J. R.

See **Schwartz, E. & Aronson, J. R.**

Arrow, K. J. Alternative Approaches to the Theory of Choice in Risk Taking Situations. Em, 19 (Oct, 1951), 404-437; -9c

Aspects of the Theory of Risk Bearing. Jahnssonin, 1965; -9a

Comment on the Portfolio Approach to the Demand for Money and other Assets. REStat, 45 (Suppl Feb, 1963), 24-27; -18a

The Role of Securities in the Optimal Allocation of Risk-Bearing. REStud, 31 (Apr, 1964), 91-96; -9d

Uncertainty and the Welfare Economics of Medical Care. AER, 53 (Dec, 1963), 941-973; -9d

& Levhari, D. Uniqueness of the Internal Rate of Return with Variable Life of Investments. EJ, 79 (Sep, 1969), 560-566; -25b

Ascher, L. W. Dollar Averaging in Theory and Practice. FAJ, 16 (Sep-Oct, 1960), 51-53; -12f

Selecting Bonds for Capital Gains. FAJ, 27 (Mar-Apr, 1971), 74-79; -19a

Ashby, A. W. On Forecasting Commodity Prices by the Balance-Sheet Approach. JFE, 46 (Aug, 1964), 633-743; -21a

Ashley, J. W. Stock Prices and Changes in Earnings and Dividends: Some Empirical Results. JPE, 70 (Feb, 1962), 82-85; -8d, 11a

Association of Certified & Chartered Accountants. Sources of Capital. The Association, nd; -23g

Atkinson, T. R. The Pattern of Financial Asset Ownership: Wisconsin Individuals. (Dist by Princeton U Pr) Natl Bur Econ Res, 1956; -3b

Trends in Corporate Bond Quality. (Dist by Columbia U Pr) Natl Bur Econ Res, 1967; -19g

Aumann, R. J. Existence of Competitive Equilibria in Markets with a Continuum of Traders. Em, 34 (Jan, 1966), 1-17; -9d

Auster, R.
See **Lerner, E. M. & Auster, R.**

Austin, D. V. The Causes of Proxy Contests: an Empirical Study, 1959-1960. PhD diss, U of Indiana, 1964; -26h
See also **Duvall, R. M. & Austin, D. V.**

Auten, J. H. Counter-Speculation and the Forward Exchange Market. JPE, 69 (Feb, 1961), 49-55; -21b

Monetary Policy and the Forward Exchange Market. JF, 16 (Dec, 1961), 546-558; -21b

Axelrad, L. I. Over-the-Counter Market: Its Organization, Its Problems. FAJ, 18 (Nov-Dec, 1962), 71-73; -2b

Ayres, H. F. Risk Aversion in the Warrant Markets. IMR, 4 (Fall, 1963), 45-53; -17b

Babcock, G. C. The Concept of Sustainable Growth. FAJ, 26 (May-Jun, 1970), 108-114; -8c

A Note on Justifying Beta as a Measure of Risk. JF, 27 (Jun, 1972), 699-702; -10b

The Trend and Stability of Earnings per Share. Paper for the Seminar on the Analysis of Security Prices, U of Chicago, Nov, 1970; -8c

Bachelier, L. Théorie de la Speculation. Docteur des Sciences Mathematiques diss, University of Paris, 1900. Originally published in Annales de l'Ecole Normale Superieure, Sec. 3, 1900, 21-86. English translation by A. J. Boness: Theory of Speculation, *in* Cootner, P. H. (Ed), The Random Character of Stock Market Prices. MIT Pr, 1964; -11c, 17a

Backer, M. Financial Reporting and Security Investment Decisions. FAJ, 27 (Mar-Apr, 1971), 67ff; -8e

Bacon, P. W. An Analysis of Bank Mergers in Marion County, Indiana, 1945 to 1960. DBA diss, U of Indiana, 1967; -26b

& Winn, E. L. The Impact of Forced Conversion on Stock Prices. JF, 24 (Dec, 1969), 871-874; -17c

Badger, R. E. & Coffman, P. B. The Complete Guide to Investment Analysis. McGraw, 1967; -4a

Baer, J. B. & Saxon, O. G. Commodity Exchanges and Futures Trading. Har-Row, 1949; -21a

Bagehot, W. (pseud for Treynor, J. L.)   The Only Game in Town. FAJ, 27 (Mar-Apr, 1971), 12ff; -2b

Risk and Reward in Corporate Pension Funds. FAJ, 28 (Jan-Feb, 1972) 80-84; -3i

Bailey, A. D. & Gray, J.   A Study of the Importance of the Planning Horizon on Reports Utilizing Discounted Future Cash Flows. JAR, 6 (Spring, 1968), 98-105; -25c

Bailey, M. J.   Formal Criteria for Investment Decisions. JPE, 67 (Oct, 1959), 476-488; -25c

& Jensen, M. C.   Risk and the Discount Rate for Public Investment, *in* Jensen, M. C. (Ed), Studies in the Theory of Capital Markets. Praeger, 1972; -25d

Bailey, W. G.   Some Points on Equity-Linked Contracts. JIA, 88 (1962); -3h

Baird, B. F.   A Simulated Sensitivity Analysis of Normative Cash Management. PhD diss, U of NC, 1967; -25a

Baker, A. W.   Sterling Certificates of Deposit. IA, 28 (Dec, 1970), 23-26; -20a

Baker, G.   The Martin Report: Blueprint for Constructive Reform. FAJ, 27 (Nov-Dec, 1971), 20 ff; -2b

Baker, J. C.   The German Stock Market. Praeger, 1970; -2c

Shareownership in Germany. BT (Winter, 1968), 46-52; -3a

Baldwin, R.   Conventional Principal and Income Accounting and Its Effect on Institutional Investment Policy. FAJ, 25 (Mar-Apr, 1970), 60-67; -3e

Baldwin, R. H.   How to Assess Investment Proposals. HBR, 37 (May-Jun, 1959), 98-104; -25c

Baldwin, R. R.   An Approximate Formula for the Yield on Bonds Selling Close to Par. AJ, 14 (Aug, 1958), 77; -19a

Baldwin, W. L. & Velk, T. J.   Uncertainty of the Income Stream in the Modigliani-Miller Model. QREB, 8 (Winter, 1968), 39-43; -23c

Ball, M.   Investment Company Performance. FAJ, 17 (Sep-Oct, 1961), 51-58; -14a

Ball, R. E. (Ed).   Readings in Investments. Allyn, 1965; -1b

& Melnyk, Z. L. (Eds).   Theory of Managerial Finance: Selected Readings. Allyn, 1967; -1b

Ball, R. J.   Some Econometric Analyses of the Long-Term Rate of Interest in the United Kingdom 1921-1961. MS, 33 (Jan, 1965), 45-96; -18b

Inflation and the Theory of Money. Allen, 1964; -18c

Ball, R. J.   Risk, Return and Disequilibrium: An Application to Changes in Accounting Techniques. JF, 27 (May, 1972), 343-354; -8e

& Brown, P.   An Empirical Evaluation of Accounting Income Numbers. JAR, 6 (Autumn, 1968), 159-178; -8d, 11a

& Brown, P.   Some Preliminary Findings on the Association Between the Earnings of a Firm, its Industry and the Economy. ERA, (1967), 55-57; -8b

& Watts, R.   Some Time Series Properties of Accounting Income. JF, 27 (Jun, 1972), 663-682; -8a

Ballam, S. H., Jr.   Preferred Stocks—They Can Be Attractive Investments. AJ, 11 (Nov, 1955), 53-57; -19i

Ballinger, W.   See **Simpson, K. & Ballinger, W.**

Bank Administration Institute.   Measuring the Investment Performance of Pension Funds. BAI, 1968; -14b

Bank of England.   The Euro-Currency Business of Banks in London. BEQB, 10 (Mar, 1970), 31-49; -20d

214

The Financial Institutions.
Part 1: BEQB, 10 (Dec, 1970), 419-431
Part 2: BEQB, 11 (Mar, 1971), 48-71
Part 3: BEQB, 11 (Jun, 1971), 199-210; -3e
The International Capital Markets of Europe. BEQB, 10 (Sep, 1970), 295-307; -20e

Barbour, J. F.   An Analysis of the Conclusions of the Cowles Studies with Respect to the Dow Theory. AJ, 4 (4th Qtr, 1948), 11-20; -12c

Barges, A.   The Effect of Capital Structure on the Cost of Capital. P-H, 1963; -23c
Growth Rates and Debt Capacity. FAJ, 24 (Jan-Feb, 1968), 100-104; -23c

Barish, N. N. & Siff, F. H.   Operational Gaming Simulation with Application to a Stock Market. MSci, 15 (Jun, 1969), B530-B541; -4f

Barker, C. A.   Effective Stock Splits. HBR, 34 (Jan-Feb, 1956), 101-106; -16c
Evaluation of Stock Dividends. HBR, 36 (Jul-Aug, 1958), 99-114; -16c
Price Changes of Stock Dividend Shares at Ex-Dividend Dates. JF, 14 (Sep, 1959), 373-378; -16c
Stock Splits in a Bull Market. HBR, 35 (May-Jun, 1957), 72-79; -16c

Barlow, R.
See **Morgan, J.; Barlow, R. & Brazer, H.**

Barnea, A. & Downes, D. H.   A Re-examination of the Empirical Distribution of Stock Price Changes. Unp ms, 1971; -11b

Barnes, L.   Is the Stock Market Getting More Stable? AJ, 12 (Feb, 1956), 21-22; -10b
Tax Relativity: The Missing 'X' Factor in Stock and Portfolio Evaluation. FAJ, 21 (Jan-Feb, 1965), 70-74; -27a
What Difference Does Knowledge Make to Investors? FAJ, 21 (Sep-Oct, 1965), 60-68; -5a

Barney, W.   An Investigation of Parametric Variations in a Moving Average Investment Rule. SM thesis, MIT, 1964; -12d

Baron, D.
See **McDonald, J. G. & Baron, D.**

Baron, D. C.   The Interrelationship between Money Supply, Interest Rates and Stock Prices. SM thesis, MIT, 1967; -6d

Barr, A.   Accounting for Business Combinations. AR, 34 (Apr, 1959), 175-181; -26d

Barrett, M. E.   APB Opinion Number 18: a Move Toward Preferences of Users. FAJ, 28 (Jul-Aug, 1972), 47-55; -8e

Barrett, R. J.; Gray, M. R. & Parkin, J. M.   The Demand for Financial Assets by the Personal Sector of the U.K. Economy. Man U mimeo, Jun, 1972; -3b

Barry, E. P.   The Financing of Stock Issues with Pre-emptive Rights, 1943-1948. Shields & Co, 1948; -16b

Bartell, R., Jr.
See **Robinson, R. I. & Bartell, R., Jr.**

Barton, A. D.
See **Wright, F. K.; Young, I. C. & Barton, A. D.**

Barton, C. E.   Equity Investment and Participating Life Assurance. JIASS, 17 (Jul, 1965); -3h

Basch, A.   Capital Markets of the European Economic Community: Problems of Integration. U of Mich Busn Res, 1965; -20e

    & Kybal, M.   Capital Markets in Latin America. Praeger, 1970; -2c

Baskin, E. F. & Crooch, G. M.   Historical Rates of Return on Investments in Flat Bonds. FAJ, 24 (Nov-Dec, 1968), 95-97; -19b

Bates, G. E.   Investment Management: a Casebook. McGraw, 1959; -1c

Baty, G. B.   Optimum Linear Prediction in Speculative Markets. PhD diss, MIT, 1967; -7a

Bauer, J.   A Diffusion Index as Applied to Price Movement in the Stock Market. SM thesis, MIT, 1964; -12e

Baughn, W. H.

    See **Walker, E. W. & Baughn, W. H.**

Baum, D. J.   Should the Size of Mutual Funds Be Limited? II, 1 (Apr, 1967); -3k

    & Stiles, N. B.   The Silent Partners—Institutional Investors and Corporate Control. Syracuse U Pr, 1965; -3e

Bauman, W. S.   Estimating the Present Value of Common Stocks by the Variable Rate Method. U of Mich Busn Res, 1963; -7b

    Evaluation of Prospective Investment Performance. JF, 23 (May, 1968), 276-295; -14a

    Investment Analysis: Science or Fiction? FAJ, 23 (Jan-Feb, 1967), 93-97; -4a

    Investment Experience with less Popular Stocks. DBA diss, Indiana U, 1961; -4a

    Investment Experience With Less Popular Common Stocks. FAJ 20 (Mar-Apr, 1964), 79-88; -7a

    Investment Returns and Present Values. FAJ, 25 (Nov-Dec, 1969), 107-120; -7b

    The Investment Value of Common Stock Earnings and Dividends. FAJ, 21 (Nov-Dec, 1965), 98-104; -7b

    The Less Popular Stocks versus the Most Popular Stocks. FAJ, 21 (Jan-Feb, 1965), 83-89; -7a

    & Klein, T. A.   Investment Profit Correlation. U of Mich Busn Res, 1968; -7c

    See also **Slovic, P.; Fleissner, D. & Bauman, W. S.**

Baumol, W. J.   An Expected Gain-Confidence Limit Criterion for Portfolio Selection. MSci, 9 (Oct, 1963), 174-182; -10f

    Mathematical Analysis of Portfolio Selection. FAJ, 22 (Sep-Oct, 1966), 95-99; -10c

    On Dividend Policy and Market Imperfection. JB, 36 (Jan, 1963), 112-115; -24b

    Stock Market and Economic Efficiency. Fordham, 1965; -2b

    Speculation, Profitability and Stability. REStat, 39 (Aug, 1957), 263-271; -9e

    The Transactions Demand for Cash: An Inventory Theoretic Approach. QJE, 80 (Feb, 1966), 48-59; -25a

    Heim, P; Malkiel, B. G. & Quandt, R. E.   Earnings Retention, New Capital and the Growth of Firms. REStat, 52 (Nov, 1970), 345-355; -23b

    & Malkiel, B. G.   The Firm's Optimal Debt-Equity Combination and the Cost of Capital. QJE, 81 (Nov, 1967), 547-578; -23c

    Malkiel, B. G. & Quandt, R. E.   The Valuation of Convertible Securities. QJE, 80 (Feb, 1966), 48-59; -17c

    & Quandt, R. E.   Investment and Discount Rates under Capital Rationing—a Programming Approach. EJ, 75 (Jun, 1965), 317-329; -25e

Baynes, T. A. H.   Share Valuations. Heinemann, 1966; -7a

Baxter, N. D.   The Commercial Paper Market. Econometric Research Program Memorandum, 69. Princeton U, 1964; -20a

     Leverage, Risk of Ruin and the Cost of Capital. JF, 22 (Sep, 1967), 395-403; -23c

     Marketability, Default Risk and Yields on Money Market Instruments. JFQA, 3 (Mar, 1968), 75-86; -20a

     & Cragg, J. G.   Corporate Choice among Long-term Financing Instruments. REStat, 52 (Aug, 1970), 225-235; -23b

     See also **Cragg, J. G. & Baxter, N. D.**

Beach, P. R.   Equity Values and Corporate Debt in the Capital Structure. PhD diss, Brown U, 1970; -23c

Beach, T. E.

     See **Miller, P. F. Jr. & Beach, T. E.**

Bear, R. M.   Martingale Movements in Commodity Markets. PhD diss, U of Indiana, 1970; -21a

     See also **Stevenson, R. A. & Bear, R. M.**

Beaver, W. H.   Financial Ratios as Predictors of Business Failure. PhD diss, U of Chicago, 1966; -26g

     The Information Content of Annual Earnings Announcements. ERA, (1968), 67-100; -8d

     Market Prices, Financial Ratios and the Prediction of Failure. JAR, 6 (Autumn, 1968), 179-192; -26g

     The Time Series Behavior of Earnings. ERA, (1970), 62-107; -8a

     & Dukes, R. E.   Interperiod Tax Allocation, Earnings Expectations and the Behavior of Security Prices. AR, 47 (Apr, 1972), 320-332; -8c

     Kettler, P. & Scholes, M.   The Association Between Market Determined and Accounting Determined Risk Measures. AR, 45 (Oct, 1970), 654-682; -10n

Beazer, W. F.   Optimization of Bank Portfolios and Response to Monetary Policy. PhD diss, Northwestern U, 1965; -10g

Becker, S. W. & Brownson, F. O.   What Price Ambiguity? Or the Role of Ambiguity in Decision Making. JPE, 72 (Feb, 1964), 62-73; -9c

     & Weil, R. L.   Experimental Determination of Risk Preferences for Portfolio Selection. Paper for the Seminar on the Analysis of Security Prices, U of Chicago, Nov, 1970; -9b

Beckhart, B. H. (Ed).   Banking Systems: a Definitive Comparison and Authoritative Account of the Banking Systems of Sixteen Countries. Columbia U Pr, 1964; -3f

Beckmann, M. J.   On the Determination of Prices in Futures Markets, *in* Brennan, M. J. (Ed), Patterns of Market Behavior. Brown U Pr, 1965; -21a

Bedford, G. L.   A Method of Estimating Price-Earnings Ratios. AJ, 3 (3rd Qtr, 1947), 14-19; -7a

Beechy, T. H.   The Effects of Financial Variables on the Cost of Capital. DBA diss, U of Wash, 1971; -23c

     Quasi-Debt Analysis of Financial Leases. AR, 44 (Apr, 1969), 375-381; -25g

Behrens, C.

     See **Ramsey, C. M. & Behrens, C.**

Beidleman, C. R.   Limitations of Price-Earnings Ratios. FAJ, 27 (Sep-Oct, 1971), 86-91; -7b

     On Growth in Share Values. JBF, 3 (Summer, 1971), 51-56; -7b

A Study of the Influence of Growth on the Valuation of Equity.
PhD diss, U of Pa, 1969; -7b

Beier, E.   An Analysis of Pension Plan Management and Its Public Policy
Implications. PhD diss, U of Wis, 1969; -3i

Beja, A.   On Systematic and Unsystematic Components of Financial Risk.
JF, 27 (Mar, 1972), 37-46; -10b

Bell, W. E.   The Price-Future Earnings Ratio. AJ, 14 (Aug, 1958), 25-28;
-7a

Bellemore, D. H. & Blucher, Mrs. L. H.   A Study of Stock Splits in the
Postwar Years. AJ, 15 (Nov, 1959), 19-26; -16c

Belveal, L. D.   Commodity Speculation: With Profit in Mind. Commodities
Pr, 1967; -21a

Bender, W.   Horizons of Security Analysis. AJ, 3 (3rd Qtr, 1947), 50-54;
-4a

Benishay, H.   Determinants of Variability in Earnings Price Ratio of
Corporate Equity. PhD diss, U of Chicago, 1960; -7c
Variability in Earnings-Price Ratios of Corporate Equities. AER,
51 (Mar, 1961), 81-94; -7c
Variability in Earnings-Price Ratios: Reply. AER, 52 (Mar, 1962),
209-216; -7c

Bennett, H.
See **Vaughn, D. E. & Bennett, H.**

Bennington, G. A.
See **Jensen, M. C. & Bennington, G. A.**

Bennion, E. G.   Capital Budgeting and Game Theory. HBR, 34 (Nov-Dec,
1956), 115-123; -25c

Ben-Shahar, H.   Capital Structure and the Cost of Capital. JF, 23 (Sep,
1968), 639-653; -23c
On the Capital Structure Theorem: Reply. JF, 25 (Jun, 1970), 678-
681; -23c
The Structure of Interest Rates, Government Financing and Econo-
mic Growth. Kyk, 20 (1967) 492-500; -18f
& Sarnat, M.   New Issues and Profitability of Investment in
Common Stock, 1959-1964. BIB, 25 (Apr, 1966), 3-31; -16a
& Sarnat, M.   Reinvestment and the Rate of Return on Common
Stocks. JF, 21 (Dec, 1966), 737-742; -5a

Benston, G. J.   Published Corporate Accounting Data and Stock Prices.
ERA, (1967), 1-54; -8d
See also **Sorter, G. H. & Benston, G. J.**

Beranek, W.   Analysis for Financial Decisions. Irwin, 1963; -25c
Common Stock Financing, Book Values and Stock Rights: the
Theory and the Evidence. U of Wis Busn, 1961; -16b
The Effect of Leverage on the Market Value of Common Stock. U
of Wis Busn, 1965; -23c
Working Capital Management. Wadsworth Pub, 1966; -25a
See also **Campbell, J. A. & Beranek, W.**
See also **Thompson, H. E. & Beranek, W.**
See also **Weston, J. F. & Beranek, W.**

Berle, A. A. & Means, G. C.   The Modern Corporation and Private Property, rev ed. HarBraceJ, 1969; -3a

Berman, A.   Regulation of Unlisted Securities, Has Time Come to End the
Double Standard? FAJ, 17 (Jul-Aug, 1961), 45-54; -2e

Berman, D. S.   Using Tax Laws to Help Finance Corporate Acquisitions.
AJ, 12 (May, 1956), 119-121; -26a

Berney, R. E.   The Auction of Long-Term Government Securities. JF, 19 (Sep, 1964), 470-482; -19b

Bernhard, A.   The Evaluation of Common Stocks. S & S, 1959; -7a

    The Valuation of Listed Stocks. AJ, 5 (2nd Qtr, 1949), 20-24; -7a

Bernhard, R. H.   Discount Methods for Expenditure Evaluation—A Clarification of Their Assumptions. JIEng, (Jan-Feb, 1962), 19-27; -25b

    Mathematical Programming Models for Capital Budgeting—a Survey, Generalization and Critique. JFQA, 4 (Jun, 1969), 111-158; -25e

    On the Consistency of the Soper and Sturm-Kaplan Conditions for Uniqueness of the Internal Rate of Return. JIEng, 18 (Aug, 1967), 498; -25b

Bernoulli, D.   Exposition of a New Theory on the Measurement of Risk. Papers of the Imperial Academy of Science in Petersburg, Vol 2 (1730), 175-192. Translated into English by Sommer, L., Em, (Jan, 1954), 23-36; -9a

Bernstein, M. C.   The Future of Private Pensions. Free Pr, 1964; -3i

Bernstein, M. H.   Regulating Business by Independent Commission. Princeton U Pr, 1955; -2e

Bernstein, P. L.   Growth Companies vs Growth Stocks. HBR, 34 (Sep-Oct, 1956), 87-98; -7a

Besser, D. E.   Tick Volume as a Means of Common Stock Selection. SM thesis, MIT, 1968; -12g

Betty, W. P.   The Valuation of Conglomerate Companies. PhD diss, N Tex St U, 1969; -26c

Bickel, S. H.   Minimum Variance and Optimal Asymptotic Portfolios. MSci, 16 (Nov, 1969), 221-226; -10c

Bicksler, J. L.   Empirical Test of Compatibility of Selected Equity Price Equations with a Descriptive Dividend Model. PhD diss, NYU, 1967; -24b

Biderman, R.

    See **Soldofsky, R. M. & Biderman, R.**

Bierman, H., Jr.   The Bond Refunding Decision as a Markov Process. MSci, 12 (Aug, 1966), B545-B551; -19h

    Discounted Cash Flows, Price Level Adjustments and Expectations. AR, 46 (Oct, 1971), 693-699; -25c

    Financial Policy Decisions. Macmillan, 1970; -23c

    The Growth Period Decision. MSci, 14 (Feb, 1968), B302-B309; -7b, 25c

    The Bond Issue Size Decision. JFQA, 1 (Dec, 1966), 1-14; -19a

    Risk and the Addition of Debt to the Capital Structure. JFQA, 3 (Dec, 1968), 415-426; -23c

    Using Investment Portfolios to Change Risk. JFQA, 3 (Jun, 1968), 151-156; -9c

    The Valuation of Stock Options. JFQA, 2 (Sep, 1967), 327-334; -17a

    Downes, D. H. & Hass, J. E.   Closed-Form Stock Price Models. JFQA, 7 (Jun, 1972), 1797-1808; -7b

    Fouraker, L. E. & Jaedicke, R. K.   Quantitative Analysis for Business Decisions, 3rd ed. Irwin, 1969; -22a

    & Hass, J. E.   Capital Budgeting Under Uncertainty—a Reformulation. JF, forthcoming; -25d

    & Hass, J. E.   Normative Stock Price Models. JFQA, 6 (Sep, 1971), 1135-1146; -7b

    & Hausman, W. H.   The Resolution of Investment Uncertainty through Time. MSci, 18 (Aug, 1972), B654-B662; -25d

    & Smidt, S.   Capital Budgeting and the Problem of Reinvesting Cash Proceeds. JB, 30 (Oct, 1957), 276-279; -25c

    & Smidt, S.   The Capital Budgeting Decision, 3rd ed. Macmillan, 1971; -25c

    & Thomas, L. J.   Ruin Considerations and Debt Issuance. JFQA, 7 (Jan, 1972), 1361-1378; -23c

    & West, R. R.   Acquisition of Common Stock by the Corporate Issuer. JF, 21 (Dec, 1966), 687-696; -16d

    See also **West, R. R. & Bierman, H., Jr.**

    See also **Alderfer, C. P. & Bierman, H., Jr.**

Bierwag, G. O. & Grove, M. A.   A Model of the Term Structure of Interest Rates. REStat, 49 (Feb, 1967), 50-62; -18f

    & Grove, M. A.   On Capital Asset Prices: Comment. JF, 20 (Mar, 1965), 89-93; -10l

    & Grove, M. A.   Portfolio Selection and Taxation. OEP, 19 (Jul, 1967), 215-221; -27b

Biggar, G. G., Jr.

    See **Buff, J. H; Biggar, G. G., Jr. & Burkhead, J. G.**

Biggs, B. M.   The Short Interest—A False Proverb. FAJ, 22 (Jul-Aug, 1966), 111-116; -13d

Bigosinski, J. T.   The Swiss Money Market. PhD diss, NYU, 1963; -20a

Bing, R. A.   Appraising Our Methods of Stock Appraisal. FAJ, 20 (May-Jun, 1964), 118-124; -7b

    Scientific Investment Analysis. FAJ, 23 (May-Jun, 1967), 97-98; -4a

    Survey of Practitioners' Stock Evaluation Methods. FAJ, 27 (May-Jun, 1971), 55-60; -7a

Bingham, A. Y.   Relative Performance—Nonsense. FAJ, 22 (Jul-Aug, 1966), 101-104; -14a

Bird, A. P.   Evaluating Warrants. IA, 31 (Dec, 1971), 17-32; -17b

Birmingham, J. M., Jr.   The Quest for Performance (Keynote Review). FAJ, 22 (Sep-Oct, 1966), 93-94; -4a

    Stock Values and Stock Prices. FAJ, 21 (Mar-Apr, 1965), 88-89; -7a

    See also **Hennis, E. A. & Birmingham, J. M., Jr.**

Birnham, E. A.

    See **Goode, R. & Birnham, E. A.**

Bishop, G. W., Jr.   Charles H. Dow and the Dow Theory. Appleton, 1960; -12c

    Evolution of the Dow Theory. FAJ, 17 (Sep-Oct, 1961), 23-26; -12c

Bittker, B. I.   Federal Income Taxation of Corporations and Shareholders, 2nd ed. Fed Tax Pr, 1966; -27a

Bizley, M. T. L.   Yields on Redeemable Securities Subject to Capital Gains Tax. JIASS, 17 (1965); -27d

Black, F.   Capital Market Equilibrium with Restricted Borrowing. JB, 45 (Jul, 1972), 444-455; -10l

    Differences in Ability among Professional Portfolio Managers. Financial Note 5A, (Sep 15, 1969), unp; -11c

    Equilibrium in the Creation of Investment Goods Under Uncertainty, *in* Jensen, M. C. (Ed), Studies in the Theory of Capital Markets, Praeger, 1972; -10l

    Implications of the Random Walk Hypothesis for Portfolio Management. FAJ, 27 (Mar-Apr, 1971), 16-22; -11c

Lifetime Investment Strategies for Individuals. Paper for the
Seminar on the Analysis of Security Prices, U of Chicago, Nov 1969;
-10j

Toward a Fully Automated Stock Exchange.
Part 1: FAJ, 27 (Jul-Aug, 1971), 29-35
Part 2: FAJ, 27 (Nov-Dec, 1971), 24ff; -2b

Jensen, M. C. & Scholes, M. The Capital Asset Pricing Model:
Some Empirical Tests. Jensen, M. C. (Ed), Studies in the Theory of
Capital Markets, Praeger, 1972

& Scholes, M. Capital Market Equilibrium and the Pricing of
Corporate Liabilities. JPE forthcoming; -17a, 19g

& Scholes, M. Dividend Yields and Common Stock Returns: a
New Methodology. Paper for the Seminar on the Analysis of Security
Prices, U of Chicago, Nov 1970; -7a

& Scholes, M. The Valuation of Option Contracts and a Test of
Market Efficiency. JF, 27 (May, 1972), 399-417; -17a

Black, H. The Watchdogs of Wall Street. Morrow, 1962; -2e

Black, J. B., Jr. The Pattern of Accumulation of Common Equity Capital
Relative to Price Earnings Relationships for Common Stocks. DBA
diss, Indiana U, 1965; -8d

Black, S. W. The Use of Rational Expectations in Models of Speculation.
REStat, 54 (May, 1972), 161-165; -9e

Bladen, A. Techniques for Investing in Convertible Bonds. New York:
Salomon Bros & Hutzler, 1966; -17c

Time to Buy? B, (Oct 10, 1966), 9ff; -17c

Blair, J. M. The Relation between Size and Efficiency of Business. REStat,
24 (Aug, 1942), 125-135; -26f

Blake, C. W. & Riegle D. W. Data Processing Key to Investment Success.
FAJ, 24 (Jan-Feb, 1968), 134-146; -4e

Blaney, T. A.
See **Olsen, J. A. & Blaney, T. A.**

Blaser, A. L. Dynamic Price Movements: the New Issue Aftermarket.
DBA diss, U of Oregon, 1971; -16a

Blattberg, R. & Sargent, T. Regression with Non-Gaussian Disturbances:
Some Sampling Results. Em, 39 (May, 1971), 501-510; -11b

Blau, G. Some Aspects of the Theory of Futures Trading. REStud, 12
(1944); -21a

Blease, J. G. Computers as an Aid to Investment Analysis. IA, 1 (Nov,
1961), 12-26; -4e

Institutional Investors and the Stock Exchange. DBR, 151 (Sep,
1964), 38-64; -3e

Blecke, C. J. Financial Analysis for Decision-Making. P-H, 1966; -25c

Bloch, E. Eurodollars: an Emerging International Money Market.
Bulletin No 39, Institute of Finance, NYU, Apr 1966; -20d

Short Cycles in Corporate Demand for Government Securities.
AER, 53 (Dec, 1963), 1058-1077); -19b

Block, F. E. Elements of Portfolio Construction. FAJ, 25 (May-Jun, 1969),
123-129; -4a

Per Share Adjustments for Rights. FAJ, 21 (May-Jun, 1965),
58-60; -16b

The Place of Book Value in Common Stock Evaluation. FAJ, 20
(Mar-Apr, 1964), 29-33; -8c

Risk and Performance. FAJ, 22 (Mar-Apr, 1966), 65-74; -14a

The Same Maturity? FAJ, 25 (Jul-Aug, 1969), 184; -18g

A Study of the Price to Book Relationship. FAJ, 20 (Sep-Oct, 1964), 108-117; -8c

Theory, Performance and Practice. FAJ, 21 (Nov-Dec, 1965), 94-95; -4a

Time Horizon. FAJ, 28 (Sep-Oct, 1972), 30ff; -4a

Block, S. B. The Effect of Mergers and Acquisitions on the Market Value of Common Stock. PhD diss, La St U, 1968; -26b

Blough, C. M. Business Combination: 'Pooling' or Purchase? JA, 104 (Jul, 1957), 55-56; -26d

Blucher, Mrs. L. H.

See **Bellemore, D. H. & Blucher, Mrs. L. H.**

Blum, J. D. An Analysis of the Price Behavior of Initial Common Stock Offerings. PhD diss, Mich St U, 1971; -16a

Blume, M. E. The Assessment of Portfolio Performance—An Application to Portfolio Theory. PhD diss, U of Chicago, 1968; -10b

On the Assessment of Risk. JF, 26 (Mar, 1971), 1-10; -10b

Portfolio Theory: A Step Toward Its Practical Application. JB, 43 (Apr, 1970), 152-173; -10c

& Friend, I. A New Look at the Capital Asset Pricing Model. JF, forthcoming; -10l

See also **Fama, E. F. & Blume, M. E.**

See also **Friend, I. & Blume, M. E.**

See also **Friend, I.; Blume, M. E. & Crockett, J.**

Blunt, R. H. & Lane, L. H. Variable Annuities. JIASS, 14 (Jul, 1957); -3h

Blyn, M. R.

See **Krooss, H. E. & Blyn, M. R.**

Bodenhammer, L. The Effect of the Size of Public Offerings of Common Stocks upon Pre-offering Stock Prices. PhD diss, Harvard U, 1968; -16b

Bodenhorn, D. A Cash-Flow Concept of Profit. JF, 19 (Mar, 1964), 16-31; -7a

On the Problem of Capital Budgeting. JF, 14 (Dec, 1959), 473-492; -25c

Boehm. G. A. W. The Science of Being Almost Certain. F, 76 (Feb, 1964), 104ff; -9c

Boehmler, E. W.

See **Robinson, R. I.; Boehmler, E. W.; Gane, F. H. & Farwell, L. C. (Eds)**

Bogen, J. I. The Changing Composition of Bank Assets. Graduate School of Business Administration. NYU, 1961; -3f

& Krooss, H. E. Security Credit, Its Economic Role and Regulation. P-H, 1960; -6e

& Shipman, S. S. (Eds). Financial Handbook, 4th ed. Ronald, 1964; -22a

Bogle, J. C. Mutual Fund Performance Evaluation. FAJ, 26 (Nov-Dec, 1970), 25ff; -14a

Bogue, M. C.

See **Robichek, A. A. & Bogue, M. C.**

Bohmfalk, J. F. The Growth Stock Philosophy. FAJ, 16 (Nov-Dec, 1960), 113-123; -7b

Bollinger, L. L.

See **Butters, J. K.; Thompson, L. E. & Bollinger, L. L.**

Bolster, R. L. The Relationship of Monetary Policy to the Stock Market:

the Experience with Margin Requirements. PhD diss, Am U, 1966; -6e

Bolten, S.   Security Analysis and Portfolio Management. HR & W, 1972; -4a

     Treasury Bill Auction Procedures: an Empirical Investigation. JF, forthcoming; -20b

     See **Mastrapasqua, F. & Bolten, S.**

Bolton, A. H.   Money and Investment Profits. Dow Jones-Irwin, 1967; -6d

Bolton, G. et al.   The European Capital Market. Fed Tst, 1967; -20e

Bomeli, E. C.

     See **Cooke, G. W. & Bomeli, E. C.**

Bomford, M. D.   Changes in the Evaluation of Equities. IA, 22 (Dec, 1968), 3-12; -7c

Bonello, F. J.   The Formulation of Expected Interest Rates: an Examination of Alternative Hypotheses. Mich St U Busn, 1970; -18b

     The Term Structure of Interest Rates, the Expectations Hypothesis, and the Formulation of Expected Interest Rates. PhD diss, Mich St U, 1968; -18f

Boness, A. J.   Elements of a Theory of Stock Option Value. JPE, 72 (Apr, 1964), 163-175; -17a

     A Pedagogic Note on the Cost of Capital. JF, 19 (Mar, 1964), 99-106; -23c

     Some Evidence on the Profitability of Trading in Put and Call Options, *in* Cootner, P. H. (Ed), The Random Character of Stock Market Prices. MIT Pr, 1964; -17a

     A Theory and Measurement of Stock-Option Value. PhD diss, U of Chicago, 1962; -17a

     & Jen, F. C.   A Model of Information Diffusion, Stock Market Behavior, and Equilibrium Price. JFQA, 5 (Sep, 1970), 279-296; -7a

Bonham, H. B., Jr.   The Use of Input-Output Economics in Common Stock Analysis. FAJ, 23 (Jan-Feb, 1967), 19-28; -6a

Bonner, G. R.   Some Notes on the Rehabilitation of Preferred Stock. AFR, (Spring, 1966), 32-37; -19i

Bonner, J.   Local Authority Investment and Debt-Financing. SJPE, 19 (Jun, 1972), 135-150; -19d

Bookbinder, A. I. A.   Investment Decision-Making. Programmed, 1948; -4a

Booth, G. G.   The Management of a Commercial Bank Portfolio: a Programming Approach. PhD diss, U of Mich, 1971; -10g

     Programming Bank Portfolios Under Uncertainty: an Extension. JBR, (Winter, 1972), 28-40; -10g

Borch, K.   The Capital Structure of a Firm. SJE, 71 (Mar, 1969); -23c

     Dividend Policies. ST, 79 (Dec, 1965), 183-201; -24a

     The Economics of Uncertainty. Princeton U Pr, 1968; -9a

     The Economic Theory of Insurance. The Astin Bulletin, (Jul, 1967), 252-264; -9d

     Equilibrium, Optimum and Prejudices in Capital Markets. JFQA, 4 (Mar, 1969), 1-14; -10*l*

     General Equilibrium in the Economics of Uncertainty, *in* Borch, K. & Mossin, J. (Eds), Risk and Uncertainty. Macmillan Int, 1968; -9d

     Indifference Curves and Uncertainty. SJE, 70 (Mar, 1968), 19-24; -9c

     A Note on Utility and Attitudes to Risk. MSci, 9 (Jul, 1963), 697-700; -9a

     Price Movements in the Stock Market. SAkt, 47 (1964), 41-50; -11c

The Theory of Risk. JRSS, 29 (1967), B432-B452;-9c

A Utility Function Derived from a Survival Game. MSci, 12 (Apr, 1966), B287-B295;-9a

& Mossin, J. (Eds).   Risk and Uncertainty: Proceedings of a Conference held by the International Economic Association. Macmillan Int, 1968;-9c

Borenstein, I.

See **Creamer, D.; Dobrovolsky, S. P. & Borenstein, I.**

Bosland, C. C.   The Common Stock Theory of Investment. Ronald, 1937; -5a

Stock Valuation in Recent Mergers. TE, 94 (Jun, 1955), 516ff; -26a

The Valuation of Public Utility Enterprises by the Securities and Exchange Commission. JF, 16 (Mar, 1961), 52-64;-7a

Valuation Theories and Decisions of the SEC. Simmons-B, 1964; -7a

Bossell, S.

See **Niederhoffer, V. & Bossell, S.**

Bothwell, J. C., Jr.   Periodic Stock Dividends. HBR, 28 (Jan, 1950), 89-100; -16c

Bottomly, A.   The Determination of Pure Rates of Interest in Underdeveloped Rural Areas. REStat, 46 (Aug, 1964), 301-304;-18b

Boulden, J. B. & Buffa, E. S.   Corporate Models: On Line, Real Time Systems. HBR, 48 (Jul-Aug, 1970), 65-83;-22c

Bowen, W. G.   The Economics of Major Universities. Berkeley, Calif, Carnegie Commission on Higher Education, 1968;-3j

Bower, D. H. & R. S.   Test of a Stock Valuation Model. JF, 25 (May, 1970), 483-492;-7c

See also **Bower, R. S. & D. H.**

Bower, J.   Investment in United States Government Securities by State Governments. NTJ, 13 (Jun, 1960), 127-140;-19b

Bower, R. S.   Comments on 'Capital Budgeting Under Uncertainty'. SJB, (Apr, 1968), 132-138; -25d

& D. H.   Risk and the Valuation of Common Stock. JPE, 77 (May-Jun, 1969), 349-362;-7c

Herringer, F. C. & Williamson, J. P.   Lease Evaluation. AR, 41 (Apr, 1966), 257-265; -25g

Myers, B. C.; Nugent, C. E. & Williamson, J. P.   A Language for the Aid of Financial Fact Finders. FAJ, 23 (Jan-Feb, 1967), 121-129; -4e

& Williamson, J. P.   Measuring Pension Fund Performance: Another Comment. FAJ, 22 (May-Jun, 1966), 143-149;-14b

Williamson, J. P. & Wippern, R. F.   Financial Research, Investment Analysis and the Computer: Work Done at the Amos Tuck School. Tuck Bulletin 31, The Amos Tuck School, 1967;-4e

Williamson, J. P. & Wippern, R. F.   Portfolio Selection and Performance Appraisal Models: the Multiperiod Case. Paper for the Seminar on the Analysis of Security Prices, U of Chicago, Nov 1970; -14a

& Wippern, R. F. (Eds).   Analytical and Quantitative Research in Finance: a Bibliography of Selected Journals, Jan 1962 to Mar 1967. Unp, 1970;-1a

& Wippern, R. F.   Risk-Return Measurement in Portfolio Selection and Performance Appraisal Models: Progress Report. JFQA, 4

(Dec, 1969), 417-448;-14a
>See also **Bower, D. H. & R. S.**
>See also **Nimrod, V. L. & Bower, R. S.**
>See also **Williamson, J. P. & Bower, R. S.**

Bowers, D. A. Investor Preference and the Structure of Interest Rates in the U.S. Government Securities Market, 1953-1961. PhD diss, S Methodist U, 1963;-18f

Bowes, A. S.
>See **Hochmuth, W. P. & Bowes, A. S.**

Bowlin, O. D. The Refunding Decision. JF, 21 (Mar, 1966), 55-68;-19h

Bowman, M. J. (Ed). Expectations, Uncertainty, and Business Behavior. Soc Sci Res, 1958;-9a

Bown, C. C. Convertible Bonds and the Cost of Capital: Some Theoretical Considerations and Empirical Findings. Paper for the Second Annual Meeting of the Western Finance Association 1966;-17c

Bowyer, J. W. Investment Analysis and Management, 3rd ed. Irwin, 1966; -4a
>See also **Plum, L. V., Humphrey, J. H. & Bowyer, J. W.**

Boylan, W. A. Endowment Funds—Collision of Corporate and Trust Standards. BL, 18 (Apr, 1963), 807-818;-3j

Bracken, J. Models for Call Options. FAJ, 24 (Sep-Oct, 1968), 149-151; -17a

Brackenburg & Co. Dealing on the London Metal Exchange. Brackenburg, 1966;-21a

Brada, J. C.; Ernst, H. & Van Tassel, J. The Distribution of Stock Price Differences: Gaussian After All? OR, 14 (Apr, 1966), 334-340;-11b

Bradley, J. F. Administrative Financial Management, 2nd ed. HR & W, 1969;-22a
>Fundamentals of Corporation Finance, rev ed. HR & W, 1959;-22a

Brand, L. Investing for Profit in Convertible Bonds. S & P, 1964;-17c

Brandt, L. K. Analysis for Financial Management. P-H, 1972;-22a
>Business Finance, a Management Approach. P-H, 1965;-22a

Branson, W. H. The Minimum Covered Interest Differential Needed for International Arbitrage Activity. JPE, 77 (Nov-Dec, 1969), 1028-1035; -21b

Bratten, H. Is the CD a Deposit or a Loan? Banking, (Mar, 1964), 46-47; -20a

Braun, M. E. Optimum Debt Financing Policy: A Linear Programming Approach. PhD diss, Ohio St U, 1967;-23c

Brauweiler, J. R.
>See **Hirschmann, W. B. & Brauweiler, J. R.**

Bray, J. N. The Risk and Use of Debt Financing. PhD diss, UCLA, 1967; -23g

Brazer, H.
>See **Morgan, J.; Barlow, R. & Brazer, H.**

Brealey, R. A. The Character of Earnings Changes. Paper for the Seminar on the Analysis of Security Prices. U of Chicago, May 1967;-8a
>The Distribution and Independence of Successive Rates of Return in the U.K. Equity Market. JBF, 2 (Summer, 1970), 29-40;-11b, 24c
>The Impact of the Market on British Share Prices. IA, 24 (Oct, 1969), 3-9;-10b
>Some Implications of the Co-movement of American Company Earnings. AE, 3 (1971), 183-196;-8a, 15b

An Introduction to Risk and Return from Common Stocks. MIT Pr, 1969; -4b

Investment Uncertainty and British Equities: a Comment. IA, 23 (Jun, 1969), 40-41; -10*l*

Managing the Research Department. Paper for the Seminar on the Analysis of Security Prices, U of Chicago, Nov, 1972; -10c

Security Prices in a Competitive Market: More about Risk and Return from Common Stock. MIT Pr, 1971; -4b

& Hodges, S. D. Playing with Portfolios. FAJ, forthcoming; -4f, 10c

& Hodges, S. D. The Valuation of British Convertibles, *in* Szego, G. P. & Shell, K. (Eds), Mathematical Methods in Investment and Finance. N-Holland, 1972; -17c

See also **Hodges, S. D. & Brealey, R. A.**

See also **Lorie, J. H. & Brealey, R. A.**

Brechling, F. P. R.

See **Hahn, F. H. & Brechling, F. P. R.**

Breen, W. J. Homogenous Risk Measures and the Construction of Composite Assets. JFQA, 3 (Dec, 1968), 405-414; -10b

Liquidity Preference, Degree of Risk Aversion and the Expected Utility Hypothosis. Unp ms, 1967; -18a

Low Price-Earnings Ratios and Industry Relatives. FAJ, 24 (Jul-Aug, 1968), 125-127; -8g

Markowitz, Sharpe, et al.: A Dissenting View. Paper for the Seminar on the Analysis of Security Prices, U of Chicago, Nov, 1966; -10c

Specific versus General Models of Portfolio Selection. OEP, 20 (Nov, 1968), 361-368; -10c

& Jackson, R. An Efficient Algorithm for Solving Large-Scale Portfolio Problems. JFQA, 6 (Jan, 1971), 627-638; -10c

& Savage, J. Portfolio Distributions and Tests of Security Selection Models. JF, 23 (Dec, 1968), 805-819; -7a

Breiman, L. Investment Policies for Expanding Businesses Optimal in a Long-Run Sense. NRLQ, 7 (Dec, 1960), 647-651; -10j, 25d

Brennan, M. J. Capital Asset Pricing and the Structure of Security Returns. Unp ms, U of BC, 1970; -10*l*

Capital Market Equilibrium with Divergent Borrowing and Lending Rates. JFQA, 6 (Dec, 1971), 1197-1206; -10*l*

Investor Taxes, Market Equilibrium and Corporate Finance. PhD diss, MIT, 1970; -24b

A Note on Dividend Irrelevance and the Gordon Valuation Model. JF, 26 (Dec, 1971), 1115-1122; -24b

Valuation and the Cost of Capital for Regulated Industries. JF, forthcoming; -23d

Brennan, M. J. The Supply of Storage. AER, 47 (Mar, 1957), 50-72; -21a

Brew, J. M. The Analysis of Split Trusts. IA, 25 (Dec, 1969), 14-20; -3m

Gilt-Edged Yield Curves. IA, 16 (Dec, 1966), 3-22; -18f

The Trustees' Meeting—a City Daydream. IA, 28 (Dec, 1970), 14-17; -14a

Brewer, D. E. & Michaelsen, J. B. The Cost of Capital, Corporation Finance and the Theory of Investment: Comment. AER, 55 (Jan, 1965), 516-524; -23c

Brewer, K. R. W. Decisions Under Uncertainty: Comment. QJE, 77 (Feb, 1963), 159-161; -9c

    & Fellner, W.   The Slanting of Subjective Probabilities—Agreement on Some Essentials. QJE, 79 (Nov, 1965), 657-663;-9c

Brickman, M.   New Federal Reserve Series Is Valuable Forecasting Tool. FAJ, 23 (Sep-Oct, 1967), 88-92;-6d

Briggs, G. C.   Performance and Portfolio Management. FAJ, 23 (Sep-Oct, 1967), 123-127;-14a

Brigham, E. F.   An Analysis of Convertible Debentures: Theory and Some Empirical Evidence. JF, 21 (Mar, 1966), 35-54;-17c

    Cases in Managerial Finance. HR & W, 1970;-1c

    The Profitability of a Firm's Repurchase of its Own Shares. CMR, 7 (Winter, 1964), 67-75;-16d

    & Gordon, M. J.   Leverage, Dividend Policy, and the Cost of Capital. JF, 23 (Mar, 1968), 85-103;-23c

    & Pappas, J. L.   Duration of Growth, Changes in Growth Rates and Corporate Share Prices. FAJ, 22 (May-Jun, 1966), 157-162;-7b

    & Pappas, J. L.   Rates of Return on Common Stock. JB, 42 (Jul, 1969), 302-316;-5a

    & Ricks, M. B. (Eds).   Readings in the Essentials of Management Finance. HR & W, 1971;-1b

    See also **Shelton, J. P.; Brigham, E. F. & Hofflander, A. E., Jr.**

    See also **Weston, J. F. & Brigham, E. F.**

    See also **Woods, D. H. & Brigham, E. F.**

Bright, C. B.

    See **Cary, W. L. & Bright, C. B.**

Briloff, A. J.   The 'Funny-Money' Game. FAJ, 25 (May-Jun, 1969), 73-79; -26b

Brimmer, A. F.   Credit Conditions and Price Determination in the Corporate Bond Market. JF, 15 (Sep, 1960), 353-370;-19g

    Foreign Banking Institutions in the United States Money Market. REStat, 44 (Feb, 1962), 76-81;-20a

    Life Insurance Companies in the Capital Markets. Mich St U Busn, 1962;-3h

    Price Determination in the United States Treasury Bills Market. REStat, 44 (May, 1962), 178-183;-20b

    Some Studies in Monetary Policy, Interest Rates and the Investment Behavior of Life Insurance Companies. DBA diss, Harvard Bus, 1956; -3h

Brinegar, C. S.   A Statistical Analysis of Speculative Price Behavior. PhD diss, Stanford U, 1954; 11c

Briscoe, G; Samuels, J. M. & Smyth, D. J.   The Treatment of Risk in the Stock Market. JF, 24 (Sep, 1969), 707-714; -10l

Briston, R. J.   The Stock Exchange and Investment Analysis. Allen, 1971;-4a

    & Herbert, P. J. A.   The Measurement of Underwriting Performance in a Depressed Market. JBF, 4 (Summer, 1972), 88-95;-16b

    & Tomkins, C. R.   Dividend Policy, Shareholder Satisfaction and the Valuation of Shares. JBF, 2 (Spring, 1970), 17-24;-24b

British Market Bureau Limited.   How Does Britain Save?—A summary of the results of a survey conducted for the London Stock Exchange. London: Stock Exchange, 1966;-3a

Brittain, J. A.   Corporate Dividend Policy. Brookings, 1966;-24a

    The Tax Structure and Corporate Dividend Policy. AER, 54 (May, 1964), 272-287;-27a

Broman, K. L.   The Use of Convertible Subordinated Debentures by Industrial Firms, 1949-1959. QREB, 3 (Spring, 1963), 65-75;-17c

Bromwich, M. Inflation and the Capital Budgeting Process. JBF, 1 (Autumn, 1969), 39-46;-25c

Brooks, J. Once in Golconda. Har-Row, 1969;-2d
    The 7 Fat Years: Chronicles of Wall Street. Magee, 1958;-2d

Brouillette, A. B.
    See **West, R. R. & Brouillette, A. B.**

Brown, B. Common-Stock Price Ratios and Long-term Interest Rates. JB, 21 (Jul, 1948), 180-182;-7d

Brown, C. V. A Theory of Interest Rates or Asset Prices? SJPE, 12 (Nov, 1965), 297-308;-18b

Brown, E. C. Mr. Kaldor on Taxation and Risk Bearing. REStud, 25 (1957), 49-52;-27b

Brown, E. E. & Vickers, D. Mutual Funds Portfolio Activity, Performance and Market Impact. JF, 18 (May, 1963), 377-391;-3k

Brown, G. C. Discounted Cash Flow Method: Circumstantial Behavior in Capital Budgeting Applications. PhD diss, Ohio St U, 1967;-25c

Brown, H. A., Jr. & Nichols, D. R. A Deterrent to Investment Mobility. FAJ, 25 (May-Jun, 1969), 131-137;-27d

Brown, J. A. The Decade Ahead in Shareownership Research. Proceedings of the Business and Economic Statistics Section, American Statistical Association, 1963;-3a
    Techniques for Measuring Share Ownership. Proceedings of the American Statistical Association, Dec, 1963;-3a

Brown, J. A. C.
    See **Aitchison, J. & Brown, J. A. C.**

Brown, J. J.
    See **Jarislowsky, S. A. & Brown, J. J.**

Brown, J. M. Post-Offering Experience of Companies Going Public. JB, 43 (Jan, 1970), 10-18;-16a

Brown, K. C. Estimating Frequency Functions from Limited Data. JFQA, 5 (Mar, 1970), 139-148;-11b
    The Significance of Dummy Variables in Multiple Regressions Involving Financial and Economic Data. JF, 23 (Jun, 1968), 515-517; -23c

Brown, P. & Kennelly, J. W. The Informational Content of Quarterly Earnings: an Extension and some Further Evidence. JB, 45 (Jul, 1972), 403-415;-8a
    & Niederhoffer, V. The Predictive Content of Quarterly Earnings. JB, 41 (Oct, 1968), 488-497;-8a
    See also **Ball, R. J. & Brown, P.**

Brown, R. Measuring Uncertainty in Business Investigations. JMS, 1 (Sep, 1964), 143-163;-9c

Browne, D. E. Analyst, Analyse Thyself! FAJ, 24 (Nov-Dec, 1968), 23-24; -4c

Brownlee, O. H. & Scott, I. O. Utility, Liquidity and Debt Management. Em, 31 (Jul, 1963), 349-362;-23c

Brownson, F. O.
    See **Becker, S. W. & Brownson, F. O.**

Broyles, J. E. A Stochastic Model of New York Stock Exchange Transactions. PhD diss, LSE, 1970;-11c

Brumberg, R.
    See **Modigliani, F. & Brumberg, R.**

Bruner, D. McD. Short Selling the USA. Winston, 1933;-13d

Bryan, W. R. & Carleton, W. T.   Short-Run Adjustments of an Individual Bank. Em, 35 (Apr, 1967), 321-347;-3f
Bryant, W. R.   Mortgage Lending: Fundamentals and Practice, 2nd ed. McGraw, 1962;-21c
Buchsbaum, M.
See **Gould, A. & Buchsbaum, M.**
Buckley, A.   The Takeover in the Context of a Capital Budgeting Framework. JBF, 4 (Summer, 1972), 37-46;-26a
Buckley, J. G.   A Method of Evaluating Growth Stocks. FAJ, 16 (Mar-Apr, 1960), 19-21;-7b
Buckley, J.
See **Loll, L. M. & Buckley, J.**
Budd, A. P. & Litzenberger, R. H.   Changes in the Supply of Money, the Firm's Market Value and Cost of Capital. JF, forthcoming; -23d
See also **Litzenberger, R. H. & Budd, A. P.**
Buek, C. W.   Managing Our Trusts as Prudent Men Would Do. CFC, (Mar, 3, 1960);-3j
Buff, J. H.; Biggar, G. G., Jr. & Burkhead, J. G.   The Application of New Decision Analysis Techniques to Investment Research. FAJ, 24 (Nov-Dec, 1968), 123-128;-9c
Buffa, E. S.
See **Reisman, A. & Buffa, E. S.**
Bulloch, J.
See **Duvall, R. M. & Bulloch, J.**
Bullock, H.   The Story of Investment Companies. Columbia U Pr, 1959; -3k
Burkhead, J. G.
See **Buff, J. H.; Biggar, G. G., Jr. & Burkhead, J. G.**
Burnham, J. M.   Conditional Chance-Constrained Programming Techniques in Portfolio Selection. PhD diss, U of Texas, 1970;-10f
Burns, R. G.
See **Midgley, K. & Burns, R. G.**
Burrell, O. K.   Dividends vs Retained Earnings as Market Force. CFC, 176 (Aug 21, 1952), 29-30;-24b
A Mathematical Approach to Growth Stock Valuation. FAJ, 16 (May-Jun, 1960), 69-76;-7b
Price Effects of Stock Dividends and Split-ups. CFC, (Dec 2, 1948), 10ff;-16c
Burtchett, F. F. et al.   Corporation Finance, rev ed. Johnsen, 1964;-22a
Burton, H. & Corner, D. C.   Investment and Unit Trusts in Britain and America. Elek, 1968;-3k
Burton, J. C.   The Management of Corporate Liquid Assets. PhD diss, Columbia U, 1962;-25a
Buse, A.   Expectations, Prices, Coupons and Yields. JF, 25 (Sep, 1970), 809-818;-18f
Interest Rates, the Meiselman Model and Random Numbers. JPE, 75 (Feb, 1967), 49-62;-18f
The Structure of Interest Rates and Recent British Experience: a comment. Ec, 34 (Aug, 1967), 298-308;-18f
Bush, R. C. et al.   Case Problems in Financial Management. Appleton, 1968;-1c
Butler, E. B.   Auction Prices: Estimated and Realized. EJ, 71 (Mar, 1961), 114-120;-21d
Butler, H. L. Jr.
See **Decker, M. G. & Butler, H. L. Jr.**

Butler, W. F. & Kavesh, R. A. (Eds).   How Business Economists Forecast. P-H, 1966;-15a

Butters, J. K. (Ed).   Case Problems in Finance. Irwin, 1969;-1c

Taxation Incentives and Financial Capacity. AER. 44 (May, 1954), 504-519;-27a

Lintner, J. & Cary, W. L.   Effects of Taxation on Corporate Mergers. Harvard Busn, 1951;-26a

Thompson, L. E. & Bollinger, L. L.   Effects of Taxation on Investments by Individuals. Harvard Busn, 1953; -27a

Byrne, R.; Charnes, A.; Cooper, W. W. & Kortanek, K.   A Chance Constrained Approach to Capital Budgeting with Portfolio Type Payback and Liquidity Constraints and Horizon Posture Controls. JFQA, 2 (Dec, 1967), 339-364;-25d

Cagan, P.   Changes in the Cyclical Behavior of Interest Rates. (Dist by Columbia U Pr) Natl Bur Econ Res, 1966;-18d

Changes in the Cyclical Behavior of Interest Rates. REStat, 48 (Aug, 1966), 219-250;-18d

Effect of Pension Plans on Aggregate Saving: Evidence from a Sample Survey. (Dist by Columbia U Pr) Natl Bur Econ Res, 1965; -3i

Calkins, D. O.   An Empirical Study of Executive Stock Options and Company Performance. DBA diss, U of S Cal, 1969;-17d

Calkins, F. J.   Cases and Problems in Investments. P-H, 1955;-1c

Call, D. V.   Accounting and Management Considerations Relative to Stock Options. PhD diss, UCLA, 1966;-17d

Calman, R. F.   Linear Programming and Cash Management—Cash Alpha. MIT Pr, 1968;-25a

Caltagirone, J. Jr.   An Econometric Analysis of Risks and Returns to Common Stock Holders: Behavior of a 65 Company Cross-Section between 1952 and 1965. PhD diss, NYU, 1970;-23d

Calvert, G. L. (Ed).   Fundamentals of Municipal Bonds, 7th ed. Inv Bankers, 1969;-19d

Campanella, F. B.   The Measurement and Use of Systematic Risk. DBA diss, Harvard Busn, 1970; -10b

The Measurement of Portfolio Risk Exposure, the Use of the Beta Coefficient. Heath, 1972;-10b

See also **Carlson, R. S. & Campanella, F. B.**

Campbell, C. D.   Investment in United States Government Securities by State and Local Government. NTS, 10 (Mar, 1957), 78-87; -19b

Campbell, E. D.   Stock Options Should Be Valued. HBR, 39 (Jul-Aug, 1961), 52-58;-17d

Campbell, J. A. & Beranek, W.   Stock Price Behavior on Ex-Dividend Dates. JF, 10 (Dec, 1955), 425-429;-24c

Canaway, E. E.

See **Page, C. S. & Canaway, E. E.**

Canterbery, E. R.   A Theory of Foreign Exchange Speculation under Alternative Systems. JPE, 79 (May-Jun, 1971), 407-436; -21b

Carleton, W. T.   An Analytical Model for Long-Range Financial Planning. JF, 25 (May, 1970), 291-315;-22c

Linear Programming and Capital Budgeting Models: A New Interpretation. JF, 24 (Dec, 1969), 825-833; -25e

& Lerner, E. M.   Measuring Corporate Profit Opportunities. JFQA, 2 (Sep, 1967), 225-240; -22a

See also **Bryan W. R. & Carleton, W. T.**

See also **Lerner, E. M. & Carleton, W. T.**

See also **Moag, J. S.; Carleton, W. T. & Lerner, E. M.**

Carlson, C. R. A Financial Efficiency Model. PhD diss, Mich St U, 1971; -22c

Carlson, R. S. Aggregate Performance of Mutual Funds. JFQA, 5 (Mar, 1970), 1-32; -14a

    & Campenella, F. B. No Load Mutual Funds—a Serendipity to Date. Harvard Bus, Jan, 1969; -3k

Carpenter, H. G. Investment Timing by Formula Plans. Har-Row, 1943; -12f

Carsberg, B. V. & Edey, H. C. (Eds). Modern Financial Management: Selected Readings. Penguin, 1969; -1b

Carson, D. (Ed). Money and Finance. Wiley, 1966; -22a

Carson, R. L. A Note on the 'Cost of Capital'. WEJ, (Jun, 1967); -23c

Carter, C. F.; Meredith, G. P. & Shackle, G. L. S. (Eds). Uncertainty and Business Decisions: The Logic, Philosophy and Psychology of Business Decision-Making Under Uncertainty: A Symposium, 2nd ed. Liverpool U Pr, 1957; -9c

Carter, E. E. A Behavioral Theory Approach to Firm Investment and Acquisition Decisions. PhD diss, Carnegie-Mellon U, 1969; -25f

    & Cohen, K. J. Bias in the DJIA caused by Stock Splits. FAJ, 22 (Nov-Dec, 1966), 90-94; -5b

    & Cohen, K. J. Stock Averages, Stock Splits, and Bias. FAJ, 23 (May-Jun, 1967), 77-81; -5b

Carter, P. Capital Structure Changes over the Life Cycle of Corporations. MBA thesis, U of Cal Berkeley, 1967; -23g

Carter, W. D. Quality of Mutual Fund Portfolio Supervision. AJ, 6 (4th Qtr, 1950), 32-36; -3k

Cary, W. L. Administrative Agencies and the Securities and Exchange Commission. LCP (Jun, 1964), 653-662; -2e

    A Review of the Work of the Securities and Exchange Commission. The Record of the Association of the Bar of the City of New York, (Nov, 1964); -2e

    & Bright, C. B. The Law and the Lore of Endowment Funds. Ford, 1969; -3j

    See also **Butters, J. K.; Lintner, J. & Cary, W. L.**

Case, F. E.

    See **Kahn, S. A.; Case, F. E. & Schimmel, A.**

Cattanach, R. L. An Inquiry into the Informational Needs of Stockholders and Potential Investors. DBA diss, Arizona St U, 1972; -8e

Cavaco Silva, A. A. Contribution to the Study of the Influence of Each of the 30 Dow Jones Industrial Stocks on the Average. AIGC, 3 (1968), 15-48; -5b

Caverly, T. A.

    See **Woods, D. H. & Caverly, T. A.**

Cerf, A. R.

    See **Wendt, P. F. & Cerf, A. R.**

Chalmers, E. R. The Gilt-edged Market: a Study of the Background Factors. Griffith, 1967; -19b

    (Ed). Readings in the Euro-dollar. Griffith, 1969; -20d

Chambers, D. J. An Approach to Capital Budgeting. EBR, (May, 1967), 7-11; -25c

    Dividend Plans and Balance Sheet Management. JBF, 4 (Autumn, 1972), 17-25; -22c

    Programming the Allocation of Funds Subject to Restrictions on Reported Results. ORQ, 18 (Dec, 1967), 407-432; -22c

      & Charnes, A.   Intertemporal Analysis and Optimization of Bank
Portfolios. MSci, 7 (Jul, 1961), 393-410; -10g
Chambers, J. C.
      See **Weekes, P. A.; Chambers, J. C. & Mullick, S. K.**
Chambers, R. J.   Financial Management. Law Book, 1967; -22a
Charnes, A.; Cooper, W. W. & Miller, M. H.   Application of Linear
Programming to Financial Budgeting and the Costing of Funds. JB, 32,
(Jan, 1959), 20-46; -25c
      & Littlechild, S. C.   Intertemporal Bank Asset Choice with
Stochastic Dependence. Paper at the TIMS/ORSA Joint Meeting, San
Francisco, May 1968; -10g
      See also **Byrne, R.; Charnes, A.; Cooper, W. W. & Kortanek, K.**
      See also **Chambers, D. J. & Charnes, A.**
Chartered Financial Analysts, Institute of.   C. F. A. Readings in Financial
Analysis. Irwin, 1970; -1b
      Investment Company Portfolio Management. Irwin, 1970; -3k
      Pension Fund Investment Management. Irwin, 1969; -3i
      Personal Trust Investment Management. Proceedings, C.F.A.
Research Seminar, May 4-6, 1967, Charlottesville, Va. Irwin, 1968;
-3j
      Property and Liability Insurance Investment Management. Irwin,
1971; -3h
Chase, D. D.   An Asset Portfolio Preference Model of Equity Valuation
with an Empirical Investigation. DBA diss, Arizona St U, 1972; -7c
Chase, R. H., Jr. et al.   Computer Applications in Investment Analysis.
Dartmouth C, 1966; -4e
Chen, A. H.-Y.   A Dynamic Programming Approach to the Valuation of
Warrants. PhD diss, U of Cal Berkeley, 1968; -17b
      A Model of Warrant Pricing in a Dynamic Market. JF, 25 (Dec,
1970), 1041-1060; -17b
      Valuation under Uncertainty. JFQA, 2 (Sep, 1967), 313-326; -9c
    Jen, F. C. & Zionts, S.   Portfolio Models with Stochastic Demands.
JF, forthcoming; -25a
Chen, H-C. (Ed).   Frontiers of Managerial Finance. Gulf Pub, 1967; -2a
Cheney, H. L.   How Good are Investment Advisory Services? FE, 37
(Nov, 1969), 30-35; -15c
Cheng, H-S.   International Bond Issues of the Less-Developed Countries:
Diagnosis and Prescription. Iowa St U Pr, 1969; -20e
Cheng, P. L.   Efficient Portfolio Selection beyond the Markowitz Frontier.
JFQA, 6 (Dec, 1971), 1207-1234; -10c
      Optimum Bond Portfolio Selection. MSci, 8 (Jul, 1962), 490-499; -19a
      & Deets, M. K.   Portfolio Returns and the Random Walk Theory.
JF, 26 (Mar, 1971), 11-30; -11c
      & Deets, M. K.   Statistical Biases and Security Rates of Return.
JFQA, 6 (Jun, 1971), 977-994; -5c
      & Savage, D. T.   Short-Run Manipulative Aspects of Common Stock
Warrants. QREB, 3 (Summer, 1963), 102-107; -17b
      & Shelton, J. P.   A Contribution to the Theory of Capital Budgeting
—the Multi-Investment Case. JF, 18 (Dec, 1963), 622-636; -25e
      & Shelton, J. P.   Capital Budgeting: Reply. JF, 19 (Dec, 1964), 671-
672; -25c
Childs, C. F.   Concerning US Government Securities. Lakeside, 1947; -19b
Childs, J. F.   Long-Term Financing. P-H, 1961; -22a
      Profit Goals and Capital Management. P-H, 1968; -22a

Chipman, J. S. The Foundations of Utility. Em, 28 (Apr, 1960), 193-224; -9a

Chisholm, R. K. The Rate of Return to Investment in Farm Land. PhD diss, U of Chicago, 1968; -21c

Choi, K. S. A Theoretical and Empirical Analysis of Convertible Bond Financing and Investment. PhD diss, U of Cincinnati, 1971; -17c

Choka, A. D. An Introduction to Securities Regulation. Twentieth Press, 1958; -2e

Chottiner, S. An Investigation of Stock Market Interactions via Computer Simulation of a Model of Idealized Behavior. PhD diss, NYU, 1968; -4a

See also **Molodovsky, N.; May, C. & Chottiner, S.**

Chown, J. F. & Valentine, R. The International Bond Market in the 1960's. Praeger, 1968; -20e

Christensen, L. R. Tax Policy and Investment Expenditures in a Model of General Equilibrium. AER, 60 (May, 1970), 18-22; -27a

Christenson, C. J. Optimal Strategies in Sealed Bidding for Corporate Debt Securities. PhD diss, Harvard U, 1961; -19e

Strategic Aspects of Competitive Bidding for Corporate Securities. Harvard Busn, 1965; -19e

Christie, H. Eurodollars and the Balance of Payments. Banker, 117 (Jan, 1967), 34-35; -20d

Christy, G. A. Capital Budgeting: Current Practices and their Efficiency. Oregon Busn, 1966; -25f

A Rationalization of the Stock-Bond Yield Spread. QREB, 7 (Spring, 1967), 63-70; -7b

Clare, R. L., Jr. (Ed). The Law, Disclosure and the Securities Markets. Pr Law Inst, 1970; -2e

Clark C. D. A Note on Investment Activities and the Graduated Corporate Tax. JF, 12 (Mar, 1957), 44-50; -27c

Clark, J. B. Insurance and Business Profit. QJE, 6 (Oct, 1892), 40-54; -9c

Clark, J. N., Jr. Common Stock Price Fluctuations. FAJ, 20 (May-Jun, 1964), 71-74; -10b

Clark, P. K. A Subordinated Stochastic Process Model with Finite Variance for Speculative Prices. Discussion Paper No. 1, Center for Economic Research, U of Minn, Apr 1971; -11b

Clarke, W. M. The City in the World Economy. Econ Affairs, 1965; -3e

Money Markets of the City: What the Future may Bring. London: Laurie Milbank, 1969; -20a

Clarkson, G. P. E. Portfolio Selection: A Simulation of Trust Investment. P-H, 1962; -4d

& **Elliott, B. J.** Managing Money and Finance. Gower, 1969; -22a

& **Meltzer, A. H.** Portfolio Selection: A Heuristic Approach. JF, 15 (Dec, 1960), 465-480; -4d

Clay, L. T. Computers in Investment Analysis. FAJ, 22 (Jan-Feb, 1966), 70-71; -4e

Clayton, G. British Financial Intermediaries in Theory and Practice. EJ, 72 (Dec, 1962), 869-886; -3e

British Insurance. Elek, 1971; -3h

& **Osborn, W. T.** Insurance Company Investment, Principles and Policy. Allen, 1965; -3h

Clendenin, J. C. Dividend Growth as Determinant of Common Stock Values. TE, (Feb, 1957); -7b

Introduction to Investments, 5th ed. McGraw, 1969; -4a

Price-Level Variations and the Tenets of High Grade Investment. JF, 14 (May, 1959), 245-262; -7b

Quality versus Price as Factors Influencing Common Stock Price Fluctuations. JF, 6 (Dec, 1951), 398-405; -7b

Theory and Technique of Growth Stock Valuation. UCLA Busn, 1957; -7b

What Do Stockholders Like? CMR, 1 (Fall, 1958), 47-55; -24b

& Van Cleave, M.   Growth and Common Stock Values. JF, 9 (Sep, 1954), 365-376; -7b

Clendenning, E. W.   Euro-dollars: the Problem of Control. Banker, 118 (Apr, 1968), 321-329; -20d

Cloos, G. W.   A Larger Role for Commercial Paper. BC (Dec, 1968), 2-12; -20a

Cobleigh, I. A. & King, H. J.   Difference Between Listed and Over-the-Counter Trading. CFC, (Oct 10, 1963) 39ff; -2f

Coen, P. J.; Gomme, E. D. & Kendall, M. G.   Lagged Relationships in Economic Forecasting. JRSS, 31 (1969), A133-A163; -7d

Coffmann, P. B.

See **Badger, R. E. & Coffman, P. B.**

Cohan, A. B.   Cost of Flotation of Long-Term Corporate Debt since 1935. U of NC Busn, 1961; -19e

Private Placements and Public Offerings: Market Shares Since 1935. U of NC Busn, 1961; -19e

Yields on Corporate Debt Directly Placed. (Dist by Columbia U Pr) Natl Bur Econ Res, 1967; -19b

Yields on New Underwritten Corporate Bonds, 1935-58. JF, 17 (Dec, 1964), 585-605; -19b

Cohan, S. B.   The Determinants of Supply and Demand for Certificates of Deposit. PhD diss, U of Mich, 1969; -20a

Cohen, B. C.   Money Market Development and the Demand for Money. JFQA, 6 (Sep, 1971), 1155-1158; -20a

Cohen, J.   Federal Reserve Margin Requirements and the Stock Market. JFQA, 1 (Sep, 1966), 30-54; -6e

Cohen, J. B. & L'Esperance, W. L.   An Econometric Analysis of the Flow of Funds in the Stock Market. Paper delivered at the Econometric Society Meeting, New York, Dec, 1965; -3c

& Robbins, S. M.   The Financial Manager — Basic Aspects of Financial Administration. Har-Row, 1966; -22a

& Zinbarg, E. D.   Investment Analysis and Portfolio Management. Irwin, 1967; -4a

Cohen, K. J.   Dynamic Balance Sheet Management: a Management Science Approach. JBR, (Winter, 1972), 9-19; -10g

& Elton, E. J.   Inter-Temporal Portfolio Analysis Based on Simulation of Joint Returns. MSci, 13 (Sep, 1967), 5-18; -10c

& Fitch, B.   The Average Investment Performance Index. MSci, 12 (Feb, 1966), B195-B215; -14a

& Hammer, F. S. (Eds).   Analytical Methods in Banking. Irwin, 1966; -3f

& Hammer, F. S.   Linear Programming and Optimal Bank Asset Management Decisions. JF, 22 (May, 1967), 147-165; -10g

& Hammer, F. S.   Optimal Coupon Schedules for Municipal Bonds. MSci, 12 (Sep, 1965), 68-82; -19d

     & Hammer, F. S.   Optimal Level Debt Schedules for Municipal Bonds. M.Sci, 13 (Nov, 1966), 161-166; -19d

     Hammer, F. S. & Schneider, H. M.   Harnessing Computers for Bank Asset Management. BM, 150 (Summer, 1967), 72-80:, -10g

     Kramer, R. L. & Waugh, W. H.   Regression Yield Curves for U S. Government Securities. MSci, 13 (Dec, 1966), B168-B175; -18e, 18f

     & Pogue, J. A.   An Empirical Evaluation of Alternative Portfolio-Selection Models. JB, 40 (Apr, 1967), 166-193; -10c

     & Pogue, J. A.   Some Comments Concerning Mutual Fund versus Random Portfolio Performance. JB, 41 (Apr, 1968), 180-190; -14a

     & Reid, S. R.   The Benefits and Costs of Bank Mergers. JFQA, 1 (Dec, 1966), 15-57; -26b

     & Rutenberg, D. P.   Toward a Comprehensive Framework for Bank Financial Planning. JBR, 2 (Winter, 1971), 41-57; -10g

     & Thore, S.   Programming Bank Portfolios Under Uncertainty. JBR, 1 (Spring, 1970), 42-61; -10g

     See also **Carter, E. E. & Cohen, K. J.**

Cohen, M. F. & Rabin, J. J.   Broker-Dealer Selling Practice Standards: the Importance of Administrative Adjudication in their Development. LCP, (Jun, 1964), 694-710; -2b

Cohn, R. A. & Pringle, J. J.   Imperfections in International Financial Markets: Implications for Risk Premia and the Cost of Capital to Firms. JF, forthcoming; -10i

     See also **Robichek, A. A.; Cohn, R. A. & Pringle, J. J.**

Colberg, M. R.

     See **Franklin, C. B. & Colberg, M. R.**

Colby, W. G.   The Management of Dealer Positions in U.S. Government Securities. PhD diss, Yale U, 1970; -19b

Coleman, A. B.

     See **Robichek, A. A. & Coleman, A. B.**

     See also **Vandell, R. F. & Coleman, A. B.**

Coleman, G. W.   Lending and Investment Practices of Commercial Banks. LCP, 17 (Winter, 1952), 108-127; -3f

Colin, J. W. & Dyl, E. A.   Calculation of Tax Effective Yields: a Correction. JFQA, 6 (Sep, 1971), 1163-1164; -27a

Colker, S. S.   An Analysis of Security Recommendations by Brokerage Houses. QREB, 3 (Summer, 1963), 19-28; -15c

Collins, C. J.   Effect of Sunspot Activity on the Stock Market. FAJ, 21 (Nov-Dec, 1965), 45-56; -12g

Comer, H. D.   Is the 'Dow' Already Above 1200? FAJ, 20 (May-Jun, 1964), 69-70; -5b

     Low Priced Versus High Priced Stocks. AJ, 1 (Apr, 1945), 15-20; -7a

Commission on Money & Credit.   Private Financial Institutions: a series of research studies prepared for the Commission. P-H, 1963; -3e

Committe, T. C.   Managerial Finance for the Seventies. McGraw, 1972; -1c

Committee on the Working of the Monetary System.   Report Command 827 (The Radcliffe Report). HMSO, 1959; -3e

Conard, J. W.   An Introduction to the Theory of Interest. U of Cal Pr, 1959; -18b

     The Behavior of Interest Rates: a Progress Report. (Dist by Columbia U Pr) Natl Bur Econ Res, 1966:, -18b

     Frankena, M. W.   The Yield Spread between New and Seasoned Corporate Bonds, 1952-63, *in* Guttentag, J. M. & Cagan, P. (Eds), Essays on Interest Rates, Vol 1. (Dist by Columbia U Pr) Natl Bur Econ Res, 1969; -19e

Conklin, G. H.   Growth Stocks—a Critical View. AJ, 14 (Feb, 1958), 49-52;-7b

Conklin, G. T., Jr.   Direct Placements. JF, 6 (Jun, 1951), 85-118; -19e

Conlong, A.   The First Eight Years of the FT Actuaries All Share Index. IA, 27 (Sep, 1970), 3-18; -5b

Conn, M. V.

See **Storer, R. W. & Conn, M. V.**

Conrad, G. R. & Plotkin, I. H.   Risk/Return: U.S. Industry Pattern, HBR, 46 (Mar-Apr, 1968), 90-99; -10o

Continental Illinois National Bank of Chicago.   The Computer Looks at the Analyst. Report prepared by D.A. Monteith and J. D. McWilliams. Chicago; Continental Illinois National Bank, 1966; -15b

The Reliability of Earnings Forecasts. Chicago: Continental Illinois National Bank, 1963; -15b

Cook, P. L.   Effects of Mergers: Six Studies. Allen, 1958; -26b

Cook, P. W.   Thinking Ahead: Trends in Merger Activity. HBR, 37 (Mar-Apr, 1959), 15-20; -26a

Cooke, G. W.   The Stock Market. Simmons-B, 1964; -2b

& Bomeli, E. C.   Business and Financial Management. HM, 1967; -22a

et al.   Financial Institutions: Their Role in the American Economy. Simmons-B, 1962; -3e

Coombs, C. H. & Pruitt, D. G.   Components of Risk in Decision-Making: Probability and Variance Preferences. JEP, 60 (1960), 265-277; -9b

Cooper, G. M.

See **Sharpe, W. F. & Cooper, G. M.**

Cooper, W. W.

See **Byrne, R.; Charnes, A.; Cooper, W. W. & Kortanek, K.**

See also **Charnes, A; Cooper, W. W. & Miller, M. H.**

Coorey, M. G.

See **Adamson, A. & Coorey, M. G.**

Cootner, P. H.   Common Elements in Futures Markets for Commodities and Bonds. AER, 51 (May, 1961), 173-183; -21a

(Ed).   The Random Character of Stock Market Prices. MIT Pr, 1964; -11c

Rationality and Risk in Financial Decision Making, *in* Fisk, G.(Ed), The Frontiers of Management Psychology. Har-Row, 1964; -9c

Returns to Speculators: Telser Versus Keynes. JPE, 68 (Aug, 1960), 396-404;-21a

Speculation and Hedging. FRIS, 7 (Suppl, 1967), 65-105; -21a

The Stochastic Theory of Bond Prices. Paper presented at the Econometric Society Meeting, Dec, 1966; -19a

Stock Market Indexes—Fallacies and Illusions. CFC, (Sep 29, 1966); -5b

Stock Prices: Random Walks vs Finite Markov Chains, IMR, 3 (Spring, 1962), 24-45; -11c

Technicians' Contribution in Selecting Undervalued Stocks. CFC (Sep 16, 1965), 5ff; -12a

& Holland, D. M.   Risk and Rate of Return, rev ed. MIT Pr, 1964; -10o

Copeman, R. C.   Attitudes to Stockmarket Investment Decisions in the City of London, August to October, 1971. Discussion paper No. 33, Graduate Centre for Mgmt Studies, U of Aston, Nov 1971;-4c

Cord, J. A Method of Allocating Funds to Investment Projects When Returns Are Subject to Uncertainty. MSci, 10 (Jan, 1964), 335-341; -25d

Corey, E. R. Direct Placement of Corporate Securities. Harvard Busn, 1951; -19e

Corley, L. Practical Investment. Arco, 1968; -4a

Cormier, F. Wall Street's Shady Side. Pub Affairs, 1962; -2b

Corner, D. C.
　　See **Burton, H. & Corner, D. C.**

Corrigan, F. J. & Ward, H. A. (Eds). Financial Management: Policies and Practices. HM, 1963; -22a

Cotter, R. V. Capital Adequacy and Commercial Bank Failures. PhD diss, U of Oreg, 1966; -3f

Cottle, S. & Whitman, W. T. Corporate Earning Power and Market Valuation, 1935-1955. Duke, 1959; -8d
　　　　& Whitman, W. T. Investment Timing. McGraw, 1953; -7d
　　See also **Graham, B.; Dodd, D. L. & Cottle, S.**

Coughtry, L. S. Computers—A Tool in Security Analysis. FAJ, 19 (Jan-Feb, 1963), 53-55; -4e

Cowing, C. B. Populists, Plungers and Progressives: Social History of Stock and Commodity Speculation. Princeton U Pr, 1965; -2d

Cowles, A. Can Stock Market Forecasters Forecast? Em, (Jul, 1933); -15c
　　　A Revision of Previous Conclusions Regarding Stock Price Behavior. Em, 28 (Oct, 1960), 909-915; -11c
　　　Stock Market Forecasting. Em, 12 (Jul-Oct, 1944), 206-214; -15c
　　　et al. Common Stock Indexes 1871-1937. Principia Pr, 1938; -5a
　　　& Jones, H. E. Some A Posteriori Probabilities in Stock Market Action. Em, (Jul, 1937), 280-294; -11c

Cox, E. B. Changes in the Size Distribution of Dividend Income. JASA, 56 (Jun, 1961), 250-260; -3a
　　　Trends in the Distribution of Stock Ownership. U of Pa Pr, 1963; -3a

Cox, R. A Counter-Example to the Random Walk Hypothesis of Stock Market Prices. PhD diss, Columbia U, 1969; -11c

Cragg, J. G. & Baxter, N. D. The Issuing of Corporate Securities. JPE, 78 (Nov-Dec, 1970), 1310-1324; -19e, 23g
　　　　Harburger, A. C. & Mieszkowski, P. Empirical Evidence on the Incidence of the Corporation Income Tax. JPE, 75 (Dec, 1967), 811-821; -27c
　　　　& Malkiel, B. G. The Consensus and Accuracy of Some Predictions of the Growth of Corporate Earnings. JF, 23 (Mar, 1968), 67-84; -15b
　　See also **Baxter, N. D. & Cragg, J. G.**

Cramer, J. J., Jr. Accounting and Reporting Requirements of the Private Pension Trust. DBA diss, Indiana U, 1964; -3i

Crane, B. The Sophisticated Investor. S & S, 1964; -4a

Crane, D. B. A Stochastic Programming Model for Commercial Bank Bond Portfolio Management. JFQA, 6 (Jun, 1971), 955-976; -10g

Cranshaw, E. T. Is Pound-Averaging a Hoax? IA, 28 (Dec, 1970), 12-13; -12f

Crary, D. T. See **Lishan, J. M. & Crary, D. T. (Eds)**

Creamer, D.; Dobrovolsky, S. P. & Borenstein, I. Capital in Manufacturing and Mining. Princeton U Pr, 1960; -23a

Cresson, G. V. The Writing of Options. AJ, 15 (May, 1959), 43-46; -17a

Cretien, P. D., Jr. Convertible Bond Premiums as Predictors of Common Stock Price Changes. FAJ, 25 (Nov-Dec, 1969), 90-95; -17c

Crick, W. F. (Ed). Commonwealth Banking Systems. Oxford U Pr, 1965;
-3f

Crockett, J. & Friend, I. Characteristics of Stock Ownership. Proceedings
of the American Statistical Association, 1963, 146-168; -3a

    & Friend, I. Some Estimates of the Cost of Capital to the Elec-
tric Utility Industry, 1954-57: Comment. AER, 57 (Dec, 1967), 1258-
1267; -23c

    See also **Friend, I., Blume, M. E. & Crockett, J.**

Crooch, G. M. An Investigation of Investors' Financial Statement Knowledge. PhD diss, Mich St U, 1970; -8e

    See also **Baskin, E. F. & Crooch, G. M.**

Cropper, P. J. The Economist in the Investment Business, *in* Alexander,
K. J. W. et al. (Eds), The Economist in Business. Blackwell, 1967; -6a

Crosse, H. D. Management Policies for Commercial Banks. P-H, 1962;
-3f

Crouch, R. L. Market Volume and Price Changes. FAJ, 26 (Jul-Aug, 1970),
104-109; -13a

    Tobin vs Keynes on Liquidity Preference. REStat, 53 (Nov, 1971),
368-371; -18f

Crowell, R. A. An Analysis of Expected Earnings. Paper for the Seminar
on the Analysis of Security Prices, U of Chicago, May 1967; -15b

    Earnings Expectations, Security Valuation and the Cost of Equity
Capital. PhD diss, MIT, 1967; -7c

Crum, C.

    See **Law, W. & Crum, C.**

Crum, M. C. Performance Investing and the Breakdown of Respect for
Authority. FAJ, 25 (May-Jun, 1969), 142-147; -4c

Crum, W. L. Analysis of Stock Ownership. HBR, 31 (May-Jun, 1953), 36-54;
-3a

Crum, W. S. Corporate Size and Earning Power. Harvard U Pr, 1939; -26f

Crysler, E. W., Jr. Growth of the Mutual Fund Industry. FAJ, 18 (Jan-Feb,
1962), 31-38; -3k

Culbertson, J. M. The Interest Rate Structure: Towards Completion of
the Classical System, *in* Hahn, F. H. & Brechling, F. P. R. (Eds), The
Theory of Interest Rates. Macmillan Int, 1965; -18f

    The Term Structure of Interest Rates. QJE, 71 (Nov, 1957), 485-
517; -18f

Cullity, J. P. An Alternative Measure of the Diffusion of Stock Prices.
QREB, 7 (Autumn, 1967), 47-55; -12e

    Stock Price Recoveries After Post-war Recessions. FAJ, 23 (Sep-
Oct, 1967), 98-100; -6b

Cuneo, L. J.

    See **Wagner, W. H. & Cuneo, L. J.**

Cunningham, N. Business Investment and the Marginal Cost of Funds.
Met, (Dec, 1958), 155-181; -23d

Curley, A. J.

    See **Stoll, H. R. & Curley, A. J.**

Curley, M. L.

    See **Johnston, G. S.; Curley, M. L. & McIndoe, R. A.**

Curran, W. S. Preferred Stock in Public Utility Finance—a Reconsideration. FAJ, 28 (Mar-Apr, 1972), 71-76; -19i

    Principles of Financial Management. McGraw, 1970; -22a

Cushing, B. E. The Effects of Accounting Policy Decisions on Trends in
Reported Corporate Earnings per Share. PhD diss, Mich St U, 1969; -8c

Dacey, W. M.   The British Banking Mechanism, 4th ed. Hutchinson, 1967; -3f

Dake, L. E.   Are Analysts' Techniques Adequate for Growth Stocks? FAJ, 16 (Nov-Dec, 1960), 45-49; -7b

Dalrymple, B. B.   Risk Analysis Applied to Commodity Speculation. PhD diss, La St U, 1970; -21a

Damant, D.   Some Aspects of Technical Analysis (II). IA, 19 (Dec, 1967), 24-28; -12a

D'Ambrosio, C. A.
See **Archer, S. H. & D'Ambrosio, C. A.**

Daniels, H. E.   Autocorrelation between First Differences of Mid-Ranges. Em, 34 (Jan, 1966), 215-219; -5c

Darkazanli, S.
See **Whitmore, G. A. & Darkazanli, S.**

Darling, P. G.   The Influence of Expectations and Liquidity on Dividend Policy. JPE, 65 (Jun, 1957), 209-224; -24a

A Surrogative Measure of Business Confidence and its Relation to Stock Prices. JF, 10 (Dec, 1955), 442-458; -24a

Dartmouth Economic Research Council.   Broadening the Base of Stock Ownership. Amos Tuck School of Business Administration, Dartmouth C, 1956; -3a

Dascher, P. E.   The Penn Central Revisited: a Predictable Situation. FAJ, 28 (Mar-Apr, 1972), 61-64; -26g

Dauten, C. A.   Business Finance: The Fundamentals of Financial Management, 2nd ed. P-H, 1956; -22a

& Welshans, M. T.   Principles of Finance: Functions, Problems, Institutions, 3rd ed. SW Pub, 1964; -22a

Davant, J. W.   The Martin Report: An Answer to the Critics. FAJ, 27 (Nov-Dec, 1971), 14ff; -2b

Davenport, M. W.   Appreciation with Safety in Convertibles. AJ, 10 (Aug, 1954), 37-39; -17c

Measuring Earnings Protection for Preferred Stocks. AJ, 12 (Aug, 1956), 31-34; -19i

Davidson, H. A.   College Endowment Fund Management. FAJ, 27 (Jan-Feb, 1971), 69-74; -3j

Davidson, S. & Drake, D. F.   Capital Budgeting and the 'Best' Tax Depreciation Method. JB, 34 (Oct, 1961), 442-452; -25c

Davis, E. W.
See **Nevin, E. & Davis, E. W.**

Davis, J. V.   The Adjustment of Stock Prices to New Information. PhD diss, Cornell U, 1967; -11a

Davis, S. C.   How U.S. Fire and Casualty Companies Invest. FAJ, 17 (Nov-Dec, 1961), 19-24; -3h

Investments in Common Stocks by Life Insurance Companies. AJ, 1 (Jul, 1945), 3-13; -3h

Dean, J.   Capital Budgeting; Top-Management Policy on Plant, Equipment, and Product Development. Columbia U Pr, 1951; -25c

Management of Capital Expenditures. U of Tex Busn, 1960; -25c

Managerial Economics. P-H, 1951; -22a

Measuring the Productivity of Capital. HBR, 32 (Jan-Feb, 1954), 120-130; -25c

Outside Directors Appraise Stock Options. FAJ, 19 (Mar-Apr, 1963), 25-31; -17d

Deane, P.   Long-Term Trends in Capital Formation and Financing. EJ, 72 (Dec, 1962), 926-930; -23a

De Bedts, R. F.   The New Deal's SEC: The Formative Years. Columbia
U Pr, 1964; -2e

Debreu, G.   New Concepts and Techniques for Equilibrium Analysis.
IntER, 3 (1962), 257-273; -9d

   Theory of Value: an Axiomatic Analysis of Economic Equilibrium.
Wiley, 1959; -9d

Decker, M. G. & Butler, H. L., Jr.   A Security Check on the Dow Jones Industrial Average. AJ, 9 (Feb, 1953), 37-45; -5b

Dedalus, A. I.   The Effect of Inflation on the Stock Market. AJ, 14 (Aug,
1958), 73-76; -6c

Deets, M. K.
   See **Cheng, P. L. & Deets, M. K.**

DeFelice, F.   Security and Investment: More Evidence. JF, 25 (Sep, 1970),
803-808; -23c

DeGroot, M. H.   Some Comments on the Experimental Measurement of
Utility. BS, 8 (Apr, 1963), 146-149; -9b

Dellenbarger, L. E., Jr.   Common Stock Valuation in Industrial Mergers.
U of Fla Pr, 1966; -26a

   A Study of Relative Common Equity Values in Fifty Mergers of
Listed Industrial Corporations, 1950-57. JF, 18 (Sep, 1963), 564-565;
-26a

De Marco, M. A.   A Computer-Aided Analysis of the Impact of Stock
Dividends and Splits on Share Price Change. SM thesis, MIT, 1967;
-16c

Demetriou, P. A.   The Present Value of Investments in Sinking Funds.
MSci, 13 (Jan, 1967), 336-343; -19g

Deming, D. D.
   See **Murdick, R. G. & Deming, D. D.**

Demsetz, H.   The Cost of Transacting. QJE, 82 (Feb, 1968), 33-53; -2b

Deslattes, V. L.   The Demand for Savings Bonds in the United States—with
Emphasis on the Significance of Interest Rates in the Postwar Period.
PhD diss, La St U, 1968; -19a

Dev, S. & Webb, M.   The Accuracy of Company Profit Forecasts. JBF, 4
(Autumn, 1972), 26-39; -15b

DeVere, C. W.
   See **Pratt, S. P. & DeVere, C. W.**

Dewey, D.   Modern Capital Theory. Columbia U Pr, 1965; -22b

Dewing, A. S.   The Financial Policy of Corporations, 2 Vols, 5th ed.
Ronald, 1953; -22a

   A Statistical Test of the Success of Consolidations. QJE, 36 (Nov,
1921), 84-101; -26b

DeWulf, L.   Taxation of Unrealized Capital Gains: Theoretical and Empirical Analysis. PhD diss, Clark U, 1970; -27d

De Zoete & Gorton.   Changes in Bank Rate since 1694 and Movements in
Long Term Interest Rates since 1731. London, de Zoete & Gorton, nd;
-18b

   Equity and Fixed Interest Investment 1919-1970. London, de Zoete
& Gorton, 1970; -19b

Dhrymes, P. J. & Kurz, M.   Investment Dividend, and External Finance
Behavior of Firms, *in* Ferber, R. (Ed), Determinants of Investment
Behavior. Natl Bur Econ Res, 1967; -24a

   & Kurz, M.   On the Dividend Policy of Electric Utilities. REStat,
46 (Feb, 1964), 76-81; -24a

Diamond, J. J.   Earnings Distribution and the Evaluation of Shares: Some Recent Evidence. JFQA, 2 (Mar, 1967), 14-29; -24b

Diamond, P. A.   On the Asset Demand for Money. Wkg Paper No. 75, Institute of Business and Economic Research, U of Cal, Berkeley, 1965; -18a

On the Cost of Tax-Exempt Bonds. JPE, 73 (Aug, 1965), 399-403; -19d

Risk Aversion and Savings. Wkg Paper No. 70, Institute of Business and Economic Research, U of Cal, Berkeley, 1965; -18a

The Role of a Stock Market in a General Equilibrium Model with Technological Uncertainty. AER, 57 (Sep, 1967), 759-776; -9d

Savings Decisions under Uncertainty. Wkg Paper No. 71, Institute of Business and Economic Research. U of Cal, Berkeley, 1965; -18a

& Yaari, M. E.   Implications of the Theory of Rationing for Consumer Choice Under Uncertainty. AER, 62 (Jun, 1972), 333-343; -9c

Diefenbach, R. E.   How Good is Institutional Brokerage Research? FAJ, 28 (Jan-Feb, 1972), 54-60; -15c

Dietz, P. O.   Components of a Measurement Model: Rate of Return, Risk and Timing. JF, 23 (May, 1968), 267-275; -14b

Evaluating the Investment Performance of Noninsured Pension Funds. PhD diss, Columbia U, 1965; -14b

Investment Goals: A Key to Measuring Performance of Pension Funds. FAJ, 24 (Mar-Apr, 1968), 133-137; -14b

Pension Fund Investment Performance—What Method to Use When. FAJ, 22 (Jan-Feb, 1966), 83-86; -14b

Pension Funds: Measuring Investment Performance. Free Pr, 1966; -14b

Diggory, T. G. & Wade, E.   Capital Expenditure. Anbar, 1967; -25c

Diller, S.   The Expectations Component of the Term Structure, *in* Guttentag, J. M. (Ed), Essays on Interest Rates, Vol 2. (Dist by Columbia U Pr) Natl Bur Econ Res, 1971; -18f

Expectations in the Term Structure of Interest Rates, *in* Mincer, J. (Ed), Economic Forecasts and Expectations. Natl Bur Econ Res, 1969; -18f

The Seasonal Variation of Interest Rates. Natl Bur Econ Res, 1970; -18d

Dince, R. R.   Another View of Formula Planning. JF, 19 (Dec, 1964), 678-688; -12f

Formula Planning. FAJ, 17 (Mar-Apr, 1961), 59-64; -12f

Portfolio Income: A Test of a Formula Plan. JFQA, 1 (Sep, 1966), 90-107; -12f

Diulio, E. A.   Fund Mobility in the Capital Markets: Interest Rate Differentials as a Measure. PhD diss, Columbia U, 1966; -18b

Dobrovolsky, S. P.   Corporate Income Retention, 1915-1943. Natl Bur Econ Res, 1962; -24a

Economics of Corporate Internal and External Financing. JF, 13 (Mar, 1958), 35-47; -23d

The Economics of Corporation Finance. McGraw, 1971; -22a

See also **Creamer, D.; Dobrovolsky, S. P. & Borenstein, I.**

Dockeray, J. C.

See **Husband, W. H. & Dockeray, J. C.**

Dodd, D. L.

See **Graham, B.; Dodd, D. L. & Cottle, S.**

Doede, R. W.   The Monopoly Power of the New York Stock Exchange. PhD diss, U of Chicago, 1967; -2b

Doenges, R. C.
>See **Wolf, H. A. & Doenges, R. C. (Eds)**

Dolley, J. C. The Price-Effect of Stock Right Issues. JB, 7 (Apr, 1934), 133-160; -16b

Domar, E. D. & Musgrave, R. A. Proportional Income Taxation and Risk-Taking. QJE, 58 (May, 1944), 388-422; -27a

Donaldson, E. F. & Pfahl, J. K. Corporate Finance: Policy and Management, 3rd ed. Ronald, 1969; -22a

Donaldson, G. Corporate Debt Capacity: A Study of Corporate Debt Policy and the Determination of Corporate Debt Capacity. Harvard Busn, 1961; -23g
>Financial Goals: Management vs Stockholders. HBR, 41 (May-Jun, 1963), 116-129; -3a
>In Defense of Preferred Stock. HBR, 40 (Jul-Aug, 1962), 123-136; -19i
>New Framework for Corporate Debt Policy. HBR, 40 (Mar-Apr, 1962), 117-131; -23g
>& **Stubbs, C.** Corporate and Business Finance: a Classified Bibliography. Baker Library, Harvard Bus, 1964; -1a
>See also **Hunt, P.; Williams, C. M. & Donaldson, G.**

Doodha, K. D. Stock Exchanges in a Developing Economy. Bombay U Pr, 1962; -2c

Dougall, H. E. Capital Markets and Institutions, 2nd ed. P-H, 1970; -2b
>Investments, 8th ed. P-H, 1968; -4a
>See also **Guthmann, H. G. & Dougall, H. E.**

Douglas, A. J. A Theory of Saving and Portfolio Selection. REStud, 35 (Oct, 1968), 453-463; -18a

Douglas, G. W. Risk in the Equity Market: An Empirical Appraisal of Market Efficiency. PhD diss, Yale U, 1967; -10*l*
>Risk in the Equity Market: an Empirical Appraisal of Market Efficiency. YEE, 9 (Spring, 1969), 3-45; -10*l*

Downes, D. H.
>See **Barnea, A. & Downes, D. H.**
>See also **Bierman, H., Jr.; Downes, D. H. & Hass, J. E.**

Drakatos, C. London Share Price Indices. BM, 193 (Jun, 1962), 465-473; -5b

Drake, D. F.
>See **Davidson, S. & Drake, D. F.**

Drayton, C. I., Jr.; Emerson, C. & Griswald, J. D. Mergers and Acquisitions: Planning and Action. Fin Exec, 1963; -26a

Drew, G. A. A Clarification of the Odd-Lot Theory. FAJ, 23 (Sep-Oct, 1967), 107-108; -13b
>New Methods for Profit in the Stock Market. Metcalf, 1955; -13b

Dreze, J. H. Endowment Income, Risk Preference and the Cost of Capital in Non-Profit Institutions. Unp ms, Apr, 1968; -3j

Driscoll, T. E. Some Aspects of Corporate Insider Stock Holdings and Trading Under Section 16(b) of the Securities Exchange Act. MBA thesis, U of Pa, 1956; -13c

Dryden, M. M. Capital Budgeting: Treatment of Uncertainty and Investment Criteria. SJPE, 11 (Nov, 1964), 235-259; -25d
>Filter Tests of UK Share Prices. AE, 1 (Jan, 1970), 261-276; -12c
>The MAPI Urgency Rating as an Investment Ranking Criterion. JB, 33 (Oct, 1960), 327-341; -25c
>Share Price Movements: A Markovian Approach. JF, 24 (Mar, 1969), 49-60; -11c

Short Term Forecasting of Share Prices: An Information Theory Approach. SJPE, 15 (Nov, 1968), 227-249; -12e

A Source of Bias in Filter Tests of Share Prices. JB, 42 (Jul, 1969), 321-325; -12c

A Statistical Study of U.K. Share Prices. SJPE, 17 (Nov, 1970), 369-389; -11c

Drzycimski, E. F. A Study of the Determinants of Common Stock Prices and Price-Relatives for a Selected Sample of Large Commercial Banks. PhD diss, Mich St U, 1966; -7c

& Frederickson, D. R. A Relative-to-Market Test of the Random Walk Theory. MVJBE, 6 (1970), 33-47; -11c

& Yudelson, J. Problems in the Measurement of Risk. FE, 37 (Sep, 1969), 32-36; -10b

Dudley, C. L., Jr. A Note on Reinvestment Assumptions in Choosing Between Net Present Value and Internal Rate of Return. JF, 27 (Sep, 1972), 907-916; -25c

Duesenberry, J. S. Criteria for Judging the Performance of Capital Markets. Commission on Money and Credit Memorandum, Apr 10, 1960; -2b

The Portfolio Approach to the Demand for Money and Other Assets. REStat, 45 (Suppl Feb, 1963), 9-24; -18a

Duff, G. M., Jr.

See **Israels, C. L. & Duff, G. M. (Eds).**

Dukes, R. E.

See **Beaver, W. H. & Dukes, R. E.**

Duncan, R. R. The Trustee's Dilemma in Growth Stock Investing. CFC (Jun 29, 1961); -3j

Dunn, M. F. Measurement of Firm Risk and Rate of Return. PhD diss, UCLA, 1971; -10o

Dunning, J. H. Profitability, Productivity and Measures of Business Performance. IA, 23 (Jun, 1969), 22-34; -8c

Durand, D. Bank Stocks and the Analysis of Covariance. Em, 23 (Jan, 1955), 30-45; -10a

Bank Stock Prices and the Bank Capital Problem. Natl Bur Econ Res, 1957; -23d

Basic Yields of Corporate Bonds 1900-1942. Natl Bur Econ Res, 1942; -18e

The Cost of Capital, Corporation Finance, and the Theory of Investment: Comment. AER, 49 (Sep, 1959), 639-655; -23c

Cost of Debt and Equity Funds for Business: Trends and Problems of Measurement, *in* Conference on Research in Business Finance, Natl Bur Econ Res, 1952; -23g

Growth Stocks and the Petersburg Paradox. JF, 12 (Sep, 1957), 348-363; -7b

A Quarterly Series of Corporate Basic Yields 1952-1957 and Some Attendant Reservations. JF, 13 (Sep, 1958), 348-356; -18e

& May, A. M. The Ex-Dividend Behavior of American Telephone and Telegraph Stock. JF, 11 (Mar, 1960), 19-31; -24c

& Winn, W. J. Basic Yields of Bonds 1920-1947: Their Measurement and Pattern. Natl Bur Econ Res, 1947; -18e

See also **Macaulay, F. R. & Durand, D.**

Dutter, P. H. Quality of Management. FAJ, 25 (Mar-Apr, 1969), 105-108

Duvall, R. M. & Austin, D. V. Predicting the Results of Proxy Contests. JF, 20 (Sep, 1965), 464-471; -26h

& Bulloch, J.   Adjusting Rate of Return and Present Value for Price Level Changes. AR, 40 (Jul, 1965), 569-573; -25c

Duvel, D.   A Dynamic Programming Model for the Evaluation of Convertible Bonds. Paper for the Seminar on the Analysis of Security Prices, U of Chicago, May 1968; -17c

Dyckman, T. R.   Allocating Funds to Investment Projects when Returns are Subject to Uncertainty: a Comment. MSci, 10 (Nov, 1964), 348; -25d

Investment Analysis and General Price-Level Adjustments: A Behavioral Study. Studies in Accounting Research No 1. Evanston, Ill.: American Accounting Association, 1969; -8e

On the Investment Decision. AR, 39 (Apr, 1964), 285-295; -25c

& Stekler, H. O.   Firm Size and Variability. JIE, 13 (Jun, 1965), 214-218; -26f

Dyl, E. A.

See **Colin, J. W. & Dyl, E. A.**

See also **McEnally, R. W. & Dyl, E. A.**

Eagly, R. V.   On Government Issuance of an Index Bond. PF, 22 (1967), 268-284; -19b

Eckel, L. G.   The Regulation of Treasury Stock Transactions. PhD diss, U of Mich; -16d

Eckstein, O.

See **Feldstein, M. & Eckstein, O.**

Edey, H. C.

See **Carsberg, B. V. & Edey, H. C.**

Edge, S. K.   Shareholders' Reaction to Rights Issues. MS, 33 (Sep, 1965), 263-284; -16b

Sources of Funds from Rights Issues and their Cost. JES, (Winter, 1965); -16b

Edmister, R. O.   An Empirical Test of Financial Ratio Analysis for Small Business Failure Prediction. JFQA, 7 (Mar, 1972), 1477-1494; -26g

Financial Ratios as Discriminant Predictors of Small Business Failure. PhD, diss, Ohio St U, 1970; -26g

Edwards, C. E. & Hilton, J. G.   High-Low Averages as an Estimator of Annual Average Stock Prices. JF, 21 (Mar, 1966), 112-115; -5c

& Hilton, J. G.   Some Comments on Short-Run Earnings Fluctuation Bias. JFQA, 5 (Jun, 1970), 187-202; -24b

Edwards, E. E.   Changing Character of the Real Estate Mortgage Markets. — JF, 19 (May, 1964), 313-320; -21c

Edwards, J. W.   The Effects of Federal Income Taxes on Capital Budgeting. PhD diss, Mich St U, 1966; -27a

Edwards, K. B.   Insider Trading. A, 81 (Jan, 1970), 46-49; -13c

Edwards, N. D.   Significance of Price Fluctuations in Securities. AJ, 14 (May, 1958), 87-90; -10b

Edwards, R. D. & Magee, J.   Technical Analysis of Stock Trends, 5th ed. Magee, 1964; -12a

Edwards, W.   Probability Preferences in Gambling. AJP, 66 (Jul, 1953), 349-364; -9b

The Theory of Decision Making. PB, (Jul, 1954), 380-417; -9c

Variance Preferences in Gambling. AJP, 67 (1954), 441-452; -9b

Edwards, W.   Study of the Management of Investment and Loan Portfolios of Selected Commercial Banks. DBA diss, Harvard Bus, 1961; -3f

Edwards, W. F.   Techniques of Investment Management. AJ, 4 (Suppl 2nd Qtr, 1948), 83-88; -4a

Egerton, R. A. D. The Holding of Assets: Gambler Preference or 'Safety First'? OEP, 8 (Feb, 1956), 51-59; -10f

    Investment Decisions Under Uncertainty. Liverpool U Pr, 1960;-9c

    Investment, Uncertainty and Expectations. REStud, 22 (Summer, 1955), 143-150; -9c

Ehrich, R. L. Cash-Futures Price Relationships for Live Beef Cattle. AJAE, 51 (Feb, 1969), 26-39; -21a

Einzig, P. A Dynamic Theory of Forward Exchange, 3rd ed. Macmillan Int, 1967; -21b

    The Eurobond Market. Macmillan Int, 1969; -20e

    The Euro-Dollar System. Practice and Theory of International Interest Rates, 3rd ed. Macmillan Int, 1967; -20d

    Foreign Exchange Crisis: an Essay in Economic Pathology, 2nd ed. Macmillan Int, 1970; -21b

    The History of Foreign Exchange, 2nd ed. Macmillan Int, 1970; -21b

    Parallel Money Markets, 2 vols. Macmillan Int, 1972; -20a

    Some Recent Changes in the Euro-Dollar System. JF, 19 (Sep, 1964), 443-449; -20d

    A Textbook of Foreign Exchange, 2nd ed. Macmillan Int, 1969; -21b

Eis, C. The 1919-1930 Merger Movement in American Industry. JLE, 12 (Oct, 1969), 267-296; -26a

    The 1919-1930 Merger Movement in American Industry. PhD diss, City U of NY, 1968; -26a

Eisenberg, E. Aggregation of Utility Functions. MSci, 7 (Jul, 1961), 337-350; -9a

Eisenstadt, S. A Mathematical Formulation of the Behavior of Stocks During the Postwar Period. Value Line Investment Survey, 19 (Apr, 1964), 1-4; -7a

Eisner, R. Determinants of Capital Expenditures: an Interview Study. U of Ill Bur of Busn, 1956; -25f

Eiteman, D. K. A Computer Program for Common Stock Valuation. FAJ, 24 (Jul-Aug, 1968), 107-111; -7a

    A Computer Program for Financial Statement Analysis. FAJ, 20 (Nov-Dec, 1964), 61-68; -8c

    A Graphic Framework for Growth Stock Selection. CMR, 8 (Winter, 1965), 39-50; -7b

    Stock Exchanges in Latin America. U of Mich Pr, 1966; -2c

    See also **Eiteman, W. J. & D. K.**

Eiteman, D. S. Are There Two Kinds of Stock Dividends? NAA, 45 (Oct, 1963), 53-58; -16c

    See **Eiteman, W. J. & D. S.**

Eiteman, S. C.

    See **Eiteman, W. J. & S. C.**

Eiteman, W. J. Yield on Common Stock Investments. AJ, 13 (Feb, 1957), 13-14; -5a

    & D. S. Common Stock Values and Yields 1950-61. U of Mich Busn Res, 1962; -5a

    & D. K. Leading World Stock Exchanges: Trading Practices and Organisation. U of Mich Pr, 1964; -2c

    & S. C. Nine Leading Stock Exchanges. Michigan International Business Studies No. 12, Graduate School of Business Administration, U of Mich, 1968; -2c

    & Smith, F. P. Common Stock Values and Yields. U of Mich Pr, 1953; -5a

Ellinger, A. G.   Security Price Behaviour. IA, 14 (May, 1966), 42-43; -12a

Elliott, B. J.
    See **Clarkson, G. P. E. & Elliott, B. J.**

Elliott, C. M.
    See **Labys, W. C.; Rees, H. J. B. & Elliott, C. M.**

Elliott, D. C.   A New Index of Equity Values. FAJ, 25 (May-Jun, 1969), 101-104; -5b

Elliott, J. W.   Control, Size, Growth and Financial Performance in the Firm. JFQA, 7 (Jan, 1972), 1309-1320; -26f
    Forecasting and Analysis of Corporate Financial Performance with an Econometric Model of the Firm. JFQA, 7 (Mar, 1972), 1499-1526; -8c

Ellis, C. D.   Institutional Investing. Dow Jones—Irwin, 1971; -4a
    New Thoughts on an Old Argument, Rebuttal to M & M. FE, (Sep, 1969), 68-74; -23c
    Portfolio Operations. FAJ, 27 (Sep-Oct, 1971), 36-46; -4a
    Repurchase Stock to Revitalize Equity. HBR, 43 (Jul-Aug, 1965), 119-128; -16d
    Will Success Spoil Performance Investing? FAJ, 24 (Sep-Oct, 1968), 117-119; -4a
    & Young, A. E.   The Repurchase of Common Stock. Ronald, 1971; -16d

Ellsberg, D.   Classic and Current Notions of 'Measurable Utility'. EJ, 64 (Sep, 1954); -9a
    Risk, Ambiguity, and the Savage Axioms. QJE, 75 (Nov, 1961), 643-669; -9a
    Risk, Ambiguity and the Savage Axioms: Reply. QJE, 77 (May, 1963), 336-342; -9a

Elsaid, H. H.   The Function of Preferred Stock in the Corporate Financial Plan. FAJ, 25 (Jul-Aug, 1969), 112-117; -19i

Elsom, H. B.   Common Stocks and the Short Term Interest Rate. FAJ, 17 (Mar-Apr, 1961), 21-26; -6e
    The Law of Trust Investment. FAJ, 16 (Jul-Aug, 1960), 27-33; -3j

Elton, E. J.   Capital Rationing and External Discount Rates. JF, 25 (Jun, 1970), 573-584; -25e
    Studies in Financial Theory. PhD diss, Carnegie-Mellon U, 1971; -22a
    & Gruber, M. J.   The Cost of Retained Earnings—Implications of Share Repurchase. IMR, 9 (Spring, 1968), 87-104; -16d
    & Gruber, M. J.   Dynamic Programming Applications in Finance. JF, 26 (May, 1971), 473-506; -22a
    & Gruber, M. J.   Earnings Estimates and the Accuracy of Expectational Data. MSci, 18 (Apr, 1972), B409-B424; -15b
    & Gruber, M. J.   The Economic Value of the Call Option. JF, 27 (Sep, 1972), 891-902; -19h
    & Gruber, M. J.   The Effect of Share Repurchases on the Value of the Firm. JF, 23 (Mar, 1968), 135-149; -16d
    & Gruber, M. J.   The Effect of Share Repurchases on the Value of the Firm: Reply. JF, 23 (Dec, 1968), 870-874; -16d
    & Gruber, M. J.   Marginal Stockholder Tax Rates and the Clientele Effect. REStat, 52 (Feb, 1970), 68-74; -24c
    & Gruber, M. J.   Prediction and Market Evaluation of Growth. Wkg paper, NYU Busn, 1969; -7b

    & Gruber, M. J. (Eds).   Security Evaluation and Portfolio Analysis. P-H, 1972; -1b

    & Gruber, M. J.   Valuation and the Cost of Capital for Regulated Industries. JF, 26 (Jun, 1971), 661-670; -23d

    See also **Cohen, K. J. & Elton, E. J.**

Emerson, C.
    See **Drayton, C. I., Jr.; Emerson, C. & Griswald, J. D.**

Emery, H. C.   Legislation Against Futures. PSQ, (Mar, 1895); -21a

Emery, J. T.   Risk, Return and the Competitive Structure of Commercial Banking. DBA diss, U of Wash, 1969; -3f

Endowment Conference.   Managing Endowment Capital. New York: Donaldson, Lufkin & Jenrette, Inc. 1969; -3j

Entine, A. D.   Government Securities Holdings of Selected Financial Intermediaries, 1954-1962. JF, 19 (Dec, 1964), 644-651; -19b

Enzer, H.   An Utility Measure Based on Time Preference. EJ, 78 (Dec, 1968), 888-897; -9a

Eppen, G. D. & Fama, E. F.   Cash Balance and Simple Dynamic Portfolio Problems with Proportional Costs. IntER, 10 (Jun, 1969), 119-133; -25a

    & Fama, E. F.   Solutions for Cash Balance and Simple Dynamic Portfolio Problems. JB, 41 (Jan, 1968), 94-112; -25a

    & Fama, E. F.   Three Asset Cash Balance and Dynamic Portfolio Problems. MSci, 17 (Jan, 1971), 320-336; -25a

Epstein, R. H.   Profits and the Size of the Firm in the Automobile Industry, 1919-1927. AER, 21 (Dec, 1931); -26f

Ernst, H.
    See **Brada, J. C.; Ernst, H., & Van Tassel, J.**

Esslen, R.   How Do Dividends Affect Price/Earnings Ratios? FE, (Feb, 1968), 45-50; -24b

European Economic Community.   The Development of a European Capital Market: Report of a Group of Experts Appointed by the E.E.C. Commission. Brussels: E.E.C., 1966; -20e

European Federation of Financial Analysts Societies.   A Concise Bibliography for Investment Analysis in Europe. Paris: The Federation, 1963; -1a

Evans, G.   Financial Life Cycle of Corporations, *in* Conference in Research in Business Finance. Natl Bur Econ Res, 1952; -22a

Evans, G. H., Jr.   The Theoretical Value of a Stock Right. JF, 10 (Mar, 1955), 55-61; -16b

Evans, J. L.   An Analysis of Portfolio Maintenance Strategies. JF, 25 (Jun, 1970), 561-572; -10c

    Diversification and the Reduction of Dispersion: an Empirical Analysis. DBA diss, U of Wash, 1968; -10e

    The Random Walk Hypothesis, Portfolio Analysis and the Buy-and-Hold Criterion. JFQA, 3 (Sep, 1968), 327-342; -11c

    & Archer, S. H.   Diversification and the Reduction of Dispersion: An Empirical Analysis. JF, 23 (Dec, 1968), 761-767; -10e

Evans, M. D.   Arbitrage in Domestic Securities in the U.S. Parker Pub, 1965; -2b

Evans, M. K.   A Study of Industry Investment Decisions. REStat, 49 (May, 1967), 151-164; -25f

Evitt, H. E.   A Manual of Foreign Exchange, 6th ed. Pitman, 1966; -21b

Ewart-James, D. O.   A Factor Analysis of Stock Market Prices. MBA thesis, Manchester Bus, 1969; -10a

Fadner, K.
　　See **Grubel, H. G. & Fadner, K.**
Faerber, L. G.　The Cost of External Common Stock Equity Capital for
　　Small Business: An Empirical Study of New Common Stock Offerings.
　　PhD diss, U of Wash, 1964; -16a
　　See also **Archer, S. H. & Faerber, L. G.**
Fairbairn, I. J. & McShane, R. W.　The Return on Equities and Fixed In-
　　terest Securities on the Australian Capital Market. ER, 45 (Mar, 1969),
　　116-123; -5a
Fama, E. F.　The Behavior of Stock Market Prices. JB, 38 (Jan, 1965), 34-
　　105; -11b, 11c
　　　Components of Investment Performance. JF, 27 (Jun, 1972), 551-
　　568; -14a
　　　The Distribution of the Daily Differences of the Logarithms of Stock
　　Prices. PhD diss, U of Chicago, 1964; -11b
　　　Efficient Capital Markets: a Review of Theory and Empirical Work.
　　JF, 25 (May, 1970), 383-417; -11c
　　　Mandelbrot and the Stable Paretian Hypothesis. JB, 36 (Oct, 1963),
　　420-429; -11b
　　　Multi-Period Consumption-Investment Decisions. AER, 60 (Mar,
　　1970), 163-174; -10k
　　　Ordinal and Measurable Utility, *in* Jensen, M. C. (Ed), Studies in
　　the Theory of Capital Markets. Praeger, 1972; -9a
　　　Portfolio Analysis in a Stable Paretian Market. MSci, 11 (Jan,
　　1965), 404-419; -10d
　　　Random Walks in Stock Market Prices. FAJ, 21 (Sep-Oct, 1965),
　　55-59; -11c
　　　Risk and Rate of Return in the Long Run. Paper for the Seminar
　　on the Analysis of Security Prices, U of Chicago, Nov 1972; -10j
　　　Risk, Return and Equilibrium. JPE, 79 (Jan-Feb, 1971), 30-55; -10*l*
　　　Risk, Return and Equilibrium: Some Clarifying Comments. JF, 23
　　(Mar, 1968), 29-40; -10*l*
　　　Tomorrow on the New York Stock Exchange. JB, 38 (Jul, 1965),
　　285-299; -12e
　　　& Babiak, H.　Dividend Policy: an Empirical Analysis. JASA,
　　63 (Dec, 1968), 1132-1161; -24a
　　　& Blume, M. E.　Filter Rules and Stock Market Trading. JB,
　　39 (Jan, 1966), 226-241; -12c
　　　Fisher, L; Jensen, M. C. & Roll, R.　The Adjustment of Stock
　　Prices to New Information. IntER, 10 (Feb, 1969), 1-21; -11a, 16c
　　　& Laffer, A. B.　Information and Capital Markets. JB, 44 (Jul,
　　1971), 289-298; -11a
　　　& Laffer, A. B.　Perfect Competition and the Market Value Rule
　　in the Two Parameter Model. Unp ms, U of Chicago, Oct 1971; -9d
　　　& Miller, M. H.　The Theory of Finance. HR & W, 1972; -4b, 22a
　　　& Roll, R.　Parameter Estimates for Symmetric Stable Distri-
　　butions. JASA, 66 (Jun, 1971), 331-338; -11b
　　　& Roll, R.　Some Properties of Symmetric Stable Distributions.
　　JASA, 63 (Sep, 1968), 817-836; -11b
　　　See also **Eppen, G. D. & Fama, E. F.**
Fand, D. I.　High Interest Rates and Inflation in the U.S.: Cause or Effect?
　　BNLQR, 25 (Mar, 1972), 23-64; -18c
　　　A Time-Series Analysis of the 'Bills-only' Theory of Interest
　　Rates. REStat, 48 (Nov, 1966), 361-371; -20b

Fanning, J. E.   How to Improve Investment Decisions. HBR, 44 (Jan-Feb, 1966), 156-168; -4a

A Four-Indicator System for Forecasting the Market. FAJ, 27 (Sep-Oct, 1971), 49-56; -7d

& Steglitz, M.   A Risk Measure for Common Stock Portfolios. Paper for the Seminar on the Analysis of Security Prices, U of Chicago, Nov, 1966; -10b

Farr, F. W. E.   The Future Level of Industrial Stock Prices. AJ, 5 (3rd Qtr, 1949), 26-27; -7d

Farrar, D. E.   The Investment Decision Under Uncertainty. P-H, 1962; -10c

Wall Street's Proposed 'Great Leap Backward'. FAJ, 27 (Sep-Oct, 1971), 14ff; -2b

See also **Allerdice, F. B. & Farrar, D. E.**

Farrell, M. J.   On the Structure of the Capital Market. EJ, 72 (Dec, 1962), 830-844; -23b

Profitable Speculation. Ec, 46 (May, 1966), 183-193; -9e

Farwell, L. C.

See **Leffler, G. L.** rev by **Farwell, L. C.**

See also **Robinson, R. I.; Boehmler, E. W.; Gane, F. H. & Farwell, L. C. (Eds)**

Federal Bar Association.   Conference on Mutual Funds, San Francisco, California, Mar, 1966. Federal Bar Association, 1966; -3k

Federal Reserve Bank of Chicago.   Bankers' Acceptance Used More Widely. Bus Cond F R Bk Chicago, (May, 1965), 9-16; -20a

Capital Markets—United States and Europe. Bus Cond F R Bk Chicago, (Sep, 1964), 9-16; -2c

Federal Reserve Bank of Cleveland. Direct Placement of Corporate Debt. MBR, (Mar, 1965); -19e

Investment Patterns of Fire and Casualty Insurance Companies. MBR, (May, 1963); -3h

Trading in Federal Funds. MBR, (Oct, 1961); -20c

Federal Reserve Bank of Kansas City.   Bank Reactions to Security Losses. Mo Rev F R Bk Kansas City, (Jun, 1960); -3f

Commercial Bank Investments in Recession and Expansion. Mo Rev F R Bk Kansas City, (Mar, 1959); -3f

Corporate Participation in the Government Securities Market. Mo Rev F R Bk Kansas City, (Dec, 1960); -19b

Taxes and the Term Structure of Yields. Mo Rev F R Bk Kansas City, (Dec, 1960); -18f

Federal Reserve Bank of New York.   Certificate of Deposits. Mo Rev F R Bk New York, (Jun, 1963), 82-87; -20a

The Financing of Government Securities Dealers. Mo Rev F R Bk New York, (Jun, 1964); -19b

Life Insurance Companies in the Postwar Capital Markets. Mo Rev F R Bk New York, (Sep, 1958); -3h

Life Insurance Companies and the Securities Markets.

Part 1: Mo Rev F R Bk New York (Mar, 1952)

Part 2: Mo Rev F R Bk New York (Apr, 1952); -3h

Federal Reserve Bank of St Louis.   The Federal Funds Market. Mo Rev F R Bk St Louis, (Apr, 1960); -20c

The Seasonal Pattern of Interest Rates. Mo Rev F R Bk St.Louis, (Nov, 1960); -18d

Federal Reserve System, Board of Governors. The Federal Funds Market. Washington, D.C.: Board of Governors, Federal Reserve System, 1959; -20c

Feeney, G. J. & Hester, D. D. Stock Market Indices: a Principal Components Analysis *in* Hester, D. D. & Tobin, J. (Eds), Risk Aversion and Portfolio Choice. Wiley, 1967; -10a

Feldstein, M. S. Corporate Taxation and Dividend Behaviour. REStud, 37 (Jan, 1970), 57-72; -24a

The Effects of Taxation on Risk Taking. JPE, 77 (Jul-Aug, 1969), 755-764; -27b

Inflation, Specification Bias and the Impact of Interest Rates. JPE, 78, (Nov-Dec, 1970), 1325-1339; -18c

Mean-Variance Analysis in the Theory of Liquidity Preference and Portfolio Selection. REStud, 36 (Jan, 1969); -10c

On the Measurement of Risk Aversion. SEJ, 35 (Jul, 1968), 58-59; -9b

Uncertainty and Forward Exchange Speculation. REStat, 50 (May, 1968), 182-192; -21b

& Eckstein, O. The Fundamental Determinants of the Interest Rate. REStat, 52 (Nov, 1970), 363-375; -18b

& Flemming, J. S. Tax Policy, Corporate Saving and Investment Behaviour in Britain. REStud, 38 (1971), 415-434; -27a

Feldstein, P. J.
See **Renshaw, E. F. & Feldstein, P. J.**

Fellner, W. Distortion of Subjective Probabilities as a Reaction to Uncertainty. QJE, 75 (Nov, 1961), 670-689; -9c

Probability and Profit. Irwin, 1965; -9c

Profit as the Risk-Taker's Surplus: A Probabilistic Theory. REStat, 45 (May, 1963), 173-184; -10o

Slanted Subjective Probabilities and Randomization: Reply to Howard Raiffa and K. R. W. Brewer. QJE, 77 (Nov, 1963), 676-690; -9c

See also **Brewer, K. R. W. & Fellner, W.**

Fenix y Pil, A. V. J., Jr. Development Finance and the Cost of Capital. PhD diss, MIT, 1968; -23d

Fenlon, P. E. Financial Management Decisions: Case Problems. Allyn, 1964; -1c

Ferber, R. (Ed). Determinants of Investment Behavior. Natl Bur Econ Res, 1967; -9d

Short-Run Effects of Stock Market Services on Stock Prices. JF, 13 (Mar, 1958), 80-95; -11a, 15c

Ferguson, R. A Nomograph for Valuing Growth Stocks. FAJ, 17 (May-Jun, 1961), 29-34; -7b

See also **Way, P. & Ferguson, R.**

Fergusson, D. A. Preferred Stock Valuation in Recapitalizations. JF, 13 (Mar, 1958), 48-69; -19i

Recent Developments in Preferred Stock Financing. JF, 7 (Sep, 1952), 447-462; -19i

Ferrara, W. L. Should Investment and Financing Decisions be Separated? AR, 41 (Jan, 1966), 106-114; -25c

Ferrari, J. R. Quantitative Decision-Making for Life Insurance Company Investments: Possibilities and Limitations. PhD diss, U of Pa, 1964; -3h

Ferreira, C. G. Quantification and Measurement of Risk: An Empirical Study of Selected Common Stocks. DBA diss, U of Wash, 1966; -10b

Ferretti, A. P.   The Economist's Role and the Stock Market. FAJ, 25
(Jan-Feb, 1969), 35-37; -4e
Ferris, P.   The City, rev ed. Penguin, 1965; -2a
Men and Money: Financial Europe Today. Hutchinson, 1968; -2c
Feuerstein, A. E. & Maggi, P. G.   Computer Investment Research. FAJ,
24 (Jan-Feb, 1968), 154-158; -4e
See also **Kisor, M., Jr. & Feuerstein, A. E.**
Feuerstein, D. M.   Toward a National System of Securities Exchanges:
The Third and Fourth Markets. FAJ, 28 (Jul-Aug, 1972), 57ff; -2b
Field, M. J.   Security Prices and Stock Exchange Holidays in Relation
to Short Selling. JB, 7 (Oct, 1934), 328; -13d
Fielitz, B. D.   On the Behavior of Stock Price Relatives as a Random
Process with an Application to New York Stock Exchange Prices. DBA
diss, Kent St U, 1969; -11c
Stationarity of Random Data: Some Implications for the Distribu-
tion of Stock Price Changes. JFQA, 6 (Jun, 1971), 1025-1034; -11b
Filer, H.   Investing in Options. AJ, 11 (Feb, 1955), 77-78; -17a
Understanding Put and Call Options. Magee, 1972; -17a
Financial Times.   Guide to the FT—Actuaries Share Indices. London:
Financial Times, 1962; -5b
Finetti, B. de.   La Prévision: ses Lois Logiques, ses Sources Subjectives.
Annales de l'Institut Henri Poincaré, 7 (1937), 1-68. Translated into
English *in* Kyburg, H. E., Jr. & Smokler, H. E., Studies in Subjective
Probability, Wiley, 1964; -9a
Finley, R. E.
See **Marting, E. & Finley, R. E. (Eds)**
Firth, M.   The Performance of Share Recommendations Made by Invest-
ment Analysts and the Effects on Market Efficiency. JBF, 4 (Summer,
1972), 58ff; -15c
Fisch, G. G.   Management in Financial Analysis. FAJ, 24 (Jul-Aug, 1968),
43-49; -4a
Fischer, D. E.   An Analysis and Evaluation of the Role of Preferred Stock
in Electric Utility Financing. PhD diss, U of Wash, 1965; -19i
& Wilt, G. A., Jr.   Non-Convertible Preferred Stock as a Financ-
ing Instrument, 1950-1965. JF, 23 (Sep, 1968), 611-624; -19i
Fischer, G. C.   American Banking Structure. Columbia U Pr 1968; -3f
& Minet, L. J.   No-Load Mutual Funds. FAJ, 20 (Jan-Feb, 1964),
64-68; -3k
Fischer, M. C.   The Relationship between Insiders' Transactions, the
Price of the Common Stock of their Respective Companies, the Stan-
dard and Poor's Stock Price Index and Price Stability. PhD diss, Am
U, 1965; -13c
Fischer, R. M.   The Accuracy of Forecasts. AJ, 10 (Feb, 1954), 73-78; -15c
Measuring Stability. AJ, 4 (3rd Qtr, 1948), 19-25; -10b
Fishburn, P. C.   Methods of Estimating Additive Utilities. MSci, 13 (Mar,
1967), 435-453; -9a
Fisher, A. K.
See **McDonald, J. G. & Fisher, A. K.**
Fisher, D.   A British Test of Recent Developments in Term Structure
Theory. PhD diss, U of Chicago, 1966; -18f
Expectations, the Term Structure of Interest Rates and Recent
British Experience. Ec, 46 (Aug, 1966), 319-329; -18f
The Structure of Interest Rates: A Comment. Ec, 44 (Nov, 1964),
412-418; -18f

Fisher, E. More about Stability of Measures of Volatility of Individual Stocks. Paper for the Seminar on the Analysis of Security Prices, U of Chicago, Nov 1968; -10b

Fisher, G. H. The Input-Output Technique as an Aid in Security Analysis. AJ, 9 (Feb, 1953), 85-92; -6a

Fisher, G. R. Some Factors Influencing Share Prices. EJ, 71 (Mar, 1961), 121-141; -24b

Fisher, I. The Nature of Capital and Income. Macmillan, 1906; -22b

The Theory of Interest: as Determined by Impatience to Spend Income and Opportunity to Invest it. Kelley, 1930; -18b

& Hall, G. R. Risk and Corporate Rates of Return. QJE, 83 (Feb, 1969), 79-92; -10o

Fisher, J. L. A Class of Stochastic Investment Problems. OR, 9 (Jan-Feb, 1961), 53-65; -25d

Fisher, L. An Algorithm for Finding Exact Rates of Return. JB, 39 (Suppl Jan, 1966), 111-118; -25b

Determinants of Risk Premiums on Corporate Bonds. JPE, 67 (Jun, 1959), 217-237; -19g

Outcomes for 'Random' Investments in Common Stocks Listed on the New York Stock Exchange. JB, 38 (Apr, 1965), 149-161; -5a

Some New Stock-Market Indexes. JB, 39 (Suppl Jan, 1966), 191-225; -5b

& Kamin, J. Good Betas and Bad Betas. Paper for the Seminar on the Analysis of Security Prices, U of Chicago, Nov 1971; -10b

& Lorie, J. H. Rates of Return on Investments in Common Stocks. JB, 37 (Jan, 1964), 1-17; -5a

& Lorie, J. H. Rates of Return on Investments in Common Stock. The Year by Year Record, 1926-65. JB, 41 (Jul, 1968), 291-316; -5a

& Lorie, J. H. Some Studies of Variability of Returns on Investments in Common Stocks. JB, 43 (Apr, 1970), 99-134; -5a, 10e

& Weil, R. L. Coping with the Risk of Interest Rate Fluctuations; Returns to Bondholders from Naive and Optimal Strategies. JB, 44 (Oct, 1971), 408-431; -18g

See also **Fama, E. F.; Fisher, L.; Jensen, M. C. & Roll, R.**

See also **Lorie, J. H. & Fisher, L.**

See also **Treynor, J. L.; Priest, W. W., Jr.; Fisher, L. & Higgins, C. A.**

Fishman, G. S. Price Behavior Under Alternative Forms of Price Expectations. QJE, 78 (May, 1964), 281-298; -9e

Fiske, H. S. The Banks Learn to Live with Report Cards. II, 2 (May, 1968); -14b

Performance Fees: Should a Manager Get a Piece of the Action? II, 2 (Mar, 1968), 23ff; -14a

Fitch, B.

See **Cohen, K. J. & Fitch, B.**

Fleissner, D.

See **Slovic, P.; Fleissner, D. & Baumann, W. S.**

Fleming, M. The Investment Trust Company. JBF, 2 (Spring, 1970), 42-45; -3k

Flemming, J. S.

See **Feldstein, M. S. & Flemming, J. S.**

Flink, S. J. Equity Financing for Small Business. Simmons-B, 1962; -16a

& Grunewald, D. Managerial Finance. Wiley, 1969; -22a

Flinn, H. M.
See **Andrew, S. L. & Flinn, H. M.**

Florence, P. S.   Reward for Risk-Bearing by Shareholders in Large
Companies. JIE, 5 (1957), 81-111; -10o
Tests of the Validity of Some Stock Exchange Folk-Lore. TBR,
37 (Mar, 1958), 3-20; -7a

Fluegel, F. K.   The Rate of Return on High and Low P/E Ratio Stocks.
FAJ, 24 (Nov-Dec, 1968), 130-133; -8g

Flynn, J.; Joseph, S.; Parker, D. & Stacey, D.   An Examination of the
Common Stock Warrant and a New Valuation Model. MBA thesis,
Harvard Bus, 1969; -17b

Fogler, H. R.   An Explanation of the Relative Decline in Common Stock
Financing, 1946-1963. PhD diss, Columbia U, 1967; -23g

Folz, D. F. & Weston, J. F.   Looking Ahead in Evaluating Proposed
Mergers. NAA, 43 (Apr, 1962), 17-27; -26a

Forbes.   That Post-Listing Tired Feeling. Forbes, (Nov 1, 1964); -2f

Ford, J. L. & Stark, T.   Long- and Short-Term Interest Rates. Blackwell,
1967; -18f

Fortune.   Buying Stocks by the Calendar. F, 71 (Jun, 1965); -12b
Hedge-Fund Miseries. F, 83 (May, 1971), 269ff; -3*l*
The Higher Meaning of NASDAQ. F, 83 (Apr, 1971), 141ff; -2b

Foster, E. M.   Analysis of Common Stock Prices. PhD diss, NYU, 1969;
-6d
Price-Earnings Ratio and Corporate Growth. FAJ, 26 (Jan-Feb,
1970), 96-103; -7b
Price-Earnings Ratio and Corporate Growth: A Revision. FAJ,
26 (Jul-Aug, 1970), 115-118; -7b

Foster, J. H. & Morgan, R.   Evaluation of Convertible Bonds. Financial
Research, Investment Analysis and the Computer, Bulletin 31, Hanover,
N.H. The Amos Tuck School, 1967; -17c

Fouraker, L. E.
See **Bierman, H., Jr.; Fouraker, L. E. & Jaedicke, R. K.**

Fox, E. A.   Comparing Performance of Equity Pension Trusts. FAJ, 24
(Sep-Oct, 1968), 121-129; -14b

Fox, G. R.   Measuring Pension Fund Performance. MBA, (Jan, 1968), 6ff;
-14b

Fox, J. S.   The Price Relationship between Purchase Warrants and
Common Stock. SB thesis, MIT, 1961; -17b

Fraedrich, K. E.   Accounting for Business Combinations. PhD diss, U of
Wis, 1969; -26d

Fraine, H. G.   Valuation of Securities Holdings of Life Insurance Com-
panies. Irwin, 1962; -3h
& Mills, R. H.   Effect of Defaults and Credit Deterioration on
Yields of Corporate Bonds. JB, 34 (Sep, 1961), 423-434; -19g

Francis, J. C.   Investments Analysis and Management. McGraw, 1972; -4b
& Archer, S. H.   Portfolio Analysis. P-H, 1971; -10c

Frank, W. G. & Weygandt, J. T.   A Prediction Model for Convertible
Debentures. JAR, 9 (Spring, 1971), 116-126; -17c

Frankena, M. W.   The Influency of Call Provisions and Coupon Rate on the
Yields of Corporate Bonds, *in* Guttentag, J. M. (Ed), Essays on Interest
Rates, Vol 2. (Dist by Columbia U Pr) Natl Bur Econ Res, 1971; -19e

Frankfurter, G. M.   The Dynamics of Corporate Debt Management. PhD
diss, St U NY Buffalo, 1971; -23c

Phillips, H. E. & Seagle, J. P.   Portfolio Selection: the Effects of Uncertain Means, Variances, and Covariances. JFQA, 6 (Dec, 1971), 1251-1262; -10c

Franklin, C. B. & Colberg, M. R.   Puts and Calls: A Factual Survey. JF, 13 (Mar, 1958), 21-34; -17a

& Colberg, M. R.   Comment on 'Puts and Calls: A Factual Survey': Reply. JF, 14 (Mar, 1959), 71-74; -17a

Fraser, H. W.   A Theory of the Optimum Time Rate of Growth of the Firm. PhD diss, Princeton U, 1961; -25c

Frazer, W. J.   Large Manufacturing Corporations as Suppliers of Funds to the United States Government Securities Market. JF, 13 (Dec, 1958), 499-509; -19b

& Yohe, W. P.   Introduction to the Analytics and Institutions of Money and Banking. Van N-Rein, 1966; -3f

See also **Terrell, W. T. & Frazer, W. J.**

Frederick, J. G.   The Real Truth about Short Selling. Bourse, 1932; -13d

Frederickson, D. R.

See **Drzycimiski, E. F. & Frederickson, D. R.**

Fredman, A. J.   The Relative Significance of Earnings and Dividends as Determinants of Stock Prices over Time and among Industries. PhD diss, UCLA, 1968; -8d

& Wert, J. E.   An Analysis of Secondary Distributions. FAJ, 24 (Nov-Dec, 1968), 165-168; -16d

Fredrikson, E. B. (Ed.)   Frontiers of Investment Analysis, rev ed. Intext, 1971; -1b

Security Analysis and the Multinational Corporation. FAJ, 21 (Sep-Oct, 1965), 109-117; -4a

Freeman, G. K.   Advance-Decline Line: a Clue to the Underlying Strength or Weakness of the Market. B, (Jan 21, 1963); -12e

Freeman, J. F.   Liquidity Preference and Loanable Funds: a New Approach to the Problem. EJ, 73 (Dec, 1963), 681-688; -18a

Freeman, P.   Some Aspects of Technical Analysis. IA, 18 (Oct, 1967), 9-19; -12a

Freeman, R. A.   Crisis in College Finance? Washington, D.C.: Institute for Social Science Research, 1965; -3j

Freimer, M. & Gordon, M. J.   Investment Behavior with Utility a Concave Function of Wealth, *in* Borch, K. and Mossin, J. (Eds), Risk and Uncertainty. Macmillan Int, 1968; -9c

Freund, R. J.   The Introduction of Risk Into a Programming Model. Em, 24 (Jul, 1956), 253-263; -9c

Freund, W. C.   An Appraisal of the Sources and Uses of Funds: Approach to the Analysis of Financial Markets. JF, 13 (May, 1958), 275-294; -3c

Investment Fundamentals. New York: American Bankers Association, 1966; -4a

Issues Confronting the Stock Market in a Period of Rising Institutionalization. JFQA, 7 (Suppl Mar, 1972), 1687-1690; -2b

Will Institutional Demands Outrun the Supply of Common Stock in the '70s? FAJ, 27 (Jul-Aug, 1971), 37-44; -3e

& Zinbarg, E. D.   Application of Flow of Funds to Interest-Rate Forecasting. JF, 18 (May, 1963), 231-248; -18b

See also **Antliff, J. C. & Freund, W. C.**

Frevert, P. W.   A Model of the Spot and Forward Markets for Foreign Exchange. PhD diss, Purdue U, 1964; -21b

A Theoretical Model of the Forward Exchange.
Part 1: IntER, 8 (Jun, 1967), 307-326,
Part 2: IntER, 8 (Oct, 1967), 153-167; -21b

Frey, T. L. Optimal Asset and Liability Decisions for a Rural Bank: an Application of Multi-Period Linear Programming. PhD diss, U of Ill, 1970; -10g

Freytag, D. C. An Investigation of the Relationship Between the Rate of Growth for the Gross National Product and the Debt to Equity Ratio for Nonfinancial Business. PhD diss, U of Cincinnati, 1966; -23g

Fricke, C. V. The Variable Annuity: its Impact on the Savings—Investment Market. U of Mich Pr, 1959; -3h

Fried, J. S. Bank Portfolio Selection. JFQA, 5 (Jun, 1970), 203-228; -10g
    Forecasting and Probability Distributions for Models of Portfolio Selection. JF, 25 (Jun, 1970), 539-554; -10c
    A Generalized Markowitz Model of Bank Portfolio Selection. PhD diss, Northwestern U, 1969; -10g

Fried, S. Investing and Speculating with Convertibles. Crown, 1969; -17c
    The Speculative Merits of Warrants. RHM, 1961; -17b

Friedland, S. The Economics of Corporate Finance. P-H, 1966; -22a

Friedman, H. C. Real Estate Investment and Portfolio Theory. JFQA, 6 (Mar, 1971), 861-874; -21c

Friedman, M. The Euro-dollar Market. Morgan Guaranty Survey, Oct 1969; -20d
    In Defense of Destabilizing Speculation, *in* Prouts, R. W. (Ed), Essays in Economics and Econometrics. U of NC Pr, 1960; -9e
    A Program for Monetary Stability. Fordham, 1959; -20b
    A Theory of the Consumption Function. (Dist by Princeton U Pr) Natl Bur Econ Res, 1957; -10j
    & Savage, L. J. The Expected Utility Hypothesis and the Measurability of Utility. JPE, 60 (Dec, 1952), 463-475; -9a
    & Savage, L. J. The Utility Analysis of Choices Involving Risk. JPE, 56 (Aug, 1948), 279-304; -9a

Friend, I. Effect of Institutionalization of Savings on the Long-Term for the Securities Industry. JFQA, 7 (Suppl Mar, 1972), 1691-1695; -2b
    The Effect of Mutual Funds on Market Performance. Paper for the Seminar on the Analysis of Security Prices, U of Chicago, May 1968; -3k
    Equity Yields, Growth and the Structure of Share Prices: Comment. AER, 54 (Dec, 1964), 1029-1035; -7b
    & Blume, M. E. Measurement of Portfolio Performance under Uncertainty. AER, 60 (Sep, 1970), 561-575; -14a
    Blume, M. E. & Crockett, J. Mutual Funds and Other Institutional Investors. McGraw, 1971; -3k
    & Herman, E. S. The S.E.C. Through a Glass Darkly. JB, 37 (Oct, 1964), 382-405; -2e, 16a
    Hoffman, G. W. & Winn, W. J. The Over-the Counter Securities Markets. McGraw, 1958; -2b
    Longstreet, J. R.; Mendelson, M.; Miller, E. & Hess, A. P., Jr. Investment Banking and the New Issues Market. World Pub, 1967; -16a 16b
    & Parker, S. A New Slant on the Stock Market. F, 68 (Sep, 1956); -7d
    & Puckett, M. Dividends and Stock Prices. AER, 54 (Sep, 1964), 656-682; -24b

    & Taubman, P.   Risk and the Rate of Return on Common Stock.
Paper for the Seminar on the Analysis of Security Prices. U of
Chicago, Nov 1966
    & Vickers, D.   Portfolio Selection and Investment Performance.
JF, 20 (Sep, 1965), 391-415; -14a
    & Vickers, D.   Re-evaluation of Alternative Portfolio Selection
Models. JB, 41 (Apr, 1968), 174-179; -10c
    See also **Blume, M. E. & Friend, I.**
    See also **Crockett, J. & Friend, I.**
Fritzemeier, L. H.   Relative Price Fluctuations of Industrial Stocks in
Different Price Groups. JB, 9 (Apr, 1936), 133-154; -10b
Frost, P. A.   Banking Services, Minimum Cash Balances and the Firm's
Demand for Money. JF, 25 (Dec, 1970), 1029-1039; -25a
Frostman, L.   The Concept of Time Centre in Investment Theory and its
Relation to the Average Period of Investment. SJE, 67 (Jun, 1965), 125-
150; -18g
Fukasawa, S.   A Variable Lag Pattern in the Formation of Expected Price
Changes. PhD diss, Columbia U, 1970; -6c
Fuller, J. G.   The Money Changers. Dial, 1962; -2b
Fullerton, D. H.   The Bond Market in Canada. Carswell, 1962; -19a
Furst, R. W.   Does Listing Increase the Market Price of Common Stocks?
JB, 43 (Apr, 1970), 174-180; -2f
    Does Listing on the Big Board Really Increase Market Price. FE,
37 (Apr, 1969); -2f
    An Investigation into the Effects of Listing on the Market Price of
Common Stocks. DBA diss, U of Wash, 1968; -2f
Gagan, L. J.   A Decision Model for Evaluating Convertible Bonds. SM
thesis, MIT, 1962; -17c
Gal, J. G.   Man-Machine Interactive Systems and their Application to
Financial Analysis. FAJ, 22 (May-Jun, 1966), 126-136; -4e
Galbraith, J. A.   The Economics of Banking Operations: a Canadian Study.
McGill-Queens U Pr, 1963; -3f
Galbraith, J. K.   The Great Crash. HM, 1955; -2d
Gane, F. H.
    See **Robinson, R. I.; Boehmler, E. W.; Gane, F. H. & Farwell, L. C.**
    (Eds)
Ganz, L. J.   An Empirical Examination of the Relation between Capital
Structure and Business Risk. PhD diss, NYU, 1968; -23b
Gardner, R. L.   How to Make Money on the Commodity Market. P-H, 1962;
-21a
Gartley, H. M.   Modern Approaches to Stock Market Analysis. AJ, 4
(Suppl, 2nd Qtr, 1948), 3-7; -12a
Gaubis, A.   Which is the Best Stock Average from a Practical Standpoint?
AJ, 8 (Nov, 1952), 70-73; -5b
Gaumnitz, E. A. (Ed).   Futures Trading Seminar: a Commodity Marketing
Forum for College Teachers of Economics. Mimir, 1966; -21a
Gaumnitz, J. E.   Appraising Performance of Investment Portfolios. JF, 25
(Jun, 1970), 555-560; 10*l*
    Investment Diversification under Uncertainty. An Examination of
the Number of Securities in a Diversified Portfolio. PhD diss, Stanford
U, 1967; -10e
    & Salabar, C. A.   The Barron's Confidence Index: an Examination
of its Value as a Market Indicator. FAJ, 25 (Sep-Oct, 1969), 16ff; -12g
    See also **Porter, R. B. & Gaumnitz, J. E.**

Gaver, D. P.   Models for Appraising Investments Yielding Stochastic Returns. MSci, 11 (Jul, 1965), 815-830; -25d

Gemmill, R. F.   The Effect of the Capital Gains Tax on Asset Prices. NTJ, 9 (1956); -27d

Interest Rates and Foreign Dollar Balances. JF, 16 (Sep, 1961), 363-376; -20d

Genillard, R. L.   The Eurobond Market. FAJ, 23 (Mar-Apr, 1967), 144-151; -20e

Gentry, J. A.   An Analysis of the Characteristics of the Common Stocks Purchased and Sold by Six Life Insurance Companies and Six Balanced Investment Companies in 1963 and 1964. DBA diss, Indiana U, 1966; -3h, 3k

Do Institutional Investors Buy and Sell Common Stocks with Similar Characteristics? QREB, 8 (Winter, 1968), 21-29; -3e

    & Pike, J. R.   Dual Funds Revisited. FAJ, 24 (Mar-Apr, 1968), 149-157; -3m

    & Pike, J. R.   An Empirical Study of the Risk—Return Hypothesis Using Common Stock Portfolios of Life Insurance Companies. JFQA, 5 (Jun, 1970), 179-186; -10l

Gershefski, G. W.   Building a Corporate Financial Model. HBR, 47 (Jul-Aug, 1969), 61-72; -22c

Gerstenberg, C. W.   Financial Organisation and Management of Business, 4th ed. P-H, 1959; -22a

Ghandhi, J. K. S.   Some Aspects of the Provincial New Issue Market. OIS (Aug, 1964), 239-263; -16a

On the Measurement of Leverage. JF, 21 (Dec, 1966), 715-726; -23c

Gibb, W. T.   Critical Evaluation of Pension Plans. JF, 23 (May, 1968), 337-343; -3i

Gibson, W. E.   Price Expectations Effects on Interest Rates. JF, 25 (Mar, 1970), 19-34; -18c

Gies, T. G.   Portfolio Regulations of Selected Financial Intermediaries: Some Proposals for Change. JF, 17 (May, 1962), 302-310; -2e

    & Apilado, V. P. (Eds).   Banking Markets and Financial Institutions. Irwin, 1971; -3f

Giguère, G.   Warrants, A Mathematical Method of Evaluation. AJ, 14 (Nov, 1958), 17-25; -17b

Gilbert, J. C.   British Investment and Unit Trusts Since the War. YB, 14 (May, 1962), 3-13; -3k

Gilbert, L. D.   Dividends and Democracy. Am Res Co, 1956; -3a

Giles, L. G.   The Function of Stock Purchase Warrants in Corporate Financing. PhD diss, U of Ill, 1971; -17b

Gilliland, A. B.   Measuring Ordinary Share Portfolio Performance. IA, 3 (Aug, 1962), 30-35; -14a

Gillis, J. G.   A Prospectus is a Prospectus. FAJ, 27 (Sep-Oct, 1971), 6ff; -2e

The Tippee in Transition. FAJ, 27 (Jan-Feb, 1971), 6-16; -2e

Girgis, N. M.   Optimal Cash Balance Levels. PhD diss, U of Cal Berkeley, 1966; -25a

Optimal Cash Balance Levels. MSci, 15 (Nov, 1968), 130-140; -25a

Glahe, F. R.   An Empirical Study of the Foreign Exchange Market: Test of a Theory. Princeton U Pr, 1967; -21b

Professional and Non-Professional Speculation, Profitability, and Stability. SEJ, 33 (Jul, 1966), 43-44; -9e

Glass, G. A.   Extensive Insider Accumulation as an Indication of Near-Term Stock Price Performance. PhD diss, Ohio St U, 1966; -13c

Glassmire, W.
See **Van Horne, J. & Glassmire, W.**
Glauber, R. R.
See **Lintner, J. & Glauber, R. R.**
See also **Meyer, J. R. & Glauber, R. R.**
Glick, I. O. A Social Psychological Study of Futures Trading. PhD diss, U of Chicago, 1957; -21a
Gnedenko, B. V. & Kolmogorov, A. N. Limit Distributions for Sums of Independent Random Variables. Addison-Wes, 1968; -11b
Godfrey, M. D.; Granger, C. W. J. & Morgenstern, O. The Random Walk Hypothesis of Stock Market Behaviour. Kyk, 17 (1964), 1-30; -11c
Goehring, E. E. An Appraisal of Some Security Price Forecasting Services. MA thesis, U of Chicago, 1938; -15c
Gold, G. Modern Commodity Futures Trading, 4th ed. Commodity R, 1966; -21a
Goldberg, M. S.
See **O'Donnell, J. L. & Goldberg, M. S. (Eds)**
Goldsmith, R. W. Financial Institutions. Random, 1968; -3e
Financial Intermediaries in the American Economy Since 1900. Princeton U Pr, 1958; -3e
Financial Structure and Development. Yale U Pr, 1969; -23c
The Flow of Capital Funds in the Postwar Economy. (Dist by Columbia U Pr) Natl Bur Econ Res, 1965; -3c
& Shapiro, E. An Estimate of Bank-Administered Personal Trust Funds. JF, 14 (Mar, 1959), 11-17; -3f
Goldstein, H. N. The Friedman Proposal for Auctioning Treasury Bills. JPE, 70 (Aug, 1962), 386-392; -20b
Should the Treasury Auction Long-term Securities? JF, 17 (Sep, 1962), 444-464; -20b
The Implications of Triangular Arbitrage for Forward Exchange Policy. JF, 19 (Sep, 1964), 544-551; -21b
Gomme, E. D.
See **Coen, P. J.; Gomme, E. D. & Kendall, M. G.**
Gonedes, N. J. Efficient Capital Markets and External Accounting. AR, 47 (Jan, 1972); -8c
Evidence on the Information Content of Accounting Numbers: Accounting-Based and Market-Based Estimates of Systematic Risk. Report No 7115, Center for Mathematical Studies in Business and Economics, U of Chicago, Mar 1971; -10n
Some Evidence on Investor Actions and Accounting Messages. Part 1: AR, 46 (Apr, 1971), 320-328
Part 2: AR, 46 (Jul, 1971), 535-551; -8d
Properties of Accounting Numbers: Models and Tests. Wkg Paper No. 64-71-2, Graduate School of Industrial Administration, Carnegie-Mellon U, Jan 1972; -8b
A Test of the Equivalent-Risk Class Hypothesis. JFQA, 4 (Jun, 1969), 159-178; -23c
Goode, R. & Birnham, E. A. The Relation between Long-term and Short-term Interest Rates in the United States. IMF, (Oct, 1959), 224-243; -18f
Goodfriend, H. E. Adjustment and Projection of Life Insurance Company Earnings Utilizing a Computer. FAJ, 22 (Nov-Dec, 1966), 57-63; -8c
Goodman, M. L.
See **Williams, W. H. & Goodman, M. L.**

Goodman, R. M. Municipal Bond Rating Testimony. FAJ, 24 (May-Jun, 1968), 59-65; -19f

Gordon, M. J. Dividends, Earnings and Stock Prices. REStat, 41 (May, 1959), 99-105; -24b

Some Estimates of the Cost of Capital to the Electric Utility Industry, 1954-57: Comment. AER, 57 (Dec, 1967), 1267-1278; -23c

European Stock Exchanges. AJ, 15 (May, 1959), 31-34; -2c

The Investment Financing and Valuation of the Corporation. Irwin, 1964; - 22a

Optimal Investment and Financing Policy. JF, 18 (May, 1963), 264-272; -23c

The Optimum Dividend Rate, *in* Churchman, C. W. & Verhulst, M. (Eds), Management Science, Models and Techniques. Pergamon, 1960; -24b

The Pay-Off Period and the Rate of Profit. JB, 28 (Oct, 1955); -25c

Risk, Debt and Share Prices. Paper presented at the meeting of the Econometric Society, MIT, Dec 1960; -23c

The Savings, Investment and Valuation of a Corporation. REStat, 44 (Feb, 1962), 37-51; -23c

Security and a Financial Theory of Investment. QJE, 74 (Aug, 1960), 472-492; -23c

Security and a Financial Theory of Investment: Reply. QJE, 76 (May, 1962), 315-319; -23c

Security and Investment: Theory and Evidence. JF, 19 (Dec, 1964), 607-618; -23c

Towards a Theory of Financial Distress. JF, 26 (May, 1971), 347-356; -26g

Variability in Earning-Price Ratios: Comment. AER, 52 (Mar, 1962), 203-209; -7c

Paradis, G. E. & Rorke, C. H. Experimental Evidence on Alternative Portfolio Decision Rules. AER, 62 (May, 1972), 107-118; -4f, 9b

& Shapiro, E. Capital Equipment Analysis: the Required Rate of Profit. MSci, 3 (Oct, 1956), 102-110; -23d

See also **Brigham, E. F. & Gordon, M. J.**

See also **Freimer, M. & Gordon, M. J.**

Gorski, R. S. Investment Security in an Uncertain World. AJ, 10 (Aug, 1954), 33-36; -9c

Gort, M. Diversification and Integration in American Industry. Princeton U Pr, 1962; -26c

An Economic Disturbance Theory of Mergers. QJE, 83 (Nov, 1969), 624-642; -26a

Systematic Errors in Budgeting Capital Outlays. REStat, 44 (Feb, 1962), 72-75; -25c

& Hogarty, T. F. New Evidence on Mergers. JLE, 13 (Apr, 1970), 167-184; -26b

Goshay, R. C.

See **Michaelson, J. B. & Goshay, R. C.**

Gottlieb, M. Cyclical Timing of Municipal Bond Issues. QREB, 1 (May, 1961), 67-75; -19d

Goudzwaard, M. B. Conglomerate Mergers, Convertibles and Cash Dividends. QREB, 9 (Spring, 1969), 53-62; -26c

See also **Smith, K. V. & Goudzwaard, M. B.**

Gould, A. & Buchsbaum, M. A Filter Approach to Stock Selection. FAJ, 25 (Nov-Dec, 1969), 61ff; -8f

Gould, E. Laggards and Swingers—Investors Should Know More About the Volatility of Stocks. B, (May 23, 1966), 9; -10b

Gould, J. P. Market Value and the Theory of Investment of the Firm. AER, 57 (Sep, 1967), 910-913; -25c

Gould, J. R. On Investment Criteria for Mutually Exclusive Projects. Ec, 39 (Feb, 1972), 70-77; -25e

Graf, T. F. Hedging—How Effective Is It? JFE, 35 (Aug, 1953), 398-413; -21a

Graham, B. The Future of Financial Analysis. FAJ, 19 (May, 1963), 65-70; -4a

The Hippocratic Method in Security Analysis. AJ, 2 (2nd Qtr, 1946), 47-50; -4a

The Intelligent Investor, 4th ed. Har-Row 1965; -4a

The New Speculation in Common Stocks. AJ, 14 (Jun, 1958), 17-21; -4a

On Being Right in Security Analysis. AJ, 2 (1st Qtr, 1946), 18-21; -4a

The S.E.C. Method of Security Analysis. AJ, 2 (3rd Qtr, 1946), 32-35; -4a

Toward a Science of Security Analysis. AJ, 8 (Aug, 1952), 96-99; -4a

Two Illustrative Approaches to Formula Valuations of Common Stocks. AJ, 13 (Nov, 1957), 11-15; -7a

Dodd, D. L. & Cottle, S. Security Analysis: Principles and Technique, 4th ed. McGraw, 1962; -4a

Graichen, R. E. Buying and Selling a Corporate Business. JA, 107 (Apr, 1959), 45-53; -26a

Granger, C. W. J. Some Aspects of the Random Walk Model of Stock Market Prices. IntER, 9 (Jun, 1968), 253-257; -11b

& Morgenstern, O. Predictability of Stock Market Prices. Heath, 1970; -11c

& Morgenstern, O. Spectral Analysis of New York Stock Market Prices. Kyk, 16 (1963), 1-27; -11c

& Rees, H. J. B. Spectral Analysis of the Term Structure of Interest Rates. REStat, 50 (Jan, 1968); -18f

See also **Godfrey, M. D.; Granger, C. W. J. & Morgenstern, O.**

See also **Labys, W. C. & Granger, C. W. J.**

See also **Niarchos, N. A. & Granger, C. W. J.**

Grant, A. T. K. A Study of the Capital Market in Britain from 1919-1936. Cass, 1967; -2a

Switching of British Government Securities. IA, 3 (Aug, 1962), 14-29; -19c

Grant, J. A. G. Meiselman on the Structure of Interest Rates: a British Test. Ec, 44 (Feb, 1964), 51-71; -18f

A Study of the London Government Securities Market. PhD diss, London U, 1963; -19c

Granville, J. E. New Key to Stock Market Profits. P-H, 1963; -12a

A Strategy of Daily Stock Market Timing for Maximum Profit. P-H, 1960; -12a

Gray, J. New Evidence on the Term Structure of Interest Rates: 1884-1900. JF, forthcoming; -18e

See also **Bailey, A. D. & Gray, J.**

See also **Simmons, J. K. & Gray, J.**

Gray, K. B., Jr. Managing the Balance Sheet: a Mathematical Approach to Decision Making. JBR, (Spring, 1970), 35-42; -10g

Griffiths, B.   The Determination of the Treasury Bill Tender Rate. Ec, 38 (May, 1971), 180-191; -20b

Griffiths, R. J.   Relative Strength—an Indicator for Investment in the Equity Market. MSc thesis, Cranfield IT, 1970; -12d

Griswald, J. D.
See **Drayton, C. I., Jr.; Emerson, C. & Griswald, J. D.**

Grossman, H. I.   Expectations, Transactions Costs, and Asset Demands. JF, 24 (Jun, 1969), 491-506; -18b

Risk Aversion, Financial Intermediation and the Term Structure of Interest Rates. JF, 22 (Dec, 1967), 611-622; -18f

Grove, M. A.
See **Bierwag, G. O. & Grove, M. A.**

Grubel, H. G.   Forward Exchange, Speculation and the International Flow of Capital. Stanford U Pr, 1966; -21b

Internationally Diversified Portfolios: Welfare Gains and Capital Flows. AER, 58 (Dec, 1968), 1299-1314; -10i

A Neglected Aspect of Forward Exchange Theory and Policy. JF, 18 (Sep, 1963), 537-548; -21b

Profits from Forward Exchange Speculation. QJE, 79 (May, 1965), 248-262; -21b

Triangular Arbitrage and Forward Exchange Policy: Reply. JF, 19 (Sep, 1964), 552-554; -21b

& Fadner, K.   The Interdependence of International Equity Markets. JF, 26 (Mar, 1971), 89-94; -10i

Gruber, M. J.   Determinants of Common Stock Prices. PhD diss, Columbia U, 1966; -7a

See also **Elton, E. J. & Gruber, M. J.**

Grunewald, A. E. & Nemmers, E. E.   Basic Managerial Finance. HR & W, 1970; -22a

Grunewald, D.
See **Flink, S. J. & Grunewald, D.**

Guild, S. E.   The Case for Stock Value Tables. FAJ, 20 (Sep-Oct, 1964), 80-97; -7b

Gumperz, J.   Machines That Analyse—or Analysts? FAJ, 23 (Jan-Feb, 1967), 113-115; -4e

Pension Funds in an Age of Discontinuity. FAJ, 26 (Nov-Dec, 1970), 20ff; -3i

Scientific Input and Economic Output. FAJ, 24 (Nov-Dec, 1968), 111-113; -6f

Gup, B. E.   The Economics of the Security Option Markets. PhD diss, U of Cincinnati, 1966; -17a

Gupta, M. C.   The Effect of Size, Growth, and Industry on the Financial Structure of Manufacturing Companies. JF, 24 (Jan, 1969), 517-529; -26f

A Synchronic Study of Corporate Financial Structures, 1961-62. PhD diss, UCLA, 1967; -23g

Gupta, S. B.   The Portfolio Balance Theory of the Expected Rate of Change of Prices. REStud, 37 (Apr, 1970), 187-203; -18c

Gupta, S. K. & Rosenhead, J.   Robustness in Sequential Investment Decisions. MSci, 15 (Oct, 1968), B18-B29; -25c

Guthart, L. A.   Corporate Repurchases of Already Outstanding Common Stock. PhD diss, Harvard U, 1966; -16d

More Companies are Buying Back their Stock. HBR, 43 (Mar-Apr, 1965), 41-53, 172; -16d

Why Companies Are Buying Back Their Own Stock. FAJ, 23 (Mar-Apr, 1967), 105-110; -16d

Guthmann, H. G.   The Jenkins Report—English Corporation Law Scrutinized for Reform, *in* Lerner, E. M. (Ed), Readings in Financial Analysis and Investment Management. Irwin, 1963; -2c

    & Dougall, H. E.   Corporate Financial Policy, 4th ed. P-H, 1962; -22a

Guttentag, J. M. (Ed).   Essays on Interest Rates, Vol 2. (Dist by Columbia U Pr) Natl Bur Econ Res, 1971; -18b

    & Cagan, P. (Eds).   Essays on Interest Rates, Vol 1. (Dist by Columbia U Pr) Natl Bur Econ Res, 1969; -18b

    & Herman, E. S.   Banking Structure and Performance. NYU, 1967; -3f

Haas, R. D.   A Portfolio Model of International Capital Flows. PhD diss, Duke U, 1971; -21b

Haavelmo, T.   A Study in the Theory of Investment. U of Chicago Pr, 1960; -22b

Hadar, J. & Russell, W. R.   Rules for Ordering Uncertain Prospects. AER, 59 (Mar, 1969), 25-34; -10h

Hagemann, H. F.   Money Market Forces. FAJ, 16 (Aug-Sep, 1960), 81-84; -20a

Hagin, R. L.   An Empirical Evaluation of Selected Hypotheses Related to Price Changes in the Stock Market. PhD diss, UCLA, 1966; -7a

Hague, D. C.

    See **Lutz, F. A. & Hague, D. C. (Eds)**

Hahn, F. H. & Brechling, F. P. R. (Eds).   The Theory of Interest Rates. Macmillan Int, 1966; -18b

Hahn, P. J.   The Capital Adequacy of Commercial Banks. Am Pr, 1966; -3f

Hakansson, N. H.   Capital Growth and the Mean-Variance Approach to Portfolio Selection. JFQA, 6 (Jan, 1971), 517-558; -10j

    An Induced Theory of the Firm Under Risk: The Pure Mutual Fund. JFQA, 5 (Jun, 1970), 155-178; -3d, 9c

    Mean-Variance Analysis of Average Compound Returns. Unp ms, 1971; -10k

    Multi-Period Mean-Variance Analysis: Toward a General Theory of Portfolio Choice. JF, 26 (Sep, 1971), 857-884; -10k

    On the Dividend Capitalization Model under Uncertainty. JFQA, 4 (Mar, 1969), 65-87; -7b

    On Optimal Myopic Portfolio Policies with and without Serial Correlation of Yields. JB, 44 (Jul, 1971), 324-334; -10k

    Optimal Investment and Consumption Strategies Under Risk, an Uncertain Lifetime and Insurance. IntER, 10 (Oct, 1969), 443-466; -10k

    Optimal Investment and Consumption Strategies for a Class of Utility Functions. PhD diss, UCLA, 1966; -10k

    Optimal Investment and Consumption Strategies under Risk for a Class of Utility Functions. Em, 38 (Sep, 1970), 587-607; -10k

    Risk Disposition and the Separation Property in Portfolio Selection. JFQA, 4 (Dec, 1969), 401-416; -10c

    Optimal Growth Portfolios When Yields are Serially Correlated. REStat, 52 (Nov, 1970), 385-394; -10j

Hale, I.   The Stock Selection 'Game Theory'. FAJ, 16 (Mar, 1960), 53-56; -7a

Haley, C. W.   The Evaluation of Investment Proposals: An Application to de-novo Branch Offices of Commercial Banks. PhD diss, Stanford U, 1968; -25c

A Note on the Cost of Debt. JFQA, 1 (Dec, 1966), 72-93; -23c

Halford, F. A.   Income Bonds. FAJ, 20 (Jan-Feb, 1964), 73-79; -19a

Hall, G. R.

See **Fisher, I. N. & Hall, G. R.**

Hall, J. P., III.   Toward Effective Portfolio Management. FAJ, 22 (Jan-Feb. 1966), 91-95; -4a

Hall, L. W.   Security Analysis from the Point of View of a Trust Company. AJ, 9 (May, 1953), 123-124; —3j

Hall, M. & Weiss, L. W.   Firm Size and Profitability. REStat, 49 (Aug, 1967), 319-331; -26f

Hall, M. G.   Industries or Shares—a Controversial Problem in Portfolio Management. 1A, 33 (Sep, 1972), 12-23; -10a

Portfolio Management Using a Computer. Unp ms, 1969; -7c

Some Thoughts on 'Higgledy Piggledy Growth'. IA, 5 (May, 1963), 3-10; -8a

See also **Weaver, D. & Hall, M. G.**

Hall, R. E. & Jorgenson, D. W.   Tax Policy and Investment Behavior. AER, 57 (Jun, 1967), 391-414; -27a

Hallingby, P., Jr.   Speculative Opportunities in Stock Purchase Warrants. AJ, 3 (3rd Qtr, 1947), 41-49; -17b

Hållsten, B. A.   A Note on Modigliani and Miller's Extension of the Theory of Investment and Financing. SJE, 68 (Jun, 1966); -23c

Halpern, P.

See **Lorie, J. H. & Halpern, P.**

Hamada, K.

See **Royama, S. & Hamada, K.**

Hamada, R. S.   An Analysis of Diffusion Indices of Insiders' Transactions. SM thesis, MIT, 1961; -13c

The Effect of the Firm's Capital Structure on the Systematic Risk of Common Stocks. JF, 27 (May, 1972), 435-452; -23c

Investment Decisions with a General Equilibrium Mean-variance Approach. QJE, 85 (Nov, 1971); -25d

Portfolio Analysis, Market Equilibrium and Corporation Finance. JF, 24 (Mar, 1969), 13-31; -23c

Hamburger, M. J.   Expectations, Long-term Interest Rates and Monetary Policy in the United Kingdom. BEQB, 11 (Sep, 1971), 354-372; -18b

Household Demand for Financial Assets. Em, 36 (Jun, 1968), 97-118; -3b

& Kochin, L. A.   Money and Stock Prices: the Channels of Influence. JF, 27 (May 1972), 231-250; -6d

Hamilton, J. D.   Stockbroking Today. Macmillan Int, 1968; -4c

Hamman, R. L.   Theory of Investment of the Diversified Corporation. PhD diss, Harvard U, 1961; -26c

Hammel, J. E. & Hodes, D. A.   Factors Influencing P/E Multiples. FAJ, 23 (Jan-Feb, 1967), 90-92; -7a

Hammer, F. S.

See **Cohen, K. J. & Hammer, F. S.**

See also **Cohen, K. J.; Hammer, F. S. & Schneider, H. M.**

Hammond, J. S., III   Better Decisions with Preference Theory. HBR, 45 (Nov-Dec, 1967), 123-141; -9c

Towards Simplifying the Analysis of Decisions Under Uncertainty Where Preference is Non-Linear. DBA diss, Harvard Bus, 1968; -9c

264

Hammonds, T. M. & Padberg, D. I.   The Risk Factor in Investment Decisions. JASA, 65 (Jun, 1970), 602-612; -25d

Handa, J. C.   A New Approach to the Theory of Portfolio Selection. PhD diss, Johns Hopkins U, 1968; -10c

Haney, L. H.   Different Values of Income from Short Loans, Bonds, and Stocks. AJ, 10 (Feb, 1954), 9-13; -5a

Hanford, L. D.   Investing in Real Estate. Inst Real Est Mgmt, 1966; -21c

Hanna, M.   Short Interest: Bullish or Bearish—Comment. JF, 23 (Jun, 1968), 520-523; -13d

A Study of Inadequate Depreciation for 1956 Due to Inflation Based Upon External Reports of Fifteen Corporations Selected from the Dow-Jones Industrial Average. PhD diss, U of NC, 1963; -6c

Hanoch, G. & Levy, H.   The Efficiency Analysis of Choices Involving Risk. REStud, 36 (Jul, 1969), 335-346; -10h

Efficient Portfolio Selection with Quadratic and Cubic Utility. JB, 43 (Apr, 1970), 181-189; -10c

See also **Levy, H. & Hanoch, G.**

Hanson, W. C.   Capital Sources and Major Investing Institutions. Simmons-B, 1963; -3e

Hanssman, F.   Operations Research Techniques for Capital Investment. Wiley, 1968; -25d

Probability of Survival as an Investment Criterion. MSci, 15 (Sep, 1968), 33-48; -10f, 25d

Harbaugh, A. W.   Operations Research in the Stock Market. El Segunda, Cal: Computer Sciences Corporation, 1963; -17b

Harberger, A. C.   The Incidence of the Corporation Income Tax. JPE, 70 (Jun, 1962), 215-240; -27c

See also **Cragg, J. G.; Harberger, A. C. & Mieszkowski, P.**

Harbrecht, P. P.   Pension Funds and Economic Power. Twentieth Fund, 1959; -3i

Hardee, C.   Stock Options and the 'Insider Trading' Provisions of the Securities Exchange Act. HLR, 65 (1952); -17d

Hardy, C. O.   Odd-Lot Trading on the New York Stock Exchange. Brookings, 1939; -13b

Haring, J. E.   The Investment Horizon. Met, 13 (Aug, 1961), 77-93; -25c

& **Smith, G. C.**   Utility Theory, Decision Theory, and Profit Maximization. AER, 49 (Sep, 1959), 566-583; -9c

Harkavy, O.   The Relationship between Retained Earnings and Common Stock Prices for Large Listed Corporations. JF, 8 (Sep, 1953), 283-297; -24b

Harkins, E. P. & Walsh, F. J., Jr.   Corporate Debt Management. Natl Ind Conf Bd, 1968; -23c

Harlan, L. M.

See **Hayes, S. L. & Harlan, L. M.**

Harlow, C. V.   An Analysis of the Predictive Value of Stock Market 'Breadth' Measurements. DBA diss, U of S Cal, 1968; -12e

An Analysis of the Predictive Value of Stock Market 'Breadth' Measurements. Inv Int, 1968; -12e

& **Teweles, R. J.**   Commodities and Securities Compared. FAJ, 28 (Sep-Oct, 1972), 64-70; -21a

See also **Teweles, R. J.; Harlow, C. V. & Stone, H. L.**

Harold, G.   Bond Ratings as an Investment Guide. Ronald, 1938; -19f

A Reconsideration of the Common-Stock Theory. JB, 7 (Jan, 1934), 42-59

Harper, A. D.   How a Professional Investor Seeks Investment Opportunities. FAJ, 19 (Nov-Dec, 1963), 47-52; -4a

Harper, D. G.
See **Vernon, R. A.; Middleton, M. & Harper, D. G.**

Harries, B. W.   Standard & Poor's Corporation New Policy in Rating Municipal Bonds. FAJ, 24 (May-Jun, 1968), 68-71; -19f

Harrington, J. J., Jr.
See **Zinbarg, E. D. & Harrington, J. J., Jr.**

Harris, J. R.   Earnings per Share, Adjusted for New Issues. IA, 5 (May, 1963), 23-27; -16b

Harris, J. T.   A Comparison of Long Term Deep Discount and Current Coupon Bonds. FAJ, 24 (Jul-Aug, 1968), 81-85; -19a

Harris (Louis) & Associates.   Managing Endowment Funds. New York: Louis Harris & Associates, 1972; -3j

Harris, R. E.   Federal Reserve Margin Requirements: a Selective Instrument of Monetary Policy. PhD diss, U of Pa, 1958; -6e

Hart, A. G.   Anticipations, Uncertainty, and Dynamic Planning. U of Chicago Pr, 1940; -9c

Risk, Uncertainty and the Unprofitability of Compounding Probabilities, *in* Studies in Mathematical Economics and Econometrics. U of Chicago Pr, 1942; -9c

Hart, O. H.   Life Insurance Companies and the Equity Capital Markets. JF, 20 (May, 1965), 358-367; -3h

Hart, P. E.   The Size and Growth of Firms. Ec, 42 (Feb, 1962), 29-39; -26f

The Time Response of Dividends to Profit. U of Reading, Discussion Papers in Economics, No 3, nd; -24a

Hartill, C.   Stock Rights Make Sense. AJ, 14 (May, 1958), 63-65; -16b

Hartley, R.   No Mean City, a Guide to the Economic City of London. Queen Anne, 1967; -2a

Hartnett, J. H.   A Survey of the Put and Call Market with a Statistical Analysis of Factors Affecting Contract Premiums. SB thesis, MIT, 1955; -17a

Harvard Business Review.   Capital Investment Decisions. (15 articles reprinted from Harvard Business Reviews, 1954 to 1964) Harvard U, 1964; -25c

Harvey, R. K.   A Portfolio Model of Capital Budgeting under Risk. DBA diss, Indiana U, 1967; -25d

Hass, J. E.
See **Bierman, H., Jr.; Downes, D. H. & Hass, J. E.**
See also **Bierman, H., Jr. & Hass, J. E.**

Hastie, K. L.   Determinants of Municipal Bond Yields. JFQA, 7 (Jun, 1972), 1729-1748; -19d

The Determination of Optimal Investment Policy. MSci, 13 (Aug, 1967), B757-B774; -10*l*

The Determinants of Municipal Bond Yields. PhD diss, Cornell U, 1970; -19d

Hastings, P. G.   The Management of Business Finance. Van N Rein, 1966; -22a

Hatfield, K.
See **Reilly, F. K. & Hatfield, K.**

Haugen, R. A.   Effects of Leverage and Dividend Policy on the Value of Equity Capital. PhD diss, U of Ill, 1968; -23c

Expected Growth, Required Return, and the Variability of Stock Prices. JFQA, 5 (Sep, 1970), 297-308; -7a

& **Kroncke, C. O.**   A Portfolio Approach to Optimizing the Structure of Assets and Claims of a Stock Insurance Company. JRI, 37 (Mar, 1970), 41-48; -3h

& **Kroncke, C. O.**   Rate Regulation and the Cost of Capital in the Insurance Industry. JFQA, 6 (Dec, 1971), 1283-1305; -23d

& **Pappas, J. L.**   A Comment on the Capital Structure and the Cost of Capital: A Suggested Exposition. JF, 25 (Jun, 1970), 674-677; -23c

& **Pappas, J. L.**   Equilibrium in the Pricing of Capital Assets, Risk-Bearing Debt Instruments and the Question of Optimal Capital Structure. JFQA, 6 (Jun, 1971), 943-954; -23c

& **Udell, J. G.**   Rates of Return to Stockholders of Acquired Companies. JFQA, 7 (Jan, 1972), 1387-1398; -26b

& **Wichern, D.**   The Diametric Effects of the Capital Gains Tax on the Stability of Stock Prices. JF, forthcoming; -27d

Hausman, W. H.   A Note on 'The Value Line Contest: A Test of the Predictability of Stock Price Changes.' JB, 42 (Jul, 1969), 317-320; -15c

& **White, W. L.**   Theory of Option Strategy under Risk Aversion. JFQA, 3 (Sep, 1968), 343-358; -17a

See also **Bierman, H., Jr. & Hausman, W. H.**

Hawk, S. L.   Comparative Investment Performance of Preferred Stocks and Bonds. PhD diss, U of Wis, 1969; -19i

Hawkins, C. A.

See **Hubbard, C. L. & Hawkins, C. A.**

Hawtrey, R. G.   A Century of Bank Rates. Longman, 1938; -18b

A Symposium on the Theory of the Forward Market: III Mr. Kaldor on the Forward Market. REStud, 7 (Jun, 1940), 196-205; -21a

Haycocks, H. W., & Plymen, J.   The Design, Application and Future Development of the Financial Times Actuaries Index. JIA, 90 (Dec, 1964); -5b

& **Plymen, J.**   Investment Policy and Index Numbers. JIA, 82 (1956), 359; -5b

Haydon, R. B. & Wicks, J. M.   A Model of Commercial Bank Earnings Assets Selection. JFQA, 1 (Jun, 1966), 99-113; -10g

See also **Peterson, D. E. & Haydon, R. B.**

Hayes, D. A.   The Dimensions of Analysis. FAJ, 22 (Sep-Oct, 1966), 81-83; -4a

Ethical Considerations in the Professional Stature of Analysts. FAJ, 18 (Sep-Oct, 1962), 53-56; -4c

Evaluating the Investment Management Record of Fire Insurance Companies. AJ, 14 (Jul-Aug, 1958), 57-59; -14a

Institutional Investors and Selection Criteria. FAJ, 21 (Jul, 1965), 86-87; -3e

Investments: Analysis and Management, 2nd ed. Macmillan, 1966; -4a

Some Reflections on Techniques for Appraising Growth Rates. FAJ, 20 (Jul-Aug, 1964), 96-101; -7b

The Undervalued Issue Strategy. FAJ, 23 (May-Jun, 1967), 121-127; -4a

See also **Adderley, T. E. & Hayes, D. A.**

Hayes, S. L., III.   New Interest in Incentive Financing. HBR, 44 (Jul-Aug, 1966), 99-112; -17d

& **Harlan, L. M.**   Real Estate as a Corporate Investment. HBR, 45 (Jul-Aug, 1967), 144-160; -21c

& **Reiling, H. B.**   Sophisticated Financing Tool: the Warrant. HBR, 47 (Jan-Feb, 1969), 137-150; -17b, 17c

See also **Taussig, R. A. & Hayes, S. L., III**

Haynes, J.   Risk as an Economic Factor. QJE, 9 (Jul, 1895), 409-449;-9c

Healy, K. T.   The Merger Movement in Transportation. AER, 52 (May, 1962), 436-444;-26a

Heckerman, D. G.   Portfolio Selection and the Structure of Capital Asset Prices when Relative Prices of Consumption Goods May Change. JF, 27 (Mar, 1972), 47-60;-10*l*

Heflebower, R. B.   Corporate Mergers: Policy and Economic Analysis. QJE, 77 (Nov, 1963), 537-558;-26a

Heilbrunn, R.   A Practical Approach to Common Stock Valuation. AJ, 14 (May, 1958), 49-51; -7b

Heim, P.
See **Baumol, W. J.; Heim, P.; Malkiel, B. G. & Quandt, R. E.**

Heins, A. J.   The Interest Rate Differential between Revenue Bonds and General Obligations: a Regression Model. NTJ, 15 (Dec, 1962), 399-405;-19d

  & Allison, S. L.   Some Factors Affecting Stock Price Variability. JB, 39 (Jan, 1966), 19-23;-10b

Heinze, D. C.   Price Spreads on the Over-the-Counter Securities Market. DBA diss, Arizona St U, 1969;-2b

Heiser, H. C.   The Application of Computers to Scientific Management. AJ, 14 (Jun, 1958), 70-72;-4e

Helfert, E. A.   Techniques of Financial Analysis, rev ed. Irwin, 1967;-4a
  Valuation: Concepts and Practice. Wadsworth Pub, 1966;-7a

Heller, H.   Integration of the Dissemination of Information Under the Securities Act of 1933 and the Securities Act of 1934. LCP, 29 (Jun, 1964), 749-776; -2e

Heller, H. R.   Foreign Bond Issues in Europe. LBR, 86 (Oct, 1967), 49-62;-20e

Heller, S.
See **Nadler, M.; Heller, S. & Shipman, S. S.**

Helm, H. M., Jr.   Technical Analysis as Applied to the 1961-1962 Stock Market Price Cycle. PhD diss, U of Tex, 1968;-12a

Helmer, B.   Perspective on Timing Equity Investments. FAJ, 21 (May-Jun, 1965), 21-25;-7d

Helpern, S. R.   An Analysis of Stock Price Movements Using Stop Orders. SB thesis, MIT, 1962;-12c

Hempel, G. H.   The Postwar Quality of State and Local Debt. Columbia U Press, 1971;-19d

Hemsted, J. R.   Probability in the Investment Field. IA, 5 (May, 1963), 11-15;-9c

Hendershott, P. H.   A Flow of Funds Model. JMCB, (1971), 815-832;-3c
  Structure of International Interest Rates: the US Treasury Bill Rate and the Eurodollar Deposit Rate. JF, 22 (Sep, 1967), 455-465; -18b

Henderson, G. D.
See **Mundheim, R. H. & Henderson, G. D.**

Henderson, R. F.   The New Issue Market and the Finance of Industry. Bowes, 1951;-16a
See also **Tew, B. & Henderson, R. F. (Eds)**

Henderson, R. H.   Ruminations on Performance. FAJ, 25 (Nov-Dec, 1969), 103ff;-7d

Henderson-Stewart, D. J.   Implications of Personal Taxation for Corporate Investment Decisions. SM thesis, MIT, 1967;-27a

Heness, S.   Measuring Investment Performance of Balanced Funds. AJ, 7 (4th Qtr, 1951), 59-60;-14a

Hennessy, J. H.   Acquiring and Merging Businesses. P-H, 1966; -26a

Henshaw, R. C., Jr.; Olson, A. C. & O'Donnell, J. L.   The Case for Public Regulation of the Securities Markets. BT, (Autumn, 1964), 69-77; -2e

Herbert, P. J. A.

　　See **Briston, R. J. & Herbert, P. J. A.**

Herman, E. S.   Mutual Fund Management Fee Rates. JF, 18 (May, 1963), 360-376; -3k

　　See also **Friend, I. & Herman, E. S.**

　　See also **Guttentag, J. M. & Herman, E. S.**

Heron, J. P.   The Capital Gearing of Companies. IA, 10 (Dec, 1964), 11-18; -23g

Herringer, F. C.

　　See **Bower, R. S.; Herringer, F. C. & Williamson, J. P.**

Hershey, R. D.   Bond Men Start Hunting. New York Times, Aug 21, 1966, 1ff; -17c

Herstein, I. N. & Milnor, J.   An Axiomatic Approach to Measurable Utility. Em, 21 (Apr, 1953), 291-297; -9a

Hertz, D. B.   Investment Policies that Pay Off. HBR, 46 (Jan-Feb, 1968), 96-103; -28d

　　　Risk Analysis in Capital Investment. HBR, 42 (Jan-Feb, 1964), 95-106; -25d

Herzog, J. P.   Investor Experience in Corporate Securities. JF, 19 (Mar, 1964), 46-62; -19b

Hespos, R. F. & Strassman, P. A.   Stochastic Decision Trees for the Analysis of Investment Decisions. MSci, 12 (Aug, 1965), B244-B259; -25d

Hess, A. C. & Winn, W. J.   The Value of the Call Privilege. JF, 14 (May, 1959), 182-195; -19h

　　　& Winn, W. J.   The Value of the Call Privilege. U of Pa Pr, 1962; -19h

Hess, A. P., Jr.

　　See **Friend, I.; Longstreet, J. R.; Mendelson, M.; Miller, E. & Hess, A. P., Jr.**

Hester, D. D.   Efficient Portfolios with Short Sales and Margin Holdings, *in* Hester, D. D. & Tobin, J. (Eds), Risk Aversion and Portfolio Choice. Wiley, 1967; -10c

　　　& Tobin, J. (Eds).   Financial Markets and Economic Activity. Wiley, 1967; -1b

　　　& Tobin, J. (Eds).   Risk Aversion and Portfolio Choice. Wiley, 1967; -1b

　　　& Tobin, J. (Eds).   Studies of Portfolio Behavior. Wiley, 1967; -1b

　　　& Zoellner, J. F.   The Relation between Bank Portfolios and Earnings: an Econometric Analysis. REStat, 48 (Nov, 1966), 372-386; -3f

　　See also **Feeney, G. J. & Hester, D. D.**

Heston, A. W.   Corporate Cash and Securities Holdings: an Empirical Study of Cash, Securities and Other Current Accounts of Large Corporations. PhD diss, Yale U, 1962; -25a

　　　An Empirical Study of Cash, Securities, and other Current Accounts of Large Corporations. YEE, 2 (Spring, 1962), 116-168; -25a

Heth, M.   The CD in American Banking: Retrospect and Prospect. BNLQR, 21 (Mar, 1968), 48-74; -20a

Hetrick, J. C.   Mathematical Models in Capital Budgeting. HBR, 39 (Jan-Feb, 1961), 49-64; -25e

Hewitt Associates.   1968 Report on the Investment Performance of Retirement Funds. Chicago: The Associates, 1968; -3i

Hey, J. D. Spectral Analysis of Stock-Market Prices. MSc diss, Edinburgh U, 1968

Hichens, A. Valuing a Company for Acquisition. IA, 17 (May, 1967), 3-10; -26a

Hickman, W. B. Corporate Bond Quality and Investor Experience. (Dist by Princeton U Pr) Natl Bur Econ Res, 1958; -19g

Corporate Bonds: Quality and Investment Performance. Natl Bur Econ Res, 1957; -19g

Statistical Measures of Corporate Bond Financing Since 1900. (Dist by Princeton U Pr) Natl Bur Econ Res, 1960; -19e

Trends and Cycles in Corporate Bond Financing. Natl Bur Econ Res, 1950; -19e

The Volume of Corporate Bond Financing Since 1900. Princeton U Pr, 1953; -19e

Hicks, C. M.

See **Burtchett, F. F. & Hicks, C. M.**

Hicks, J. R. Inflation and Interest. BNLQR, 23 (Sep, 1970), 261-275; -18c

Liquidity. EJ, 72 (Dec, 1962), 787-802; -18a

Mr. Hawtrey on Bank Rates and the Long Term Rate of Interest. MS, 10 (No 1, 1939), 21-37; -18b

The Pure Theory of Portfolio Selection, *in* Hicks, J. R., Critical Essays in Monetary Theory. Oxford U Pr, 1967; -10c

Value and Capital: An Inquiry Into Some Fundamental Principles of Economic Theory, 2nd ed. Oxford U Pr, 1946; -22b

Hieronymus, T. A. Economics of Futures Trading: for Commercial and Personal Profit. Commodity R, 1971; -21a

Higgins, C. A.

See **Treynor, J. L.; Priest, W. W., Jr.; Fisher, L. & Higgins, C. A.**

Higgins, H. B.

See **Horowitz, I. & Higgins, H. B.**

Higgins, L. R. The Put-and-Call. Effingham, 1906; -17a

Higgins, R. C. The Corporate Dividend-Saving Decision. JFQA, 7 (Mar, 1972), 1477-1494; -24a

Dividend Policy and Increasing Discount Rates. JFQA; forthcoming; -24b

Dividend Policy and the Valuation of Corporate Shares under Uncertainty. PhD diss, Stanford U, 1969; -24b

See also **Robichek, A. A.; McDonald, J. G. & Higgins, R. C.**

Hill, H. G., Jr. Capital Expenditures Management. JB, 28 (Oct, 1955), 285-290; -25c

Hill, R. W. Cash Management Techniques. Am Mgmt, 1970; -25a

Hillier, F. S. Derivation of Probabilistic Information for the Evaluation of Risky Investments. MSci, 9 (Apr, 1963), 443-457; -25d

Supplement to the Derivation of Probabilistic Information for the Evaluation of Risky Investments. MSci, 11 (Jan, 1965), 485-487; -25d

Hilton, J. G.

See **Edwards, C. E. & Hilton, J. G.**

Hirsch, J. H. An Effective Yardstick of Common Stock Value. FAJ, 17 (May-Jun, 1961), 13-20; -7a

Improved Yardstick of Common Stock Value. FAJ, 19 (Sep-Oct, 1963), 60-69; -7a

Hirschmann, W. B. & Brauweiler, J. R. Investment Analysis: Coping with Change. HBR, 43 (May-Jun, 1965), 62-72; -25c

Hirshleifer, J. Efficient Allocation of Capital in an Uncertain World. AER, 54 (May, 1964), 77-85; -25d

Investment Decision Under Uncertainty: Applications of the State—
Preference Approach. QJE, 80 (May, 1966), 252-277;-9c
    Investment Decision Under Uncertainty: Choice—Theoretic Ap-
proaches. QJE, 79 (Nov, 1965) 509-536;-9c
    Investment, Interest and Capital. P-H, 1969;-25c
    On the Theory of Optimal Investment Decisions. JPE, 66 (Aug,
1958), 329-352;-25c
    Risk, the Discount Rate, and Investment Decisions. AER, 51 (May,
1961), 112-120;-25d
Hirst, F. W.   The Stock Exchange; A Short Study of Investment and Specu-
lation, 4th ed. Oxford U Pr, 1948;-2a
Hoagland, H. E. & Stone, L. D.   Real Estate Finance, 4th ed. Irwin, 1969;-21c
Hobson, O.   How the City Works: Dickens, 1966;-2a
Hochmuth, W. P. & Bowes, A. S.   Investment Companies: Performance vs
Charges. FAJ, 17 (Jan-Feb, 1961), 43-49; -14a
Hodes, D. A.
    See Hammel, J. E. & Hodes, D. A.
Hodges, S. D. & Brealey, R. A.   Portfolio Selection in a Dynamic and Un-
certain World. FAJ, 28 (Nov-Dec, 1972), 58-70; -10c
    & Brealey, R. A.   Using the Sharpe Model. IA, 27 (Sep, 1970),
41-50; -10c
    & Moore, P. G.   The Consideration of Risk in Project Selection.
JIA, 94 (1968), 355-378; -9c
    & Moore, P. G.   Mathematical Models in Portfolio Selection.
JBF, 3 (Spring, 1971);-10c
    See also Brealey, R. A. & Hodges, S. D.
Hodgman, D. R.   Commercial Bank Loan and Investment Policy. U of Ill
Pr, 1963;-3f
Hoffland, D. L.   The Folklore of Wall Street. FAJ, 23 (May-Jun, 1967),
85-88; -4a
    The Price-Rating Structure of the Municipal Bond Market. FAJ,
28 (Mar-Apr, 1972), 65-70;-19f
Hofflander, A. E., Jr.
    See Shelton, J. P.; Brigham, E. F. & Hofflander, A. E., Jr.
Hoffman, G. W.
    See Friend, I.; Hoffman, G. W., & Winn, W. J.
Hogarty, T. F.   The Profitability of Corporate Mergers. JB, 43 (Jul, 1970),
317-327;-26b
    See also Gort, M. & Hogarty, T. F.
Holbrook, R. & Stafford, F.   The Propensity to Consume Separate Types of
Income: a Generalized Permanent Income Hypothesis. Em, 39 (Jan,
1971), 1-22;-10k
Holland, D. M.   Dividends Under the Income Tax. Princeton U Pr, 1962;-
27a
    The Income-Tax Burden on Stockholders. (Dist by Princeton U
Pr) Natl Bur Econ Res, 1958; -27a
    Private Pension Funds: Projected Growth. (Dist by Columbia U
Pr) Natl Bur Econ Res, 1966;-3i
    & Lewellen, W. G.   Probing the Record of Stock Options. HBR,
40 (Mar-Apr, 1962), 132-150;-17d
    See also Cootner, P. H. & Holland, D. M.
Holland, T. E.   Cyclical Movements of Interest Rates, 1948-61. JB, 37
(Oct, 1964), 364-369;-18d
    Forecasting Interest Rate Movements: Time Series Analyses and

271

Functional Relationships. PhD diss, Duke U, 1963;-18b

Holmes, A. R. & Klopstock, F. H. The Market for Dollar Deposits in Europe. Mo Rev F R Bk New York, (1960);-20d

Holmes, J. M. A Direct Test of Friedman's Permanent Income Hypothesis. JASA, 65 (Sep, 1970), 1159-1162;-10k

Holmes, L. M. Corporate Acquisition Patterns. SM thesis, MIT, 1967;-26a

Holsen, R. C. Another Look at Business Combinations. JA, 116 (Jul, 1963), 67;-26a

Holt, C. C. The Influence of Growth Duration on Share Prices. JF, 17 (Sep, 1962), 465-475;-7b, 18g

    & Shelton, J. P. The Implications of the Capital Gains Tax for Investment Decision. JF, 16 (Dec, 1961), 559-580;-27d

    & Shelton, J. P. The Lock-in Effect of the Capital Gains Tax. NTJ, 15 (Dec, 1962), 337-352;-27d

Homa, K. E. & Jaffee, D. M. The Supply of Money and Common Stock Prices. JF, 26 (Dec, 1971), 1045-1066; -6d

Homer, S. Distortions Within Bond and Money Markets. FAJ, 24 (Jul-Aug, 1968), 77-79;-19a

    A Dynamic Approach to Institutional Investment. New York: Salomon Bros, & Hutzler, 1961; -19a

    A History of Interest Rates. Rutgers U Pr, 1963;-18a

    Inflation and the Capital Markets. FAJ, 25 (Jul-Aug, 1969), 143-145;-6c

    Stocks Versus Bonds: a Comparison of Supply and Demand Factors. II, 2 (Aug, 1968), 45ff; -19a

    & Johannesen, R. I., Jr. The Price of Money, 1946-1969: an Analytical Study of United States and Foreign Interest Rates. Rutgers U Pr, 1969;-18b

Hood, O. The Science of Volatility. AJ, 14 (Aug, 1958), 35-37;-10b

Hooper, L. O. Should Security Analysts Have a Professional Rating? The Negative Case. AJ, 1 (Jan, 1945), 41-44;-4c

    The Specialist Should Be a Generalist Too. FAJ, 21 (Nov-Dec, 1965), 33-35;-4c

Hoos, S. & Working, H. Price Relations of Liverpool Wheat Futures with Special Reference to the December-March Spread. Wheat Studies of the Food Research Institute, 16 (Nov, 1940), 101-143;-21a

Hoover, E. M. Some Institutional Factors in Business Investment Decisions. AER, 44 (May, 1954), 201-213;-25c

Hoppes, H. N. An Evaluation of Selected Normative Models of Equity Valuation. PhD diss, Am U, 1968; -7a

Horiguchi, Y. Corporate Financial Decisions: General Equilibrium Approach. PhD diss, Rice U, 1971;-22c

Horowitz, I. A Model for Mutual Fund Evaluation. IMR, 6 (Spring, 1965), 81-92;-14a

    Popularity Versus Performance: The Mutual Funds. QREB, 6 (Spring, 1966), 45-57; -14a

    A Rating of Mutual Fund Managements' Investment Ability. IMR, 7 (Fall, 1965), 65-76;-14a

    The Reward-to-Variability Ratio and Mutual Fund Performance. JB, 39 (Oct, 1966), 485-488;-14a

    The Varying (?) Quality of Investment Trust Management. JASA, 58 (Dec, 1963), 1011-1032;-14a

    & Higgins, H. B. Some Factors Affecting Investment Fund Performance. QREB, 3 (Spring, 1963), 41-50;-14a

Horrigan, J. O.   The Determination of Long-Term Credit Standing with Financial Ratios. ERA (1966);-19f

An Evaluation of Financial Ratio Analysis. PhD diss, U of Chicago, 1968;-19f

Horton, J. J. Jr.   Statistical Classification of Municipal Bonds. JBR, (Autumn, 1970), 29-40;-19d

A Statistical Rating Index for Municipal Bonds. FAJ, 25 (Mar-Apr, 1969), 72-75;-19d

Horwich, G.   Real Assets and the Theory of Interest. JPE, 70 (Apr, 1962), 157-169; -18b

Horwitz, R. M.   Arrearages on Cumulative Preferred Stocks Listed on the New York Stock Exchange: an Analysis of Experiences, 1935-62. PhD diss, Mich St U, 1964; -19i

Houck, J. P.   A Statistical Model of the Demand for Soybeans. JFE, 46 (May, 1964), 366-374; -21a

House, W. C.   Sensitivity Analysis in Making Capital Investment Decisions. National Association of Accountants, 1968; -25c

Houthakker, H. S.   Commodity Futures IV: an Empirical Test of the Theory of Normal Backwardation. Cowles Commission Discussion Paper, Economics, No. 2124, (22 Jun, 1955); -21a

Restatement of the Theory of Normal Backwardation. Cowles Foundation Discussion Paper, No 44, (18 Dec, 1957); -21a

The Scope and Limits of Futures Trading, *in* Abromovitz, M. (Ed), Allocation of Economic Resources. Stanford U Pr, 1959; -21a

Can Speculators Forecast Prices? REStat, 39 (May, 1957), 143-151; -21a

Systematic and Random Elements in Short-Term Price Movements. AER, 51 (Mar, 1961), 164-172; -21a

& Telser, L. G.   Commodity Futures II: Gains and Losses of Hedgers and Futures Speculators. Cowles Commission Discussion Paper, Economics, No. 2090, (7 Dec, 1952); -21a

Howard, B. B. & Jones, S. L. (Eds).   Managerial Problems in Finance; Cases in Decision Making. McGraw, 1964; -1c

& Upton, M.   Introduction to Business Finance. McGraw, 1953; -22a

Howard, E. D.   The Relative Vulnerability of Growth and Income Stocks. AJ, 11 (Aug, 1955), 19-23; -7b

Howard, G. G.   Investment Research in the 1970's. FAJ, 24 (May-Jun, 1968), 120-123; -4a

Howe, M.

See **Merrett, A. J.; Howe, M. & Newbould, G. D.**

Howell, L. D.   Analysis of Hedging and Other Operations in Grain Futures. US Dept of Agriculture Technical Bulletin No. 971, Aug 1948; -21a

Howell, P. L.   Common Stocks and Pension Fund Investing. HBR, 36 (Nov-Dec, 1958), 92-106; -3i

A Re-examination of Pension Fund Investment Policies. JF, 13 (May, 1958), 261-274; -3i

Howrey, E. P.   Are Stock Prices Random or Predictable? BE, 1 (Summer, 1965); -11c

Huang, S. S. C.   Study of the Performance of Rapid Growth Stocks. FAJ, 21 (Jan-Feb, 1965), 58-59; -7b

Hubbard, C. L.   An Operational Stock Valuation Model Based on Multiple Growth Horizons. PhD diss, St U NY Buffalo, 1965; -7b

& Hawkins, C. A.   Theory of Valuation. Intext, 1969; -7a

    & Johnson, T.   Writing Calls with Convertible Bonds. FAJ, 25 (Nov-Dec, 1969), 78-79; -17a

Hubbard, P. M., Jr.   Hard Look at Secondaries. B, (Nov 23, 1963), 18; -16e
    Short Term Impact of Secondary Distributions. CFC, (Apr 28, 1960), 11ff; -16e

Huefner, R. J.   Capital Investment Decisions and Uncertainty: Sensitivity Analysis of the Present Value Model and Evaluation of the Treatment of Uncertainty. PhD diss, Cornell U, 1968; -25d

Hughes, P. F. & Tingley, K. R.   Taxation of Capital Gains, 2nd ed. Taxation, 1969; -27d

Hugon, J. H.   Past and Future of the Euro-money Market. FAJ, 27 (Sep-Oct, 1971), 21-24; -20d

Hulett, D. T.   A Short-Run Model of Commercial Bank Portfolio Behavior. PhD diss, Stanford U, 1966; -10g

Humphrey, J. H.
    See **Plum, L. V.; Humphrey, J. H. & Bowyer, J. W.**

Hunt, P.   Financial Analysis in Capital Budgeting. Harvard Busn, 1965; -25c
    Portfolio Policies of Commercial Banks in the United States, 1920-1939. Harvard Busn, 1940; -3f
    A Proposal for Precise Definitions of 'Trading on the Equity' and 'Leverage'. JF, 16 (Sep, 1961), 377-386; -23c
    & Andrews, V. L.   Financial Management: Cases and Readings. Irwin, 1968; -1c
    Williams, C. M. & Donaldson, G.   Basic Business Finance: Text and Cases, 4th ed. Irwin, 1971; -22a
    See also **Masson, R. L.; Hunt, P. & Anthony, R. N.**

Hunt Commission Report.   The Report of the President's Commission on Financial Structure and Regulation (The Hunt Commission Report). Washington, DC: Supt. of Documents, Dec 1971; -3e

Hunter, A.   Mergers and Industry Concentration in Britain. BNLQR, 22 (Dec, 1969), 372-394; -26a

Hunter, J.
    See **Jorgenson, D. W.; Hunter, J. & Nadir, M. I.**

Hurwicz, L.   Optimality Criteria for Decision Making Under Ignorance. Cowles Commission Discussion Paper, No. 370, (1951); -9a

Husband, W. H. & Dockeray, J. C.   Modern Corporation Finance, 6th ed. Irwin, 1966; -22a

Hutchins, R. C.   Measurement of Multicompany Diversification. PhD diss, U of S Cal, 1971; -26c

Hutchinson, G. S. (Ed).   The Business of Acquisitions and Mergers. Presidents, 1968; -26a

Ibbotson, R.   Price Performance of New Unseasoned Common Stock Issues. Paper for the Seminar on the Analysis of Security Prices, U of Chicago, Nov 1972; -16a

Iglehart, D. L.   Capital Accumulation and Production for the Firm: Optimal Dynamic Policies. MSci, 11 (Nov, 1965); -25d

Ijiri, Y.   On the Convergence of Periodic Reinvestments by an Amount Equal to Depreciation. MSci, 13 (Jan, 1967), 321-335; -25c
    Levy, F. K. & Lyon, R. C.   A Linear Programming Model for Budgeting and Financial Planning. JAR, 1 (Autumn, 1963), 198-212; -22c

Imai, Y.   An Integration of Neo-classical Theory of Optimal Accumulation and Corporate Financial Theory. PhD diss, Rice U, 1971; -9d

Innes, J. T.   The Role of Capacity Utilization in the Investment Decision. PhD diss, U of Oreg, 1967; -25c

Innocenti, R. E.   The Stock-Bond Split Decision for Pension Funds. FAJ, 25 (Nov-Dec, 1969), 97-101; -3i

Institute of Chartered Financial Analysts
    See **Chartered Financial Analysts, Institute of**

Institutional Investor.   Can Our Non-Profit Institutions be Saved?—Special Issue. II, 6 (Aug, 1972), 33ff; -3j¡

Investment Bankers Association of America.   A Study of the Market Effects of Cash Equity Financing, Jan 1, 1958-Jun 30, 1960. Report of the Industrial Securities Committee, 1960; -16b

Investment Company Institute.   Management Investment Companies. P-H, 1962; -3k

The Money Managers: Professional Investment through Mutual Funds. McGraw, 1967; -3k

Investors' Chronicle.   All About Options.
    Part 1: IC, (Sep 1, 1961),
    Part 2: IC, (Sep 8, 1961),
    Part 3: IC, (Sep 15, 1961); -17a

Beginners Please. Eyre & S, 1967; -2a

Irwin, H. S.   Seasonal Cycles in Aggregates of Wheat Futures Contracts. JPE, 43 (1935), 278-288; -21a

Ishaq, T.   The Capital Market in Pakistan. PEJ, 2 (Jan, 1969), 102-111; -2c

Israels, C. L. & Duff, G. M., Jr. (Eds).   When Corporations Go Public. Pr Law Inst, 1962

Istvan, D. F.   Capital-Expenditures Decisions: How They Are Made in Large Corporations. Ind U Busn Res, 1961; -25f

Jääkeläinen, V.   Growth of Earnings and Dividend Distribution Policy. SJE, 69 (Sep, 1967), 184-195; -24a

Jack, A. B.   The Capital Expenditure Function. MS, 34 (May, 1966), 133-158; -25c

Jackson, A. S. & Townsend, E. C.   Financial Management. Harrap, 1970; -22a

Jackson, D. F.   The Variable Annuity and its Investment Performance. PhD diss, U of Tex, 1968; -3h

Jackson, J. T. R.   Some Speculative Strategies in the Stock Market. PhD diss, Case IT, 1964; -11c

Jackson, R.   The Consideration of Economies in Merger Cases. JB, 43 (Oct, 1970), 439-447; -26a

See also **Breen, W. & Jackson, R.**

Jacob, N. L.   The Measurement of Market Similarity for Securities Under Uncertainty. JB, 43 (Jul, 1970), 328-340; -10b

The Measurement of Systematic Risk for Securities and Portfolios: Some Empirical Results. JFQA, 6 (Mar, 1971), 815-834; -10b

& Smith, K. V.   The Value of Perfect Market Forecasts in Portfolio Selection. JF, 27 (May, 1972), 355-370; -10c

Jacobs, D. P.   The Marketable Security Portfolios of Non-Financial Corporations, Investment Practices and Trends. JF, 15 (Sep, 1960), 341-352; -3a

Jacoby, N. H. & Weston, J. F.   Factors Influencing Managerial Decisions in Determining Forms of Business Financing: An Exploratory Study. Conference on Research in Business Finance. Natl Bur Econ Res, 1952; -23g

Jaedicke, R. K.
    See **Bierman, H., Jr.; Fouraker, L. E. & Jaedicke, R. K.**

Jaenicke, H.R.   Business Combinations: The Criteria for Distinguishing
   Purchases from Poolings of Interests and their Present Day Appli-
   cability. PhD diss, U of Pa, 1963; -26d
      Management's Choice to Purchase or Pool. AR, 37 (Oct, 1962),
   758-765; -26d
Jaffe, L.H.   A Study of Stock Splits, 1946-1956. MBA thesis, NYU, 1957; -16c
   See Blucher, L.H.
Jaffee, D.M.
   See Homa, K.E. & Jaffee, D.M.
James, E.
   See James, R. & E.
James, F.E., Jr.   The Implications of Trend Persistency in Portfolio
   Management. PhD diss, Rensselaer, 1967; -12d
      Monthly Averages—An Effective Investment Tool? JFQA, 3 (Sep,
   1968), 315-326; -12d
James, R. & E.   Disputed Role of the Stock Exchange Specialists. HBR,
   40 (May-Jun, 1962), 133-146; -2b
Jamison, D.   Time Preference and Utility: a Comment. EJ, 80 (Mar, 1970),
   179-180; -9a
Jaretzki, A., Jr.   Duties and Responsibilities of Directors of Mutual Funds.
   LCP, 29 (Jun, 1964), 777-794; -3k
Jarislowsky, S.A. & Brown, J.J.   A Statistical Approach to Security Analy-
   sis. AJ, 10 (Nov, 1954), 79-83; -7a
Jarrett, F.G.   Short Term Forecasting of Australian Wool Prices. AEP,
   4 (Jun-Dec, 1965), 93-102; -21a
Jean, W.H.   The Analytical Theory of Finance: a Study of the Investment
   Decision Process of the Individual and the Firm. HR & W, 1970; -22a
      Capital Budgeting: the Economic Evaluation of Investment Projects.
   Intext, 1969; -25c
      The Extension of Portfolio Analysis to Three or More Parameters.
   JFQA, 6 (Jan, 1971), 505-516; -10m
      On Multiple Rates of Return. JF, 23 (Mar, 1968), 187-191; -25c
      Terminal Value or Present Value in Capital Budgeting Programs.
   JFQA, 6 (Jan, 1971), 649-652; -25c
Jehring, J.J.   The Investment and Administration of Profit Sharing Trust
   Funds: a research study of 208 profit sharing trust funds. Profit Shar-
   ing, 1957; -3j
Jen, F.C. & Wert, J.E.   Effect of Call Risk on Corporate Yields. JF, 22
   (Dec, 1967), 637-651; -19h
      & Wert, J.E.   The Effect of Sinking Fund Provisions on Cor-
   porate Bond Yields. FAJ, 23 (Mar-Apr, 1967), 125-131; -19h
      & Wert, J.E.   Imputed Yields of Sinking Fund Bonds and the
   Term Structure of Interest Rates. JF, 21 (Dec, 1966), 697-714; -18f
      & Wert, J.E.   The Value of the Deferred Call Privilege. NBR,
   (Mar, 1966); -19h
      See also Boness, A.J., Jr. & Jen, F.C.
      See also Chen, A.H.Y.; Jen, F.C. & Zionts, S.
Jenks, J.C.   Investing in Growth Stock. AJ, 3 (2nd Qtr, 1947), 38-53; -7b
Jennings, E.H.   An Empirical Analysis of Some Aspects of Common Stock
   Diversification. JFQA, 6 (Mar, 1971), 797-814; -10e
Jennings, R.W.   The New York Stock Exchange and the Commission Rate
   Struggle. BL, (Nov, 1965), 159-183; -2b
      Self-Regulation in the Securities Industry: The Role of the Securi-
   ties and Exchange Commission. LCP, 29 (Jun, 1964), 663-690; -2e

Jensen, J. E.   A Pricing Model for the Convertible Debenture: A Selective Study. PhD diss, U of Pittsburgh, 1966; -17c

Jensen, K. R.   A Critical Analysis of Measures of Income for the Endowment Funds of Universities and Colleges Invested in Common Stock: their Empirical Utility and Accounting Acceptability. Unp ms, Mar 1968; -3j

Jensen, M. C.   The Foundations and Current State of Capital Market Theory, *in* Jensen, M. C. (Ed), Studies in the Theory of Capital Markets. Praeger, 1972; -10*l*

   Optimal Utilization of Market Forecasts and the Evaluation of Investment Performance. Unp ms, 1971; -14a

   The Performance of Mutual Funds in the Period 1945-64. JF, 23 (May, 1968), 389-416; -14a

   Random Walks: Reality or Myth—Comment. FAJ, 23 (Nov-Dec, 1967), 77-85; -12d

   Risk, the Pricing of Capital Assets, and the Evaluation of Investment Portfolios. JB, 42 (Apr, 1969), 167-247; -10*l*

   (Ed).   Studies in the Theory of Capital Markets. Praeger, 1972; -10*l*

   & Bennington, G. A.   Random Walks and Technical Theories: Some Additional Evidence. JF, 25 (May, 1970), 469-482; -12d

   See also **Bailey, M. J. & Jensen, M. C.**
   See also **Black, F; Jensen, M. C. & Scholes, M.**
   See also **Fama, E. F.; Fisher, L.; Jensen, M. C. & Roll, R.**
   See also **Long, J. B., Jr. & Jensen, M. C.**
   See also **Meckling, W. H. & Jensen, M. C.**

Jensen, R. E.   An Experimental Design for Study of Effects of Accounting Variations in Decision Making. JAR, 4 (Autumn, 1966), 224-238; -8e

Jervis, F. R.   The Economics of Mergers. Routledge, 1971; -26a

Jessup, P. F.
   See **Upson, R. B. & Jessup, P. F.**

Jeynes, P. H.   Evaluating Cost of Capital. FAJ, 20 (Jul, 1964), 102-108; -23d

Jicha, O.   A Conceptual Approach to Securities Valuation and Analysis. PhD diss, U of Mich, 1963; -7a

Jiler, H. (Ed).   Guide to Commodity Price Forecasting. Commodity R, 1965; -21a

Jiler, W. L.   How Charts Can Help You in the Market. Commodity R, 1962; -12a

Joehnk, M. D.   The Call-Risk Protection of the Seasoned Issue. PhD diss, U of Arizona, 1971; -19h

Johannesen, R. I., Jr.   The Effect of Coupon on Bond Price Fluctuations. FAJ, 24 (Sep-Oct, 1968), 89-91; -19a
   See also **Homer, S. & Johannesen, R. I., Jr.**

Johnson, A.
   See **Smidt, S. & Johnson, A.**

Johnson, A. W.   The Interpretation of Financial Statements. FAJ, 24 (Nov-Dec, 1968), 75ff; -8c

Johnson, C. R.
   See **Soldofsky, R. M. & Johnson, C. R.**

Johnson, D. G.   Forward Prices for Agriculture. U of Chicago Pr, 1947; -21a

Johnson, G. L.; Reilly, F. K. & Smith, R. E.   Individual Common Stocks as Inflation Hedges. JFQA, 6 (Jun, 1971), 1015-1024; -6c

Johnson, H. W. & Simon, J. L.   The Success of Mergers: the Case of Advertising Agencies. OIS, 31 (1969), 139-144; -26b

Johnson, K. B.   An Analysis of the Permanent Price Change Associated with Common Stock Splits. PhD diss, U of Wash, 1963; -16c

Stock Splits and Price Change. JF, 21 (Dec, 1966), 675-686; -16c

Johnson, L. L.   Hedging and Speculation and Futures Trading in the Futures Market since World War II. PhD diss, Yale U, 1957; -21a

Price Instability, Hedging and Trade Volume in the Coffee Market. JPE, 65 (Aug, 1957); -21a

The Theory of Hedging and Speculation in Commodity Futures. REStud, 27 (Jun, 1960), 139-151; -21a

Johnson, L. R.; Shapiro, E. & O'Meara, J.   Valuation of Closely-Held Stock for Federal Tax Purposes: Approach to an Objective Method. U of Pa Law Rev, 100 (Nov, 1951), 166-195; -24b

Johnson, N. O.   Euro-dollars in the New International Money Market. New York: First National City Bank, 1964; -20d

Johnson, R. D.   The Extinguishment of Convertible Bonds: a Theoretical and Empirical Analysis. PhD diss, St U NY Buffalo, 1970; -17c

Johnson, R. E.   Term Structures of Corporate Bond Yields as a Function of Risk of Default. JF, 22 (May, 1967), 313-345; -18f

Johnson, R. L.   The Value of the Call Privilege. FAJ, 23 (Mar-Apr, 1967), 134-140; -19h

Johnson, R. W.   Capital Budgeting. Wadsworth Pub, 1970; -25c

Financial Management, 4th ed. Allyn, 1971; -22a

Subordinated Debentures: Debt that serves as Equity. JF, 10 (Mar, 1955), 1-16; -17c

& Lewellen, W. G.   Analysis of the Lease-or-Buy Decision. JF, 27 (Sep, 1972), 815-824; -25g

See also **Robinson, R. I. & Johnson, R. W.**

Johnson, T.

See **Hubbard, C. L. & Johnson, T.**

Johnston, G. S.; Curley, M. L. & McIndoe, R. A.   Dual-Purpose Funds Undervalued? FAJ, 24 (Nov-Dec, 1968), 157-164; -3m

Johnston, R.   Rebirth of Commercial Paper. Mo Rev F R Bk San Francisco, (Jul, 1968), 137-142; -20a

Jolivet, V.   The Weighted Average Marginal Tax Rate on Dividends Received by Individuals in the U.S. AER, 56 (Jun, 1966), 473-477; -27a

Jones, C. H., Jr.   The Growth Rate Appraiser. FAJ, 24 (Sep-Oct, 1968), 109-111; -7b

Jones, C. P.   The Value of Quarterly Information in Predicting Future Stock Price Changes. PhD diss, U of NC, 1969; -8f

& Litzenberger, R. H.   Earnings Seasonality and Stock Prices. FAJ, 25 (Nov-Dec, 1969), 57-59; -12b

& Litzenberger, R. H.   Quarterly Earnings Reports and Intermediate Stock Price Trends. JF, 25 (Mar, 1970), 143-148; -8f

See also **Joy, O. M. & Jones, C. P.**

See also **Latané, H. A.; Joy, O. M. & Jones, C. P.**

See also **Latané, H. A.; Tuttle, D. L. & Jones, C. P.**

See also **Litzenberger, R. H. & Jones, C. P.**

See also **Litzenberger, R. H.; Joy, O. M. & Jones, C. P.**

Jones, D. L.   Stock Options—An Incentive in Reverse? FAJ, 18 (Nov, 1962), 33-39; -17d

Jones, H. E.

See **Cowles, A. & Jones, H. E.**

Jones, I. E.   Performance Measurement: Are We Lacking Critical Data? Paper for the Seminar on the Analysis of Security Prices, U of Chicago,

Nov 1970; -14a

Jones, J. M.
    See **Robichek, A. A.; Teichroew, D. & Jones, J. M.**

Jones, L. D.   Some Contributions of the Institutional Investor Study. JF, 27 (May, 1972), 305-318; -2b
    Investment Policies of Life Insurance Companies. Harvard Busn, 1968; -3h

Jones, O.   Private Secondary Market Facilities. JF, 23 (May, 1968), 359-366; -21c

Jones, S. L.
    See **Howard, B. B. & Jones, S. L. (Eds).**

Jones-Lee, M. W.   Portfolio Adjustment and Capital Budgeting Criteria. JBF, 1 (Autumn, 1969), 47-54; -25d
    Some Portfolio Adjustment Theorems for the Use of Non-Negativity Constraints on Security Holdings. JF, 26 (Jun, 1971), 763-776; -10c
    A Risk Model of Equilibrium Equity Price Determination. JES, 4 (Nov, 1969); -10l

Jordan, R. J.   An Empirical Investigation of the Adjustment of Stock Prices to New Quarterly Earnings Data. PhD diss, NYU, 1971; -8d

Jorgenson, D. W.   Capital Theory and Investment Behavior. AER, 53 (May, 1963), 247-259; -22b
    Hunter, J. & Nadir, M. I.   The Predictive Performance of Economic Models of Quarterly Investment Behavior. Em 38 (Mar, 1970), 213-224; -15a
    & Siebert, C. D.   A Comparison of Alternative Theories of Corporate Investment Behavior. AER, 58 (Sep, 1968), 681-772; -25f
    & Siebert, C. D.   Optimal Capital Accumulation and Corporate Investment Behavior. JPE, 76 (Nov-Dec, 1968), 1123-1151; -25f
    & Siebert, C. D.   Theories of Corporate Investment Behavior. AER, 58 (Sep, 1968), 681-712; -25f
    See also **Hall, R. E. & Jorgenson, D. W.**

Joseph, A. W.   The Yield on a Loan Subject to Capital Gains Tax. JIASS, 18 (Oct, 1966); -27d

Joy, O. M.   The Value of Limited Monthly Information in Forecasting Airline Price Relatives. PhD diss, U of NC, 1969; -11a
    & Jones, C. P.   Predictive Value of P/E Ratios. FAJ, 26 (Sep-Oct, 1970), 61-68; -8g
    See also **Latané, H. A.; Joy, O. M. & Jones, C. P.**
    See also **Litzenberger, R. H. & Joy, O. M.**
    See also **Litzenberger, R. H.; Joy, O. M. & Jones, C. P.**

Joyce, J. M. & Vogel, R. C.   The Uncertainty in Risk: Is Variance Unambiguous? JF, 25 (Mar, 1970), 127-134; -10b

Kabak, I. W. & Owen, J.   Random Variables, the Time Value of Money and Capital Expenditures. MSci, 17 (Nov, 1970), 142-145; -25d

Kahl, A. L.   Investment Management and the Computer: Limitations and Prospects. PhD diss, U of Fla, 1969; -4e

Kahn, S. R.   An Evaluation of the Real Estate Investment Trust. PhD diss, U of Cincinnati, 1967; -21c
    Case, F. E. & Schimmel, A.   Real Estate Appraisal and Investment. Ronald, 1963; -21c

Kaish, S.   Odd Lotter Trading of High and Low Quality Stocks. FAJ, 25 (Mar-Apr, 1969), 88-91; -13b
    Odd Lot Profit and Loss Performance. FAJ, 25 (Sep-Oct, 1969), 83-92; -13b

Kaldor, N. A Note on the Theory of the Forward Markets. REStud, 7 (Oct, 1939), 196-201; -21a

Speculation and Economic Stability. REStud, 7 (Oct, 1939), 13-16;-9e

Kalecki, M. The Principle of Increasing Risk. Ec, 4 (Nov, 1937), 440-447; -9c

Kalymon, B. A. Bond Refunding with Stochastic Interest Rates. MSci, 18 (Nov, 1971), 171-183; -19h

Estimation Risk in the Portfolio Selection Model. JFQA, 6 (Jan, 1971), 559-582; -10c

Kamien, M. I. & Schwartz, N. L. A Direct Approach to Choice Under Uncertainty. MSci, 18 (Apr, 1972), B470-B477; -9c

Kane, E. J. The Term Structure of Interest Rates: An Attempt to Reconcile Teaching with Practice. JF, 25 (May, 1970), 361-374; -18f

& Malkiel, B. G. Bank Portfolio Allocation, Deposit Variability and the Availability Doctrine. QJE, 79 (Feb, 1965), 113-134; -10g

& Malkiel, B. G. The Term Structure of Interest Rates: An Analysis of a Survey of Interest Rate Expectations. REStat, 49 (Aug, 1967), 343-355; -18f

See also **Malkiel, B. G. & Kane, E. J.**

Kantor, M. Market Sensitivities. FAJ, 27 (Jan-Feb, 1971), 64-68; -10b

See also **Treynor, J. L.; Shelton, J. & Kantor, M.**

Kaplan, A. D. H. The Current Merger Movement Analysed. HBR, 33 (May-Jun, 1955), 391-398; -26a

Kaplan, M. Yields on Recently Issued Corporate Bonds: A New Index. JF, 17 (Mar, 1962), 81-109; -19b

Kaplan, R. S. & Roll, R. Investor Evaluation of Accounting Information: some Empirical Evidence. JB, 45 (Apr, 1972), 225-257; -8e

Kaplan, S. Computer Algorithms for Finding Exact Rates of Return. JB, 40 (Oct, 1967), 389-392; -25b

A Note on a Method for Precisely Determining the Uniqueness or Non-uniqueness of the Internal Rate of Return for a Proposed Investment. JIEng, 16 (Jan-Feb, 1965); -25b

Solution of the Lorie-Savage and Similar Integer Programming Problems by the Generalized Lagrange Multiplier Method. OR, 14 (Nov-Dec, 1966), 1130-1136; -25b

Kaplan, S. A. Piercing the Corporate Boilerplate: Anti-Dilution Clauses in Convertible Securities. U of Chicago Law Rev, 33 (Autumn, 1965), 1-30; -17b, 17c

Karnosky, D. W.

See **Yohe, W. P. & Karnosky, D. W.**

Kartchner, E. C. A Distributed Lag Analysis of the Dividend-Earnings Relationship of Some Listed, Non-Financial U.S. Corporations. PhD diss, U of Wash, 1966; -24a

Kassouf, S. T. An Econometric Model for Option Price With Implications for Investors' Expectations and Audacity. Em, 37 (Oct, 1969), 685-694; -17b

The Evaluation of Convertible Securities. Analytical Inv, 1966; -17b, 17c

Stock Price Random Walks: Some Supporting Evidence. REStat, 50 (May, 1968), 275-278; -17b

A Theory and an Econometric Model for Common Stock Purchase Warrants. PhD diss, Columbia U, 1965

Warrant Price Behavior, 1945-1964. FAJ, 24 (Jan-Feb, 1968), 123-126; -17b

See also **Thorp, E. O. & Kassouf, S. T.**

Katz, R. C.   Profitability of Put and Call Option Writing. SM thesis, MIT, 1962; -17a

      The Profitability of Put and Call Option Writing. IMR, 5 (Fall, 1963), 55-69; -17a

Kaufman, G. M.   Sequential Investment Analysis under Uncertainty. JB, 36 (Jan, 1963), 39-65; -25d

Kaufman, H.   The Changing Dimensions of the Corporate Bond Market. New York: Salomon Bros, & Hutzler, 1967; -19e

Kavesh, R. A.

      See **Butler, W. F. & Kavesh, R. A. (Eds).**

Keane, S. M.   The Significance of the Issue Price in Rights Issues. JBF, 4 (Autumn, 1972), 40-45; -16b

Keefe, W. C.   Cost of Capital—Rate of Return. FAJ, 24 (Jul-Aug, 1968), 113-116; -23d

Keeler, E.

      See **Zeckhauser, R. & Keeler, E.**

Keeley, R. H.   Pension Plan Decisions and Corporate Financial Policy. PhD diss, Stanford U, 1969; -3i

      & Westerfield, R.   A Problem in Probability Distribution Techniques for Capital Budgeting. JF, 27 (Jun, 1972), 703-710; -25d

Keenan, W. M.   The State of the Finance Field Methodology Models of Equity Valuation: the Great Serm Bubble. JF, 25 (May, 1970), 243-274; -7b

      Towards a Positive Theory of Equity Valuation. PhD diss, Carnegie IT, 1967; -7a

Kekish, B. J.   Moody's Averages. FAJ, 23 (May-Jun, 1967), 65-69; -5b

Keller, F. R.   The Behavior of Individuals in Security Investment Decisions. DBA diss, Harvard Bus, 1967; -4d

Kellett, R.   The Merchant Banking Arena. Macmillan Int, 1967; -3g

Kelly, E. M.   The Profitability of Growth Through Mergers. Pa St U, Center for Research of the College of Business Administration, 1967; -26b

Kelly, J.   A New Interpretation of Information Rate. BellSys, 35 (Jul, 1956), 917-926; -10j

Kemmerer, D. L.   For Long-Term Investment: Stocks or Bonds. CFC, (Feb 1, 1951); -5a

Kemp, A. G. & Reid, G. C.   The Random Walk Hypothesis and the Recent Behaviour of Equity Prices in Britain. Ec, 38 (1971), 28-51; -11c

Kemp, M. C.   Speculation, Profitability and Price Stability. REStat, 45 (May, 1963), 185-189; -9e

Kenadjian, V. H.   Constant Safety versus Sound Profitability. AJ, 11 (Aug, 1955), 77-80; -9c

Kendall, L. T.

      See **Ketchum, M. D. & Kendall, L. T. (Eds).**

Kendall, M. G.   The Analysis of Economic Time Series, Part I. JRSS, 96 (1953), 11-25; -11c

      & Stuart, A.   Measuring Share Price Changes. Times, (Apr 20, 1960), 13; -5b

      See also **Coen, P. J.; Gomme, E. D. & Kendall, M. G.**

Kennedy, C. M.   Inflation and the Bond Rate. OEP, 12 (Oct, 1960), 269-273; -18c

Kennedy, M.   A Critique of Game Theory for Capital Budgeting. NAA, 44 (May, 1963); -25c

Kennedy, R. E., Jr.   An Approach to Pricing Growth Stocks. AJ, 13 (Aug, 1957), 31-33; -7b

Growth Stocks: Opportunity or Illusion. FAJ, 16 (Mar-Apr, 1960), 27-31; -7b

Kennelly, J. W.

See **Brown, P. & Kennelly, J. W.**

Kent, R. P.   Corporate Financial Management, 3rd ed. Irwin, 1969; -22a

Keran, M. W.   Expectations, Money and the Stock Market. Mo Rev F R Bk St Louis, (Jan, 1971), 16-31; -6d

Kerchner, D. H.   Some Limitations on the Usefulness of Investors' Services. PhD diss, U of Chicago, 1936; -15c

Kessel, R. A.   The Cyclical Behavior of the Term Structure of Interest Rates. (Dist by Columbia U Pr) Natl Bur Econ Res, 1965; -18f

A Study of the Effects of Competition in the Tax-Exempt Bond Market. JPE, 79 (Jul-Aug, 1971), 706-738; -19d

& Alchian, A. A.   Effects of Inflation. JPE, 70 (Dec, 1962), 521-537; -6c

& Alchian, A. A.   Inflation and Stock Prices. Paper for the Seminar on the Analysis of Security Prices, U of Chicago, May 1965; -6c

See also **Alchian, A. A. & Kessel, R. A.**

Ketchum, M. D.   Is Financial Analysis a Profession? FAJ, 23 (Nov-Dec, 1967), 33-37; -4c

& Kendall, L. T. (Eds).   Readings in Financial Institutions. HM, 1965; -3e

Kettler, P.

See **Beaver, W.; Kettler, P. & Scholes, M.**

Kewley, T. J. & Stevenson, R. A.   The Odd-Lot Theory as Revealed by Purchase and Sales Statistics for Individual Stocks. FAJ, 23 (Sep-Oct, 1967), 103-106; -13b

& Stevenson, R. A.   The Odd-Lot Theory for Individual Stocks: A Reply. FAJ, 25 (Jan-Feb, 1969), 99-104; -13b

Keynes, J. M.   A Treatise on Money. Macmillan Int, 1930; -18a

Kiese, D. E.

See **Wyatt, A. R. & Kiese, D. E.**

Kiger, J. E.   An Empirical Investigation of the Use of Interim Reports. PhD diss, U of Mo, 1971; -8d

Kimball, M.   Corporate Finance. Littlefield, 1962; -22a

Kimball, P. & Papera, D. R.   Effect of Stock Splits on Short-Term Market Prices. FAJ, 20 (May-Jun, 1964), 75-80; -16c

Kimmel, L. H.   Share Ownership in the United States; A Study Prepared at the Request of the New York Stock Exchange. Brookings, 1952; -3a

Kinard, H. Y.   Financing Mergers and Acquisitions. FE, 31 (Aug, 1963), 13-16; -26a

Kindleberger, C. P.   The Euro-Dollar and the Internationalization of United States Monetary Policy. BNLQR, 22 (Mar, 1969), 3-15; -20d

King, B. F.   The Latent Statistical Structure of Security Price Changes. PhD diss, U of Chicago, 1964; -10a

Market and Industry Factors in Stock Price Behavior. JB, 39 (Jan, 1966), 139-190; -10a

King, H. J.

See **Cobleigh, I. A. & King, H. J.**

King, M. J.   Puts, Calls and Straddles: a Study. MBA thesis, NYU, 1954; -17a

Kinney, W. R.   Predicting Earnings: Entity versus Subentity Data. JAR, 9 (Spring, 1971), 127-136; -8c

See also **Pinches, G. E. & Kinney, W. R.**

Kirkham, P. G.   The Portfolio Behavior of Selected Canadian Financial Intermediaries: an Econometric Analysis. PhD diss, Princeton U, 1970; -3e

Kisor, M., Jr.   The Financial Aspects of Growth. FAJ, 20 (Mar-Apr, 1964), 46-51; -8c

Quantitative Approaches to Common Stock Selection. BE, 2 (Spring, 1966); -8f

& Feuerstein, A.   Towards a Valuation Model Employing Historical Constructs as Proxies for Analysts' Expectations. Paper for the Seminar on the Analysis of Security Prices, U of Chicago, May 1967; -7c

& Messner, V. A.   The Filter Approach and Earnings Forecasts. FAJ, 25 (Jan-Feb, 1969), 109-116; -8f

& Niederhoffer, V.   Odd-Lot Short Sales Ratio: It Signals a Market Rise. B, (Sep 1, 1969), 8; -13b

See also **Whitbeck, V. & Kisor, M., Jr.**

Kitching, J.   Why Do Mergers Miscarry? HBR, 45 (Nov-Dec, 1967), 84-101; -26b

Klammer, T.   Empirical Evidence of the Adoption of Sophisticated Capital Budgeting Techniques. JB, 45 (Jul, 1972), 387-397; -25f

Klein, D. J.   The Odd-Lot Stock Trading Theory. PhD diss, Mich St U, 1964; -13b

Klein, M. A.   Differential Commercial Bank Portfolio Allocation. PhD diss, Northwestern U, 1968; -10g

Klein, S.   How to Play the New Issues Game. F, 74 (Jan, 1962); -16a

Klein, T. A.

See **Bauman, W. S. & Klein, T. A.**

Klemkosky, R. R.   An Analysis of a Strategy for Purchasing Straddle Options. PhD diss, Mich St U, 1971; -17a

Klevorick, A. K.   Capital Budgeting Under Risk: a Mathematical-programming Approach. PhD diss, Princeton U, 1967; -25d

Klopstock, F. H.   The Euro-Dollar Market: Some Unresolved Issues. International Finance Section, Princeton U, Mar 1968; -20d

The International Money Market: Structure, Scope and Instruments. JF, 20 (May, 1965), 182-208; -20d

See also **Holmes, A. R. & Klopstock, F. H.**

Knaus, R. L.   A Reappraisal of the Role of Disclosure. Mich Law Rev, (Feb, 1964), 607-648; -2e

Knight, F. H.   Risk, Uncertainty and Profit. Kelley, 1921; -9c

Knodel, H. W.   A Method of Appraising the Stock Market. AJ, 4 (4th Qtr, 1948), 43-53; -7d

Kochin, L. A.

See **Hamburger, M. J. & Kochin, L. A.**

Kogan, N. & Wallach, M. A.   Risk Taking: a Study in Cognition and Personality. HR & W, 1964; -9b

Kogiku, K. C.   A Model of the Raw Materials Market. IntER, 8 (Feb, 1967), 116-120; -21a

Kohlmeier, J. M.   An Analysis of Some Aspects of Capital Budgeting Policy, a Simulation Approach. PhD diss, Harvard U, 1964; -25c

Kolb, B. A.   Problems and Pitfalls in Capital Budgeting. FAJ, 24 (Nov-Dec, 1968), 170-174; -25c

Research, Development and Common Stock Values. FAJ, 18 (Sep-Oct, 1962), 9-16; -6f

Kolin, M. The Relative Price of Corporate Equity with Particular Attention to Investor Valuation of Retained Earnings and Dividends: Tests on Cross-Sections of Industrials, 1951-1957. PhD diss, U of Chicago, 1965; -24b

Kolmogorov, A. N.
See **Gnedenko, B. V. & Kolmogorov, A. N.**

Koopmans, T. C. Stationary Ordinal Utility and Impatience. Em, 28 (Apr, 1960), 287-309; -9a

Kopp, B. S. Conglomerates in Portfolio Management. FAJ, 24 (Mar-Apr, 1968), 145-148; -3e

Korkie, R. M.
See **Mumey, G. A. & Korkie, R. M.**

Korsvold, P. E. The Cost of Raising New Private Debt Capital and Capital Market Efficiency. JBF, 3 (Summer, 1971), 3-9; -23c

Kortanek, K.
See **Byrne, R.; Charnes, A.; Cooper, W. W. & Kortanek, K.**

Kost, W. E. Rates of Return for Farm Real Estate and Common Stock. AJAE, 50 (May, 1968), 213-224; -21c

Kotler, P. Elements in a Theory of Growth Stock Valuation. FAJ, 18 (May-Jun, 1962), 35-44; -7b

Kottke, F. J. Mergers of Large Manufacturing Companies: 1951 to 1959. REStat, 41 (Nov, 1959), 430-433; -26a

Kourday, M. A Method of Outperforming the Market. FAJ, 19 (Nov-Dec, 1963), 35-44; -7a

Krainer, R. E. Financial Institutions and the Struggle for Primary Securities. SEJ, 30 (Apr, 1964), 362-376; -3e

Interest Rates, Investment Decisions and External Financing. OEP, 18 (Nov, 1966), 304-312; -23d

Liquidity Preference and Stock Market Speculation. JFQA, 4 (Mar, 1969), 89-98; -18a

A Pedagogic Note on Dividend Policy. JFQA, 6 (Sep, 1971), 1147-1154; -24b

Kramer, R. L. Arbitrage in U.S. Government Bonds: a Management Science Approach. JBR, 1 (Summer, 1970), 30-44; -19c
See also **Cohen, K. J.; Kramer, R. L. & Waugh, W. W.**

Krantz, D. H.
See **Luce, R. D. & Krantz, D. H.**

Kraus, A. & Litzenberger, R. H. A State-Preference Model of Optimal Financial Leverage. JF, forthcoming; -23c

& Stoll, H. Price Impacts of Block Trading on the New York Stock Exchange. JF, 27 (Jun, 1972), 569-588; -16d

Kreag, M. A. The Market as a Function of Time, Price, and Volume. AJ, 9 (Jul-Aug, 1953), 81-86; -12a

Kreger, H. R.
See **Starkweather, L. P.; Otto, E. A. & Kreger, H. R.**

Kreinin, M. E. Factors Associated with Stock Ownership. REStat, 41 (Feb, 1959), 12-23; -3a

Kripotos, S. L.
See **Levy, R. A. & Kripotos, S. L.**

Kriss, H. The Convertible Bond as a Capital Raising Instrument. SM thesis, MIT, 1961; -17c

Kroncke, C. O.
See **Haugen, R. A. & Kroncke, C. O.**

Krooss, H. E. & Blyn, M. R.   A History of Financial Intermediaries. Random, 1971; -3e

See **Bogen, J. I. & Kroos, H. E.**

Krouse, C. G.   Financial Planning: a Dynamic Multi-objective Framework. PhD diss, UCLA, 1969; -22c

A Model for Aggregate Financial Planning. MSci, 18 (Jun, 1972), B555-B566; -22c

Optimal Financing and Capital Structure Programs for the Firm. JF, forthcoming; -23c

Portfolio Balancing Corporate Assets and Liabilities with Special Application to Insurance Management. JFQA, 5 (Mar, 1970), 77-104; -10c

Krow, H. A.   Forecasting Stock Market Fluctuations by Technical Methods. PhD diss, U of Pittsburgh, 1964; -12a

Kruizenga, R. J.   Comment on 'Puts and Calls: A Factual Survey'. JF, 14 (Mar, 1959), 67-70; -17a

Put and Call Options: A Theoretical and Market Analysis. PhD diss, MIT, 1956; -17a

Krzyzaniak (Ed).   Effects of Corporation Income Tax. Wayne St U Pr, 1966; -27c

& Musgrave, R. A.   The Shifting of the Corporation Income Tax: an Empirical Study of its Short Run Effect upon the Rate of Return. Johns Hopkins, 1963; -27c

Kuehn, D. A.   Stock Market Valuation and Acquisitions: an Empirical Test of One Component of Managerial Utility. JIE, 17 (Apr, 1969), 132-144; -26b

Kuehner, C. D.   Underwritten Common Stock Rights Offers; 1955-64; Considerations and a Descriptive Under-pricing Model. PhD diss, NYU, 1966; -16b

Kuh, E.   Capital Stock Growth: A Micro-econometric Approach. N Holland, 1963; -22b

Capital Theory and Capital Budgeting. Met, 12 (Aug-Dec, 1960), 64-80; -25c

See also **Meyer, J. R. & Kuh, E.**

Kulp, C. A.   The Discounting of Dividends by the Stock Market. U of Pa Pr. 1924; -24b

Kumar, P.   Market Power, Growth, Leverage and the Valuation of the Firm. PhD diss, U of Wis, 1970; -23c

Kurz, M.

See **Dhrymes, P. J. & Kurz, M.**

Kuznets, S.   Capital in the American Economy: Its Formation and Financing. (Dist by Princeton U Pr) Natl Bur Econ Res, 1961; -23a

Kybal, M.

See **Basch, A. & Kybal, M.**

Labys, W. C.   Commodity Price Fluctuations: A Short-Term Explanation for Selected Commodities on the American Market. PhD diss, U of Nottingham, 1968; -21a

& Granger, C. W. J.   Speculation, Hedging and Commodity Price Forecasts. Heath, 1970; -21a

Rees, H. J. B. & Elliott, C. M.   Copper Price Behaviour and the London Metal Exchange. AE, 3 (Jun, 1971), 99-114; -21a

Ladendorf, J. W.   The Stockholder Interest: a Study of Over-the-Counter Corporations. PhD diss, Harvard U, 1966; -3a

La Farge, F. W.   Methods of Evaluating Future Price Levels of the Dow-Jones Industrial Average. AJ, 1 (Oct, 1945), 49-55; -7d

Timing Common Stock Purchases and Sales. AJ, 10 (Feb, 1954), 47-49; -7d

Laffer, A. B.
    See **Fama, E. F. & Laffer, A. B.**

Laidler, D.   The Rate of Interest and the Demand for Money—Some Empirical Evidence. JPE, 74 (Dec, 1966), 543-555; -18b

Lambert, W. R.   Evidence of Risk Aversion in the Stock Market. DBA diss, U of Indiana, 1970; -10*l*

Lamberton, D. L.   Economic Growth and Stock Prices: the Australian Experience. JB, 31 (Jul, 1958), 200-212; -7d

Lamberton, D. M.   The Theory of Profit. Blackwell, 1965; -22b

Lane, L. H.
    See **Blunt, R. H. & Lane, L. H.**

Langer, L. C. R.   The Use of Stock Subscription Rights in the Financing of Gas and Electric Utility Companies. DBA diss, Harvard Bus, 1958; -16a

Langmuir, D.   Common Sense and Investment Techniques. AJ, 3 (1st Qtr, 1947), 3-10; -4a

La Noue, B. E.   Analysis of the Factors which Affect the Investment Decision: a Case Study. PhD diss, St Louis U, 1968; -25f

Laporte, L.   Dividend Policy in the Smaller Company. Natl Ind Conf Bd, 1969; -24a

Largay, J. A.   100% Margins: Combating Speculation in Individual Security Issues. JF, forthcoming; -6e
    Some Tests of the Relationship between Margin Requirements and Stock Market Activity. PhD diss, Cornell U, 1971; -6e

Larkin, E. L., Jr.   Accounting for the Realities of Bank Portfolio Management. New York: Haskins & Sells, Feb, 1970; -3f

Larner, R. J.   Ownership and Control in the 200 Largest Nonfinancial Corporations, 1929 and 1963. AER, 56 (Sep, 1966), 777-787; -3a

Larson, A. B.   Estimation of Hedging and Speculative Positions in Futures Markets. FRIS, 2 (Nov, 1961), 203-212; -21a
    Evidence on the Temporal Dispersion of Price Effects of New Market Information. PhD diss, Stanford U, 1960; -21a
    Measurement of a Random Process in Futures Prices. FRIS, 1 (Nov, 1960), 313-324; -21a
    Price Prediction on the Egg Futures Market. FRIS, 7 (Suppl, 1967), 49-64; -21a

Larson, R. B.   The Optimal Choice of Corporate Growth Plans Under Risk. PhD diss, Case WR U, 1971; -25d

Larson, R. C.   Self-Administered Pension Funds and Performance. FAJ, 25 (Jul-Aug, 1969), 135-137; -3i

Latané, H. A.   Criteria for Choice among Risky Ventures. JPE, 67 (Apr, 1959), 144-155; -10j
    Individual Risk Preference in Portfolio Selection. JF, 15 (Mar, 1960), 45-52; -9b
    Investment Criteria—A Three Asset Portfolio Balance Model. REStat, 45 (Nov, 1963), 427-430; -10j
    Portfolio Balance—the Demand for Money, Bonds, and Stock. SEJ, 29 (Oct, 1962), 71-76; -19a

    Price Changes in Equity Securities. JF, 9 (Sep, 1954), 252-264; -7a
    Rational Decision Making in Portfolio Management. PhD diss, U of NC, 1957; -10j
        Joy, O. M. & Jones, C. P.   Quarterly Data, Sort-Rank Routines, and Security Evaluation. JB, 43 (Oct, 1970), 427-438; -8f

    & Tuttle, D. L.   An Analysis of Common Stock Price Ratios.
SEJ, 33 (Jan, 1967), 343-354; -8d
    & Tuttle, D. L.   Annual Changes in Prices of Equity Securities.
Paper presented at Southern Economic Association meeting, Miami,
Florida, 1965; -5a
    & Tuttle, D. L.   Criteria for Portfolio Building. JF, 22 (Sep, 1967),
360-361; -10j
    & Tuttle, D. L.   Decision Theory and Financial Management.
JF, 21 (May, 1966), 228-244; -9c
    & Tuttle, D. L.   Framework for Forming Probability Beliefs.
FAJ, 24 (Jul-Aug, 1968), 51-61; -9c
    & Tuttle, D. L.   Pure Risk Yields and the Cost of Capital. Paper
presented at the Eastern TIMS meeting, Oct 1965; -23d
    & Tuttle, D. L.   Security Analysis and Portfolio Management.
Ronald, 1971; -4b
    Tuttle D. L. & Jones, C. P.   E/P Ratios v Changes in Earnings.
FAJ, 25 (Jan-Feb, 1969), 117-120; -8g
    Tuttle, D. L. & Young, W. E.   Market Indexes and their Implica-
tions for Portfolio Management. FAJ, 27 (Sep-Oct, 1971), 75-85; -5b
    & Young, W. E.   Test of Portfolio Building Rules. JF, 24 (Sep,
1969), 595-612; -10j
Lau, S. C.
    See **Wagner, W. H. & Lau, S. C.**
Laughhunn, D. J. & Peterson, D. E.   Computational Experience with Capital
    Expenditure Programming Models under Risk. JBF, 3 (Winter, 1971),
    43-48; -25d
    See also **Peterson, D. E. & Laughhunn, D. J.**
Laughlin, E. J.   Creditors' Rights in Corporate Reorganization: a Finan-
    cial Approach. PhD diss, U of Ill, 1965; -26g
Lauver, R. C.   The Case for Pooling. AR, 41 (Jan, 1966), 65-74; -26d
Lavely, J. A.   Comparative Usage of Bond-Warrant and Convertible Bond
    Issues. PhD diss, U of Iowa, 1970; -17c
Law, W. & Crum, C.   New Trend in Finance, the Negotiable Certificate of
    Deposit. HBR, 41 (Jan-Feb, 1963), 113-126; -20a
Lawson, G. H.   The Cost of Ploughed-Back Profits. BM, 201 (Feb, 1966),
    103-113; -24b
    & Windle, D. W.   Capital Budgeting in the Corporation Tax
    Regime. JMS, 4 (May, 1967), 189-203; -25c
    & Windle, D. W.   Capital Budgeting and the Use of DCF Criteria
    in the Corporation Tax Regime. Oliver, 1967; -25c
Laya, J. C.   A Cash Flow Model and the Rate of Return: the Effect of Price
    Level Change and other Factors on Book-Yield. PhD diss, Stanford U,
    1966; -25c
    See also **Solomon, E. & Laya, J. C.**
Lazarcik, G.   Scientific Research and Its Relation to Earnings and Stock
    Prices. FAJ, 18 (Jan-Feb, 1962), 49-53; -6f
Leach, J. H. C.   Institutional Role in United Kingdom Ordinary Share
    Market. FAJ, 25 (Jul-Aug, 1969), 163-166; -3e
    The Role of the Institutions in the UK Ordinary Share Market. IA,
    31 (Dec, 1971), 33-35; -3e
Leach, W. A. & Wenman, E. G.   Investments in Land and Property: a Guide
    for Investors and Those Responsible for Investment Policy. Estates
    Gazette, 1964; -21c

Lee, R. E., Jr.   Acquisition of a Business: Accounting and Financial Aspects. Taxes, 49 (Feb, 1962), 147-152; -26d

Lee, T. H.   Alternative Interest Rates and the Demand for Money: the Empirical Evidence. AER, 57 (Dec, 1967), 1168-1181; -18b

Leenders, C. T.
    See **Theil, H. & Leenders, C. T.**

Leeuw, F. De.   Financial Markets in Business Cycles: a Simulation Study. AER, 54 (May, 1964), 309-323; -6b

Leffler, G. L.   Seasonal Patterns. B (Mar 30, 1953), 27; -12b
    Stock Rights. B, (Sep 16, 1957), 15ff; -16a
    rev. by Farwell, L. C.   The Stock Market, 3rd ed. Ronald, 1963; -2b

Lehane, J. F.   Comparative Analyses of the Underlying Characteristics for Risk Performance Measures of No-Load Mutual Funds in the 1950-1969 Period. PhD diss, U of Santa Clara, 1971; -3k

Lehr, M. E. & Newbould, G. D.   New Issues—Activity and Pricing Performance, 1964-1967. IA, 18 (Oct, 1967), 20-23; -16a

Leland, H. E.   Dynamic Portfolio Theory. PhD diss, Harvard U, 1968; -10k

Lempert, L. H.   Forecasting the Leading Indicator of Stock Prices. FAJ, 17 (Sep-Oct, 1961), 13-21; -6b
    The Use of Composite Indicators. FAJ, 21 (Nov-Dec, 1965), 57-59; -6b

Leonard, W. R. & Shapiro, L. A.   Heavy-Duty Tools for the Market Analyst. AJ, 8 (May, 1952), 73-76; -6a

Lepper, S. J.   Effects of Alternative Tax Structures on Individuals' Holdings of Financial Assets, *in* Hester, D. D. & Tobin, J. E. (Eds), Risk Aversion and Portfolio Choice. Wiley, 1967; -27a

Lerner, A. P.   A Note on the Rate of Interest and the Value of Assets. EJ, 71 (Sep, 1961), 539-543; -18b

Lerner, E. M.   Managerial Finance: a Systems Approach. HarBraceJ, 1971; -22a
    Model of Security Price Determination. Paper for the Seminar on the Analysis of Security Prices, U of Chicago, Nov 1965; -7a
    Rate of Return on Common Stocks. FAJ, 16 (Sep-Oct, 1960), 47-50; -5a
    Readings in Financial Analysis and Investment Management. Irwin, 1963; -1b
    & Auster, R.   Does the Market Discount Potential Dilution? FAJ, 25 (Jul-Aug, 1969), 118-121; -17c
    & Carleton, W. T.   The Capital Structure Problem of a Regulated Public Utility. PUF, 76 (Jul 8, 1965), 24-32; -23c
    & Carleton, W. T.   Financing Decisions of the Firm. JF, 21 (May, 1966), 202-214; -23d
    & Carleton, W. T.   The Integration of Capital Budgeting and Stock Valuation. AER, 54 (Sep, 1964), 681-702; -25i
    & Carleton, W. T.   The Integration of Capital Budgeting and Stock Valuation: Reply. AER, 57 (Mar, 1967), 220-221; -25c
    & Carleton, W. T.   A Theory of Financial Analysis. HarBraceJ, 1966; -22a
    & Rappaport, A.   Limit DCF in Capital Budgeting. HBR, 46 (Sep-Oct, 1968), 133-139; -25c
    See also **Carleton, W. T. & Lerner, E. M.**
    See also **Machol, R. E. & Lerner, E. M.**
    See also **Moag, J. S.; Carleton, W. T. & Lerner, E. M.**
    See also **Moag, J. S. & Lerner, E. M.**

Leroy, S. F.   The Determination of Stock Prices. PhD diss, U of Pa, 1971;
-7d

L'Esperance, W. L.
         See **Cohen, J. & L'Esperance, W. L.**

Lessard, D. R.   International Portfolio Diversification: a Multivariate
Analysis for a Group of Latin American Countries. JF, forthcoming;
-10i
         Multinational Portfolio Diversification for Developing Countries.
PhD diss, Stanford U, 1970; -10i

Letwat, M.
         See **Williams, B. S. & Letwat, M.**

Leuthold, R. M.   Random Walk and Price Trends: the Live Cattle Futures
Market. JF, 27 (Sep, 1972), 879-890; -21a

Lev, B. & Mandelker, G.   The Microeconomic Consequences of Corporate
Mergers. JB, 45 (Jan, 1972), 85-104; -26b

Leverett, E. J., Jr.   A Simulation of the Financial Operations of a Life
Insurance Company under Various Operating Assumptions with Special
Emphasis on Solvency and Paid-in Surplus and Capital. DBA diss,
Indiana U, 1967; -3h

Leveson, S. M.   Money and Stock Prices. BE, 3 (Summer, 1968); -6d

Levhari, D. & Srinivasan, T. N.   Optimal Savings under Uncertainty.
REStud, 36 (Apr, 1969), 363-379; -10k
         See also **Arrow, K. G. & Levhari, D.**

Levin, J.   Prophetic Leaders. FAJ, 26 (Jul-Aug, 1970), 87-90; -6b

Levine, J. M.
         See **Safer, A. E. & Levine, J. M.**

Levine, S.   Heuristic Determination of Optimum Filters for Use in a Rule
for Speculative Market Action. SM thesis, MIT, 1962; -12c

Levy, F. K.   An Application of Heuristic Problem Solving to Accounts
Receivable Management. MSci, 12 (Feb, 1966), B236-B244; -25a
         See also **Ijiri, Y.; Levy, F. K. & Lyon, R. C.**

Levy, H.   The Demand for Assets Under Conditions of Risk. JF, forthcoming; -10l
         A Note on the Payback Method.   JFQA, 3 (Dec, 1968), 433-444;
-25c
         Portfolio Performance and the Investment Horizon. MSci, 18
(Aug, 1972), B645-B653; -10l
         Portfolio Selection and Optimal Capital Structure. PhD diss, Heb-
rew U, 1969; -23c
         & Arditti, F. D.   Valuation, Leverage, and the Cost of Capital in
the Cost of Depreciable Assets. JF, forthcoming; -23d
         & Hanoch, G.   Relative Effectiveness of Efficiency Criteria for
Portfolio Selection. JFQA, 5 (Mar, 1970), 63-76; -10h
         & Sarnat, M.   Alternative Efficiency Criteria: an Empirical
Analysis. JF, 25 (Dec, 1970), 1153-1158; -10h
         & Sarnat, M.   Diversification, Portfolio Analysis and the Uneasy
Case for Conglomerate Mergers. JF, 25 (Sep, 1970), 795-802; -26c
         & Sarnat, M.   International Diversification of Investment Port-
folios. AER, 60 (Sep, 1970), 668-675; -10i
         & Sarnat, M.   Investment and Portfolio Analysis. Wiley, 1972;
-4b
         & Sarnat, M.   Investment Performance in an Imperfect Securities
Market and the Case for Mutual Funds. FAJ, 28 (Mar-Apr, 1972), 77-
81; -3k

    & Sarnat, M.   A Note on Portfolio Selection and Investors' Wealth. JFQA, 6 (Jan, 1971), 639-642; -10c

    & Sarnat, M.   Portfolio Selection and Investor's Utility: a Graphical Analysis. AE, 2 (1970), 113-120; -10c

    & Sarnat, M.   Safety First—an Expected Utility Principle. JFQA, 7 (Jun, 1972), 1829-1834; -10f

    & Sarnat, M.   Two-Period Portfolio Selection and Investor Discount Rates. JF, 26 (Jun, 1971), 757-762; -10c

    See also **Hanoch, G. & Levy, H.**

    See also **Sarnat, M. & Levy, H.**

Levy, M. E.   Cycles in Government Securities: Determinants of Changes in Ownership. Natl Ind Conf Bd, 1965; -19c

    Cycles in Government Securities: Federal Debt and Its Ownership. Natl Ind Conf Bd, 1962; -19c

Levy, R. A.   Conceptual Foundations of Technical Analysis. FAJ, 22 (Jul-Aug, 1966), 83-89; -12a

    An Evaluation of Selected Applications of Stock Market Timing Techniques, Trading Tactics and Trend Analysis. PhD diss, Am U, 1966; -12d

    Is Performance Fund Trading Gainful or Wasteful? II, 1 (Dec, 1967): -14a

    Measurement of Investment Performance. JFQA, 3 (Mar, 1968), 35-57; -14a

    On the Short-Term Stationarity of Beta Coefficients. FAJ, 27 (Nov-Dec, 1971), 55-62; -10b

    The Predictive Significance of Five-Point Chart Patterns. JB, 44 (Jul, 1971), 316-323; -12g

    The Principle of Portfolio Upgrading. IMR, 7 (Fall, 1967), 82-96; -12d

    Random Walks: Reality or Myth. FAJ, 23 (Nov-Dec, 1967), 69-77; -12d

    Random Walks: Reality or Myth—Reply. FAJ, 24 (Jan-Feb, 1968), 129-133; -12d

    Relative Strength as a Criterion for Investment Selection. JF, 22 (Dec, 1967), 595-610; -12d

    The Relative Strength Concept of Common Stock Price Forecasting. Inv Int, 1968; -12d

    The Theory of Random Walks: A Survey of Findings. AmE, 11 (Fall, 1967), 34-48; -11c

    & Kripotos, S. L.   Sources of Relative Price Strength. FAJ, 25 (Nov-Dec, 1969), 60 ff; -12d

Lewellen, W. G.   The Cost of Capital. Wadsworth Pub, 1969; -23d

    A Pure Financial Rationale for the Conglomerate Merger. JF, 26 (May, 1971), 521-537; -26c

    See also **Holland, D. M. & Lewellen, W. G.**

    See also **Johnson, R. W. & Lewellen, W. G.**

Lietaer, B. A.   Financial Management of Foreign Exchange. MIT Pr, 1971; -21b

Life Insurance Association of America.   Life Insurance Companies as Financial Institutions. P-H, 1962; -3h

Light, J. U.   The Effect of News of General Interest on Stock Market Prices. PhD diss, U of Wash, 1971; -7d

Lindsay, R. & Sametz, A. W.   Financial Management—An Analytical Approach, rev ed. Irwin 1967; -22a

Linowes, D. F. Managing Growth Through Acquisition. Am Mgmt, 1968; -26a

Lintner, J. The Aggregation of Investor's Diverse Judgments and Preferences in Purely Competitive Security Markets. JFQA, 4 (Dec, 1969), 347-400; 10*l*

The Cost of Capital and Optimal Financing of Corporate Growth. JF, 18 (May, 1963), 302-310; -23d

The Determinants of Corporate Savings, *in* Heller, W. W. et al, Savings in the Modern Economy. U of Minn Pr, 1953; -24a

Distribution of Incomes of Corporations Among Dividends, Retained Earnings and Taxes. AER, 46 (May, 1956), 97-113; -24a

Dividends, Earnings, Leverage, Stock Prices and the Supply of Capital to Corporations. REStat, 44 (Aug, 1962), 243-269; -24b

Effect of Taxation on Real Investment. AER, 44 (May, 1954), 520-534; -27a

The Effects of Short Selling and Margin Requirements in Perfect Capital Markets. JFQA, 6 (Dec, 1971), 1173-1196; -101

The Financing of Corporations, *in* Mason, E. S. (Ed), The Corporation in Modern Society. Harvard U Pr, 1961; -22a

The Market Price of Risk, Size of Market and Investor's Risk Aversion. REStat, 52 (Feb, 1970), 87-99; -10*l*

Optimal Dividends and Corporate Growth Under Uncertainty. QJE, 78 (Feb, 1964), 68-71; -24b

Security Market Equilibrium with Increasing Costs of Debt, Restrictions on Total Debt and Imperfect Markets for Short Sales. JFQA, forthcoming; -10*l*

Security Prices and Risk; The Theory and a Comparative Analysis of AT&T and Leading Industrials. Paper at the Conference on 'The Economics of Regulated Public Utilities', sponsored by the Bell System and the U of Chicago Business School, Jun 1965; -10*l*

Security Prices, Risk and Maximal Gains from Diversification. JF, 20 (Dec, 1965), 587-615; -10*l*

The Valuation of Risk Assets and the Selection of Risky Investments in Stock Portfolios and Capital Budgets. REStat, 47 (Feb, 1965), 13-37; -10*l*

   & Glauber, R. R. Higgledy Piggledy Growth in America. Paper for the Seminar on the Analysis of Security Prices, U of Chicago, May 1967; -8a

   & Glauber, R. R. Further Observations on Higgledy Piggledy Growth. Paper for the Seminar on the Analysis of Security Prices, U of Chicago, May 1969; -8a

   See also **Butters, J. K.; Lintner, J. & Cary, W. L.**

Lishan, J. M. & Crary, D. T. (Eds). The Investment Process. Intext, 1970; -1b

Little, A. D., Inc. Studies of the Mutual Fund Industry. Report to the Investment Company Institute, Jun 1967; -3k

Little, I. M. D. Higgledy Piggledy Growth. OIS, 24 (Nov, 1962), 387-412; -8a

   & Rayner, A. C. Higgledy Piggledy Growth Again. Blackwell, 1966; -8a

Littlechild, S. C.
   See **Charnes, A. & Littlechild, S. C.**

Litts, R. N. Another Interesting Tool for Stock Appraisal. AJ, 10 (Nov, 1954), 59-62; -7b

Litzenberger, R. H.   Allocation of Corporate Capital Under Uncertainty. PhD diss, U of NC, 1969; -25d

Equilibrium in the Equity Market under Uncertainty. JF, 24 (Sep, 1969), 663-671; -10l

& Budd, A. P.   Corporate Investment Criteria and the Valuation of Risk Assets. JFQA, 5 (Dec, 1970), 395-420; -25d

& Budd, A. P.   A Note on Geometric Mean Portfolio Selection and the Market Prices of Equities. JFQA, 6 (Dec, 1971), 1263-1276; -10j

& Budd, A. P.   Secular Trends in Risk Premiums. JF, 27 (Sep, 1972), 857-864; -10l

& Jones, C. P.   The Capital Structure and the Cost of Capital: Comment. JF, 25 (Jun, 1970), 669-673; -23c

& Joy, O. M.   Target Rates of Return and Corporate Asset and Liability Structure under Uncertainty. JFQA, 6 (Mar, 1971), 675-686; -25d

Joy, O. M. & Jones, C. P.   Ordinal Predictions and the Selection of Common Stocks. JFQA, 6 (Sep, 1971), 1059-1068; -8f

& Rao, C. U.   Estimates of the Marginal Rate of Time Preference and Average Risk Aversion of Investors in Electric Utility Shares, 1960-1966. BellJ, (Spring, 1971), 265-277; -23d

& Rao, C. U.   Portfolio Theory and Industry Cost-of-Capital Estimates. JFQA, 7 (Mar, 1972), 1443-1462; -23d

& Rutenberg, D. P.   Size and Timing of Corporate Bond Flotations. JFQA, 7 (Jan, 1972), 1343-1360; -19e, 23b

See also **Budd, A. & Litzenberger, R. H.**

See also **Jones, C. P. & Litzenberger, R. H.**

See also **Kraus, A. & Litzenberger, R. H.**

See also **Rao, C. U. & Litzenberger, R. H.**

See also **Tuttle, D. L. & Litzenberger, R. H.**

Liu, T-C.

See **Hakansson, N. H. & Liu, T-C.**

Livermore, S.   The Success of Industrial Mergers. QJE, 49 (Nov, 1935), 68-95; -26b

Value of Stock Dividends. AER, 20 (Dec, 1930), 687-691; -16c

Liviatan, N.   Multiperiod Future Consumption as an Aggregate. AER, 56 (Sep, 1966), 828-840; -10k

Lloyd, C.; Rohr, R. J. & Walker, M.   A Calculus Proof of the Existence of a Continuous Utility Function. Met, 19 (1967), 103-112; -9a

Lockett, A. G. & Tomkins, C.   The Discount Rate Problem in Capital Rationing Situations: a Comment. JFQA, 5 (Jun, 1970), 245-260; -23d

Lockhart, J. A.   Secondary Euro-Dollar Bonds. FAJ, 25 (Mar-Apr, 1969), 128-132; -20e

Loeb, G. M.   The Battle for Investment Survival, rev ed. S & S, 1965; -4a

Battle for Stock Market Profits. S & S, 1971; -4a

Logue, D. E.   An Empirical Appraisal of the Efficiency of the Market for First Public Offerings of Common Stock. PhD diss, Cornell U, 1971; -16a

Loll, L. M. & Buckley, J.   Over-the-Counter Securities Markets, 2nd ed. P-H, 1967; -2b

Lombourne, R. W.   Institutional Investing. FAJ, 17 (Nov-Dec, 1961), 61-70; -3e

Long, J. B., Jr.   Consumption-Investment Decisions and Equilibrium in the Securities Market, *in* Jensen, M. C. (Ed), Studies in the Theory of Capital Markets. Praeger, 1972; -10l

Wealth, Welfare and the Price of Risk. JF, 27 (May, 1972), 419-433; -9d

    & Jensen, M. C.   Corporate Investment Under Uncertainty and Pareto Optimality in the Capital Markets. BellJ, 3 (Apr, 1972); -9d

Longstreet, J. R.   Cases in Financial Management. Wadsworth Pub, 1961; -1c

    See also **Friend, I.; Longstreet, J. R.; Mendelson, M.; Miller, E. & Hess, A. P. Jr.**

    See also **Norgaard, R. L. & Longstreet, J. R.**

Loomis, C. J.   A Case for Dropping Dividends. F, (Jun 15, 1968), 181 ff; -24b

    Fortune's Guide to Personal Investing.   McGraw, 1963; -3b

    Hard Times Come to the Hedge Funds. F, 81, (Jan, 1970), 100 ff; -3e

Lorie, J. H.   NABAC Study on Measuring Investment Performance of Pension Funds. FAJ, 24 (Mar-Apr, 1968), 139-143; -14b

    & Brealey, R. A. (Eds).   Modern Developments in Investment Management: a Book of Readings. Praeger, 1972; -1b

    & Fisher, L.   Knowledge Makes a Difference—a Reply to Dr. Leo Barnes. FAJ, 21 (Nov-Dec, 1965), 118-120; -5a

    & Halpern, P.   Conglomerates: The Rhetoric and the Evidence. JLE, 13 (Apr, 1970), 149-166; -26c

    & Niederhoffer, V.   Predictive and Statistical Properties of Insider Trading. JLE, 11 (Apr, 1968), 35-53; -13c

    & Savage, L. J.   Three Problems in Rationing Capital. JB, 28 (Oct, 1955), 229-239; -25b, 25e

    See also **Fisher, L. & Lorie, J. H.**

Loss, L.   Securities Regulation, Vols 1-3. Little, 1961; -2e

Lucas, W. H.   An Entity Theory of Capital Budgeting. PhD diss, U of Ala, 1966; -25c

Luce, R. W. & Krantz, D. H.   Conditional Expected Utility. Em, 39 (Mar, 1971), 253-272; -9a

Luckett, D. G.   Bills Only: a Critical Appraisal. REStat, 41 (Aug, 1960), 301-306; -20b

    Compensatory Cyclical Bank Asset Adjustments. JF, 17 (Mar, 1962), 53-62; -3f

    Multi-Period Expectations and the Term Structure of Interest Rates. QJE, 81 (May, 1967), 321-329; -18f

    Professor Lutz and the Structure of Interest Rates. QJE, 73 (Feb, 1959), 131-144; -18f

Ludtke, J. B.   The American Financial System: Markets and Institutions, 2nd ed. Allyn, 1961; -2b

Lusher, D. W.   The Structure of Interest Rates and the Keynsian Theory of Interest. JPE, 50 (Apr, 1942), 272-279; -18f

Lusztig, P. & Schwab, B.   A Note on the Application of Linear Programming to Capital Budgeting. JFQA, 3 (Dec, 1968), 427-432; -25e

    See also **Schwab, B. & Lusztig, P.**

Lutgert, S.   Risk and Convertible Bonds. Unp ms, U of Chicago, 1968; -17c

Lüthi, J. E.   The Problem of Corporate Debt Capacity. SM thesis, MIT, 1968; -28c

Lutz, F. A.   The Structure of Interest Rates. QJE, 55 (1940-1941), 36-63; -18f

The Theory of Interest. Reidel, 1968; -18b

   & Hague, D. C. (Eds).   The Theory of Capital. Macmillan, 1963; -22b

   & V. C.   The Theory of Investment of the Firm. Princeton U Pr, 1951; -22a

Lutz, V. C.

   See **Lutz, F. A. & V. C.**

Lynch, H. H.   Financial Performance of Conglomerates. Harvard Busn, 1971; -22c

Lynch, M.

   See **Thornber, E. H. & Lynch, M.**

Lyon, R. A.   Investment Portfolio Management in the Commercial Bank. Rutgers U Pr, 1960; -3f

Lyon, R. C.

   See **Ijiri, Y.; Levy, F. K. & Lyon, R. C.**

Lyons, J. F.   What Happens When Liquidity Disappears? II, 3 (Nov, 1969), 29 ff; -16d

McCahan, D. (Ed).   Investment of Life Insurance Funds. Irwin, 1953; -3h

McCain, W. G.   Price Effects of Margin Changes in Commodity Futures Markets. PhD diss, Stanford U, 1969; -21a

McCall, J. J.   Difference between the Personal Demand for Money and the Business Demand for Money. JPE, 68 (Aug, 1960), 358-368; -25a

McCandlish, R. W., Jr.   Some Methods for Measuring Performance of a Pension Fund. FAJ, 21 (Nov-Dec, 1965), 105-110; -14b

   Portfolio Evaluation: An Approach. FAJ, 23 (Nov-Dec, 1967), 147-150; -14b

McCarroll, J. C.

   See **Von Mehren, R. B. & McCarroll, J. C.**

McCarthy, G. D.   Acquisitions and Mergers. Ronald, 1963; -26a

   Premeditated Merger. HBR, 39 (Jan-Feb, 1961), 74-82; -26a

Macaulay, F. R.   Some Theoretical Problems Suggested by the Movements of Interest Rates, Bond Yields and Stock Prices in the United States Since 1856. Natl Bur Econ Res, 1938; -19b

   & Durand, D.   Short Selling on the New York Stock Exchange. Twentieth Fund, 1951; -13d

McCloy, H. F.   Managing Corporate Real Estate. Am Mgmt, 1967; -21c

McClung, N.   The Distribution of Capital Gain on Corporate Shares by Holding Time. REStat, 48 (Oct, 1966), 40-50; -27d

MacCrimmon, K. R.   Descriptive and Normative Implications of the Decision—Theory Postulates, *in* Borch, K., & Mossin, J. E. (Eds), Risk and Uncertainty. Macmillan Int, 1968; -9c

McCue, G. A.   An Econometric Equity-Market Model: Cobwebs in the Stock Market. PhD diss, U of Cal Irvine, 1970; -7d

McCullers, L. D.   Convertible Securities—Debt or Equity? PhD diss, U of Fla, 1969; -17c

McCulloch, J. H.   Measuring the Term Structure of Interest Rates. JB, 44 (Jan, 1971), 19-31; -18e

McDiarmid, F. J.   Some Broader Aspects of the Insurance Investment Problem. AJ, 1 (Oct, 1945), 39-48; -3h

   Investing for a Financial Institution. New York: Life Office Management Association Institute, 1961; -3e

McDonald, J. G.   Valuation of Common Stock and the Cost of Equity Capital. PhD diss, Stanford U, 1967; -23d

   & Baron, D.   Risk and Return on Short Position in Common

Stocks. JF, forthcoming; -13d

    & Fisher, A. K.   New Issue Stock Price Behavior. JF, 27 (Mar, 1972), 92-102; -16a

     See also **Robichek, A. A.; McDonald, J. G. & Higgins, R. C.**

     See also **Van Horne, J. C. & McDonald, J. G.**

MacDougal, G. E. & Malek, F. V.   Master Plan for Merger Negotiations. HBR, 48 (Jan-Feb, 1970), 71-82; -26a

McEnally, R. W.   An Investigation of the Extrapolative Determinants of Short-Run Earnings Expectations. JFQA, 6 (Mar, 1971), 687-706; -15b

    & Dyl, E. A.   Risk of Selling Short. FAJ, 25 (Nov-Dec, 1969), 73-77; -13d

McEvoy, R. H.   Variation in Bank Asset Portfolios. JF, 11 (Dec, 1956), 463-473; -3f

McFarlane, D. D.   Application of the Markowitz Portfolio Selection Model as a Managerial Tool. DBA diss, Indiana U, 1965; -10c

McGill, D. M.   Fulfilling Pension Expectations. Irwin, 1962; -3i

McGuigan, J. R.   Timing Strategies in the Call Option Market. PhD diss, U of Pittsburgh, 1971

Machol, R. E. & Lerner, E. M.   Risk, Ruin and Investment Analysis. JFQA, 4 (Dec, 1969), 473-492; -9c

McIndoe, R. A.

     See **Johnston, G. S.; Curley, M. L. & McIndoe, R. A.**

McKenzie, L. W.   On the Existence of General Equilibrium for a Competitive Market. Em, 27 (Jan, 1959), 54-71; -9d

McKenzie, P. B.   The Relative Usefulness to Investors of Price-Level Adjusted Financial Statements: an Empirical Study. PhD diss, Mich St U, 1970; -8e

McKenzie, R. R.   A Computer Simulation Used to Evaluate Alternative Financial Strategies. PhD diss, UCLA, 1965; -22c

     Convertible Debentures, 1956-65. QREB, 6 (Winter, 1966), 41-51; -17c

McKeon, J. J.   Structure of Corporate External Financing. FAJ, 25 (Sep-Oct, 1969), 25-28; -23g

McKibben, W.   Econometric Forecasting of Common Stock Investment Returns: a New Methodology Using Fundamental Operating Data. JF, 27 (May, 1972), 371-380; -7c

McKinnon, R.   Futures Markets, Buffer Stocks, and Income Stability for Primary Producers. JPE, 75 (Dec, 1967), 844-861; -21a

Mackintosh, G.   A Method of Valuing Growth Stocks. AJ, 1 (Jan, 1945), 6-14; -7b

McLaughlin, C. W.   An Analysis of the First Public Stock Issues of New Technical Enterprises. SM thesis, MIT, 1967; -16a

McLean, J. G.   How to Evaluate New Capital Investments. HBR, 36 (Nov-Dec, 1958), 59-69; -25c

McMichael, S. L.   How to Operate a Real Estate Business, rev ed. P-H, 1967; -21c

    & O'Keefe, P. T.   How to Finance Real Estate, 3rd ed. P-H, 1967; -21c

McQuown, J. A.   The Nature, Measurement, and Meaning of Investment Performance. Paper for the Seminar on the Analysis of Security Prices, U of Chicago, May 1966; -14a

     See also **Vasicek, O. A. & McQuown, J. A.**

Macrae, N.   The London Capital Market. Staples, 1964; -2a

McShane, R. W.

See **Fairbairn, I. J. & McShane, R. W.**

McWilliams, J. D.   Prices, Earnings and P-E Ratios. FAJ, 22 (May-Jun, 1966), 137-142; -8g

Mace, M. L. & Montgomery, G. E., Jr.   Management Problems of Corporate Acquisitions. Harvard Busn, 1962; -26a

Machlup, F.   The Stock Market, Credit and Capital Formation. Translated from a revised version of the German edition by V. C. Smith. Macmillan, 1940; -22b

Madden, J. T. & Nadler, M.   The International Money Markets. Greenwood, 1968; -20d

Magee, J.

See **Edwards, R. D. & Magee, J.**

Magee, J. F.   How to Use Decision Trees in Capital Investment. HBR, 42 (Sep-Oct, 1964), 79-96; -25d

Magen, S. D.   Cost of Capital and Dividend Policies in Commercial Banks. JFQA, 6 (Mar, 1971), 733-746; -24b

Maggi, P. G.

See **Feuerstein, A. E. & Maggi, P. G.**

Maher, C. L.   Corporate Acquisitions—Tax Accounting Consequences. NAA, 46 (Mar, 1965), 50-54; -26d

Maheshwari, A.

See **Green, P. E. & Maheshwari, A.**

Maine, R. F.   My Attitude Toward Institutional Investment Attitudes. AJ, 4 (Suppl, 2nd Qtr, 1948), 31-36; -3e

Maisel, S. J.   Financing Real Estate. McGraw, 1965; -21c

Majumdar, T.   The Measurement of Utility. St Martin, 1958; -9a

Makridakis, S. G. & Wheelwright, S. C.   Predicting European Stock Indices from Movements in the New York Stock Exchange Index. JBF, 4 (Autumn, 1972), 65-69; -10i

Maledon, E. N., Jr.   Toward a Theory of Investment Decision Making. PhD diss, U of Tex, 1968; -4a

Malek, F. V.

See **MacDougal, G. E. & Malek, F. V.**

Malkiel, B. G.   Equity Yields, Growth and the Structure of Share Prices. AER, 53 (Dec, 1963), 1004-1031; -7b

Expectations, Bond Prices and the Term Structure of Interest Rates. QJE, 76 (May, 1962), 197-218; -18f

Problems in the Structure of Financial Markets. PhD diss, Princeton U, 1964; -2b

The Term Structure of Interest Rates. AER, 54 (May, 1964), 532-543; -18f

The Term Structure of Interest Rates: Expectations and Behavior Patterns. Princeton U Pr, 1966; -18f

The Definition of Endowment Income. Report of a special faculty-administrative committee, Princeton U, unp, 1969; -3i

& Cragg, J. G.   Expectations and the Structure of Share Prices. AER, 60 (Sep, 1970), 601-617; -7b

& Kane, E. J.   Expectations and Interest Rates: a Cross-sectional Test of the Error-learning Hypothesis. JPE, 77 (Jul-Aug, 1969), 453-470; -18f

U.S. Tax Law and the Locked-In Effect. NTJ, 16 (Dec, 1963), 389-396; -27d

& Quandt, R. E.   Can Options Improve an Institution's Performance? II, 2 (Nov, 1968), 55 ff; -17a

Strategies and Rational Decisions in the Securities Option Market. MIT Pr, 1969; -17a

The Supply of Money and Common Stock Prices: Comment. JF, 27 (Sep, 1972), 921-926; -6d

See also **Baumol, W. J. & Malkiel, B. G.**

See also **Baumol, W. J.; Malkiel, B. G. & Quandt, R. E.**

See also **Baumol, W. J.; Heim, P.; Malkiel, B. G. & Quandt, R. E.**

See also **Cragg, J. G. & Malkiel, B. G.**

See also **Kane, E. J. & Malkiel, B. G.**

Mampe, E. P., Jr. The Impact of Interest Rates on Share Prices: the Influence of Expectation, Growth and Leverage. PhD diss, U of Ill, 1968; -7b

Mandelbrot, B. Some Aspects of the Random Walk Model of Stock Market Prices: Comment. IntER, 9 (Jun, 1968), 258-259; -11b

Forecasts of Future Prices, Unbiased Markets, and Martingale Models. JB, 39 (Suppl Jan, 1966), 242-255; -11c

Is There Persistence in Stock Price Movements? Paper for the Seminar on the Analysis of Security Prices. U of Chicago, Nov, 1964; -11c

New Methods in Statistical Economics. JPE, 71 (Oct, 1963), 421-440; -11b

Paretian Distributions and Income Maximization. QJE, 76 (Feb, 1962), 57-85; -11b

The Stable Paretian Income Distribution When the Apparent Exponent is Near Two. IntER, 4 (Jan, 1963), 111-115; -11b

The Variation of Certain Speculative Prices. JB, 36 (Oct, 1963), 394-419; -11b

The Variation of Some Other Speculative Prices. JB, 40 (Oct, 1967), 393-413; -11b

When Can Price be Arbitraged Efficiently? A Limit to the Validity of the Random Walk and Martingale Models. REStat, 53 (Aug, 1971), 225-236; -11c

& Taylor, H. M. On the Distribution of Stock Price Differences. OR, (Nov-Dec, 1967), 1057-1062; -11b

Mandelker, G.

See **Lev, B. & Mandelker, G.**

Manes, P. The Structure of the Italian Stock Market. BNLQR, 53 (Jun, 1960), 171-208; -2c

Manne, A. S. (Ed). Investments for Capacity Expansion: Size, Location and Time Phasing. Allen, 1967; -25c

Optimal Dividend and Investment Policies for a Self Financing Business Enterprise. MSci, 15 (Nov, 1968), 119-129; -25d

Manne, H. G. (Ed). Economic Policy and the Regulation of Corporate Securities. Am Ent, 1969; -2e

Insider Trading and the Stock Market. Free Pr, 1966; -2e

Merger and the Market for Corporate Control. JPE, 73 (Apr, 1965), 110-120; -26a

Mantripragada, K. G. Stable Dividends and Share Prices. PhD diss, U of Minn, 1971; -24b

Mao, J. C. T. Essentials of Portfolio Diversification Strategy. JF, 25 (Dec, 1970), 1109-1122; -10c

Models of Capital Budgeting, E-V vs E-S. JFQA, 4 (Jan, 1970), 657-676; -25d

Quantitative Analysis of Financial Decisions. Macmillan, 1969; -22a

Security Pricing in an Imperfect Capital Market. JFQA, 6 (Sep, 1971), 1105-1116; -10b

Survey of Capital Budgeting: Theory and Practice. JF, 25 (May, 1970), 349-360; -25f

The Valuation of Growth Stocks. JF, 21 (Mar, 1966), 95-102; -7b

& Särndal, C. E.   A Decision Theory Approach to Portfolio Selection. MSci, 12 (Apr, 1966), B323-B333; -10c

& Wallingford, B. A.   An Extension of Lawler and Bell's Method of Discrete Optimization with Examples from Capital Budgeting. MSci, 15 (Oct, 1968), B51-B60; -25e

Marcis, R. G.
See **Smith, K. V. & Marcis, R. G.**

Marcus, M.   Profitability and Size of the Firm: Some Further Evidence. REStat, 51 (Feb, 1969), 104-107; -26f

Marglin, S. A.   Approaches to Dynamic Investment Planning. N Holland, 1963; -25c

Margoshes, S. L.   Cost of Capital. FAJ, 19 (Jul, 1963), 49-53; -23d

Debt Financing and Investment Value of Common Stock. FAJ, 18 (Jul, 1962), 67-72; -23c

'Present Value' Techniques of Common Stock Valuation. FAJ, 17 (Mar, 1961), 37-42; -7b

Price-Earnings Ratio in Financial Analysis. FAJ, 16 (Nov, 1960), 125-130; -7b

Profitability, Probability and 'The Modified Present Value Profile' FAJ, 24 (Mar-Apr, 1968), 97-104; -7b

Markham, J. W.   Survey of the Evidence and Findings on Mergers. (Dist by Princeton U Pr) Natl Bur Econ Res, 1955; -26b

Markowitz, H. M.   The Optimization of a Quadratic Function Subject to Linear Constraints. NRLQ, (Mar & Jun, 1956), 111-133; -10c

Portfolio Selection. JF, 7 (Mar, 1952), 77-91; -10c

Portfolio Selection: Efficient Diversification of Investments. Wiley, 1959; -10c

The Utility of Wealth. JPE, 60 (Apr, 1952), 151-158; -9a

Marks, L. J.   In Defense of Performance. FAJ, 23 (Nov-Dec, 1967), 135-137; -4a

Marks, P. & Stuart, A.   An Arithmetic Version of the FT Index. J1A, 97 (Dec, 1971), 297-324; -5b

Marris, R. & Singh, A.   A Measure of a Firm's Average Share Price. JRSS, 129 Series A (1966), 74-97; -5c

Marschak, J.   Rational Behavior, Uncertain Prospects and Measurable Utility. Em, 18 (Apr, 1950), 111-141; -9a

Marshall, D. C.   Federal Income Tax Treatment of Capital Gains and Losses. PhD diss, La St U, 1967; -27d

Marshall, W. S. & Young, A. E.   A Mathematical Model for Re-Acquisition of Small Shareholdings. JFQA, 3 (Dec, 1968), 463-470; -16d

Martenson, G. C.   The Euro-dollar Market. Bankers, 1964; -20d

Martin, A.   The Decision-Relevance of Reported Accounting Information: an Empirical Perspective. PhD diss, Northwestern U, 1971; -8e

Martin, A. D., Jr.   Mathematical Programming of Portfolio Selections. MSci, 1 (Jan, 1955), 152-166; -10c

Martin, T. J.
See **Plum, L. V. & Martin, T. J.**

Martin, W. McC., Jr.   The Securities Markets. A Report with recommendations submitted to the Board of Governors of the New York Stock

Exchange, Aug 5, 1971; -2b

Marting, E. & Finley, R. E. (Eds).   The Financial Manager's Job. Am Mgmt, 1964; -22a

Mascia, J. S.   Corporate Earnings Predictions. FAJ, 25 (Jul-Aug, 1969), 107-110; -8c

Masera, R. S.   Least-Squares Construction of the Yield Curves for Italian Government Securities, 1957-1967.
Part 1: BNLQR, 22 (Dec, 1969), 347-371,
Part 2: BNLQR, 23 (Mar, 1970), 82-102; -18e
The Term Structure of Interest Rates—an Expectations Model Tested on Post-War Italian Data. Oxford U Pr, 1972; -18f

Mason, S.   Information for Investment Decisions. How Efficiently is it Used? IA, 30 (Sep, 1971), 3-16; -4a
Merchant Banking Today and in the Future. JBF, 3 (Winter, 1971), 4-28; -3g

Massé, P.   Optimal Investment Decisions: Rules for Action and Criteria for Choice. Translated by Scripta Technica, Inc. P-H, 1962; -9a

Masson, R. L.; Hunt, P. & Anthony, R. N.   Cases in Financial Management. Irwin, 1960; -1c

Masson, R. T.   The Creation of Risk Aversion by Imperfect Capital Markets AER, 62 (Mar, 1972), 77-86; -10*l*

Mastrapasqua, F. & Bolten, S.   A Note on Financial Analyst Evaluation: a Statistical Approach. JF, forthcoming; -14c

Masui, M.   Bibliography of Finance. Kobe University of Commerce, 1935; -1a

Mathews, R.   Inflation and Company Finance. AR, 35 (Jan, 1960), 8-18; -22a

Mathur, G.   Investment Criteria in a Platinum Age. OEP, 19 (Jul, 1967), 199-214; -25c

Mattessich, R.   Budgeting Models and System Simulation. AR 36 (Jul, 1961), 384-397; -22c
Simulation of a Firm through a Budget Computer Program. Irwin, 1964; -22c

Mattlin, E.   How Do You Measure an Analyst's Performance? II, 3 (Jul, 1969), 37 ff; -14c

Mauer, L. J.   Commercial Bank Maturity Demand for United States Government Securities and the Determinants of the Term Structure of Interest Rates. JFQA, 4 (Mar, 1969), 37-52; -18f
The Term Structure of Interest Rates. PhD diss, U of Tenn, 1967; -18f

Maw, J. F.   Return on Investment; Concept and Application. Am Mgmt, 1968; -25c

May, A. M.
See **Durand, D. & May, A. M.**

May, C.
See **Molodovsky, N.; May, C. & Chottiner, S.**

May, M. M.   The Earnings per Share Trap. FAJ, 24 (May-Jun, 1968), 113-117; -26c

Mayer, M.   Wall Street: Men and Money, rev ed. Macmillan, 1966; -2b

Mayer, R. R.   Financial Analysis of Investment Alternatives. Allyn, 1966; -25c

Mayer, R. W.   Analysis of the Flow of Funds Through the Capital Market. FAJ, 17 (Jan, 1961), 71-76; -3c
Analysis of Internal Risk in the Individual Firm. AJ, 15 (Sep, 1959),

91-95; -10n

Business Risk and the Earnings Multiplier. FAJ, 21 (Sep-Oct, 1965), 19-21; -10*l*

Performance and its Measurement. FAJ, 22 (Mar-Apr, 1966), 54-55; -14a

Mayer, T. Is the Portfolio Control of Financial Institutions Justified? JF, 17 (May, 1962), 311-317; -3e

& Sonenblum, S. Lead Times for Fixed Investment. REStat, 37 (Aug, 1955), 300-304; -25c

Mayers, D. Non-Marketable Assets and Capital Market Equilibrium under Uncertainty, *in* Jensen, M. C. (Ed), Studies in the Theory of Capital Markets. Praeger, 1972; -10*l*

Maynard, J. The Most Rapidly Changing Industry of All. FAJ, 27 (Nov-Dec, 1971), 41-47; -2b

Maynard, W. Problems of Investing in Growth Stocks. AJ, 12 (Aug, 1956), 27-28; -7b

Mayor, T. H. Short Trading Activities and the Price of Equities: Some Simulation and Regression Results. JFQA, 3 (Sep, 1968), 283-298; -13d

Mazuy, K.

See **Treynor, J. L. & Mazuy, K.**

Mead, S. B. Mutual Fund and Investment Company Performance in the 1950's. Mich St U Busn, 1962; -14a

Meade, J. Degrees of Competitive Speculation. REStud, 17 (1949-1950); -9e

Means, G. C.

See **Berle, A. A. & Means, G. C.**

Mears, E. G. Stockholders' Privileged Subscriptions, 1906-1911 Inclusive: Their Effect on the Market Price of the Stocks. MBA thesis, Harvard Bus, 1912; -16b

Meck, J. F. A New Investment Concept: Total Returns. Dartmouth Alumni Magazine, (Jul, 1969); -3i

Meckling, W. H. & Jensen, M. C. University Endowments and Spending Policies. U of Rochester, Jan 1970; -3i

Meek, P. Open Market Operations. New York: Federal Reserve Bank, 1969; -18f

Meigs, J. A. The Changing Role of Banks in the Market for Equities. JF, 20 (May, 1965), 368-378; -3f

Meiselman, D. Bond Yields and the Price Level: the Gibson Paradox Regained, *in* Carson, D. (Ed), Banking and Monetary Studies. Irwin, 1963; -18c

The Term Structure of Interest Rates. P-H, 1962; -18f

Melicher, R. W. An Analysis of Changes in the Merger Valuation Process of Listed Industrial Corporations during the Current Merger Movement (1950-1960). DBA diss, U of Wash, 1968; -26a

Melnik, A. Short Run Determinants of Commercial Bank Investment Portfolios: An Empirical Analysis. JF, 25 (Jun, 1970), 639-649; -3f

Melnyk, Z. K.

See **Ball, R. E. & Melnyk, Z. K.**

Meltzer, A. H. & Von der Linde, G. A Study of the Dealer Market for Federal Government Securities. US Govt, 1960; -19c

See also **Clarkson, G. P. E. & Meltzer, A. H.**

See also **Ott, D. J. & Meltzer, A. H.**

Mendelson, M. A Comment on Payback, JFQA, 6 (Sep, 1971), 1159-1160; -25c

300

London's Many Money Markets. Banker, 117 (May, 1967), 411-417; -20a

Security and a Financial Theory of Investment: Comment. QJE, 76 (May, 1962), 311-315; -23c

See also **Friend, I.; Longstreet, J. R.; Mendelson, M.; Miller, E. & Hess, A. P. Jr.**

Menger, K. Das Unsicherheitsmoment in der Wertlehre. Zeitschrift für Nationalökonomie, 51 (1934), 459-485; -9a

Menippus (pseud). Some Self-Criticism of Institutional Investing. AJ, 6 (4th Qtr, 1950), 29-31; -3c

Mennis, E. A. The Investment Manager of the Future. FAJ, 16 (Mar-Apr, 1960), 23-24; -4c

Investment Policy for a Growing Pension Fund. FAJ, 24 (Mar-Apr, 1968), 122-131; -3i

New Tools for Profits Analysis. FAJ, 25 (Jan-Feb, 1969), 25-33; -6a

New Trends in Institutional Investing. FAJ, 24 (Jul-Aug, 1968), 133-138; -3e

Security Prices and Business Cycles. AJ, 11 (Feb, 1955), 79-86; -6b

& Birmingham, J. M., Jr. Diffusion Analysis as an Investment Guide. AJ, 13 (May, 1957), 47-56; -12e

Meredith, G. G. Capital Investment Decisions: a Manual for Managerial Planning and Control. U of Queensland Pr, 1966; -25c

Meredith, G. P.
See **Carter, C. F.; Meredith, G. P. & Shackle, G. L. S.**

Merjos, A. Broken Mergers: A Security Analyst Adds Up the Gains and Losses. B, 36 (Mar 21, 1966), 5 ff; -26a

Going on the Big Board. B (May 1, 1967), 9-10; -2f

Going on the Big Board: Stocks Act Better Before Listing than Right Afterward. B (Jan 29, 1962), 54 ff; -2f

Into the Treasury. B (Aug 17, 1964), 9-12; -16d

Like Money in the Bank: Big Board Listing, the Record Suggests, is a Valuable Asset. B, (Jul 8, 1963), 94 ff; -2f

Lunch at the Analysts. B (Oct 9, 1961), 5 ff; -11a

Reverse Stock Splits. B (May 28, 1962); -16c

Treasury Stock: Many Companies Are Regular Buyers of Their Own Shares. B, (Aug 29, 1960), 11-12; -16d

Mermelstein, D. Large Industrial Corporations and Asset Share Maintenance, 1909-1964. PhD diss, Columbia U, 1967; -26f

Merrett, A. J. The Capital Gains Tax. LBR, 78 (Oct, 1965), 1-14; -27d

Net Present Value versus the Internal Rate of Return Yet Again. SJPE, 12 (Feb, 1965), 116-118; -25c

Valuation of Ordinary Shares. Gower, 1970; -7b

Howe, M. & Newbould, G. D. Equity Issues and the London Capital Market. Longman, 1967; -16a

& Newbould, G. D. The Comparative Efficiency of Methods of Issues. MS, 34 (Jan, 1966), 1-14; -16a

& Sykes, A. Capital Budgeting and Company Finance. Longman, 1966; -25c

& Sykes, A. The Finance and Analysis of Capital Projects. Longman, 1963; -25c

& Sykes, A. Rates of Return Standards: The Cost of Capital. A, 77 (Jan, 1966), 7-14; -23d

& Sykes, A. Return on Equities and Fixed Interest Securities

1919-1963. DBR, (Dec, 1963); -5a, 19b

    & Sykes, A.   Return on Equities and Fixed Interest Securities 1919-1966. DBR, 158 (Jun, 1966), 29-45; -5a, 19b

Merriman, C. O.   Mutual Funds and Unit Trusts; a Global View. Pitman, 1965; -3k

Merton, R. C.   A Dynamic General Equilibrium Model of the Asset Market and its Application to the Pricing of the Capital Structure of the Firm. Wkg paper No. 497-70, Alfred P. Sloan School of Management, MIT, 1970; -10l

    An Intertemporal Capital Asset Pricing Model. Wkg paper No. 588-72, Alfred P. Sloan School of Management, MIT, Feb, 1972; -10l

    Lifetime Portfolio Selection under Uncertainty. REStat, 51 (Aug, 1969), 247-257; -10k

    See also **Samuelson, P. & Merton, R. C.**

Messner, V. A.

    See **Kisor, M., Jr. & Messner, V. A.**

Meyer, A. H.   Designing a Convertible Preferred Issue. FE, 36 (Apr, 1968) 42 ff; -17c

Meyer, J. R. & Glauber, R. R.   Investment Decisions, Economic Forecasting and Public Policy. Harvard Busn, 1964; -25f

    & Kuh, E.   The Investment Decision: An Empirical Study. Harvard U Pr, 1957; -25f

Meyer, P. A. & Pifer, H. W.   Prediction of Bank Failures. JF, 25 (Sep, 1970), 853-868; -26g

Meyer, R. L.   The Rationale and an Empirical Test of a Model to Determine the Intrinsic Value of Call Options. PhD diss, U of Wis, 1971; -17a

Meyerholz, J. C.   Competition and Investment Management. FAJ, 22 (Jan-Feb, 1966), 97-105; -3k

Meyers, S. L.   A Factor Analysis Approach to Studying the Structure of the Stock Market. PhD diss, U of Pa, 1970; -10a

Michaelsen, J. B.   The Determinants of Dividend Policies: A Theoretical and Empirical Study. PhD diss, U of Chicago, 1961; -24a

    The Term Structure of Interest Rates: a Comment. QJE, 77 (Feb, 1963), 166-174; -18f

    The Term Structure of Interest Rates and Holding-Period Yields on Government Securities. JF, 20 (Sep, 1965), 444-463; -18f

    & Goshay, R. C.   Portfolio Selection in Financial Intermediaries: A New Approach. JFQA, 2 (Jun, 1967), 116-199; -3d

    See also **Brewer, D. E. & Michaelsen, J. B.**

Middleton, M.

    See **Vernon, R. A.; Middleton, M. & Harper, D. G.**

Midgley, K. & Burns, R. G.   Business Finance and the Capital Market. Macmillan Int, 1969; -22a

Midler, J. L.   A Dynamic Portfolio Selection Model. Paper for the Seminar on the Analysis of Security Prices, U of Chicago, Nov, 1965; -10k

Mieszkowski, P.

    See **Cragg, J. P.; Harberger, A. C. & Mieszkowski, P.**

Miles, J. E.   Discount Bonds. PhD diss, NYU, 1966; -19a

    Formulas for Pricing Bonds and Their Impact on Prices. FAJ, 25 (Jul-Aug, 1969), 156-161; -19a

    Investment Management: Strategies in Ferment. FAJ, 23 (Sep-Oct, 1967), 147-154; -4a

Millar, J. A.   The Effect of Stock Splits and Stock Dividends on the Monthly Price Relatives of Common Stocks. PhD diss, U of Ok, 1971; -16c

Miller, A. B.   The Standby Purchase Agreement. FAJ, 27 (Jul-Aug, 1971), 71ff; -17c

Miller, E.   Trends in Private Pension Funds. JF, 16 (May, 1961), 313-327; -3i

    See also **Friend, I.; Longstreet, J. R.; Mendelson, M.; Miller, E. & Hess, A. P., Jr.**

Miller, F. B. & Robinson, R. S.   A Management Summary of 'Measuring the Investment Performance of Pension Funds'. BAI, 1968; -14b

Miller, J. D.   Effects of Longevity on Values of Stock Purchase Warrants. FAJ, 27 (Nov-Dec, 1971), 78-85; -17b

Miller, M. H.   The Corporation Income Tax and Corporate Financial Policies, *in* Stabilization Policies. CMC Supporting Papers, P-H, 1963; -23b

    & Modigliani, F.   The Cost of Capital, Corporation Finance and the Theory of Investment: Reply. AER, 49 (Sep 1959), 655-668; -23c

    & Modigliani, F.   Dividend Policy, Growth, and the Valuation of Shares. JB, 34 (Oct, 1961), 411-433; -7b, 24b

    & Modigliani, F.   Dividend Policy and Market Valuation: A Reply. JB, 36 (Jan, 1963), 116-119; -24b

    & Modigliani, F.   Some Estimates of the Cost of Capital to the Electric Utility Industry, 1954-57. AER, 56 (Jun, 1966), 333-391; -23c

    & Modigliani, F.   Some Estimates of the Cost of Capital to the Electric Utility Industry, 1954-57: Reply. AER, 57 (Dec, 1967), 1288-1300; -23c

    & Orr, D.   The Demand for Money by Firms: Extensions of Analytical Results. JF, 23 (Dec, 1968), 735-759; -25a

    & Orr, D.   A Model of the Demand for Money by Firms. QJE, 80 (Aug, 1966), 413-435; -25a

    & Scholes, M.   Rates of Return in Relation to Risk: a Re-examination of some Recent Findings, *in* Jensen, M. C. (Ed), Studies in the Theory of Capital Markets. Praeger, 1972; -10*l*

    See also **Charnes, A.; Cooper, W. W. & Miller, M. H.**

    See also **Fama, E. F. & Miller, M. H.**

    See also **Modigliani, F. & Miller, M. H.**

Miller, N. C.   The Great Salad Oil Swindle. Gollancz, 1966; -21a

Miller, N. C. & Whitman, M. v. N.   A Mean-Variance Analysis of United States Long-Term Portfolio Foreign Investment. QJE, 84 (May, 1970), 175-196; -10i

Miller, P. F., Jr. & Beach, T. E.   Recent Studies of P/E Ratios—A Reply. FAJ, 23 (May-Jun, 1967), 109-110; -8g

Miller, R. L.
    See **Solodfsky, R. M. & Miller, R. L.**

Mills, H. D.   On the Measurement of Fund Performance. JF, 25 (Dec, 1970), 1125-1132; -14a

Mills, R. H.
    See **Fraine, H. G. & Mills, R. H.**

Milne, R. D.   Benchmarks for a Diversified Portfolio. AJ, 14 (Nov, 1958), 51-54; -10d

    The Dow-Jones Industrial Average Re-examined. FAJ, 22 (Nov-Dec, 1966), 83-88; -5b

Milnor, J.
    See **Hertstein, I. N. & Milnor, J.**

Mincer, J. (Ed).   Economic Forecasts and Expectations: Analyses of Forecasting Behavior and Performance. (Dist by Columbia U Pr) Natl Bur Econ Res, 1969; -15a

Mindell, J.   How News Affects Market Trends. FAJ, 17 (Jan-Feb, 1961), 17-22; -11a

Minet, L. J.
    See **Fischer, G. C. & Minet, L. J.**

Mingo, K.
    See **Pinches, G. E. & Mingo, K.**

Minto, G. S.   The Flow of Funds through the Capital Market. IA, 9 (Sep, 1964), 11-20; -3c

    Some Suggestions Relating to the Assessment of Investment Performance in Multi-Asset Funds Subject to Decentralised Control. IA, 28 (Dec, 1970), 7-11; -14a

Mirman, L. J.   Uncertainty and Optimal Consumption Decisions. Em, 36 (Jan, 1971), 177-183; -10k

Misawa, M.   The Historical and Comparative Study of the Post-War Japanese Securities Markets in the Light of Law and Business Practice. PhD diss, U of Mich, 1967; -2c

Mitchell, G. B.   After-Tax Cost of Leasing. AR, 45 (Apr, 1970), 308-314; -25g

Mitchell, W. C.   A Critique of Index Numbers of the Prices of Stocks. JPE, 24 (Jul, 1916), 685; -5b

Mlynarczyk, F. A., Jr.   An Empirical Study of Accounting Methods and Stock Prices. ERA, (1969), 63-89; -8e

Moag, J. S.; Carleton, W. T. & Lerner, E. M.   Defining the Finance Function: a Systems Approach. JF, 22 (Dec, 1967), 543-555; -22c

    & Lerner, E. M.   Capital Budgeting Decisions Under Imperfect Market Conditions—a Systems Framework. JF, 24 (Sep, 1969), 613-622; -25c

Mock, E. J.   An Evaluation of Borrower Risk in Industrial Companies Employing Convertible Subordinated Debentures. PhD diss, Ohio St U, 1964; -17c

    Financial Decision-Making. Intext, 1967; -22a

    The Investment of Corporate Cash. MServ, 4 (Sep-Oct, 1967); -25a

    (Ed).   Readings in Financial Management. Intext, 1964; -1b

    Short Problems in Business Finance and Financial Management. Intext, 1964; -1c

Modigliani, F. & Brumberg, R.   Utility Analysis and the Consumption Function: an Interpretation of Cross Section Data, *in* Kurihara, K. (Ed), Post-Keynsian Economics. Rutgers U Pr, 1954; -10k

    & Miller, M. H.   Corporate Income Taxes and the Cost of Capital: A Correction. AER, 53 (Jun, 1963), 433-443; -23c

    & Miller, M. H.   The Cost of Capital, Corporation Finance and the Theory of Investment. AER, 48 (Jun, 1958), 261-297; -23c

    & Sutch, R.   Debt Management and the Term Structure of Interest Rates. JPE, 75 (Suppl Aug, 1967), 569-589; -18f

    & Sutch, R. C.   Innovations in Interest Rate Policy. AER, 56 (May, 1966), 178-197; -18f

    et al.   Efficiency of European Capital Markets and Comparison with American Markets. Unp ms, 1972; -10i

    See also **Miller, M. H. & Modigliani, F.**

Mokkelbost, P. B.   Unsystematic Risk Over Time. JFQA, 6 (Mar, 1971), 785-796; -10b

Molodovsky, N.   Some Aspects of Price-Earnings Ratios. AJ, 9 (May, 1953), 65-78; -7b
Building a Stock Market Measure—A Case Story. FAJ, 23 (May-Jun, 1967), 43-46; -5b
'It's Good to Own Growth Stocks!' FAJ, 19 (Mar-Apr, 1963), 75ff; -7b
The Many Aspects of Yields. FAJ, 18 (Mar-Apr, 1962), 49ff; -7d
Recent Studies of P/E Ratios. FAJ, 23 (Mar-Apr, 1967), 101-108; -8g
Selecting Growth Stocks. FAJ, 24 (Sep-Oct, 1968), 103-106; -7b
Stock Prices and Current Earnings. AJ, 11 (Aug, 1955), 83-94; -7b
Stock Values and Stock Prices.
Part 1: FAJ, 16 (May-Jun, 1960), 9ff,
Part 2: FAJ, 16 (Jul-Aug, 1960), 53-64; -7b
Stock Values and Stock Prices. FAJ, 24 (Nov-Dec, 1968), 134-148; -7b
A Theory of Price-Earnings Ratios. AJ, 9 (Nov, 1953), 65-80; -7b
Valuation of Common Stocks. AJ, 15 (Jan-Feb, 1959), 23-44; -7b
May, C. & Chottiner, S.   Common Stock Valuation.
Part 1: FAJ, 21 (Mar-Apr, 1965), 104-123,
Part 2: FAJ, 21 (Sep-Oct, 1965), 135; -7b
Money Which.   Share Tipsters. Money Which, (Sep, 1968); -15c
Montalbano, M.
See **Teichroew, D.; Robichek, A. A. & Montalbano, M.**
Montgomery, G. E., Jr.
See **Mace, M. L. & Montgomery, G. E., Jr.**
Moody, P. E.   The Market Price of Convertible Loan Stocks. JIASS, 15 (Mar, 1959), 295-298; -17c
Moon, R. W.   Business Mergers and Take-over Bids: a Study of the Post-war Pattern of Amalgamations and Reconstructions of Companies, 3rd ed. Gee, 1968; -26a
Moor, R. E.   The Use of Economics in Investment Analysis. FAJ, 27 (Nov-Dec, 1971), 63-69; -6a
Moore, A. B.   Some Characteristics of Changes in Common Stock Prices, *in* Cootner, P. H. (Ed), The Random Character of Stock Market Prices. MIT Pr, 1964; -11c
A Statistical Analysis of Common Stock Prices. PhD diss, U of Chicago, 1962; -11c
Moore, B. J.   An Introduction to the Theory of Finance—Assetholder Behavior Under Uncertainty. Free Pr, 1968; -22a
Moore, D. M.   The Price Behavior of Convertible Preferred Stock. DBA diss, Georgia St C, 1971; -17c
Moore, G. H. & Shiskin, J.   Indicators of Business Expansion and Contractions. (Dist by Columbia U Pr) Natl Bur Econ Res, 1967; -6b
Moore, P. G.
See **Hodges, S. D. & Moore, P. G.**
Moore, T. G.   Stock Market Margin Requirements. JPE, 74 (Apr, 1966), 158-167; -6e
Morgan, B. W.   Corporate Debt and the Evaluation of Corporate Earnings. PhD diss, Yale U, 1966; -23c
Corporate Debt and Stockholder Portfolio Selection. YEE, 7 (Fall, 1967), 201-261; -23c
Morgan, E. V. & Taylor, C.   The Relationship between Size of Joint Stock Companies and the Yield of their Shares. Ec, 24 (1957), 116-127; -26f

    & Thomas, W. A.   The Stock Exchange, Its History and Functions, 2nd ed. Elek, 1970; -2d

Morgan Guaranty Trust Company.   Money Market Investments, The Risk and the Return. New York: Morgan Guaranty Trust Company, 1964; -20a

Morgan, J.; Barlow, R. & Brazer, H.   A Survey of Investment Management and Working Behavior among High-Income Individuals. AER, 55 (May, 1965), 252-264; -3b

Morgan, R.
    See **Foster, J. H. & Morgan, R.**

Morgenstern, O.
    See **Godfrey, M. D.; Granger, C. W. J. & Morgenstern, O.**
    See also **Granger, C. W. J. & Morgenstern, O.**
    See also **Von Neumann, J. & Morgenstern, O.**

Morgner, A.   Security Analysis in a Science-Oriented Society. AJ, 11 (Aug, 1955), 59-61; -6f

Morris, E. L.   Agent-Aided Private Placements. FAJ, 27 (May-Jun, 1971), 83-88; -19e

Morris, W. T.   Diversification. MSci, 4 (Jul, 1958), 382-391; -10e

Morrison, G. R.   Liquidity Preferences of Commercial Banks. U of Chicago Pr, 1966; -3f

Morrison, R. J.   The Bullish Bias. FAJ, 20 (Mar-Apr, 1964), 77-78; -4a
    The Warrants or the Stock? AJ, 13 (Nov, 1957), 51-52; -17b

Moses, E. A.   Seasonal Variations in Common Stock Prices. PhD diss, U of Ga, 1971; -12b

Mosich, A. N.   An Evaluation of Purchase and Pooling Concepts of Accounting for Corporate Mergers and Acquisitions. PhD diss, UCLA, 1963; -26d
    Impact of Merger Accounting on Post-Merger Financial Records. MA, 97 (Dec, 1965), 21-28; -26d

Mossin, J.   Equilibrium in a Capital Asset Market. Em, 34 (Oct, 1966), 768-783; -10*l*
    Merger Agreements: Some Game-theoretic Considerations. JB, 41 (Oct, 1968), 460-471; -26a
    Optimal Multiperiod Portfolio Policies. JB, 41 (Apr, 1968), 215-229; -10k
    Security Pricing and Investment Criteria in Competitive Markets. AER, 59 (Dec, 1969), 749-756; -10*l*
    Studies in the Theory of Risk-bearing. PhD diss, Carnegie-Mellon U, 1968; -9c
    Taxation and Risk-Taking: an Expected Utility Approach. Ec, 35 (Feb, 1968), 74-82; -27b
    See also **Borch, K. & Mossin, J. (Eds).**

Mosteller, F. & Nogee, P.   An Experimental Measurement of Utility. JPE, 59 (Oct, 1951), 371-404; -9b

Mottram, R. H.   A History of Financial Speculation. Chatto, 1929; -2d

Moyle, J.   The Pattern of Ordinary Share Ownership 1957-1970. Cambridge U Pr, 1971; -3a
    See **Stone, R.; Revell, J. & Moyle, J.**

Moynihan, E. O.   The Financial Analyst and the Computer. FAJ, 20 (Mar-Apr, 1964), 115-119; -4e

Mueller, D. C.   A Theory of Conglomerate Mergers. QJE, 83 (Nov, 1969), 643-659; -26c

Mueller, W. F.   A Comment on the FTC's Report on Mergers with Special
   Reference to Dairy Mergers. JFE, 39 (Feb, 1957), 140-152; -26a
Mullick, S. K.
         See **Weekes, P. A.; Chambers, J. C. & Mullick, S. K.**
Mumey, G. A.   Earnings Probabilities and Capital Costs. JB, 40 (Oct,
   1967), 450-461; -23d
         Theory of Financial Structure. HR & W, 1969; -23c
         & Korkie, R. M.   Balance Sheet Additivity of Risk Measures.
   JFQA, 6 (Sep, 1971), 1123-1134; -10b
Mundell, R.   Inflation and Real Interest. JPE, 71 (Jun, 1963), 280-283; -18c
Mundheim, R. H. (Ed).   Conference on Securities Regulation. Commerce,
   1965; -2e
         & Henderson, G. D.   Applicability of the Federal Securities Laws
   to Pension and Profit Sharing Plans. LCP, 29 (Jun, 1964), 795-841; -3i
Munn, G. G.   Encyclopedia of Banking and Finance, 6th ed rev. Bankers,
   1962; -3f
Murdick, R. G. & Deming, D. D.   The Management of Capital Expenditures.
   McGraw, 1968; -25c
Murphy, G. W. & Prussman, D. F.   Equity Issues and the London Capital
   Market. MS, 35 (May, 1967), 167-184; -16a
Murphy, J. E., Jr.   Earnings Growth and Price Changes in the Same Time
   Period. FAJ, 24 (Jan-Feb, 1968), 97-99; -8d
         Some Effects of Leverage. FAJ, 24 (Jul-Aug, 1968), 121-123; -23c
         Relative Growth of Earnings per Share—Past and Future. FAJ,
   22 (Nov-Dec, 1966), 73-76; -8a
         Return, Payout and Growth. FAJ, 23 (May-Jun, 1967), 91-96; -24b
         & Nelson, J. R.   Five Principles of Financial Relationships.
   FAJ, 27 (Mar-Apr, 1971), 38-52; -8c
         & Nelson, J. R.   A Note on the Stability of P/E Ratios. FAJ, 25
   (Mar-Apr, 1969), 77-80; -8d
         & Nelson, J. R.   Random and Nonrandom Relationships Among
   Financial Variables: a Financial Model. JFQA, 6 (Mar, 1971), 875-886;
   -8c
         & Stevenson, H. W.   Price/Earnings Ratios and Future Growth
   of Earnings and Dividends. FAJ, 23 (Nov-Dec, 1967), 111-114; -8d
Murphy, J. S.   An Empirical Investigation of the Relationships between
   Interest Rates and Changes in the Stock of Money. PhD diss, St U NY
   Buffalo, 1968; -23d
Murphy, J. T.
         See **Soldofsky, R. M. & Murphy, J. T.**
Murray, R. F.   Economic Aspects of Pensions: A Summary Report. (Dist
   by Columbia U Pr) Natl Bur Econ Res, 1968; -3i
         Institutional Influences on the Stock Market. FAJ, 14 (May, 1958),
   15-16; -3e
         Interest Rates and their Influence on Equity Prices. FAJ, 12 (Jun,
   1956), 15-17; -6e
         Pension Funds in the American Economy. JF, 23 (May, 1968), 331-
   336; -3i
         Urgent Questions About the Stock Market. HBR, 42 (Sep-Oct, 1964),
   53-59; -2b
Musgrave, R. A.
         See **Krzyzaniak, M. & Musgrave, R. A.**
Muth, J. F.   Rational Expectations and the Theory of Price Movements.
   Em, 29 (Jul, 1961), 315-335; -9e

                                                                      307

Myers, B. C.
> See **Bower, R. S.; Myers, B. C.; Nugent, C. E. & Williamson, J. P.**

Myers, J. H.   The Effect of Issuing Securities for New Capital upon the Company's Common Stock Price. CFC, (Nov 18, 1943), 1991ff; -16b
> The Effect of Raising New Capital by Security Issues upon the Company's Common Stock Price. PhD diss, Northwestern U, 1943; -16b

Myers, S. C.   Effects of Uncertainty on the Valuation of Securities and the Financial Decisions of the Firm. PhD diss, Stanford. U, 1967; -9c
> Effects of Uncertainty on the Valuation of Securities and the Financial Decisions of the Firm. JF, 23 (Mar, 1968), 205-206; -9c
> Procedures for Capital Budgeting under Uncertainty. IMR, 9 (Spring, 1968), 1-20; -25d
> A Note on Linear Programming and Capital Budgeting. JF, 27 (Mar, 1972), 89-92; -25e
> A Time-State Preference Model for Security Valuation. JFQA, 3 (Mar, 1968), 1-34; -9c
> See also **Robichek, A. A. & Myers, S. C.**

Myers, T. S.   A Leading Indicator Approach to Stock Selection. Financial Research, Investment Analysis and the Computer, The Amos Tuck School, Hanover, NH, 1967; -8f

Nadir, M. I.
> See **Jorgenson, D. I.; Hunter, J. & Nadir, M. I.**

Nadler, M.   Corporate Consolidations and Reorganization. New York: Alexander Hamilton Institute, 1930; -26g
> **Heller, S. & Shipman, S. S.**   The Money Market and Its Institutions. Ronald, 1955; -20a
> See also **Madden, J. T. & Nadler, M.**

Naess, R. D.   Changing Patterns of Individual Equity Investment. FAJ, 20 (Jul-Aug, 1964), 74-83; -3b
> The Enigma of Investment Management. AJ, 5 (3rd Qtr, 1949), 5-9; -4a

Narver, J. C.   Conglomerate Mergers and Market Competition. U of Cal Pr, 1967; -26c

Naslund, B.   Some Effects of Taxes on Risk-Taking. REStat, 35 (1968), 289-306; -27b
> Mathematical Programming under Risk. SJE, 67 (Sep, 1965), 240-255; -9c
> A Model of Capital Budgeting Under Risk. JB, 39 (Apr, 1966), 257-271; -25d
> **& Whinston, A.**   Model of Decision-Making under Risk. Met, 16 (May-Aug, 1964), 81-94; -9c
> **& Whinston, A.**   A Model of Multi-Period Investment Under Uncertainty. MSci, 8 (Jan, 1962), 184-200; -10f, 10k

Nassar, J. I.
> See **Williams, A. C. & Nassar, J. I.**

National Bureau of Economic Research.   Corporate Bond Project: Organisation and Methods. Parts 1-5, 1942-1944; -19e
> Research in the Capital Markets. JF, 19 (Suppl May, 1964), 1-43; -2b

National Economic Development Corporation.   Investment Appraisal, 2nd ed. HMSO, 1967

National Industrial Conference Board.   Bibliography on Diversification and Mergers. Natl Ind Conf Bd, 1962; -1a
> Mergers and Markets: An Economic Analysis of the First Fifteen

Years under the Merger Act of 1950, 5th ed. Natl Ind Conf Bd, 1966;
-26a

Naylor, G.   Guide to Shareholders' Rights.   Allen, 1969; -2e

Naylor, J. A.   Some Theoretical and Empirical Considerations Relative to the Term Structure of Interest Rates. PhD diss, U of Ill, 1968;
-18f

Neave, E. H.   The Stochastic Cash Balance Problem with Fixed Costs for Increases and Decreases. MSci, 16 (Mar, 1970), 472-490; -25a

Neenan, W. B.   Review of Institutional Activity in the Equity Market, 1951-54. JF, 12 (Dec, 1957), 468-488; -3e

Neill, H. B.   The Inside Story of the Stock Exchange. Forbes B C, 1950;
-2d

Nelkin, M. C.
>   See **Underwood, E. F. & Nelkin, M. C.**

Nelson, C. R.   A Model of the Term Structure of Interest Rates. JASA, 65 (Sep, 1970), 1163-1179; -18f
>   The Term Structure of Interest Rates. Basic, 1972; -18f

Nelson, J. R.   The Role of Stock Rights in Corporate Financial Policy. PhD diss, UCLA, 1962; -16b
>   See **Murphy, J. E., Jr. & Nelson, J. R.**

Nelson, R. L.   The Investment Policies of Foundations. Russell Sage, 1967;
-3j
>   Merger Movements in American Industry 1895-1956. (Dist by Princeton U Pr) Natl Bur Econ Res, 1959; -26a

Nelson, W. G.   Could Game Theory Aid Capital Budgeting? NAA, 43 (Jun, 1962); -25c

Nemmers, E. E.
>   See **Grunewald, A. E. & Nemmers, E. E.**

Nerlove, M.   Factors Affecting Differences among Rates of Return on Investments in Individual Common Stocks. REStat, 50 (Aug, 1968), 312-331; -7b

Netter, J., II.   Dual-Purpose Funds: One Month Later. FAJ, 23 (Jul-Aug, 1967), 85-87; -3m

Neveu, R. P.   Constraints on the Risk Behavior of Commercial Banks. PhD diss, U of Pittsburgh, 1968; -3f

Nevin, E.   Some Reflections on the New York New Issue Market. OEP, 13 (Feb, 1961), 84-102; -16a
>   **& Davis, E. W.**   The London Clearing Banks. Elek, 1970; -3f

Nevins, A. J.   Some Effects of Uncertainty: Simulation of a Model of Price. QJE, 80 (Feb, 1966), 73-87; -9c

Newbould, G. D.   The Benefits and Costs of a Stock Exchange Quotation. BM, 203 (Jun, 1967), 359-365; -2f
>   Business Finance. Harrap, 1970; -22a
>   Management and Merger Activity. Guthstead, 1970; -26a
>   See also **Lehr, M. E. & Newbould, G. D.**
>   See also **Merrett, A. J.; Howe, M. & Newbould, G. D.**
>   See also **Merrett, A. J. & Newbould, G. D.**
>   See also **Rose, H. B. & Newbould, G. D.**

Newell, G. E.   Published Quarterly Financial Data: Their Adequacy for Investment Decision Making. PhD diss, Mich St U, 1969; -8d

Newman, M.
>   See **Wherry, R. H. & Newman, M.**

New York Stock Exchange.   Comparative Price Performance of New 1959 and 1960 Listings on the New York Stock Exchange. New York Stock

Exchange, Department of Research and Statistics, 1962; -2f

Institutional Shareownership. The New York Stock Exchange, Jun 1964; -3e

The 17 Million: 1962 Census of Shareowners in America. The New York Stock Exchange, 1962; -3a

Und^rstan^ing Preferred Stocks and Bonds. The New York Stock Exchange, 1966; -19i

New York University. The Capital Market in Japan. NYU, C.J.Devine Institute of Finance, 1962; -2c

Newell, G. E. Revisions of Reported Quarterly Earnings. JB, 44 (Jul, 1971), 282-285; -8c

Niarchos, N. A. Statistical Analysis of Transactions of the Athens Stock Exchange. PhD diss, Nottingham U, 1971; -11c

& Granger, C. W. J. The Gold Sovereign Market in Greece—An Unusual Speculative Market. JF, forthcoming; -21d

Nichols, A. The Optimal Rate of Investment in a Firm: Comment. JF, 25 (Jun, 1970), 682-684; -25c

Nichols, D. A. A Note on Inflation and Common Stock Values. JF, 23 (Sep, 1968), 655-657; -6b

Nichols, D. M. Trading in Federal Funds. Washington, D.C.: Board of Governors of the Federal Reserve System, 1965; -20c

Nichols, D. R. See **Brown, H. A., Jr. & Nichols, D. R.**

Nicholson, G. A. Jr. & O'Hara, T. E. Investment Clubs. FAJ, 24 (May-Jun, 1968), 141-146; -3b

Nicholson, S. F. Price-Earnings Ratios. FAJ, 16 (Jul-Aug, 1960, 43-45; -8g

Price Ratios in Relation to Investment Results. FAJ, 24 (Jan-Feb, 1968), 105-109; -8g

Niebuhr, W. D. See **Robichek, A. A. & Niebuhr, W. D.**

Niederhoffer, V. Alphabetical Properties of Stock Prices. FAJ, 24 (Mar-Apr, 1968), 105-111

The Analysis of World Events and Stock Prices. JB, 44 (Apr, 1971), 193-219; -11a

Clustering of Stock Prices. OR, 13 (1959), 258-265; -11b

The Predictive Content of First-Quarter Earnings Reports. JB, 43 (Jan, 1970), 60-62; -8a

World Events and Stock Prices: a Study of Large New York Times Headlines and Subsequent Movements in the Standard and Poor's Composite Index. PhD diss, U of Chicago, 1969; -11a

& Bossell, S. Effect of Quantitative Federal Reserve Actions on the Bond and Stock Market. Paper for the Seminar on the Analysis of Security Prices, U of Chicago, Nov 1969; -6e

& Osborne, M. F. M. Market Making and Reversal on the Stock Exchange. JASA, 61 (Dec, 1966), 897-916; -11c

& Regan, P. J. Earnings Changes, Analysts' Forecasts and Stock Prices. FAJ, 28 (May-Jun, 1972), 65-71; -8d

See also **Brown, P. & Niederhoffer, V.**

See also **Lorie, J. H. & Niederhoffer, V.**

Nielsen, E. S. Market Value and Financial Structure in the Railroad Industry. PhD diss, MIT, 1961; -23c

Market Value and Financial Structure in the Railroad Industry. The Travelers Insurance Company, Occasional Paper No. 4, Mar 1961; -23c

Niendorf, R. J. Changes in the Price Relationship between Investment-Grade Bonds and Preferred Stocks. PhD diss, U of Wis, 1969; -19i

Nightingale, R. D.   Money Supply and the Stock Market. IA, 23 (Jun, 1969), 5-10;-6d

Nimaroff, S.   See **Seghers, P. D.; Reinhart, W. J. & Nimaroff, S.**

Nimrod, V. L. & Bower, R. S.   Commodities and Computers. JFQA, 2 (Mar, 1967), 58-73;-21a

Nogee, P.   See **Mosteller, F. & Nogee, P.**

Norby, W. C.   Some Contrary Views On the Professional Status of Financial Analysis. FAJ, 24 (Mar-Apr, 1968), 11-13;-4c
> Profile of the Financial Analyst. FAJ, 24 (Jul-Aug, 1968), 11-15;-4c
> See also **Stern, W. P. & Norby, W. C.**

Norgaard, R. L.   Evaluating Intercorporate Risk, Returns, and Trends. JFQA, 6 (Sep, 1971), 1069-1082;-10o
> & Longstreet, J. R.   Cases in Financial Management, 2nd ed. Wadsworth Pub 1964; -1c
> > & Vaughn, D. E.   Cases in Financial Decision Making. P-H, 1967;-1c
> See also **Thompson, F. C. & Norgaard, R. L.**

Noritake, Y.   The Japanese Capital Market. BM, 205 (May, 1968), 287-291;-2c

Norr, D.   Investment Theories and Applications. FAJ, 16 (Jul-Aug 1960), 121-124;-4a

Norstrøm, C. J.   A Mathematical Connection Between the Present Value, the Rate of Return and the Scale of an Investment. JBF, 4 (Summer, 1972), 75-77; -25b
> A Sufficient Condition for Nonnegative Internal Rate of Return. JFQA, 7 (Jun, 1972), 1835-1840;-25b

Norton, F. E.   Administrative Organization in Capital Budgeting. JB, 28 (Oct, 1955), 291-295;-25c

Nugent, C. E.
> See **Bower, R. S.; Myers, B. C.; Nugent, C. E. & Williamson, J. P.**

Nursaw, W. G.   The Art and Practice of Investment. Hutchinson, 1963; -4a
> Principles of Pension Fund Investment. Hutchinson, 1965;-3i

Nutter, G. W.   Growth by Merger. JASÁ, 49 (Sep, 1954), 448-466;-26a

Oakford, R. V.   Capital Budgeting—a Quantitative Evaluation of Investment Alternatives. Ronald, 1970;-25c

Oakland, W. H.   Corporate Earnings and Tax Shifting in U.S. Manufacturing, 1930-1968. REStat, 54 (Aug, 1972), 235-244;-27c

O'Brien, J. W.   How Market Theory Can Help Investors Set Goals, Select Investment Managers and Appraise Investment Performance. FAJ, 26 (Jul-Aug, 1970), 91-103;-14a
> & Tito, D.   The Implications of Pension Fund Investment Policy. Paper for the Seminar on the Analysis of Security Prices, U of Chicago, Nov 1972;-3i

O'Brien, R. J.   See **Rowan, D. C. & O'Brien, R. J.**

Obst, N. P.   A Connection Between Speculation and Stability in the Foreign Exchange Market. SEJ, 34 (Jul, 1967), 146-149; -21b

Ochs, J. N.   The Appropriate Set of Discount Rates for Public Investment Decisions. PhD diss, Indiana U, 1966;-23d

O'Connor, J. J.   An Investment Analysis of the Office Building. PhD diss, NYU, 1964;-21c

O'Donnell, J. L.   Case Evidence on the Value of a New York Stock Exchange Listing. BT, 17 (Summer, 1969);-2f
> Relationships between Reported Earnings and Stock Prices in the

Electric Utility Industry. AR, 40 (Jan, 1965), 135-143; -8d

    & Goldberg, M. S. (Eds).   Elements of Financial Administration. Merrill, 1962; -22a

    See also **Henshaw, R. C., Jr.; Olson, A. C., & O'Donnell, J. L.**

O'Donnell, T. M.   The Stock Market Activity of the Corporate Insider and Future Price Movements of the Stock. MBA thesis, U of Pa, 1960; -13c

O.E.C.D. Committee for Invisible Transactions.   Capital Markets Study: Structure of Interest Rates in Some OECD Countries. O.E.C.D., 1967; - 18b

    Capital Markets Study: Utilization of Savings. O.E.C.D., 1967; -2c

    Functioning of Capital Markets. O.E.C.D., 1968; -2c

    The Supply of Capital Funds for Industrial Development in Europe: Resources, Structure and Methods. O.E.C.D., 1957; -2c

O'Hanlon, T.   The Odd News about Conglomerates. F, (Jun 15, 1967), 175-177; -26c

O'Hara, T. E.

    See **Nicholson, G. A., Jr. & O'Hara, T. E.**

O'Keefe, P. T.

    See **McMichael, S. L. & O'Keefe, P. T.**

Oliver, R. B.   Cash Tender Offers. MBA thesis, NYU, 1969; -26e

Olney, P.   Some Observations on Pension Fund Property Unit Trusts. IA, 33 (Sep, 1972), 32-41; -21c

Olsen, J. A. & Blaney, T. A.   Forecasting by Probabilities: the Copper Industry. FAJ, 24 (Mar-Apr, 1968), 36-40; -8c

Olson, A. C.   An Analysis of the Impact of Valuation Requirements on the Preferred Stock Investment Policies of Life Insurance Companies. PhD, diss, U of Minn, 1962; -19i

    See also **Henshaw, R. C., Jr.; Olson, A. C. & O'Donnell, J. L.**

O'Meara, J.

    See **Johnson, L. R.; Shapiro, E. & O'Meara, J.**

Ophir, T.

    See **Aharoni, Y. & Ophir, T.**

Orgler, Y. E.   An Unequal-Period Model for Cash Management Decisions. MSci, 16 (Oct, 1969), B77-B92; -25a

    Cash Budgeting, the Payment Schedule and Short Term Financing by Business Firms. PhD diss, Carnegie-Mellon U, 1967; -25a

    Cash Management. Methods and Models. Wadsworth Pub, 1970; -25a

    Joint Demand and Time Deposits: an Application of Inventory Control. NBR, 4 (Sep, 1966), 73-80; -25a

Orr, D.   Cash Management and the Demand for Money. Praeger, 1971; -25a

    See also **Miller, M. H. & Orr, D.**

Ortner, R.   The Concept of Yield on Common Stock. JF, 19 (May, 1964), 186-198; -5a

    An Estimate of the Time Horizon and Expected Yield for a Selected Group of Common Shares, 1935-1955. IntER, 2 (May, 1961), 179-198; -7a

Osborn, R.   The Mathematics of Investment. Har-Row, 1957; -25c

Osborn, R. C.   Business Finance: the Management Approach. Appleton, 1965; -22a

    Corporation Finance. Har-Row, 1959; -22a

    Effects of Corporate Size on Efficiency and Profitability. U of Ill Bur of Busn, 1950; -26f

    Efficiency and Profitability in Relation to Size. HBR, 29 (Mar, 1951), 82-94; -26f

    The Relative Profitability of Large, Medium Sized and Small Business. AR (Oct, 1956); -26f

Osborn, W. T.
    See **Clayton, G. & Osborn, W. T.**

Osborne, M. F. M.   Brownian Motion in the Stock Market. OR, 7 (Mar-Apr, 1959), 145-173;-11c
    The Dynamics of Stock Trading. Em, 33 (Jan, 1965), 88-113;-11c
    Periodic Structure in the Brownian Motion of Stock Prices. OR, 10 (May-Jun, 1962), 345-379;-11c, 12b
    Some Quantitative Tests for Stock Price Generating Models and Trading Folklore. JASA, 62 (Jun, 1967), 321-340;-11c
    See also **Niederhoffer, V. & Osborne, M. F. M.**

Oster, R. J.   The Cost of Capital and Investment Behavior: A Study of the Opportunity Cost of Investment, its Determinants, and its Determination of Business Investment Behavior. PhD diss, U of Cal Berkeley, 1967;-23d

O.T.C. Information Bureau.   Considerations in Listing on a Stock Exchange. New York: Arthur Schmidt & Associates Inc, 1965;-2f
    Supplement to Considerations in Listing on a Stock Exchange. New York: Arthur Schmidt & Associates Inc, 1966;-2f

Ott, D. J. & Meltzer, A. H.   Federal Tax Treatment of State and Local Securities. Brookings, 1963;-27a

Otto, E. A.
    See **Starkweather, L. P.; Otto, E. A. & Kreger, H. R.**

Oudet, B. A.   Returns on Financial Assets in Periods of Inflation. PhD diss, Indiana U, 1972;-6c

Owen, J.   Analysis of Variance Tests for Local Trends in the Standard and Poor's Index. JF, 23 (Jan, 1968), 509-514;-11c
    An Investor in the Stock Market. PhD diss, Harvard U, 1966;-11c
    See also **Kabak, I. W. & Owen, J.**

Oxenfeldt, A. R.   Valuation of Untraded and Closely Held Securities. AJ, 9 (Aug, 1953), 33-37;-7a

Ozga, S. A.   Expectations in Economic Theory. Weidenfeld & N, 1965; -9a

Packer, S. R.   Municipal Bond Ratings. FAJ, 24 (Jul-Aug, 1968), 93-97; -19f

Page, A. N.   The Variation of Mortgage Interest Rates. JB, 37 (Jul, 1964), 280-294;-21c

Page, C. S. & Canaway, E. E.   Finance for Management. Heinemann, 1966;-22a

Pain, N. R.   A Case Study in Mathematical Programming of Portfolio Selection. AS, 15 (1966), 24-36; -10c
    Uncertainty and Capital Budgeting. AR, 39 (Apr, 1964), 330-332;-25d

Paine, R. H.   Convertible Debentures. IA, 9 (Sep, 1964), 21-25; -17c

Paish, F. W.   Business Finance, 4th ed. Pitman, 1968; -22a
    Factors Determining the Long-Term Rate of Interest. IA, 4 (Dec, 1962), 20-23;-18b
    Long-Term and Short-Term Interest Rates in the United Kingdom. Man U Pr, 1966;-18b

Palance, D.   Mutual Funds—Legal Pickpockets? Vantage, 1963; -3k

Palmer, G. A.   An Approach to Stock Valuation. AJ, 12 (May, 1956), 17-19;-7b

Palmer, G. F. D.   The Majority and Minority Reports of the Commission of Inquiry into the Stock Exchange. SAJE, 34 (Jun, 1966), 93-112;-2c

Palmer, M.   Money Supply, Portfolio Adjustments and Stock Prices. FAJ, 26 (Jul-Aug, 1970), 19-22;-6d

P. A. Management Consultants Ltd.   Expenditure Evaluation Using Discounted Cash Flows: a Course of Programmed Instruction. Business Bks, 1966;-25c

Pankoff, L. D. Market Efficiency and Football Betting. JB, 41 (Apr, 1968), 203-214; -21d

The Quantification of Judgment: a Case Study. PhD diss, U of Chicago, 1967; -21d

& Virgil, R. L. Some Preliminary Findings from a Laboratory Experiment on the Usefulness of Financial Accounting Information to Security Analysts. ERA, (1970), 1-61; -8e

Papera, D. R.
See **Kimball, P. & Papera, D. R.**

Pappas, J. L.
See **Brigham, E. F. & Pappas, J. L.**
See also **Haugen, R. A. & Pappas, J. L.**

Paradis, G. E.
See **Gordon, M. J.; Paradis, G. E. & Rorke, C. H.**

Park, Y. S. Financing Operations of U.S. Firms in the Euro-bond Market. DBA diss, Harvard Bus, 1970; -20e

Parker, G. G. C.
See **Van Horne, J. C. & Parker, G. G. C.**
See also **Seelenfreund, A.; Parker, G. G. C. & Van Horne, J. C.**

Parker, H. J. The Euro-Dollar Market. Detroit: City National Bank of Detroit, 1964; -20d

Parker, J. A. An Investigation of the Ten Most Active Acquisitors in the Paper and Allied Products Industry, 1950-1965. PhD diss, U of Ok, 1968; -26a

Parker, S.
See **Friend, I. & Parker, S.**

Parker, W. M. Business Combinations and Accounting Valuation. JAR, 4 (Autumn, 1966), 149-154; -26d

Parkin, J. M.
See **Barrett, R. J.; Gray, M. R. & Parkin, J. M.**

Parks, R. H. Income and Tax Aspects of Commercial Bank Portfolio Operations in Treasury Securities. NTJ, 11 (Mar, 1958), 21-34; -3f

Portfolio Operations of Commercial Banks and the Level of Treasury Security Prices. JF, 14 (Mar, 1959), 52-66; -3f

Parr, A. F. Theory of the Capital Decision in the Regulated Firm. PhD diss, U of Ok, 1968; -25c

Pastoriza, H. Valuing Utility Earnings, Distributed and Retained. AJ, 1 (Jul, 1945), 14-18; -24b

Patinkin, D. An Indirect-Utility Approach to the Theory of Money, Assets and Savings, *in* Hahn, F. H. & Brechling, F. P. R. P. (Eds), The Theory of Interest Rates. Macmillan Int, 1966; -18a

Money, Interest and Prices, 2nd ed. Har-Row, 1964; -18a

Patni, N. K. Empirical Evaluation of Combined Fundamental and Technical Models for Stock Prices. SM thesis, MIT, 1968; -12a

Patrick, R. B. The Life Insurance Company Portfolio. AJ, 10 (Jun, 1954), 54-57; -3h

Pattison, J. C. Stock Market Prices and Economic Activity: an Empirical Examination. JBF, 3 (Autumn, 1971), 13-17; -7c

Paukert, F. The Value of Stock Exchange Transactions in Non-Government Securities, 1911-1959. Ec, 28 (Aug, 1961), 303-309; -2a

Paxson, D. A. The International Monetary Fund for Commercial Banks. DBA diss, Harvard Bus, 1969; -20d

Pease, F. The Warrant—Its Powers and its Hazards. FAJ, 19 (Jan-Feb, 1963), 25-32; -17b

Peck, L. G.   A Critique of the Filter Technique. FAJ, 22 (May-Jun, 1966), 156; -8f

Pecora, F.   Wall Street Under Oath.   S & S, 1939; -2b

Peet, C. H.   Relative Strength—a Review and Some New Results. Paper delivered to the Financial Analysts Federation, Baltimore, Oct 21, 1969; -23g

Pellatt, P. G. K.   The Analysis of Real Estate Investments Under Uncertainty. JF, 27 (May, 1972), 459-472; -21c

Pember and Boyle   British Government Securities in the 20th Century: Supplement 1950-1972. London: Pember and Boyle, 1972; -19c

Penner, R. G.   A Note on Portfolio Selection and Taxation. REStud, 31 (Jan, 1964), 83-86; -27b

Pennypacker, J. C.
        See **Zakon, A. J. & Pennypacker, J. C.**

Pepper, G. T.   The Selection and Maintenance of a Gilt-edged Portfolio. JIA, 90 (1964); -19c

Pepper, N. A.   The Money Demand and Supply Determinants of Stock Prices. PhD diss, UCLA, 1971; -6d
        & Zwick, B.   Liquidity and Income Effects of Monetary Changes on Stock Prices. UCLA, (1971), mimeo; -6d

Percus, J. & Quinto, L.   The Application of Linear Programming to Competitive Bond Bidding. Em, 24 (Oct, 1956), 413-429; -19e

Perez, R. C.   A Critical Appraisal of the Marketing Structure and Techniques Used in Distributing Mutual Fund Shares to the Investing Public. PhD diss, NYU, 1966; -3k

Persons, R. H.   Handbook of Formula Plans in the Stock Market. Am Res Co, 1967; -12f

Pesek, B.   Equilibrium Level of Transaction Services of Money. JF, forthcoming; -18a

Peston, M. H. & Yamey, B. S.   Inter-Temporal Price Relationships with Forward Markets: a Method of Analysis. Ec, 27 (Nov, 1960), 355-367; -21a

Peters, J. R.   Economics of the Canadian Corporate Bond Market. McGill-Queens U Pr, 1971; -19e

Petersen, H. A.   Risk and the Capital Structure of the Firm. PhD diss, Brown U, 1963; -23c

Peterson, D. E.   Corporate Investment Decisions and Financial Planning PhD diss, U of Ill, 1963; -25c
        & Haydon, R. B.   A Quantitative Framework for Financial Management. Irwin, 1969; -22a
        & Laughhunn, D. J.   Capital Expenditure Programming and some Alternative Approaches to Risk. MSci, 17 (Jan, 1971), 320-336; -25d
        See also **Laughhunn, D. J. & Peterson, D. E.**

Pettit, R. R.   Dividend Announcements, Security Performance and Capital Efficiency. JF, forthcoming; -11a
        & Westerfield, R.   A Model of Capital Asset Risk. JFQA, 7 (Mar, 1972), 1649-1668; -10n

Pettway, R. H.   Interest Rates on Direct Leases and Secured Term Loans. NBR, 3 (Jun, 1966), 533-537; -25g
        & Weinraub, H. J.   Profitable Bond Trading Among Bonds of the Same Risk Class and Maturity. FAJ, 25 (Nov-Dec, 1969), 125-128; -19a

Pfahl, J. K.
        See **Donaldson, E. F. & Pfahl, J. K.**

Phelps, E. S.   The Accumulation of Risky Capital: a Sequential Utility Analysis. Em, 30 (Oct, 1962), 729-743; -10k

Phillips, H. E.
    See **Frankfurter, G. M.; Phillips, H. E. & Seagle, J. P.**

Phillips, J.   The Theory and Practice of Futures Trading. Review of Marketing and Agricultural Economics (Jun, 1966);-21a

Pierce, J. L.   An Empirical Model of Commercial Bank Portfolio Management, *in* Hester, D. D. & Tobin, J. (Eds), Studies of Portfolio Behavior. Wiley, 1967; -10g

Pierce, S.   Mutual Funds—a Growth Business. AJ, 7 (4th Qtr, 1951), 23-25;-3k

Pierson, G.   Effect of Economic Policy on the Term Structure of Interest Rates. REStat, 52 (Feb, 1970), 1-11;-18f

    The Effect of Economic Policy on the Term Structure of Interest Rates. PhD diss, U of Mich, 1968;-18f

    Why Have Interest Rates Risen? REStat, 53 (Feb, 1971), 89-100; -18b

Pifer, H. W.
    See **Meyer, P. A. & Pifer, H. W.**

Pike, J. R.
    See **Gentry, J. A. & Pike, J. R.**

Pilcher, J. C.   Raising Capital with Convertible Securities. U of Mich Pr, 1955

Pinches, G. E.   Financing with Convertible Preferred Stock, 1960-1967. JF, 25 (Mar, 1970), 53-63;-17c

    Financing Corporate Mergers and Acquisitions with Convertible Preferred Stock. PhD diss, Mich St U, 1968; -17c

    & Kinney, W. R.   The Measurement of the Volatility of Common Stock Prices. JF, 26 (Mar, 1971), 119-126;-10b

    & Mingo, K.   A Multivariate Analysis of Industrial Bond Ratings. JF, forthcoming;-19e

    & Simon, G.   An Analysis of Portfolio Accumulation Strategies Employing Low-Priced Common Stocks. JFQA, 7 (Jun, 1972), 1773-1796;-5a

Pinney, A.   The Plight of the Stock Exchange. AJ, 10 (Aug, 1954), 99-102;-2b

Pippenger, J. E.   The Behavior of Flexible Exchange Rates: Theory and Evidence. PhD diss, UCLA, 1966;-21b

Platt, R. B.   The Interest Rate on Federal Funds: an Empirical Approach. JF, 25 (Jun, 1970), 585-598;-20c

Platt, S. D. & Rosen, D. A.   Put and Call Options Under Section 16 of the Securities Exchange Act. YLJ, (Apr, 1960);-17a

Plattner, R. H.   Fund Administration and Dividend Policy. QREB, 9 (Summer, 1969), 21-29; -24b

Plotkin, I. H.
    See **Conrad, G. R. & Plotkin, I. H.**

Plum, L. V.; Humphrey, J. H. & Bowyer, J. W.   Investment Analysis and Management, 2nd ed. Irwin, 1961;-4a

    & Martin, T. J.   The Significance of Conversion Parity in Valuing Common Stock Warrants. FR, 1 (Feb, 1966), 21-31;-17b

Plymen, J.
    See **Haycocks, H. W. & Plymen, J.**

Poe, J. B.   An Analysis of the Stock Dividend Distributions of New York Stock Exchange Listed Corporations. PhD diss, Harvard U, 1963;-16c

Poensgen, O. H.   The Valuation of Convertible Bonds,
    Part I: IMR, 7 (Fall, 1965), 77-92
    Part II: IMR, 7 (Spring, 1966), 83-98; -10m, 17c

Pogue, J. A.   An Inter-Temporal Model for Investment Management.

JBR, 1 (Spring, 1970), 17-34; -10k

An Adaptive Model for Investment Management. PhD diss, Carnegie IT, 1967; -10c

An Extension of the Markowitz Portfolio Selection Model to Include Variable Transactions Costs, Short Sales, Leverage Policies and Taxes. JF, 25 (Dec, 1970), 1005-1028; -10c

See also **Cohen, K. J. & Pogue, J. A.**

Pogue, T. F. The Corporate Dividend Decision: A Cross-Section Study of the Relationship between Dividends and Investment. PhD diss, Yale U, 1968; -24a

A Cross-Section Study of the Relationship between Dividends and Investment. YEE, 11 (1971), 181-218; -24a

& Soldofsky, R. M. What's in a Bond Rating? JFQA, 4 (Jun, 1969), 201-228; -19f

Polakoff, M. E. Public Pension Funds. FAJ, 22 (May-Jun, 1966), 75-81; -3i

et al. Financial Institutions and Markets. HM, 1970; -3e

Pollak, R. A. Additive Von-Neumann-Morgenstern Utility Functions. Em, 30 (Oct, 1962), 729-743; -9a

Poole, W. McKinnon on Futures Markets and Buffer Stocks. JPE, 78 (Sep-Oct, 1970), 1185-1190; -21a

Speculative Prices as Random Walks: an Analysis of Ten Time Series of Flexible Exchange Rates. SEJ, 33 (Apr, 1967), 468-478; -21b

Poore, D. M. A Behavioral Analysis of the Short-Range Capital Budgeting Decision Process. PhD diss, U of Pittsburgh, 1966; -25c

Popovic, M. D. A Case for Security Analysis. AJ, 2 (1st Qtr, 1946), 31-36; -4a

Porter, R. B. Application of Stochastic Dominance Principles to the Problem of Asset Selection Under Risk. PhD diss, Purdue U, 1971; -10h

& Gaumnitz, J. E. Stochastic Dominance vs. Mean-Variance Portfolio Analysis: an Empirical Evaluation. AER, 62 (Jun, 1972), 438-446; -10h

Porter, R. C. A Model of Bank Portfolio Selection. YEE, 1 (Fall, 1961), 323-359; -10g

Porter, S. Regulation of Financial Analysis. FAJ, 19 (May-Jun, 1963), 104; -4c

Porterfield J. T. S. Dividends, Dilution, and Delusion. HBR, 37 (Nov-Dec, 1959), 56-61; -24b

Investment Decisions and Capital Costs. P-H, 1965; -25c

Powers, M. J. An Economic Analysis of the Futures Market for Pork Bellies. PhD diss, U of Wis, 1966; -21a

Praetz, P. D. Australian Share Prices and the Random Walk Hypothesis. AJS, 11 (1969), 123-129; -11c

The Distribution of Price Changes. JB, 45 (Jan, 1972), 49-55; -11b

Prais, S. J. The Financial Experience of Giant Companies. EJ, 67 (Jun, 1957), 249-264; -26f

Prather, C. L. Financing Business Firms, 3rd ed. Irwin, 1966; -22a

Money and Banking, 9th ed. Irwin, 1969; -3f

Pratt, J. W. Risk Aversion in the Small and in the Large. Em, 32 (Jan-Apr, 1964), 122-136; -9a

Raiffa, H., & Schlaifer, R. The Foundations of Decision Under Uncertainty. JASA, 59 (Jun, 1964), 353-375; -9c

Pratt, S. P. Bibliography on Risks and Rates of Return for Common Stocks. FAJ, 24 (May-Jun, 1968), 151-166; -1a

Relationship Between Risk and Rate of Return for Common Stocks. DBA diss, Indiana U, 1967; -10l

Relationship between Variability of Past Rates of Return and Levels of Future Rates of Return for Common Stocks, 1926-60. Paper for the Seminar on the Analysis of Security Prices, U of Chicago, May 1967; -10*l*

    & DeVere, C. W.   Relationship between Insider Trading and Rates of Return for NYSE Common Stocks, 1960-1966. Paper for the Seminar on the Analysis of Security Prices. U of Chicago, May 1968; -13c

Pratten, C. F.   A Case Study of a Conglomerate Merger. Moorgate,(Spring, 1970), 27-54; -26c

    The Merger Boom in Manufacturing Industry. LBR, 90 (Oct, 1968), 39-55; -26a

Prentice-Hall Editorial Staff   Encyclopedic Dictionary of Business Finance. P-H, 1960; -22a

Press, S. J.   A Compound Events Model for Security Prices. JB, 40 (Jul, 1968), 317-335; -11b

Priest, W. W., Jr.   Rate of Return as a Criterion for Investment Decisions. FAJ, 21 (Jul-Aug, 1965), 109-113; -25c

    See also **Treynor, J. L.; Priest, W. W., Jr.; Fisher, L. & Higgins, C. A.**

Pringle, J. J.

    See **Robichek, A. A.; Cohn, R. A. & Pringle, J. J.**

Pringle, J. M.   The Mortgage Market and Its Relationship to Markets for Government, High-Grade Corporate and Municipal Bonds. FAJ, 22 (May-Jun, 1966), 105-106; -21c

Prochnow, H. V. (Ed).   American Financial Institutions. P-H, 1951; -3e

Pruitt, D. G.

    See **Coombs, C. H. & Pruitt, D. G.**

Prussman, D. F.

    See **Murphy, G. W. & Prussman, D. F.**

Puckett, M.

    See **Friend, I. & Puckett, M.**

Puu, T.   A Simple Graphic Method for Estimating the Yield of Bonds, *in* Hahn, F. M. & Brechling, F. P. R. (Eds), The Theory of Interest Rates. Macmillan Int, 1966; -19a

    Some Reflections on the Theories of Choice Between Alternative Investment Opportunities. WA, 99 (1967), 107-123; -9c

Pye, G.   A Markov Model of the Term Structure. QJE, 80 (Feb, 1966), 60-72; -18f

    Minimax Policies for Selling an Asset and Dollar Averaging. MSci, 17 (Mar, 1971), 379-393; -12f

    Minimax Portfolio Policies. FAJ, 28 (Mar-Apr, 1972), 56-60; -10f

    On the Tax Structure of Interest Rates. QJE, 83 (Nov, 1969), 562-579; -18f

    Portfolio Selection and Security Prices. REStat, 49 (Feb, 1967), 111-115; -10c

    Preferential Tax Treatment of Capital Gains, Optimal Dividend Policy, and Capital Budgeting. QJE, 86 (May, 1972), 226-242; -25c

    Value of Call Deferment on a Bond: Some Empirical Results. JF, 22 (Dec, 1967), 623-636; -19h

    The Value of a Call Option on a Bond. JPE, 74 (Apr, 1966), 200-205; -19h

Pyle, D. H.   Asset Substitution, Inflation and Interest Rates. Wkg paper No. 2, Institute of Business and Economic Research, U of Cal Berkeley, 1971; -18c

    Observed Price Expectations and Interest Rates. REStat, 54 (Aug, 1972), 275-280; -18c

On the Theory of Financial Intermediation. PhD diss,MIT,1968;-3d

On the Theory of Financial Intermediation. JF, 26 (Jun, 1971), 737-747;-3d

    & Turnovsky, S. J.   Risk Aversion in Chance Constrained Portfolio Selection. MSci, 18 (Nov, 1971), 218-225;-10f

    Safety-First and Expected Utility Maximization in Mean-Standard Deviation Portfolio Analysis. REStat, 52 (Feb, 1970), 75-81;-10f

Quandt, R. E.   On the Size Distribution of Firms. AER, 56 (Jun, 1966), 416-432;-26f

    See also **Baumol, W. J.; Heim, P.; Malkiel, B. G., & Quandt, R. E.**

    See also **Baumol, W. J.; Malkiel, B. G., & Quandt, R. E.**

    See also **Baumol, W. J. & Quandt, R. E.**

    See also **Malkiel, B. G. & Quandt, R. E.**

Que, A.

    See **Walter, J. E. & Que, A.**

Quinto, L.

    See **Percus, J. & Quinto, L.**

Quirin, G. D.   The Capital Expenditure Decision. Irwin, 1967;-25c

Quirk, J. P.   The Capital Structure of Firms and the Risk of Failure. IntER, 2 (May, 1961), 210-228;-23c

    & Saposnik, R.   Admissibility and Measurable Utility Functions. REStud, 29 (Feb, 1962), 140-146;-9a, 10h

Qureshi, M. A.   Mutuality as a Factor in the Growth of the Mutual Fund Industry. PhD diss, U of S Cal, 1965;-3k

Rabin, J. J.

    See **Cohen, K. J. & Rabin, J. J.**

Radcliffe, Lord

    See **Committee on the Working of the Monetary System**

Radner, R.   Competitive Equilibrium under Uncertainty. Em, 36 (Jan, 1968), 31-58;-9d

    Equilibrium of Spot and Futures Markets Under Uncertainty. Technical Report No. 24, Center for Research in Management Science, U of Cal Berkeley, Apr 1967;-21a

    Problems in the Theory of Markets under Uncertainty. AER, 60 (May, 1970), 454-464;-9d

Raiffa, H.   Decision Analysis: Introductory Lectures on Choices Under Uncertainty. Addison-Wes, 1968;-9c

    Risk, Ambiguity and the Savage Axioms: Comment. QJE, 74 (Nov, 1961), 690-694;-9a

    See also **Pratt, J. W.; Raiffa, H. & Schlaifer, R.**

Ramanathan, K. V. & Rappaport, A.   Size, Growth Rates and Merger Valuation. AR, 46 (Oct, 1971), 733-745; -26a

Ramsey, C. M. & Behrens, C.   Analysing the Performance of Security Analysts. Paper for the Seminar on the Analysis of Security Prices, U of Chicago, Nov 1969;-14c

Ramsey, F. P.   Truth and Probability, *in* The Foundations of Mathematics and Other Logical Essays. Paul Trench, 1931;-9a

Randell, D. H.   Evolution of the Analyst. FAJ, 17 (Mar-Apr, 1961), 67-75;-4c

Rankin, D. F.   Security-based Conglomerate Acquisitions: the Effect on Residual Ownership. PhD diss, U of Miss, 1970;-26c

Rao, C. U., & Litzenberger, R. H.   Leverage and the Cost of Capital in a Less Developed Capital Market: Comment. JF, 26 (Jun, 1971), 777-782; -23c

Rao, K.

    See **Sarma, L. & Rao, K.**

Rao, N. K.   Equivalent-Risk Class Hypothesis. JFQA, 7 (Jun, 1972), 1763-1772; -23c

Rapp, W. A.   The Role of Reacquired Common Stock in Financial Management. PhD diss, Northwestern U, 1966; -16d

Rappaport, A.
  See **Lerner, E. M. & Rappaport, A.**
  See also **Ramanathan, K. V. & Rappaport, A.**

Rappaport, L. H.   SEC Accounting Practice and Procedure, 3rd ed. Ronald, 1971; -2e

Ravenscroft, E. A.   Return on Investment: Fit the Method to Your Need. HBR, 38 (Mar-Apr, 1960), 97-109; -25c

Ray, H. C.   Pros and Cons of Timing Methods. AJ, 9 (Jun, 1953), 52-54; -7d

Rayner, A. C.
  See **Little, I. M. D. & Rayner, A. C.**

Readett, P. B., Jr.   The Price Behavior of Stocks on Their Ex-Dividend Dates. SM thesis, MIT, 1956; -24c

Reading, B.   The Forward Pound, 1951-1959. EJ, 70 (Jun, 1960), 304-319; -21b

Reddaway, W. B.   An Analysis of Take-Overs. LBR, (Apr, 1972), 8-19; -26a

Redlich, F.   Towards a Better Theory of Risk. Explorations in Entrepreneurial History, (Oct, 1957), 33-39; -9c

Redwood, H.   The Fisons Shareholder Survey. LRP, 3 (Apr, 1971), 2-6; -3a

Reed, E. W.   Commercial Bank Management. Har-Row, 1963; -3f
  & Woodland, D. L.   Cases in Commercial Banking. Appleton, 1970; -3f

Rees, G. L.   Britain's Commodity Markets. Elek, 1972; -21a

Rees, H. J. B.
  See **Granger, C. W. J. & Rees, H. J. B.**
  See also **Labys, W. C.; Rees, H. J. B., & Elliott, C. M.**

Reeves, J. P.   Tax Aspects of Corporate Mergers, Exchanges, Redemptions, Liquidations, and Reorganisations. Vantage, 1967; -27a

Regan, P. J.
  See **Niederhoffer, V. & Regan, P. J.**

Reid, G. C.
  See **Kemp, A. G. & Reid, G. C.**

Reid, S. R.   Corporate Mergers and Acquisitions Involving Firms in Missouri: Some Economic Results and Administrative Policies and Procedures. PhD diss, St Louis U, 1962; -26b
  Mergers, Managers, and the Economy. McGraw, 1968; -26b
  See also **Cohen, K. J. & Reid, S. R.**

Reierson, R. L.   The Euro-Dollar Market. New York: Bankers Trust Co., 1964; -20d
  New Forces in the Money Market. JF, 17 (May, 1962), 220-229; -20a

Reiling, H. B.
  See **Hayes, S. L. III & Reiling, R. B.**

Reilly, F. K.   Evidence Regarding a Segmented Stock Market. JF, 27 (Jun, 1972), 607-626; -10*l*
  First Look at O-T-C Volume. FAJ, 25 (Jan-Feb, 1969), 124-128; -13a
  Our Misnamed Stock Price Indicators. KanBR, 20 (Jan, 1967), 4-9; -5b
  Price Changes in NYSE, Amex and OTC Stocks Compared. FAJ, 27 (Mar-Apr, 1971), 54-59; -5a
  What Determines the Ratio of Exchange in Corporate Mergers. FAJ, 18 (Nov-Dec, 1962), 47-50; -26a

& Hatfield, K. Experience with New Stock Issues. FAJ, 25 (Sep-Oct, 1969), 73-82; -16a

See also **Johnson, G. L.; Reilly, F. K. & Smith, R. E.**

Reinhart, W. J.

See **Seghers, P. D.; Reinhart, W. J. & Nimaroff, S.**

Reisman, A. On the Valuation of Growth Equity Shares. Paper for the 12th International Meeting of TIMS, Vienna, Sep 1965; -7b

& Buffa, E. S. A General Model for Investment Policy. MSci, 8 (Apr, 1962), 304-310; -25c

See also **Sloane, W. R. & Reisman, A.**

Rejda, G. E. Dollar Averaging and Other Formula Plans: Their Role in the Investment Operations of Insurance Companies. PhD diss, U of Pa, 1962; -3h

The Role of Dollar Averaging in the Common Stock Investment Operations of Life Insurance Companies. JI, (Dec, 1962); -3h

Remaley, W. A. Suboptimization in Mean-Variance Efficient Set Analysis. PhD diss, NYU, 1971; -10c

Renshaw, E. F. Estimating the Return on S & P's Industrial Price Index. FAJ, 25 (Jan-Feb, 1969), 121-123; -7d

Foundations of Security Analysis. AJ, 14 (Feb, 1958), 57-61; -4a

A Note on the Arithmetic of Capital Budgeting Decisions. JB, 30 (Jul, 1957), 193-201; -20c

A Note on Behavior in the Stock Market. AJ, 14 (Aug, 1958), 19-23; -12f

Portfolio Balance Models in Perspective: Some Generalizations That Can Be Derived From the Two-Asset Case. JFQA, 2 (Jun, 1967), 123-149; -10c

The Random Walk Hypothesis, Performance Measurement, and Portfolio Theory. FAJ, 24 (Mar-Apr, 1968), 114-119; -11c

Stock Market Instability. FAJ, 23 (Jul-Aug, 1967), 80-83; -10b

The Theory of Financial Leverage and Conglomerate Mergers. CMR, 11 (Fall, 1968), 79-84; -26c

& Feldstein, P. J. The Case for an Unmanaged Investment Company. FAJ, 16 (Jan-Feb, 1960), 43-46; -3k

& Renshaw, V. D. Some Notes on the Rationality Model. SEJ, 36 (Jan, 1970), 244-251; -10j

& Renshaw, V. D. Test of the Random Walk Hypothesis. FAJ, 26 (Sep-Oct, 1970), 51-60; -11c

Renshaw, V. D.

See **Renshaw, E. F. & Renshaw, V. D.**

Rentz, W. F. Optimal Consumption and Investment Policies. PhD diss, U of Rochester, 1971; -10k

Renwick, F. B. Economic Growth and Distributions of Change in Stock Market Prices. IMR, 9 (Spring, 1965), 39-68; -11b

Introduction to Investments and Finance: Theory and Analysis. Macmillan, 1971; -4a

Theory of Investment Behavior and Empirical Analysis of Stock Market Price Relatives. MSci, 15 (Sep, 1968), 57-71; -11b

et al. Portfolio Management for Commercial Banks. Presidents, 1971; -3f

Repsold, G. J. The Relationship Between the Rate of Return and Risk. Unp ms, May 1964; -10*l*

Resek, R. W. Multidimensional Risk and the Modigliani-Miller Hypothesis. JF, 25 (Mar-Apr, 1970), 47-51; -23c

Reul, R. I. Profitability Index for Investments. HBR, 35 (Jul-Aug, 1957), 116-132; -25c

Revell, J.
    See **Stone, R.; Revell, J. & Moyle, J.**

Revsine, L.   Predictive Ability, Market Prices and Operating Flows. AR, 46 (Jul, 1971), 480-489; -8d

Rich, C. D.   The Rationale of the Use of the Geometric Average as an Investment Index. JIA, 74 (1948), 338-339; -5b

Richardson, D.   Investment Companies Throughout the Free World. FAJ, 21, (Jan-Feb, 1965), 90-91; -3k

Richardson, L. K.   Misconceptions About Earnings Dilution in Electric Utility Analysis. FAJ, 20 (Sep-Oct, 1964), 58-62; -23d

Richardson, R. A.   Financial Forecasting for Capital Budgeting. DBA diss, U of S Cal, 1968; -25c

Richebächer, K.   Structural Weaknesses of Europe's Capital Markets. Banker 117, (Dec, 1967), 1048-1055; -2c

Richter, M. K.   Cardinal Utility, Portfolio Selection and Taxation. REStud, 27 (Jun, 1960), 152-166; -27b

Ricks, M. B.
    See **Brigham, E. F. & Ricks, M. B.**

Ricks, R. B.   Imputed Returns on Real Estate Financed with Life Insurance Company Loans. JF, 24 (Dec, 1969), 921-937; -21c
    Recent Trends in International Real Estate Investment. Research Report 23, Center for Real Estate and Urban Economics, U of Cal Berkeley, 1964; -21c
    & Weston, J. F.   Land as a Growth Investment. FAJ, 22 (Jul-Aug, 1966), 69-78; -21c

Rie, D.   Preliminary Test of a Theory of Market Returns when Capitalization Rates are Variable. Unp ms, Wharton School of Finance and Commerce, U of Pa, 1970; -10l

Rieber, M.   Bids, Bid Patterns and Collusion in the Auction Market for Treasury Bills. JLE, 10 (Oct, 1967), 149-168; -20b
    Collusion in the Auction Market for Treasury Bills. JPE, 72 (Oct, 1964), 509-512; -20b
    The Primary Market for United States Treasury Bills. PhD diss, MIT, 1963; -20b

Riefler, W. W.   Money Rates and Money Markets in the United States. Har-Row, 1930; -20a

Riegle, D. W. & Blake, C. W.
    See **Blake, C. W. & Riegle, D. W.**

Riehle, R. C.   Moody's Municipal Ratings. FAJ, 24 (May-Jun, 1968), 71-73; -19f

Riggs, H. E.   The Economics of 'Tax Switching' FAJ, 19 (Sep-Oct, 1963), 25-31; -27a

Rinfret, P. A.   Investment Managers Are Worth Their Keep. FAJ, 24 (Mar-Apr, 1968), 163-170; -11c

Ring, A. A.   The Valuation of Real Estate, 2nd ed. P-H, 1970; -21c

Rischer, G.   Computers and the Stock Market. FAJ, 17 (Jul-Aug, 1961), 91-93; -4e

Rix, M. S.   Stock Market Economics. Pitman, 1963; -4a

Robbins, S. M.   A Bigger Role for Income Bonds. HBR, 33 (Nov-Dec, 1955), 100-115; -19e
    The Securities Markets, Operations and Issues. Free Pr, 1966; -2b
    & Terleckyj, N. E.   Money Metropolis; a Locational Study of Financial Activities in the New York Region. Harvard U Pr, 1960; -2b
    & Werner, W.   Professor Stigler Revisited. JB, 37 (Oct, 1964), 406-413; -2e

See also **Cohen, J. B. & Robbins, S. M.**

Roberts, H. V.   Probabilistic Prediction. JASA, 60 (Mar, 1965), 50-62; -9c

Risk, Ambiguity and the Savage Axioms: Comment. QJE, 77 (May, 1963), 327-336; -9a

Stock Market 'Patterns' and Financial Analysis: Methodological Suggestions. JF, 14 (Mar, 1959), 1-10; -11c

Robichek, A. A. (Ed).   Financial Research and Management Decisions. Wiley, 1967; -22a

Risk and the Value of Securities. JFQA, 4 (Dec, 1969), 513-538; -10*l*

& Bogue, M. C.   A Note on the Behavior of Expected Price/Earnings Ratios over Time. JF, 26 (Jun, 1971), 731-736; -7b

Cohn, R. A. & Pringle, J. J.   Returns on Alternative Investment Media and Implications for Portfolio Construction. JB, 45 (Jul, 1972), 427-443; -5a

& Coleman, A. B.   Management of Financial Institutions: Notes and Cases. HR & W, 1967; -1c

McDonald, J. G. & Higgins, R. C.   Some Estimates of the Cost of Capital to the Electric Utility Industry, 1954-57: Comment. AER, 57 (Dec, 1967), 1278-1288; -23c

& Myers, S. C.   Conceptual Problems in the Use of Risk Adjusted Discount Rates. JF, 21 (Dec, 1966), 727-730; -23d

& Myers, S. C.   Optimal Financing Decisions. P-H, 1965; -23c

& Myers, S. C.   Problems in the Theory of Optimal Capital Structure. JFQA, 1 (Jun, 1966), 1-35; -23c

& Myers, S. C.   Valuation of the Firm: Effects of Uncertainty in the Market Context. JF, 21 (May, 1966), 215-227; -9c

& Niebuhr, W. D.   Tax-Induced Bias in Reported Treasury Yields. JF, 25 (Dec, 1970), 1081-1090; -20b

Teichroew, D. & Jones, J. M.   Optimal Short-Term Financing Decision. MSci, 12 (Sep, 1965), 1-36; -25a

& Van Horne, J. C.   Abandonment Value and Capital Budgeting. JF, 22 (Dec, 1967), 577-589; -25c

See also **Myers, S. C. & Robichek, A. A.**

See also **Teichroew, D.; Robichek, A. A. & Montalbano, M.**

Robinson, F. A., Jr.   An Inquiry into the Dividend Practices of Industrial Corporations. PhD diss, NYU, 1951; -24b

Robinson, G. J.   Going Public—Successful Securities Underwriting, 2nd ed. Boardman, 1971; -16a

Robinson, J.   The Rate of Interest. Em, 19 (Apr, 1951), 92-111; -18b

Forecasting Interest Rates. JB, 27 (Jan, 1954), 87-100; -18b

Robinson, R. I.   The Management of Bank Funds, 2nd ed. McGraw, 1962; -3f

Money and Capital Markets. McGraw, 1964; -2b

Postwar Market for State and Local Government Securities. Princeton U Pr, 1970; -19d

& Bartell, R., Jr.   Uneasy Partnership SEC/NYSE. HBR, 43 (Jan-Feb, 1965), 76-88; -2e

Boehmler, E. W.; Gane, F. H. & Farwell, L. C. (Eds).   Financial Institutions, 3rd ed. Irwin, 1960; -3e

& Johnson, R. W.   Self Correcting Problems in Finance, 2nd ed. Allyn, 1970; -22a

Robinson, R. S.   Measuring the Risk Dimension of Investment Performance. JF, 25 (May, 1970), 455-468; -14b

See also **Miller, F. B. & Robinson, R. S.**

Robson, P.   Index-Linked Bonds. REStud, 28 (Oct, 1960), 57-68; -19a

Rockley, L. E.   Capital Investment Decisions: a Manual for Profit Planning.

Business Bks, 1968; -25c

Rockwell, C. S.   Normal Backwardation, Forecasting and the Return to Commodity Futures Traders. FRIS, 7 (Suppl 1967), 107-130; -21a

Profits, Normal Backwardation and Forecasting in Commodity Futures. PhD diss, U of Cal Berkeley, 1964; -21a

Rogers, A. Y.   Management of Trusteed Pension Funds; Review of Fiduciary Responsibility. TE, (Mar, 1967); -3i

Rogoff, D. L.   The Forecasting Properties of Insiders' Transactions. DBA diss, Mich St U, 1964; -13c

Rohr, R. J.

See **Lloyd, C.; Rohr, R. J. & Walker, M.**

Rolen, C. O.   An Analysis and Evaluation of Earnings per Share. PhD diss, U of Ark, 1969; -8c

Rolfe, S. E.   Capital Markets in Atlantic Economic Relationships. The Atlantic Institute, 1967; -2c, 20d

Roll, R.   The Behavior of Interest Rates: an Application of the Efficient Market Model to U.S. Treasury Bills. Basic, 1970; -18f

Bias in Fitting the Sharpe Model to Time Series Data. JFQA, 4 (Sep, 1969), 271-289; -10c

The Efficient Market Model Applied to U.S. Treasury Bill Rates. PhD diss, U of Chicago, 1968; -18f

Interest Rates on Monetary Assets and Commodity Price Index Changes. JF, 27 (May, 1972), 251-278; -18c

Investment Diversification and Bond Maturity. JF, 26 (Mar, 1971), 51-56; -18f

Some Preliminary Evidence on the 'Growth Optimum' Model. Wkg Paper No. 3-71-2, Graduate School of Industrial Administration, Carnegie-Mellon U, Jul 1971; -10j

See also Fama, E. F.; Fisher, L.; Jensen, M. C. & Roll, R.

See also Fama, E. F. & Roll, R.

See also Kaplan, R. S. & Roll, R.

Roosa, R. V.   Federal Reserve Operations in the Money and Government Securities Markets. New York: Federal Reserve Bank, 1956; -20b

Root, C. D., Jr.   Importance of Investment Yield (in Pension and Profit-Sharing Plans). TE, (Jul, 1967); -3i

Rorke, C. H.

See **Gordon, M. J.; Paradis, G. E. & Rorke, C. H.**

Rose, A. M.   A Social Psychological Approach to the Study of the Stock Market. Kyk, 19 (1966), 267-287; -4d

Rose, H. B.   Corporation Tax and Share Prices—Some Reflections on 'Supply' Factors. IA, 19 (Dec, 1967), 3-9; -27c

Disclosure in Company Accounts (Eaton Paper No. 1). Econ Affairs, 1963; -2e

The Economic Background to Investment. Cambridge U Pr, 1960; -6a

Industry, New Issues and the Equity Market. DBR, 149 (Mar, 1964), 19-37; -16b

Investment Policy and Capital Gains Tax. IA, 20 (Jun, 1968), 3-14; -27d

Price-Earnings Multiples and Long Term Rates of Return. IA, 21 (Oct, 1968), 15-23; -7d

Reflections on the Equity Boom, 1966-69. TBR, 82 (Jun, 1969), 4-24; -7d

Share Price Indices and the Measurement of Investment Performance. IA, 31 (Dec, 1971), 3-9; -5b

Some Aspects of the New Tax System. IA, 33 (Sep, 1972), 3-11; -27a

    & Newbould, G. D.   The 1967 Take-over Boom. Moorgate,(Autumn, 1967); -26a

Rose, J. R.   The Cost of Capital, Corporation Finance, and the Theory of Investment: Comment. AER, 49 (Sep, 1959), 638-639; -23c

Rose, P. J.   Some Aspects of Private Pension Funds and the Capital Market. ER, 43 (Sep, 1967), 354-370; -3i

Rosen, D. A.

    See **Platt, S. D. & Rosen, D. A.**

Rosen, L. R.   Go Where the Money Is: a Guide to Understanding and Entering the Securities Business. Dow Jones-Irwin, 1969; -4c

Rosen, M. N.   Strategies for Writers of Puts and Calls. SM thesis, MIT, 1965; -17a

Rosenberg, B.   Statistical Analysis of Price Series Obscured by Averaging Measures. JFQA, 6 (Sep, 1971), 1083-1094; -5b

Rosenberg, M.   A Study of the Risk Factor Implicit in Securities Prices. PhD diss, Columbia U, 1968; -10b

Rosenfeld, L.   Electronic Computers and Their Place in Security Analysis. AJ, 13 (Feb, 1957), 51-53; -4e

Rosenhead, J.

    See **Gupta, S. K. & Rosenhead, J.**

Rosett, R. N.   Estimating Time Horizons and Expected Yields: A Comment. IntER, 4 (Jan, 1963), 105-107; -7a

    Estimating the Utility of Wealth from Call Option Transactions, *in* Hester, D. D. & Tobin, J. (Eds), Risk Aversion and Portfolio Choice. Wiley, 1967; -10m, 17a

    Gambling and Rationality. JPE, 73 (Dec, 1965), 595-607; -9a

    Measuring the Perception of Risk, *in* Borch, K. & Mossin, J. E.(Eds), Risk and Uncertainty. Macmillan Int, 1968; -9c

Roskamp, K. W.   Factors Influencing Portfolio Selection: A Simple Model. Kyk, 20 (1967), 502-510; -10g

Rotnem, R. A.   Methods for Determining Stock Market Trends. AJ, 2 (3rd Qtr, 1946), 12-21; -7d

Rowan, D. C. & O'Brien, R. J.   Expectations, the Interest Rate Structure and Debt Policy, *in* Hilton, K. & Heathfield, D. F., The Econometric Study of the United Kingdom. Macmillan Int, 1970; -18f

Roy, A. D.   Safety First and the Holding of Assets. Em, 20 (Jul, 1952), 431-449; -10f

Royama, S. & Hamada, K.   Substitution and Complementarity in the Choice of Risky Assets, *in* Hester, D. D. & Tobin, J. E. (Eds), Risk Aversion and Portfolio Choice. Wiley, 1967; -9a

Rozen, M. E.   The Changing Structure of Financial Institutions. QREB, 2 (Nov, 1962), 69-80; -3e

Rubinstein, M.   A Synthesis of Corporate Financial Theory. JF, forthcoming; -22a

Rubner, A.   The Ensnared Shareholder. Macmillan Int, 1965; -24b

Rudolph, J. A.   The Money Supply and Common Stock Prices. FAJ, 28 (Mar-Apr, 1972), 19-25; -6e

Rueschhoff, N. G.   Treasury Stock Practices of Industrial Corporations with Listed Common Stocks. PhD diss, U of Neb, 1968; -16d

Ruff, R. T.   The Effect of Selection & Recommendation of a Stock of the Month. FAJ, 19 (Mar-Apr, 1963), 41-43; -15c

Ruffin, R. J.   Free Reserves, Vault Cash and the Portfolio Behavior of Banks. JPE, 75 (Dec, 1967), 889-892; -3f

Rush, D. F.   Corporate Risk-Rate of Return Performance, 1948-1966. DBA diss, Indiana U, 1971; -10o

Russell, A. & Taylor, B. F.   Investment Uncertainty and British Equities. IA, 22 (Dec, 1968), 13-22; -10*l*

Russell, W. R.   Commercial Bank Portfolio Adjustments. PhD diss, U of Wash, 1964; -3f

    Commercial Bank Portfolio Adjustments. AER, 56 (May, 1964), 547-550; -3f

    & Smith, P. E.   A Comment on Baumol (E,L) Efficient Portfolios. MSci, 12 (Mar, 1966), 619-621; -10f

    See also **Hadar, J. & Russell, W. R.**

Rutenberg, D. P.

    See **Litzenberger, R. H. & Rutenberg, D. P.**

Rutherford, R. W.   Ranking Correlation of Unit Trust Performance, 1963-1968. IA, 25 (Dec, 1969), 21-24; -14a

Safer, A. E. & Levine, J. M.   How Fast Are the Institutions Accumulating Equity Shares? FAJ, 26 (Jul-Aug, 1970), 74-86; -3e

Safian, K.

    See **Smilen, K. B. & Safian, K.**

St. Laurent, A. G.   Comments on 'Brownian Motion in the Stock Market'. OR, 7 (1959), 806-807; -11c

    A Stochastic Model for the Behavior of a Set of Price Index—Numbers and its Application. Michigan St U Research Memo No. 37, 1957; -5b

Salabar, C. A.

    See **Gaumnitz, J. E. & Salabar, C. A.**

Salazar, R. C. & Sen, S. K.   A Simulation Model of Capital Budgeting Under Uncertainty. MSci, 15 (Dec, 1968), B161-B179; -25d

Sametz, A. W.   Trends in the Volume and Composition of Equity Finance. JF, 19 (Sep, 1964), 450-469; -23g

    See also **Lindsay, R. & Sametz, A. W.**

Sampson, A. A.   Measuring the Rate of Return on Capital. JF, 24 (Mar, 1969), 61-74; -23d

Samuels, J. M.   An Empirical Study of the Cost of Equity Capital. BR, (Summer, 1968), 12-15; -23d

    The Measurement of the Performance of Unit Trusts. IA, 27 (Sep, 1970), 34-40; -14a

    The Performance of Unit Trusts. BM, 206 (Aug, 1968), 80-87; -14a

    Readings on Mergers and Takeovers. Elek, 1972; -26a

    & Smyth, D. J.   Profits, Variability of Profits and Firm Size. Ec, 35 (May, 1968), 127-139; -26f

    See also **Briscoe, G.; Samuels, J. M. & Smyth, D. J.**

    See also **Tzoannos, J. & Samuels, J. M.**

Samuelson, P. A.   Some Aspects of the Pure Theory of Capital. QJE, 51 (1937), 469-496; -22b, 25b

    An Exact Consumption-Loan Model of Interest with or without the Social Contrivance of Money. JPE, 66 (Dec, 1958), 467-482; -18b

    Efficient Portfolio Selection for Pareto-Levy Investments. JFQA, 2 (Jun, 1967), 107-122; -10d

    The 'Fallacy' of Maximizing the Geometric Mean in Long Sequences of Investing or Gambling. PNAS, (Oct, 1971), 2493-2496; -10j

    The Fundamental Approximation Theorem of Portfolio Analysis in Terms of Means, Variances and Higher Moments. REStud, 37 (Oct, 1970), 537-542; -10c

General Proof that Diversification Pays. JFQA, 2 (Mar, 1967), 1-13; -10e

Intertemporal Price Equilibrium: A Prologue to the Theory of Speculation. WA, 79 (1957), 181-221; -11c

Lifetime Portfolio Selection by Dynamic Stochastic Programming. REStat, 51 (Aug, 1969), 239-246; -10k

Probability, Utility and the Independence Axiom. Em, 20 (Oct, 1952); -9a

Proof That Properly Anticipated Prices Fluctuate Randomly. IMR, 6 (Spring, 1965), 41-49; -11c

A Random Theory of Futures Prices. IMR, 6 (Jun, 1965); -21a

Rational Theory of Warrant Pricing. IMR, 6 (Spring, 1965), 13-31; -17b

& Merton, R. C. A Complete Model of Warrant Pricing that Maximises Utility. IMR, 10 (Winter, 1969), 17-46; -17b

Sandmo, A. Capital Risk, Consumption and Portfolio Choice. Em, 37 (Oct, 1969), 586-599; -10l

Equilibrium and Efficiency in Loan Markets. Ec, 37 (Feb, 1970), 23-38; -9d

Portfolio Choice in a Theory of Saving. SJE, 70 (1968), 106-122; -18a

Santow, L. J. Cost of Long-Term Capital from a Corporate Point of View. FAJ, 19 (May-Jun 1963), 43-50; -23c

Ultimate Demise of Preferred Stock as a Source of Corporate Capital. FAJ, 18 (May-Jun, 1962), 47-54; -19i

Sapienza, S. R. Business Combinations: A Case Study. AR, 91 (Jan, 1963), 91-101; -26b

Distinguishing Between Purchase and Pooling. JA, 111 (Jun, 1961), 35-40; -26d

Saposnik, R.
See **Quirk, J. P. & Saposnik, R.**

Sarachman, E. T. A Study of Rights Offerings on the New York Stock Exchange from 1950 to 1961. MBA thesis, NYU, 1963; -16b

Sargent, T. J. The Structure of Interest Rates. PhD diss, Harvard U, 1968; -18f

Commodity Price Expectations and the Interest Rate. QJE, 83 (Feb, 1969), 127-140; -18c

Expectations at the Short End of the Yield Curve: An Application of Macaulay's Test, *in* Guttentag, J. M. (Ed), Essays on Interest Rates, Vol 2. (Dist by Columbia U Pr) Natl Bur Econ Res, 1971; -18d, 18f

Interest Rates and Prices in the Long Run: a Study of the Gibson Paradox. Unp ms, 1971; -18c

See also **Blattberg, R. & Sargent, T. J.**

Sarma, L. & Rao, K. Leverage and the Value of the Firm. JF, 24 (Sep, 1969), 673-677; -23c

Sarnat, M. The Development of the Securities Market in Israel. Kyklos, 1966; -2c

The Gains from Risk Diversification on the London Stock Exchange. JBF, 4 (Autumn, 1972), 54-64; -10e

A Note on the Prediction of Portfolio Performance from Ex Post Data. JF, 27 (Sep, 1972), 903-906; -10h

& Levy, H. The Relationship of Rules of Thumb to the Internal Rate of Return: a Restatement and Generalization. JF, 24 (Jun, 1969),

Schlarbaum, G. G. The Investment Performance of Stock Property-Liability Insurance Companies: 1948-1967. PhD diss, U of Pa, 1971; -3h

Schloss, W. J. The Dow-Jones Industrial Average Amended. AJ, 9 (Feb, 1953), 35-36; -5b

Schmeidler, D. Competitive Equilibria in Markets with a Continuum of Traders and Incomplete Preferences. Em, 37 (Oct, 1969), 578-585; -9d

Schmidt, C. H. & Stockwell, E. J. The Changing Importance of Institutional Investors in the American Capital Markets. LCP, 17 (Winter, 1952), 3-25; -3e

Schneider, C. W. SEC Filings—Their Content and Use. FAJ, 21 (Mar-Apr, 1965), 42-48; -2e

SEC Filings—Their Use to the Professional. FAJ, 21 (Jan-Feb, 1965), 33-38; -4a

Schneider, H. M. & Wintrub, W. G. Tax Savings Opportunities in Securities Transactions. Lybrand, 1966; -27a

See also **Cohen, K. J.; Hammer, F. S. & Schneider, H. M.**

Schneider, T. H. Measuring Performance. FAJ, 25 (May-Jun, 1969), 105-111; -14a

The Smaller Institution. FAJ, 24 (Sep-Oct, 1968), 9-11; -3e

A Worksheet Technique for Measuring Performance. FAJ, 25 (May-Jun, 1969), 105-111; -14b

Schoeplein, R. N. The Effect of Pension Plans on Other Retirement Saving. JF, 25 (Jun, 1970), 633-638; -3i

Scholes, M. The Market for Securities: Substitution versus Price Pressure and the Effects of Information on Share Prices. JB, 45 (Apr, 1972), 179-211; -11a, 16e

The Relationship Between the Returns on Bonds and the Returns on Common Stocks. Paper for the Seminar on the Analysis of Security Prices, U of Chicago, Nov 1971; -19a

A Test of the Competitive Market Hypothesis: the Market for New Issues and Secondary Offerings. PhD diss, U of Chicago, 1969; -11a, 16e

See also **Beaver, W.; Kettler, P. & Scholes, M.**

See also **Black, F.; Jensen, M. C. & Scholes, M.**

See also **Black, F. & Scholes, M.**

Schoomer, B. A., Jr. American Stock Exchange Index Systems. FAJ, 23 (May-Jun, 1967), 57-61; -5b

Schreiner, J. Graphical Comparisons of Actual and Proposed Brokerage Commission Schedules. FAJ, 27 (Jul-Aug, 1971), 75-84; -2b

Historically Successful Portfolio Selection Rules. PhD diss, UCLA, 1970; -10c

See also **Smith, K. V. & Schreiner, J. C.**

Schrieber, A. N. (Ed). Corporate Simulation Models. U of Washington Pr, 1970; -22c

Schrock, N. W. Asset Choice Under Uncertainty with Borrowing Introduced. WEJ, (Mar, 1967), 201-209; -10c

A Portfolio Analysis of Straddle Operations in the Futures Markets: An Application of the Expected Returns—Variance of Returns Hypothesis. PhD diss, U of Oreg, 1967; -21a

Schulkin, P. A. Real Estate Investment Trusts. FAJ, 27 (May-Jun, 1971), 33 ff; -21c

Schultz, B. E. The Securities Market, and How it Works, rev ed. Har-Row, 1963; -2b

Schultz, T. W. Spot and Futures Prices as Production Guides. AER, 39 (May, 1949); -21a

Schumacher, A. C. The Relationship of Money Forces to Equity Prices. AJ, 11 (Feb, 1955), 15-18; -6d

Schutt, L. D. Investment Policy and Portfolio Considerations for a Mutual Life Insurance Company. FAJ, 22 (Mar-Apr, 1966), 105-112; -3h

Schwab, B. & Lusztig, P. A Comparative Analysis of the Net Present Value and the Benefit-Cost Ratio as Measures of the Economic Desirability of Investments. JF, 24 (Jun, 1969), 507-516; -25c

    & Lusztig, P. A Note on Investment Evaluation in the Light of Uncertain Future Opportunities. JF, forthcoming; -25d

    See also **Lusztig, P. & Schwab, B.**

Schwartz, E. A Contribution to the Theory of Capital Budgeting—the Multi-Investment Case—a Comment. JF, 19 (Dec, 1964), 668-670; -25e

    Corporation Finance. Macmillan Int, 1962; -22a

    The Cost of Capital and Investment Criteria in the Public Sector. JF, 25 (Mar, 1970), 135-142; -23d

    Theory of the Capital Structure of the Firm. JF, 14 (Mar, 1959), 18-39; -23c

    & Aronson, J. R. Some Surrogate Evidence in Support of the Concept of Optimal Financial Structure. JF, 22 (Mar, 1967), 10-18; -23c

Schwartz, N. L.

    See **Kamien, M. I. & Schwartz, N. L.**

Schwartz, R. A. & Altman, E. I. Volatility Behavior of Industrial Stock Price Indices. JF, forthcoming; -10b

    See also **Altman, E. I. & Schwartz, R. A.**

Schwartz, W. Convertibles Get Realistic Image. FAJ, 23 (Jul-Aug, 1967), 55-57; -17c

    Warrants: a Form of Equity Capital. FAJ, 26 (Sep-Oct, 1970), 87-101; -17b

    & Spillman, J. Guide to Convertible Securities. Convertible S Pr, nd; -17c

Scott, D. F. An Inquiry into the Existence of Optimum Financial Structures. PhD diss, U of Fla, 1970; -23c

Scott, I. O., Jr. The Changing Significance of Treasury Bill Obligations in Commercial Bank Portfolios. JF, 12 (May, 1957), 213-222; -3f

    European Capital Markets. NBR, (Dec, 1966), 131-144; -20e

    Government Securities Markets. McGraw, 1965; -19c

    The Implications of the Changing Ownership of Federal Securities. Proceedings of the Business and Economic Statistics Section, American Statistical Association, 1957, 154-158; -19c

    See also **Brownlee, O. H. & Scott, I. O., Jr.**

Scott, M. F. G. Relative Share Prices and Yields. OEP, 14 (Oct, 1962), 218-250; -7c

Scott, R. H. A Conditional Theory of Banking Enterprise, *in* Pontecorvo, G. et al (Eds), Issues in Banking and Monetary Analysis. HR & W, 1967; -3f

    Liquidity and the Term Structure of Interest Rates. QJE, 79 (Feb, 1965), 135-145; -18f

Scott, W. P.

    See **Williams, B. R. & Scott, W. P.**

Scoville, J. A. An Exercise in Common Stock Selection. FAJ, 12 (Nov, 1956), 99-103; -7a

Seager, S. E.   Leverage and the Cost of Capital. NBR, (Jun, 1966), 497-508;-23c

Seagle, J. P.
    See **Frankfurter, G. M.; Phillips, H. E. & Seagle, J. P.**

Securities & Exchange Commission.   Cost of Flotation of Corporate Securities, 1951-1955. US Govt, 1957;-16a
    Institutional Investor Study Report of the Securities and Exchange Commission. US Govt, 1971;-2b, 3e
    Public Policy Implications of Investment Company Growth. US Govt, 1966;-3k
    Report of the Special Study of the Securities Markets. US Govt, 1963;-2b
    Report on Put and Call Options. US Govt, 1961;-17a
    Stock Trading on the New York Stock Exchange. US Govt, Sep 3 1946;-2b
    Study of Mutual Funds Prepared for the Securities and Exchange Commission by the Wharton School of Finance and Commerce. House Report No 2274. US Govt, 1962;-3k, 14a
    A 25 Year Summary of the Activities of the Securities and Exchange Commission, 1934-1959. US Govt, 1961;-2e

Seelenfreund, A.; Parker, G. G. C. & Van Horne, J. C.   Stock Price Behavior and Trading. JFQA, 3 (Sep, 1968), 263-282;-23g

Segall, J. E.   The Effect of Maturity on Price Fluctuations. JB, 29 (1950), 202-206;-18f
    Merging for Fun and Profit. IMR, 9 (Winter, 1968), 17-30;-26b
    See also **Alberts, W. W. & Segall, J. E.**
    See also **Green, D., Jr.,** & **Segall, J. E.**
    See also **Weil, R. L.; Segall, J. E. & Green, D., Jr.**

Seghers, P. D.; Reinhart, W. J. & Nimaroff, S.   Essentially Equivalent to a Dividend. Ronald, 1960;-16c

Selden, R. T.   Trends and Cycles in the Commercial Paper Market. (Dist by Columbia U Pr) Natl Bur Econ Res, 1963;-20a

Seligman, D.   The Mystique of Point-and-Figure. F, 67 (Mar, 1962);-12a
    Playing the Market with Charts. F, 67 (Feb, 1962);-12a
    & Wise, T. A.   New Forces in the Stock Market. F, 69 (Feb, 1964), 92ff;-3e

Semah, J.; Serres, C. & Tessier, B.   L'Ordinateur Speculateur. Dunod, 1970; -11c

Sen, S. K.
    See **Salazar, R. C. & Sen, S. K.**

Seneca, J. J.   Short Interest: Bearish or Bullish? JF, 22 (Mar, 1967), 67-70; -13d
    Short Interest: Bullish or Bearish?—Reply. JF, 23 (Jun, 1968), 524-527;-13d

Serres, C.
    See **Semah, J.; Serres, C. & Tessier, B.**

Shackle, G. L. S.   Decision Order and Time in Human Affairs, 2nd ed. Cambridge U Pr, 1970;-9a
    Expectations in Economics. Cambridge U Pr, 1949;-9a
    Uncertainty in Economics and Other Reflections. Cambridge U Pr, 1955;-9a
    See also **Carter, C. F.; Meredith, G. P. & Shackle, G. L. S.**

Shapiro, D. L.   Conglomerate Mergers and Optimal Investment Policy. JFQA, 4 (Jan, 1970), 643-656;-26c

Shapiro, E.   The Postwar Market for Corporate Securities: 1946-55. JF, 14 (May, 1959), 196-217;-19e

    See also **Goldsmith, R. W. & Shapiro, E.**

    See also **Gordon, M. J. & Shapiro, E.**

    See also **Johnson, L. R.; Shapiro, E. & O'Meara, J.**

Sharpe, W. F.   Addendum to 'A Simplified Model for Portfolio Analysis'. MSci, 9 (Apr, 1963), 498;-10c

    Capital Asset Prices: A Theory of Market Equilibrium Under Conditions of Risk. JF, 19 (Sep, 1964), 425-442;-10*l*

    A Linear Programming Algorithm for Mutual Fund Portfolio Selection. MSci, 13 (Mar, 1967), 499-510;-10c

    A Linear Programming Approximation for the General Portfolio Analysis Problem. JFQA, 6 (Dec, 1971), 1263-1276;-10c

    Mathematical Investment Portfolio Selection: Some Early Results. UWBR, (Apr, 1963);-10c

    Mean-Absolute-Deviation Characteristic Lines for Securities and Portfolios. MSci, 18 (Oct, 1971), B1-B13;-10b

    Mutual Fund Performance. JB, 39 (Jan, 1966), 119-138;-14a

    Mutual Fund Performance and the Theory of Capital Asset Pricing: Reply. JB, 41 (Apr, 1968), 235-236;-14a

    Portfolio Analysis. JFQA, 2 (Jun, 1967), 76-84;-10c

    Portfolio Theory and Capital Markets. McGraw, 1971;-10*l*

    Reply (to Bierwag and Grove). JF, 20 (Mar, 1965), 94-95;-10*l*

    Risk Aversion in the Stock Market: Some Empirical Evidence. JF, 20 (Sep, 1965), 416-422;-10*l*

    Risk, Market Sensitivity and Diversification. FAJ, 28 (Jan-Feb, 1972), 74-79;-10e

    Security Prices, Risk and Maximal Gains from Diversification: Reply. JF, 21 (Dec, 1966), 743-744;-10*l*

    A Simplified Model for Portfolio Analysis. MSci, 9 (Jan, 1963), 277-293;-10c

    & Cooper, G. M.   Risk-Return Class of New York Stock Exchange Common Stocks, 1931-1967. FAJ, 28 (Mar-Apr, 1972), 46ff; -10*l*

Shaw, D. C.   The Performance of Primary Common Stock Offerings: a Canadian Comparison. JF, 26 (Dec, 1971), 1101-1114;-16a

Shaw, R. B.   The Dow Jones Industrials vs. the Dow Jones Industrial Average. AJ, 11 (Nov, 1955), 37-40;-5b

    Justifiable Invasion of Principal. AJ, 12 (Nov, 1956), 65-67;-24b

Shell, K.

    See **Szego, G. P. & Shell, K.**

Shelton, J. P.   An Evaluation of Merger Hedges. FAJ, 21 (Mar-Apr, 1965), 49-52;-26a

    Influence of the Six-Month Capital Gains Rule on Short Term Transactions. FAJ, 18 (Sep-Oct, 1962), 99-101;-27d

    The New Research and the Investment Profession. FAJ, 22 (Nov-Dec, 1966), 65-67;-4e

    The Relation of the Price of a Warrant to the Price of the Associated Stock.

    Part 1: FAJ, 23 (May-Jun, 1967), 143-151,

    Part 2: FAJ, 23 (Jul-Aug, 1967), 88-99; -17b

    The Value Line Contest: A Test of the Predictibility of Stock Price Changes. JB, 40 (Jul, 1967), 251-269;-15c

    Brigham, E. F. & Hofflander, A. E., Jr.   Dual Funds. FAJ, 23 (May-Jun, 1967), 131-139;-3m

See also **Cheng, P. L. & Shelton, J. P.**

See also **Holt, C. C. & Shelton, J. P.**

See also **Treynor, J. L.; Shelton, J. P. & Kantor, M.**

See also **Warren, J. M. & Shelton, J. P.**

Sheppard, C. S. The Professionalization of the Financial Analysts. FAJ, 23 (Nov-Dec, 1967), 39-41; -4c

Sheppard, D. K. The Growth and Role of U.K. Financial Institutions 1880-1962. Methuen, 1971; -3e

Sherman, J. C. A Device to Measure Portfolio Performance. FAJ, 22 (Jan-Feb, 1966), 106-108; -14a

Sherr, L. A. The Value of the Delayed Call Provision. PhD diss, U of Mich, 1967; -19h

Shibata, A. N. Effects of Taxation on Risk Taking. AER, 59 (May, 1969), 553-561; -27b

Shick, R. A. The Analysis of Mergers and Acquisitions. JF, 27 (May, 1972), 495-502; -26a

Shillinglaw, G. Residual Values in Investment Analysis. JB, 28 (Oct, 1955), 275-284; -25c

Shin, S. K. Relative Importance of Cash Flow as a Criterion of Dividend Policy. PhD diss, U of Ill, 1970; -24a

Shipman, S. S.

See **Nadler, M.; Heller, S. & Shipman, S. S.**

Shiskin, J. Systematic Aspects of Stock Price Fluctuations. Paper for the Seminar on the Analysis of Security Prices, U of Chicago, May 1967; -6b, 12b

See also **Moore, G. H. & Shiskin, J.**

Short, R. A. Business Mergers: How and When to Transact Them. P-H, 1967; -26a.

Siebert, C. D.

See **Jorgenson, D. W. & Siebert, C. D.**

Sieff, J. A. Construction of a Retirement Fund Portfolio. FAJ, 21 (Jul-Aug, 1965), 89-94; -3i

Measuring Investment Performance: the Unit Approach. FAJ, 22 (Jul-Aug, 1966), 93-99; -14a

Siff, F. H.

See **Barish, N. N. & Siff, F. H.**

Sihler, W. W. The Capital Investment Analysis and Decision Process at the Plant Level of a Large, Diversified Corporation. PhD diss, Harvard U, 1965; -25c

Silber, W. L. Portfolio Behavior of Financial Institutions. HR & W, 1970; -3e

See also **Keare, D. H. & Silber, W. L.**

Silberman, I. H. A Note on Merger Valuation. JF, 23 (Jun, 1968), 528-534; -26a

Silberman, L. Critical Examination of S.E.C. Proposals. HBR, 42 (Nov-Dec, 1964), 121-132; -2e

Silverberg, S. Bank Trust Investments: Their Size and Significance. NBR, (Jun, 1964), 577-598; -3f

Silvers, J. B. An Alternative Analysis of Bond Risk. PhD diss, Stanford U, 1971; -19g

An Alternative to the Yield Spread as a Measure of Risk. JF, forthcoming; -19g

Simmons, J. K. Comparability in Financial Reporting: the Concept and its Application to Financial Analysts. PhD diss, Ohio St U, 1967; -8e

& Gray, J.   An Investigation of the Effect of Differing Accounting
Frameworks on the Prediction of Net Income. AR, 44 (Oct, 1969),
757-776;-8a

Simon, G.
See **Pinches, G. E. & Simon, G.**

Simon, J. L.   Does 'Good Portfolio Management' Exist? MSci, 15 (Feb,
1969), B308-B319;-14a
See also **Johnson, H. W. & Simon, J. L.**

Simonson, D. G.   The Speculative Behavior of Mutual Funds. JF, 27 (May,
1972), 381-391;-3k

Simpson, K. & Ballinger, W.   The Feasibility and Advisability of the
Complete Separation of the Functions of Dealer and Broker.
Washington D.C.: Securities & Exchange Commission, 1936;-2b

Sims, E. C.   A Critical Analysis of Yields and Rates of Return Received
from the Investment of Educational Endowments. PhD diss, U of Mo,
1971;-3i

Singh, A.   Take-overs: their Relevance to the Stock Market and the
Theory of the Firm. Cambridge U Pr, 1971;-26a
& Whittington, G.   Growth, Profitability and Valuation: A Study
of United Kingdom Quoted Companies. Cambridge U Pr, 1968;-8c
See also **Marris, R. & Singh, A.**

Singhvi, S. S.   Disclosure to Whom? Annual Financial Reports to Stockholders and to the Securities and Exchange Commission. JB, 41 (Jul,
1968), 347-351;-2e

Sinkey, J. F.   The Term Structure of Interest Rates: Theory, Models of
Interest-Rate Forecasting, and Empirical Evidence. PhD diss, Boston
C, 1971;-18c

Sitt, I.   Mechanical Investment Plans Versus Judgment. AJ, 2 (2nd Qtr,
1946), 30-38;-12f

Sjogren, P. H.   Enterprise Valuation by the Securities and Exchange .
Commission under Chapter X of the Bankruptcy Act. PhD diss,
Columbia U, 1964;-7a

Skelly, W. S.   Convertible Bonds: A Study of the Suitability for Commercial
Bank Bonds Portfolios. New York: Salomon Bros. & Hutzler, 1959;-17c

Sloane, P. E.   Determinants of Bond Yield Differentials, 1954-1959. YEE,
3 (Spring, 1963), 3-55;-19a

Sloane, W. R.   Earnings, Dividends and Stock Prices: Review and General
Model. MarqBR, (Fall, 1967);-7a
& Reisman, A.   Stock Evaluation Theory: Classification, Recon-
ciliation and General Model. JFQA, 3 (Jun, 1968), 171-203;-7a

Slovic, P.   Psychological Study of Human Judgment: Implications for
Investment Decision Making. JF, 27 (Sep, 1972), 779-800;-4d
Fleissner, D. & Baumann, W. S.   Analysing the Use of Information in Investment Decision Making: a Methodological Proposal. JB,
45 (Apr, 1972), 283-301;-4d

Smeets, M. J. H.   The Influence of Taxes on the Capital Market. ABQR,
133, (1961), 3-16;-27a

Smerling, S. A.   Found: a Realistic Market Measure. AJ, 13 (May, 1957),
59-62;-5b

Smidt, S.   A New Look at the Random Walk Hypothesis. JFQA, 3 (Sep,
1968), 235-262;-11c
A Test of the Serial Independence of Price Changes in Soybean
Futures. FRIS, 5 (1965), 117-136;-21a

Which Road to an Efficient Stock Market? FAJ, 27 (Sep-Oct, 1971), 18ff;-2b

    & Johnson, A. Expectations and Information: A Study of Pork Inventory Behavior. Graduate School of Business and Public Administration, Cornell U, 1962;-21a

    See also **Bierman, H., Jr. & Smidt, S.**

Smilen, K. B. & Safian, K. Relative Earnings: a Fresh Approach. FAJ, 20 (Sep-Oct, 1964), 104-107;-8d

Smith, A. (pseud). The Money Game. Random, 1968;-4a

Smith, D. T. Corporate Taxation and Common Stock Financing. NTJ, 6 (Sep, 1953), 209-225;-27c

    Effects of Taxation: Corporate Financial Policy. Harvard Busn, 1952;-27a

Smith, E. L. Common Stocks as Long Term Investments. Macmillan, 1924;-5a

Smith, E. L. Low Tide in Sunspots—1964. FAJ, 19 (Jul-Aug, 1963), 91-92; -12g

Smith, E. P. Markov Processes and Investment Behaviour. Met, 18 (Jan-Apr, 1966), 15-30;-11c

    Reporting Requirements and Standards for Stock Option Plans. FAJ, 25 (Sep-Oct, 1969), 64-68;-17d

Smith, F. P. Management Trading, Stock-Market Prices and Profits. Yale U Pr, 1941;-13c

    See also **Eiteman, W. J. & Smith, F. P.**

Smith, G. C.

    See **Haring, J. E. & Smith, G. C.**

Smith, J. M., Jr. Financial Information Conversion: Analysis and Evaluation. PhD diss, Stanford U, 1965;-8c

Smith, K. V. Alternative Procedures for Revising Investment Portfolios. JFQA, 3 (Dec, 1968), 371-403;-10c

    Needed: A Dynamic Approach to Investment Management. FAJ, 23 (May-Jun, 1967), 115-117;-4a

    Option Writing and Portfolio Management. FAJ, 24 (May-Jun, 1968), 135-138;-17a

    Portfolio Management. HR & W, 1971;-4b

    Selection and Revision Decision Rules for Portfolio Management. PhD diss, Purdue U, 1967;-10c

    Stock Price and Economic Indexes for Generating Efficient Portfolios. JB, 42 (Jul, 1969), 326-336;-10c

    A Transition Model for Portfolio Revision. JF, 22 (Sep, 1967), 425-439;-10c

    & Goudzwaard, M. B. Survey of Investment Management: Teaching versus Practice. JF, 25 (May, 1970), 329-348;-4a

    & Schreiner, J. C. A Portfolio Analysis of Conglomerate Diversification. JF, 35 (Jun, 1969), 413-427;-26c

    & Tito, D. A. Risk-Return Measures of Ex Post Portfolio Performance. JFQA, 4 (Dec, 1969), 449-472;-14a

    See also **Jacob, N. L. & Smith, K. V.**

Smith, P. E.

    See **Russell, W. R. & Smith, P. E.**

Smith, P. F. Economics of Financial Institutions and Markets. Irwin, 1971;-3e

Smith, R. Cost of Capital in the Oil Industry. Hectograph, Carnegie IT, 1955;-23c

Smith, R. D.   Short Interest and Stock Market Prices. FAJ, 24 (Nov-Dec, 1968), 151-154;-13d

Smith, R. E.

See **Johnson, G. L.; Reilly, F. K. & Smith, R. E.**

Smith, R. G. E.   The Appraisement, Valuation and Selection of Security Investments and the Theory of Price Determination in Securities Markets. DBA diss, La St U, 1968;-7a

The 'Marginal Opinion' Theory of Stock Prices. FAJ, 23 (Nov-Dec, 1967), 127-132;-7a

Uncertainty, Information and Investment Decisions. JF, 26 (Mar, 1971), 67-82;-4d

Smith, R. L.   The Grim Truth about Mutual Funds. Putnam, 1963;-3k

Smith, V. K. & Marcis, R. G.   A Time Series Analysis of Post-Accord Interest Rates. JF, 27 (Jun, 1972), 589-606;-18f

Smith, V. L.   Default Risk, Scale, and the Homemade Leverage Theorem. AER, 62 (Mar, 1972), 66-76;-23c

Time Preference and Risk in Investment Theory. AER, 51 (May, 1961), 124-127;-9c

Smith, W. L.   Debt Management in the United States, Study Paper No. 19. Paper prepared for the Joint Economic Committee, Congress of the United States, Jan 1960;-23g

Smith, W. P.   Commercial Bank Entry into Revenue Bond Underwriting: an Appraisal of the Public Benefits of S 1306. Washington, D.C.: Dept of Banking & Currency, Office of the Controller of the Currency, 1967;-19d

Smyth, D. J.

See **Briscoe, G.; Samuels, J. M. & Smyth, D. J.**

See also **Samuels, J. M. & Smyth, D. J.**

Snape, R. H.   Price Relationships on the Sydney Wool Futures Market. Ec, 35 (May, 1968);-21a

& Yamey, B. S.   Test of the Effectiveness of Hedging. JPE, 73 (Oct, 1965), 540-544;-21a

Snyder, G. L.   Alternative Forms of Options. FAJ, 25 (Sep-Oct, 1969), 93-100;-17a

A Look at Options. FAJ, 23 (Jan-Feb, 1967), 100-103;-17a

Sobel, R.   The Big Board, A History of the New York Stock Market. Free Pr, 1965;-2d

The Great Bull Market: Wall Street in the 1920's. Norton, 1968; -2d

Panic on Wall Street: a History of America's Financial Disasters. Macmillan, 1968;-2d

Society of Investment Analysts.   A Bibliography for Investment and Economic Analysis. London: Society of Investment Analysts, 1965;-1a

Sohmen, E.   Flexible Exchange Rates. Theory and Controversy, rev ed. U of Chicago Pr, 1969;-21b

The Theory of Forward Exchange. International Finance Section, Department of Economics, Princeton U, 1966;-21b

Soldofsky, R. M.   Growth Yields. FAJ, 17 (Sep-Oct, 1961), 43-47;-7b

Growth Yields on Common Stock Since 1900. QREB, 5 (Winter, 1965), 51-61;-5a

The Industry of Bond Tables and Stock Valuation Models. JF, 21 (Mar, 1966), 103-111;-7b

Institutional Holdings of Common Stock 1900-2000. U of Mich Busn Res, 1971;-3e

The Size and Maturity of Direct-Placement Loans. JF, 15 (Mar, 1960), 32-44;-19e

Yield-Risk Performance Measurements. FAJ, 24 (Sep-Oct, 1968), 130-139;-10*l*

Yield Risk Performance of Convertible Securities. FAJ, 27 (Mar-Apr, 1971), 61ff;-17c

   & Biderman, R.   Yield-Risk Measurements of the Performance of Common Stocks. JFQA, 3 (Mar, 1968), 59-74;-10*l*

   & Johnson, C. R.   Rights Timing. FAJ, 23 (Jul-Aug, 1967), 101-104;-16b

   & Miller, R. L.   Risk Premium Curves for Different Classes of Long-Term Securities, 1950-1966. JF, 24 (Jun, 1969), 429-445;-19g

   & Murphy, J. T.   Growth Yields on Common Stock: Theory and Tables. Iowa St Busn, 1963;-7b

   See also **Pogue, T. F. & Soldofsky, R. M.**

Solomon, E.   The Arithmetic of Capital Budgeting Decisions. JB, 29 (Apr, 1956), 124-129;-25c

Economic Growth and Common-Stock Value. JB, 28 (Jul, 1955), 213-221;-7d

Leverage and the Cost of Capital. JF, 18 (May, 1963), 273-279; -23c

The Management of Corporate Capital. Free Pr, 1959;-22a

Measuring a Company's Cost of Capital. JB, 28 (Oct, 1955), 240-252;-23d

The Theory of Financial Management. Columbia U Pr, 1963;-22a

   & Laya, J. C.   Measuring Profitability. P-H, 1969;-8c

Solomon, M. B., Jr.   Investment Decisions in Small Business. U of Ky Pr, 1963;-25c

Uncertainty and its Effect on Capital Investment Analysis. MSci, 12 (Apr, 1966), B334-B339;-25d

Solow, R. M.   Capital Theory and the Rate of Return. N-Holland, 1963;-22b

Somers, H. B.   A Comparison of Rates of Earnings of Large Scale and Small Scale Industries. QJE, 46 (May, 1932), 465-479;-26f

Sommers, H. M.   Estate Taxes and Business Mergers. JF, 13 (May, 1958), 201-210;-26a

Sonenblum, S.

   See **Mayer, T. & Sonenblum, S.**

Sophian, T. J.   The Taxation of Capital Gains. Butterworth, 1967;-27d

Sorter, G. H. & Benston, G.   Appraising the Defensive Portion of a Firm: The Interval Measure. AR, 35 (Oct, 1960), 633-640;-8c

Sosnick, S. H.   Stock Dividends Are Lemons, Not Melons. CMR, 3 (Winter, 1961), 61-82;-16c

Sosnoff, M. T.   Hedge Fund Management. FAJ, 22 (Jul-Aug, 1966), 105-108;-3*l*

Soule, R. P.   Trends in the Cost of Capital. HBR, 31 (Mar-Apr, 1953), 33-47;-23d

Sowards, H. L.   Comments, Cases and Materials on Securities Regulation. Dennis, 1966;-2e

Spacek, L.   Are Double Standards Good Enough for Investors But Unacceptable to the Securities Industry? FAJ, 21 (Mar-Apr, 1965), 17ff;-2e

Business Success Requires an Understanding of Unsolved Problems of Accounting and Financial Reporting. Address presented at Harvard U, Sep 1959;-8c

Spano, A. T.   The Accuracy of Stock Market Forecasts, 1947-52. Senior thesis, Princeton U, 1954; -15c

Sparrow, J.   Convertible Loan Stocks. JBF, 1 (Spring, 1969), 24-31; -17c

Spear, R. E.   Constant Dividends Plus Good Appreciation through Fast Stocks versus Slow Stocks. FAJ, 7 (3rd Qtr, 1951), 47-50; -10b

Spencer, M. H.   Studies in the Determination of Specific Interest Rates. EE, 8 (Oct-Nov, 1962), 17-32; -19a

Spetzler, C. S.   The Explicit Consideration of Uncertainty in Capital Investment Analysis. PhD diss, Ill IT, 1968; -25d

Spiegelglas, S.   Changes in Margin Requirements and Stock Market Prices. FAJ, 16 (Nov-Dec, 1960), 35-37; -6e

Spillman, J.   See **Schwartz, W. & Spillman, J.**

Spitz, A. E.   Mutual Fund Performance and Cash Inflows. AE, 2 (Aug, 1970), 141-145; -3k, 14a

Some Determinants of Investing in Load or No-Load Mutual Funds: A Statistical Analysis. PhD diss, U of Ky, 1969; -3k

Spray, D. E. (Ed).   The Principal Stock Exchanges of the World—Their Operation, Structure and Development. Int Econ, 1964; -2c

Sprecher, C. R.   A Note on Financing Mergers with Convertible Preferred Stock. JF, 26 (Jun, 1971), 683-686; -17c

Sprenkle, C. M.   The Uselessness of Transactions Demand Models. JF, 24 (Dec, 1969), 835-847; -25a

Warrant Prices as Indicators of Expectations and Preferences. YEE, 1 (Fall, 1961), 179-231; -17b

Sprinkel, B. W.   Money and Markets. Irwin, 1971; -6d

Money and Stock Prices. Irwin, 1964; -6d

& West, B. K.   Effects of Capital Gains Taxes on Investment Decisions. JB, 35 (Apr, 1962), 122-134; -27d

Sprowls, J. S.   Short Term Investment Practices of Large Non-Financial Corporations. Masters thesis, U of Pittsburgh, 1953; -3e

Squier, A. P.   Training Prospective Security Analysts. AJ, 10 (May, 1954), 39; -4c

Srinivasan, T. N.

See **Levhari, D. & Srinivasan, T. N.**

Stacey, N. A. H.   Mergers in Modern Business. Hutchinson, 1966; -26a

Stafford, F.

See **Holbrook, B. & Stafford, F.**

Stalker, A. C.   Frequency Distributions of Investment Index Yields. JIA, 93 (1967), 113-118; -11b

Standard & Poor's Corporation.   Bond Quality Ratings. AJ, 2 (1st Qtr, 1946), 9-17; -19f

Stapleton, R. C.   Portfolio Analysis, Stock Valuation and Capital Budgeting Decision Rules for Risky Projects. JF, 26 (Mar, 1971), 95-118; -25d

The Theory of Corporate Finance. Harrap, 1970; -22a

Stark, T.

See **Ford, J. L. & Stark, T.**

Starkweather, L. P.; Otto, E. A. & Kreger, H. R.   Policies and Practices in Corporate Finance; an Application of Principles and Techniques. New York: New York University Book Store, 1951; -22a

Staubus, G. J.   Earnings Periods for Common Share Analysis. JB, 41 (Oct, 1968), 472-476; -8d

Steglitz, M.

See **Ahlers, D. M. & Steglitz, M.**

See also **Fanning, J. E. & Steglitz, M.**

Steiger, W. Non-Randomness in the Stock Market: A New Test on an Existent Hypothesis. SM thesis, MIT, 1963; -11c

The Taxation of Unrealized Capital Gains and Losses: A Statistical Study. NTJ, 10 (Sep, 1957); -27d

A Test of Nonrandomness in Stock Price Changes, *in* Cootner, P. H. (Ed), The Random Character of Stock Market Prices. MIT Pr, 1964; -11c

Destabilizing Speculative Activity Can Be Profitable. REStat, 43 (Aug, 1961), 301-302; -9d

International Short-Term Capital Movements. AER, 55 (Mar, 1965), 40-66; -20d

The Nature and Efficiency of the Foreign Exchange Market. Princeton U Intl Fin, Oct 1962; -21b

The Optimum Foreign Exchange Market. AER, 53 (Jun, 1963), 384-402; -21b

The Simultaneous Determination of Spot and Future Prices. AER, 51 (Dec, 1961), 1012-1025; -21a

Steindl, J. On Risk. OEP, (Jun, 1941), 43-53; -9c

Random Processes and the Growth of Firms. Griffin, 1965; -26f

Steinhaus, H. W. The Effect of Pension Fund Investments on Common Stock Funds. AJ, 14 (Feb, 1958), 63-64; -3i

Stekler, H. O. An Evaluation of Quarterly Judgmental Economic Forecasts. JB, 41 (Jul, 1968), 329-339; -15a

Economic Forecasting. Praeger, 1970; -15a

Profitability and the Size of Firm. U of Cal Pr, 1963; -26f

The Variability of Profitability with Size of Firm, 1947-1958. JASA, 59 (Dec, 1964), 1183-1193; -26f

Stern, W. P. Performance-Transitory or Real? FAJ, 24 (Jan-Feb, 1968), 110-113; -14a

& Norby, W. C. Investment Research and Market Structure— Today and Tomorrow. FAJ, 28 (Jan-Feb, 1972), 24ff; -4a

Stetson, W. B. Price Yield Relationships. AJ, 10 (Nov, 1954), 67-68; -18f

Stevens, G. Corporation Dividend Payout Ratios and Target Ratios. Cowles Foundation Discussion Paper, Cowles Commission for Research in Economics, Dept. of Economics, Yale U, 1961; -24a

Stevens, G. G. V. Two Problems in Portfolio Analysis: Conditional and Multiplicative Random Variables. JFQA, 6 (Dec, 1971), 1235-1250; -10c

Stevenson, H. W. Common Stock Financing. U of Mich Busn Res, 1957; -16b

See also **Murphy, J. E., Jr. & Stevenson, H. W.**

Stevenson, R. A. Retirement of Non-Callable Preferred Stock. JF, 25 (Dec, 1970), 1143-1152; -19i

The Variability of Common Stock Quality Ratings. FAJ, 22 (Nov-Dec, 1966), 97-101; -19f

& Bear, R. M. Commodity Futures: Trends or Random Walks? JF, 25 (Mar, 1970), 65-81; -21a

See also **Kewley, T. J. & Stevenson, R. A.**

Stewart, B. An Analysis of Speculative Trading in Grain Futures. U.S. Dept of Agriculture Technical Bulletin No. 1001, Oct 1949; -21a

Stewart, S. S. An Econometric Model of the Stock Market. PhD diss, Stanford U, 1970; -3e

Stewart, T. H. Can Technical Analysis Help? IA, 8 (May, 1964), 29-34; -12a

Stigler, G. J.   Capital and Rates of Return in Manufacturing. (Dist by Princeton U Pr) Natl Bur Econ Res, 1963; -23a

The Development of Utility Theory. JPE, 58 (Aug, 1950), 307-327; -9a

The Economics of Information. JPE, 69 (Jun, 1961), 213-225; -11a

Imperfections in the Capital Market. JPE, 75 (Jun, 1967), 287-292; -23c

Monopoly and Oligopoly by Merger. AER, 40 (May, 1950); -26a

Public Regulation of the Securities Markets. JB, 37 (Apr, 1964), 117-142; -2e, 16a

The Statistics of Monopoly and Merger. JPE, 64 (Feb, 1956), 33-40; -26a

Stiglitz, J. E.   Behavior Towards Risk with Many Commodities. Em, 37 (Oct, 1969), 660-667; -9a

On the Optimality of Stock Market Allocation. QJE, 86 (Feb, 1972), 25-60; -9d

A Re-Examination of the Modigliani-Miller Theorem. AER, 59 (Dec, 1969), 784-793; -23c

Taxation, Risk Taking and the Allocation of Investment in a Competitive Economy, *in* Jensen, M. C. (Ed), Studies in the Theory of Capital Markets. Praeger, 1972; -27b

Stignum, B. P.   Competitive Equilibria under Uncertainty. QJE, 83 (Nov, 1969), 533-561; -9d

Stiles, N. B.

See **Baum, D. J. & Stiles, N. B.**

Stitzel, T. E.   Investing in Intrastate Issues of Common Stock. JFQA, 4 (Jan, 1970), 697-706; -5a

Stockfisch, J. A.   Common Stock Financing and Tax Capitalization. NTJ 7 (Jun, 1954), 182-186; -27a

Stockwell, E. J.

See **Schmidt, C. H. & Stockwell, E. J.**

Stoffels, J. D.   Stock Recommendations by Investment Advisory Services: Immediate Effects on Market Pricing. FAJ, 22 (Mar-Apr, 1966), 77-86; -15c

The Use of Margin Credit in the Trading of Securities. PhD diss, Mich St U, 1969; -6c

Stoll, H. R.   An Empirical Study of the Forward Exchange Market under Fixed and Flexible Exchange Rate Systems. CJE, 1 (Feb, 1968), 55-78; -21b

The Determinants of Forward Exchange Rates. PhD diss, U of Chicago, 1967; -21b

The Relationship between Put and Call Option Prices. JF, 24 (Dec, 1969), 801-824; -17a

& Curley, A. J.   Small Business and the New Issues Market for Equities. JFQA, 5 (Sep, 1970), 309-322; -16a

Stone, B. K.   A General Class of Three-Parameter Risk Measures. JF, forthcoming; -10m

Risk, Return and Equilibrium. MIT Pr, 1970; -10*l*

Stone, D. E.   Computer-Aided Financial Analysis. FAJ, 24 (Jan-Feb, 1968), 149-153; -4e

Stone, D. G.   A Price Model for Common Stock Warrants. PhD diss, NYU, 1971; -17b

Stone, G. R.   An Analysis of the Investment Nature of Convertible Bonds. PhD diss, Stanford U, 1968; -17c

340

Stone, H. L.
> See Teweles, R. J.; Harlow, C. V. & Stone, H. L.

Stone, L. D.
> See Hoagland, H. E. & Stone, L. D.

Stone, R.; Revell, J. & Moyle, J. The Ownership of Quoted Ordinary Shares —a Survey for 1963. Chapman, 1966; -3a

Stone, R. W. The Changing Structure of the Money Markets. JF, 20 (May, 1965), 229-238; -20a

Storer, R. W. The Effects of the Yield-Maturity Curve on True Yields. AJ, 5 (2nd Qtr, 1949), 29-33; -19a

> A Stock-Price Yardstick. AJ, 10 (Aug, 1954), 51-56; -7d

> **& Conn, M. V.** Stock Market Leading Indicators. FAJ, 17 (Sep-Oct, 1961), 61-64; -6b

Straley, J. A. What About Mutual Funds?, 2nd ed. Har-Row, 1967; -3k

Strauss Turnbull. A Technical Study of Convertible Euro-bonds. London: Strauss Turnbull, Mar 1967; -17c, 20d

Streeten, P. The Effect of Taxation on Risk Bearing. OEP, 5 (1953), 271-287; -27b

Strotz, R. H. Cardinal Utility. AER, 43 (May, 1953), 390-391; -9a

Struble, F. M. The Commercial Paper Boom in Perspective. Mo Rev F R Bk Kansas City, (Nov, 1968), 3-10; -20a

> The Current Debate on the Term Structure of Interest Rates. Mo Rev F R Bk Kansas City, (Jan-Feb, 1966); -18f

Stuart, A.
> See Kendall, M. G. & Stuart, A.
> See also Marks, P. & Stuart, A.

Stubbs, C.
> See Donaldson, G. & Stubbs, C.

Stubbs, F. G., Jr. An Evaluation of the Risk Management Practices in Selected Corporations. PhD diss, U of Ill, 1966; -10o

Studness, C. M. New York Stock Exchange Trading in Perspective. FAJ, 24 (Nov-Dec, 1968), 26-36; -2b

Stuebner, E. A. The Role of the Investment Banker in Arranging Private Financing. BL (Jan, 1961); -19e

Stutchbury, O. P. The Management of Unit Trusts. Skinner, 1964; -3k

Sullivan, J. W. A Central Market for Stock Options: the Problems and the Promise. Paper for the Seminar on the Analysis of Security Prices, U of Chicago, Nov 1969; -17a

Summers, G. W. Financing and Initial Operations of New Firms. P-H, 1962; -22a

Summers, R. A Peek at the Trade off Relationship between Expected Return and Risk. QJE, 81 (May, 1967), 437-456; -10*l*

Sunbury, D. H. & Thompson, G. C. Improving Control over Capital Expenditures. Natl Ind Conf Bd, Conference Board Business Record, 18 (Oct, 1961), 22-33; -25c

Supel, T. M. A Two-Period Balance Sheet Model for Banks. PhD diss, U of Minn, 1969; -10g

Suppes, P. Behavioristic Foundations of Utility. Em, 29 (Apr, 1961), 186-202; -9a

Sussman, M. R. The Stock Dividend. U of Mich Busn Res, 1962; -16c

Sutch, R. C. Expectation, Risk and the Term Structure of Interest Rates. PhD diss, MIT, 1968; -18f

> See also Modigliani, F. & Sutch, R. C.

Sutton, S. S.   An Evaluation of Investment Criteria. PhD diss, G Wash U, 1968; -25c

Swalm, R. O.   Utility Theory—Insights into Risk Taking. HBR, 44 (Nov-Dec, 1966), 123-136; -9a

Swoboda, A. K.   The Euro-Dollar Market: An Interpretation. Princeton U Intl Fin, Feb 1968; -20d

Sykes, A.   Optimum Company Financing-Debt versus Equity. IA, 15 (Sep, 1966), 3-9; -23c

See also **Merrett, A. J. & Sykes, A.**

Synnott, T. W., III.   Time Series Analysis for Investment Decisions. Paper for the Seminar on the Analysis of Security Prices, U of Chicago, Nov 1968; -13b

Szatrowski, Z.   A Statistical Approach to Formula Planning, AJ, 11 (May, 1955), 65-69; -12f

Szego, G. P. & Shell, K. (Ed).   Mathematical Methods in Investment and Finance. N-Holland, 1972; -1b

Tabell, A. W.
See **Tabell, E. W. & A. W.**

Tabell, E. W.   Technical Approach to the Market. AJ, 7 (2nd Qtr, 1951), 49-56; -12a

& A. W.   An Introduction to Technical Analysis. IA, 6 (Sep, 1963), 15-26; -12a

& A. W.   The Case for Technical Analysis. FAJ, 20 (Mar-Apr, 1964), 67-76; -12a

Taff, C.   Dividend Omission as a Buying Signal. AJ, 10 (Feb, 1954), 67-70; -24b

Tambini, L.   Financial Policy and the Corporation Income Tax. PhD diss, U of Chicago, 1968; -27c

Tatham, C.   Common Stock Dividend Yields and Total Return. New York: Bache & Co., 1961; -5a

Taubman, P.
See **Friend, I. & Taubman, P.**

Taussig, F. W.   Is Market Price Determinate? QJE, 35 (May, 1921), 394-411; -11c

Taussig, R. A. & Hayes, S. L., III.   Are Cash Takeover Bids Unethical? FAJ, 23 (Jan-Feb, 1967), 107-111; -26a

Taylor, B. F.   Financing Tables and the Future. IA, 19 (Dec, 1967), 29-35; -8c

(Ed).   Investment Analysis and Portfolio Management: Readings from British Publications. Elek, 1970; -1b

See also **Russell, A. & Taylor, B. F.**

Taylor, C.
See **Morgan, E. V. & Taylor, C.**

Taylor, D. H.   Capital Budgeting Theory as Applied to the Leasing or Purchasing of Capital Assets—with the Emphasis on Computer Equipment. PhD diss, La St U, 1967; -25c

Taylor, H. M.   Evaluating a Call Option and Optimal Timing Strategy on the Stock Market. MSci, 14 (Sep, 1967), 111-120; -17a

See also **Mandelbrot, B. & Taylor, H. M.**

Taylor, J. H.   Wartime Finance and the Term Structure of Interest Rates. PhD diss, Iowa State U, 1969; -18f

Taylor, L. H.   When to Go Public for the Acquisition of Capital. CFC (Feb 1, 1962); -16a

Taylor, M.   General Financing Knowledge: the Principles and Practice of Finance. Textbooks, 1964; -22a

Taylor, R. G.   An Examination of the Evaluation, Content, Utility and Problems of Published Interim Reports. PhD diss, U of Chicago, 1964; -8c

Teichmoeller, J.   A Note on the Distribution of Stock Price Changes. JASA, 66 (Jun, 1971), 282-284; -11b

Teichroew, D.; Robichek, A. A. & Montalbano, M.   An Analysis of Criteria for Investment and Financing Decisions Under Certainty. MSci, 11 (Nov, 1965), 151-179; -25c

    Robichek, A. A. & Montalbano, M.   Mathematical Analysis of Rates of Return Under Certainty. MSci, 11 (Jan, 1965), 395-403; -25b

    See also **Robichek, A. A.; Teichroew, D. & Jones, J. M.**

Telser, L. G.   A Critique of Some Recent Empirical Research on the Explanation of the Term Structure of Interest Rates. JPE, 75 (Suppl Aug, 1967), 546-561; -18f

    Futures Trading and the Storage of Cotton and Wheat. JPE, 66 (Jun, 1958), 233-255; -21a

    Safety-First and Hedging. REStud, 23 (1955-1956), 1-16; -10f

    The Supply of Speculative Services in Wheat, Corn and Soybeans. FRIS, 7 (Suppl 1967), 131-176; -21a

    The Supply of Stocks, Cotton and Wheat. PhD diss, U of Chicago, 1956; -21a

    A Theory of Speculation Relating Profitability and Stability. REStat, 41 (Aug, 1959), 295-301; -9e, 21a

    See also **Houthakker, H. S. & Telser, L. G.**

Templeton, J. M.   Practical Methods to Test Analysts' Ability to Select Stocks for Appreciation. AJ, 2 (3rd Qtr, 1946), 51-52; -14c

Tennican, M. L.   The Valuation of Convertible Debentures. DBA diss, Harvard Bus, 1970; -17c

Tepper, I.   Revealed Preference Methods and the Pure Theory of the Cost of Capital. JF, forthcoming; -23d

Terborgh, G. W.   Business Investment Management. Machinery and Allied Products Institute and Council for Technological Advancement, 1967; -25f

    An Introduction to Business Investment Analysis. Machinery and Allied Products Institute and Council for Technological Advancement, 1958; -25c

    Studies in the Analysis of Business Investment Projects. Machinery and Allied Products Institute and Council for Technological Advancement, 1960-61; -25c

Terleckyj, N. E.

    See **Robbins, S. M. & Terleckyj, N. E.**

Terrell, J. H.   Mergers and Consolidations: The Role of Accounting in the Management-Decision Process. PhD diss, U of Tex, 1966; -26d

Terrell, W. T. & Frazer, W. J.   Interest Rates, Portfolio Behavior and Marketable Government Securities. JF, 27 (Mar, 1972), 1-36; -18f

Tersine, R. J.   Analysis of the Effect of 100 Per Cent Margin Requirement on Certain Common Stocks in 1967 Listed on the New York Stock Exchange. DBA diss, Fla St U, 1969; -6e

Tessier, B.

    See **Semah, J.; Serres, C. & Tessier, B.**

Tew, B. & Henderson, R. F. (Eds).   Studies in Company Finance. Cambridge U Pr, 1959; -22a

Teweles, R. J.; Harlow, C. V. & Stone, H. L.   The Commodity Futures Trading Guide. McGraw, 1969; -21a

    See also **Harlow, C. V. & Teweles, R. J.**

Theil, H. Optimal Decision Rules for Government and Industry. N-
Holland, 1964; -25c

The Use of Information Theory Concepts in the Analysis of Financial Statements. MSci, 15 (May, 1969), 459-481; -8c

& Leenders, C. T. Tomorrow on the American Exchange. JB,
38 (Jul, 1965), 277-284; -12e

Theilman, W. A General Theory of the Optimum Plan of Financing. PhD
diss, U of Ill, 1964; -23c

Thomas, L. J.

See **Bierman, H., Jr. & Thomas, L. J.**

Thomas, W. A. An Analysis of the Part Played by the Stock Exchange in
the Post War Financial System. MA thesis, Swansea U, 1961; -2a

Jobbing in the Regional Stock Exchanges. BM, 206 (Aug, 1968),
90-94; -2a

See also **Morgan, E. V. & Thomas W. A.**

Thompson, E. A. Debt Instruments in Both Macroeconomic Theory and
Capital Theory. AER, 57 (Dec, 1967), 1196-1210; -19a

Thompson, F. C. & Norgaard, R. L. Sinking Funds. Fin Exec, 1967; -19h

Thompson, G. C. & Walsh, F. J., Jr. Companies Stress Dividend Consistency. Natl Ind Conf Bd Management Record, 25 (Jan, 1963) 30-36; -24a

See also **Sunbury, D. G. & Thompson, G. C.**

Thompson, H. A Note on the Value of Rights in Estimating the Investor
Capitalization Rate. JF, forthcoming; -16b

Thompson, H. E. & Beranek, W. The Efficient Use of an Imperfect Forecast. MSci, 13 (Nov, 1966), 233-243; -9c

Thompson, L. E.

See **Butters, J. K.; Thompson, L. E. & Bollinger, L. L.**

Thomson, T. D. The Demand of Commercial Banks for Cash Assets: a
Cross Sectional Analysis. PhD diss, U of Chicago, 1967; -3f

Thore, S.

See **Cohen, K. J. & Thore, S.**

Thornber, E. H. & Lynch, M. A Workable Procedure for Optimizing the
Value of a Portfolio. Paper for the Seminar on the Analysis of Security
Prices, U of Chicago, Nov 1968; -10c

Thornton, J. E. Financial Characteristics of Firms Following a Policy of
Paying Small, Periodic Stock Dividends. PhD diss, U of NC, 1967; -16c

Thorp, G. O. & Kassouf, S. Beat the Market. Random, 1967; -17b

Tilney, N. S. Security Selection During a Period of Inflation. Bernhard,
1969; -6c

The Times. The Times Share Indices. Times, 1964; -5b

Tinbergen, J. The Dynamics of Share Price Formation. REStat, 21
(Nov, 1939), 153-160; -7a

Statistical Testing of Business Cycle Theories II; Business Cycles
in the United States of America, 1919-1932. Geneva: League of Nations
Economic Intelligence Service, 1939 (No. 6 in 1939 Volume); -24a

Tingley, K. R.

See **Hughes, P. F. & Tingley, K. R.**

Tinic, S. M. E. The Economics of Liquidity Services. QJE, 86 (Feb, 1972)
79-93; -2b

The Value of Time Preferences and the Behavior of Liquidity
Costs in the New York Stock Exchange. PhD diss, Cornell U, 1970; -2b

& West, R. R. Competition and the Pricing of Dealer Service in
the Over-the-Counter Market. JFQA, 7 (Jun, 1972), 1707-1728; -2b

See also **West, R. R. & Tinic, S. M.**

Tinsley, P. A.   Capital Structure, Precautionary Balances, and Valuation of the Firm: The Problem of Financial Risk. JFQA, 5 (Mar, 1970), 33-64; -23c

Tintner, G.   A Contribution to the Non-Static Theory of Choice. QJE, 55 (Feb, 1942), 274-306; -9a

The Theory of Choice Under Subjective Risk and Uncertainty. Em, 9 (Jul-Oct, 1941), 298-304; -9a

Tisdell, C.   Notes upon Some of the Present Theories of Choice under Uncertainty. Met, 15 (Aug-Dec, 1963), 125-135; -9c

Tito, D.
>   See **O'Brien, J. & Tito, D.**
>   See also **Smith, K. V. & Tito, D. A.**

Tobin, J.   The Interest Elasticity of Transactions Demand for Cash. REStat, 38 (Aug, 1956), 241-247; -25a

Liquidity Preference as Behavior Toward Risk. REStud, 25 (Feb, 1958), 65-86; -10c, 18a

The Theory of Portofolio Selection, *in* Hahn, F. H. & Brechling, F. P. R. (Eds), The Theory of Interest Rates. Macmillan Int, 1966; -10k
>   See also **Hester, D. D. & Tobin, J. (Eds)**

Tomkins, C.
>   See **Lockett, A. G. & Tomkins, C.**
>   See **Briston, R. J. & Tomkins, C. R.**

Tomlinson, L.   Appraising the Risk Factor in Investment Company Leverage Shares. AJ, 2 (1st Qtr, 1945), 52-62; -10b

Torrance, G.   Investing Life Insurance Funds. AJ, 11 (Feb, 1955), 45-48; -3h

Townsend, E. C.   Investment and Uncertainty: a Practical Guide. Oliver, 1970; -25d
>   See also **Jackson, A. S. & Townsend, E. C.**

Treadway, P. T.   An Explanation of the Conglomerate Merger Movement— the Conglomerate as a Result of Forces Arising in the Capital Markets. PhD diss, U of NC, 1971; -26c

Treasury Department et al.   A Description and Analysis of Certain European Capital Markets, prepared for the Joint Economic Committee by the Treasury Dept and various European Consulates. US Govt, 1964; -2c

Trent, R. H.   Corporate Growth Rates: An Analysis of Their Intertemporal Association. PhD diss, U of NC, 1968; -5d
>   See also **Young, W. E. & Trent, R. H.**

Treynor, J. L.   The Coming Revolution in Investment Management. Unp ms, 1971; -10c

How to Rate Management of Investment Funds. HBR, 43 (Jan-Feb, 1965), 63-75; -14a

On the Quality of Municipal Bonds. Paper for the Seminar on the Analysis of Security Prices, U of Chicago, Nov 1972; -19d

Towards a Theory of Market Value of Risky Assets. Unp ms, nd

The Trouble with Earnings. FAJ, 28 (Sep-Oct, 1972), 41-43; -8d
>   **& Black, F.**   Using Security Analysis to Improve Portfolio Selection. JB, forthcoming; -10c
>   **& Mazuy, K.**   Can Mutual Funds Outguess the Market? HBR, 44 (Jul-Aug, 1966), 131-136; -14a
>   **Priest, W. W., Jr.; Fisher, L. & Higgins, C. A.**   Using Portfolio Composition to Estimate Risk. FAJ, 24 (Sep-Oct, 1968), 93-100; -10b
>   **Shelton, J. & Kantor, M.**   Is Rate of Return Influenced More by

Systematic Risk than by Unique Risk? An Empirical Test of the Asset-Pricing Model. Paper for the Seminar on the Analysis of Security Prices, U of Chicago, Nov 1969; -10*l*

See also **Bagehot, W. (pseud for Treynor, J. L.)**

Trowbridge, C. L. ABC's of Pension Funding. HBR, 44 (Mar-Apr, 1966), 115-126; -3i

Tsiang, S. C. The Rationale of the Mean-Standard Deviation Analysis, Skewness Preference and the Demand for Money. AER, 62 (Jun, 1972), 354-371; -18a

A Theory of Foreign-Exchange Speculation under a Floating Exchange System. JPE, 66 (Oct, 1958), 399-418; -21b

Tucker, R. D. A Discussion of Benjamin Graham's Central Value Concept. AJ, 13 (May, 1957), 93-95; -7a

Tuite, M. F. An Analysis of Variables which are Associated with the Sensitivity of Common Stock Prices to News. DBA, diss, Indiana U, 1967; -10b

Turner, B. The Federal Funds Market. P-H, 1931; -20c

Turner, D. F. Conglomerate Mergers and Section 7 of the Clayton Act. HLR, 78 (May, 1965), 1313-1395; -26c

Turnovsky, S. J. The Allocation of Corporate Profits between Dividends and Retained Earnings. REStat, 49 (Nov, 1967), 583-589; -24a

Financial Structure and the Theory of Production. JF, 25 (Dec, 1970), 1061-1080; -22b

See also **Pyle, D. H. & Turnovsky, S. J.**

Turvey, R. The Economics of Real Property: an Analysis of Property Values and Patterns of Use. Allen, 1957; -21c

Present Value versus Internal Rate of Return: an Essay in the Theory of the Third Best. EJ, 73 (Mar, 1963), 93-98; -25c

Tuttle, D. L. An Analysis of Annual Changes in Prices of Equity Securities. PhD diss, U of NC, 1965; -7a

The Implications for Portfolio Management of Different Measures of Market Performance. Paper for the Seminar on the Analysis of Security Prices, U of Chicago, Nov 1969; -5b

& Litzenberger, R. H. Capital Budgeting Under Uncertainty. SJB, (Apr, 1968), 119-131; -25d

& Litzenberger, R. H. Leverage, Diversification and Capital Market Effects on a Risk-Adjusted Capital Budgeting Framework. JF, 23 (Jun, 1968), 427-443; -25d

& Wilbur, W. L. A Multivariate Time-Series Investigation of Annual Returns on Highest Grade Corporate Bonds. JFQA, 6 (Mar, 1971), 707-722; -19e

See also **Latané, H. A. & Tuttle, D. L.**
See also **Latané, H. A., Tuttle, D. L. & Jones, C. P.**

Twentieth Century Fund The Security Markets. Twentieth Fund, 1935; -2b

Tyler, P. (Ed). Securities, Exchanges and the S.E.C. Wilson, 1965; -2e

Tysseland, M. S. Further Tests of the Validity of the Industry Approach to Investment Analysis. JFQA, 6 (Mar, 1971), 835-848; -10a

Tzoannos, J. & Samuels, J. Mergers and Takeovers—the Financial Characteristics of Companies Involved. JBF, 4 (Autumn, 1972), 5-16; -26a

Udell, J. G.

See **Haugen, R. A. & Udell, J. G.**

Underwood, E. F. & Nelkin, M. C. Brokerage House Opinion at Turning Points in the Stock Market. AJ, 2 (4th Qtr, 1946), 39-43; -15c

Ungar, M.   Rational Entrepreneurial Behavior and the Demand for Investment and Borrowing. PhD diss, Columbia U, 1970; -25c

United States Securities & Exchange Commission
        See **Securities and Exchange Commission**

United States Trade Commission   The Merger Movement: A Summary Report. US Govt, 1948; -26a
        Present Trend of Corporate Mergers and Acquisitions. US Govt, 1947; -26a

Upson, R. B. & Jessup, P. F.   Risk-Return Relationships in Regional Securities. JFQA, 4 (Jan, 1970), 677-696; -10*l*

Upton, M.
        See **Howard, B. B. & Upton, M.**

Usher, D.   The Debt/Equity Ratio. PhD diss, U of Chicago, 1960; -23c

Vaile, R.   Cash and Futures Price of Corn. JM, 9 (Jul, 1944); -21a
        Inverse Carrying Charges in Futures Markets. JFE, 30 (Aug, 1948), 574-575; -21a

Valenta, J. R.   Capital Equipment Decisions: A Model for Optimal Systems Interfacing. SM thesis, MIT, 1968; -25c

Valentine, R.
        See **Chown, J. F. & Valentine, R.**

Van Alstyne, D. T.   Models of Option Writer Portfolios. PhD diss, Northwestern U, 1966; -17a

Van Arsdell, P. M.   Considerations Underlying Cost of Capital. FAJ, 19 (Nov-Dec, 1963), 69-76; -23d
        Corporation Finance. Ronald, 1968; -22a

Vance, L.   Grain Market Forces in the Light of Inverse Carrying Charges. JFE, 28 (Nov, 1946), 1036-1040; -21a

Vancil, R. F.   Lease or Borrow—New Method of Analysis. HBR, 39 (Sep, 1961), 122-136; -25g
        See also **Vandell, R. F. & Vancil, R. F.**

Van Cleave, M.
        See **Clendenin, J. C. & Van Cleave, M.**

Vandell, R. F. & Coleman, A. B.   Case Problems in Finance, 4th ed. Irwin, 1962; -1c
        & Vancil, R. F.   Cases in Capital Budgeting. Irwin, 1962; -25c

Van Den Dool, P.   Forward Exchange Transactions and Some Theoretical Implications. DBA diss, U of Oreg, 1968; -21b

Vanderford, D. E.   An Econometric Evaluation of Alternative Models of the Term Structure of Interest Rates. PhD diss, U of Cal Berkeley, 1970; -18f

Van Horne, J. C.   The Analysis of Uncertainty Resolutions in Capital Budgeting for New Products. MSci, 15 (Apr, 1969), B376-B386; -25d
        Capital-Budgeting Decisions Involving Combinations of Risky Investments. MSci, 13 (Oct, 1966), B84-B92; -25d
        Financial Management and Policy, 2nd ed. P-H, 1971; -22a
        Foundations for Financial Management: A Book of Readings. Irwin, 1966; -1b
        The Function and Analysis of Capital Market Rates. P-H, 1970; -18b
        Fundamentals of Financial Management. P-H, 1971; -22a
        Interest-Rate Expectations, the Shape of the Yield Curve, and Monetary Policy. REStat, 48 (May, 1966), 211-215; -18f
        Interest-Rate Risk and the Term Structure of Interest Rates. JPE, 73 (Aug, 1965), 344-351; -18f

A Linear Programming Approach to Evaluating Restrictions Under Bond Indenture or Loan Agreement. JFQA, 1 (Jun, 1966), 68-83; -19e

New Listings and their Price Behavior. JF, 25 (Sep, 1970), 783-784; -2f

A Note on Biases in Capital Budgeting Introduced by Inflation. JFQA, 6 (Jan, 1971), 653-658; -25c

Warrant Valuation in Relation to Volatility and Opportunity Costs. IMR, 10 (Spring, 1969), 19-32; -17b

& Glassmire, W.   The Impact of Unanticipated Changes in Inflation on the Value of Common Stocks. JF, forthcoming; -6c

& McDonald, J. G.   Dividend Policy and New Equity Financing. JF, 26 (May, 1971), 507-520; -24b

& Parker, G. G. C.   The Random Walk Theory: An Empirical Test. FAJ, 23 (Nov-Dec, 1967), 87-92; -23g

& Parker, G. G. C.   Technical Trading Rules: a Comment. FAJ, 24 (Jul-Aug, 1968), 128-132; -23g

See also **Robichek, A. A. & Van Horne, J. C.**

See also **Seelenfreund, A.; Parker, G. G. C. & Van Horne, J. C.**

Van Houten, J. F.   The Euro-Dollar Market and Monetary Policy. PhD diss, Georgetown U, 1966; -20d

Van Tassel, J.

See **Brada, J. C.; Ernst, H. & Van Tassel, J.**

Vasicek, O. A.   Capital Asset Pricing Model with No Riskless Borrowing. Unp ms, Wells Fargo Bank, 1971; -10l

& McQuown, J. A.   The Efficient Market Model. FAJ, 28 (Sep-Oct, 1971), 71-84; -11c

Vatter, W. J.   Income Models, Book Yield and Rate of Return. AR, 41 (Oct, 1966), 681-698; -8c

Vaughn, D. E.   Combining the Undervaluation, Fundamental, and Technical Approaches to Security Selection. SWSSQ, 48 (Jun, 1967), 79-85; -4a

Investment Principles, Practices and Techniques. HR & W, 1965; -4a

Survey of Investments. HR & W, 1967; -4a

& Bennett, H.   Adjusting for Risk in the Capital Budget of a Growth-Oriented Company. JFQA, 3 (Dec, 1968), 445-462; -25d

See also **Norgaard, R. L. & Vaughn, D. E.**

Vawter, J.   The Role of Formula Timing Plans in Investment Analysis. FAJ, 15 (Feb, 1959), 67-68; -12f

Velk, T. J.

See **Baldwin, W. L. & Velk, T. J.**

Venkataramanan, L. S.   The Theory of Futures Trading. Asia, 1965; -21a

Vernon, R. A.; Middleton, M. & Harper, D. G.   Who Owns the Blue Chips? A Study of Shareholding in a Leading Company. Gower, forthcoming; -3b

Vickers, D.   The Cost of Capital and the Structure of the Firm. JF, 25 (Mar, 1970), 35-46; -23d

Elasticity of Capital Supply, Monopsonistic Discrimination and Optimal Capital Structure. JF, 22 (Mar, 1967), 1-9; -23c

Profitability and Reinvestment Rates: A Note on the Gordon Paradox. JB, 39 (Jul, 1966), 366-370; -25c

The Theory of the Firm; Production, Capital and Finance. McGraw, 1968; -22b

See also **Brown, E. E. & Vickers, D.**

See also **Friend, I. & Vickers, D.**

Vickrey, W. S.   Measuring Marginal Utility by Reactions to Risk. Em, 13

(Oct, 1945), 319-333; -9a

Vidger, L. P. Selected Cases and Problems in Real Estate. Wadsworth Pub, 1963; -21c

Vinson, C. E. Investing and Hedging Techniques in the Convertible Bond Market. PhD diss, N Tex St U, 1969; -17c

    Rates of Return on Convertibles. FAJ, 25 (Jul-Aug, 1970), 110-114; -17c

Virgil, R. L.

    See **Pankoff, L. D. & Virgil, R. L.**

Vogel, R. C.

    See **Joyce, J. M. & Vogel, R. C.**

Von der Linde, G.

    See **Meltzer, A. H. & Von der Linde, G.**

Von Mehren, R. B. & McCarroll, J. C. The Proxy Rules: A Case Study in Administrative Process. LCP, 29 (Jun, 1964), 728-748; -26h

Von Neumann, J. & Morgenstern, O. Theory of Games and Economic Behavior, 3rd ed. Princeton U Pr, 1953; -9c

Von Szeliski, V. Predicting Stock Market Trends by Structure Analysis. AJ, 12 (May, 1956), 51-61; -7d

Voorheis, F. L. Bank Trustees and Pension Fund Performance. FAJ, 28 (Jul-Aug, 1972), 60-64; -3i

    Investment Policy and Performance of Bank Administered Pooled Equity Funds for Employee Benefit Plans. PhD diss, Mich St U, 1966; -3i

Vowels, R. C. An Evaluation of Equity and Economic Effects in Capital Gains Taxation. PhD diss, Am U, 1964; -27d

Wacht, R. F. The Derivation and Testing of a Normative Portfolio Balance Model for Allocating Commercial Bank Funds among Alternative Assets. PhD diss, U of NC, 1966; -10g

Wade, E.

    See **Diggory, T. G. & Wade, E.**

Wagle, B. The Use of Models for Environmental Forecasting and Corporate Planning. ORQ, 20 (Sep, 1969), 327-336; -22c

Wagner, W. H. & Cuneo, L. J. Stock Trading Costs. Paper for the Seminar on the Analysis of Security Prices, U of Chicago, May 1972; -2b

    & Lau, S. C. The Effect of Diversification on Risk. FAJ, 27 (Nov-Dec, 1971), 48-53; -10e

Wahlstrom, K. A Study and Analysis of the Bond Market in 1962 and 1963 Concerning the Value Placed on the Call Privilege. U of S Dak, unp monograph, 1966; -19h

Wakefield, B. R. Mergers and Acquisitions. HBR, 43 (Sep-Oct, 1965), 6ff; -26a

Wakeley, M. A. H. et al. (Eds). Federal Income Taxation of Banks and Financial Institutions. Boston: The Banking Law Journal, 1963; -27a

Walker, C. E. Federal Reserve Policy and the Structure of Interest Rates on Government Securities. QJE, 68 (Feb, 1954), 19-42; -18f

Walker, E. W. Essentials of Financial Management. P-H, 1965; -22a

    & Baughn, W. H. Financial Planning and Policy. Har-Row, 1964; -22a

Walker, M.

    See **Lloyd, C.; Rohr, R. J. & Walker, M.**

Walker, R. G. The Judgment Factor in Investment Decisions. HBR, 39 (Mar-Apr, 1961), 93-99; -25c

Walker, W. B. A Re-examination of Common Stocks as Long Term Investments. Anthoensen, 1954; -5a

Wallace, E.   Appraisal of Stock Options as an Incentive Device—A Study of Their Use and Abuse. PhD diss, Columbia U, 1961; -17d

Wallace, N.   Term Structure of Interest Rates and the Maturity Composition of the Federal Debt. JF, 22 (May, 1967), 301-312; -18f

The Term Structure of Interest Rates and the Maturity Composition of the Federal Debt. PhD diss, U of Chicago, 1964; -18f

Wallach, M. A.

See **Kogan, N. & Wallach, M. A.**

Wallingford, B. A.   An Inter-Temporal Approach to the Optimization of Dividend Policy with Predetermined Investments. JF, 27 (Jun, 1972), 627-636; -24b

A Survey and Comparison of Portfolio Selection Models. JFQA, 2 (Jun, 1967), 85-106; -10c

See also **Mao, J. C. T. & Wallingford, B. A.**

Walsh, F. J., Jr.

See **Harkins, E. P. & Walsh, F. J., Jr.**

See also **Thompson, G. C. & Walsh, F. J., Jr.**

Walter, J. E.   A Discriminant Function for Earnings—Price Ratios of Large Industrial Corporations. REStat, 41 (Feb, 1959), 44-52; -7a

Dividend Policies and Common Stock Prices. JF, 11 (Mar, 1956), 29-41; -24b

Dividend Policy and Enterprise Valuation. Wadsworth Pub, 1967; -24b

Dividend Policy: its Influence on the Value of the Enterprise. JF, 18 (May, 1963), 280-291; -24b

The Information Content of Stock Prices. BE, 1 (Summer, 1965); -7a

The Investment Process, as Characterized by Leading Life Insurance Companies. Harvard Busn, 1962; -3h

The Role of Regional Security Exchanges. U of Cal Pr, 1957; -2b

The Use of Borrowed Funds. JB, 28 (Apr, 1955), 138-147; -23c

& **Que, A.**   The Valuation of Convertible Bonds. JF, forthcoming; -17c

& **Williamson, J. P.**   Organized Securities Exchanges in Canada. JF, 15 (Sep, 1960), 307-324; -2c

Walter, R. G.   The Effects of Corporate Financial Policy on Shareholder Expectations. PhD diss, Mich St U, 1970; -23c

Walters, A. A.   The Demand for Money, Expectations, and Short and Long Rates, *in* Wolfe, J. N. (Ed), Value, Capital and Growth. Edinburgh U Pr, 1968; -18f

Monetary Policy, Gilts and Equities. IA, 28 (Dec, 1970), 3-6; -6d

Ward, H. A.

See **Corrigan, F. J. & Ward, H. A.**

Ward, K.   Number of Analysts Increasing in Field of Investment Research. FAJ, 19 (Jul, 1963), 84-85; -4c

Warren, J. M. & Shelton, J. P.   A Simultaneous Equation Approach to Financial Planning. JF, 26 (Dec, 1971), 1123-1142; -22c

Warren, R. A.   Formula Plan Investing. HBR, 31 (Jan-Feb, 1953), 57ff; -12f

Wasson, H. C.   Some Investment Policies for Commercial Banks. FAJ, 22 (May-Jun, 1966), 83-91; -3f

Waterman, M. H.   Investment Banking Functions, their Evolution and Adaptation to Business Finance. U of Mich Busn Res, 1958; -16a

Watson, R. D.   Tests of Maturity Structure for Commercial Bank Securities Portfolios—a Simulation Approach. DBA diss, Indiana U, 1971; -3f

Watts, R.   The Information Content of Dividends. JB, forthcoming; -24a

Waud, R. N.   Public Interpretation of Discount Rate Changes: Evidence on the 'Announcement' Effect. Em, 38 (Mar, 1970), 231-250; -6e, 11a

Small Sample Bias Due to Misspecification in the 'Partial Adjustment' and 'Adaptive Expectation' Models. JASA, 61 (Dec, 1966), 1130-1152; -24a

Waugh, W. W.

See **Cohen, K. J.; Kramer, R. L. & Waugh, W. W.**

Way, P. & Ferguson, R.   The Role of Simulation in Measuring Investment Performance. Paper for the Seminar on the Analysis of Security Prices, U of Chicago, Nov, 1969; -14a

Weaver, A. R. H.   The Uncertainty of the Expectations Theory of the Term Structure of Interest Rates. WEJ, 4 (1966), 122-134; -18f

Weaver, D.   Investment Analysis. Longman, 1971; -4a

& **Hall, M. G.**   The Evaluation of Ordinary Shares Using a Computer. JIA, 93 (1967), 165-203; -7c

Weaver, M.   The Technique of Short Selling. Inv Pr, 1963; -13d

Weaver, R. A., Jr.   Equity Financing for the Small Firm. HBR, 34 (Mar-Apr, 1956), 91-102; -16b

Webb, M.

See **Dev, S. & Webb, M.**

Wechsberg, J.   The Merchant Bankers. Weidenfeld & N, 1967; -3g

Weedin, D. E.   Competition: Key to Market Structure. JFQA, 7 (Suppl Mar, 1972), 1699-1701; -2b

Wehrle, L. S.   Life Insurance Investment: the Experiences of Four Companies. YEE, 1 (Spring, 1961), 70-136; -3h

A Theory of Life Insurance Portfolio Selection. Cowles Foundation Discussion Paper No. 60, Dec, 1958; -3h

Weil, R. L.   Realized Interest Rates and Bondholders' Returns. AER, 60 (Jun, 1970), 502-511; -19b

Segal, J. E. & Green, D., Jr.   Premiums on Convertible Bonds. JF, 23 (Jun, 1968), 445-463; -17c

See also **Becker, S. W. & Weil, R. L.**

See also **Fisher, L. & Weil, R. L.**

Weinberg, M. A.   Take-overs and Amalgamations. Sweet, 1963; -26a

Weiner, J. M.   Developing a European Capital Market. LBR, 85 (Jul, 1967), 16-28; -20e

Weingartner, H. M.   Capital Budgeting of Interrelated Projects: Survey and Synthesis. MSci, 12 (Mar, 1966), 485-516; -25e

Criteria for Programming Investment Project Selection. JIE, 15 (Nov, 1966), 65-76; -25e

The Generalized Rate of Return. JFQA, 1 (Sep, 1966), 1-29; -25b

Mathematical Programming and the Analysis of Capital Budgeting Problems. P-H, 1963; -25e

Some New Views on the Payback Period and Capital Budgeting Decisions. MSci, 15 (Aug, 1969), B594-B607; -25c

Optimal Timing of Bond Refunding. MSci, 13 (Mar, 1967), 511-524; -19h

Weinraub, H. J.

See **Pettway, R. H. & Weinraub, H. J.**

Weintraub, R. E.   On Speculative Prices and Random Walks: A Denial. JF, 18 (Mar, 1963), 59-66; -11c

Weisman, B. B.   An Empirical Study of 21 Investment Criteria Employed in Common Stock Selection. PhD diss, NYU, 1970; -7a

Weiss, L. W.   An Evaluation of Mergers in Six Industries. REStat, 47 (May, 1965), 172-181; -26b

See also **Hall, M. & Weiss, L. W.**

Welfling, W.   Financing Business Enterprise. New York: American Institute of Banking, 1960; -22a

Weller, K. J.   An Analysis and Appraisal of Rights Offerings as a Method of Raising Equity Capital. PhD diss, U of Mich, 1961; -16b

Welles, C.   The Unions: $4 Billion Goes to Work. II, 2 (Jun, 1968); -3i

The Beta Revolution: Learning to Live with Risk. II, 5 (Sep, 1971), 21ff; -10b

University Endowments: Revolution Comes to the Ivory Tower. II, 1 (Sep, 1967); -3j

Welshans, M. T.

See **Dauten, C. A. & Welshans, M. T.**

Wendel, H. F.   Short-Run Interest-Rate Expectations in the Government Securities Market. PhD diss, Columbia U, 1967; -19c

Wendt, P. F.   Current Growth Stock Valuation Methods. FAJ, 21 (Mar-Apr, 1965), 91-103; -7b

What Should We Teach in an Investment Course? JF, 21 (May, 1966), 416-422; -4c

& Cerf, A. R.   Real Estate Investment Analysis and Taxation. McGraw, 1969; -21c

& Wong, S. N.   Investment Performance: Common Stocks versus Apartment Houses. JF, 20 (Dec, 1965), 633-646; -21c

Wenglowski, G. M.   Estimates of the Cost of Capital and the Market's Valuation of the Average Utility Firms, 1954-1964. PhD diss, U of Pa, 1967; -23d

Wenman, E. G.

See **Leach, W. A. & Wenman, E. G.**

Wentz, A. G.   Intrinsic Value and Its Use as a Determinant of Cost of Capital: A Test. PhD diss, Ohio St U, 1969; -23d

Werner, F.   A Study of the Predictive Significance of Two Income Measures. JAR, 7 (Spring, 1969), 123-136; -8a

Werner, W.

See **Robbins, S. M. & Werner, W.**

Wert, J. E.

See **Fredman, A. J. & Wert, J. E.**

See also **Jen, F. C. & Wert, J. E.**

West, B. K.

See **Sprinkel, B. W. & West, B. K.**

West, D. A.   The Investor in a Changing Economy. P-H, 1968; -3e

Risk Analysis in the Sixties. FAJ, 23 (Nov-Dec, 1967), 124-126; -10b

West, R. R.   An Alternative Approach to Predicting Bond Ratings. JAR, 8 (Spring, 1970), 118-125; -19f

Conflicts of Interest: Substance or Subterfuge? FAJ, 27 (Nov-Dec, 1971), 31-39; -2e

Determinants of Underwriters' Spreads on Tax Exempt Issues. JFQA, 2 (Sep, 1967), 241-264; -19d

'Homemade' Diversification vs. Corporate Diversification. JFQA, 2 (Dec, 1967), 417-420; -26c

Institutional Trading and the Changing Stock Market. FAJ, 27 (May-Jun, 1971), 17ff; -2b

More on the Effects of Municipal Bond Monopsony. JB, 39 (Apr, 1966), 305-308; -19d

352

Mutual Fund Performance and the Theory of Capital Asset Pricing: some Comments. JB, 40 (Apr, 1968), 230-234; -14a

New Issue Concession on Municipal Bonds: a Case of Monopolistic Pricing. JB, 38 (Apr, 1965), 135-148; -19d

Should Commercial Banks be Allowed to Underwrite Municipal Bonds? NBR, 3 (Sep, 1965), 35-44; -19d

Simulating Securities Markets Operations; Some Examples, Observations, and Comments. JFQA, 5 (Mar, 1970), 115-138; -11c

& **Bierman, H., Jr.** Corporate Dividend Policy and Preemptive Security Issues. JB, 41 (Jan, 1968), 71-75; -24b

& **Brouillette, A. B.** Reverse Stock Splits—Harbinger of Bad Times or Valid Management Technique? FE, (Jan, 1970), 12-17; -16c

& **Tinic, S. M. E.** The Economics of the Stock Market. Praeger, 1971; -2b

See also **Bierman, H. Jr. & West, R. R.**

See also **Tinic, S. M. E. & West, R. R.**

West, S. & Miller, N. Why the NYSE Common Stock Indexes? FAJ, 23 (May-Jun, 1967), 49-54; -5b

Westerfield, R. Capital Assest Pricing Model: an Analysis of the Performance of Conglomerates. U of Pa Pr, 1969; -26c

See also **Pettit, R. R. & Westerfield, R.**

Weston, J. F. An Appraisal of Recent Contributions to the Theory of the Cost of Capital. Proceedings of the 34th Annual Conference of the Western Economic Association, 1959, 19-22; -23d

Norms for Debt Levels. JF, 9 (May, 1954), 124-135; -23c

A Note on Merger Valuation: Reply. JF, 23 (Jun, 1968), 535-536; -26a

(Ed). Readings in Finance from Fortune. HR & W, 1958; -1b

The Recent Merger Movement. JB, 25 (Jan, 1952), 30-38; -26a

The Role of Mergers in the Growth of Large Firms. U of Cal Pr, 1953; -26a

The Stock Market in Perspective. HBR, 34 (Mar-Apr, 1956), 71-80; -4a

A Test of Cost of Capital Propositions. SEJ, 30 (Oct, 1963), 105-112; -23d

& **Beranek, W.** Programming Investment Portfolio Construction. FAJ, 11 (May, 1955), 51-55; -10c

& **Brigham, E. F.** Managerial Finance, 3rd ed. HR & W, 1969; - 22a

& **Woods, D. H. (Eds).** Basic Financial Management: Selected Readings. Wadsworth Pub, 1967; -1b

& **Woods, D. H. (Eds).** Theory of Business Finance: Advanced Readings. Wadsworth Pub, 1967; -1b

See also **Ansoff, H. I. & Weston, J. F.**

See also **Folz, D. F. & Weston, J. F.**

See also **Jacoby, N. H. & Weston, J. F.**

See also **Ricks, R. B. & Weston, J. F.**

Westwick, C. A. The Accuracy of Profit Forecasts in Bid Situations. A, 83 (Jul, 1972), 10-16; -15b

Weygandt, J. T.

See **Frank, W. G. & Weygandt, J. T.**

Weymar, F. H. The Dynamics of the World Cocoa Market. MIT Pr, 1968; - 21a

The Supply Storage Revisited. AER, 56 (Dec, 1966), 1226-1234; -21a

Whalen, E. L.   Extension of the Baumol-Tobin Approach to the Transactions Demand for Cash. JF, 23 (Mar, 1965), 113-134; -25a

Wheeler, A. C. & K. A. C.   Some Views on Property Investment. JIASS, 12 (Nov, 1953); -21c

Wheeler, K. A. C.

See **Wheeler, A. C. & K. A. C.**

Wheelwright, S. C.

See **Makridakis, S. G. & Wheelwright, S. C.**

Wherry, R. H. & Newman, M.   Insurance and Risk. HR & W, 1964; -3h

Whinston, A.

See **Naslund, B. & Whinston, A.**

Whitbeck, V. S.   An Iterative Version of a Stock Valuation Model. Paper for the Seminar on the Analysis of Security Prices, U of Chicago, May 1968; -7c

    & Kisor, M.   A New Tool in Investment Decision-Making. FAJ, 19 (May-Jun, 1963), 55-62; -7c

Whitcomb, H. C.

See **Greiner, P. P. & Whitcomb, H. C.**

White, W. H.   Interest Inelasticity of Investment Demand: The Case from Business Attitude Surveys Re-examined. AER, 46 (Sep, 1956), 565-587; -25f

Interest Rate Differences, Forward Exchange Mechanism and Scope for Short-Term Capital Movements. IMF, (Nov, 1963); -21b

White, W. L.   The Debt-Equity Ratio, the Dividend-Payment Ratio, Growth and the Rate at which Earnings are Capitalized. An Empirical Study. PhD diss, MIT, 1963; -23c, 24b

See also **Hausman, W. H. & White, W. L.**

Whiting, R.   Profitable Trading with Puts and Calls. RHM, 1959; -17a

Whitman, W. T.

See **Cottle, C. S. & Whitman, W. T.**

Whitmarsh, T. F.   When to Sell Securities Short Against the Box. FAJ, 28 (May-Jun, 1972), 80ff; -13d

Whitmore, G. A.   Diversification and the Reduction of Dispersion: a Note. JFQA, 5 (Jun, 1970), 263-264; -10e

Market Demand Curve for Common Stock and the Maximization of Market Value. JFQA, 5 (Mar, 1970), 105-114; -22a

    & Darkazanli, S.   A Linear Risk Constraint in Capital Budgeting. Msci. 18 (Dec, 1971), B155-B157; -25d

Whitney, A. D.   Odd Lot Trading as a Market Barometer. AJ, 4 (1st Qtr, 1948), 58-66; -13b

Whitney, J. M., II.   The S.E.C. and the Financial Analyst. FAJ, 19 (Jul-Aug, 1963), 11-16; -2e

Whittaker, J.   The Evaluation of Warrants. IA, 18 (Oct, 1967), 39-47; -17b

Minimising the Burden of the Dollar Premium. IA, 24 (Oct, 1969), 26-33; -27a

How High is High?-the Market's Required Return in America and in Britain. IA, 20 (Jun, 1968), 15-19; -7d

The Relevance of Duration. JBF, 2 (Spring, 1970), 34-41; -18g

What Level for Share Prices? LBR 87 (Jan, 1968), 1-14; -7d

Whittall, D.   A Simulation Model for Estimating Earnings. FAJ, 24 (Nov-Dec, 1968), 115-118; -8c

Whittington, G.   The Prediction of Profitability and Other Studies of Company Behaviour. Cambridge U Pr, 1971; -8c

The Profitability of Retained Earnings. REStat, 54 (May, 1972),

152-160; -23b

of College and University Endowment Funds. Unp, Oct 1968; -1a
>   See also **Bower, R. S.; Herringer, F. C. & Williamson, J. P.**
>   See also **Bower, R. S.; Myers, B. C.; Nugent, C. E. & Williamson, J. P.**
>   See also **Bower, R. S. & Williamson, J. P.**
>   See also **Bower, R. S.; Williamson, J. P. & Wippern, R. F.**
>   See also **Walter, J. E. & Williamson, J. P.**

Willis, P. B.   The Federal Funds Market. The Federal Reserve Bank of Boston, 1964; -20c

Wilson, J. S. G.   Some Aspects of the Development of Capital Markets. BNLQR, 19 (Dec, 1966), 263-310; -2c
>   Monetary Policy and the Development of Money Markets. Allen, 1966; -20a
>   The New Money Markets. LBR, 64 (Apr, 1962), 31-45; -20a
>   See also **Whittlesey, C. R. & Wilson, J. S. G. (Eds)**

Wilson, R.   A Pareto-Optimal Dividend Policy. MSci, 13 (May, 1967), 756-764; -24b

Wilson, S. J.   Public Participation in the Stock Market: an Analysis of Long-Term Market Trends. Fraser, 1962; -3b

Wilt, G. A. Jr.
>   See **Fischer, D. E. & Wilt, G. A. Jr.**

Windle, D. W.
>   See **Lawson, G. H. & Windle, D. W.**

Winer, L.   Growth Rate Graph and Nomograph. FAJ, 25 (Jan-Feb, 1969), 105-108; -7b

Winn, E. L.
>   See **Bacon, P. W. & Winn, E. L.**

Winn, W. J.
>   See **Durand, D. & Winn, W. J.**
>   See also **Friend, I.; Hoffman, G. W. & Winn, W. J.**
>   See also **Hess, A. C. & Winn, W. J.**

Winter, E. L.   A Complete Guide to Making a Public Stock Offering. P-H, 1962; -16a
>   Cost of Going Public. FE, 31 (Sep, 1963); -16a

Winthrop, J.   Layman's View of Computer Power. FAJ, 25 (Sep-Oct, 1969), 101-103; -4e

Wintrub, W. G.
>   See **Schneider, H. M. & Wintrub, W. G.**

Wippern, R. F.   Earnings Variability, Financial Structure and the Value of the Firm. PhD diss, Stanford U, 1964; -23c
>   Financial Structure and the Value of the Firm. JF, 21 (Dec, 1966), 615-634; -23c
>   A Note on the Equivalent Risk Class Assumption. EE, (Spring, 1966), 13-22; -23c
>   Portfolio Selection: the Multiperiod Case. Wkg paper, Amos Tuck School of Business Administration, Dartmouth C, Apr 1971; -10k
>   The Significance of Dummy Variables in Multiple Regressions Involving Financial and Economic Data: Reply. JF, 23 (Jun, 1968), 518-519; -23c
>   Utility Implications of Portfolio Selection and Performance Appraisal Models. JFQA, 6 (Jun, 1971), 913-924; -10c
>   See also **Bower, R. S.; Williamson, J. P. & Wippern, R. F.**
>   See also **Bower, R. S. & Wippern, R. F.**

Wise, J.   Linear Estimators for Linear Regression Systems Having Infinite Residual Variances. Paper presented to the Berkeley-Stanford

Mathematical Economics Seminar, Oct 1963; -11b

Wise, T. A. Wall Street's Main Event: S.E.C. vs. the Specialist. F, 76 (May, 1964), 149-152; -2e

    & the Editors of Fortune. The Insiders. Doubleday, 1962; -4a

    See also **Seligman, D. & Wise, T. A.**

Wolf, C. R. Bank Preferences and Government Security Yields. QJE, 85 (May, 1971), 283-303; -19c

    The Management of Commercial Bank Government Bond Portfolios. PhD diss, Harvard U, 1965; -3f

    A Model for Selecting Commercial Bank Government Security Portfolios. REStat, 51 (Feb, 1969), 40-52; -3f

Wolf, H. A. & Doenges, R. C. (Eds). Readings in Money and Banking Appleton, 1968; -3f

    & Richardson, L (Eds). Readings in Finance. Appleton, 1966; -1b

Wong, C-H. Capital Structure and Investment Behavior. PhD diss, U of Minn, 1970; -23c

Wong, S. N.

    See **Wendt, P. F. & Wong, S. N.**

Wood, J. H. Expectations and the Demand for Bonds. AER, 59 (Sep, 1969), 522-530; -18f

    Expectations, Errors, and the Term Structure of Interest Rates. JPE, 71 (Apr, 1963), 160-171; -18f

    The Expectations Hypothesis, the Yield Curve and Monetary Policy. QJE, 78 (Aug, 1964), 457-470; -18f

    The Term Structure of Interest Rates: A Theoretical and Empirical Study. PhD diss, Purdue U, 1962; -18f

Wood, R. N. Measurement of Investment Performance. Alexander, 1967; -14a

    Measuring the Investment Yield of Pension Funds. Alexander, 1965; -14b

Wood, T. D. A Study of the Behavioral Characteristics of Conglomerates. PhD diss, U of Fla, 1971; -26c

Woodfield, L. W. An Experiment in Application of Monte Carlo Method for Simulating Capital Budgeting Decisions under Uncertainty. PhD diss, Mich St U, 1966; -25d

Woods, D. H. Decision-Making in Investment Management Institutions. FAJ, 23 (Jul-Aug, 1967), 73-75; -2e

    & Brigham E. F. Stockholder Distribution Decisions: Share Repurchases or Dividends. JFQA, 1 (Mar, 1966), 15-25; -16d

    & Caverly, T. A. Development of a Linear Programming Model for the Analysis of Merger/Acquisition Situations. JFQA, 4 (Jan, 1970), 627-642; -26a

    See also **Weston, J. F. & Woods, D. H.**

Woods, I. R. Financial 'Leverage' and 'Gearing' in Perspective. SAJE, 32 (Mar, 1964), 26-35; -23c

    Price Behavior of Ordinary Shares on Ex Div Dates on the Johannesburg Stock Exchange, July 1, 1959 to June 30, 1961. SAJE, 31 (Mar, 1963), 38-59; -24c

Woodward, B. M. The Dow Theory and the Management of Portfolios. PhD diss, U of Fla, 1969; -12c

Working, H. Cycles in Wheat Prices. Wheat, 7 (Nov, 1931); -21a

    Financial Results of Speculative Holdings in Wheat. Wheat, 7 (Jul, 1931); -21a

    Futures Markets Under Renewed Attack. FRIS, 5 (Feb, 1963), 13-

Some Financial Aspects of Recent Corporation Mergers and
Consolidations. PhD diss, Am U, 1962; -26a

Discounted Cash Flow. McGraw, 1968; -25c

Financial Management. McGraw, 1970; -22a

Wrightsman, D. Pension Funds and Economic Concentration. QREB, 7
(Winter, 1967), 29-36; -3i

Wu, H. K. Corporate Insider Trading, Profitability and Stock Price
Movement. PhD diss, U of Pa, 1963; -13a

Odd-Lot Trading in the Stock Market and its Market Impact.
JFQA, 7 (Jan, 1972), 1321-1342; -13b

& Zakon, A. J. (Eds). Elements of Investments: Selected Readings.
HR & W, 1965; -1b

Wyatt, A. R. A Critical Study of Accounting for Business Combinations,
Accounting Research Study No. 5. New York: American Institute of
Certified Public Accountants, 1963; -26d

& Kieso, D. E. Mergers, Acquisitions and Consolidations. Intext,
1968; -26a

Wyckoff, P. G. Dictionary of Stock Market Terms. P-H, 1964; -2b

The Method and Motives of Selling Short. AJ, 15 (May, 1959),
101-104; -13d

The Psychology of Stock Market Timing. P-H, 1963; -7d

Yaari, M. E. Convexity in the Theory of Choice under Risk. QJE, 79
(May, 1965), 278-290; -9a

Uncertain Lifetime. Life Insurance and the Theory of the Consumer. REStud, 32 (1965), 137-150; -10k

See also **Diamond, P. A. & Yaari, M. E.**

Yager, C. A.

See **Young, R. A. & Yager, C. A.**

Yamashita, G. A. Cash Tender Offers: a Predictive Model. PhD diss,
Columbia U, 1970; -26e

Yamey, B. S. An Investigation of Hedging on an Organized Produce
Exchange. MS, 19 (Sep, 1951); -21a

See also **Peston, M. H. & Yamey, B. S.**

See also **Snape, R. H. & Yamey, B. S.**

Ying, C. C. Are There Any Relationships Between Stock Price and
Volume? PhD diss, Harvard U, 1964; -13a

Stock Market Prices and Volume of Sales. Em, 34 (Jul, 1966), 676-
685; -13a

Yohe, W. P. & Karnosky, D. W. Interest Rates and Price Level Changes,
1952-69. Mo Rev F R Bk St Louis, (Dec, 1969), 18-38; -18c

See also **Frazer, W. J. & Yohe, W. P.**

Yohn, C. B. An Investigation of the Covariance of Stock Prices. SB thesis
MIT, 1962; -10a

Young, A. E. Financial, Operating and Security Market Parameters of
Repurchasing. FAJ, 25 (Jul-Aug, 1969), 123-128; -16d

Managerial, Market and Investor Problems Associated with the
Cash Tender Offers of Corporations for their Own Common Stocks.
PhD diss, Columbia U, 1967; -16d

The Performance of Common Stocks Subsequent to Repurchase.
FAJ, 23 (Sep-Oct, 1967), 117-121; -16d

See also **Ellis, C. D. & Young, A. E.**

See also **Marshall, W. S. & Young, A. E.**

Young, G. K. Merchant Banking: Practice and Prospects. Weidenfeld & N,
1966; -3g

Young, G. R. et al.   Mergers and Acquisitions: Planning and Action. Routledge, 1965; -26a

Young, I. C.
  See **Wright, F. K.; Young, I. C. & Barton, A. D.**

Young, R. A. & Yager, C. A.   The Economics of 'Bills Preferably'. QJE, 74 (Aug, 1960), 341-373; -20b

Young, W. E.   Common Stock Ex Post Holding Period Returns and Port-folio Selection. PhD diss, U of NC, 1969; -10c
  Random Walk of Stock Prices: a Test of the Variance-Time Function. Em, 39 (Sep, 1971), 797-812; -11c
  & Trent, R. H.   Geometric Mean Approximations of Individual Security and Portfolio Performance. JFQA, 4 (Jun, 1969), 179-200; -10j
  See also **Latané, H. A. & Young, W. E.**
  See also **Latané, H. A.; Tuttle, D. L. & Young, W. E.**

Youngblood, C. E.   A Publicly Owned Stock Exchange? FAJ, 25 (Nov-Dec, 1969), 104A-104D; -2b

Youssef, A. A.   The Predictive Power of Corporate Interim Earnings Reports. PhD diss, U of Minn, 1971; -8a

Yudelson, J.
  See **Drzycimiski, E. F. & Yudelson, J.**

Zaentz, N.   Relative Price Performance Among Coupon Areas in Corporate Bonds. FAJ, 25 (Jul-Aug, 1969), 146-155; -19e

Zakon, A. J.
  See **Wu, H-K. & Zakon, A. J. (Eds)**
  & Pennypacker, J. C.   An Analysis of the Advance-Decline Line as a Stock Market Indicator. JFQA, 3 (Sep, 1968), 299-314; -12e

Zarnowitz, V.   An Appraisal of Short-Term Economic Forecasts. Natl Bur Econ Res, Occasional Paper No. 104, 1967; -15a
  Prediction and Forecasting, Economic, *in* International Encyclo-pedia of the Social Sciences, Vol 12. Macmillan, 1968; -15a

Zausner, M.   Corporate Policy and the Investment Community. Ronald 1968; -22a

Zdanowicz, J. S.   Investment Risk Considering Intraperiod Liquidation: a Re-evaluation of Price Variance. PhD diss, Mich St U, 1971; -10b

Zeckhauser, R. & Keeler, E.   Another Type of Risk Aversion. Em, 38 (Sep, 1970), 661-665; -9a

Zeikel, A.   Group Dynamics. FAJ, 27 (Jan-Feb, 1971), 30-34; -4d

Zieg, K. C., Jr.   A Study of Common Stock Options from the Standpoint of the Returns Accruing to the Buying and Selling Sides. PhD diss, Ohio St U, 1969; -17a

Ziemba, W. T.   A Myopic Capital Budgeting Model. JFQA, 4 (Sep, 1969), 305-328; -25d

Zinbarg, E. D.   Price-Earnings Ratios and Yields. AJ, 15 (Aug, 1959), 35-42; -8d
  Supply and Demand Factors in the Stock Market. FAJ, 20 (Jul-Aug, 1964), 84-88; -23b
  & Harrington, J. J., Jr.   The Stock Market's Seasonal Pattern. FAJ, 20 (Jan-Feb, 1964), 53-56; -12b
  See also **Cohen, J. B. & Zinbarg, E. D.**
  See also **Freund, W. C. & Zinbarg, E. D.**

Zionts, S.
  See **Chen, A. H. Y.; Jen, F. C. & Zionts, S.**

Zobian, S. P.   Investment Decision Modelling. FAJ, 22 (May-Jun, 1966), 151-155; -25c

Zoellner, J. F.
    See **Hester, D. D. & Zoellner, J. F.**

Zweig, M. E.   An Analysis of Risk and Return on Put and Call Option Strategies. PhD diss, Mich St U, 1969; -17a
    An Investor Expectations Stock Price Predictive Model Using Closed-End Fund Premiums. JF, forthcoming; -7a

Zwick, B.   An Equilibrium Model of Interest Rate Determination. PhD diss, Carnegie-Mellon U, 1969; -18b
    See also **Pepper, N. & Zwick, B.**